POLITICAL SCIENCE

To Chris Bailey,

Whose comments are a valuable if uncredited addition to this volume

Jerry Scott

Oct. '96

POLITICAL SCIENCE
Foundations for a Fifth Millennium

Gregory M. Scott

University of Central Oklahoma

Foreword by Charles O. Jones

PRENTICE HALL
Upper Saddle River, New Jersey 07458

Library of Congress Cataloging-in-Publication Data

Scott, Gregory M.
    Political science : foundations for a fifth millennium / Gregory M.
  Scott ; foreword by Charles O. Jones.
      p. cm.
    Includes bibliographical references and index.
    ISBN 0–13–207572–5
    1. Political science.   2. Political science—Study and teaching.
  I. Title.
  JA71.S323 1996
  320—dc20   96–33648
                                          CIP

This book was set in 10/12 Baskerville by ElectraGraphics, Inc.
and was printed and bound by R. R. Donnelley & Sons.
The cover was printed by Lehigh Press.

Editor in Chief: Nancy Roberts
Acquisitions editor: Michael Bickerstaff
Editorial assistant: Anita Castro
Editorial/production supervision
  and interior design: Mary McDonald
Copy editor: Ann Donahue
Cover design: Bruce Kenselaar
Buyer: Bob Anderson

© 1997 by Prentice-Hall, Inc.
Simon & Schuster/A Viacom Company
Upper Saddle River, New Jersey 07458

Printed in the United States of America
10 9 8 7 6 5 4 3 2 1

ISBN 0-13-207572-5

Prentice-Hall International (UK) Limited, *London*
Prentice-Hall of Australia Pty. Limited, *Sydney*
Prentice-Hall Canada Inc., *Toronto*
Prentice-Hall Hispanoamericana, S.A., *Mexico*
Prentice-Hall of India Private Limited, *New Delhi*
Prentice-Hall of Japan, Inc., *Tokyo*
Simon & Schuster Asia Pte. Ltd., *Singapore*
Editora Prentice-Hall do Brasil, Ltda., *Rio de Janeiro*

TO

Stephen Wayne
Tom Rossetti
Michael Smith
Hubert Morken
Michael Brint
Dante Germino
Kenneth Thompson

and to the memory of Jacques Ellul

WITH APPRECIATION FOR THE SUPPORT, ENCOURAGEMENT,
AND EFFORTS OF

Jill MacKay Scott

Steve Garrison

John George
Randall Jones
Louis Furmanski
Youngtae Shin

AND FOR THE CONTRIBUTIONS OF

Be Reasonable: Selected Quotations for Inquiring Minds
(Laird Wilcox & John George, Prometheus Books, 1994)

and

Stephen E. Bennett
John C. Berg
Mary Dietz
Christine Di Stefano
Michael Dukakis
Miriam Golden
Susan Hekman
Charles O. Jones
Nolan Jones
Michael Kantor

Joyce Kaufman
Richard Lau
David Mares
Sam Nunn
David O'Brien
Edward Portis
Paul Quirk
Yitzhak Shamir
Stephen Skowronek
John M. Strate

James Swanson
Katherine Tate
Kenneth Wald
Michael Ward
Stephen Wayne
Richard Worthington
Vladimir Zhirinovsky
Catherine Zuckert

Contents

Foreword

Charles O. Jones
University of Wisconsin—Madison

Political Science: Foundations for a Fifth Millennium, by Gregory M. Scott, is more than a textbook; it is a substantial achievement. Professor Scott has undertaken an awesome task—that of introducing students to how politics has been studied and explored through time, indeed, virtually from the beginning of human relationships. The obstacles to such a feat are many: loss of continuity, overwhelming detail, imbalances of various kinds, creating an encyclopedia rather than a text. He has avoided these pitfalls through a prodigious effort of selecting signal developments in the growth and maturity of political scholarship, being ever sensitive to the need for integration.

Scott identifies creativity as a central feature of political science. In doing so, he has clearly challenged himself to be inventive. He has met that challenge; evidence for this conclusion is found in the distinctive features of the book. He associates what political science is today with what it has been through time by identifying the larger questions of state building and social relations that have faced the designers of governments and the practitioners of politics. Therefore the reader can relate contemporary political science, as displayed in the annual meetings of the American Political Science Association as well as in its organized sections, to antecedent developments.

The best textbooks influence the curriculum. That will be the case with *Political Science: Foundations for a Fifth Millennium.* The book requires teachers and students to make connections and seek generalizations beyond those that are common in introductory courses. The historical, contextual, and theoretical features of the book are central to this effect, as is the scope and sweep of the undertaking.

Finally, I admire the author's nerve in writing this book. It suits his accent on creativity as characteristic of political inquiry. But I have another reason for my respect. We are at a time in history when many of the fundamental questions of government and politics identified by Professor Scott form the agenda in many, perhaps most, political systems. Yet we are told that apathy about politics is common throughout the world and among our audience as teachers, *i.e.,* college-age students in the United States.

Political scientists typically have been indifferent about promoting their discipline, perhaps even defensive in the face of criticism of methods by those in the so-called "hard" sciences. Professor Scott's book audaciously boosts our craft as treating the truly important issues. There was a time when I was quite casual about fostering study of my particular corner of the discipline, more or less assuming a "take it or leave it" approach. I am no longer diffident. I strongly believe that college students must benefit from the product of the systematic study of politics. We have ourselves learned much in recent decades about the enduring questions. It is our obligation as teachers to transmit this knowledge to the students, who will be the active citizens and future leaders of government. Among its many fine contributions, Professor Scott's book shows why.

Preface

Political science, the creative, thoughtful study of political behavior, has enriched human understanding for four millennia. At least as early as 2000 BCE, people were recording the motives, strategies, and actions of political leaders and commenting upon the efficiency, effectiveness, and ethics of rulers and regimes.

Unlike other introductions to political science, which only survey or compare forms of government or focus primarily upon ideologies, *Political Science: Foundations for a Fifth Millennium* is about the progress, accomplishments, and challenges of the *discipline* of political science. Introducing political science as an expression of human creativity, this text covers the full span of the discipline's history, subject matter, methods, and creative accomplishments, not only in the United States but around the world.

The scope of *Political Science: Foundations for a Fifth Millennium* is unique among introductions to the study of politics. The text proceeds in five parts. Part I begins by introducing political science as an expression of creativity and encourages students to think imaginatively and precisely about politics. It then surveys the development of the study of politics from its origins at about 2000 BCE to the 1990s. Part II explains the subject matter of the discipline, discussing the great issues of politics (freedom, equality, justice) and the varieties of political ideologies that have developed in response to these issues. Part II then demonstrates the application of the comparative method to the study of political behavior by comparing the political systems first of the United States and Israel and then those of North and South Korea. Part III explains how political scientists study politics, examining general approaches and schools of thought and explaining the most widely used quantitative methods in the discipline, including surveys, experiments, case studies, and content analysis. Part IV introduces six subfields of the discipline, each in its own chapter: American government—political analysis, American government—policy analysis, American constitutional law, comparative government and politics, international relations, and political theory. Each chapter provides a general introduction to the subfield followed by a recently published article in that subfield. The chapter on international relations, for example, prepares the student for a discussion of the relationship of war to democracy and then presents Mansfield and Snyder's "Democratization and War," an article arguing that, contrary to popular perceptions, democracies in their early phases are more likely to go to war than long-established and stable nondemocratic states. Finally, Part V surveys the development of the discipline of political science in twelve foreign countries, and then discusses some recent developments in each of the forty-seven program divisions of the American Political Science Association.

In addition to the wide variety of topics covered within the text, *Political Science: Foundations for a Fifth Millennium* includes several letters written specifically to its student readers by such noted personalities as former Israeli Prime Minister Yitzak Shamir, Russian dissident Vladimir Zhirinovsky, U.S. Trade Representative Mickey Kantor, Democratic presidential candidate Michael Dukakis, and United States Senator Sam Nunn.

Political Science: Foundations for a Fifth Millennium has been written to inspire students to engage the study politics creatively and thoughtfully, and in so doing to join the magnificent multimillennial quest for enlightenment that constitutes the discipline of political science.

Gregory M. Scott

POLITICAL SCIENCE

1 Welcome to the Creative Study of Politics

Much may be expected from the progress and diffusion of political science.
—James Madison

What do you already know about political science? You know it is an academic discipline, something taught in college—and something you are beginning to study. Something you may not yet know is that political science affects your daily life, directly and indirectly, in countless ways. Your freedom to select the school you want to attend, your confidence in the quality of the canned tuna that you buy, the amount that is taken from your paycheck every week, all these aspects of your life and many more are determined by presidents, members of congress, justices, and hundreds of other government officials. Many of these individuals gained their knowledge of politics and government directly from political science. Consider, for example, that America's Founding Fathers were avid students of some of history's greatest political analysts, whom we shall discuss, and constructed a constitution based upon what they had learned from their studies. Consider further that attorneys are represented more than any other profession, not only in the leadership of the court system, but in national and state legislatures as well. What did these attorneys major in, as undergraduate students, more than any other college major? The answer is political science. Even most of those who did not major in political science have had courses in politics and government in high school or college.

Whether it is being taught in a college classroom, formulated in a position paper, or practiced in a professional conference, political science is always a search for enlightenment. It is the energy, work, and product of a world-wide community of scholars, teachers, practitioners, researchers, and consultants engaged in a quest for understanding and answers. It is an organized academic discipline with deep divisions, debts to other fields, controversies, aspirations, opportunities, and challenges, tied together by a common purpose: understanding politics. Political scientists today draw upon a distinguished heritage of four millenniums of thoughtful observation of politics, and they invite you to participate with them in one of humanity's most stimulating intellectual adventures.

The Dynamics of *Politics*

What has your own experience told you about the political aspects of life? We seem to know politics when we see it, but we often find it hard to define. Some things appear to be very political, and others not at all. What quality makes some things political and others not? Consider the following:

- President Clinton's State of the Union Address
- A letter from Senator Edward Kennedy to the citizens of Massachusetts
- The 1996 Platform of the Republican Party
- A political cartoon by Doonesbury
- A campaign speech by Phil Gramm
- An editorial in the *New York Times*

The items above are obviously political. We readily understand that they are for the purpose of expressing or furthering one person's or a group of people's views or interests. Now examine the following list:

- *Anonymously* donating to the American Lung Association
- Reading a bedtime story to a child
- Giving blood to the Red Cross
- Refinishing an old table
- Dancing in the rain
- Cooking fettucine

Although there may possibly be something political about the items on the list above, we do not normally think about them as being political. These activities do not involve people who are attempting to further their own political interests. There are many aspects of life that are not political. Look at this list:

- A teacher's attempt to get you to learn
- Your attempt to influence a teacher to get a better grade
- An argument with your brother or sister over who gets to drive the car, with an appeal to your parents
- A sermon
- A conversation at a cocktail party
- A speech at a meeting of the Rotary Club

Reprinted by permission: Tribune Media Services.

What is it that makes each of these situations at least potentially political? What quality do they all share? To answer this question is to understand the fundamental nature of politics.

Politics: A Definition

Politics has been defined by many people in many different ways. According to some of the more popular definitions, politics is:

- The science of "who gets what, when, and how" (Harold Lasswell, *Politics: Who Gets What, When and How,* 1936)
- The authoritative allocation of values (David Easton, *The Political System,* 1953, 129)
- The activity by which differing interests within a given unit of rule are conciliated by giving them a share in power proportional to their importance to . . . the whole community (Bernard Crick, *In Defense of Politics,* 1962, 21)
- The process of making government policies (Austin Ranney, *Governing: An Introduction to Political Science,* 1990, 25)
- The art of looking for trouble, finding it everywhere, diagnosing it incorrectly, and applying the wrong remedies (Groucho Marx)

In spite of the differences among these definitions, however, several qualities are common to them all:

- Politics is *relational,* that is, it has to do with relationships among people or groups of people.
- Politics concerns *interests and power.* The signature of political activity is the attempt on someone's part to further his own interest, increase her own power, or to reduce the influence of someone else.
- Politics is *dynamic.* This means that politics is not a snapshot of an event or a place in time, nor is it a collection of snapshots. It is a process or an activity that is perpetually in motion; constantly changing; and continually expressing, transforming, and conforming to the people, trends, and events through which it operates.

The immediate connotation of the word "politics" is usually negative. We typically see politicians as manipulators who do things for people to get something from them. The fact is, however, that politics is absolutely necessary to our lives. Think about it. As human beings we find ourselves in a world in which we have many physical and emotional needs and desires but insufficient resources to meet all of them. In such a situation, we have perhaps three basic alternatives for getting our needs met. We can:

1. Deny our needs in favor of the needs of others.
2. Attempt to take what we need by force.

3. Attempt to communicate our needs to others to resolve need conflicts through nonviolent processes, often in procedures established to promote participation and fairness.

The first alternative is *altruism*. When we act altruistically, we abandon politics by declining to further our own self-interest, giving preference instead to the needs of others. We are all altruistic to a certain extent, but consistent altruism surpasses our normal desires and capabilities. Mother Theresa, for example, has spent most of her life caring for sick and dying people in conditions that pose a threat to her health, but most of us are not willing to follow her example, at least for any extended period.

The second alternative, taking what we need by force, is *coercion*. As with the first course of action, it ultimately abdicates politics. In a superficial sense, force is the quintessential political act because its intent is furthering one's self-interest. On the other hand, an act of force destroys relationships and exchanges normal political channels—communication, bargaining, manipulation, and compromise—for physical compulsion.

The third course of action described above is what we usually mean by the term *politics:* a method of mediation that meets our needs and does not lead to such undesirable consequences as war or neglect of the self. Perhaps politics may, therefore, be best understood as a quality of the interactions that spring directly from our attempts to meet our own needs without coercion. Viewed in this way, politics occupies the center of a spectrum, the polarities of which are coercion and altruism:

altruism   politics   coersion
|———|

The Eternal Paradox

Two basic emotional needs figure prominently in politics because they are fundamental aspects of human interaction in society: the need for *community* (or unity) and the need for *individuality*. We emerge from the womb with a sense, even if not understood intellectually, of being separate, cut off from others. Studies have shown that infants who are not held or given human interaction in the days following birth may actually die of emotional deprivation. As the years go by we try to overcome this sense of separation in a number of ways, including bonding with our mothers and families, making friends, and getting married. We also seek acceptance in larger communities. We join a church, a sorority, a bowling league, the Kiwanis Club, or a political party, or we experience community when we share a sense of national pride or make a contribution to a candidate who articulates our views.

While we seek community with others in some or all of these ways, we simultaneously exhibit an opposing impulse: individuality. To feel unique, to desire recognition as a special human being unlike any other individual, is as deep a human need as the desire for unity and community. Much of the energy we devote to our careers is motivated by a need for recognition of our personal talents and contributions.

The behavior that often results from simultaneously responding to these two opposing drives (community and individuality) sometimes appears odd and contradictory, perhaps most noticeably during adolescence. Teenagers conform desperately to norms set by their peers. Having the right brand of clothing, the right style of shoes, the right group of friends, becomes vitally important to students in junior high and high school. At the same time, however, adolescents express their individuality continuously by breaking rules or norms set by the adult world and by demonstrating in many large and small ways their independence from their parents.

It is not an exaggeration to say that the primary task of the founding fathers in writing the Constitution of the United States was to construct a government system that simultaneously maximizes opportunities for both individuality and community. In fact, the entire history of politics is largely the story of how communities and nations resolved the inherent conflict between the universal needs for community and individuality. Consider a few examples.

- Ancient Athenians built an empire and history's first democracy at least partly upon a strong loyalty, a bonded unity, to their city. When asked to identify themselves, they did not hesitate to respond "We are Athenians." This sense of loyalty to the polis ironically allowed Athenians to express their personal views strongly within the citizens' Assembly.
- Citizens of Rome proclaimed the innate natural rights of citizens to equal treatment before the law (individuality), while seeking to bring the world together under the Roman Empire (community).
- American patriots adopted a constitution to bind the states together in a document that established majority rule (community) in a new society while insisting upon a bill of rights (individuality).
- In virtually every case it decides, the United States Supreme Court is called upon to consider the interests of individual citizens (individuality) in relationship to the interests of the society as a whole (community).

Governments deal in many ways with the tension between the competing needs for community and individuality, attempting to satisfy both. Congress struggles every year with the rights of businesses to operate free from government interference and with the need of the public to be assured of product quality and safety. The president, in times of war and national emergency, must balance the lives of individual members of the armed services against the need of the country to be secure from terrorism or assaults against our national interests. Politics is in large part the story of how people resolve conflicts such as these. When politicians attempt to strike a balance between the individual and the community, they are attempting to bring order to society. Perhaps, then, it is most appropriate to say that

Politics is ordering societal relations

Politics is an often chaotic clash of interests and values, striving for acceptance or dominance. In other words, people in politics strive toward constructing an order conducive to the goals they seek. Political action aims at order at all levels, including the micro (small groups such as family members), the medial (larger groups like community associations), and the macro (states, provinces, and nations) levels. This means that politics is a way in which we meet our emotional needs for unity and individuality, as well as our physical needs.

Having established a definition of politics, it is relatively easy to define *government*, the arena in which politics is most visible, and, therefore, most intensively studied. Government is a forum and authoritative structure for making, interpreting, and enforcing the rules through which politics operates in society. Government is the laws, institutions, and processes that set the rules and create the mechanisms through which human relations are publicly carried out. Governments make laws about the limits of marriage, proper conduct in family life, business relations, use of the physical environment, national defense, and other matters. In its most basic sense, government is the set of rules and institutions that establish the order within which politics is conducted in society. In most simple terms, then,

Government is ordering politics.

The Focus of Political Science

It is important to understand that *politics* and *political science* are not exactly the same things. While politics operates in all levels of life (family, community, and government), political science as a discipline focuses mostly upon the more complex levels of political interaction, and especially upon governments and activities related to them. While economists direct their attention to money and finance and sociologists are primarily interested in aspects of social life such as the family and cultural norms, political scientists analyze *public* relationships. The phenomena of most interest to political scientists involve the activities of people in their communities and their private activities as they affect governments.

Three Activities of Political Science

Political science, the quest for knowledge about politics, is conducted through *three basic activities:*

- *Investigation:* finding the facts
- *Interpretation:* discerning patterns in the facts
- *Application:* putting the patterns to use

Investigation means finding the facts. For example, to investigate the attitudes of voters in Ohio, a survey might be designed which would identify characteristics of people who vote in Ohio primary elections.

Interpretation means discerning patterns in the facts, and the processes that cause, control, or affect these patterns. For example, interpreting the results of an investigation into the attitudes of Ohio voters might lead us to the following conclusion: "Voting in primaries in Ohio increases as voter knowledge of economic issues increases."

Application means putting the knowledge gained through investigation and interpretation to use. Applying the information gained in our example, we might establish a program designed to educate Ohio voters about economic issues, and begin a study to determine the effects of the program upon voting behavior.

The methods political science uses to conduct these three activities are discussed in detail in Part III of this book, "*How* to Study Politics." It is only relatively recently that all three of these activities have gained acceptance as components of political science. For centuries people have debated which of the three activities ought properly to be included within the discipline, and the debate is not entirely over, as we shall see in later chapters of this text. The table below illustrates some of the ways in which political scientists perform these activities.

	Investigation	Interpretation	Application
Definition →	*Finding the facts*	*Discerning patterns in the facts, and the processes that cause, control, or affect these patterns*	*Putting the knowledge gained through investigation and interpretation to use*
Example 1: Political Participation →	A survey designed to identify characteristics of people who vote in primary elections in Ohio	Analysis of the survey data; drawing conclusions such as "voting in primaries in Ohio increases as education on economic issues increases"	A program designed to educate Ohio voters about economic issues, accompanied by a study to determine the effects of the program upon voting behavior
Example 2: Public Administration →	A study which identifies both personnel procedures and administrative problems in the Department of Defense	An examination of the relationship between personnel procedures and administrative problems, which concludes that some personnel policies are causing problems	A revision of personnel policies accompanied by a study to determine if the revisions actually solve administrative problems
Example 3: International Relations →	A study which identifies the amount, value, and types of economic interaction between Japan and the United States	An estimation of the relative benefits of economic interdependence to Japan and the United States, which concludes that Japan benefits more than the United States	Recommendations for altering trade agreements between Japan and the United States, followed by an assessment of the results of changes caused by altering the trade agreements

Political Science as Creativity

In *The Courage to Create* (1975, 71–72), psychologist Rollo May describes the relation between science and creativity:

> Scientists themselves, particularly the physicists, have told us that the creativity of a science is bound up with the freedom of human beings to create in the free, pure sense. In modern physics it is very clear that the discoveries that later become utilized for our technological gains are generally made in the first place because a physicist lets his imagination go and discovers something simply for the joy of discovery. . . . I am proposing that . . . creativity . . . is not only important for art and poetry and music; but is essential in the long run also for our science.

Creativity is the heart of political science, as it is of all science. Creativity is the essential common element and primary driving force in all three major activities of the discipline. Investigation is the attempt to gain new knowledge, and to gain knowledge in new ways. Interpretation is the attempt to make sense out of the knowledge that is gained, to derive meaning from it. Application is the attempt to apply new understandings to the problems and opportunities of our lives.

This notion of the importance of creativity in political science is so important and so complex that it is worth exploring a little further. If we continue to view political science as a creative, dynamic process, one that actively helps people to establish an understanding of the way their world works, we can make an analogy between the world of the political scientist and the world of the artist. When an artist paints a picture of a tree, the painting creates an interpretive image of the tree, a representation of the tree as perceived by the artist. In the same way, political science creates interpretive images of the phenomena of politics as perceived by the political scientist. The goal, for both artist and political scientist, is the same: to make us *see*, to help us *understand*.

Speaking of the great French Impressionist painter Paul Cezanne, Rollo May (1975, 77–78) provides a clear explanation of the process of creative representation:

> Cezanne sees a tree. He sees it in a way no one else has ever seen it. He experiences, as he no doubt would have said, "being grasped by the tree." The arching grandeur of the tree, the mothering spread, the delicate balance as the tree grips the earth—all these and many more characteristics of the tree are absorbed into his perception and are felt throughout his nervous structure. These are part of the vision he experiences. This vision involves an omission of some aspects of the scene and a greater emphasis on other aspects and the ensuing rearrangement of the whole; but it is more than the sum of all these. Primarily it is a vision that is now not the tree, but Tree; the concrete tree Cezanne looked at is formed into the essence of tree. However original and unrepeatable his vision is, it is still a vision of all trees triggered by his encounter with this particular one.

The painting that issues out of this encounter between a human being,

Cezanne, and an objective reality, the tree, is literally new, unique, and original. Something is born, comes into being, something that did not exist before—which is as good a definition of creativity as we can get. Thereafter, everyone who looks at the painting with intensity of awareness and lets it speak to him or her will see the tree with the unique powerful movement, the intimacy between the tree and the landscape, and the architectural beauty which literally did not exist in our relation with trees until Cezanne experienced and painted them. I can say without exaggeration that I never really *saw* a tree until I had seen and absorbed Cezanne's paintings of them.

Political science does for our understanding of politics what Cezanne's representation of a tree does for our perception of trees. As thousands of readers can attest, the following works, all written by incisive, keenly observant political scientists, will help you to *see,* as if for the first time, the meanings behind the most fundamental of political concepts. You may not yet have read any of these works, but if you continue your exploration of political science, you will. And you have a marvelous adventure in store for you.

Once you read . . .	you will gain a new understanding of . . .
Plato's allegory of the cave	democracy
Machiavelli's *Prince*	political strategy
David Easton's *The Structure of Political Systems*	the interrelationships of political phenomena
Richard Flathman's *The Philosophy and Politics of Freedom*	freedom
James MacGregor Burns' *Leadership*	political leadership
Gabriel Almond's *The Civic Culture*	political socialization

When you do political science and do it well, you participate in this drama of creativity.

This book cannot tell you exactly how to be creative. You must try it yourself, and persevere until you succeed. There is available, however, some information on the traits and characteristics of creative people that you may find helpful. Psychologists have studied creativity intensively, and John Dacey has summarized the findings of many of their studies. Dacey finds agreement in the scientific literature that eight personal qualities are strongly associated with creativity:

- Tolerance of ambiguity
- Stimulus freedom
- Functional freedom
- Flexibility

- Androgyny
- Delay of gratification
- Preference for disorder
- Risk taking

Tolerance of ambiguity is, according to the literature, the most important characteristic of creative people. An ambiguous situation is one in which there are no clear indications about how to respond, no rules or guidelines for conduct. Imagine, for example, that you are middle-aged, newly divorced, and about to go out on your first date in twenty years. Again, perhaps you are visiting a religious shrine in Japan, and you have no knowledge of the practices and customs of the religion, but you do not wish to offend anyone. People who can tolerate ambiguity do not refrain from entering situations in which they do not know the rules. They do not attempt to escape but rather become inquisitive and attempt to find their own ways of dealing with the situation.

Stimulus freedom has to do with following rules. According to Dacey, "When the stated rules of a situation interfere with the creative ideas of people who have stimulus freedom, those people are likely to bend the rules to their needs. More important, they do not assume that rules exist when the situation is ambiguous" (Dacey 1989, 22). Creative people have a way of doing what intuitively makes sense, rather than attempting to follow the rules. Thomas Jefferson, for example, broke the rules of previous diplomatic understandings when he arranged for the Louisiana Purchase.

Functional freedom concerns learning how to make things work in new ways. As our experiences in life teach us how things work, we begin to think that the patterns we observe are unchangeable, and we become "functionally fixed," which is the opposite of being functionally free. Functionally free people can find new uses for things. For functionally free people, garden implements become sculptures, and armies undertake humanitarian missions.

Flexibility is the ability to see an entire situation, not just parts of it. People without flexibility seize one aspect of a problem and take it as far as they can go while ignoring many other possibilities. Flexibility is, therefore, the ability to change one's focus to new aspects of a situation. If you are observing political candidates speak, for example, do you focus only upon their words, or do you also note their body language, their dress, their mannerisms, their tone, and other things?

Risk taking is a trait shared by creative people, who tend to take moderate risks more consistently than people who are not creative. Less creative people are more prone to take only minimal risks, or to take risks wherein the chance of failure is excessively high. Moderate risk taking, as Dacey notes, correlates highly with a tolerance for ambiguity (Dacey 1989, 30). People who seek political office, for example, risk time and effort, not knowing many of the factors that will eventually determine the results of the election.

It seems strange that people who are creative have a preference for disorder, but in fact disorder presents opportunities for creating order, and this is the challenge that creative people gladly accept. Complexity in relationships and asymmetry in design make for different and, therefore, intriguing matters with which the creative mind can grapple.

The ability to delay gratification is what enables some people to work quietly and carefully for years on something they consider to be important, without any reward in the meantime. Dacey notes that Thomas Edison had to conduct 2,004 laborious experiments before he found the right filament for a light bulb.

Androgyny is the final item on Dacey's list. It means that creative people, either men or women, have a combination of what have been conventionally known as masculine and feminine traits. They may be assertive (masculine) and sensitive (feminine), for example, in their attitudes, likes, and dislikes. Men who tend to be extremely masculine in their attitudes and women who tend to be extremely feminine are not as likely to be creative as those who have characteristics of both genders. Thinking about the characteristics of creative people may help you to become more creative as you pursue the study of politics and do other things in your life.

The Creative Approach:
Thinking like Einstein

At one point early in his career, Albert Einstein (1879–1955) became fascinated with tea leaves. For several days he sat, hour after hour, watching tea leaves fall to the bottom of a tea cup. Einstein would stir the cup and watch the tea leaves fall over and over again, enchanted by the simplicity of the motion he observed. Furthermore, when he commuted to work on a train he sat motionless for hours, concentrating all his thought on the image of telegraph poles going past the window. Fixing his gaze on tea leaves falling to the bottom of a cup and telegraph lines whizzing past a train window, Einstein began to see both motion and time in a whole new way, a way which eventually revolutionized scientific concepts of time, motion, and matter. Einstein is by no means the only great scientist or thinker to have made important discoveries after painstaking observation of what seems common and obvious. Jean Piaget (1896–1980), for example, one of this centuries greatest psychologists, wrote some of the most important works in the field of developmental psychology after spending weeks watching children play in a playground.

Great discoveries often have small and ordinary beginnings. A succession of careful, seemingly insignificant observations may lead to a new vision of political life. Einstein and Piaget drew much of their inspiration from:

- Intense, prolonged, repeated observation of the most elementary phenomena;
- Systematic examination and analysis of what they observed; and
- Creative thinking about the results of their observations.

The author asks you to consider that the great future discoveries of political science may well be made in exactly this manner. The history of political science, like the history of any science, is normally written as the story of the great advances, the great discoveries. Most people think of great scientific discoveries being made by geniuses who grasp complexities far beyond the capabilities of people of average intelligence, and there is certainly truth in this. Some of the greatest scientific discoveries, however, have been made not only by attempting to assemble complex patterns, but by clearly perceiving the ordinary, the simple, and the obvious. In fact, we are all able, in a very important respect, to think like Albert Einstein. As a student of political science you may find that your most meaningful discoveries come from intense, prolonged observation of simple things; from carefully discovering, sorting, and examining the political phenomena you encounter. *To think like Einstein, oddly enough, is to be fascinated with the most fundamental aspects of life, to examine them closely and systematically, and to think creatively about them.*

This book is written to help you to "think like Einstein." It provides the introductory materials necessary for you to begin to become a political scientist. Its chapters provide what may seem a bewildering array of topics to study. Its discussions of research methods introduce you to the basic means of conducting investigations into the world of politics. It challenges you to supply the single most important ingredient in the process of making discoveries about politics: creativity.

Creativity for Understanding or Creativity for Change?

As you begin to study politics, be aware that there are two schools of thought regarding the uses to which political science should be put. Some political scientists claim that political science should only describe and interpret reality in a strictly objective manner. Others believe that such objectivity is neither possible nor desirable, and that the greatest potential benefit of political science is its potential for changing society. The controversy which engendered these viewpoints will be explained in detail in Chapter 6. At this point, however, let's look at option two: the potential of political science, as an expression of creativity, to change society. Rollo May (1975, 71–73) captures the potential of political insights in the form of poetry to change political systems:

> The creativity of the spirit does and must threaten the structure and presuppositions of our national, orderly society and way of life. . . . Just as the poet is a menace to conformity, he is also a constant threat to political dictators. He is always on the verge of blowing up the assembly line of political power. We have had powerful and poignant demonstrations of this in Soviet Russia. It appeared chiefly in the prosecution and purge of artists and writers under Stalin, who was pathologically anxious when faced with the threat that the creative unconscious posed to his political system. Indeed, some students believe that the . . . situation in [Soviet] Russia shows an ongoing struggle between rationality and what we have been calling "free creativity."

Changes brought about by the release of creativity may be chaotic yet peaceful, as in the collapse of the Soviet Union, or violent, as in the French and Russian Revolutions. Creativity expressed in new political ideas may constructively transform the course of history. Beliefs are powerful. The history of political science is the history of how politics has been studied. Because some students of politics, like Karl Marx, have founded vastly influential intellectual movements, the history of political science is also in part the history of beliefs that have changed the world. Beliefs have legitimized slavery and freed the slaves, instigated the holocaust and inspired the liberation of India, reinforced the Holy Roman Empire and spurred the civil rights movement.

Political science is not only the discovery of facts about politics; it is the process of creatively using those facts. James Madison studied political science and creatively applied the lessons he learned from Roman statesman Cicero (106–43), English philosopher John Locke (1632–1704), and French political and legal historian Charles Secondat, Baron de Montesquieu (1689–1755), to build a constitution that has lasted more than two hundred years. Martin Luther King (1929–1968) studied Mohandas Gandhi's (1869–1948) liberation movement in India and creatively applied the lessons he learned to lead the American civil rights movement.

We live in a world of a dialectic of belief and action. This means that people who define politics change the course of the world, and the change in the world, in turn, defines politics anew. Examine the following examples:

- In 508–507 BCE, Cleisthenes believed that personal action of citizens makes a difference in politics, and with this belief he founded the world's first democracy.
- In 1787, James Madison, Thomas Jefferson, and others, accepting Montesquieu's idea that the legislative, executive, and judicial powers of government should be placed in separate offices held by separate people, founded what has become one of the world's oldest continuous democracies.
- In 1848, Karl Marx believed that class struggle is the most important motive in political life, and his philosophy became the driving force behind a world-wide communist movement.

Creative ideas that accurately describe some aspect of political existence can revolutionize life.

The Creative Attitude

You may believe that the proper role of political science is only to discover the facts, and that to interpret the facts involves the application of values beyond the range of science. On the other hand, you may believe that the very purpose of political science is to change society. The author is not interested in supporting either point of view but rather wishes to suggest that both viewpoints are accepted (and debated) today within the discipline of political science. In any case, however you interpret the role and work of political science, do it with passion! Theodore Lowi (1993, 394), a former president of the American Political Science Association, spoke with vision and wisdom when he said:

> [A]mong the sins of omission of modern political science, the greatest of all has been the omission of passion. There are no qualifications for membership in the APSA, but if I had the power to establish such standards they would be something like this: one must love politics, one must love a good constitution, one must take joy in exploring the relation between the two, and one must be prepared to lose some domestic and even some foreign policy battles to keep alive a positive relation between the two. I do not speak for the passion of ideology, though I don't count it out. I speak for the pleasure of finding a pattern, the inspiration of a well-rounded argument, the satisfaction in having made a good guess about what makes democracy work, and a good stab at improving the prospect of rationality in human behavior. . . . This is not an opportunity to play philosopher king. It is an opportunity to meet our own intellectual needs while serving the public interest. And we need not worry how to speak truth to power. It is enough to speak truth to ourselves.

As you begin your adventure in political science, take up Professor Lowi's challenge. The men and women who, in the second half of the twentieth century, transformed the study of politics from a fledgling offshoot of history and economics into a substantial and powerful influence in academics and public life are now fading away. According to one prominent historian of the discipline, because of retirements, half the people who were practicing political science in 1990 will not be practicing it by the year 2000 (Leftwich 1991). A new generation will do political science for the first half of the twenty-first century, a generation who will continue to devote themselves to traditional tasks but will do so in creative ways with new results.

What kind of attitude will you need in order to participate in the creation of the next generation's contribution to political science? You will need an attitude that starts in the classroom with a desire to participate earnestly and actively. You will need an attitude that carries your research in the library and amidst the turmoil of actual politics with dignity, perseverance, honesty, and a passion for accuracy. And, if you are to make a significant contribution to the study of politics, which some of you will do, you will need to learn to develop and apply your ability to think creatively.

Grasping the Future of Political Science

This book will introduce you to the history of past controversies and the status of some present challenges to political science. Although political science, as the study of politics, is now four millenniums old, the answers to the following questions are still investigated and debated—and, perhaps, always will be:

- What are our strengths and limitations as human beings?
- What factors govern political behavior?

- How can we maintain diversity and community?
- How can we maintain group discipline and still encourage creativity?
- What role does/should the state play in history?
- What should be done about poverty and the creation of wealth?
- What is the meaning of equality and inequality?
- What are the causes of violence and extremism?
- What can be done about violence/extremism?
- What is efficiency in government?
- What is effectiveness in government?
- What have we learned about the nature of politics?
- Who are we as political beings? What are our capabilities and limitations?
- What sources of information can we depend upon?
- What common values can we adopt?
- How can we make better government policy?
- How can we make a better government policy-making process?

As political scientists, we accept the search for answers to these questions and many more. As creative political scientists, we know no bounds in asking questions about politics. As responsible political scientists, we are bounded in our investigations by integrity, ethics, openness, sincerity, faith in ourselves, and respect both for our own limitations and for the perspectives of others.

In 1925, APSA President Charles Merriam in his paper entitled "Recent Advances in Political Methods" (1993, 129–146) had these words to say about the importance of political science, words as meaningful today as they were more than seventy years ago:

> Social science and political science are urgently needed for the next great stage in the advancement of the human race. As custodians of the political science of our time, the responsibility rests upon us to exhaust every effort to bring the study of government in its various stages to the highest possible degree of perfection, to exhaust every effort to obtain effective knowledge of political forces, to bring to bear every resource of science and prudence at our command.

In a letter written specifically for the readers of this book, United States Senator Sam Nunn notes the price to be paid for success in politics. His well-considered comments apply to the discipline of political science as well.

Sam Nunn
United States Senator
Washington, D.C. 20510-1001

July 7, 1995

Dear Mr. Scott:

In answering your request for some thoughts to share with your students, I would tell them what my high school basketball coach always told us, "You have to pay the price." He was also our principal, and he held the record, until just a few years ago, for the most wins of any high school basketball coach in the nation. But the example he set and what he taught us about life were far more important.

At the time we thought of his words in terms of the self-discipline to practice and get in shape to do our best on the basketball court. Later we realized that every worthwhile thing has a price -- in time spent studying or putting in long hours of hard work, giving up comforts or pleasures to help others or to achieve a long-term goal. The price to be paid for things like drug and alcohol abuse was far too high to justify any temporary pleasure. The price for doing the right thing can be high, but the price for losing your self-respect, can be even higher.

Sincerely,

Sam Nunn

Prof. Greg Scott
University of Central Oklahoma
100 North University Drive
Edmond, Oklahoma   73034

2

Four Millenniums: A History of Political Science

The first key to wisdom is this—constant and frequent questioning . . . for by doubting we are led to question and by questioning we arrive at the truth.

—Peter Abelard

Political Science as the Continuing Creative Search for Truth

Whatever else it might be, political science is a creative expression of our attempt to understand how we relate to each other in communities larger than the family, in other words, tribes, counties, states, nations, and international organizations. An examination of the history of political science reveals much about how people have answered the questions that continually arise when they relate to each other within their own communities and with other societies in the world.

If we define political science as thoughtful consideration of politics, then political science began at least as early as 2000 BCE, as recorded in the Old Testament and other ancient writings. The history of political science has been detailed in numerous volumes, and classifications of time periods have appeared from time to time. Each of these classifications interprets political history in a unique way. For example, in his study "Recent Advances in Political Methods" (1993, 137), the leading political scientist of the 1920s, Charles Merriam, classified four eras of political science according to the predominant method of inquiry which scholars used in each period:

1. The *a priori* and deductive method down to 1850
2. The historical and comparative method, 1850 to 1900
3. The tendency toward observation, survey, and measurement, 1900 to the present
4. The beginnings of the psychological treatment of politics

We introduce Merriam's classification to provide a contrasting example to the one developed by David Easton. Probably the most well-known recent classification system, Easton's analysis in his book *Political Science in the United States: Past and Present* (1993, 292) divides the history of political science into four stages:

- *Formal,* which emphasized the study of laws and constitutions
- *Traditional,* which focused on informal political processes, political parties, pressure groups

- *Behavioral,* which described and collected information about political processes
- *Postbehavioral,* which, as a reaction to behavioralism, has not yet achieved a central focus

Easton's categories are insightful and serve to illustrate trends in the development of political science in the United States for the past two centuries. They do not, however, comprehend the long and complex history of political science. In particular, they do not adequately reflect three characteristics of the discipline. First, contemporary political science is the product of centuries of development which cannot be reflected adequately in a framework that addresses only more recent periods. A typology that is comprehensive in chronological scope, therefore, is needed. Second, the discipline today addresses the same essential questions that it addressed millenniums ago, if in a different manner, and a typology that is comprehensive in conceptual scope would be more descriptive of the discipline as a whole. Finally, although American political science generates the largest share of published works today, political scientists around the world have contributed in many ways to the discipline. A new set of categories is needed, therefore, which is comprehensive not only in chronological and conceptual scope, but in geographic scope as well. This new set of categories will help us see more clearly the whole history of the discipline, which will in turn enable us to think more creatively about the discipline and to identify its significant moments.

To begin to construct this new and more comprehensive set of categories, let us look back across the history of the discipline. We find that the careful and systematic study of politics has progressed through seven great eras, each defined by two characteristics: (1) the objectives of the people who studied politics, and (2) the methods they employed to meet their objectives. A summary of the seven eras is presented in the following table:

Era	Time Span	Name of the Era:	The Objective of Observers of Politics . . .	The Predominant Method of Observers of Politics
❶	To 2000 BCE	Myth	Unity	Denial of Politics
❷	2000 BCE to 400 BCE	Politics	Individuality	Participation in Politics
❸	400 BCE to 400 CE	Philosophy	Good Government	Logic and Observation of Politics
❹	400 to 1500	Theology	Godly Government	Revelation and Reason about Politics
❺	1500 to 1900	History	Consensual Government	Rational Analysis of Political Experience
❻	1900 to 1970	Science	Facts	Observing Political Behavior
❼	1970 to ?	Eclecticism	Disciplinary Identity	Creative Synthesis of Methods & Data

The seven eras have been given the following names: Myth, Politics, Philosophy, Theology, History, Science, and Eclecticism. Placed on a time line continuum, the seven eras appear like this:

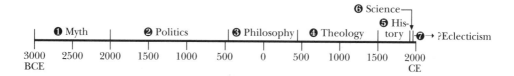

The Era of Myth (to 2000 BCE)

Archaeologists and anthropologists have discovered evidence for the proposition that there was once a time before politics, when a consciousness of politics, at least as we know it today, did not exist. At this early moment in history, human consciousness did not perceive social interactions as political in the way we do today. We will call this period the era of myth, because people lived according to myths, that is, narratives wherein gods expressed the creative forces of the universe. We use the term "myth" here in its classical sense rather than in its contemporary meaning. Today, a myth is a fictional story, something that is not true. In a classical sense, however, a myth is the opposite: it is complete or ultimate truth. In this sense, myth is a story that expresses our perception of an ultimate truth that is beyond our limited human capacity to understand fully.

Mircea Eliades' classic anthropological study *The Myth of the Eternal Return* (1971) explains that primitive people had a consciousness of the world around them that is much different from ours today. In this consciousness, life seemed to be "eternally returning" in cycles of day-night-day and spring-summer-fall-winter, instead of progressing from one point to another. Ancient religious practices, living patterns, and art have revealed patterns of consciousness which deny or reject three fundamental facets of political life as we know them:

- The existence of human beings as autonomous individuals
- A sense of time and of history
- A sense of the difference between good and evil

According to Eliade, "The chief difference between the man of the archaic and traditional societies and the man of the modern societies, with their strong imprint of Judeo-Christianity, lies in the fact that the former feels himself indissolubly connected with the Cosmos and the cosmic rhythms, whereas the latter insists that he is connected only with History" (Eliade 1971, iii). When a primitive person, for example, emerged from her cave in the morning, she experienced herself as an undifferentiated part of the cosmos as it unfolded around her. She was, along with the

rocks, the trees, the river, the sun, and the stars, an inseparable part of the continuing flow of life and death. According to Eliade, it would not have occurred to our
primitive woman to think of herself as an individual human being, distinct from
the motion and processes of life. She had no concept of time or of history, for life
appeared as an unending series of cycles, and, therefore, night turned to day and
back to night; winter, spring, summer, and fall followed winter, spring, summer,
and fall; and all life flowed and cycled in an uninterrupted rhythm.

According to Eliade, what is "real" to us today was not meaningful to primitive people, for whom there were two planes of existence: (1) a higher, transcendent, "sacred" realm of existence in which the gods are in the perpetual process of
creating the world, and (2) a lower realm, the "profane" world, made up of only
the ordinary acts of existence that had not been sanctified by ritual. Only the first,
the higher realm, constituted what was, for primitive people, truly real. Dances and
feasts, for example, were religious ritual activities that sanctified hunting, birth,
death, and other important aspects of life. As Eliade explains (1971, 3–27):

> Evidently, for the archaic mentality, reality manifests itself as force, effectiveness,
> and duration. Hence the outstanding reality is the sacred; for only the sacred *is*
> in an absolute fashion, acts effectively, creates things and makes them endure.
> . . . If we observe the general behavior of archaic man, we are struck by the fol-
> lowing fact: neither the objects of the external world nor human acts, properly
> speaking, have any autonomous intrinsic value. Objects acquire a value, and in
> so doing become real, because they participate, after one fashion or another, in
> a reality that transcends them. . . . We might say that the archaic world knows
> nothing of 'profane' activities: every act has a definite meaning—hunting, fish-
> ing, agriculture; games, conflicts, sexuality—in some way participates in the sa-
> cred. . . . The only profane activities are those which have no mythical meaning,
> that is, which lack exemplary models.

The real world, then, for primitive people, was the world of the sacred, which
they entered psychologically and spiritually by performing rituals. Every time they
performed a ritual, they recreated one of the original acts of the gods by which the
universe was created. Primitive people were, therefore, continually engaged, as
they performed their daily rituals, in participating in the original creative acts of
the universe. Eliade observes that "[I]n the particulars of his conscious behavior,
the 'primitive,' the archaic man, acknowledges no act which has not been previously posited and lived by someone else, some other being who was not a man.
What he does has been done before. His life is a ceaseless repetition of gestures initiated by others" (Eliade 1971, 4).

Since their true reality consisted in recreating original acts of the gods, primitive people did not perceive the passage of time as we do today. "Through repetition of the cosmogonic act, concrete time, in which the construction takes place,
is projected into mythical time, *in illo tempore* when the foundation of the world occurred" (Eliade 1971, 20). In this primitive consciousness, people saw the sun, the
moon, artifacts, and animals as deities. The creation of the universe was the center
of their religious concern. The only acts which had meaning were the original creative acts which brought the universe into being. The gods' creation of the universe
was a continuous process with no beginning and no end. Primitive people could

participate in the process of creation through religious ceremonies which reenacted the creative acts of the gods.

Because for primitive people reality consisted of being one with the universe, and because the only meaningful acts were those which repeated the cosmological creations of the gods, there was no conception of good and evil, no idea of morality. Trees, animals, the acts of the gods, other people were neither good nor evil. They simply existed. Primitive people, in this respect, were like newborn infants are today. In their first months of life, infants have no conception of good or bad. They see, hear, think, respond, explore, but they have no idea that things are good or bad until those concepts are taught to them.

When a consciousness of politics first began to appear to primitive people, it was perceived as a threat to their existence. To act politically, that is, to assert rights or attempt to claim power, was to be an individual, isolated from God and the warmth of life in the unified community, and operating in the realm of profane existence was unfamiliar and frightening. Primitive people, therefore, rejected politics in two primary ways. The first was to continue to seek unity through religion. Priesthoods developed to lead people in religious ceremonies that celebrated the creative acts of the gods, and many of these rituals continue today. Christian celebrations of the birth of Christ at Christmas and the resurrection of Christ at Easter, for example, are contemporary parallels to these rituals.

The second method of rejecting politics was and continues to be organizational hierarchy. Hierarchy is a method of arranging an organization in a strict configuration of leadership so that there is a definite chain of command in which every participant has a defined place. In a hierarchy, workers report to a supervisor, supervisors report to managers, managers report to executives, and executives report to a chief executive. Politics has to do with making decisions, with the struggle with others to help make the decisions that affect the life of the community; to the extent that everyone in a hierarchy obeys the orders of the person above him or her, politics is eliminated. No hierarchical organization can eliminate politics completely, of course, but hierarchy reduces the free flow of political action, and, in extreme cases, such as military operations in time of war, politics may be largely eliminated from daily life.

In comparison even with corporate life today, ancient organizations were strongly hierarchical. Emperors and kings ruled with divine sanction and with authority of life and death over their subjects. The greatest part of daily politics was eliminated.

The Era of Politics (2000 to 400 BCE)

We will call this time period the era of politics, not because it was more political than other eras, but because it was the era in which a consciousness of the nature, power, value, and dangers of politics, as we know them today at all levels of life (family, community, nation, world), was conceived.

During the previous period, the period of myth, people rejected the personal responsibility that comes through free and open politics and attempted to eradicate politics in society both through religious ceremony, which tied politics to their primitive consciousness, and through organizational hierarchy. The era of mythical consciousness came to an end in various places in the world at different times, but our most clearly recorded early examples are from Israel and Greece.

A consciousness of politics as we understand it first appeared as people developed an awareness of morality, of personal responsibility for good and evil. One of the earliest symbolic expressions of this dawning awareness was recorded by the ancient Hebrews in the Book of Genesis. The Garden of Eden was a world without good or evil. Adam and Eve were at peace with God, and the animal world knew no competition and strife. Then the world of peace with God was shattered. Adam and Eve ate the forbidden fruit, the fruit of the tree of the *knowledge of good and evil.* Symbolically, the knowledge of good and evil is the central dilemma of humanity. If we have no knowledge of good and evil, we cannot be held accountable for our actions. Because Adam and Eve received this knowledge, they were then responsible for the morality of their actions. Their moral eyes were opened. Their struggle began when they came to know good from evil but were not always capable of doing good. And so their children, Cain and Abel, fully possessed of human consciousness, struggled for power and for recognition from God, and politics was conceived. The story of Adam, Eve, Cain, and Abel tells symbolically how the transformation from nonpolitical consciousness to political consciousness took place.

Old Testament stories about the patriarchs (Abraham, Isaac, Jacob, Joseph) are full of political intrigue. In the story of Joseph, for example, Jacob's favorite son is sold into slavery by his jealous brothers and thrown into prison, only eventually to become, by interpreting dreams for the pharaoh, administrator of the Egyptian empire. Several generations later, the descendants of the Hebrews whom Joseph brought to Egypt become so powerful that the Egyptians, reacting from fear, enslave them and make them build the pyramids. Hearing the people cry out for freedom, God calls Moses to lead them out of Egypt to the promised land.

In his book *Exodus and Revolution* (1985), political scientist Michael Walzer explores the political implications of the biblical story of the Exodus. For Walzer (1985, 12–13), Exodus, perhaps the most famous and often repeated political liberation story of all time, marks the end of the mythical consciousness of cyclical time and the beginning of the modern concept of linear or historical time:

> A political history with a strong linearity, a strong forward movement, the Exodus gives permanent shape to Jewish conceptions of time; and it serves as a model, ultimately, for non-Jewish conceptions too. We can think of it as the crucial alternative to all mythic notions of eternal recurrence—and hence to those cyclical understandings of political change from which our word "revolution" derives. The idea of eternal recurrence connects the social to the natural world and gives to political life the simple closure of a circle: birth, maturity, death, and rebirth. The same story is enacted again and again; men and women and the timely deeds of men and women alike lose their singularity; one represents another in a system of correspondences that extends upward, hierarchically, into the mythic realm of nature and nature's gods. Biblical narrative generally, Exodus more particularly, breaks in the most decisive way with this kind of cos-

mological story-telling. In Exodus historical events occur only once, and they take on their significance from a system of backward- and forward-looking interconnections, not from the hierarchical correspondences of myth.

In the book of Exodus, the Hebrew God demands that the Hebrews reject the myth and rituals of primitive consciousness and look to a God who helped them create singular, nonrepeatable events that became chapters of a history of a progressive time in which the same creative events are not repeated over and over. The God of the Hebrews also demanded that the people take moral responsibility for their actions, to realize that their true humanity was fulfilled in being moral actors in an ongoing history which had a beginning and an end. Inasmuch as the Hebrews were now to accept the challenge of making their own history and to help decide their fates communally, the Hebrews were called by God to accept the challenge of politics: to treat each other morally while consciously accepting their individual and collective responsibility for building a society that would reflect the will of God in a new land. In *The Myth of the Eternal Return,* Mircea Eliade (1971, 104), anticipating Walzer, says of the God of Exodus:

> This God of the Jewish people is no longer an Oriental Divinity, creator of archetypal gestures, but a personality who ceaselessly intervenes in history, who reveals his will through events. . . . It may be said with truth that the Hebrews were the first to discover the meaning of history as the epiphany of God, and this conception, as we should expect, was taken up and amplified by Christianity.

Political consciousness in Israel developed, therefore, through a religious tradition in which individuals and the community as a whole were responsible to God for making moral choices. In Greece, consciousness of a political way of life had arrived by the time of the Homeric epics. Written probably around 1000 BCE, the Odyssey and the Iliad tell tales of the great Greek heroes of the Trojan War. In the following centuries, Greeks viewed these poetic renderings of heroism as expressing essential qualities of life, and together they constituted a sort of Greek historical bible, a new myth by which to live. In the Odyssey, Odysseus has a series of adventures in which he encounters multiheaded creatures, a Cyclops, and other supernatural beings. Constantly in the background are the "fates," which shape important aspects of the story, but which are entirely beyond human control. The Greeks of the Homeric era viewed life in the same way. Supernatural forces, the gods, the forces of nature, were believed to shape human life in important ways. The moral message of Homer's stories is that guidance from the gods was necessary for success in life.

The implications of the Homeric perspective on life are profound. To the extent that external forces control our lives, politics is irrelevant, for all our political efforts may come to nothing. Homer's characters are not entirely directed by fate, however, and the beginnings of political consciousness appear particularly in an emerging new view of hierarchy. There is an ongoing academic debate about the strength of hierarchy and the extent of democracy in the Greek army as it is portrayed in the Homeric poems. One side of the argument, which is propounded later by the fifth century BCE philosopher Socrates, holds that military life in

Homer's epics is authoritarian. When his rule is challenged by someone under his command, Odysseus says, in Book II of the Iliad, "Surely not all of us Achaians can be kings here. Lordship for many is no good thing. Let there be one ruler, one king, to whom the son of devious king Kronos gives the scepter and the right of judgment to watch over his people" (Illiad 2:204–6). But one proponent of the opposing interpretation, the idea that the Greek military exhibited definite democratic features, is American journalist I.F. Stone, who writes in *The Trial of Socrates* (1988, 34–35):

> When Odysseus has finally prevailed on everyone else to sit down at the assembly, only Thersites refuses to be silent. Despite Homer's invidious description of Thersites as a man of disorderly speech, he speaks here not only boldly, but succinctly and to the point. Odysseus replies with violence. In front of the whole assembly, he beats Thersites until he bleeds, humiliating him and threatening that if Thersites ever again dares "take the name of kings in your mouth," Odysseus will strip him naked before the assembly and send him "wailing to the swift ships."

In reply to Stone it may be noted, of course, that to be beaten bloody by a king is not exactly a sign of a vital democracy. Stone responds (1988, 21) to this point, however, by noting other features of Greek army organization:

> Agamemnon was not the absolute king the Socratics idealized. Instead, the Greek host before Troy already exhibited in embryo the features common to the polis and modern parliamentary and presidential systems. Agamemnon was the presiding officer. He was advised by a council of elders made up of aristocratic landowners and warriors. Below this council, there was a general assembly of the warriors. So the Iliad shows us not absolute kingship but a government of three branches, an Executive, a Senate, and an assembly of the "Commons."

Although the debate concerning the democratic features of Greek life around 1000 BCE may never be conclusively resolved, there is little doubt that a variety of conditions and trends in the following five hundred years led to the establishment of democracy in Athens in the century after 508 BCE. The first of these trends was that Greece, which had been ruled by Crete and other empires previous to this time, was left for long periods without interference from outside empires. A series of city states (polis) emerged, each developing a strong sense of independence. The typical Greek polis had a free market economy, few government agencies to interfere with trade, and a military based primarily on an independent militia comprised of citizens. The farmers of Athens, who became the backbone of the citizen class, were sufficiently wealthy to acquire their own shield and lance. Known as hoplites, these militia men fought fiercely in war and then returned immediately to their farms and families. Developing a sense of self-sufficiency within the unity of the polis, the hoplites attempted to gain from the oligarchic (wealthy, aristocratic) families a greater voice in making decisions in government.

Scientific discovery also fanned the emergent flames of democracy in Greece. Several influential philosopher-scientists came to Greece from Ionia, which is presently the nation of Turkey, and other areas of the Mediterranean. Thales of

Miletus became known as the first scientific philosopher. Accurately predicting an eclipse on May 25, 585 BCE, he introduced to the Greek world the idea that Homer did not adequately describe reality. For Thales (640–546 BCE) it was natural phenomena, rather than the activities of the gods, which explained events in the world. Accurate measurement and calculation were important for Thales, and he calculated the circumference of the world. Looking for the essential components of existence, Thales said the ground of the universe is water, which is fluid and changes into many forms.

A number of other sixth and fifth century (BCE) scientists, asking many of the same questions Thales had raised, came up with different answers. Anaximander (611–547 BCE) said that the fire in the physical universe and the fire of life in the human soul are of the same essential substance, and that the energy represented by fire is the basic element of existence. Anaximenes proposed that air, which can be visible as clouds or invisible, was the fundamental substance. Democritus provided an important concept for science when he developed atomic theory, claiming that atoms are those particles which are not divisible; have motion, extension, and mass; and are infinitely small.

The result of all these investigations was that the universe began to look less and less like the product of the actions of the gods and more and more like the result of the interaction of natural elements. This perception had theological and political consequences. Zenophenes, for example, who became known as the first major skeptic, reached the conclusion that we anthropomorphize our deities. In other words, we create gods in our minds who resemble human beings. Zenophanes claimed that there is only one god, and this god was essentially unlike man. Protagoras (500–430 BCE) rejected a theocentric view of the universe and declared that "man is the measure of all things."

These discoveries may appear inconsequential today, but at the time their political implications were revolutionary. If "man is the measure of all things," if "he" is in control of at least the social if not the physical environment, then "he" may have a sense of political efficacy. Efficacy is the belief that one's actions do actually make a difference. Voting studies in America and elsewhere have demonstrated that groups who have a high sense of political efficacy, in other words, groups of people who believe that their activities and votes count, are much more active in politics and have a much greater effect on the political system than those who believe their efficacy is limited. The Athenian hoplites began to believe that they could have a major and effective role in the governmental decisions that affected them. If they, not the gods, were the measure of all things, they were individually important. So in 508 and 507 BCE, when the Athenian aristocrat Cleisthenes offered the hoplites a strong role in government in return for their support, the hoplites were ready to accept.

From 508 to 507 BCE, Cleisthenes instituted a number of reforms which completed some developments already in progress. One of these was to give substantial power to a popular assembly. Any Athenian citizen could attend the assembly, and it was often crowded with as many as 6,000 citizens. Athens' poets and playwrights enjoyed freedom of speech similar to that of modern day political cartoonists, and the typical Greek democrat, always open to spoof and ridicule, is caricatured by Aristophanes (1969, 9–10) in his play *The Acharnians*. In the following sequence, a citizen waiting for the Assembly to convene complains about the leadership:

> There's a stated meeting of the Assembly called for dawn, and here's the Pnyx [the forum in which the assembly was held]—completely empty! Everybody's down at the Agora [the marketplace], gabbing, cackling, running away from the Masters-at-arms. Nobody's going to rope them into their civic duty. No, sir! The Executive Board hasn't come! Oh, it will, shoving and jostling—you know how—streaming down in a bunch to get the first bench; but they don't give a damn for peace and how to get it. Oh, Athens, Athens! So I come to the Assembly—as usual, first—and sit. But what's to do when you're all alone? Well, I sigh, I yawn, I stretch, sometimes I fart. I try to think of things to do. I write, I pluck out my hairs, I balance my books. I fix my eyes upon my fields and lust for peace. I loathe the stingy, greedy city. I long for my own ungrudging countryside, my generous village. . . . Good-bye to that! So here I am. By god, I'm ready, to boo, to interrupt, to heckle every speaker who dares to say a word on any subject but peace. Well, look! Here's the Executive Board—and it's noon. Didn't I tell you? Just what I was saying; every last one of them pushing to sit up front.

The reforms of Cleisthenes were both broad and deep. In addition to the popular assembly of all the citizens, a council of 500 was established as a permanent legislative body which could debate and formulate policy. Cleisthenes accomplished a major political reform when, overlooking the potentially divisive tribal groups that formed Athens, he established a system of ten new tribes, not defined by the old geographic boundaries but constituting new political units, each of which contained elements from the countryside and the city. By this reorganization, Cleisthenes was able to break down traditional political antagonisms and form a new sense of unity in which citizenship in the polis of Athens was the most important factor. In the Athenian process, members of the Council of 500 were chosen not by election, but by lot, 50 from each tribe, for one-year terms so that every citizen had the opportunity to share leadership at some time in his life. Ten archons, or administrative rulers, and 10 strategos, or generals, were also chosen. In addition, the heliaea became the centerpiece of the judicial system. It consisted of 6,000 jurors from whom juries of 51 to 1,501 were chosen.

Pericles (495–429 BCE), Cleisthenes' nephew, who became Athens' leader in the mid-fifth century, expanded democratic reforms and led Athens to the height of its wealth and power. Among the interesting procedures developed in classical Athens was *ostracism*, which means to banish. *Ostracism* comes from the word *ostraka*, which refers to shards of pottery on which the names of people to be ostracized could be scratched. When an ostracism was called, citizens would gather and write on an ostrakon the name of a person whom they wanted to ostracize. If at least 6,000 ostraka were cast, the person whose name most frequently appeared upon them was sent out of Athens for a period of ten years. The ostracized person could retain property but could not come to Athens or participate in its politics. Today, this procedure sounds almost barbaric, but at the time, ostracism was a solid step forward from the normal method of changing political regimes in the ancient world, which was violent revolution. Under ostracism a leader could be voted out of town so that an opposition group could install its leaders without problems caused by the former leadership, and the former leader retained his life. Ostracism is, therefore, an innovation in nonviolent regime change.

In some ways, such as citizens taking turns holding office, Athens was the most democratic government ever to exist in history. In other ways, however, the democracy was very limited. Citizenship was restricted to males born to citizen parents. Not only women, but large numbers of resident aliens and slaves, were excluded from any effective political participation. Citizens, in fact, made up less than twenty percent of the people of Athens.

The Era of Philosophy (400 BCE to 400 CE)

Among those enjoying democratic freedom of speech in fifth century BCE Athens was Socrates (480–399 BCE), a balding philosophic gadfly whose influence, along with his student, Plato's (427–347 BCE), upon the history of philosophy is difficult to overestimate. Socrates was democracy's greatest philosophic enemy (since Plato wrote the dialogues in which Socrates is the speaker, it is difficult to tell whose views are being recorded, so we shall treat the two philosophers as if they are the same author). Socrates (Plato) believed that democracy violated all principles of reason. He compared the Greek democrats to residents of a cave, chained to a wall, allowed to see only the shadows cast on the opposite wall by marionettes manipulated by politicians. Socrates believed that democratic freedom was merely an illusion. Greek democrats believed that in their assembly they could openly debate the great issues of the day and that they, as citizens, had the capacity to make intelligent decisions based on the struggle of competing ideas voiced in public. Socrates scoffed at this notion, arguing that the citizens were merely deluding themselves, deceived by great orators into thinking they were making decisions, whereas in reality they were merely manipulated into thinking what those in power wanted them to think.

Socrates proposed that the value of life was the human ability to seek and find the truth. Plato records in *The Republic* that Socrates was fond of saying "the unexamined life is not worth living." Truth could be found not through democratic discussion, but through a method known as the Socratic dialectic. The dialectic is a process of asking questions and testing the answers. Someone, for example, would propose a question to Socrates, such as, "Does not the worst evil for a state arise from anything that tends to rend it asunder and destroy its unity, while nothing does it more good than whatever tends to bind it together and make it one?" Socrates would then test this statement through a process of deductive logic in which statements are measured against their conformance to general principles. If a statement appeared to be true, Socrates might exclaim, "That is true!" Then, as other speakers added subsequent statements, a philosophy developed. The participants in this dialogue would reject statements which appeared to be false, in a process similar to the reasoning that occurs in mathematics. Socrates' knowledge of and affinity for geometry and similar forms of mathematical reasoning are evident in his remarks.

Socrates asserted that a higher realm, beyond the physically perceptible aspects of daily life, exists in which "forms," that is, perfect representations of physical objects, may be found. In other words, in this higher realm, there are forms of chairs, trees, animals, and people. A form of a person is a perfect person, more real than people on earth. It is almost as if forms are ideas in the mind of God, who then creates earthly men, women, trees, and animals, which are imperfect imitations of the forms. The function of philosophy, for Plato, is to develop wisdom, and the purpose of wisdom is the use of reason to perceive the forms. Only those in society who are the most intelligent, and who have been suitably educated, are able to perceive the forms, the perfect manifestations of all things. Since there is a form for everything that exists, there is a form for government. Since only a few select people can perceive the form for government and, therefore, know best how to rule, these gifted people should be made philosopher-kings. Plato's most famous dialogue, *The Republic,* contains Socrates' dialectical quest to define both justice and the best form of government, one which will result in a just society.

For Socrates and Plato, the best government is one which reflects the natural capacities and inclinations of humanity. People are composed of body, mind, and spirit (a spirited or courageous nature). Those ruled by their bodies seek sensual satisfaction first. Those ruled by their spiritedness seek military conquest. Those ruled by their minds, a small minority, seek the height of reason, and these obviously should rule the others. For Socrates, according to *The Republic,* everyone had a proper role to fill in society, and only those who were qualified, by virtue of their intelligence and leadership skills, could rule. When the proper people ruled, society experienced justice.

In a world in which everyone knows his or her place, and one person or a few make the decisions for all the rest, politics ceases to exist, and this is precisely what Plato intends. Rejecting the politics of Greek democracy of his day, Plato attempts to revive the conditions of the myth, the mental framework of primitive man, to build a more modern society. With an absolute hierarchy and a belief in forms—which take the place of the gods in a more sophisticated mind—Plato accomplishes an astounding feat: he translates the powerful primal needs of primitive psychology, which remain with us today as manifestations of the subconscious mind, into a rational mental framework acceptable to the modern world. For this accomplishment Plato is read with intense interest almost two and a half millenniums after his death. As Mircea Eliade has noted in *The Myth of the Eternal Return,* "Plato could be regarded as the outstanding philosopher of primitive mentality," that is, as the thinker who succeeded in giving philosophic currency and validity to the modes of life and behavior of archaic humanity (Eliade 1971, 34).

Aristotle was a student of Plato, but the differences perhaps more than the similarities between the approaches of the younger philosopher and his mentor have fascinated students for centuries. In a lecture on Aristotle, Barnard College political science professor Dennis Dalton points out how wonderfully the Renaissance painter Raphael captures the dispute between Plato and Aristotle in his famous painting "School of Athens."

In the center of this painting, Plato extends an index finger towards the heavens, indicating that truth and wisdom are to be found in the world of the forms.

Aristotle, to the contrary, extends his hand outward directly from his waist, indicating that truth is found not in the heavenly world of the forms but in the observation of physical reality in this world, and comes through living life in moderation. For Aristotle, Plato was guilty of going to extremes. In attempting to imitate the ideal world of the forms, Plato's philosophy led to the sanctioning of what seemed at the time to be outrageous concepts, such as communal property for the military class and even political equality for women.

While Plato had based his concept of human reasoning on mathematics, Aristotle (384–322 BCE), a physician and the son of a physician, based his philosophy on the natural sciences and observation of nature. Aristotle developed the system of classification of living organisms into phylums, genuses, and species that is still used in the science of biology, and as we can see in this excerpt from his *Politics* (1290b), he used the same methods to investigate government.

> If we aimed at a classification of the different kinds of animals, we should begin by enumerating the parts, or organs, which are necessary to every animal. These will include, for example, some of the sensory organs: they will also include the organs for getting and digesting food. . . . They will further include the organs of locomotion. . . . States too, as we have repeatedly noticed, are composed not of one but of many parts. One of these parts is the group of persons concerned with the production of food. . . . A second . . . is . . . occupied in the various arts and crafts. . . . A third part is what may be termed the marketing class; it includes all those who are occupied in buying and selling. . . . A fourth part is the serf class composed of agricultural laborers; and a fifth element is the defense force.

Rather than looking to the power of deductive reasoning to find the ideal form of government, Aristotle turned to inductive reasoning, beginning with observation. Recording features of some 350 Greek governments, both historical and contemporary, Aristotle sought to discover how existing forms of government worked and how their structures related to their strengths and weaknesses. Aristotle employed the same methods that he used in his investigation of biological organisms, classing governments into two types, each having three manifestations. Aristotle observed that there are (1) good governments, those that rule in the interest of all the classes of people in society, and (2) bad governments, those that rule in the interest of the ruling class only. Further, both good and bad governments may be composed of (a) one person, (b) a few persons, or (c) a majority, the poor masses of society. Good governments ruled by one person he called monarchies, good governments ruled by a few persons he called aristocracies, and good governments ruled by many he called polities or constitutional governments. Bad governments ruled by one person were tyrannies, bad governments ruled by a few persons were oligarchies, and bad governments ruled by many persons were democracies. Why did Aristotle consider democracy to be a bad form of government? He perceived democracies as governments run by the masses of the poor, who ruled in their own interests only. Polities, however, which were ruled by the majority and considered the interests of all classes, were rare, but could be the best form of government. As he says in the *Politics,* "We have now to consider what is the best constitution and the best way of life for the *majority* of states and men. . . . It is clear from our argument, first, that the best form of political society is one where power is vested in the middle class" (*Politics* 1295a). For Aristotle, the middle class was composed of those who had neither too much nor too little. Versed in the ways of moderation, they were best suited to govern the society as a whole.

Continuing to classify his observations carefully, Aristotle investigated many matters pertaining to political theory, including the causes of revolution (*Politics* 1302a):

> The principal and general cause of mind which disposes men towards change is the cause of which we have just spoken. There are some who stir up sedition because their minds are filled by a passion for equality, which arises from their thinking that they have the worst bargain in spite of being the equals of those who have got the advantage. There are others who do it because their minds are filled with a passion for inequality (i.e., superiority), which arises from their conceiving that they get no advantage over others (but only an equal amount, or even a smaller amount) although they are really more than equal to others. (Either of these passions may have some justification; and either may be without any.) Thus inferiors become revolutionaries in order to be equals, and equals in order to be superiors. (Aristotle 1302a)

Although to this point we have confined our discussion to Western thinkers, it is important to note that much was happening in the Eastern countries throughout the history of political thought as well. An interesting example of an Eastern political philosopher is Mencius (372–289 BCE), second only to Confucius in his philosophical leadership of Confucianism. Mencius was concerned to establish the principle, which also became the cornerstone of Western political thought in the Middle Ages, that the state is the product of divine inspiration. When asked who gave the Chinese empire to the emperor, Mencius answered, "Heaven gave it to him" (Bary 1966, 110). Reasoning much as Aristotle had about the origin of the state, Mencius asserted: "Men are in the habit of speaking of the world, the state. As a matter of fact, the foundation of the world lies in the state, the foundation of the state lies in the family, and the foundation of the family lies in the individual" (Bary 1966, 110). Mencius advocated humane government, and presaged Jesus' emphasis on service to humanity when he declared that in the affairs of the state, "the people rank the highest, the spirits of land and grain come next, and the ruler counts the least" (Bary 1966, 110).

The era of philosophy began as an attempt by Plato to eradicate democratic politics, if not all features of political life. Ironically, politics flourished throughout the era, finding eloquent theorists such as Cicero during the period of the Roman Republics and then coming under attack again during the time of the Roman empires.

The Era of Theology (400 to 1500)

In the fourth era of the development of political science, Western civilization in all its aspects reflected the social, philosophical, moral, and often the political dominance of the Roman Catholic Church. This period was marked by momentous theological struggles in which church leaders attempted to come to terms with both the spirituality of their faith and the hard realities of the world of practical politics.

From the beginning of the Middle Ages, the Catholic Church decisively rejected the apolitical and antipolitical implications and lessons of the teachings of Jesus Christ in favor of a philosophy, implied in the Old Testament and in the New Testament writings of the apostle Paul, which embraced political power. Because the theology of the Catholic Church dominated the study of politics in the Middle Ages in Europe, it is necessary to understand the Church's perspective on politics. To do this, we must first examine the teachings of Jesus, as presented in the four Gospels, and the way these teachings were understood by the early church.

Early in his ministry, according to the Gospel of Luke, Jesus announced that his primary mission was to announce the kingdom of God (or kingdom of heaven):

> And he came to Nazareth, where he had been brought up; and he went to the synagogue, as his custom was, on the Sabbath day. And he stood up to read; and there was given to him the book of the prophet Isaiah. He opened the book and found the place where it was written,
>
>> "The spirit of the Lord is upon me to preach good news to the poor.
>> He has sent me to proclaim release to the captives
>> and recovering of sight to the blind,
>> to set at liberty those who are oppressed,
>> to proclaim the acceptable year of the Lord."
>
> And he closed the book, and gave it back to the attendant, and sat down; and the eyes of all in the synagogue were fixed on him. And he began to say to them, "Today this scripture has been fulfilled in your hearing." (NIV Luke 4:16–22)

Most of the teachings of Jesus, as they are recorded in the Gospels, are in the form of parables about the qualities of the kingdom of God. In his actions, in his parables, and in his teaching, Jesus decisively announces that the kingdom of God is not of this world; it is not a political kingdom. At the end of his forty days in the wilderness, Jesus decisively rejects the "political temptation" to rule the political kingdoms of the world:

> And the devil took him up, and showed him all the kingdoms of the world in a moment of time, and said to him, "To you I will give all this authority and their glory; for it has been delivered to me, and I give it to whom I will. If you, then, shall worship me, it shall all be yours." And Jesus answered him, "It is written 'You shall worship the Lord your God and him only shall you serve.'" (NIV Luke 4:5–8)

Thereafter, Jesus purposely refutes any suggestion that he was attempting to seek political power. If the kingdom of heaven is not political, then what is it? According to Jesus' parables, one participates in the kingdom of heaven when one acts like the good Samaritan, when one gives his or her wealth to the poor, when one forgives debts, when one claims the lowest seat at the banquet table, when one washes another's feet, when one seeks humble service to others rather than honor. The kingdom of God, then, is everything that political kingdoms are not. The kingdom of heaven is not the struggle for power; it is the absence of the struggle for power. The kingdom of heaven is not jostling for privilege and the protection of one's interests; it is, in fact, a spiritual state in which one is indifferent to political power and its privileges. When the Pharisees approached Christ, attempting to trap him into either supporting tax payments to the Roman Empire (which the Jewish people abhorred) or rebelling against Roman authority, and thereby becoming a political figure, Jesus said "Render unto Caesar that which is Caesar's." This statement indicates that a coin bearing Caesar's image is of no special consequence to the kingdom of heaven, which recognizes neither wealth nor poverty as merit, but is concerned with things which the power of money does not represent. When one renders unto God that which is God's, one gives up one's political ambition, for what is owed to God is to love him with all one's heart, soul, and mind. There is little room left for accumulating political power when one is this dedicated to God.

This interpretation of the Gospels, which presents Jesus as a figure who cut though politics because he denied the eternal importance of politics, was prevalent in the early church during the first four centuries of the Christian era. Most Christians in these centuries declined to initiate rebellions, for they did not aim to seize political power. On many occasions, however, they refused to carry out acts of the Roman state which they believed contrary to the Kingdom of God. They refused to worship Caesar or to recognize any god but their own. For this lack of allegiance to the Roman state, they were often persecuted. Christians were not purposefully rebellious because rebellion was also a political act, and they were normally obedient to the Roman regime when it required things of them that did not conflict with their worship of God. The strongest biblical injunction to obey the laws of the state is found in Romans 13, verses 1–7: "All souls must place themselves in submission to the governing authorities. For there is no authority except by God" (Romans 13:1). Paul apparently did not intend this command to imply absolute obedience for two obvious reasons. First, he ends this passage with an admonition: "Pay back to everyone that which is owed: to one (owed) taxes, the taxes, to the one (owed) duty, the duty, to the one (owed) respect, the respect, to the one (owed) honor, the honor" (Romans 13:7). The implication of this statement is that loyalty to the state is limited to that which is owed, and that the state is not owed loyalty which conflicts with the will of God.

But while Paul insists that followers of Jesus fulfill certain civic duties, he strongly implies that the emperor is *not* owed worship, which is reserved for God; nor is the centurion owed obedience when he demands that a Christian stop believing or preaching the gospel. In fact, Paul, Peter, and other apostles spent much time in jail, where they were often placed for disobedience and where they wrote some their most famous letters; and all of the apostles but John reportedly were killed at the hands of those who were acting for the governing authorities. One of the most famous stories of the death of martyrs is that of the burning at the stake of Polycarp, an aging but courageous gentleman of Smyrna:

> And when the governor insisted, saying, "Take the oath, and I will let you go; revile Christ," Polycarp said,
> "For eighty-six years I have been his slave, and he has done me no wrong; how can I blaspheme my king who has saved me?"

When he (the governor) still insisted, and said, "Swear by the fortune of Caesar,"

"If you imagine that I will swear by the fortune of Caesar, as you say, and pretend not to know who I am, let me tell you plainly, I am a Christian. And if you want to learn the doctrine of Christianity, set a day and hear me."

The governor said, "Convince the people."

Polycarp said, "I thought you worth reasoning with; for we have been taught to pay suitable honor to governments and authorities, appointed by God, if it does us no harm; but as for these others, I do not think they are worth defending myself before them." (Goodspeed 1950, 250–251)

The kingdom of God, therefore, as seen by most of its early adherents, was not political, and the new religion was, therefore, apolitical or overtly antipolitical. Tertullian, a leading theologian of the first three centuries of Christianity, summed up his belief in the apolitical nature of the kingdom of God by asking, "What indeed has Athens to do with Jerusalem?" a question which contrasts Athens, the symbol of politics, with Jerusalem, the holy city.

But herein lies a paradox. The existence in society of an antipolitical religion had serious political implications. Society was concerned that people whose first loyalty was to God, people who refused to take up the sword and instead followed Christ's admonitions to nonviolence, might be unreliable citizens, especially in times of emergency or war, when their loyalty and help were needed by their fellow citizens.

In the year 325 CE, an unexpected event occurred. The Roman emperor Constantine converted to Christianity. Whereas previously Christians had been officially persecuted, now they found themselves enjoying the official endorsement of the Roman Empire. They began to believe that, perhaps, now that the Empire was officially Christian, the long awaited return of Christ would unfold before their eyes. But their enthusiasm was short lived. In 410, Alaric and the Goths conquered Rome, and Roman Christians, who had been reluctant to fight in any political cause, were blamed for the disaster. It was said that they were not good citizens because they gave allegiance first to their God and only second, if at all, to the state.

The very vitality of the Catholic Church itself seemed at stake. The Church, with its tradition of pacifism and indifference to politics, had no apparent basis upon which to respond to this threat. At this critical point, a Catholic Bishop in the town of Hippo in North Africa wrote a work that was to reject the antipolitical teachings of Jesus and permanently revolutionize and politicize the Church. Shortly after the fall of the empire, Augustine published *City of God*, in which he divided human experience into two cities, the city of God and the city of this world. According to Augustine, two cities have been formed by two loves: "love of self, even to the contempt of God; the heavenly by the love of God, even to the contempt of self." The city of God was the spiritual realm in which the virtues of Jesus were practiced. Only Christians, selected by God through his grace, were citizens of this realm. Only Christians could know the joy of the love of God. Everyone else, excluded from the kingdom of God for reasons known only to God, were citizens only of this world, in which the bitter conflicts of politics were fought. The critical point of Augustine's theology is that Christians, though they are citizens of the city of God, are also citizens of the kingdoms of this world. They are placed in this world by God to interact in it. As citizens of this world, they are good and loyal subjects of the governments whose protection they enjoy. As such, they must fight to defend their earthly kingdoms when it is just to do so. Augustine then develops a doctrine of a just war. Rejecting Christ's admonition to his disciples to reject violent conflict, Augustine asserts that wars may be justly waged by Christians under several specific conditions, including self-protection, the correcting of wrongs, and the establishment of peace.

The Catholic Church warmly received Augustine's doctrine, because through it the Church gained a rationale for exercising political power. In the minds of many people, however, the Church paid a high price for this power, gaining the kingdom of the world, the kingdom of politics, but losing the kingdom of God. Although there have been individuals throughout the history of the Church who practiced the apolitical faith of Christ, the Church establishment followed Augustine's doctrine and pursued political power.

For the next 1,000 years, the Church increased its financial and political power. At a time when land was the primary source of wealth, the Church was the largest land owner in Europe. The year 1000 was important, for many Christians believed references in the Book of Revelation suggesting that Jesus would return at the time of the millennium (one thousand years). When he did not return, and when feudal wars and plagues added to their desperation, many began to question their faith and the Church. "Millenarian" movements, which claimed the coming of the millennium signaled the return of Christ, spread across Europe, taking many forms but sharing some common themes. They would often begin, for example, when someone emerging from contemplation in a wilderness claimed to be the resurrected Christ or John the Baptist or another prophet with a mission from God. The millenarian prophets would march from town to town, gaining bands of followers as they preached a coming transformation of the world. Some of these prophets and their followers became flagellants, who would bloody themselves in public, repenting of their sins before God and crying out for his mercy. Others turned their anger outward, killing village priests they thought, in their resentment at the wealth and power of the church, were agents of Satan. The millenarians also robbed and burned Jewish settlements, killing many along the way. The millenarian prophets justified their actions by claiming to have received direct revelation from God.

Alarmed by these developments, the Church nevertheless could not reject revelation as a source of morality. To counter the depredations of the millenarians, the Church fathers claimed that reason was also the voice of God and that mob violence violated the bounds of reason. Thomas Aquinas, one of the scholars helping to start Europe's great universities, provided a rationale by which the Church could integrate reason into its doctrine of revelation. In his *Summa Theologica,* Aquinas argued that the ability to reason is a gift from God for human use to understand his purpose. Revelation, whether in the form of scripture or voiced announcements of God's appointed speakers in the Church, is completely compatible with reason. Aquinas thereby maintained the Church's claim to revelation while allowing it to develop a reasoned philosophy which helped to consolidate the Church's power.

Aquinas's philosophic method is of great importance. He was a leading figure in the scholastic movement, which in the thirteenth century discovered for Christianity the manuscripts of Aristotle that Islamic scholars had known for years. Aquinas combined Aristotle's scientific-dialectical method of reasoning with Christ's revelation of the kingdom of heaven. Aristotle believed that human beings are inherently political and that developing their political talents was the essence of social behavior. In combining Aristotle's politics with the New Testament, Aquinas integrated into the Church's theology a rationale for Christians to be highly political and, at the same time, obedient to the authority of government. In the following passage from the *Summa Theologica,* Aquinas presents his rationale for monarchy. His argument sounds very much like Aristotle, and his political goal, which is unanimity and peace, is directly inspired by Jesus, the "Prince of Peace."

> The aim of any ruler should be directed towards securing the welfare of that which he undertakes to rule. . . . Now the welfare and safety of a multitude formed into a society lies in the preservation of unity, which is called peace. If this is removed, the benefit of social life is lost and, moreover, the multitude in its disagreement becomes a burden to itself. The chief concern of the ruler of a multitude, therefore, is to procure the unity of peace. . . . Now it is manifest that what is itself one can more efficaciously bring about unity than several— just as the most efficacious cause of heat is that which is by nature hot. Therefore the rule of one man is more useful than the rule of many. . . . This is also evident from experience. For provinces or cities which are not ruled by one person are torn with dissensions and tossed about without peace. (De Regime Principum 1267, II)

Because the Church represents a higher realm (spirituality), reasoned Aquinas, the Church should be able at least to advise secular leaders strongly upon important temporal political questions, if not actually settle them.

The Era of History (1500 to 1900)

> *History without political science has no fruit;*
> *Political science without history has no root.*
> —Sir John Robert Seeley (1896)

In 1858, in an address he made upon assuming the first chair in political science at an American university, Francis Lieber had this to say about the importance of history to political science (1881, 23):

> Political science treats of man in his most important earthly phase; the state is the institution which has to protect or check all his endeavors, and, in turn, reflects them. It is natural, therefore, that a thorough course of this branch should become, in a great measure, a delineation of the history of civilization, with all the undulations of humanity. . . . Need I add that the student, having passed

through these fields and having viewed these regions, will be the better prepared for the grave purposes for which this country destines him, and as a partner in the great commonwealth of self-government? If not, then strike these sciences from your catalog.

We designate the fifth era of political science (1500–1900) the era of history
because the primary method of understanding politics throughout this period was
to learn lessons from history and then attempt to apply them to politics. Further,
the goal of most serious students of politics during this period was not the study of
politics for its own sake but, rather, the study of politics for a purpose: applying the
lessons of history to achieve better government. Many of the most important works
of the period were philosophical in approach, and focused on legal issues, but
these discussions were almost always tested by the lessons of history. For the most
important thinkers of this period, the type of government sought is consensual government, that is, government in which the people who are ruled agree to the extent, limits, and character of the power given to the authorities.

This era begins with the person often credited with ushering in modernity,
Nicolo Machiavelli (1469–1527). "Modernity" is the period marked by the end of
the Church's domination of thought and institutions that defined the Middle Ages,
and the beginning of the time when secular or nonreligious thought and institutions became preeminent. Machiavelli's work *The Prince* (1513) is a classic of modern political realism. Machiavelli, a senior government official in Florence, Italy,
who had lost his position when the Medicis came to power, wrote *The Prince* for
Lorenzo de Medici in hopes of gaining the ruler's favor and being reinstated in his
previous position. Rejecting the works of Thomas Aquinas and the scholastic movement, which speak about government only as it *should* be, *The Prince* talks about government as it *is*. Machiavelli advises Lorenzo to rule with calculating shrewdness,
to appear to be the champion of virtues such as honesty and fairness, but never to
draw back from being deceitful and ruthless when it is necessary. Machiavelli provides many lessons from history to support his advice, such as the following one
about an Italian Machiavelli admired, the Duke of Milan (1979, 99–100):

> After the Duke had taken Romagna and had found it governed by powerless
> lords who had been more anxious to plunder their subjects than to govern
> them, and had given them reason for disunity rather than unity, so that the en-
> tire province was full of thefts, fights, and of every other kind of insolence, he
> decided that if he wanted to make it peaceful and obedient to the ruler's law it
> would be necessary to give it good government. Therefore, he put Messer
> Remirro de Orco, a cruel and able man, in command there and gave him com-
> plete authority. This man, in little time, made the province peaceful and united,
> and in doing this he had made for himself a great reputation. Afterward, the
> Duke decided that such excessive authority was no longer required, for he was
> afraid that it might become despised; and he set up in the middle of the
> province a civil court with a very distinguished president, wherein each city had
> its own counselor. And because he realized that the rigorous measure of the past
> had generated a certain amount of hatred, he wanted to show, in order to purge
> men's minds and to win them to his side completely, that if any form of cruelty
> had arisen, it did not originate from him but from the harsh nature of his min-

ister. And having come upon the opportunity to do this, one morning at Cesena he had Messer Remirro placed on the piazza in two pieces with a block of wood and a bloody sword beside him. The ferocity of such a spectacle left those people satisfied and amazed at the same time.

In the midst of the English Civil War of the 1640s, yet another prominent political scholar arose. Thomas Hobbes wrote *Leviathan* as a systematic examination of the origin of government and the proper approach to rule. Written midst a violent conflict in which life indeed seemed "solitary, poore, nasty, brutish and short," Hobbes proposed that maintaining order in society was the primary role of government. Contrary to theologians who had assumed that government is ordained and established by God, Hobbes said that government comes not from God but from men. Human beings, in their natural condition before they become civilized, which Hobbes called a state of nature, are characteristically in conflict with one another. They come together and form a government in order to protect themselves from violence. Hobbes proposed that citizens should enter into what he termed a social contract with a leviathan, a powerful ruler who would provide security in return for their pledge of allegiance and assignment of the right to rule. For Hobbes, as with Machiavelli, human history, not the action of God, provides the framework for understanding politics.

Half a century after Hobbes published *Leviathan*, John Locke further developed Hobbes' concept of the social contract. For Locke, government was established by the consent of the people it rules in order to secure "life, liberty, and property." Writing during the nonviolent English revolution of 1688, Locke had much more faith than Hobbes did that people could secure a wide range of rights, especially those that allowed them to prosper economically. Locke argued that a social contract is no longer valid if broken by the ruler, and that, once the ruler violates his people's trust, they have the right of revolution—a concept which had a substantial influence on Thomas Jefferson and the signatories to the American Declaration of Independence. Locke's approach to the study of politics, like that of Hobbes before him, was to draw lessons from history and construct a philosophy of government based upon the consent of the people.

Karl Marx, the founding father of communism, is discussed in more detail in Chapter 4. It is important to note here, however, that Marx proclaimed he was the first, Machiavelli, Hobbes, and Locke notwithstanding, to base his analysis of politics not upon deductive philosophy but upon observation of what was actually going on in history. Marx reported that he had perceived the major trend of history, a dialectical movement of change propelled by class conflict in which the proletariat (the working class) would eventually overthrow the bourgeoisie (the middle class) just as the bourgeoisie had overthrown the feudal aristocracy centuries earlier. Marx's most lasting contribution to the development of political science is his emphasis on class conflict as the fundamental cause of political events.

An examination of many other theorists such as Edmund Burke, John Stuart Mill, and Friedrich Nietzsche, who have made important contributions to our understanding of politics, will be included under a variety of appropriate headings in the upcoming chapters. Before proceeding with our discussion of them, however, we shall complete our overview of the history of the development of the study of politics by turning to a discussion of the teaching of politics in American universities in the years leading to recognition of political science as a discipline.

According to Anna Haddows' *Political Science in American Colleges and Universities: 1636–1900* (1969), a remarkable study of the early history of the discipline, "Ethicks" and "Politicks" were discussed in Harvard classes as early as 1642. Politics was a topic of discussion in history classes throughout the colonial period, and one of the earliest texts was Grotius' *De Jure Belli et Pacis,* published in 1625, "in which," so Grotius claims, "are explain'd the Laws and Claims of Nature and Nations, and the Principal Points that relate either to Publick Government, or the Conduct of Private Life." The writings of French political theorist Jean Jacques Rousseau were assigned in classes at the College of William & Mary in 1798, and not long after that Locke and Hobbes were being read there, and, as Haddow notes, "The College of William and Mary claims the distinction of having actually established the first American professorship of law, as a result of the changes instituted by Governor Jefferson and President Madison in 1779" (Haddow 1969, 87). Masters theses at Harvard from 1770 to 1791 included the following titles (Haddow 1969, 107):

- Is the Federal System the Best Fitted, Above All Other Human Institutions, for Fighting a Royal Tyrant?
- Does a Democratic Form of Government Contribute More Than Any Other to Preserve the Liberty of the People?
- Is It More Necessary in a Republic Than in Any Other Form of Government that Young Men Should Be Instructed in Political Science?
- Is Public Virtue the Best Security of Republican Liberty?
- Is a Government Despotic in Which the People Have No Check on the Legislative Power?

The first chair of history and political science at an American university was awarded to Francis Lieber at Columbia University in May 1857. In 1876, Johns Hopkins became the first university to establish a political science department. In 1880, a graduate school of political science began to enroll students at Columbia University, and when the University of Chicago opened in 1892 the Department of Political Science was one of its original twenty-three departments. Finally, in 1903, the American Political Science Association was established at the annual meeting of the American Historical Association at Tulane University.

From earliest conception, the role of political science at American universities was not only to advance the knowledge of politics, but also to equip students to be good citizens and to resolve the many difficult issues that politics entail. As Francis Lieber put it in 1858,

> One of the means to insure liberty—that difficult problem in history . . . is the earnest bringing up of the young in the path of political truth and justice, the necessity of which is increased by the reflection that in our period of large cities man has to solve, for the first time in history, the problem of making a high degree of general and individual liberty compatible with populous cities (Lieber 1993, 26–27).

Haddow (1969, 249–251) notes that some of the most popular political science textbooks of the nineteenth century included:

The Federalist Papers
Alexis de Tocqueville's *Democracy in America* (1935)
Theodore Dwight Woolsey's *Political Science* (1878)
Woodrow Wilson's *The State* (1889)
John W. Burgess' *Political Science and Comparative Constitutional Law* (1890).
Woodrow Wilson, *The State: Elements of Historical and Practical Politics* (1918)
Woodrow Wilson, *Congressional Government* (1885)
James Bryce, *The American Commonwealth* (1912)
Frank J. Goodnow, *Politics and Administration* (1900)

The first major political science journals appeared during this period. *The Political Science Quarterly* was established at Columbia University in 1886; the University of Pennsylvania began publishing *Annals of the American Academy of Political and Social Science* in 1890. The *American Political Science Review* began publication in 1906. By the turn of the twentieth century, several departments were issuing doctoral degrees, and today they number one hundred and seventeen.

The Era of Science (1900 to 1970)

By the turn of the century, the goal of many leading political scientists in the country was to establish political science as an independent, scientifically acceptable discipline within the social sciences. Through inductive, accurate observation of political behavior, they ushered in the discipline's sixth era: the era of science. Their first task was to gain a new perspective on politics and political movements. Their second task was to break away from confinement to the methods of their parent discipline, history, and to seek a new place among the other disciplines—philosophy, law, and economics—from which they had borrowed much.

Gaining a new perspective on politics entailed seeing things differently from both European political scientists and American politicians. Some of the most interesting commentaries on American politics and political scientists have been written by Europeans. Political science students today normally become familiar with Alexis de Tocqueville's *Democracy in America* (1835), for example, at some time in their undergraduate studies. In courses in American Political Thought they are often introduced to James Bryce's *The American Commonwealth* (1912). Following in the tradition established by Tocqueville and Bryce, British political analyst Bernard Crick, in his book *The American Science of Politics* (1960), points out that the development of political science at the beginning of the twentieth century was in part a response to the progressive agrarian, labor, and educational reform movements which characterized the era. Crick notes how the reform movements of American politics constituted a development that was fundamentally different from the ideological and doctrinal struggles of Europe. Whereas the European movements sought to create collective national identities under strong dictatorial communist regimes, American progressives directed their energies to an ideal of individualism. Even so, says Crick (1960, 188), American political scientists, reacting to the reforms, began to see the political process differently from the ways in which the leaders of the movements viewed them: "Progressive reformers might still try to hold fast to the ultra-individualism of direct democracy, but the new political scientists began to see politics as a contest for marginal privilege by a great many pressure groups, mostly regional and economic rather than primarily ideological and doctrinal."

Because American political scientists were beginning to see politics differently both from Europeans and from the leaders of the reform movements, American political science began to develop a unique character. As Farr and Seidleman note in their thorough history of the discipline, turn-of-the-century political scientists did share with reformers a desire to have the knowledge they gained become "an instrument for change in society" (Farr & Seidelman 1993, 107–112).

In the first decade of this century, political scientists spent much of their energies in comparing the histories of civic and cultural institutions, a method of studying politics which became known as "formalism." They believed themselves to be focusing upon the same general phenomena that were studied by historians and economists, but from a different perspective, which was described by W.W. Willoughby in 1903. Willoughby noted that the discipline at that time was composed of three studies: (1) political theory or philosophy, (2) public law, and (3) forms and functions of government and administration (Willoughby 1993, 60). All three of these areas of study were grounded in the methods of historians. In fact, the APSA had its origins in the American Historical Association, many of whose members taught political history and political science courses. The founding of the APSA occurred at a joint meeting of the American Historical Association and the American Economic Association on December 30, 1903. At this meeting Frank J. Goodnow, professor of administrative Law at Columbia University, was elected President. The first vice-presidents were Woodrow Wilson (later President of the United States), Paul S. Reinsch, and Simeon E. Baldwin.

By 1908, however, a reaction against formalism began to brew. Arthur Bentley, one of the leaders of the "revolt against formalism," proposed that the proper focus of the discipline is upon the political process, that is, the competition for power and influence among interest groups. From the founding of APSA to the end of the first World War, two notable developments within the discipline took place.

The first trend of the World War I period was a direct result of the war itself. Championed most notably by Woodrow Wilson, a movement for world peace started that became known as political idealism. World War I was far more gruesome and deadly than any previous war in history. For the first time, submarines roamed unseen beneath the seas, sinking passenger, freight, and military vessels. Tanks appeared on the battlefield, and the force of artillery became far more effective and deadly. The technology of the machine gun far exceeded the intelligence of the general officers of armies on both sides, who sent their soldiers in wave after wave up over the tops of the trenches into the face of machine gun fire for no effective purpose. Political idealists such as Woodrow Wilson believed that the technology of war was advancing so quickly that soon there would be weapons capable of destroying the entire human race. They were correct in their predictions, for it was only twenty-seven years after the signing of the treaty of Versailles, ending the First World War, that the first atomic bombs were dropped on Hiroshima and Nagasaki, effectively marking the end of the second World War.

The idealists reasoned that, if war would shortly be so destructive as to end humanity altogether, an alternative to war must be found. The League of Nations was Wilson's answer. Wilson hoped that a community of national leaders, led by the Western democracies, could come together to resolve disputes peacefully and enforce a ban on war. Wilson's hopes, of course, were not to be realized. Wilson failed to gain the Senate's approval for United States' participation, and the League that was established was far less effective than it would have been with strong American support. By the late 1930s, Germany, Italy, and Spain had installed Nazi or Fascist regimes, and the Soviet Union's communist government was well entrenched and carrying out a campaign of terror against its own citizens. One effect of these events upon the discipline of political science was to cast doubt, in the minds of American political scientists, on the heretofore unassailable notion of the permanence of democracy. Under the weight of these disappointments, political idealism faded, and by the mid-1950s the American realist movement, which believed in a strong military and active intervention in world affairs, had secured its domination of international political thought.

The second notable development after World War I was a quest for the basis for a scientific method of political study. Overshadowed by the events surrounding the war, the quietly developing strategies of political scientists blossomed in the 1920s in a series of activities.

Three national conferences on the Scientific Study of Politics were held in the early 1920s. Research into political attitudes began to reveal that, when it came to politics, the average citizen was neither very rational nor very well-informed. Political attitudes became the primary focus of research, and as political science began producing information of interest to practical politics, political scientists began to have a more active role in government. Charles Merriam, for example, the most prominent political scientist of the 1920s, became an advisor to President Roosevelt. An early leader of what became known as the behavioralist movement, Merriam taught many of the twentieth century's leading political scientists during his tenure at the University of Chicago.

In an article entitled "Recent Advances in Political Methods," published in 1923 in *American Political Science Review* (APSR 1923, 17:274–95) Merriam noted several trends in political science at that time:

- A shift from philosophical *a priori* or deductive reasoning to pragmatism
- Generation of scientific studies in criminology
- A continuation of historical inquiry into the development of political institutions
- Comparative descriptions of political institutions
- Increased observation and description of the actual processes of government

• Increased use of surveys as an instrument of data collection
• New interest in the political applications of psychology

For many political scientists, the period from 1920 to 1950 was a struggle to determine what political *science* was all about, to develop a consensus on a concept of the science of politics and a set of methods such as had been achieved in other social sciences, especially economics. It was a task that called for imagination, energy, and a certain boldness of thought—qualities that, unfortunately, seemed in short supply in the country's universities during the middle years of the century. In *The Bias of American Political Science* (1940), Benjamin E. Lippincott described the reluctance among conservative faculty members, who felt vulnerable from a lack of financial independence, to bring forth new ideas. Lippincott complained also that far too little of the knowledge gained in the study of economics was being integrated into the study of political science. A third problem with the discipline, as Lippincott (1993, 157) explained, was that an extreme adherence to empiricism had led to a dearth of theory:

> In view of our conception of the scientific method, it is hardly surprising that political science has restricted its scope so largely to the study of law, organization, structure, and machinery of government. Most political scientists have been exponents in some degree or other of empiricism, and empiricism leads to a concentration on these aspects. Empiricism worships two doctrines: first, that if you collect all the relevant facts and classify them, they will speak for themselves (i.e., laws or principles will emerge somehow automatically); second, that preconceived theories or ideas about the facts are not only unnecessary but positively dangerous. . . . Hostility to theory has meant that political scientists would describe our legal and political arrangements rather than explain them. . . . The truth is the empiricist is a victim of the illusion of objectivity, which must prevent him from being a thoroughgoing scientist. . . . The political scientist, to speak in more general terms, is guilty of two sins: a sin against reason and imagination, and a sin against courage. His sin against reason and imagination explains his failure to search beyond empiricism to a more creative scientific method, it explains his failure to widen the scope of his inquiries, and it explains his failure to transcend his middle-class assumptions. His sin against courage explains his easy acceptance of an autocratic system of government in his own bailiwick, although such government is contrary to the best thought of his science.

Criticisms such as this led to the birth of a new movement in political science called behavioralism. From 1950 to 1970 political science was dominated by the debate between the behavioralists and the traditionalists. Leading traditionalists, who preferred the historical, philosophical, and institutional approaches of previous generations, will be discussed in detail in Chapter 8, and, therefore, will not be discussed here.

Leading behavioralist David Easton notes in *Political Science in the United States Past and Present* (1991) that *behavioralism* should not be confused with *behaviorism:* "Political science has never been behavioristic, even during the height of its behavioralistic phase. Behaviorism refers to a theory in psychology about human behavior and has its origins in the work of J.B. Watson" (Easton 1991, 278).

Describing the behavioral movement in which he had played an important role, Easton identifies several characteristics of behavioralism which make it distinct from earlier developments in the history of political science. Behavioralism believes, according to Easton (1991, 278–79), that "discoverable uniformities in human behavior" can be "confirmed by empirical tests," including "quantification whenever possible," which are "value-free or value-neutral" and place "emphasis on pure theory as against applied research."

In 1961, prominent behavioralist and Yale political scientist Robert Dahl, in an article entitled "The Behavioral Approach in Political Science: Epitaph for a Monument to a Successful Protest," noted the success of the behavioralist revolution in political science and outlined some of the causes for its rise. Among these were the efforts of Charles Merriam, the influx of European scholars in the 1930s, the practical experiences of scholars who worked in government positions in World War II, the Social Science Research Council, the survey as a research tool, and philanthropic foundations (Dahl 1961).

The Era of Eclecticism (1970 to Present)

"a new political science for a world itself quite new"
—Tocqueville, *Democracy in America* (1835)

In the 1960s, political science entered an era that Easton (1969, 61) has called the postbehavioral era:

> What I have called the postbehavioral revolution—a name generally used for this next phase—began during the 1960s and is still with us today. It represents a deep dissatisfaction with the results of behavioralism but has not led to the abandonment of scientific method in political science. The postbehavioral movement, in its broadest meaning, represented the awakening of the modern world to the dangers of rapid and unregulated industrialization, ethnic and sexual discrimination, worldwide poverty, and nuclear war.

Although David Easton has called the present period in the development of political science the postbehavioral era, the time has come to give this era a new name. Political science is now in the process of attempting to define its own identity, to understand its place and role in the world. The label "postbehavioral" does not describe the character of the present era, except to say that it falls chronologically after the behavioral era. A more specific term, which aptly describes the character of the present stage of development of the discipline, can help political scientists better understand their challenges and opportunities for contributing to the broader human search for knowledge.

Anyone who studies the vast array of subjects being studied and methodologies employed within what is called political science will quickly see that the one term which most accurately describes the present state of the discipline is *eclectic*. This means that, instead of having a single method and focus, political science is currently reaching out to virtually every branch of knowledge, borrowing ideas, combining concepts in new ways, and creating a study which is fascinating in its variety and fantastic in its creative breadth. In the pages that follow, in which only a small and roughly representative sample of studies being conducted in the discipline are described, you will read about many ideas that have originated in political science, but also about many more that were first given expression in economics, history, psychology, education, business, biology, sociology, literature, physics, philosophy, law, and other disciplines.

Some political scientists will be hesitant to adopt the term *eclectic* for fear it might imply a lack of internal cohesion and originality on the part of political scientists. But this hesitation must be overcome for two reasons. First, it is more honest to describe the discipline as it is than to avoid what at first may appear to be an unfavorable label. Second, and more important, eclecticism is a powerful approach to developing a discipline. Astronomers have told us that over the span of thousands of centuries galaxies expand and contract in regular cycles. Shrinking to small masses with incredible densities, they then explode in a myriad of new constellations. Studies of the history of science show that academic disciplines also expand and contract in reasonably predictable cycles. As established methods or approaches (called "paradigms") become accepted, disciplines contract in the types of studies that are conducted. As paradigms fall apart, a flood of new ideas compete to build the new accepted method. For example, while historical formalism was the dominant mode of study of politics early in this century, it fell to scientific challenges in the 1920s. Behavioralists gained ascendancy in the 1950s, but by the 1990s a new profusion of approaches and concerns had emerged.

We are now in a period between paradigms, which is to say there is no dominant accepted method or approach but rather many that are competing for attention. While this transitional period may appear to be a state of confusion, it is actually vibrant with creative potential. In fact, no period in the history of the study of politics has been more challenging or exciting. This period, the Era of Eclecticism, is the subject of much of the remainder of this book. It is well under way. You are invited to participate.

3

The Great Issues of Political Science

The issues can be stated very briefly: Who will be controlled? Who will exercise control? What type of control will be exercised? Most important of all, toward what end or purpose, or in the pursuit of what value, will control be exercised?

—Carl Rogers

How Shall We Get Along Together?

The great issues of politics, from one generation to the next, continue to evolve from attempts to answer one simple question: how shall human beings get along together? The question may be simple, but attempts to answer it are not, because this question immediately raises several other fundamental questions:

Who are we? (the question of identity)
What are our capabilities and limitations? (the question of human nature)
When do we need to cooperate? (the question of unity)
How shall we cooperate? (the question of community)
What aspects of life belong to each of us alone? (the question of individuality)
What should we be able to do or decide for ourselves? (the question of freedom)
What decisions are to be made that will affect us all? (the question of authority)
Who will make the decisions that affect us all? (the question of representation)
What must we do as citizens? (the question of responsibility)
How shall we preserve what we value? (the question of order)
What is fair? (the question of justice)
Shall some have more benefits from society than others? (the question of equality)

Many similar questions may be asked, but most questions about government and politics relate directly to one of the items on this list. Systematic inquiries into the great issues of politics often begin with a discussion of political identity, that is, the attempt to define who and what we are as human beings.

Politics and Human Nature

Historically, the discussion of the great issues of politics is filled with reasoned commentaries, violent arguments, analytical dissertations, and vituperative ideological harangues. Reading these discussions, we immediately become aware that people have different views of what politics should be all about because they hold different assumptions concerning what people are all about. Are people basically good, and only occasionally greedy and selfish, or are people mostly self-centered, and occasionally altruistic? Are people born open, kind, and generous, only to be subsequently corrupted by dysfunctional families and corrupt social institutions, or are they born with such acquisitive, selfish natures, that they have to be taught civility and "socialized" in order to get along with others? The manner in which one answers these questions will determine one's views toward a wide range of political issues.

These questions about the essential character of humanity have been discussed for centuries. The Old Testament declares that we are born into sin and separation from God because we are children of Adam, who violated God's will and sowed the seed of sin into all generations. Philosopher Jean Jacques Rousseau, to the contrary, declared that we are "born free," yet, because of faulty societal institutions and cultural practices, we are "everywhere in chains."

One of the most interesting recent explanations of the differences between these two perspectives has been written by political commentator Thomas Sowell. Underlying the varying discussions of political ideology and philosophy, says Sowell, are two different visions of human nature: the constrained vision and the unconstrained vision.

The constrained vision sees people as fundamentally limited in terms of their abilities to live peaceful, cooperative, public-spirited lives. People are morally limited, and therefore, although they may do a good deed, they are not to be trusted to act as they ought to toward one another. If we hear of a disaster in another part of the world, we may take a moment to feel sorry for the victims, but then we proceed with our lives as if nothing had happened. When philosopher Edmund Burke spoke of "a radical infirmity in all human contrivances," he was expressing the constrained view that we should not expect very much from people, especially in regard to their social morality. Sowell cites Alexander Hamilton, who, in the Federalist Papers, wrote that government must allow for human imperfections. Adam Smith, who wrote *The Wealth of Nations,* is an excellent example of someone who extolled the constrained vision. Sowell quotes Smith, saying "Nature, it seems, when she loaded us with her sorrows, thought that they were enough, and therefore did not command us to take any further share in those of others, than what was necessary to prompt us to relieve them." Smith believed that we are creatures who meet our own needs first, and that a free market is the best economic system because it recognizes our inherent selfishness and allows us to pursue our own individual gain in a manner that mysteriously results in the advantage of all. According to Smith, an "invisible hand" moves behind market forces, and as we pursue our own interests, we produce more products of all kinds, which eventually benefits us all. The important element of Smith's attitude, according to Sowell, is that Smith did not want to try to change human nature, but instead wanted to create a system that would take advantage of it. According to Sowell, "Instead of regarding man's nature as something that could or should be changed, Smith attempted to determine how the moral and social benefits desired could be produced in the most efficient way, *within* that constraint" (Sowell 1987, 21).

Opposing the constrained vision is the unconstrained vision, which views people as moral agents capable of creating and sustaining values such as justice, welfare, and social and political equality. The great philosophical proponent of the unconstrained vision was the Englishman William Godwin, who became famous for publishing *Enquiry Concerning Political Justice* in 1793. For Godwin, people are capable of intending to benefit others, and this intention is the essential moral virtue. People naturally have not only this virtue, but the intelligence to find the ways to fulfill it. Advances in science make it possible, if we will only apply them, to solve fundamental social problems. For the people who hold the unconstrained vision, the essential task is not to live with selfishness and other less beneficial aspects of our natures, but to overcome them. Since we have the ability and the will to solve social problems, we must simply set our minds and energies to solving them. The difference between the two visions is perhaps best explained in the analogy of two people looking at the same glass, halfway filled with water. For some it is half full (society is basically good, but there are problems to be solved), and for others it is half empty (society is evil, but there are opportunities for improvement). As Sowell explains, "While believers in the unconstrained vision seek the special causes of war, poverty, and crime, believers in the constrained vision seek the special causes of peace, wealth, or a law-abiding society" (Sowell 1987, 31).

Your view of the nature of humanity is fundamental to your view of government. If you see people as dangerous, you will want a government to protect you from danger. If you view people as capable of fulfilling their own creative potential, you may want a government that protects individual liberties. John Adams, second President of the United States, wrote about the emotional needs of people that serve as the basis for constitutions:

> Fear is the foundation of most governments; but it is so sordid and brutal a passion, and renders men ill whose breasts it predominates so stupid and miserable, that Americans will not be likely to approve of any political institution which is founded on it.
>
> Honor is truly sacred, but holds a lower rank in the scale of moral excellence than virtue. Indeed, the former is but a part of the latter, and consequently has not equal pretensions to support a frame of government productive of human happiness.
>
> The foundation of every government is some principle or passion in the minds of the people. The noblest principles and most generous affections in our nature, then, have the fairest chance to support the noblest and most generous models of government. (Adams 1851, 193)

Community and Individuality

In the long history of commentaries about politics, the tension between the basic needs of unity and individuality has been discussed and analyzed in thousands of different ways, and virtually every political discussion is in some way related to it.

When we speak of freedom, we speak of what an individual can do within the constraints of a community. When we speak of justice, we speak of what is fair for individual members of a community as opposed to the interests of other members or of the community as a whole. When we speak of democracy, we discuss how individuals may be heard in the society's process of making decisions.

The overwhelming body of these discussions is oppositional. In other words, issues of individual and community are almost always raised in terms of individual rights *against* society's interests, or community values *opposed to* individual freedoms. The public debate is normally dominated by disputes between those, for example, who would use government to force women to carry a pregnancy to term as opposed to those who champion an individual woman's right to have an abortion, or by those who claim that the community is not safe because individuals are allowed to carry guns against those who demand a constitutional right to bear arms. You will read much more about such controversies in your political science classes.

In all this discussion surprisingly little is said about the compatibility of individuality with community. It is important to note that there are those who believe, in spite of all the discussion to the contrary, that individuality and community are not necessarily oppositional values. In fact, not only are they both necessary, but each one is a necessary condition for the other. In other words, individuals can only be truly actualized within a community, and a political community can only be healthy and strong, if it supports the creative individuality of its members.

At the level of family and intimate relationships, the symbiotic relationship between unity and individuality has been substantiated by psychologists, especially in the work of a founding father of developmental psychology, Erik H. Erikson. Erikson demonstrates that as we live we go through emotional and cognitive developmental stages, each of which presents a special challenge. He identifies eight such stages, and each stage presents each individual with a primary challenge that has to do with simultaneously attaching to others (unity) and gaining a secure sense of the self (individuality). In each stage the two elements, unity and individuality, depend on each other; that is, failure to attach properly to others results in an incomplete sense of the self, and the development of an incomplete sense of the self leads to a failure to attach.

Erikson's first stage is infancy. In the first months of life a child gains either a sense of security or insecurity that is at least partly permanent. The infant acquires a sense of basic trust or develops a deep seated mistrust of others and thereafter either views life with a sense of hope or approaches it with the defense of withdrawal. Basic trust allows the child both to bond with parents, family, and friends, and to feel a confidence in being special, in being different from others as a unique human being.

The second stage, the early childhood years, finds the child either building a sense of autonomy, of genuine independence from parents in walking and moving, or being overcome with a sense of shame and doubt. Either a strong, independently directed will begins to form, or the child finds herself afraid and may begin acting out various compulsions.

The third stage, play age, presents the challenge of taking initiative with peers as opposed to operating from a sense of guilt. The child then either exhibits a sense of self-directed purpose or merely responds to inhibitions placed upon her, perhaps by domineering or abusive parents.

The fourth stage, school age, sees the same struggles being waged in the milieu of teachers and peers who challenge the child to grasp hold of school work and thereby accept the challenge of industry, or, failing the challenge, to take on a sense of inferiority. One possible result of this phase is competence in living life and doing work. Another potential result is a sense of inertia in which little seems possible.

Erikson's fifth stage, adolescence, is the one wherein a newly developing adult either gains a sense of identity or falls into identity confusion. Here relationships with others are intense, and a child learns the fidelity of friends and members of the opposite sex or experiences their repudiation.

Young adulthood, stage six, continues this struggle. Genuine intimacy with a long-term partner or, for some, with friends and relatives is usually the successful resolution of this stage, but isolation is the consequence of failure. Love, the ultimate bond of unity, and exclusivity, the ultimate statement of rejection of others, await the resolution of this phase.

Stage seven, adulthood, finds persons interacting with others in creative caring generativity or enduring stagnation and rejectivity. The final stage is the one in which persons look back on their lives with a sense of wisdom, wholeness, and integrity, or else in the darkness of despair, experience disdain for the products of their lives.

There is, of course, no set pattern to these events. Each individual goes through them in a different way. Erikson's message, however, is clear. At each stage in life, if we develop a secure sense of unity with others, we are able to find the strength to be genuine, unique individuals, and as we become whole individuals, we are more capable of responding in beneficial ways to others.

The feeling of security, of having a place where one belongs, is a permanent feature of human life and is mirrored in virtually every aspect of ancient political life. For the cultures of Egypt, Babylon, and Assyria, reaching back at least 3,000 years before the birth of Christ, the emperor, king, or tribal chieftain was a father figure, who was typically believed to be either the incarnation of a god or the descendant of a god. For his subject children, the ruler held the unquestioned authority of the father in a family and symbolically linked all the community together in a sense of togetherness that mirrors family unity today.

In his *Republic,* Plato's blueprint for society, Plato defined three classes of people, the largest and lowest of which was comprised of tradespeople and workers of all sorts. The upper classes of society were divided among the very few philosopher kings, and the guardians, the warriors who protected the community. Plato admired the military society of Sparta, the male citizens of which lived military communal lives, being obliged to service in the army or navy from ages 18 to 60. Plato proposed that the guardian class of Athens should be set aside for constant training and readiness for war. This class was to be comprised of both men and women, and women were to have equal opportunity to become philosopher kings. The guardians would make up a large family. Children would be raised in common, and no one would know the identity of her or his own child. Communal property, meals, festivities, and military exercises, Plato believed, would help the guardian class achieve the absolute unity needed to protect the society as a whole:

> First, none of them must posses any private property beyond the barest necessities. Next, no one is to have any dwelling or store-house that is not open for all to enter at will. Their food, in the quantities required by men of temperance and courage who are in training for war, they will receive from the other citizens as the wages of their guardianship, fixed so that there shall be just enough for the year with nothing over; and they will have meals in common and all live together like soldiers in a camp. Gold and silver, we shall tell them, they will no need. . . . They alone of all the citizens are forbidden to touch or handle silver or gold. . . . This manner of life will be their salvation and make them the saviours of the commonwealth. (*Republic* 10:3)

As in Plato's guardian class, we also see a sense of family unity in early religious communities of all faiths. Some early Christians, according to the accounts in the book of Acts, brought their possessions to a common storehouse to be shared by all. Their highest goal, as a community, was to live "in one accord," placing the needs of others above their own, and avoiding internal strife:

> All the believers were together and had everything in common. Selling their possessions and goods, they gave to anyone as he had need. Every day they continued to meet together in the temple courts. They broke bread in their homes and ate together with glad and sincere hearts, praising God and enjoying the favor of all the people. And the Lord added to their number daily those who were being saved. (NIV Acts 2:44–47)

Communal societies were a standard feature of life throughout the Middle Ages. Following practices established by their founding saints, Benedictine, Franciscan, and Jesuit monks secluded themselves in monasteries for lives which included long hours of fasting, prayer, and manual labor. At the end of the Middle Ages, new communities sprang up composed of those who despaired of the inequalities of the industrial revolution and the fragmentation and competitiveness of life. In England Robert Owen and in France Pierre Joseph Proudhon established utopian communes in which people attempted to create an atmosphere of family unity in community life. Few of these experiments were successful for any length of time, but some religious movements, such as the Shakers in America and the monastic orders of the Roman Catholic church and other faiths, have successfully operated communal societies for successive decades or centuries.

Contemporary communitarians see society as fragmented, and they perceive that people are alienated and estranged from one another. This estrangement, they believe, is the cause of poverty, crime, and despair. To overcome these problems communitarians believe that people need to commit themselves voluntarily to look beyond individual fulfillment, to seek the good of the community as a whole, and to participate. Community is more than society. It implies that the members of a society have a concern for each other and for the community as a whole that transcends their individual interests. Communitarians find society insufficient. They find their lives actualized in sharing: sharing accomplishments, sharing challenges, and doing things together in peace and harmony.

In a way, communitarians are attempting to regain a sense of community that until recently was a part of daily life in America. A sense of personal honor and trust in small closely knit communities made possible a way of life that seems remarkable to us today. Consider, for example, a person not remarkable in other respects, who lived not long ago within the ideals of an earlier America. Ransford Tidd lived in the small Canadian border town of Hodgdon, Maine, from his birth in August 1895, to the day he died peacefully during a service in the Methodist church at the age of ninety-two. Having lived in Hodgdon all his life and knowing many of the people in the region, he was able to walk into some of the local stores and carry out anything he wanted without paying or even signing his name. The store owners knew him and had no doubt that they would be paid. When he wanted to buy a car, he would call a couple of local automobile dealers on the phone and tell them what he was looking for. They would drive several cars to his house and let him test drive them for a few days until he selected the one he wanted. Tidd was a respected member of a community that valued personal commitments and trust. He could be counted upon to help those less fortunate without being asked. He represents a style of community life that seems lost to America today, a style of mutual trust and concern that communitarians would like to restore.

A cohesive communitarian movement has emerged in this country which has a recognized spokesperson, sociologist Amitai Etzioni. In *Rights and the Common Good: The Communitarian Perspective* (1995), Etzioni explains that, as communitarians see it, the universal central political problem is finding the right amount of togetherness and common concern. If people are too individualistic, they fail to support each other's efforts and to respect each other's needs. If people are too unified, they become authoritarian and attempt to use the state to impose a common set of beliefs and practices. Like ancient and medieval philosophers, communitarians find the lack of unified purpose and direction in society to be a crucial problem. As Etzioni explains:

> The communitarian movement seeks to shore up the moral, social, and political foundations of society. It builds on the elementary social science observation that people are born without any moral or social values. If they are to become civil, they must acquire values. Later, they may rebel against these values or seek to modify them, but first they must have them. Historically, the family was the societal entity entrusted with laying the foundation for moral education. Schools were the second line of defense. Community bonds—whether centered around religious institutions, schools, town meetings, or other establishments— served to reinforce values that had been previously acquired. These social institutions were the seedbeds of virtue in which values were planted and cultivated. (Etzioni 1995, iv)

At the other end of the unity-individuality spectrum is a vast array of people who speak of the joys, not of associating with others, but of being left alone by them. Perhaps their most eloquent spokesperson is author and abolitionist Henry David Thoreau (1817–1862), who, observing the pressures, expectations, and demands made upon us by the societies in which we live, concluded that "the mass of men lead lives of quiet desperation." Not wanting to be one of them, he opted to live according to the beat of "a different drum." In 1845, he withdrew for two years to then secluded Walden Pond near Concord, Massachusetts. Here he lived as simply as possible, desiring to free himself as much as possible from dependence on others. He recorded his experience in *Walden, or Life in the Woods* (Thoreau 1965, 67):

> I went to the woods because I wished to live deliberately, to front only the essential facts of life, and see if I could not learn what it had to teach, and not, when I came to die, discover that I had not lived. I did not wish to practice resignation, unless it was quite necessary. I wanted to live deep and suck out all the marrow of life, to live so sturdily and Spartan-like as to put to rout all that was not life, to cut a broad swath and shave close, to drive into a corner, and reduce it to its lowest terms, and if it proved to be mean, why then to get the whole and genuine meanness of it, and publish its meanness to the world; or if it were sublime, to know it by experience, and be able to give a true account of it.

Thoreau did not lead all of his life in seclusion, but he consistently wrote about standing alone against the common acts of society. To be truly alive, he believed, is to test oneself against the challenges of life and to find one's own way of doing it, not someone else's (1965, 52):

> I would not have any one adopt my mode of living on any account; for, beside that before he has fairly learned it I may have found out another for myself. I desire that there may be as many different persons in the world as possible; but I would have each one be very careful to find out and pursue his own way, and not his father's or his mother's or his neighbor's instead.

Authority, Order, and Freedom

Much of what motivates individualists is a strong desire for freedom, and consequently they reject all but minimal government authority. For example, in a letter to James Madison, Thomas Jefferson wrote:

> I own that I am not a friend to a very energetic government. It is always oppressive. The late [Shays] rebellion in Massachusetts has given more alarm than I think it should have done. Calculate that one rebellion in thirteen states in the course of eleven years, is but one for each state in a century and a half. No country should be so long without one. Nor will any degree of power in the hands of government prevent insurrections.

Jefferson would not, however, disagree with his good friend and political ally James Madison, who, at the very beginning of his discussion of the need for a constitution, in Federal Paper No. 10, cites the need to bring order from the chaos of competing factions in society:

> Among the numerous advantages promised by a well-constructed Union, none deserves to be more accurately developed than its tendency to break and control the violence of faction. . . . By a faction, I understand a number of citizens, whether amounting to a majority or minority of the whole, who are united and actuated by some common impulse of passion, or of interest, adverse to the rights of other citizens, or to the permanent and aggregate interests of the community . . .

Authority is the right to use force or to regulate the affairs of others. The need to keep order amidst the sparring of factions and the tendency of some human beings to dominate others are two of the leading factors in establishing government authority. Robert Michaels has explained that the will to dominate others is naturally expressed whenever people form an association. He called this principle, in which a hierarchy always forms, the "iron law of oligarchy." As Michaels explains, the need for administrative order, and the fact that leadership talents are not evenly distributed, assures that when people come together some will dominate the others to further their own personal interests (Michaels 1915).

Authority is often justified by the need to bring order amidst dissent and controversy. To create order from the multitude of competing, disagreeing individuals was the primary concern of ancient societies and ancient and medieval political thought. Some people believe that order is the primary concern for society today. They see crime, substance abuse, and the deterioration of traditional family values largely as a function of a loss of order in society.

Some want to return to the order of an earlier time and see order as consisting of a strict adherence to law, in particular the law of God. Rousas John Rushdoony, a Christian fundamentalist, believes that God's law as it is expressed in the Old Testament is the ultimate expression of God's will for man. Rushdoony advocates that Christians reestablish a biblical society in which the Old Testament, especially the Ten Commandments, will become the primary guiding force in life, and be binding on all members of the community. In *The Institutes of Biblical Law* he notes that the Puritans of the New Haven Colony created such a community in the 1600s, and that "colony records show that the law of God, without any sense of innovation, was made the law of the colony" (Rushdooney 1973, 1–2).

Rushdoony explains that much of modern Christianity misunderstands Biblical teaching and thereby rejects the idea that adherence to Old Testament law is necessary (1973, 2–3):

> A central characteristic of the churches and of modern preaching and Biblical teaching is antinomianism, an anti-law position. The antinomian believes that faith frees the Christian from the law, so that he is not outside the law but rather dead to the law. There is no warrant whatsoever in Scripture for antinomianism.

Rushdoony, like other authoritarians, believes that the rule of law is the foundation of order in society and if the authority of law is questioned, anarchy and chaos will result. For many others, however, excessive government authority is the greatest danger to community life, and they seek ways to expand human freedom.

Freedom

So much has been written on the subject of freedom that it would consume this entire chapter merely to list the most famous works. This is true partly because freedom is a fascinating and difficult subject. On one level, everyone knows what freedom is, and everyone wants it. Once we look closer, however, we find that what one person calls freedom may be bondage for someone else. In fact, as Michael Walzer points out, one of the paradoxes of freedom is that there is freedom in bondage and bondage in freedom. In his discussion of the Bible, Walzer reminds us of the moment when the Hebrew slaves are led by Moses out of bondage in Egypt to freedom in the promised land. At one point the Hebrews aroused God's wrath because they began complaining about the food in the desert and were speaking nostalgically about the certainty of life in Egypt. The wrath of God was directed at their inability to accept the challenges of their freedom, especially their moral obligations to treat each other kindly and fairly. In the desert they realized that, paradoxically, slavery in Egypt offered them a certain type of freedom. In Egypt they did only what they were told. They were, therefore, free from making decisions, free from taking responsibility for their own lives, free from the civic responsibilities that life in the promised land would demand.

Life in society today is full of the same types of choices the Hebrews were forced to make. Ask yourself what kind of freedom you really want. Some people want to be free *to* make decisions, to join a country club, to succeed in a business they own for themselves. Others want to be free *from* the pressures of hiring and firing. They want to be free from having to work late into the night. They want to be free *from* getting yet another college degree. They want to be free *to* go home at five o'clock and not think about work until eight o'clock the next morning. Sir Isaiah Berlin calls the freedom *to* do things *positive* freedom, while he calls freedom *from* things or doing things *negative* freedom.

Of the many summaries and compendiums available, one of the very best is *The Philosophy and Politics of Freedom* (1987) by John Hopkins University political science professor Richard Flathman. Flathman reviews the history of the discussion of political freedom and finds five basic conceptions discussed in the literature. Throughout his discussion, Flathman designates the lack of freedom, or the opposite of freedom, as "unfreedom." For each of Falthman's categories, we shall first describe his concept and then present his definition of it.

Question: Can a rock that is rolling down a hill be said to be free? The answer of the vast majority of writers to this question is "no." Freedom, they contend, requires at least this: the ability to move. If you cannot move by yourself, if you are moved only by natural or other external forces, then you cannot be said to be free. What about a quadraplegically disabled person? Can that person be free? Only if she can, from her initiative, cause herself to move or act. Technology or the willingness of others to help may make this possible. The bare minimum requirement for freedom, then, is the ability to move or act, based upon your own initiative. For some philosophers this is sufficient. You are free to the extent you can move and act, and you are unfree to the extent that things (impediments) prevent you from moving or acting. Seventeenth century philosopher Thomas Hobbes, as we mentioned in Chapter 2 of this text, wrote the earliest modern version of social contract theory, in which he proposed that people voluntarily assign all rights to a sovereign king, a leviathan, in exchange for which the leviathan would protect lives and property and keep order in society. As Flathman explains (1987, 16–23):

> Thomas Hobbes portrayed not just human beings but all higher animals as *self-activated* in a very strong sense. Impulses that originate within these creatures are the necessary and . . . sufficient conditions of their movements. He contended that these creatures should be said to be free just insofar as those movements are effectively impeded or prevented. Information about the two condi-

tions is all that is needed, indeed all that can properly [be] employed, in discourse about their freedom and unfreedom. . . . Hobbes is famous for the argument that subjects or citizens are at liberty just insofar as their sovereign has not promulgated laws or commands requiring or forbidding modes of conduct. Freedom consists of the absence of rules; their presence is a sufficient condition of unfreedom.

Thomas Hobbes, therefore, falls into Flathman's first category of definitions of freedom: $Freedom_1$ and $Unfreedom_1$, or Freedom and Unfreedom of Movement. $Freedom_1$ involves "Self-activated movement plus the possibility of impediments to the movement in question" (Flathman 1987, 322). If we follow Hobbes, we believe that self-activated things such as animals are free. His position has been called "pure negative freedom" by some, because it consists of freedom *from* impediments. Political freedom, for Hobbes, consisted essentially in being free from government rules or laws.

Suppose, however, that we raise an objection to Hobbes' definition. Although animals exhibit responses to external stimuli, can they really make decisions for themselves, or are they merely reacting according to instinct? Further, even one-celled animals—amoebas—move by themselves. Can an amoeba be free? Some commentators say "no," insisting that to be free requires the ability consciously to intend to take an action. How can you be free if you merely automatically react to things in your environment? People who raise this objection may subscribe to Flathman's second category (1987, 322):

> $Freedom_2$ and $Unfreedom_2$ or Freedom and Unfreedom of Action.
> Action attempted by an agent plus the possibility of impediments to that action placed or left by another agent or agents acting with the intention of placing or leaving those impediments.

$Freedom_2$ theorists believe that to be free or unfree requires the existence of some desire that remains unfulfilled. Without a desire and an intent to act upon it, they say, the concept of freedom has no significant political meaning. These writers acknowledge that a desire in itself does not necessarily bring freedom. One may be obstructed from fulfilling a desire, or one may be said to be so controlled by desire, such as in alcohol or drug addiction, that the desire results in unfreedom.

A third group of thinkers claims that even conscious intent is not a sufficient basis for freedom. Genuine freedom, they insist, means being able to act upon a consciously reasoned set of values that the person holds. To be free, in other words, you need not only to be able to act on a desire, but to act after having concluded that the objective of the action is good or beneficial. To be free means doing what is good, because to do what is harmful reflects a lack of ability to determine one's true interests. I may think that I am free if I take heroin, but since I cannot defend the use of this drug within a consciously established value system, I have actually further enslaved myself to things that are against my interest. The key to this concept is self-selection of the values that may be supported by rational argument. My ability to chose what is good for me and the lack of impediments to carrying out my choice are the two factors that make me free. The definition for Flathman's $Freedom_3$ is as follows (1987, 322):

Freedom$_3$ and Unfreedom$_3$ or Autonomy or Heteronomy.

Action attempted by an agent in the pursuit of a self-critically self-chosen plan or project that the agent has reason to believe is consonant with defensible norms or principles, plus the possibility of impediments to that action placed or left by another agent or other agents acting with the intention of placing or leaving those impediments.

We have already mentioned Henry David Thoreau as an example of an individualist, and it is important to cite him again here, for he is perhaps the most famous proponent of Flathman's Freedom$_3$. For Thoreau, an individual's conscience is his or her guide to action in life. Law represents merely the rules of the community, and to be tied slavishly to these rules is the essence of unfreedom (Thoreau 1965, 243):

> It is not desirable to cultivate a respect for the law, so much as for the right. The only obligation which I have a right to assume is to do at any time what I think right. It is truly enough said, that a corporation has no conscience; but a corporation of conscientious men is a corporation with a conscience. Law never made men a whit more just; and, by means of their respect for it, even the well-disposed are daily made the agents of injustice. A common and natural result of an undue respect for law is, that you may see a file of soldiers, colonel, captain, corporal, privates, powder-monkeys, and all, marching in admirable order over hill and dale to the wars, against their will, ay, against their common sense and consciences, which makes it very steep marching indeed, and produces a palpitation of the heart. . . . In most cases there is no free exercise whatever of the judgment or of the moral sense; but they put themselves on a level with wood and earth and stones; and wooden men can perhaps be manufactured that will serve the purpose as well.

Many objections, however, are also raised to Thoreau's concept of conscience and to the lack of concern for the needs of others exhibited by the adherents to Freedom$_3$. Communitarians, among others, believe that genuine freedom exists only within a community which has established a common set of values. Without these values we may damage ourselves and alienate other members of the community, a situation which prevents us from actualizing our potential in life. These people want freedom to associate in an atmosphere of common caring and concern, to find the values in which the community agrees, and to live according to those values. This type of life style brings maximum freedom to enjoy the life of the community, a freedom Flathman (1987, 322) calls:

Freedom$_4$ and Unfreedom$_4$ or Communal Freedom and Unfreedom.

Action attempted by an agent in pursuit of a plan or project chosen to satisfy, and in fact satisfying norms or principles that are authoritative in the agent's community, plus the possibility of impediments to that action placed or left by another agent or other agents acting with the intention of placing or leaving those impediments.

Amitai Etzioni and the communitarians described earlier subscribe to Freedom$_4$. They hope to create a situation in which people will agree upon basic values. Some have contended, however, that this quest for shared values can lead to the negation of freedom, or what Flathman would call unfreedom. In *Democracy in America,* Alexis de Tocqueville notes that in the America he explored in the 1830s and 1840s there existed a strong consensus on basic religious and political values, so much so that anyone who disagreed with these fundamental values lost credibility and became an outcast from society. He observed that in Europe, where kings then reigned with the help of authoritarian regimes, there was actually greater freedom of expression, for the regimes allowed the quiet discussion of a wide range of views as long as rebellion was not being planned. In America, to the contrary, a "tyranny of the majority" had formed precisely because there was so much general agreement on acceptable religious and political values (Tocqueville 1945, 273–4):

> I know of no country in which there is so little independence of mind and real freedom of discussion as in America. . . . In America, the majority raises formidable barriers around the liberty of opinion: within these barriers, an author may write what he pleases; but woe to him if he goes beyond them. . . . His political career is closed forever, since he has offended the only authority which is able to open it.

But many other people would disagree with Tocqueville and find the unity of belief a haven wherein the good life is finally possible. For some of these people, even choosing values in agreement with those of the community is not enough to ensure freedom for other people. For Freedom$_5$ people, the values that are chosen must be objectively certifiable as well as accepted by the community. This type of freedom is often held by religious groups and expounded by people like R.J. Rushdoony, the fundamentalist we discussed earlier in this chapter. Theologies written for many faiths often assert that to be free is to follow the will of God. To be unfree, therefore, is to violate or be ignorant of the will of God. Since the will of God is what is best for us, we would always follow it if we could. To do anything else, whether we realize it or not, is to be enslaved to desire, illusion, or the winds of passion. The definition of freedom which contends that true freedom is acting in conformance to principles that are certifiably, objectively true is what Flathman (1987, 322) calls:

> Freedom$_5$ and Unfreedom$_5$ or Fully Virtuous Freedom and Unfreedom.
> Action attempted by an agent in pursuit of a plan or project self-critically chosen to satisfy, and in fact satisfying, certifiably worthy norms or principles, plus the possibility of impediments to that action placed or left by another agent or other agents acting with the intention of placing or leaving those impediments.

Equality

As citizens of modern democracies, we champion freedom. We abhor the thought of someone else telling us what to do. We demand a voice in the decisions that affect us. True? Not really. Think about it. How much time does the average person spend participating in the political process? Studies have shown that less than five percent of the population does anything more than occasionally vote in any given year. What, then, do we spend most of our time doing? We work. We work in jobs that are not, for the most part, democracies. We have a boss, or we are the boss, but there is virtually always a boss. Even artists working alone depend upon customers to buy their art, and, therefore, even they are not free from the whims and dictates of other people. And although a recent compulsion to imitate the success of the Japanese in their participatory management practices has lead to some increased responsiveness on the part of management, most American businesses, which employ Americans, are hierarchies, little different in their channels of control from the empires of the ancient Orient or kingdoms of medieval Europe. We love hierarchy. We demand hierarchy. We insist upon knowing our place in the organization and the specific duties to which we are assigned. We cherish what little privilege our station brings us, hold steadfastly to the prerogatives of our offices, and cannot for a moment imagine a working situation in which there is no one person at any particular level who is designated to make decisions. We may want to be consulted, and often are, but if our boss fails to make decisions promptly and efficiently, we blame her or him for being an ineffective leader. We talk all day about freedom, but give us real freedom in our working lives and most of us shrink away in terror, demanding instead the order and authority of the modern corporation. In the modern corporation we each have a specialized and specific job to do, and we follow the rules established for doing it. Just as Plato envisioned social life 2,400 years ago, each person in society has a specified role to play within a tightly organized hierarchy.

The wedding of hierarchy and efficiency in administration achieved by reformers at the beginning of this century (and now under heavy attack), was carefully detailed in the 1920s (and published in English in the 1940s) by German sociologist Max Weber. Weber (1946, 196–198) outlined the rules by which the modern corporation is run:

I. There is the principle of fixed and official jurisdictional areas, which are generally ordered by rules, that is, by laws or administrative regulations.
II. The principles of office hierarchy and of levels of graded authority mean a firmly ordered system of super- and subordination in which there is a supervision of the lower offices by the higher ones.
III. The management of the modern office is based upon written documents ("the files"), which are preserved in their original or draught form.
IV. Office management, at least all specialized office management—and such management is distinctly modern—usually presupposes thorough and expert training.
V. When the office is fully developed, official activity demands the full working capacity of the official, irrespective of the fact that his obligatory time in the bureau may be firmly delimited.
VI. The management of the office follows general rules, which are more or less exhaustive, and which can be learned.

If we consider how pervasive authoritarian structures seem so natural to us, it is less difficult to understand how Aristotle came to his opinion about a deeper level of authoritarianism, an enshrinement of inequality: slavery. Aristotle provided a philosophic justification of slavery that fit very well with his conception of the universe. Trained as a physician, the son of a physician, Aristotle looked to nature, the biological realm, to discover the principles of existence. There he discovered inequality, a natural hierarchy of rulers and ruled. Throughout the natural world and among the various species, especially humans, some are more intelligent than others, and they are by nature designed to rule over their inferiors (*Politics* 1252a):

> [T]here must necessarily be a union of the naturally ruling element with the element which is naturally ruled, for the preservation of both. The element which is able, by virtue of its intelligence, to exercise forethought, is naturally a ruling or master element; the element which is able, by virtue of its bodily power, to do what the other element plans, is a ruled element, which is naturally in a state of slavery.

Aristotle believed that slaves were necessary to society and that those who were slaves were naturally inferior. He seemed to be oblivious to the fact, well known in his day, that the ruling classes of conquered cities, often highly intelligent and cultured people, made up a substantial number of the slaves of Athens.

Many definitions of political equality have been written throughout history. In an essay entitled *Equality versus Solidarity*, Paul Spicker explains what the word "equality" means when used in political discussions (Spicker 1992, 66):

> Equality refers, in a social context, to the removal of disadvantage. A number of critics tend to confuse "equality" with "sameness" or "uniformity;" but people are not considered "unequal" simply because their hair is a different color, because some are fat or some are thin. . . . People are unequal because there is something which leads to their being advantaged or disadvantaged in terms of treatment, opportunities, or circumstances. . . . [T]he objective of policies concerned with equality is not to remove differences, but to change the relationships which the differences imply.

One of the most common distinctions among types of equality distinguishes equality of opportunity from equality of condition. People who argue for equality of condition do not normally argue that everyone should have exactly the same amount of property or wealth, but that society should regulate distribution of benefits in order that extremes of wealth and poverty disappear, so that the poorest members of society may live in reasonable security and health. People who champion equality of opportunity believe that guaranteeing benefits to those who may not have earned them is unfair and discourages initiative, but that everyone should get an equal chance to earn a good living.

In *Rival Visions of Equality in American Political Culture*, Richard J. Ellis, describing these two types of equality further, identifies two different American concepts of *equality* (Ellis 1992, 254):

> The first, the competitive individualist definition of equality, conceives of equality in terms of *process;* the second, the egalitarian definition, conceives of equality in terms of *results*. . . . What differentiates the egalitarian vision from the individualist vision is that the former focuses on equalizing outcomes while the latter focuses on equalizing processes.

It has often been noted that America, unlike European nations, seems to lack a strong tradition of equality of results. Americans are noted as rugged individualists who are inclined to leave people to achieve their own rewards, whereas in Europe the conditions that make equality of opportunity more fiction than fact, such as monopolies of industry and land, have been given more attention. While this difference between the two continents has been explained in different ways, Ellis believes that what makes America different is that many Americans once believed that, if people are actually given the opportunity to succeed, they will do so, and the gap between rich and poor will become more narrow. A free market was, therefore, expected to bring greater actual economic equality. But over the course of two centuries in which racial discrimination did not fade away and economic equality did not materialize, people concerned about equality finally gave up faith in the free market and adopted an attitude that was essentially the opposite. As Ellis explains (1992, 275–6):

> In early American history, egalitarians assumed that equal process was sufficient to produce equal results. In contemporary America, the presumption among egalitarians has become entirely different. If the outcomes are unequal, the process must be unequal. Are minorities and the poor more likely to end up in prison, then incarceration is discriminatory. Are blacks more likely to be sentenced to death, then the death penalty must be racist. . . . Egalitarians have tried to reverse the burden of proof: the process is assumed to be unequal until the results are equal.

As Ellis points out, this new approach on the part of egalitarians, who have championed programs such as affirmative action, has led to a great split with the individualists who, feeling forced to choose between equality and freedom from government regulation, choose the latter. In recent years individualists have pushed hard to revoke affirmative action and other government initiatives which they regard as interfering with every individual's opportunity to succeed.

Egalitarians have not given up, however. Political scientist Robert Dahl is among those who point out that radical inequalities of condition can be dangerous for the health of politics in a democracy. Dahl and many others have pointed out that in today's political world, campaigns for office are very expensive, and campaign advertising is highly influential. Those who have money can buy advertising for their candidates, which gives them an unfair advantage over those who cannot. Dahl's concern, how to achieve substantive *political* equality in society, introduces another distinction, one that suggests three types of equality which are of concern to political scientists: political, social, and economic.

Political equality begins with establishing equal rights as citizens, something which is still a goal rather than a reality for many people all over the world. Although American history provides evidence of many types of inequality, the first American battle for political equality was the fight against slavery. The man who signed the Emancipation Proclamation, Abraham Lincoln, denounced slavery on many occasions, and the simplicity of his argument makes the anti-slavery case very clear (1990, 62–3):

> The ant, who has toiled and dragged a crumb to his nest, will furiously defend the fruit of his labor, against whatever robber assails him. So plain, that the most

dumb and stupid slave that ever toiled for a master, does constantly know that he is wronged. So plain that no one, high or low, ever does mistake it, except in a plainly selfish way; for although volume upon volume is written to prove slavery a very good thing, we never hear of the man who wishes to take the good of it, by being a slave himself.

At one time in history, a distinction was made between political equality and social equality. In the case of *Plessy v. Ferguson* (1896), the Supreme Court was asked to review a Louisiana law that mandated separate railway cars for blacks and whites. In a decision that upheld the Louisiana law, and thereby legalized discrimination in public accommodations for another half century, Justice Brown maintained that, while the Constitution (which by 1896 included the Thirteenth, Fourteenth, and Fifteenth amendments) had established *political* equality, it did not establish *social* equality:

> The object of the [fourteenth] amendment [which guarantees equal protection of the laws to all citizens] was undoubtedly to enforce the absolute equality of the two races before the law, but in the nature of things it could not have been intended to abolish distinctions based upon color, or to enforce social, as distinguished from political equality, or a commingling of the two races upon terms unsatisfactory to either. . . . We consider the underlying fallacy of the plaintiff's [Plessy's] argument to consist in the assumption that the enforced separation of the two races stamps the colored race with a badge of inferiority. If this be so, it is not by reason of anything found in the act, but solely because the colored race chooses to put that construction upon it.

Reprinted by permission: Tribune Media Services.

This distinction between social and political equality was erased by *Sweatt v. Painter* (1948) and *Brown v. Board of Education* (1954) in which the Court declared that government acts which enforce social distinctions based upon race violate the Fourteenth Amendment's provision for equal protection of the law.

America has been ambivalent about the third type of equality, economic equality. Both during the days of the great depression, when America's economy was at its lowest point, and during the 1960s, when it had by far the strongest economy in the world, America's leaders have successfully raised the call of economic equality by instituting programs for the poor. Franklin D. Roosevelt's "New Deal" meant government jobs for millions of unemployed people, and Lyndon Johnson's "Great Society" initiated many programs in job training, housing, health, and welfare for those who had no had such opportunities in the past. Roosevelt's vision, however, as he proclaimed it in his *Economic Bill of Rights,* has never been completely realized, either by champions of equality of results or by supporters of equal opportunity (Roosevelt 1990, 298–99):

> The Republic had its beginning, and grew to its present strength, under the protection of certain inalienable political rights—among them the right of free speech, free press, free worship, trial by jury, freedom from unreasonable searches and seizures. They were our rights to life and liberty.
>
> As our nation has grown in size and stature, however—as our industrial economy expanded—these political rights proved inadequate to assure us equality in the pursuit of happiness.
>
> We have come to a clear realization of the fact that true individual freedom cannot exist without economic security and independence. "Necessitous men are not freemen." People who are hungry and out of a job are the stuff of which dictatorships are made.
>
> In our day these economic truths have become accepted as self-evident. We have accepted, so to speak, a second Bill of Rights under which a new basis for security and prosperity can be established for all—regardless of station, race, or creed.
>
> Among these are—
>
>> The right to a useful and remunerative job in the industries, or shops or farms or mines of the Nation;
>>
>> The right to earn enough to provide adequate food and clothing and recreation;
>>
>> The right of every farmer to raise and sell his products at a return which will give him and his family a decent living;
>>
>> The right of every businessman, large and small, to trade in an atmosphere of freedom from unfair competition and domination by monopolies at home and abroad;
>>
>> The right of every family to a decent home;
>>
>> The right to adequate medical care and the opportunity to achieve and enjoy good health;
>>
>> The right to adequate protection from the economic fears of old age, sickness, accident, and unemployment;
>>
>> The right to a good education.
>>
>> All of these rights spell security. And after this war is won we must be prepared to move forward, in the implementation of these rights, to new goals of human happiness and well-being.

Justice

The most famous discussion of justice ever written is Plato's *Republic,* in which Socrates discusses popular definitions of justice with his contemporaries and then provides one of his own. Socrates speaks to Cephalus, an eminent Athenian of advanced age, who declares that justice involves honesty and repaying debt. Socrates, however, is not satisfied with this answer, and replies:

> But take this matter of doing right: can we say that it really consists in nothing more nor less than telling the truth and paying back anything we may have received? Are not these actions sometimes right and sometimes wrong? Suppose, for example, a friend who had lent us a weapon were to go mad and then ask for it back, surely anyone would say we ought not to return it. It would not be 'right' to do so; nor yet to tell the truth without reserve to a madman. (Republic I:331)

Having disposed of Cephalus' definition, Socrates moves on to the next, which is posed by Polemarchus. Polemarchus proposes "That it is just to render every man his due," which in practice means helping friends and harming enemies. But Socrates maintains that it can never be just to harm someone, because to do so makes the harmed person less than she or he was, and thereby makes that person less just. To make someone less just is not justice.

Thrasymachus then presents the famous argument that justice is the will of the stronger, or might makes right. The point of this argument is that justice is actually no more nor less than what those in power say that it is. Socrates again turns the tables on his opponent. He gets Thrasymachus to admit that the strong are not perfect and that they sometimes order things to be done that harm themselves. If justice is always that which is in the interest of the stronger, than it is not always just to obey the commands of the strongest: might does not necessarily make right.

Having eliminated the most popular definitions of justice of his time, Socrates then proposes a new definition. He compares the parts of society to the parts of each human being, which are three: body (physical appetites), spirit (courage), and mind (intelligence, or rationality). In each human being, justice occurs when the rational faculty, the mind, rules the spirited nature and the physical appetites. When either of the other two rules the person, the result is excessive indulgence in physical pleasure or excessive courage that leads to unnecessary conflict. When the mind rules, the intellect, which is naturally superior, can lead the spirit and body to the appropriate balance, and justice is achieved. The same is true of society. When those with the best minds, those who understand how best to govern, rule over those with courage or strength as their primary virtues, justice in society is achieved. It only makes sense, therefore, that a philosopher king, one who has the highest educated intelligence for governing, should rule society in the interests of everyone in society. The rule of the philosopher is the foundation of justice in society.

Many other definitions of justice have been proposed throughout history. Every country's system of law is based upon certain basic concepts of justice, and the legal community is the guardian of justice in society. One of the continuing controversies in the legal community is the distinction between substantive justice and procedural justice. To understand the difference between these two concepts, consider the following story:

> John Doe broke into a house and stole a VCR and stereo, which he took to his apartment. Later that week, a policeman who stopped Doe for a speeding ticket near Doe's apartment felt suspicious about the way Doe was acting and, calling another officer, entered Doe's apartment without a warrant. The police found the stolen VCR and stereo in Doe's apartment and charged Doe with burglary. When the case came to court the judge disallowed introduction of the VCR and stereo as evidence against Doe because they had been obtained without a warrant. Doe, who was guilty, was acquitted of the crime.

Was justice done in this case? If you answer "yes," you are likely to be an advocate of procedural justice, which means that if the rules of law have been followed, justice has been achieved. If you answer "no," you may be a proponent of substantive justice, which declares that, regardless of whether or not the rules have been followed, if the guilty person goes free or an innocent person is convicted, justice has not been done. Most of the time, one hopes, procedural justice and substantive justice go hand in hand. Many times, however, they do not. The problem is that procedures and rules are normally the basic requirement to ensure that justice is achieved in society, but following them does not guarantee fairness. If police disregard the need for a warrant, then basic liberties are at risk. If people start to believe, however, that someone with influence can use the rules to get away with doing wrong, then the system loses the confidence of the people, who may then tend to go around it or ignore it.

Harvard professor John Rawls' *A Theory of Justice* (1971) is often credited with inspiring much of the enthusiasm for a revival of normative political thought in recent years. *A Theory of Justice* is a rich, complex work, and we shall only point to some of its most basic principles here. Rawls begins by defining justice as fairness and by defining fairness as a fundamental equality with respect to the political and social privileges of people in society. Rawls (1971, 3–4) maintains that

> Each person possesses an inviolability founded on justice that even the welfare of society as a whole cannot override. For this reason justice denies that the loss of freedom for some is made right by a greater good shared by others. It does not allow that the sacrifices imposed on a few are outweighed by the larger sum of advantages enjoyed by many. Therefore in a just society the liberties of equal citizenship are taken as settled; the rights secured by justice are not subject to political bargaining or to the calculus of social interests.

In order to determine the principles of justice for society, Rawls proposes that an "original agreement" be made by the people who form the society, an agreement containing "principles that free and rational persons concerned to further their own interests would accept in an initial position of equality as defining the fundamental terms of the association" (Rawls 1971, 11). Rawls' fame is derived in large part from his concept of how this "original agreement" is to be formulated. If any group of people should come together today to set up the rules for a new society, each person would naturally strive to protect her or his own interests. In the struggle to preserve privileges or advantages that already exist, valid principles of fairness would be lost. Rawls proposes, therefore, that people come together under a "veil of ignorance" in which they can design the rules of society as if they were yet unborn, in other words, as if they did not know in advance who they would be or what attributes they would have in the society that they construct. Since they would not know in advance whether they personally will be rich or poor, mentally impaired or highly intelligent, attractive or unattractive, healthy or physically impaired, they will design principles that will be fair to anyone under any of these circumstances. As Rawls explains, the veil of ignorance is not an actual historical condition or a "state of nature" such as Hobbes and Locke proposed. It is a hypothetical condition that allows people to deduce a superior conception of justice.

Having established the process of selecting principles by which to govern society, Rawls (1971, 60) explains the kinds of principles that he expects this process to bring forth:

> I shall now state in a provisional form the two principles of justice that I believe would be chosen in the original position. . . . First: each person is to have an equal right to the most extensive basic liberty compatible with similar liberty for others. Second: social and economic inequalities are to be arranged so that they are both (a) reasonably expected to be to everyone's advantage, and (b) attached to positions and offices open to all.

This is merely the beginning of the discussion, for Rawls himself, and commentators responding to his work, hash out the many fascinating implications of what is a relatively new way of conceiving justice in society. In the course of this discussion, many alternative definitions of justice have been proposed. One of the most prominent alternative views is that of Robert Nozick. Whereas fairness and equality are Rawls' primary concerns, Nozick believes that the central issue is the role of the state. While Rawls' desire for equality leads to an active welfare state, Nozick takes an extreme individualist view, contending that an active state is dangerous to freedom and justice, and that only a minimal state is in accord with justice. Nozick calls his version of justice the "entitlement view." As he explains in *Anarchy, State, and Utopia* (1974, ix):

> Individuals have rights, and there are things no person or group may do to them (without violating their rights). So strong and far-reaching are these rights that they raise the question of what, if anything, the state and its officials may do. How much room do individuals leave for the state? . . . Our main conclusions about the state are that a minimal state, limited to the narrow functions of protection against force, theft, fraud, enforcement of contracts, and so on, is justified; that any more extensive state will violate person's rights not to be forced to do certain things, and is unjustified; and that the minimal state is inspiring as well as right. Two noteworthy implications are that the state may not use its coercive apparatus for the purpose of getting some citizens to aid others, or in order to prohibit activities to people for their *own* good or protection.

According to the entitlement view, therefore, individuals are entitled to the protection of fundamental natural rights, and this protection is the purpose of the state. In society, conflicts of interest arise, requiring an agency to protect individual rights. Various agencies evolve, and eventually a minimal state arises from consolidating protective power. This minimal state only keeps peace and compensates people for loss of benefits incurred in resolving disagreements wherein some gain more than others. Justice is established by the minimal state when the state enables maximum freedom for individuals who have differing desires. Within this minimal state, people may form utopian communities if they desire. In this version of justice, the state only redistributes the minimal quantities of goods that are necessary to ensure the protection of all. The open marketplace within the society, wherein people can freely exchange as they choose, is the vehicle for the redistribution of goods, and this just marketplace is guaranteed by the state. If some accumulate more than others, this is just (morally correct) because the *process* of exchange was justly conducted. We can see, therefore, that Nozick has a process view of justice and political equality.

Democracy

Democracy (literally "the people rule") has had many meanings throughout the centuries, and it has come, by the end of the twentieth century, to represent humanity's best hope for freedom, equality, justice, and many other political values. In ancient usage it has two meanings. The first, as understood by Aristotle, meant rule by the largest and poorest class in its own interest. This use of the term associated democracy with mob rule. The second and more positive connotation of the term was used by Perikles, leader of Athens in that city's golden age. Perikles' definition emphasizes the point that in a democracy everyone has a chance to rule:

> Let me say that our system of government does not copy the institutions of our neighbors. It is more the case of our being a model to others, than of our imitating anyone else. Our constitution is called a democracy because power is in the hands not of a minority but of the whole people. When it is a question of settling private disputes, everyone is equal before the law: when it is a question of putting one person before another in positions of public responsibility, what counts is not membership of a particular class, but the actual ability that the man possesses.

In 1946, Winston Churchill, who led Great Britain through its most perilous hours in World War II, defined democracy in opposition to the "iron curtain" which fell between Eastern and Western Europe as a consequence of Soviet domination of the Eastern Bloc after the war (1992, 87):

> All this means that the people of any country have the right, and should have the power by constitutional action, by free unfettered elections, with secret ballot, to choose or change the character or form of government under which they dwell; that freedom of speech and thought should reign; that courts of justice, independent of the executive, unbiased by any party, should administer laws which have received the broad assent of large majorities or are consecrated by time and custom. Here are the title deeds of freedom which should lie in every cottage home. Here is the message of the British and American peoples to mankind. Let us preach what we practice—let us practice what we preach.

In *The Third Wave* (1991), Harvard political scientist Samuel Huntington has adopted a definition of democracy and then attempted to understand the process of democracy as it has become established in more and more nations around the world. Huntington adopts two criteria for determining when a country is qualified to be called democratic. The first is that at least half of the adult males are allowed to vote, and the second is "a responsible executive who either must maintain majority support in an elected parliament or is chosen in periodic popular elections." Applying these two criteria to the history of the nations of the world, Huntington finds that "the United States began the first wave of democratization roughly about 1828" (Huntington 1991, 16). In his succeeding analysis, Huntington finds that there have been three great waves of democratization around the world, with two intervening periods of "reverse waves" when democracies lost ground to authoritarian regimes. We are now in the midst of the third great historical wave of democratization. His series of waves and reverse waves is as follows:

First, long wave of democratization	1828–1926
First reverse wave	1922–42
Second, short wave of democratization	1943–62
Second reverse wave	1958–75
Third wave of democratization	1974–

Jan-Erik Lane and Svante Ersson (1991, 65–67) have examined many studies of democracies and found that many indices have been constructed to determine the extent of democracy in any particular country. Each index focuses on a different aspect of democracy. Some of the indices are:

Cutright's index of political development
Smith's index of aggregate degree of political democracy
Neubauer's index of democratic political development
Jackman's index of democratic performance
Bollen's index of political democracy
Vanhanen's index of democratization
Humana's index of human rights
Gastil's index of freedom

How much participation is needed from citizens in order to have a viable democracy? Must this participation be based upon a certain minimum knowledge and competence on the part of the citizens? For several decades Robert Dahl has been a leading student of the problem of citizen participation in democracy. The problem is that theoretically democracy will work well only if those who have the ultimate responsibility for making political decisions, the voters, are competent to make those decisions. Classical democratic theory claims that citizens can become knowledgeable enough and will participate sufficiently to make the quality of decisions that is required for good government. Dahl (1965, 263) explains, however, that political science has discovered a great deal of evidence that the traditional assumptions about voters in democracies are not grounded in fact:

Although there are variations among democratic countries (notably on turnout in elections), the evidence seems to show that in all democratic countries the average citizen falls far short of the standards of the good citizen as portrayed in either the classical or modern version. Only a minority of citizens are deeply interested in politics, and, except for voting, even fewer are actively engaged in political life.

A common response to the problem that most citizens are neither well informed nor politically active is that, although ideal citizens are few and far between, there are enough active and informed citizens to make the system work. This explanation, Dahl (1965, 264) says, goes like this:

> Most citizens receive a level of formal education sufficient to ensure political literacy. Their political understanding is further increased by the widespread availability of relevant and low-cost information supplied by the media and political leaders competing for office and organized political parties. In their adversarial competition for votes, leaders are compelled to supply information on which citizens can make informed judgments about the policies, programs, and proposals of parties and elected leaders, as well as the trustworthiness, honesty, ability, and other relevant personal organizational characteristics of political leaders. Armed with information of this kind, citizens may hold elected officials or parties accountable in a succeeding election.

Dahl believes, however, that this solution faces three important problems. The first is that *changes in scale* have altered the nature of the problems that must be solved. No longer are the populations of democratic communities figured in the hundreds of thousands; now they are present in the hundreds of millions. This causes the centers of power for making decisions to become increasingly remote from the people themselves and for representation to be far less direct. The American Founders originally planned for there to be one member of the House of Representatives for every 30,000 people. If that standard had been maintained, there would now be 8,666 members of the House. That formula was changed, so that now each member of the House represents about 600,000 people, and each member of the Senate represents between 227,000 (Wyoming) to 14.9 million (California), an average of about 2.6 million people per senator.

The second problem that Dahl mentions is *complexity,* which means that the complexity of the problems that government must face has increased at a faster rate than the level of education needed to deal with these problems among average citizens. Dahl complains that even the availability of experts does not solve the problem because the experts may be less knowledgeable than even average citizens on the wider range of problems that must be faced together.

The third problem is *communications*. While it is true that information technology has increased the availability of information in astounding ways in the past half century, information alone does not automatically lead to understanding.

Representation

One of the most important problems of democracy is representation. Although only the adult male citizens of ancient Athens could participate in government and only a minority of the population were qualified to be citizens, that ancient city-state was in some ways more democratic than modern democracies because all of the citizens could sit in the Assembly and help make the most important decisions of the society. In addition, citizens took turns holding many of the public offices. Today's democracies are much larger, and they have turned to representation to allow the citizens a role while limiting the number of actual decisionmakers.

What does it mean to be an elected representative in a modern democracy? Should she or he merely voice the demands of her or his constituents and be a delegate of their wishes only, or has the representative been elected to fulfill a public trust wherein she or he exercises conscience or judgment to do what is best for people? A related question also arises. Does a member of the House of Representatives represent the interests of her or his constituency, or the nation as a whole? These questions are answered by representatives every day in a variety of ways. One of the most famous answers was given by conservative British philosopher Edmund Burke. Speaking about British government near the end of the eighteenth century, Burke (1992, 50–51) explained that

> To deliver an opinion is the right of all men; that of constituents is a weighty and respectable opinion, which a representative . . . ought always most seriously to consider. But authoritative instructions, mandates issued, which the member is bound blindly and implicitly to obey . . . though contrary to the clearest convictions of his judgment and conscience—these are things utterly unknown to the laws of this land, and which arise from a fundamental mistake of the whole order and tenor of our constitution. Parliament is not a congress of ambassadors from different and hostile interests, which interests each must maintain, as an agent and advocate, against other agents and other advocates; but parliament is a deliberative assembly of one nation, with one interest, that of the whole—where not local purposes, not local prejudices, ought to guide, but the general good, resulting from the general reason of the whole. You choose a member, indeed; but when you have chosen him, he is not a member of Bristol, but he is a member of Parliament.

German-American philosopher Eric Voegelin believed that the problem of representation in society is much deeper than it first appears. He believed that there are several levels of the meaning of representation that have important consequences for society. The first level of meaning he called the *elemental type.* Considerations of the elemental type refer to the normal actions that are taken when elections are conducted, such as voting and counting ballots (Voegelin 1952).

This simple concept of representation, however, does not account for important facts. For example, during the Cold War, Americans denied that the Soviet government actually represented the people living within the Soviet Union. Americans pointed to the fact that there was only one legitimate party, the Communist Party. The American view was that there must be an actual choice to be made by the electorate if elections are to be meaningfully representative. Suppose that the American view is correct. A problem still remains. The Soviet government may not have *represented* the Russian and other people in the sense that its representatives were selected on the basis of free choice, but nonetheless the Soviet government *represents* the people within its jurisdiction on the stage of history, in diplomatic decisions, and before the people of the world in international affairs. Further, there is another important meaning to the concept of representation. Government officials articulate the goals, dreams, intent, and character of the people within their jurisdictions. Articulation is vastly important because it expresses the meaning of life for the culture in symbols that people understand. The effectiveness of political leadership in large part depends upon the ability of leadership to represent the people accurately by articulating their dreams, their hopes, their fears, and their common purpose. Voegelin (1952, 40–41) cites as an example of effective leadership and representation Lincoln's powerful description of American government as government "of the people, by the people, for the people."

> The symbol "people" in this formula means successively the articulated political society, its representative, and the membership that is bound by the acts of the representative. The unsurpassable fusion of democratic symbolism with theoretical content in this formula is the secret of its effectiveness. . . . Articulation, thus, is the condition of representation. In order to come into existence, a society must articulate itself by producing a representative that will act for it.

Perhaps we consider how we represent ourselves as Americans today. What do we say about ourselves as a people? Does it matter? Consider, for a moment, the manner in which Native American Luther Standing Bear articulated the character of his people in a speech he made in 1933 (247):

> The feathered and blanketed figure of the American Indian has come to symbolize the American continent. He is the man who through centuries has been molded and sculpted by the same hand that shaped its mountains, forests, and plains, and marked the course of its rivers.
>
> The American Indian is of the soil, whether it be the region of forests, plains, pueblos, or mesas. He fits into the landscape, for the hand that fashioned the continent also fashioned the man for his surroundings. He once grew as naturally as the wild sunflowers; he belongs just as the buffalo belonged. . . .
>
> The white man does not understand the Indian for the reason that he does not understand America. He is too far removed from its formative processes. The roots of the tree of his life have not yet grasped the rock and soil. The white man is still troubled with primitive fears; he still has in his consciousness the perils of this frontier continent, some of its fastness not yet having yielded to his questing footsteps and inquiring eyes. He shudders still with the memory of the loss of his forefathers upon its scorching deserts and forbidding mountain-tops. The man from Europe is still a foreigner and an alien. And he still hates the man who questioned his path across the continent.

Consider the power in which the United States of America was symbolically born when Thomas Jefferson wrote the following words: "We hold these truths to be self-evident; that all men are created equal, that they are endowed by their creator with certain unalienable rights, that among these are life, liberty and the pursuit of happiness" (*The Declaration of Independence*). Is this a genuine representation of who we are today, or have we unfinished business before we can proclaim these ideals as reality?

If Jefferson's statement is true today, it is only because it became true after a long and difficult battle. Consider the following passage from *Dred Scott v. Sanford* (1857) written by Justice Taney and expressing the law of the land as interpreted by the Supreme Court on the eve of the Civil War. Taney first quotes Jefferson's famous lines on equality from the Declaration of Independence, and then proceeds to say:

> The general words above quoted would seem to embrace the whole human family, and if they were used in a similar instrument at this day would be so understood. But it is too clear for dispute that the enslaved African race were not intended to be included, and formed no part of the people who framed and adopted this declaration. . . . The unhappy black race were separated from the white by indelible marks, and laws long before established and were never thought of or spoken of except as property, and where the claims of the owner or the profit of the trader were supposed to need protection.

The Dred Scott decision upheld the practice of slavery in the South, inflamed abolitionists in the North, and failed to avert the Civil War. It represented a dying vision of America.

Our brief survey of the great issues of politics has merely introduced a few of the deep and abiding controversies of politics. The next chapter extends the discussion of the great issues by describing the manner in which ideologies have formed which contain combinations of beliefs about freedom, equality, justice, democracy, and more.

4

Political Ideologies ˙

The whole history of civilization is strewn with creeds and institutions that were invaluable at first, and deadly afterward.

—Walter Bagehot, *Physics and Politics*, 1869

The Nature of Ideology

"Ideology" is a loaded word. For the last 150 years, it has been used most often by political theorists in a negative way. To be an "ideologue," in the thinking of most analysts, is to be willfully narrow-minded, to choose to interpret the world in only one way. And yet, if we consider another, nonprejudicial definition of the word, we have to admit that, in a very real sense, we all have an ideology; we are all ideologues. Because ideologies are basically systems of beliefs, it may indeed be true to say that there are as many ideologies as there are people. Most personal belief systems, however, follow a somewhat limited set of variations, and it is, therefore, possible to classify most belief systems in a definite, if long, list. The variety of belief patterns is fascinating, as indicated by the following list, which is by no means complete.

101 Ideologies

Anarchism, individualist
Anarchism, socialist
Anarchocapitalism
Anarchoenvironmentalism
Anarchosyndicalism
Anticolonialism
Anticommunism
Antidisestablishmentarian-
  ism
Antisemitism
Apartheid
Authoritarianism
Bolshevism
Calvinism
Capitalism, laissez faire
Capitalism, welfare state
Catholicism

Collectivism
Colonialism
Communalism
Communism, Vietnamese
Communism, war
Conservatism, economic
Conservatism, progressive
Conservatism, religious
Conservatism, moral
Constitutionalism
Corporatism
Democratic Centralism
Determinism, economic
Ecosocialism
Egalitarianism
Eurocommunism
Elitism

Environmentalism
Fabianism
Fascism
Federalism
Feminism, liberal
Feminism, radical
Feminism, socialist
Fidelismo
Fundamentalism, Hindu
Fundamentalism,
  Protestant
Fundamentalism, Shiite
Fusionism
Holism
Humanism, messianic
Humanism, secular
Humanism, theocentric

101 Ideologies—*Continued*

Idealism	National Chauvinism	Realism
Imperialism	Nationalism	Relativism
Individualism	Nazism	Republicanism
Internationalism	Neocolonialism	Revisionism
Irrationalism	Neoconservatism	Social Darwinism
Keynesianism	Neoliberalism	Socialism, democratic
Liberalism, classical	Nihilism	Socialism, scientific
Liberalism, McGovernite	Pacifism	Socialism, state
Liberalism, New Deal	Paleolibertarianism	Stalinism
Libertarianism	Panafricanism	Statism
Maoism	Patriotism	Syndicalism
Marxism	Pluralism	Titoism
Marxism-Leninism	Positivism	Totalitarianism
Materialism	Progressivism	Ujamaa
Mercantilism	Protestantism	Utilitarianism
Militarism	Racism	Zionism
Multiculturalism	Radicalism	
Mutualism	Rationalism	

The number of variations in ideologies is virtually limitless. The list above contains only 101 examples of the hundreds of ideologies and versions of ideologies that you will find discussed if you review the literature of political science for the twentieth century. To give you a sense of the diversity of opinion that you will discover upon further investigation, the second part of this chapter will discuss a few important current ideologies, focusing on one or two of the leading characteristics of each. Our present focus, however, is to define the term "ideology" clearly, yet in a way that does justice to the variety of uses to which it is put in today's world. Lyman Tower Sargent (1993, 3) has constructed an excellent definition of ideology

> An ideology is a value system or belief system accepted as fact or truth by some group. It is composed of sets of attitudes toward the various institutions and processes of society. An ideology provides the believer with a picture of the world both as it is and as it should be, and, in doing so, organizes the tremendous complexity of the world into something simple and understandable.

An ideology, most basically, is a set of beliefs that orients us towards the challenges and opportunities of life. The term *ideology* combines two Greek roots, *eidos* or "knowledge," and *logos* or "word." Literally, ideology means "words of knowledge." Antoine Louis Claude Destutt de Tracy (1754–1836) popularized and may have originated the term. In *Elements d'Ideologie* (1826), Tracy proposed ideology as a formal and accurate method of inquiry into the truth, in fact a "science of ideas" to be sharply distinguished from religion or metaphysical philosophy.

For Tracy, ideology was an empirical method of discerning the principles through which the mind operates, of using sense perception as a verification of belief, a way of distinguishing false from true ideas. Tracy's followers, who proudly proclaimed themselves ideologues, set out to free humanity from religion through a new scientific way of thinking. According to H. M. Drucker in *The Political Uses of Ideology* (1974, 4), "what the Ideologues did was to take the anti-metaphysical arguments which had been articulated in the past, whether by the British empiricists or the French Philosophes, and use them to attack the established institutions of French society, and as a guide towards creating new 'scientific institutions.'"

For Tracy, then, an ideology was a useful tool for expanding the boundaries of political thought. The now more familiar pejorative use of the term ideology began when Napoleon, defending the institutions of postrevolutionary France, accused the ideologues of spreading beliefs destructive to the nation's welfare. Marx and Engels permanently defamed the term in *The German Ideology* by defining ideology as *false belief* as opposed to *correct belief*, which is gained through observation of society.

Whether you consider them generally benign or dangerous, ideologies may be relatively simple, or extremely complex. Consider the following statement:

> The fruit of SILENCE is Prayer
> The fruit of PRAYER is Faith
> The fruit of FAITH is Love
> The fruit of LOVE is Service
> The fruit of SERVICE is Peace
>
> —Mother Theresa

In this simple but profound statement, Mother Theresa presents a basic component of ideology: a prescription for action beneficial to human life. It is difficult to consider Mother Theresa's formula to be a politically threatening one. Here is another example of a benign ideology:

> ALL I REALLY NEED TO KNOW about how to live and what to do and how to be I learned in kindergarten. Wisdom was not at the top of the graduate-school mountain, but there in the sand pile at Sunday School. These are things I learned:
>
> > Share everything.
> > Play fair.
> > Don't hit people.
> > Put things back where you found them.
> > Clean up your own mess.
> > Don't take things that aren't yours.
> > Say you're sorry when you hurt somebody.
> > Wash your hands before you eat.
> > Flush.
> > Warm cookies and cold milk are good for you.
> > Live a balanced life—learn some and think some and draw and paint and sing and dance and play and work every day some.
> > Take a nap every afternoon.
> > When you go out into the world, watch out for traffic, hold hands, and stick together.

> Be aware of wonder. Remember the little seed in the Styrofoam cup: the
> roots go down and the plant goes up and nobody really knows how or
> why, but we are all like that.
> Goldfish and hamsters and white mice and even the little seed in the
> Styrofoam cup—they all die. So do we.
> And then remember the Dick-and-Jane books and the first word you
> learned—the biggest word of all—LOOK.

This passage from Robert Fulghum's best-selling book *All I Really Need to Know I Learned in Kindergarten* (1988, 4–6) presents a simple but perhaps profound ideology. It sets forth a basic set of beliefs that describe reality and how to approach reality. When considered thoughtfully, Fulghum's formula has many social and political implications.

As our ideologies develop, they become our compass, our map, and our sextant. First and foremost, they perform one primary function: they help us find our way through life. Ideologies come in many forms; there are practical, psychological, and religious ideologies.

The above statements by Mother Teresa and Robert Fulghum differ from each other in tone and intent. They share, however, an essential characteristic of ideology: a set of beliefs that orient their holders to personal and social life in the world. They contain explicitly social but only implicitly political ideology. Consider, however, the following statement from the *Communist Manifesto* (1848):

> The history of all hitherto existing society is the history of class struggles. Free man and slave, patrician and plebeian, lord and serf, guild master and journeyman, in a word, oppressor and oppressed, stood in constant opposition to one another, carried on an uninterrupted, now hidden, now open fight, a fight each time ended either in a revolutionary constitution of society at large or in the common ruin of contending classes.

In the *Communist Manifesto* we have the full political expression of an ideology which interprets the history of the world as the history of class struggle. The Manifesto depicts humanity's present and past existences as corrupt and details a vision of a new, better existence to come.

These statements by Mother Theresa, Robert Fulghum, and Marx & Engels all fall within our definition of ideology: a set of beliefs, neither necessarily false nor true, which helps guide our thoughts and actions. We create ideologies by accepting or rejecting the beliefs of others and by drawing our own conclusions about how things operate in the world.

Ideologies begin with basic perceptions and progress in more or less structured patterns to a set of beliefs that encompass specific ideas about what people are like and how society should operate. When you attempt to grasp reality, you combine several basic belief statements and take them as guides to your life. You thereby create an ideology. Ideology is in part the search for certainty, which some call "truth." Ideology serves an essential purpose: it enables us to draw conclusions upon which we can take action. Ideology, in this definition, is harmful when it contains destructive or false beliefs, or when it becomes rigid, that is, the person holding it refuses to consider information that may contradict it.

In *Ideology and the Ideologists* (1975, 17), Lewis Feuer defines ideology as "a myth written in the language of philosophy and science." Feuer uses the word myth, in its classical sense, that is, not as something that is untrue, but as a story, metaphor, or analogy that expresses a truth that is beyond our human perceptive capabilities. According to Feuer, every political ideology includes one "invariant ingredient," which is some form of repetition of the Mosaic myth, the story told in the biblical book of Exodus of how Moses liberated the ancient Hebrews from their slavery in Egypt. According to Feuer (56–58):

> The Mosaic myth can be stated in its most elemental form as a series of situations and incidents:
>
> 1. A people is oppressed;
> 2. a young man, not himself of the oppressed, appears;
> 3. moved by sympathy, he intervenes and strikes down an oppressor's henchman;
> 4. he flees, or goes into exile;
> 5. he experiences the call to redeem the oppressed people;
> 6. he returns to demand freedom for the oppressed;
> 7. he is spurned by the tyrannical ruler;
> 8. he leads the actions, which, after initial defeats, overwhelm the oppressor;
> 9. he liberates the oppressed people;
> 10. he imparts a new sacred doctrine, a new law of life, to his people;
> 11. the newly liberated people relapse from loyalty to their historical mission;
> 12. almost disillusioned, their leader imposes a collective discipline on the people to re-educate them morally for their new life;
> 13. a false prophet arises who rebels against the leader's authoritarian rule, but he is destroyed;
> 14. the leader, now the revered lawgiver, dies, as he glimpses from afar the new existence.

Feuer's point is that the essentials of this pattern, established first by Moses, are found in the political liberation stories of persons like George Washington, Mohandas Gandhi, and Martin Luther King. For Feuer (1975, 17), however, a myth is not all there is to ideology. An ideology "incorporates a myth but what it adds is distinctive; it tries to demonstrate the truth of its contained myth from basic philosophical and scientific premises." Further, the "ideologist wishes to derive that myth from the nature of the universe itself."

For Karl Marx, the founder of modern communism, ideologies are philosophical illusions constructed by one social class to justify its oppression of another. Marx proclaimed that the religious leaders and philosophers before him had constructed ideologies. They were in fact philosophical illusions that attempt to deduce political events from abstract, illusory principles, designed by some social classes to legitimize oppressing others. Marx claimed that his own approach, as opposed to that of ideologists like Hegel, was to identify political actions as they occur in the real world, and then decipher patterns among them. This kind of inductive thinking led Marx, and other theorists, to a profound skepticism regarding the belief systems by which Western civilization maintained its structure.

Sigmund Freud, the father of modern psychology, agreed with Marx that religion and political ideology are illusions. Rather than originating in class struggles, however, ideologies in Freud's view are expressions of a need to repress the powerful psychological forces within us. Victorian conservatism, for example, was an expression of a desire to repress the need for sex. Freud recognized, however, that, although ideologies are illusions, they are necessary for giving people a perspective on how to understand human life and how it works. Later authors have in fact claimed that Freud's ideas have themselves been made into an ideology, a closed system of thought that finds a way to explain everything that might appear to be an inconsistency.

While Marx believed that ideologies derive from class conflict and Freud maintained that they came from inner psychological needs, Karl Mannheim asserted that ideology, and in fact all thought, is socially determined. The meaning of what a person says can be understood in terms of childhood conflicts. Mannheim calls incongruous thoughts, which are inconsistent with helping the person to understand himself, ideologies. For other thinkers like H.M. Drucker, ideologies are attempts to escape reality. According to Drucker (1974, 21), thoughts that "enable men to break through the status quo and satisfy the needs of the thinker, are called utopias. . . . In effect a utopia is a progressive prejudice and ideology is a conservative one."

In 1960, Daniel Bell generated a controversy when he asserted, in *The End of Ideology* (1968, 99) that he believed that the development of new political ideologies had come to an end:

> [F]or the radical intelligentsia, the old ideologies have lost their "truth" and their power to persuade. Few serious minds believe any longer that one can set down "blueprints" and through "social engineering" bring about a new utopia of social harmony. . . . In the Western world, therefore, there is today a rough consensus among intellectuals on political issues: the acceptance of a Welfare State; the desirability of decentralized power; a system of mixed economy and of political pluralism. In that sense too, the age of ideology has ended.

Bell's book elicited an immediate controversy in which many writers disputed his claim. By the end of the 1960s, it is probably fair to say that most students of ideology agreed with noted Italian political scientist Giovanni Sartori that the dissolution of some ideologies does not necessarily indicate the end of the needs which gave rise to ideologies and to efforts to develop new ones. Agreeing with Sartori, H. M. Drucker writes in *The Political Uses of Ideology* (1974, xi):

> The powerful political ideas of our time are almost all part of some ideology or other. . . . But most of us come to grips with the political world, and commit what paltry political acts we do commit under the influence of some ideology or other. . . . Specific ideologies come and go. This does not affect the issue. Particular ideologies seem to arise to meet some new-felt need and disappear the next day. Like Marxism, they splinter off into a dozen warring factions.

Ideologies share a set of common characteristics. As you examine the differences between the ideologies in this chapter, bear in mind the following similarities.

- Ideology is the *quest for certainty*. It differs from philosophy in that, while philosophy can be defined as the open search for truth, in which new questions are constantly being asked, ideology is a set of beliefs which, if they do not contain all truth, at least claim to have the definitive formula for finding it.

- Ideology purports to *describe and prescribe reality*. Every ideology claims to tell us first what reality is like, and then how we should approach and change it.

- Ideology *addresses basic human psychological needs* such as safety, freedom, love, community. Our social ideology in itself satisfies many basic human needs by telling us how to meet them. It tells us how to relate to others. It may tell us, for example, that to be loved we need to be attractive, or that, to be financially secure, we must be aggressive.

- Ideology is *essential*. It is a yardstick, a reference point. Without a perspective with which to grasp the world, we cannot operate within it.

- Political ideology is concerned with *political and governmental systems*. In *Contemporary Ideologies*, Lyman Sargent proposes eleven categories of questions designed to analyze, fairly completely, the assumptions underlying any ideology. The topics dealt with by these categories include human nature, the origin of society and government or the state, political obligation, law, freedom, equality, community, power, justice, the end of society or government, and the structural characteristics of government

- Ideology is in a *dialectical relationship with interests*. That is to say there is an ongoing dispute between those who believe that our interests create our beliefs, and those who believe that our beliefs create our interests. Perhaps both phenomena occur within ideologies simultaneously, alternately affecting each other.

- Ideology is *powerful*. Ideologies have provided the inspiration to sweep some governments into power and others out of power. This is not to say that interests are not important, but that ideologies give effective expression to interests.

- The power of ideology may serve to *overthrow domination or to maintain it, or to first overthrow and then maintain domination*.

- Ideology reflects *deep and permanent antagonisms*. A national survey, which described the differences between conservatives and liberals within each of the major American religious denominations, reached the following conclusions:

  > Liberals regarded conservatives as rigid, intolerant, and fanatical. Conservatives described liberals as shallow, morally loose, unloving, and unsaved. The study also demonstrated that, unlike other kinds of prejudice and hostility, the ill feelings separating religious liberals and religious conservatives *did not mitigate* as the two groups came into greater contact with one another. The more each side came into contact with the other, and the more knowledge it gained about the other, the less it liked the other. (Wuthnow 1990, 80)

Every ideology is the expression of two mental pictures of the human condition. The first picture is of the world as it is, with its gravest problems. The second picture is of the world as it should or could be. In the remainder of this chapter, we shall describe some of the most famous ideologies and the social and historical conditions from which they have grown.

The Political Spectrum, Liberalism, and Conservatism

Complete the following exercise. There are no right or wrong answers. Indicate your opinion regarding each of the following statements by placing a number from 1 to 5 in the open column to the right of the statement, according to the following numbers:

1 = strongly agree   2 = agree   3 = uncertain   4 = disagree   5 = strongly disagree

Statement	Column 1	Column 2
If given a chance, most people will do the right thing.	█	
The rich do not pay their fair share of taxes.	█	
Inequalities in public schools need to be rectified.	█	
Better law enforcement is the best way to reduce crime.		█
The unborn child has a fundamental individual right to life.		█
Government should work actively to benefit society.	█	
Sexual orientation should not be protected by civil rights legislation.		█
Economic growth is not opposed to environmental protection.		█
Public support for the arts strengthens freedom of expression.	█	
The right to bear arms is a fundamental freedom.		█
Society would be better off if people followed the rules.		█
A lot of people on welfare could be earning their own living.		█
We need more choice in where to send our children to school.		█
Better programs aimed at *prevention* of social problems are the best way to reduce crime.	█	
Every woman has a fundamental right to choose whether or not to continue a pregnancy.	█	
Government that governs least governs best.		█
Sexual preference should be given the same legal protection as other civil rights.	█	
The environment needs more governmental protection.	█	
No artist has a right to claim public support for his or her art.		█
Gun control legislation will help reduce crime.	█	
Totals		

Total the numbers in each column. Calculate your score as follows:

Total for column 2: _____ minus (−) Total for column 1: _____ = _____.

Now mark the point where your score falls on the following contemporary American political ideology spectrum:

Very Liberal   Liberal   Moderate   Conservative   Very Conservative

(−40)—(−30)—(−20)—(−10)———(0)———————(+10)—(+20)———(+30)————(+40)

A spectrum is a device for illustrating relative differences. An optical spectrum, for example, is visible as bands of color when light is refracted from a prism. A political spectrum illustrates differences in political ideologies by placing them in relationship to each other along a line from right to left. The more conservative an ideology, the farther to the right it will be on a spectrum, while the more liberal ideologies fall on the left. Political scientists have devised many spectrums, but a typical simple political spectrum looks like this:

Left ←   Center   → Right

Radical   Liberal   Moderate   Conservative   Reactionary

●- - - - - - - - - - - -●- - - - - - - - - - - -●- - - - - - - - - - - -●- - - - - - - - - - - -●

The terms *left* and *right,* in connection with political ideas, are believed to have originated during the French Revolution, when relatively conservative delegates sat on the right side of the assembly hall and liberal delegates sat to the left. Although there are many differences among ideologies, the position that each ideology holds on the above spectrum is determined by dispositions towards three basic factors:

• The amount of change that is desirable for society
• The predisposition of human nature to good and evil
• The need for individuality and the need for community

It must be remembered that few individuals in any society hold views that fall clearly into any of the categories on the spectrum, and two individuals who are both called "moderates" may actually agree on very little, but their views, taken as a whole, may both be unlike those on either end of the spectrum.

The desire to change the institutions of society increases as one moves to the left of the spectrum. *Moderates* want modest, gradual change in society. *Liberals* are inclined to see injustice in current conditions and desire significant but not revolutionary change to correct perceived inequities. *Conservatives,* as their name suggest, want to conserve the current system, which, though it may be imperfect, has developed from experience, and should, they believe, be changed very gradually and with caution. Radicals, on the far left of the spectrum, want extreme change, and reactionaries, on the far right, want to return to a previous condition of society.

According to Lewis Feuer's *Ideology and the Ideologists,* ideologies conform to the "principle of wings," which "affirms that every philosophic unit-idea in the course of its career makes the passage through the whole spectrum of ideological affiliations. A philosophical doctrine which begins at the left will move rightward, and if at the right, will diffuse toward the left" (Feuer 1975, 57). For example, an idea such as progressivism may start at the left of the spectrum, where it will be seen as a tool of liberals who wish to change certain aspects of their society. As the idea becomes socially acceptable, it moves toward the center, and when new ideas replace it, for most members of society, it ends up at the right. There its intellectual force is eventually spent and it dies, to be replaced by a new ideology entering at the left end of the spectrum.

Liberalism

American liberalism accepts democratic principles of freedom and political equality, constitutional government, and an essentially free market economy. Today, liberalism in America is normally associated with the proposition that government should:

- Actively undertake to reduce poverty;
- Insure at least adequate levels of health, safety, and economic security;
- *Not* interfere with a woman's reproductive freedom;
- Protect the environment; and
- Reduce defense spending in comparison to domestic spending.

These beliefs have developed to their present status in the 1990s through a series of twentieth century political movements, most notably those connected with Presidents Franklin Roosevelt and Lyndon Johnson and presidential candidate George McGovern. Franklin Roosevelt assumed the presidency amidst the country's worst depression. Twenty-five percent of the work force would at times be unemployed before the depression began to lift at the end of the 1930s. Roosevelt introduced a series of programs that he called the "New Deal." They included an impressive array of activities such as Social Security and public employment in public works through agencies like the Civilian Conservation Corps. Accepting much of the economic philosophy of John Maynard Keynes, followers of Roosevelt adopted a policy of deficit spending, at first, just to get the country through the depression, but later as a method of stimulating economic growth.

In the 1960s, following President Kennedy's support for the civil rights movement, President Johnson initiated programs of the "Great Society." In his efforts to redirect some of the wealth of America to solving problems of poverty and racial inequality, Johnson launched programs such as the "war on poverty," which included the establishment of the Job Corps and housing assistance for the poor. Johnson's efforts to reduce poverty, however, were overshadowed by the war in Vietnam. As the war progressed without any apparent means of American victory, Johnson was challenged by Senators Eugene McCarthy and Robert Kennedy. Surprising everyone, Johnson announced that he would not seek a second full term as president in 1968. His Vice President and fellow Great Society liberal Hubert Humphrey was defeated by Richard Nixon in that year's presidential election. Senator George McGovern won the Democratic nomination in 1972. McGovern strongly protested the war and advocated a minimum income, to be provided by the government, for the poor.

McGovern's defeat in the election has been viewed as the turning point for contemporary liberals. Since McGovern, Democratic presidential candidates have found it necessary to place comparatively moderate social proposals before the American public, for the simple reason that the American voters regularly reject candidates endorsing what are perceived to be traditional liberal views. Democrats widely perceived as moderates, such as Jimmy Carter and Bill Clinton, have won election, while presidential candidates who have been successfully labeled "liberals" by Republicans, such as Walter Mondale and Michael Dukakis, have lost elections.

Today's American liberalism, however, has developed within a rich and complex tradition. Two other varieties of liberalism deserve special note. The first is what is sometimes called "classical liberalism," or "nineteenth century liberalism," which emphasized individual freedom and a free market economy. Many of the ideas of classical liberals would today be associated with conservatism. Two writers from the tradition of classical liberalism, Adam Smith and John Stuart Mill, are worthy of special note. In 1776, Adam Smith published *The Wealth of Nations,* which became the seminal work for American capitalism. Smith extolled the free market system as the solution to the problem of how best to encourage the creation of wealth in society. Smith proposed that, when each individual pursued his own economic interest, the unintended but natural result was that society as a whole also benefited. Smith proposed that an "invisible hand" guided the activities of people serving their own interests to promote the interests of the whole.

John Stuart Mill was the son of utilitarian James Mill who believed that the good of society could be determined by calculating the "greatest good for the greatest number." The younger Mill's essay *On Liberty* is the most famous treatise written on its subject. In this essay, Mill attempts to expand the concept of individual freedom as far as possible within modern society (1951, 95):

> The object of this essay is to assert one very simple principle, as entitled to govern absolutely the dealings of society with the individual in the way of compulsion and control, whether the means used be physical force in the form of legal penalties, or the moral coercion of public opinion. That principle is, that the sole end for which mankind are warranted, individually or collectively, in interfering with the liberty of action of any of their number, is self-protection.

Contemporary liberal groups focus much of their energy on helping the poor. One group, for example, that has periodically issued statements in support of liberal economic social policy is the National Conference of Catholic Bishops. In *Economic Justice for All: Pastoral Letter on Catholic Social Teaching and the U.S. Economy* (1984, 38), the Bishops stress the need for human dignity and society's obligation to provide everyone with the resources to attain the minimum standard of living necessary for dignity:

> Basic justice also calls for the establishment of a floor of material on which all can stand. This is a duty of the whole society and it creates particular obligations for those with greater resources. This duty calls into question extreme inequalities of income and consumption when so many lack basic necessities. Catholic social teaching does not maintain that a flat, arithmetical equality of income and wealth is a demand of justice, but it does challenge economic arrangements that leave large numbers of people impoverished.

Neoliberalism

Neoliberalism is an offshoot of contemporary liberalism. It arose from the frustrations of liberals who believe in the basic values of liberalism (justice, equality) but have lost faith in the government's ability to solve all social problems within responsible financial means. Sometimes called "pragmatic idealism" or "compassionate realism," neoliberalism wants to meet the most pressing social needs of society primarily through reducing the adversarial spirit in society, by promoting cooperation, and through encouraging incentives to economic growth. Neoliberals see themselves as wanting to help society while being practical and goal-oriented. Michael Dukakis, former governor of Massachusetts and 1988 Democratic presidential candidate, is a distinguished neoliberal who has written some of his thoughts concerning the importance of government service, specifically for the students reading this book. They are presented in the letter on page 84.

Conservatism

> *To design a personal plan for a new society is a pleasant form of madness; it is in imagination to play at being God and Caesar to the human race. Any such plan must implicitly assume that the visionary or someone else might find the power, to shape society to the plan; all such general plans of social reconstruction are merely the rationalization of the will to power. For that reason they are the subjective beginnings of fanaticism and tyranny. In these utopias the best is the enemy of the good, the heart's desire betrays the interests of man.*
>
> —Walter Lippman, *The Good Society,* 1947

Like liberalism, conservatism appears in many varieties. This discussion will describe three types that significantly influence American life today: classical conservatism, contemporary American conservatism, and neoconservatism.

Classical conservatism has one preeminent spokesman: Edmund Burke. Most famous for his treatise *Reflections on the Revolution in France* (1790), Burke believes that the best society is founded upon experience and custom. Abhorring the violence of the French Revolution, Burke defends the established aristocratic order of British society as a reflection of the natural order of things. Privilege and

FLORIDA ATLANTIC UNIVERSITY
P.O. BOX 3091
BOCA RATON, FLORIDA 33431-0991

DEPARTMENT OF POLITICAL SCIENCE
(407) 367-3210
FAX: (407) 367-2744

March 10, 1995

Dear Greg:

Thanks for your letter. Feel free to use whatever part
of this letter you think might be valuable in any publication.

I would say two things to a group of first year political
science students.

First, there is nothing in this world that can give one
more personal satisfaction or fulfillment than the opportunity
public service gives one to make a difference in one's community
or state or country. Unfortunately, the way the media cover
American politics these days, people have no sense of how
many good citizens are making a difference every day all across
this country. If your students get involved in the political
process, they will meet and work with some of the best and most
dedicated people in this country and have a much better appreciation
of just what is possible when good people work together for common
goals in politics.

Second, the best way to learn about politics is to get
involved. What makes that so easy in the United States is that
we have the most open political system in the world. You don't
need a ticket of admission other than your voter registration.
You don't need a famous name. It doesn't make any difference
where you were born or what your family status is. You have just
as good a shot at making a real contribution as anyone else.
And the careers of people like Bill Clinton and myself are as
good a testimonial to that fact as any I know. Of course, it
requires a lot of hard work and an enthusiasm for the task and
many, many citizen volunteers who are willing to work hard.
But succeeding in politics and public service is something
worth working for, and I want to see young people in this
country get involved a lot more actively than many of them are
these days.

I hope these comments are helpful.

Sincerely,

Michael S. Dukakis

position in society, according to Burke, are not only necessary to maintain order, but are most likely to produce legal, economic and social systems conducive to harmony and peace. In *Reflections on the Revolution in France* (1961, 45), Burke scorns what he calls innovation, a spirit of rapid change. Social customs and conventions, after all, have developed after many years of experience tested by trial and error:

> You will observe, that from Magna Charta to the Declaration of Right, it has been the uniform policy of our constitution to claim and assert . . . our liberties, as an entailed inheritance. . . . We have an inheritable crown; an inheritable peerage; and an house of commons and a people inheriting privileges, franchises, and liberties from a long line of ancestors. This policy appears to me to be the result of profound reflection; or rather the happy effect of following nature. . . . A spirit of innovation is generally the result of selfish temper and confined views.

Contemporary conservatism has two faces: economic and moral. Economic conservatives stress reducing government spending on social programs in favor of spending on defense, or reducing taxes. Moral conservatives emphasize traditional family values, such as heterosexuality, fidelity within marriage, refraining from premarital sex, and encouraging women to raise their children at home.

When Ronald Reagan, who was philosophically an economic and moral conservative, began his two terms in the White House, he recommended that people read George Gilder's *Wealth and Poverty*, which became known as the "economic Bible" of the Reagan administration. In *Wealth and Poverty*, Gilder says that, in regard to poverty, liberals focus on the wrong issues. Rather than attempting to reduce poverty, government should encourage the creation of wealth. According to Gilder (1981, 67–83):

> THE ONLY dependable route from poverty is always work, family, and faith. The first principle is that in order to move up, the poor must not only work, they must work harder than the classes above them. Every previous generation of the lower class has made such efforts. But the current poor, white even more than black, are refusing to work hard. . . . The poor choose leisure not because of moral weakness, but because they are paid to do so. . . . Indeed, after work the second principle of upward mobility is the maintenance of monogamous marriage and family. . . . [M]arried men work between two and one-third and four times harder than married women, and more than twice as hard as female family heads. . . . [H]usbands work 50 percent harder than bachelors. . . . The effect of marriage, thus, is to increase the work effort of men by about half. . . . [I]t is manifest that the maintenance of families is the key factor in reducing poverty. . . . [A] married man . . . is spurred by the claims of family to channel his otherwise disruptive male aggressions into his performance as a provider for a wife and children. . . . Faith in man, faith in the future, faith in the rising returns of giving, faith in the mutual benefits of trade, faith in the providence of God are all essential to successful capitalism.

Rush Limbaugh and Newt Gingrich represent economic conservatives today. The *Contract with America*, introduced by the Republicans during the 1994 congressional elections, not only represents the social agenda of the Republican Party, it exemplifies conservative aims, translated into political action. The *Contract with America* has the following ten goals:

1. To pass a balanced budget amendment and create line-item veto authority for the president
2. To strengthen enforcement measures to reduce crime
3. To reduce welfare amounts, eligibility, and term of benefits
4. To strengthen enforcement of paternal child support laws
5. To provide tax cuts for the middle class
6. To restrict command of U.S. troops to U.S. (not U.N.) commanders
7. To raise earnings for senior citizens
8. To cut the capital gains tax
9. To limit law suit awards in product liability and medical malpractice cases
10. To limit House of Representatives member terms to 6 years and Senators to 12 years

Neoconservatism

Neoconservatism, which has had such a large influence upon contemporary American conservatism that the two are now difficult to tell apart, arose in the 1960s as a reaction against the civil rights movement and protests of the Vietnam War. Although neoconservatives disdain the label "reactionary," their core beliefs form a statement which is largely a collection of negative reactions to the liberal and radical movements of the 1960s and which indicate a desire to return to the traditional values of the 1950s. Neoconservatives believe that society, led by liberals and radicals, has gone too far in:

- Redistributing income and other attempts to create equality of condition in society,
- Practicing social planning or social engineering,
- Protesting and disrespect for authority,
- Supporting multiculturalism and affirmative action, and
- Tolerating moral permissiveness and the "counterculture."

Neoconservatives accept social security and other basic features of the welfare state, but they insist that, rather than pursuing the above goals, Americans ought to restore traditional family and religious values, have more respect for authority, and leave economic activity as much as possible to the free market. Neoconservatives believe that society is now being directed by a "New Class" of professionals who have discarded traditional values. According to one of neoconservatism's most prominent spokespersons, Irving Kristol (1978, 171):

> We have a "New Class" of self-designated "intellectuals" who . . . pursue power in the name of equality. And then we have the ordinary people, working-class and lower-middle class, basically loyal to the bourgeois order but confused and apprehensive at the lack of clear meaning in this order. . . . All of these discon-

tents tend to express themselves in terms of "equality"—which is in itself a quintessentially bourgeois ideal and slogan.

Kristol claims that neoconservatism is not an organized movement, but its adherents share a number of beliefs. These beliefs include confidence in a free market economy, acknowledgment of the importance of economic growth, and reliance upon stable families and religion to help produce a healthy society. Harvard professor Samuel Huntington, another leading neoconservative, has argued that democracy, reacting to the social turmoil of the 1960s, has gone too far in allowing freedom to demonstrate and protest, and that more government authority is needed.

Radicalism and Reactionism

At opposite poles of our political spectrum lie radicalism, on the left or liberal end, and reactionism, on the right or conservative end. The word *radical* is derived from the Latin word *radix*, which means *root*. Radicals want to get to the root of society's ills by making basic, fundamental changes in the way society operates. They want to change the form of political representation or they want to change the economic system to redistribute society's wealth. A radical pronouncement known as the Port Huron Statement was issued in 1962 by the Students for a Democratic Society (SDS), an organization of college students committed to changing America:

> We would replace power rooted in possession, privilege, or circumstance by power and uniqueness rooted in love, reflectiveness, reason, and creativity. As a social system we seek the establishment of a democracy of individual participation, governed by two central aims: that the individual share in those social decisions determining the quality and direction of his life; that society be organized to encourage independence in men and provide the media for their common participation. In political democracy, the political life would be based in several root principles:
>
>> the decision-making of basic social consequence be carried on by public groupings;
>>
>> that politics be seen positively, as the art of collectively creating an acceptable pattern of social relations;
>>
>> that politics has the function of bringing people out of isolation and into community, thus being a necessary, though not sufficient, means of finding meaning in personal life;
>>
>> that the political order should serve to clarify problems in a way instrumental to their solution; it should provide outlets for the expression of personal grievance and aspiration; opposing views should be organized so as to illuminate choices and facilitate the attainment of goals; channels should be commonly available to relate men to knowledge and to power so that private problems—from bad recreation facilities to personal alienation—are formulated as general issues.

James Cone, a radical of a different sort, espoused Black Liberation Theology, which he defines in his book *God of the Oppressed* (1969, 54–57):

> To put it simply, Black Theology knows no authority more binding than the experience of oppression itself. This alone must be the ultimate authority in all religious matters. Concretely, this means that Black Theology is not prepared to accept any doctrine of God, man, Christ, or Scripture which contradicts the black demand for freedom now. It believes that any religious idea which exalts black dignity and creates a restless drive for freedom must be affirmed. All ideas which are opposed to the struggle for black self-determination or are irrelevant to it must be rejected as the work of the Antichrist.

At the other pole of the political spectrum stands the reactionary. Students should note that some books in recent years have referred to reactionaries as "the radical right." To be *reactionary* is to react negatively to the current system and desire a return to a previous condition of society. Reactionaries may call for a return to the social conditions of times such as the Roman Empire, the New Testament, the Victorian Age, the era of America's Founding Fathers, or the 1950s. White racists calling for a return to subjugation of African-Americans in the South are expressing reactionary views.

Radicals, liberals, moderates, conservatives, and reactionaries have different attitudes toward human capacity for good and evil. The farther one moves to the left of the spectrum, the more one is likely to believe that human beings are basically good and that the primary source of violence and corruption in society is faulty social, economic, and political institutions. The more conservative a person is, the more likely she or he is to believe that people are inherently sinful or evil, that social institutions are primarily for the purpose of restraining unacceptable behavior, and that prospects of reforming humanity through changing society are doubtful at best and probably dangerous.

On the whole, liberals tend to emphasize the need for stronger community ties and unified efforts, while conservatives are more inclined to champion the rights of individuals in opposition to the interference of the government. Liberals stress the manner in which people can come together to eliminate crime, racism, and poverty. Conservatives are more likely to seek ways to increase an individual's freedom to use fire arms, spend less on taxes, and operate a business without government interference. Referring to the spectrum we have been discussing, Kenneth Hoover offers this summary in *Ideology and Political Life* (1994, 7): "[T]hose on the *left* are associated with the belief that *similarities between people are more important than differences,* and those on the *right* are associated with the conviction that *differences are more important than similarities.*"

Spectrums like the one on the following page, drawn to differentiate liberal from conservative views, are useful for illustrating other political concepts. Many other ideological spectrums could be drawn. A spectrum for economic ideologies, for example, would have pure or unregulated capitalism on the far right and communism on the far left. This *political economy* spectrum would compare views on how much involvement government should have in business and economic matters. It might look like the following:

In the spectrum above, the far right (*unregulated capitalism*) represents a lack of government involvement in business affairs. In *welfare state capitalism,* a free market economy is not only regulated, but some income is redistributed from some members of society (the rich) to others (the poor). *Socialism* means that the means of production, such as factories and farms, are owned by the government. Theoretically, since everyone in a socialist system owns a share of the government, everyone owns a share of all the major industries. *Communism,* theoretically, distributes goods according to Marx's formula: "from each according to his abilities, to each according to his needs."

A governmental activism spectrum, which measures the amount of desired government involvement in people's lives, might look like this:

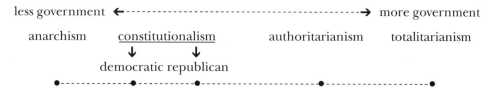

In the spectrum above, *anarchism* is the ideology that advocates minimum government. *Constitutionalism* supports governments the powers of which are carefully described and limited. *Authoritarianism* supports governments which require obedience to law as the ruling regime propogates it. *Totalitarianism* insists upon not only obedience but *active* support of the existing regime.

Anarchism

American patriot Thomas Paine's *Common Sense* (1776) is a classic example of anarchical thought:

> Some writers have so confounded society with government as to leave little or no distinction between them, whereas they are not only different but have different origins. Society is produced by our wants, and government by our wickedness; the former promotes our happiness *positively* by uniting our affections, the latter *negatively* by restraining our vices. The one encourages intercourse, the other creates distinction. The first is a patron, the last a punisher.
>
> Society in every state is a blessing, but government even in its best state is but a necessary evil, in its worst state an intolerable one; for when we suffer or are exposed to the same miseries by a government which we might expect in a country *without government,* our calamity is heightened by reflecting that we furnish the means by which we suffer.

Socialist anarchists like Emma Goldman (writing in 1907) believe that not only government but the institution of private property ought to be abolished:

> ANARCHISM:—The philosophy of a new social order based on liberty unrestricted by man-made law; the theory that all forms of government rest on violence, and are therefore wrong and harmful, as well as unnecessary. . . . [A]narchism is the great liberator of man from the phantoms that have held him captive; it is the arbiter and pacifier of the two forces for individual and social harmony. To accomplish that unity, anarchism has declared war on the pernicious influences which have so far prevented the harmonious blending of individual and social instincts, the individual and society. Religion, the dominion of the human mind; Property, the dominion of human needs; and Government, the dominion of human conduct, represent the stronghold of man's enslavement and all the horrors it entails. (Goldman 1907, 392–393)

When we hear the word "anarchy" today, we are most likely to think of disorder, of violence, of society out of control. "Anarchy" is an English word built from Greek roots which mean "no rule" or "no ruler." Anarchists believe that government, by its very existence and by its actions, restricts the freedom of individuals. Although most anarchists do see the need for some ordering institutions in society, they wish to limit government to its essential activities only. They all agree with Henry David Thoreau that "That government which governs least, governs best."

Peter Kropotkin (1842–1921) was history's most famous anarchist. Defeated by Lenin's Bolsheviks by 1919, Kropotkin failed in his attempt to establish an anarchical society in Russia. Kropotkin had seen the sufferings of the Russian people under the czars in the last half of the nineteenth century. He borrowed some of his ideas from Pierre Joseph Proudhon, a French utopian socialist, who popularized the term "anarchy" earlier in the century. Proudhon had believed that federations of voluntary associations, established to produce the material needs of society, could eventually replace government. The property arrangements which characterized postmedieval Europe could be abolished, and land and resources distributed to clusters of small associations, which would work together to coordinate activities but which would not be under any central control.

In the mid-1800s, Charles Darwin had written in *The Origin of the Species* that conflict and competition were the central processes of nature, and that humanity had evolved from natural selection, which meant that, in the competition for survival, the strongest individuals in each species had overcome the weak and learned to adapt to new conditions. Kropotkin, however, studied nature and came to an entirely different conclusion: the life of the various species is cooperative rather than competitive. Further, for Kropotkin, liberty was essential to well-being, and freedom from coercion is the essence of liberty. Government is inherently coercive and must, therefore, be abolished. Only when people are free to choose to live together without coercion can harmony, peace, and social well-being be established. A new society could be achieved if it were to be composed of small communes. Membership in the communes would be completely voluntary. Each commune would elect delegates to higher levels of association, but these delegates would have no authority other than the ability to support policies mandated by the people in the communes. Kropotkin at first advocated and later rejected the use of violence for the overthrow of the state. Like other anarchists, Kropotkin wanted an orderly society, but believed governments make peace and order difficult to achieve.

Nazism

Nazism would now be an historical curiosity if neonazis in Germany, the United States, and other countries were not attempting to resurrect an ideology that once terrorized the world. The evil genius of nazism was Adolph Hitler. Exploiting German resentment to the 1919 Treaty of Versailles, which ended World War I and exacted large war reparations payments from Germany to the victorious British and French, Hitler became Chancellor in 1933. Soon after, he proclaimed himself Führer, or leader, and attached to this title the status of the heroes of German myth. Proceeding to rearm a nation whose spirit was taking a further beating from the Great Depression, Hitler's National Socialist (Nazi) Party led Germany eventually to initiate World War II, which Hitler hoped would result in German conquest of the world. Even more horrible than the war was his plan to eliminate Jews from Europe. The Holocaust was the ghastly expression of an ideology the central core of which is racial hatred.

Nazi ideology is the accumulated expression of a series of ideas that begins with German mythology and the mythical notion of *volk*. Literally meaning "folk" or "people," volk implies a much more complex and irrational force, a power residing within Germans which comes from the land, with its deep forests and rich soil. Every nation has produced literature in which it is extolled as having a special place among the nations of the world. German tradition, however, more than most, held its people to be not only superior, but destined to rule others.

This aspect of German thought was developed by a series of thinkers over the course of two centuries before it was seized by Hitler as a rationale for bringing the Nazi Party to power. More than a century before Hitler was born, Johann Fichte (1762–1814) asserted that Germans constitute a superior race and that one day, under a strong leader, they would dominate the entire earth. Throughout the nineteenth century, German writers amplified this theme. Some of the most prominent of these writers were known as irrationalists for their emphasis on the idea that people act from their emotions or from some natural impulse other than reason. Arthur Schopenhauer (1788–1860), a leading irrationalist, wrote that, contrary to popular belief, life is not the manifestation of God's plan unfolding in the universe. Instead, life is the expression of a mysterious force or energy which Schopenhauer called the will. The will is uncontrollable, beyond prediction, and defies rational analysis. Agreeing with Schopenhauer that life is irrational, Heinrich von Treitschke (1834–1896) asserted that Germans, as the superior race, would be the ultimate expression of the irrational will.

The writings of Friedrich Nietzsche (1844–1900) lent further support to what eventually became Nazi ideology. Nietzsche predicted that a race of supermen would one day rule the earth. These supermen would recognize that conflict leads to the purification of humanity by eliminating the weak and leaving the strong to procreate. Pain is good, kindness is folly. Driven by a will to power, supermen would declare any attempt to help the weak to be immoral. Nietzsche criticized Christianity for its advocacy of the weak and oppressed. He claimed that democracy irresponsibly allowed the weak and mediocre to rule.

Hitler was particularly fond of the works of composer Richard Wagner (1813–1883), whose grand and majestic operas brought traditional German mythic heroes to life. The greatest of these heroes was Siegfried, who dominated others with courage and strength. Wagner became the center of a group who idealized the German state and propagated racism and antisemitism.

German folk myth, irrationalism, and a will to power were all added to antisemitism, which became the central element of the Nazi creed. While Nietzsche was writing philosophy, other scholars, studying linguistics, helped to lay the foundation for the Nazi belief in the superiority of the German race. Discovering similarities among the many European and Asian languages, these scholars assumed, on scant evidence, that there must have been a common source for these languages, and they conjectured that an undiscovered people, called Aryans, had originated a language whose features were now evident in many areas of the world.

This speculative Aryan soon began to take on a life of its own. Arthur de Gobineau became famous by asserting that Aryans were a group of nomads who had once dominated all other people through superiority of skill and strength. It was actually an Englishman, ironically, who took this myth to its tragic conclusion. Houston Stewart Chamberlain (1855–1927) asserted that intermarriage with inferior tribes had corrupted the Aryans everywhere, but they were less corrupt in northern Europe and least corrupt of all in the German people. For Chamberlain there were only two pure races, the Germans, who were purely good, and the Jews, who were purely evil. More ominous still, Chamberlain predicted that a great German leader would arise who would purify Germany, ridding the Aryan race of contamination from the weak, the impure, and, especially, the Jews. In *Mein Kampf* (1939, 406–420) a combination autobiography and manifesto written when he was in prison in the early 1920s, Adolph Hitler echoed Chamberlain's sentiments:

> The Aryan gave up the purity of his blood and therefore he also lost his place in the Paradise he had created for himself. . . . All that is not race in this world is trash. All world historical events, however, are only the expression of the race's instinct of self-preservation in its good or in its evil meaning. . . . In the Jew's life as a parasite in the body of other nations and States, his characteristic is established which once caused Schopenhauer to pronounce the sentence, already mentioned, that the Jew is the 'great master of lying.' Life urges the Jew towards the lie, that is, to a perpetual lie, just as it forces the inhabitants of northern countries to wear warm clothes.

Antisemitism was by no means new in twentieth century Europe. Throughout the middle ages atrocities were committed periodically against Jews, who were, at one time or another, blamed for everything from disease to crop failure. Hitler's destruction of several million Jews, however, is still history's foremost example of the decimation of a people as the gruesome expression of an explicitly detailed and carefully, if irrationally formulated, ideology.

Communism

We are engaged today in a class war; and why? For the simple reason that in the evolution of the capitalist system in which we live, society has been mainly divided into two economic classes—a small class of capitalists who own the tools with which work is done and wealth is produced, and a great mass of workers who are compelled to use those tools. Between these two classes there is an irrepressible economic conflict. Unfortunately for himself, the workingman does not yet understand the nature of this conflict, and for this reason has hitherto failed to accomplish any effective unity of his class. . . . [I]n the capitalist system in which we live today the worker who produces all wealth receives but enough of his product to keep him working and producing order. His wage, in the aggregate, is fixed by his living necessities. . . . He receives, as a matter of fact, but about 17 percent of what his labor produces. . . . By virtue of his private ownership of the social tool—made and used by the cooperative labor of the working class—the employer has the economic power to appropriate to himself, as a capitalist, what is produced by the social labor of the working class. This accounts for the fact that the capitalist becomes fabulously rich, lives in a palace where there is music and singing and dancing, and where there is luxury of all climes, while the workingmen who do the work and produce the wealth and endure the privations and make sacrifices of health and limb and life, remain in a wretched state of poverty and dependence. The exploiting capitalist is the economic master and the political ruler in capitalist society, and as such holds the exploited wage worker in contempt.

—Eugene V. Debs, "Revolutionary Unionism," 1905

Today, after the collapse of the Soviet Union, communism is often spoken of as a misguided, destructive, and dying dream of people who allowed their radical fantasies to overcome their sense of reality, and who set the stage for murderous dictators to enslave and kill whole populations. Perhaps this will be the final verdict of history for the communist movement. To understand how communism arose, however, it is necessary to consider the world as its founding fathers viewed it. Of the many communist authors, none is more important than Karl Marx. To see the world through Marx's eyes, imagine that you lived in England in the middle of the nineteenth century. If you had, you might have described your life in terms such as the following:

God cursed the day I was born; Poor and short on all the things that bring comfort is my lot in life. It is 1865, and for twelve years I have labored in the woolen mill and now, at age 20 I am, because I am still alive, one of the fortunate ones. My four brothers and sisters, all of whom entered the mills before age ten, child laborers trying in vain to help sustain a family indentured to the owner of the mill, are all dead. The dust from the mills, the noise of the machines, the lack of enough food and good water, all these have brought them to an early end. I have survived by becoming a part of the loom I tend. I live to work. I work seven days a week, sleeping at night under the machine I tend. I leave the mill only occasionally to try to get a breath of fresh air. As my pay does not cover the barest necessities, I owe more each year to the company store. Should I try to flee, the police, agents of the mill owners, would clasp me in arms, and, if I survived their beatings, I would be dragged back to my place, tending, adjusting these levers and gears. I take no pride in the product of my work, for it is not mine. It is the property of the factory owner, and I am but another piece of his machinery, to be discarded, when I no longer function well. My grandfather, a mere half century ago, so I am told, worked a different sort of loom. At its wooden frame he would spin the natural-dyed wool of his own sheep into patterns fit for kings. An artist at form and texture, he sold the richly textured product of his cottage home with pride. It was his offering to humanity, his sense of life breathed through it, and his name was spoken with respect. As he tended his sheep in the evening air on the family farm, the satisfactions of hearth and home were his daily pleasure. But I am a child my grandfather would not recognize. The farm is long gone, victim of crop failure and foreclosure, and I am a slave in this industrial hell.

This story, a fictional composite exposition of the actual misfortunes of thousands of real people, represents, unfortunately, a typical experience for workers in industrialized nations in the nineteenth century. Child labor was extensive, working conditions were deplorable, and many died before a normal working life today would begin. Conditions such as these inspired the writing of Karl Marx (1818–1883) and his friend and associate Friedrich Engels (1820–1895).

Trained in the German philosophic tradition of G.W.F. Hegel (1770–1831), Marx viewed the condition of the urban factory workers as the decisive fact of history. The proletariat, the oppressed class that actually made the products of society, had been robbed by the techniques of mass production of their ability to produce individually products in which they could take pride. They were thereby alienated from the products of their labor. To Marx, the ability to create something with pride and contribute it to society's needs was the essence of human dignity. Factory workers, mere cogs in industrial machines, had been robbed of their dignity, alienated from their labor by the distribution of tasks mandated by capitalism. According to Marx and Engels (1959, 254), a dignified and gratifying life came only when an individual was able to actuate all of his or her talents, desires, and abilities in the manner which that person saw as appropriate:

> For as soon as labor is distributed, each man has a particular, exclusive sphere of activity which is forced upon him and from which he cannot escape. He is a hunter, a fisherman, a shepherd, or a critical critic, and must remain so if he does not want to lose his means of livelihood; while in communist society, where nobody has one exclusive sphere of activity but each can become accomplished in any branch he wishes, society regulates the general production and thus makes it possible for me to do one thing today and another tomorrow, to hunt in the morning, fish in the afternoon, rear cattle in the evening, criticize after dinner, just as I have a mind, without ever becoming hunter, fisherman, shepherd, or critic.

This communist vision of life would be accomplished through a revolution of the proletariat against the ruling class. The proletariat would eventually rise up against the bourgeoisie, the middle class, and create a new society in which the vast discrepancies between the massive wealth of the few and the desperate poverty of the many would be relieved. Eventually, the state, with its various government agencies, would, in Marx's phrase, "wither away." This revolution was not just something communists hope for; according to Marx's theory, it would happen as a part of the natural processes of history.

Marx's theory, which predicted these events, is known as *dialectical materialism*. A dialectic is a process of change which governs how regimes change. Developed by German philosophers G.W.F. Hegel and J.G. Fichte (1762–1814), the theory of dialectic proposed that an existing regime (*thesis*) would gradually generate sufficient resistance so that an opposing regime (*antithesis*) would replace it. Changes in the second regime would cause it to be replaced by a new form of rule (*synthesis*), which would become the new dominant regime (*thesis*). In this manner, feudalism, or rule by the nobility, was replaced by capitalism, the rule of the middle class, which in turn would be replaced, according to Marx, by the reign of the proletariat.

Marx incorrectly predicted that communism would inevitably develop in industrialized capitalist countries. Instead, the first stronghold of communism was in Russia which, in the second decade of the twentieth century, had not yet become industrialized. In 1917, V.I. Lenin led a revolutionary communist party known as the Bolsheviks into power. Lenin had long advocated communism as an answer to capitalist imperialism. Lenin argued that capitalism, which theoretically operated as an open market system characterized by free competition, had been corrupted by great monopolies which controlled trade in basic commodities and services such as oil, sugar, steel, and transportation. As these monopolies grew, they took control of the international banking system and began stripping nations across the world of natural resources and leaving them little in return. "In other words," wrote Lenin (1939, 40), "the old capitalism, the capitalism of free competition, and its indispensable regulator, the Stock Exchange, are passing away. A new capitalism has come to take its place, which bears obvious features of something transitory, which is a mixture of free competition and monopoly."

Lenin envisioned the international expansion of communism as predicted by Karl Marx. Eventually, both men believed, workingmen of the world would unite in an international society. But that vision was not held by Joseph Stalin (1879–1953), who succeeded Lenin in 1924 as head of the Soviet State. In an attempt to consolidate power in the Soviet Union, Stalin changed the focus of communism from internationalism to a policy of "building socialism in one country." Lenin had successfully completed a violent revolution which installed a dictatorship. Stalin completed the transformation of communism from Marx's vision of the withering away of the state to a totalitarian government which ruled the Soviet Union until 1991.

Under the leadership of Stalin and his successors, totalitarianism became Karl Marx's unwitting legacy. According to Hanna Arendt in *The Origins of Totalitarianism* (1958, 438),

Total domination, which strives to organize the infinite plurality and differentiation of human beings as if all of humanity were just one individual, is possible only if each and every person can be reduced to a never-changing identity of reactions, so that each of these bundles of reactions can be exchanged at random for any other. The problem is to fabricate something that does not exist, namely, a kind of human species resembling other animal species whose only "freedom" would consist in "preserving the species." Totalitarian domination attempts to achieve this goal both through ideological indoctrination of the elite formations and through absolute terror in the camps; and the atrocities for which the elite formations are ruthlessly used become, as it were, the practical application of the ideological indoctrination—the testing ground in which the latter must prove itself—while the appalling spectacle of the camps themselves is supposed to furnish the "theoretical" verification of the ideology.

The camps are meant not only to exterminate people and degrade human beings, but also serve the ghastly experiment of eliminating, under scientifically controlled conditions, spontaneity itself as an expression of human behavior and of transforming the human personality into a mere thing, into something that even animals are not; for Pavlov's dog, which, as we know, was trained to eat not when it was hungry but when a bell rang, was a perverted animal.

Fundamentalism

Before his death in 1984, Francis Schaeffer, the American director of Labri, a center of Christian thought and education in Switzerland, became through his films and books a guru of the religious right. In *A Christian Manifesto* (1981, 17–30) Schaeffer expounds upon the central themes of contemporary American fundamentalism:

> The basic problem of the Christians in this country in the last eighty years or so, in regard to society and in regard to government, is that they have seen things in bits and pieces instead of totals. They have very gradually become disturbed over permissiveness, pornography, the public schools, the breakdown of the family, and finally abortion. But they have not seen . . . that all of this has come about due to a shift in world view—that is, through a fundamental change in the overall way people think and the view of the world as a whole. This shift has been away from a world view that was at least vaguely Christian . . . toward a world view based upon the idea that the final reality is impersonal matter or energy shaped into its present form by impersonal chance. . . . These two world views stand as totals in complete antithesis to each other in content and also in their natural results—including sociological and governmental results, and specifically including law. . . . Humanism is the placing of Man at the center of all things and making him the measure of all things. . . . Humanism, with its lack of any final base for values or law, always leads to chaos. It naturally then leads to some form of authoritarianism to control the chaos.

Fundamentalists like Schaeffer, seeing society as morally corrupt, wish to return to the "fundamentals" of the faith. The most famous American statement of the fundamentals of the Christian faith was composed at the Niagara Bible Conference in 1878:

We believe "that all Scripture is given by inspiration of God," by which we understand the whole of the book called the Bible. . . . We believe that the Godhead eternally exists in three persons, the Father, the Son, and the Holy Spirit; and that these three are one God. . . . We believe that man, originally created in the likeness of God, fell from his high and holy estate by eating the forbidden fruit, and . . . he totally lost all spiritual life, becoming dead in trespasses and sins, and subject to the power of the devil. . . . We believe that this spiritual death . . . has been transmitted to the entire race of man. . . . We believe that, owing to this universal depravity and death in sin, no one can enter the kingdom of God unless born again. . . . We believe that our redemption has been accomplished solely by the blood of our Lord Jesus Christ.

James Davidson Hunter's book *Culture Wars* (1991, 42–44) maintains that the American fundamentalist movement represents one side of a deep division in the basic belief systems of the American people:

[T]he cleavages at the heart of the contemporary culture war are created by what I would like to call *the impulse toward orthodoxy* and the *impulse toward progressivism*. . . . What is common to . . . orthodoxy . . . *is the commitment on the part of adherents to an external, definable, and transcendent authority*. . . . Within cultural progressivism, by contrast, moral authority tends to be defined by the spirit of the modern age, a spirit of rationalism and subjectivism.

Leading American fundamentalists like Jerry Falwell tend to be politically and economically, as well as morally, conservative. According to Falwell, for example, capitalism is biblical because it challenges people to develop their own capabilities, relying upon faith in God instead of the handouts of others. Fundamentalists have arisen in many places and in many religions, but they all share at least three common beliefs:

- Contemporary society is morally corrupt and the source of the corruption is identifiable.
- A return to God is necessary.
- The will of God is known through "the book," which explains God's plan for individuals and society.

In his book *The Revenge of God: The Resurgence of Islam, Christianity and Judaism in the Modern World* (1994, 11), Gilles Kepel, an expert on Islamic fundamentalism, concludes that fundamentalism "is the undeniable evidence of a deep malaise in society that can no longer be interpreted in terms of our traditional categories of thought." Although fundamentalist ideas have developed gradually over many decades, Kepel believes that contemporary movements gained influence as a reaction to the explosion of secular values, including sexual permissiveness, that gained popularity in the 1960s.

An example of Islamic fundamentalism that Kepel reports is in India, where the Jama'at al Tabligh (Society for the Propagation of Islam) was founded by Muhammed Ilyas, who thought Muslims in India were being contaminated by the Hindu society. Tabligh's followers try to imitate Mohammed, founder of Islam, in every little detail of life. People who do not abide by Tabligh's strict standards of conduct are said to be "straying." Salman Rushdie, denounced by an Ayatollah in

Iran for his novel *The Satanic Verses,* became the target of Tabligh groups in England. In France, in what was known as the affair of "the Islamic veil," Islamic fundamentalists demanded that Islamic girls in school be allowed to wear veils and not
participate in physical education and in music. This policy was called "positive discrimination."

Feminism

Feminism's long history in the United States began with women's efforts to secure
basic political rights. In 1776, Abigail Adams wrote to her husband John, later to
be the second President of the United States, "[I]n the new code of laws which I
suppose it will be necessary for you to make, I desire you would remember the
ladies and be more generous and favorable to them than your ancestors." For centuries, women could not vote, had limited property rights, and were excluded from
many occupations open to men. George Sand, whose loves included a long relationship with Frederick Chopin and who assumed a man's name in order to get her
novels published, described women's relationships with men in her journal (*The
Intimate Journal of George Sand,* entry for 13 June 1837) in these terms, which struck
a responsive chord with many women:

> Most women, whether from avarice, or sexual desire, or vanity, are so desperate
> not to lose the men they love, that they allow these men to rule their lives ab-
> solutely. There is but one way for a woman to both hold onto her tyrant and at
> the same time to lighten her oppression: by flattering him shamelessly. Her sub-
> mission, loyalty, tenderness and devotion are received by him as his due.
> Unless a woman treats him this way, he will not deign to put up with her at all.
> Still more, however, is required of her. She must prostrate herself before him
> and say—"You are great, you are sublime, you are incomparable! You are more
> perfect than God. Your face is radiant; in your footsteps, nectar is distilled; you
> are without a single failing and every virtue is yours. No individual is your
> equal."

Among the many important moments in the American woman's movement
was the convention at Seneca Falls, New York, in the summer of 1848. The convention adopted a Declaration of Sentiments which announced: "We hold these
truths to be self-evident: that all men *and women* are created equal. . . . The history
of mankind is a history of repeated injuries and usurpation's on the part of man
toward woman, having in direct object the establishment of an absolute tyranny
over her."

Feminism developed in the midst of a vast array of social changes that transpired in the ninetieth and twentieth centuries. The efforts of Susan B. Anthony
and others to secure the right to vote for women finally succeeded in 1920 with the
ratification of the 19th amendment to the Constitution. Advances in technology
made house keeping far less arduous, freeing women's time for leisure and education. Families, through the aid of birth control, became smaller. Women began to
enter areas of the work force from which they had been excluded in the past. Writ-

ing books that expressed the growing frustration of women, new leaders arose to the forefront of the feminist movement. Among them are Simone de Beauvoir, author of *The Second Sex;* Betty Friedan, who wrote *The Feminine Mystique* (1962); and Gloria Steinhem. As Betty Friedan (1962, 362) describes the unsettling experience of women in the 1950s:

> The problem lay buried, unspoken, for many years in the minds of American women. It was a strange stirring, a sense of dissatisfaction, a yearning that women suffered in the middle of the twentieth century in the United States. Each suburban wife struggled with it alone. As she made the beds, shopped for the groceries, matched slipcover material, ate peanut butter sandwiches with her children, chauffeured cub scouts and brownies, lay beside her husband at night, she was afraid to ask even of herself the silent question—is this all?

In order to organize a movement for social and political equality, Friedan founded the National Organization for Women (NOW) in 1966. NOW's *Organizing Statement* describes it principles and goals:

> NOW is dedicated to the proposition that women, first and foremost, are human beings, who, like other people in our society, must have the chance to develop their fullest human potential. We believe that women can achieve such equality only by accepting to the full the challenges and responsibilities they share with all other people in our society, as part of the decision-making mainstream of American political, economic and social life.

Of note is the reaction the feminist movement caused, not only among men, but among women themselves. Phyllis Schlafly has been a leading spokesperson for women who believe that traditional family values—values challenged by the women's movement—are best for them and for society as a whole. In *The Power of the Positive Woman* (1977), Schlafly describes the objectives of women who prefer traditional values. These objectives include the ability of women to be full-time wives and mothers, to take care of their preschool-age children, to have voluntary prayer in their neighborhood schools, and to encourage moral lifestyles in the community.

Contemporary feminism comes in many forms. Consider the following passage from Clarissa Pinkola Estes' book *Women Who Run with the Wolves: Myths and Stories of the Wild Woman Archetype* (1992, 4–78):

> Healthy wolves and healthy women share certain psychic characteristics: keen sensing, playful spirit, and a heightened capacity for devotion. Wolves and women are relational by nature, inquiring, possessed of great endurance and strength. They are deeply intuitive, intensely concerned with their young, their mate, and their pack. They are experienced in adapting to constantly changing circumstances, they are fiercely stalwart, and very brave. . . . I call her [the woman with the wildish nature, the woman who possesses these wolf-like qualities] Wild Woman. . . . No matter by which culture a woman is influenced, she understands the words *wild* and *woman,* intuitively. When women hear those words, an old, old memory is stirred and brought back to life. The memory is of our absolute, undeniable, and irrevocable kinship with the wild feminine, a relationship which may have become ghostly from neglect, buried by over domestication, outlawed by the surrounding culture, or no longer understood any-

more. . . . Once women have lost her and then found her again, they will contend to keep her for good. Once they have regained her, they will fight and fight hard to keep her, for with her their creative lives blossom; their relationships gain meaning and depth and health; their cycles of sexuality, creativity, work and play are re-established; they are no longer marks for the predations of others; they are entitled equally under the laws of nature to grow and thrive.

Estes probably did not intend her book, *Women Who Run with the Wolves,* to be a statement of politics, ideology, or feminism. The book was at the top of the bestseller list for weeks, however, because it accomplishes so well some of the aims of feminist ideology. It helps women to understand themselves and their world, to utilize their talents with a new sense of confidence, to apply their rich and uniquely feminine perceptions to the challenges of life, and to relate with each other and with men in ways that bring fulfillment and dignity. While the book's content is not directly political, its descriptions of women have significant political implications.

Feminism has many other expressions. Socialist feminism, noting that women experience a disproportionate share of poverty, attempts to restructure society so that women will receive a more equal share of the value of commercial, industrial, and agricultural production. Socialist feminists see class oppression as the root of gender inequality.

Radical feminism rejects the belief of other feminists that inequality is derived from dysfunctional social attitudes. Radical feminists assert that oppression of women by men is the most salient feature of society. Men are the enemy, using rape and other forms of violence to enforce their will, and power must be seized from men. Radical lesbian feminists advocate separating men and women into different societies. They claim that women are physically (they live longer), intellectually, and morally superior to men. A world dominated by women would be less violent and more humane than the male-dominated planet we now inhabit. Most moderate feminists reject the extreme claims of the radical feminist movement. Feminism as an approach to the study of politics is discussed in Chapter 6.

Environmentalism

In 1962 Rachel Carson sounded an environmental alarm in her book *The Silent Spring* (15–16):

> For the first time in the history of the world, every human being is now subjected to contact with dangerous chemicals, from the moment of conception until death. In the less than two decades of their use, the synthetic pesticides have been so thoroughly distributed throughout the animate and inanimate world that they occur virtually everywhere. They have been recovered from most of the major river systems and even from streams of groundwater flowing unseen through the earth. They have entered and lodged in the bodies of fish and birds, reptiles, and domestic and wild animals. . . . They occur in the mother's milk, and probably in the tissues of the unborn child.

In the industrial countries of the world, environmentalism appears most commonly as the Green Movement. In many European countries, Green parties have elected their members to national legislatures. Greens have many different ideas and goals, but they all believe (1) that we can understand our existence as human beings only if we see ourselves as part of the natural environment, and (2) that we are not responding responsibly to our environment. In his book *Environmentalism and the Future of Progressive Politics* (1989, 144), Robert Paehlke notes thirteen of the central concepts of environmentalism, including:

- An appreciation of all life forms and a view that the complexities of the ecological web of life are politically salient
- A sense of humility regarding the human species in relation to other species and to the global ecosystem
- A global rather than a nationalist or isolationist view
- A sense of urgency regarding the survival of life on earth, both long-term and short-term

Environmentalism's principal framework and method for understanding the world is ecology, the study of the relationships among animals, plants, and their environments. Environmentalists insist that, instead of being above nature, we are a part of it, and that if we are to survive as a species, we must become aware of the fragile, self-regulating natural structures—ecosystems—in which all living things operate. Rather than using science to conquer nature, rather than trying to bring all living resources under our command, we should assume a posture of humility and recognize our indebtedness to many natural forces for the vitality of our lives.

In his 1979 book, *Gaia: A New Look at Life on Earth,* James Lovelock, a leading environmentalist, set forth what he termed the Gaia Hypothesis. According to Lovelock, the earth itself has life, just as living organisms within it are alive. "Gaia" (the name of the Greek Goddess of the Earth) is "Earth's biosphere, atmosphere, oceans, and soil." The earth, as Gaia, is itself a living organism and acts as all living organisms do in order to maintain its existence. Humanity, unfortunately, has violated its trust, its responsible role in caring for the Gaia earth (1979, 150):

> What should we have thought of an early race of hunters who developed a taste for horse meat and then proceeded to eliminate the horse from the earth by systematically hunting and killing every one, merely to satisfy their appetite? It is bad enough to cull or farm the whale. . . . If we hunt them heedlessly to extinction it must surely be a form of genocide, and will be an indictment of the indolent and hidebound national bureaucracies, Marxist and capitalist alike. . . . Yet perhaps it is not too late for them to see the error of their ways. Perhaps one day the children we shall share with Gaia will peacefully co-operate with the great mammals of the ocean and use whale power to travel faster and faster in the mind, as horse power once carried us over the ground.

Challenges for Political Science

Ideologies present some unique problems for political science. Ideologies are powerful. They help us simplify the complexities of life so that we may deal with them. But this is also, according to Daniel Bell in *The End of Ideology* (1968, 102), the danger of ideology:

The point is that ideologists are "terrible simplifiers." Ideology makes it unnecessary for people to confront individual issues on their individual merits. One simply turns to the ideological vending machine, and out come the prepared formulae. And when these beliefs are suffused with apocalyptic fervor, ideas become weapons, and with dreadful results.

Another problem for the study of ideology is the question of whether all ideas are ideological. H.M. Drucker (Drucker 1974, xii). proposes that our thinking is so ideological that we cannot objectively evaluate ideology. "[O]ur several notions of ideology are each of them appropriate to our own ideology. That is, we disagree because we see ideology from an ideological point of view. We see it as Conservatives, Liberals, or Marxists."

On the other hand, we may be able to mitigate the effects of our own ideologies when we study ideology. Two possibilities come to mind. First, we should honor the integrity, power, and seductive potential of ideology, both our own and others. If we remain open to the possibility that our own investigative patterns of thought may be ideological, we may avoid entrapment by our own rigid thinking. One of the surest ways to fall into the trap of ideology is to use the term ideology in its common mode: as a pejorative term. In other words, we denigrate the term "ideology" when we use it to refer to ideas that conflict with our own.

What distinguishes ideological thinking from nonideological thinking is not so much the content of the ideology but the attitude with which its content is viewed. Ideological thinking, presuming infallibility, is closed to question, while nonideological thinking, presuming fallibility, is open to additional or conflicting information and is responsive to pressure for revision. Ideological thinking, therefore, is a characteristic of the way we hold a set of beliefs rather than the content of the beliefs themselves. Ideas are not necessarily ideological. The way we believe them is. If we hold them as closed truth not to be questioned, we hold them ideologically. If we hold them as possibilities to be questioned, we hold them as philosophy. Perhaps, therefore, the antidote for the negative side, the excessive closure of ideology, is what is known in religious terms as faith, or in secular terms as philosophy.

Having discussed the perennial issues of politics, and some of the ideologies that have formed in response to them, we now proceed to examine the topics that have dominated political science in the twentieth century: political behavior and institutions.

5

Political Institutions and Behavior in Comparative Perspective

I believe the British government forms the best model the world ever produced . . . [it] has for its object public strength and individual security.

—Alexander Hamilton

The best political community is formed by the citizens of the middle class.

—Aristotle

We compare governments to learn what works and what does not work. We hope to use this knowledge to improve government for ourselves and mankind. The American Founding Fathers, following in the path of Aristotle, were masters at the art of comparative government. They compared the governments of their day to one another and to the governments of history, and from the lessons they learned in these comparisons they built the world's longest lasting democracy. When we compare governments and political systems, we learn many lessons about different peoples, cultures, values, and institutions that may be applied directly in our own efforts to build a better society. We may learn, for example, why some people prefer parliamentary democracy while others with different cultures and values appear content in a theocracy (government by religious authorities). We may also be able to assess the effects of two or more different types of governments upon a set of people who share the same cultures and values.

Giovanni Sartori, a well-known Italian political scientist, voices the view of many when he declares that comparative political science is effectively informative when it follows the scientific method. Using the scientific method, social scientists control some variables in order to identify the effects of other variables, and then draw generalizations from the behavior that they observe about the variables whose activities have been isolated. For Sartori, the primary reason we compare nations is to *control* variables. Sartori points out that, when we compare a number of cases of a political phenomenon, such as parliaments or revolutions or elections, we are able to see whether the generalizations we have made are valid in a variety of circumstances. When, for example, we ask a question such as, "Is a democratic government more likely than an authoritarian government to have peaceful relations with other regimes?" we compare numerous cases, controlling variables such as the form of government, as we examine other variables such as history, culture, geopolitical position, natural resources, and so forth.

In this chapter we will illustrate, in an elementary way, how such comparisons are made, and point out some lessons we may learn from them. We shall first define political culture and behavior and describe types of institutions in general. Second, we shall examine some of the ways that political scientists compare governments. Finally, we shall, for purposes of example, make two sets of comparisons: The United States and Israel, and North and South Korea.

Political Culture and Socialization

Gabriel Almond and G. Bingham Powell define political culture as the "pattern of individual attitudes and orientations toward politics among the members of the political system" (Almond and Powell 1966, 50). Political culture is a broader concept than ideology. It includes people's political ideologies but goes on to incorporate unexamined attitudes that affect patterns of campaign behavior or voting, plus perceptions about how the political system works and the benefits to be achieved from participating in it. Political attitudes come and go, and ideologies can change with some frequency, but political culture is a broad and enduring pattern of behavior which defines the way people in politics relate to each other.

Political scientists have classified many types of political cultures. *Democratic* political cultures, such as those of the United States, Canada, and Europe, feature a willingness to follow the will of the majority along with respect for the rights of minorities. *Authoritarian* political cultures such as those in Iran, Cuba, and Guatemala support governmental systems in which decisions are made by a few for the whole people, and in which dissent is not tolerated. In *conflictual* political cultures such as Ireland, violence is a normal method of solving problems. In *consensual* political cultures such as Japan, a sense of the will of the community as a whole is considered necessary or highly desirable for conducting the nation's business.

In *The Civic Culture,* Gabriel Almond and Sidney Verba identify three types of political culture: parochial, subject, and participant. *Parochial* political cultures are dominated by people who are concerned almost entirely with local issues. They may be found in isolated villages in extreme climates where what goes on in the nation or the world seems to have little daily relevance. *Subject* political cultures are found in the slums of major South American and other cities. In these places a small wealthy minority dominates a large poor majority. People there often feel as if they have little influence upon the political process and therefore find themselves subject to whatever rules are made for them. *Participant* cultures are those of the major Western democracies. In participant cultures, people feel free to participate, believing that their participation will count, and they have enough information available to make sense of at least some of the major issues.

Political socialization is the process by which individuals learn the values and norms of their society, and by which political culture is passed from one generation to the next. It is the series of influences that shapes our attitudes and opinions from the first moment that we are able to perceive them. While the socialization process in general is the series of people, events, and other influences that show us how to relate to others in our families, schools, and communities, political socialization helps form our ideologies, our political attitudes and beliefs, and our approach to the political process. Political socialization takes place in our families, as we talk about political issues around the dinner table. It continues in school, where we are taught about our rights as citizens and our laws and constitution. Our friends, churches, newspapers, television, and social clubs all influence the way in which we relate to the political culture around us. Government institutions have much at stake in political socialization and the building of the political culture, for it is through these processes that governments derive their legitimacy.

Political Institutions

Thousands of different kinds of political institutions are to be found within the countries of the world at all levels of government. From local school boards to the Supreme Court, from state highway safety commissions to the United Nations, political institutions attempt to serve, in one way or another, basic human needs such as safety, health, environmental protection, and education. Political scientists have long noted that all such institutions serve one or more primary *functions*. The most basic of functions of government are legislative (making the rules for society), executive (carrying out and enforcing the rules), and judicial (interpreting the rules in specific cases to settle disputes). All governments carry out these same basic three functions, but each government carries them out in different ways. Examining the way the same functions are carried out in different countries provides a basis of comparison. In comparing countries according to function, we shall be applying what is known as structural-functional analysis, which is explained in greater detail in the next chapter. The present chapter examines some of the basic functions of the governments of the United States, Israel, the Democratic People's Republic of Korea (North Korea), and the Republic of Korea (South Korea), but first we shall explain what we mean when we speak of the three basic functions.

The *legislative* function is, most simply, making the rules for society. Society's rules are most often expressed as constitutions, treaties, and laws. Looking back to Aristotle's methods, we may say that the legislative function may be carried out by one person, by a few persons, or by many persons. Ancient kingships and modern totalitarian states invest most of the legislative power in the king or dictator. In fifth century BCE Athens, the citizens held the legislative power directly, for they could attend the meetings of the Assembly and vote on the most important policy matters of the day.

Modern democracies have found it practically impossible to assemble millions of citizens and engage them in meaningful debate, and so the legislative power has been invested in assemblies, the members of which are elected by the people and charged with the responsibility of representing the people, for whom they make the laws. Democratic legislative systems are parliamentary, presidential, or mixed. In parliamentary systems, the members of the legislature select from among themselves the nation's chief executive. In presidential systems a chief executive, who is not a member of the legislature, is elected by the people in a separate election. Some mixed systems, like the government of France, have both a president and a prime minister, each of whom has substantial executive authority.

Legislative systems may be either unicameral (one house) or bicameral (two houses). The American bicameral legislature resulted from a compromise between states with large populations, which wanted representation based on population, and small population states, which wanted each state to have an equal number of representatives. The American states have bicameral legislatures with the exception of Nebraska, which elects 49 Senators on nonpartisan ballots (party affiliations are not identified) to a unicameral assembly. The British Parliament is formally bicameral, but in practice it is unicameral. The British House of Lords has some legislative review functions but is largely ceremonial, while the House of Commons selects the prime minister and is the final authority in matters of law.

The primary function of *executives* is to provide leadership. This normally means not only seeing that the laws are implemented, but also initiating programs for the legislature to adopt. National chief executives come in many forms. The oldest form is hereditary monarchy, wherein power is passed from one generation to the next and kings and queens rule by virtue of their birth. Britain's Queen Victoria, last monarch of the British House of Hanover, reigned from 1837 to 1901. Some of today's remaining monarchies, like Britain under Queen Elizabeth II, the Netherlands, Norway, and Belgium, are merely ceremonial; heads of state have no actual governmental power. In other monarchies like Morocco, Saudi Arabia and Jordan, kings are the actual rulers of their countries.

Presidential governments, in which the chief executive is elected separately from the legislature, are to be found in the Philippines, Mexico, France, and Columbia as well as in the United States. Presidents may claim that their election by all the people gives them a strong base of support when they are confronted with the opposing power of legislatures. By contrast, prime ministers in countries such as Britain, Israel, and Japan derive their power from leading the legislature and must convince the members of parliament to maintain coalitions sufficiently strong to support their programs.

Dictators depend primarily upon two factors to keep themselves in power. The first is their personal leadership ability, and the second is the cadre of devoted supporters who normally form the core of the state's only legal political party. Dictators such as Fidel Castro in Cuba, General Lansana Conte of Guinea, and General Kolingba of the Central African Republic are concerned with maintaining party loyalty and eliminating dissent. In most cases, resources needed for economic development are used to maintain support of the regime, and as economic conditions grow worse, dictators attempt to tighten their control, thus making matters even worse. This phenomenon will be evident when we examine North Korea in this chapter.

Presidents, prime ministers, and dictators do the same types of things. The differences among them are the amount of power they hold in their offices, the restrictions upon their actions, and the amount and types of power they must share with other parts of government. Executive responsibilities include, first of all, administration. Administration means assigning duties to the members of an organization and guiding it to the accomplishment of its assigned tasks. If the task of the Department of Defense is to maintain an army, navy, and air force, then the role of the president, prime minister, or dictator is to oversee the plans, programs, and progress of the armed forces in defending the nation.

Executives have other duties as well. In diplomacy, they conduct negotiations with other nations, receive ambassadors, and help formulate foreign policy. Most chief executives command the armed forces, making major decisions upon the advice of a staff of generals and admirals. Since the national budget determines how many of society's benefits are distributed, the chief executive normally plays a prominent role in formulating the budget. Executives also increase their control in times of emergency and, as heads of state, personally symbolize the character of their respective nations.

The judiciary fulfills several essential roles in any society, but the most important is the nonviolent resolution of conflict. When people disagree about how the law should be carried out, or when an offense has been committed by an individual against another person or the society as a whole, the courts provide an arena in which the government, through the public prosecutor, may take the part of the injured party and decide the issue according to rules and procedures known to both sides. The courts play an invaluable role in protecting the rights of minorities, securing government authority, and, in the case of judicial review, making policy in support of the constitution.

To a large extent, courts define justice for society. Concepts of justice vary from one society to another, but they all contain notions of fairness and human rights. Courts in most countries operate under one of two systems: adversarial and inquisitorial. In adversarial systems such as that of the United States, each case is decided by setting up trials in which adversaries (lawyers representing each side) make arguments. The jury decides who has made the better case, and the judge ensures that proper procedures are followed. In inquisitorial systems like the judicial system in France, the judge inquires about the evidence to determine if the defendant (accused person) is guilty. Only if the judge decides the defendant is guilty does the case go to trial, and cases going to trial rarely result in acquittal.

Justices decide matters of *civil* law (law governing suits between private parties in which there is no criminal penalty, such as libel or slander cases) and *criminal* law, according to which a crime such as extortion is considered an offense against the state as well as the person or organization against which it was committed. *Basic law,* which concerns constitutions or the most fundamentally observed customs of a nation, is normally interpreted by a country's highest courts, whereas interpretation of statutory law (law passed by legislatures) is a part of every case that comes before the lower courts.

National court systems all follow some sort of hierarchy. Higher courts review the decisions of lower courts. Decisions of the 91 United States District Courts, for example, may be appealed to one of the 12 United States Courts of Appeal for the Federal Circuit. Specialty courts are instituted for all types of special purposes. Examples include the Court of Military Appeals (for all matters arising under military law), Court of Claims (for property damage suits), and bankruptcy courts.

Political Behavior

Political behavior provides a third measure by which political systems are often compared. When we study political behavior we want to know about participation in the political process, specifically:

- How many people participate in politics?
- Who participates?
- To what extent do they participate?
- In what way(s) do they participate?
- For what purposes do they participate?

To answer these questions, political scientists study public opinion, campaigns and elections, political parties, and interest groups. Many factors influence political behavior. *Ideology* often has a significant role to play, especially for people who have clearly defined their own ideologies. *Socioeconomic status* not only affects ideology but also determines how some people vote, especially on economic issues. For example, Americans who are in professional occupations and make substantial incomes tend to have conservative ideologies and more often vote for Republican candidates, whereas voters with less than average incomes are more often inclined to vote for Democratic candidates. One factor that has less effect upon political behavior in the United States than in many other Western democracies is *party identification,* which is the strength of the loyalty that people feel towards their political parties. Early in this century, many Americans were so loyal to their party that they would vote a "straight ticket" (vote for only members of their party) election after election. This loyalty has declined in recent decades and now split-ticket voting is common in America. Party identification is likely to be stronger in nations such as France or Israel where each political party has a well defined ideology to which all the major candidates in the party subscribe. In America, Democrats and Republicans may be conservative, moderate, or liberal even if Republicans on the whole tend to be more conservative than Democrats. Other factors influencing political behavior include the personality of candidates, political advertising, and the state of the economy.

Political parties provide the arena for much political participation in democratic countries. The electoral system of the United States favors the formation of two large parties. Only a large diverse political party will be able to win enough votes for a presidential candidate to get a majority of the votes in the electoral college (270 out of 538), and smaller parties, therefore, usually fade away if they are not immediately successful in winning an election. In addition, Americans elect members of the House of Representatives from single-member districts. This means that a party has to be large enough to get the greatest number of votes cast within a district in order to elect a single representative. Other countries, by contrast, have multimember districts. When several members are elected from the same (multimember) district, the party that gets the greatest number of votes elects a representative, but the parties whose candidates receive the second, third or fourth largest number of votes may also elect representatives. The multimember district system thus allows parties with much smaller numbers of voters actually to elect representatives and thereby encourages the development of small parties.

Interest groups (also called pressure groups) are associations organized to promote a particular political, social, economic, or environmental issue, interest, or cause. If you think about the number of interests most of us have, it is easy to understand how thousands of interest groups have become active today. Mr. Brown (a hypothetical example) is a dentist who is married, has three children, attends church, enjoys hiking, owns stock in Texaco, plays golf, and drives a BMW. Among the organizations he has joined are Marriage Encounter, the American Dental Association, the Parent-Teacher's Association, the Presbyterian Church, the Sierra Club, the Republican Party, and the American Automobile Association. Not all of these organizations hire lobbyists or are directly involved in political action, but some of them are highly active, and *most* of them take a direct interest in specific selected political issues. Furthermore, some of the groups Mr. Brown has joined may actually be working against each other on some issues!

We have mentioned a few of the many elements of political culture, institutions, and behavior that political scientists consider when comparing political systems. We now proceed to examine some of the ways in which governments may be compared.

Methods of Comparing Governments and Political Systems

The Basics of Making Comparisons

Consider the statement, "You can't compare oranges and apples." In his discussion of comparative method, Giovanni Sartori (1994, 16) invites us to consider an interesting reply to such questions: "How do you know unless you compare them?" Sartori's point is that things are comparable in some respects, but not others. We may easily see that the apple is red and the orange is orange, and furthermore that their shapes are similar in some ways and different in others. But how do we compare their tastes? How can we say that one is better than the other, except by stating that we personally prefer one to the other? A large part of the difficulty in comparing nations is in deciding what is appropriately compared and what is not. To begin to resolve this difficulty, we must examine the process of making comparisons.

Making comparisons involves identifying similarities and differences among the objects of our study. To identify similarities and differences, we must establish mutually exclusive and exhaustive categories and then assign specific cases to the categories. Concerning apples and oranges, for example, we may first establish two such categories: fruit and nonfruit. Since all existing objects are either fruit or nonfruit, and no object is both at the same time, our categories are both exhaustive and mutually exclusive. Since both apples and oranges are fruits, we have identified a similarity. If we establish another set of categories, the colors of the visual spectrum, we may place oranges in the orange category and (red) apples in the red category, and we will have established a difference. Continuing in this process, we can control some variables to determine the effects of other variables, and thus derive generalizations. For example, if we find that all oranges are orange but that they have different levels of sugar content, we have controlled the variable "orange color," and may continue to seek other explanations of the level of sugar content, such as the amount of sun the orange receives.

Comparing the apples and oranges according to the simple categories of fruit/nonfruit, and red/orange is, therefore, relatively simple, but how do we compare their value to us or their taste? These tasks are more difficult precisely because constructing exhaustive and mutually exclusive categories for comparison of taste and value is much more difficult. What does this discussion about fruit have to do with comparing governments? The same problem that we have in comparing apples and oranges applies to comparing governments. We find it relatively easy to establish exhaustive and mutually exclusive categories for things such as structures of governments (democracy vs. dictatorship) and electoral systems (single member districts vs. multimember districts). The task becomes more difficult when we begin to compare such important matters as the quality of political discourse or the openness of the political environments produced by different government structures. But this is not to say that meaningful complex comparisons cannot be made. By carefully constructing categories in a progressive fashion, we can identify more similarities and differences, and the complex picture of the relationship of political systems to the quality of political life gradually unfolds.

Approaches to Comparative Politics

The part of the discipline of political science that concerns making comparisons is called either *comparative government,* which compares the institutions, constitutions, processes, and functions of governments, or *comparative politics,* which is a broader term that includes not only the politics that happens within governments but other things such as voting, elections, campaigns, and interest groups.

Interest in comparing governments in the nineteenth century began with the works of French aristocrat Alexis de Tocqueville, British scholar James Bryce, and American President Woodrow Wilson. This interest intensified in the twentieth century, at least in part because of the violence of totalitarian movements and the ferocity of large scale wars. Like much work that has been done in the field of international politics and foreign relations, comparisons among governments are sometimes made from a desire to shed light upon questions such as "Are democratic governments more peaceful or stable than authoritarian regimes?" or "What kinds of government structures tend to be successful in heterogeneous political environments?" There is practical value in finding the answers to these questions. In order to find accurate answers, however, political scientists attempt to frame and focus their work in an objective manner. That is, they attempt to understand what *does* happen in politics, apart from the problem of what *ought* to happen in politics.

In *Theories of Comparative Politics, The Search for A Paradigm Reconsidered* (1994, 7), Ronald Chilcote describes five different schools of thought or approaches to the study of comparative politics. Most of the methods Chilcote mentions are explained in more detail in Chapters 6 and 15, and, therefore, will be described only briefly here. The five approaches are "state [and systems] theories, culture theories, developmental theories, class theories, and theories of political economy."

State theorists start with the modern nation-state as the basic unit of analysis, as opposed to the individual, local community, region, province, or set of government institutions. As the totality of political processes within national communities, states have identifiable impacts upon politics. In the 1950s, systems theorists such as David Easton convinced most of the profession that political *systems,* which include many features of internal politics in addition to the state, revealed more information than states when subjected to political analysis, but by the mid-1980s theorists such as Theda Skocpol were trying to "bring the state back in" to the center of attention for political science.

The discipline of sociology has always provided many concepts useful to the study of politics, and sociology's influence is perhaps most pronounced in studies of *political culture.* As Chilcote points out, sociologists like Max Weber (1881–1961) and Emile Durkheim (1858–1917) made particularly important contributions. Max Weber's *The Protestant Ethic and the Spirit of Capitalism* (1958) demonstrated how a set of Protestant Christian beliefs, such as belief in the benefits of hard work and the right of individuals to the fruits of their labor, formed the basis of an ideology that propelled the free capitalist economies of Western nations to success during the industrial revolution. In *The Rules of Sociological Method* (1938), Emile Durkheim established procedures for collecting facts about social and political behavior and events that are still used, if in modified form, in sociology and political science today.

The most influential proponent of developmental theories has been Gabriel Almond, whose *Politics of Developing Areas* (1966) and *Comparative Politics: A Developmental Approach* (1959) (with G. Bingham Powell, later editor of the *American Political Science Review*) discuss how nations develop their political systems. Some development studies have defined stages that nations go through on their way to becoming industrial democracies, and the reforms in government that accompany these stages. Others concentrate on the effects of other trends upon political development, such as communications, modernization, or nationalism. Some theorists, such as American political scientists Andre Frank, Walter Rodney, and Malcolm Caldwell, have argued that capitalism actually undermines political and economic development in what are known as "underdeveloped" countries.

Class theories discuss which group rules society; that is, they try to determine who actually makes the important decisions that direct politics and economics. Class theory became an indelible part of political discourse upon the publication in 1848 of Karl Marx and Friedrich Engels' *The Communist Manifesto,* which outlined the manner in which the proletariat was to seize power from the bourgeoisie. Although communism has lost much of its influence in the wake of the fall of the former Soviet Union, so long as wide disparities exist between the rich and the poor (such as those in many South American, African, and Asian nations), class analysis will be a part of political science. In the 1950s, sociologist C. Wright Mills' *The Power Elite* (1956) claimed that combinations of influential people in large corporations, the government, and the military form an elite that effectively governs

America. Yale University political scientist Robert Dahl, to the contrary, argued that America has a pluralist system, governed not by a small group of elites but by a plurality of many small and large interest groups, each concerned with only a limited segment of public policy such as defense, welfare, or gun control. Elites, as Holloway and George (1979) point out, therefore, are plural and constrained.

Theories of *political economy* began with eighteenth and nineteenth century British writers such as Adam Smith and John Stuart Mill, who advocated a free market (capitalist) economy. The study of political economy looks for links between economic and political conditions and events, such as the relationship of capitalism to democracy. V.I. Lenin, the Russian Revolutionary who founded the Soviet Union's communist regime, blamed political economists like Smith and Mill for creating an ideology in support of a capitalist economic system that was supposedly democratic but, in fact, which led to the domination of the world economy by a small group of influential bankers. Today political economists are concerned with the political effects of free trade agreements, technology transfer, and world monetary systems.

Having discussed some of the basic concepts necessary to compare nations, and some of the major approaches by which nations are compared, we turn now, by way of example, to two elementary comparisons. We shall first compare the politics and governments of the United States and Israel, and then make similar comparisons between North and South Korea. The United States and Israel will be compared because they are both pluralist democracies but with different governmental systems. The United States is a federal republic with separation of powers, whereas Israel is a unitary republic with a centralized parliamentary system. The Koreas have been selected because, while they share the same relatively homogeneous population and culture, North Korea's government is a dictatorship while South Korea, after having experienced several types of regimes since 1950, has a parliamentary democracy. The brief comparisons that follow shall not attempt to compare nations comprehensively. They shall, however, describe some of the same elements of political culture, institutions, and behavior in each country to show both the features common to all nations and the aspects of their political systems that make them unique.

Comparison 1: The United States and Israel

History, Political Culture, and Political Behavior

United States

American history abounds with stories of wars at home and abroad, the settlement of the West, and the growth of the cities. The most notable aspects of American history, for the purpose of comparison with other countries in this chapter, are the long continuous process of immigration and the political battles that have helped extend the rights and privileges of citizenship first to immigrants, then to slaves, and finally to women and other minorities. Several waves of immigration have brought people from all over the world. The first wave of immigration into what is now the territorial United States was probably the ancient movement of the ancestors of Native Americans from Asia, across the area now occupied by the Bering Strait. Viking explorers appeared along the Eastern coast of North America in the century before Columbus. Spanish missions and military expeditions traveled north from Mexico in the 1500s. French fur trappers and traders and English settlers then vied for control of the continent from the time of the first English settlements at Jamestown (1607) and Plymouth (1620) until the French and Indian Wars established English dominance (1756–1753). Until the Civil War, the slave trade brought Africans under compulsion to work the plantations of the Southern states, while famines in Ireland and wars in other northern European countries brought millions of people to American shores. In the last half of the nineteenth century, immigrants from Eastern Europe and China came in great numbers, and the twentieth century has seen immigrants from virtually every corner of the earth. These waves of immigration account for much of the cultural pluralism evident in American life today. Today, census classifications designate the population as about eighty percent "white," twelve percent "black," three percent "Asian," one percent "Native American," and four percent "Other."

Much of the drama of American political life has centered on the struggle each succeeding group has had to find its place in the political system. Native Americans, driven from their ancestral lands and relegated to reservations in the nineteenth century, have gained some attention for their problems in the last decade but have not yet been able to affect the national political agenda in any substantial way. African Americans have made substantial progress since the days of slavery in the last century and the formal segregation of the present one, but the current controversy over Affirmative Action indicates that discrimination in many areas of life has by no means disappeared. Women are now accepted in almost every profession, but they do not yet occupy a share of leadership positions in those professions that is comparable to their share of the general population membership. Gays and lesbians have come "out of the closet" in the last half of the twentieth century, but antagonism towards their sexual orientations remains strong, especially among conservative religious groups. The continual struggle of group against group is the heart of the story of American politics: the struggles of the poor against the wealthy, of labor against management, of environmentalists against corporations, and of less privileged minorities against those who have more of the benefits of American life.

While almost half of America's 260 million population is associated with one of the many sects within Protestantism, and another quarter of the population is Roman Catholic, the rest of the population holds to a wide variety of religious beliefs. Class distinctions in America are not rigid, but exist nonetheless. The richest fifth of the population controls nearly half of the nation's wealth, while the poorest fifth of the population controls only about four percent of the wealth. Perhaps one feature of American life that is found in European nations, but not in most countries of the southern hemisphere, is the size and influence of the middle class. In 1990, two-thirds of Americans were members of families whose incomes fell between $15,000 and $75,000.

American political culture expresses the pluralism of American society. Polls consistently show that Americans are patriotic and religious, that they see traditional family and marriage structures as important, and distrust government and large corporations. If any one feature of the American system of values stands out from the rest, it is individualism, which finds expression in many, sometimes paradoxical, ways. Americans are family-centered and concerned about crime in their communities but want individuals to have the right to carry a registered gun. Most Americans are concerned about the high rate of abortion but do not want government to limit legally the individual woman's right to choose whether or not to have an abortion. Three-quarters of Americans say that prayer is important in their lives, yet most are not willing to make individuals join in public prayer at school. Most Americans indicate, when asked in polls, that they believe the government should help those who cannot help themselves, yet they value a capitalist system in which some individuals are able to accumulate far more than others. These values are all part of what has become known as the "American Dream," in which everyone has the *opportunity* to build a happy and prosperous life.

In the previous chapter, we explored the varieties of ideology. Although Americans may be found at all points along any ideological spectrum, the most visible and active political forces moving in the country today fit into one of four major groups: economic conservatives, economic liberals, social conservatives, and social liberals. Although each of these four groups are concerned with all the major issues, each group focuses its concern on a different set of issues.

Economic conservatives are concerned with limiting government expenditures for social programs, increasing defense expenditures, lowering taxes, and balancing the budget. The Republican Party's *Contract With America* (1994) has expressed some of these goals. Economic liberals want new government initiatives to deal with problems of drugs, crime, teenage pregnancy, and other problems, and want government to control practices of corporations that adversely affect the environment. Social conservatives want to strengthen traditional family values such as monogamous marriage and care of children by their mothers in the home. Social liberals want to increase opportunities for women in the business world and secure rights for gay men and lesbian women. Although conservative views on economic issues often coincide with conservative views on social issues, the two areas of ideology do not always coincide. Many Americans call themselves "moderates," which means they are neither conservative nor liberal. Since moderates most often have liberal views on some issues and conservative views on others, and the mixture of these views varies widely, two people, each calling him- or herself a "moderate" may not agree with each other on anything.

Since the Civil War (1861–1865), the history of political parties in the United States has been dominated by two parties: Republican and Democratic. Third parties have made noticeable gains at times, such as Theodore Roosevelt's Bull Moose Party during the election of 1912, but the rules of the electoral system, which encourage large, broad-based parties, have eventually led to the demise of them all. The Democratic party dates its founding to the presidency of Thomas Jefferson (1801–1809). The Democratic coalition formed by Franklin Roosevelt after the 1932 election, which included labor organizations, minorities, intellectuals, and the Southern states (which had become Democratic in reaction to Republican re-construction programs after the Civil War), has survived at least in part into the 1990s, but it is increasingly challenged by conservatives, especially in the South, who have become Independents or have converted to the Republican party. The Republican party won its first presidency after nominating Abraham Lincoln in 1860 and was the dominant party until Franklin Roosevelt's New Deal converted many to the Democratic party during the Great Depression of the 1930s. From 1952 until 1994, when they gained control of both houses of Congress, the Repub-licans were successful in winning the presidency seven times, as opposed to only four times for the Democrats. During the same period, however, the Democrats lost control of the House just once and the Senate only twice. Now that the Republi-cans have gained both houses, they will attempt to solidify that control.

A topic of particular importance to students of political behavior is tolerance, the ability to accept that others have views that differ from your own. Attitudes about race is a tolerance-related issue which is currently under investigation in public opinion studies. One hypothesis about racism is that it is no longer overt in most of the population, as it was up to the 1970s, but that today a form of "symbolic racism" has developed which is nearly as detrimental to society. Symbolic racism means that white Americans continue discriminatory practices against black Amer-icans, using as a rationale a perception that whites place a higher value upon indi-vidual initiative and achievement.

Americans participate in politics indirectly through membership in thou-sands of interest groups, but relatively few Americans get involved directly in poli-tics, or even go out to vote. In fact, among the world's major democracies, only Switzerland has had a lower rate of voter turnout (44%) in the last decade than the United States (54%). Some democracies, such as Australia, Belgium, and Italy, pe-nalize voters for not voting, and manage to achieve voter turnout rates as high as 94%, but other countries such as Austria and Sweden achieve a rate of 88% with-out fines or other penalties (Powell 1986, 38). Political analysts have given many reasons for low voter turnout in the United States, including the difficulty of reg-istration and the lack of difference among candidates as a result of the broad-based, two-party system. The research of Donald Kinder (1983), for example, indi-cates that the American public is largely "innocent of ideology." This means that Americans do not understand and use the more complicated and abstract ideas that make up most major ideologies. James Stimson (1985) has pointed out, how-ever, that the small proportion of the people who are politically active also tends to be more ideologically astute, and, therefore, judging the whole population by the average voter is very misleading.

Israel

Israel today is the product of Zionism, the political, social, cultural, and religious movement to build a homeland for the Jews. Modern Zionism grew out of a spiri-tual and psychological identification with Zion, the Jewish name for territory that has been known to Arabs for centuries as Palestine. Palestine, on the eastern end of the Mediterranean, was controlled by Arabs during the Middle Ages and was ruled by the Turkish Ottoman Empire from 1517 until the outbreak of World War I, when Great Britain assumed control.

Ancient Zionism, which originated as a movement of resistance to Roman occupation in the century before Christ, was effectively crushed in CE 70 when the Romans destroyed the Jewish Temple and dispersed the Jews to locations all around the Mediterranean, a relocation known as the Diaspora. Even before the Diaspora, the land known as Palestine had held a powerful cultural and spiritual significance for the Jews. According to the Torah, their sacred law, Palestine was promised to them by God, and their founding father Abraham established his family there in contentment and abundance two millenniums before Christ. Genesis and Exodus recount the story of how Abraham's great grandson Joseph was sold into slavery in Egypt by his brothers, became administrator of Egypt, and brought in his family, where they prospered until the Egyptians enslaved them. Delivered four centuries later by Moses back to Palestine, they spent the next millennium in and out of captivity to neighboring empires such as Assyria and Babylon. Palestine, the "Promised Land," therefore, had for centuries an undiminished, deeply spiritual significance for Jews around the world.

Over the course of the 1,800 years following the Diaspora, substantial Jewish communities were established in Asia, Africa, and Europe. In most places during the Middle Ages, Jews were persecuted and kept from participating in national life, and in Europe, where the largest Jewish settlements were located, they were barred from owning land. Therefore, they dwelled in closely knit communities in which they developed trades available to them such as merchandising, skilled crafts, and banking. They continued ancient religious ceremonies and observed traditional Hebrew law and customs.

Amidst the turbulence in Europe that began with the French Revolution, formal barriers to Jewish economic activity were removed, and Jews entered many areas of business, academic, and community life. At the same time, a reaction to the Jews intensified persecution in some areas, most notably in Eastern Europe and Russia. Throughout the nineteenth century, pogroms, organized attacks on Jews and their property, drove many Jews out of Russia to new homes in Western Europe and the United States. Some Jews began to encourage a new sense of Jewish nationalism and to advocate finding a home for a Jewish nation, which they called Zion. The problem was that the proposed homeland to be regained was located in an area already inhabited by several million Arabs, who had claimed the land as their own for centuries and who had ties to Palestine reaching as far back in history as did the Jews.

The modern Zionist movement was inspired by authors such as the German socialist Moses Hess (1812–1875), who wrote *Rome and Jerusalem* (1862), in which he envisioned a "national renaissance" for Jews. Another author, Russian Leo Pinsker (1821–1891), wrote *Autoemancipation* (1882), in which he coined the term "anti-Semitism" and described Jews living everywhere as distrusted minorities in the lands of others, needing a national homeland. Inspired by these and other works, a few small groups of Jews from various nations traveled to Palestine and managed to create a few modest settlements. By 1914, there were only 12,000 Jewish residents of Israel, who together made up a community known as the Yishuv, which was not located in one place but was composed of groups of Jews in Jerusalem and in numerous cities and towns. Some of these Jews were new to Palestine, and some were descendants of people who had lived there for most periods of recorded history.

In 1917, British forces took control of Jerusalem, and the Zionist movement, then headed by Chaim Weizmann, urged Britain to assist in establishment of a Jewish state in Palestine. These efforts resulted, on November 2, 1917, in the Balfour Declaration. Written by Lord Alfred Balfour, England's Foreign Minister, the Declaration promised support for a Jewish homeland in Palestine which would have due regard for Palestinians already in residence there, without specifying exactly how this would be accomplished. For the next thirty years, British administrations attempted to balance the competing interests of the Yishuv and the Palestinian Arabs, the largest number of whom considered themselves to be Syrians.

The person known as the founder of modern Zionism is Theodore Herzel, who was born in Budapest, Hungary, in 1860. A newspaper reporter, Herzel personally witnessed expressions of hatred against Jews in Germany and France, and in 1896, he published *The Jewish State*, which outlined plans for a new Jewish nation.

Not particularly religious, Herzel proposed that the national powers of Europe designate a homeland somewhere in the world in which Jews could be resettled. Attracting the support of Jews across Europe, he convened, in Basle, Switzerland, in 1897, the First World Zionist Congress, which launched the world Zionist movement. Rejected by the Germans in his endeavor to secure a homeland, he turned to Great Britain and attempted to secure territory in Uganda. This effort failed partly because a large religious faction of the Zionist movement demanded that only Palestine would be satisfactory as the new homeland.

The Holocaust, in which about five million Jews throughout Europe were killed by the German Nazi regime during World War II (Hilberg 1985), cemented sentiment for a national homeland among Jews around the world. By 1948, the Jewish population in Palestine had risen to about 650,000, most of whom were immigrants from Europe. A United Nations mandate to partition Palestine into Jewish and Arab sectors allowed Jewish leaders to declare the first government of Israel on May 14, 1948. This declaration immediately led resident Arab Palestinians, joined by Egypt, Syria, Jordan, and Lebanon, to declare a war which became known to the Israelis as the War of Liberation. Ending with armistice agreements among the contending parties, this war was the first of several between Israel and neighboring states, including substantial engagements in 1967 and 1973, in which Israeli victories allowed for expansion of the country's boundaries. The efforts of U.S. President Jimmy Carter led to a peace treaty signed by Egypt's Anwar Sadat and Israel's Menachim Begin in 1979. The Palestine Liberation Organization (PLO), the largest and most influential of Palestinian resistance groups, continued attacks on Israel throughout the 1980s, and the Israelis retaliated by bombing PLO encampments in Lebanon. Many similar conflicts, some violent and some diplomatic, continue among Israeli and Palestinian extremist groups and neighboring Arab states today, although an historic peace agreement between the PLO and Israel was reached in 1995. His efforts to secure this agreement cost Yitzak Rabin, Israeli Prime Minister his life. He was assassinated not by an Arab, but by a member of an extreme Jewish religious sect who accused him of betraying Israel. Yitzhak Shamir, who was Prime Minister of Israel from 1990 to 1992, and who participated in the effort to build and maintain the nation of Israel throughout its history, has written the letter on the following page especially for political science students who read this book. His letter expresses the commitment and determination that have brought Israelis through almost five decades of struggle.

In his book, *Israel, Building a New Society* (1986, 251), American political scientist Daniel Elazar describes the character of today's Israel.

> Israel's polity and society are still raw, still emergent in a certain sense. There is much about it that appears shrill and ugly, aggressive and uncouth. Its drivers are reckless, its mass housing unattractive. Casual interpersonal contacts can be abrasive. Knesset [the Israeli parliament] debates often give the appearance that there is no culture of public discourse. Strikes and demonstrations are commonplace. The country has an unfinished look at every turn.
>
> Yet paradoxically Israel is one of the most conservative of states. Israelis behave in ways that make them appear quite wedded to existing forms and practices. They show little inclination to change or experiment. . . . Israel's conser-

י צ ח ק   ש מ י ר
Yitzhak Shamir

Tel Aviv, 7 March, 1995

Professor Greg Scott
University of Central Oklahoma
Department of Political Science
100 North University Drive
Edmond, Oklahoma 73034-5209

Dear Professor Scott,

Thank you for your letter of 17 February. I wish you success in
your publishing efforts, and am sure that your students will
benefit from your initiative.

As requested, I give you below a brief statement on my own early
life, and the vision and thoughts which motivated me and my
friends:

"Twice in my life - the first in Warsaw and then in Jerusalem –
I had to interrupt my university studies for the higher purpose
of participating in our People's struggle for survival, freedom
and independence. A part of my generation was inspired by the
precept and example of the great leader and teacher, Ze'ev
Jabotinsky, and we were willing to forget all personal interests
and ambitions in order to devote ourselves totally to the
national need.

"He gave us the vision and the hope that we would succeed. He
taught us the simple lesson that a nation will achieve normality
and security only if its sons are ready to fight, to endure
suffering, to sacrifice, and if need be, to die for it.

"We accepted this philosophy and from that time onward,   I have endeavoured to serve our People to the utmost,   for the liberation of our People, and to make our State and Nation stronger and safer."

"I believe in the ongoing and constantly improving relationship between Israel and the United States, the leader of the Free World and Democratic Nations.

"I believe that Democracy will prevail everywhere in the world, including the Middle East. It is very difficult for our friends in the free democratic world to accept that we are the only democratic country in the region. Indeed, we have experienced the loneliness of democracy. Our way of life - government of the people, by the people, and for the people - is not understood by the states in our region, which prefer the leadership of one man or one family, and which interpret democracy as weakness. Naturally, this complicates our relationship with them.

Sincerely,

Yitzhak Shamir

בית אמות משפט, שד' שאול המלך 8, תל־אביב 64733. טל' 03-6951166, פקס' 03-260480

Beit Amot Mishpat, 8 Shaul Hamelech Blvd., Tel Aviv 64733. Tel: 972-3-6951166, Fax: 972-3-260480

vatism is not in support of ancient tradition but in support of the new ways of Zionism.

Israel's population in 1990 was approximately 4,371,000. Of this number, about 83% (3,600,000) are Jewish. Israel holds about 24% of the world's fifteen million Jews. The non-Jewish community of approximately 715,000 includes about 550,000 Muslims, 100,000 Christians, and 65,000 Druze, a religious sect that split off from Islam in the early Middle Ages.

Israeli political culture represents the intermingling of many beliefs, traditions, and ideologies, but perhaps two divisions of the people best define the culture's national character. The first division is between the Jews of European origin (called Ashkenazic) and those from North Africa (called Sephardic). The Ashkenazic Jews have dominated the class structure and the political system since the country's founding. They bring European values and customs, including an emphasis on the development of technology and social services, into the culture. The Sephardic Jews have taken up the less prestigious occupations in the country and struggle to retain cultural attributes from their many countries of origin. The second major division is religious. Among both Arabs and Jews in Israel there are divisions among the deeply religious, the moderately religious, and the purposefully secular. The Hasidic Jews, for example, hold tenaciously to ancient religious rituals and customs. Those who are more religious have tended to align with the political right, but not in all situations.

Because many dominant Israeli groups came from Eastern Europe, Israel adopted an Eastern European conception of nationalism, which is based upon ethnicity, as opposed to a Western version, which is based upon allegiance to a politically defined state (Aronoff 1993, 66). This type of nationalism emphasizes communal identity rather than individualism and was a major influence in the adoption of many socialist policies by the early Israeli governments.

Political participation in Israel is high compared to that in the United States. Eighty percent of the voters normally go to the polls in national elections. The high level of participation is at least partly a result of the development of a diverse array of ideologically oriented political parties. The two major parties are the Labor party, which is liberal, and the Likud Party, which is conservative. The Israeli Labor party (known as Mapai until 1968) achieved dominance in Zionist politics in the 1930s and maintained it until 1977. During that time it established wide ranging programs, including state supported health care, education, and social services.

In 1977, the Likud gained control, and in 1984 and 1988, the Labor party shared power with the Likud as a National Unity coalition against vying Arab and Jewish religious groups. In 1990, Likud leader Yitzhak Shamir was forced to form a coalition with Moledet, an extremist party which wanted to move Arabs from their homes in occupied territories into Jordan. Arabs have become increasingly unhappy with Zionist parties in the last two decades, and have formed new small parties of their own.

In the 1992 elections, ten parties won seats, while fifteen others listed on the ballot received no seats. In these elections, Labor party leader Yitzak Rabin was able to form a bare minimum coalition government with sixty-one members, composed of forty-four from the Labor party, twelve from Meretz, six from the Shas, and five from other Arab parties.

Political Party	Number of Seats in the Knesset, 1992
Labor (left)	44
Likud (right)	32
Meretz (left)	12
Tzomet (right)	8
National Religious (right)	6
Shas (Orthodox)	6
Four Other Parties	12

Rabin's coalition won the 1992 elections on a platform which included plans to reduce support of Israeli settlements in disputed territories, to be more open to Arab proposals, to build better relations with the United States, and to pay more attention to economic problems and immigration than had the Likud.

Political Institutions

United States

The political institutions of the United States are familiar to all students of American government, but for purposes of comparison, we shall summarize their main features. Rejecting the British parliamentary model, which combines legislative, executive, and judicial functions within the House of Commons, the American founding fathers adopted Montesquieu's concept of separation of the three powers and reinforced the separation with provision for the three branches to check and balance the operations of each other. The first three articles of the Constitution of the United States of America are written in an order intended by the delegates to the Constitutional Convention to imply the relative importance of the three branches of government. The first article defines the legislative branch, the second article defines the executive branch, and the third article defines the judicial branch.

Article I describes Congress, which is composed of a Senate and a House of Representatives. Two senators who must be at least thirty years old are elected from each of the fifty states. They serve six-year terms. Representatives are elected from districts the lines of which may be redrawn after each census (every ten years) to allow reapportionment of the 435 seats from states who have lost population, relative to the population of the whole country, to states which have had a greater population gain. Representatives, who serve two-year terms, must be at least twenty-five years old when they take office. Congress is empowered to pass laws, raise taxes, appropriate public moneys, regulate commerce, establish a court system, declare war, and perform many other activities. The Senate confirms presidential appointments and ratifies treaties.

Article II asserts that the President of the United States must be at least thirty-five years old when assuming office, and may serve for two four-year terms. The president is chief executive, head of state, and commander-in-chief of the armed forces. He or she negotiates treaties, presents legislation to Congress, hosts foreign heads of state, and conducts many other official duties. The President may veto legislation, and appoints justices of the Supreme Court and other courts, as well as the secretaries of State, Defense, Transportation, etc., which make up his cabinet and administer the departments of government.

The Supreme Court, described in Article III, consists of nine justices appointed for life terms (during good behavior), who together constitute the final appeal in cases arising under the Constitution. The Supreme Court has the power of judicial review. District and Circuit courts of appeal and many special purpose other courts, such as maritime courts, are also established by Congress.

American government is a federal system, which is to say that all states have their own constitutions, which establish executive (governors), legislative (state assemblies), and judicial (state courts) powers. Local governments are set up according to charters granted by the state governments. Over 80,000 different "governments" exist within the United States, including planning districts, school boards, counties, cities, townships, among others. A prominent feature of the American system of government is decentralization of political power. This means that power is not concentrated in the hands of a few people but is dispersed over hundreds of officials and agencies at local, regional, state, national, and international levels.

Israel

Accurately viewing themselves as surviving within a hostile geopolitical context, the Israelis purposely designed perhaps the most highly centralized state authority of any democracy. Local administrative bodies do exist in Israel, but they are concerned mainly with carrying out nationally determined policies.

Israel has a parliamentary system of government. This means that its people elect representatives to a legislative body called the Knesset, but do not directly elect a chief executive. The chief executive in a parliamentary system is the Prime Minister, who is elected by the members of Parliament. Israel's constitution is found in what is known as the Basic Law. Members of the Knesset are chosen in a general election in which voters do not vote for candidates directly, although they know who the leading candidates for each party are, but for the political party that they wish to support. The 120 seats in the Knesset are divided among the parties according to the percentage of votes that each party receives. A party that gets 10% of the votes, therefore, gets 10% (12) of the seats. Any party that gets at least 40,000 votes gets at least one seat. Each political party draws up a list of candidates for the election. The Labor Party holds a primary election, but the other parties have their leaders draw up the lists. On each party's list, candidate names appear in priority order. If a party wins thirty seats, for example, then the first thirty persons named on that party's list get a seat. That it is necessary to get only about 1% of the popular vote to gain a seat in the Knesset encourages small parties to arise. This makes it hard for any one party to receive the majority of seats (61 out of 120) necessary to form a government. To form a government, therefore, party leaders must usually form coalitions with other parties.

Comparing Politics in the United States and Israel

To make the comparison process clear, we shall compare the governments and politics of Israel and the United States of America by making comparisons in two steps. We shall first summarize the features of both countries, placing descriptions of major factors side by side in a table so that similarities and differences may be noted. Then we shall draw conclusions from our summary. Examine the entries in the table on the next page.

Having summarized the main features of the two political systems, we may now draw some conclusions or implications of the comparison. While many more comparisons could be made, a few observations will provide examples of the insights about the interaction of political institutions, culture, and behavior that may be gained from comparative analysis.

Category	United States	Israel
Ethnicity	Heterogeneous: European, African, Asian, and others.	Heterogeneous by nationality but with largely common Jewish heritage, also Arabs, including Christians and Druze
History to 1945	Successive waves of immigration, democratic republic since 1788	Arab-occupied British Protectorate from World War I until 1948
History since 1945	Evolving civil rights movements, Cold War conducted and concluded	Independent state, series of wars, and internal violence; attempts to make peace with neighbors and Palestinians
Political Culture and Behavior	Individualism, two broad-based parties, dominance of Democratic Party to 1994, low voter turnout	Consensual government, multiple ideological parties in shifting coalitions, high voter turnout
Government Structure	Federal, decentralized, presidential system, separation of powers, separate elections for Congress and President	Unitary, centralized, parliamentary government with party-list electoral system.

First, the electoral systems of the two countries have important implications for the manner in which conflict among competing interests is handled in society. In the United States, two large nonideological parties produce candidates who each attempt to gain the center of the spectrum to get the votes of moderates. This move to the middle of the spectrum produces less ideological elections and less voter interest and turnout than in Israel. Second, the major political-cultural problem for both countries has been the struggle to incorporate minorities into national life. In the United States, minorities, especially African-Americans, have waged a long struggle for equality. In Israel, the struggle of the Zionists to establish a homeland has created an ongoing problem with providing opportunities for Palestinians within and without the country's borders, and with opposition from sympathizers to the Palestinian cause. Third, the heightened need for internal cohesion due to external threats to national existence has brought about a political culture in Israel that is much more inclined to strive for consensus. Although the variety of ideologies and parties in Israel is great, the value that is placed upon individualism per se, as it is expressed in the United States, is likely to be viewed in Israel more as an aggravation than as a solution to political problems. In the United States, conformity is feared and individualism is prized, whereas in Israel, individualism, as expressed in a panoply of ideologies, is a fact of daily life that is viewed as an obstacle to the cohesion that is necessary for survival in a hostile environment.

Comparison 2: North and South Korea

North and South Korea are compared in this text for two reasons. First, they allow students to encounter briefly examples of Asian political culture and to note how it compares to American, Canadian, or European political culture. Second, the two Koreas present a unique opportunity for political scientists to compare the effects of two exceedingly different political systems upon what is essentially the same culturally homogeneous people. If the cultures of the two countries are essentially the same, then culture may be eliminated as a variable in the comparison, and the effects of the two governmental systems upon political behavior may be clearly identified. Korean political scientist Sung Chul Yang (1994, v) notes that the political cultures of North and South Korea are so similar that, "The two systems and two states presently existing in the Korean Peninsula are like the two bowls molded out of the same clay."

History, Political Culture, and Political Behavior in Korea

Scholars have records of Korean society as old as two millenniums before Jesus (BCE). Political unification as a nation dates back to 676 CE when the Silla Dynasty combined the territories of several rival kingdoms, but subsequent intradynastic feuds left Korea's northern boundary unsettled until the mid-fifteenth century, when the Yi Dynasty consolidated power. The Yi Dynasty reigned until the Japanese occupation began in 1910. The Japanese protectorate had profound effects upon Korea. According to University of Chicago professor Bruce Cumings (1990), the Japanese attempted to replace Korea's ruling elite, educational system, banking and economic system, government bureaucracy, and language with Japanese practices. Never accepted and bitterly contested, Japanese innovations were so humiliating to the Koreans that animosity to the Japanese remains to this day.

During World War II, Korea was freed from Japanese occupation, not by its own efforts, but by the Soviet Union and the United States. In the Potsdam Conference of July 1945, and the Moscow Conference of December 1945, Korea was divided into North Korea, under Soviet control, and South Korea, under United States control. The boundary between the two countries, which is still in force today, was set along a military demarcation line, which runs roughly along the 38th parallel.

Immediately after World War II, the Soviets denied Korean revolutionaries in the North the right to rule, and the United States hindered the attempt by the Korean Provisional Government (KPG) to return to South Korea from its exile in China. The Americans and Soviets each succeeded in seeing installed governments that were friendly to themselves in their respective areas of interest. During the next five years (1945–1950), Koreans were increasingly ideologically polarized as either communists (the North) or anti-Communists (the South). From 1950 to 1953, the two sides, each attempting to control the entire country, fought the Korean War. United Nations forces, combining 40,000 United States troops with those of fifteen other nations, fought alongside South Korean troops against the North

Koreans, who were assisted by China and several other communist countries. More than three million Koreans died in the conflict, along with thousands of foreign troops on both sides. Since the war, many attempts at unification have been unsuccessful, and today plans by the North to test nuclear weapons pose a recurrent problem for Western democracies.

Korean political culture, like that of many nations, has for most centuries featured a distinct division of two classes: a small ruling elite and the majority of the people. This class division has its roots in a feudal system established as far back as the third century CE. The Korean feudal system was similar to European feudalism in that large numbers of serfs worked land owned by nobles in return for protection. Unlike the European system, however, in which there were many local Kings, Dukes, and Barons, the Korean system was centralized under one king who ruled through a strong bureaucracy and maintained control of the population through his army and his proclaimed, although not always actual, ownership of land. Heredity determined class membership, and marriages and class interactions were strictly controlled. In the last of the great dynasties, the Yi Dynasty (1450–1910), a four-class system divided people permanently by birth into four groups: ruling elite; artisans, merchants and peasants; laborers; and slaves. The upper layers of the bureaucracy were controlled exclusively by the ruling elite, who composed only about one percent of the population. The Yi bureaucracy required examinations for administrative positions, but membership in the highest class was necessary to take the exams. The stratification of society has historically been directly related to internal violence. Periodic peasant uprisings and military coups have erupted in response to abuses of authority.

A long tradition of authoritarianism has shaped Korean society and is expressed in Korean law. Whereas in Western tradition the law is a means for protecting the rights of individuals against the encroachment of government, as well as a vehicle for protecting society against offenses by individuals, the Eastern tradition is to regard the law as an instrument for "chastising the vicious and depraved" (Yang 1994, 15). The differences between the Eastern and Western concepts is clearly illustrated if one compares the development of law in Britain and Korea. British law is intentionally an expression of custom in which the naturally evolving practices of a people are systematically codified; Korean law, on the other hand, focuses on forceful punishment for something disallowed by a ruler, an act of an authoritarian figure which had nothing to do with custom (Pyong-Choon Hahm 1967). Yang points out that authoritarianism, most often expressed in the form of hereditary monarchy with a centralized bureaucracy, has pervaded all aspects of Korean politics for centuries. Ideas of pluralism, of civil liberties, of decentralized power, came only after World War II, and then only to South Korea.

Authoritarian rule was also maintained traditionally through a state religion, which provided a theological justification for political rule. The state and ecclesiastical powers, as two sources of authority, became so completely fused that the concept of separation of church and state would not have been an intelligible notion until this century. For several centuries leading up to the Yi Dynasty, Confucianism and Buddhism combined in different patterns, largely in support of im-

The Korean Peninsula

perial power. However, during the Yi Dynasty Buddhism was suppressed by Confucianists and Neo-Confucianists, who quarreled over the correct interpretation of religious texts. The introduction of Christianity in the seventeenth century enlivened religious debates, which continue to be of interest in the South, but the banning of most religious practices by the communist North Korean regime has practically eliminated these controversies, at least publicly, in the North. In North Korea, authority has been transferred from religion to the Marxist-Leninist ideology of the state.

Students of Korean political culture should not underestimate the pride that Koreans hold in their nationality. Over the centuries, Koreans have successfully fought off several foreign invasions, and their national identity as Koreans is as strong as ever. As Yang (1994, 93) has noted, "That Korea has survived as a nation and has maintained its independent political entity, national identity, and high degree of cultural homogeneity despite incessant foreign invasions and domination by the Chinese, Khitans, Jurchens, Mongols, Manchus and Japanese is indeed extraordinary."

Yang notes further, following recent scholarship, that in the world today two seemingly oppositional but actually complementary trends are occurring: integration and disintegration. While, for example, the former Soviet Bloc is disintegrating into many small ethnically homogeneous units, West European countries are increasingly integrating their economic development efforts, much to their mutual benefit. The dialectical process of integration and disintegration is a natural response to changing conditions and assists in the gradual attainment of a sense of national maturity and security. In other words, from 1945 to 1990, peoples of Eastern Europe and Yugoslavia were unified artificially under authoritarian regimes to which they did not consent. Upon achieving independence, these nations have been able to choose associations with other nations freely upon their own terms. Within this international framework of integration and disintegration, Korea lags behind. It is still in a situation of artificial division and separation. Yang believes that once it is internally unified, which is likely to happen eventually, Korea will be more free to associate with other nations. At the moment the North is especially constricted in its foreign relations, enjoying good relations with only a few authoritarian states. In view of its national pride and deep-seated desire for unity on both sides, however, the artificial but powerful political division of North and South makes for a potentially explosive situation.

North Korea is in much worse shape economically than its southern neighbor. Unable to feed its citizens, it imports grains and other essential commodities, and the South has sent the North rice in large quantities as foreign aid. People in Japan and South Korea sometimes send money to their relatives in the North, who then use the money to pay off state officials in order to keep their jobs or stay out of jail. Dictator Kim Jong Il's regime is suspected of dealing in illicit drugs and counterfeiting money to pay foreign bills, and the repression of the people has not lifted in recent years. Foreign visitors to North Korea are closely watched, and their activities and travels restricted. Whereas in the capital city of Pyongyang, the governmental elite drive about in Mercedes, few ordinary North Koreans have cars or many other basic necessities that are common in the South.

The government of North Korea is believed to organize and house families in groups of five, who spy on each other. Loyalty to the state is rewarded by party membership, which brings privileges and luxuries, while disloyalty is punished by imprisonment in labor camps. Under these circumstances, it is little wonder that virtually no criticism of the government is heard.

Regimes that are "merely" *authoritarian* require only that citizens do their jobs, obey the laws, and refrain from being disruptive. *Totalitarian* regimes, on the other hand, are those for which passive acceptance of the government is not enough; these regimes require actively demonstrated support of the party and regime. Following these two definitions, North Korea is a totalitarian regime. In their free time North Koreans are expected to volunteer to contribute their own manual labor to public works projects. The Korean Workers Party (KWP), which supports the dictatorship, has an active party organization, including a Youth League which numbers three million teenagers and young adults.

South Koreans are living in an economic boom which some of them believe will allow them to overtake Japan as economic leader of the Far East by the year 2000. They produce $8,500.00 in gross national product per person, which, for example, is thirty times what the average Indian produces (*Economist* 1995a, 3). Much of this success is based on a trade policy that strongly encourages exports and strongly discourages imports. In addition, this success has been generated by a regime that in many ways is still authoritarian, and this condition may cause problems in the years ahead. Under Park Chung Hee's repressive regime in the 1970s, the Korean Central Intelligence Agency (KCIA) had substantial power and used it to arrest and torture people suspected of being opposed to the government. In 1987, factory and office workers and student groups led the first substantial moves towards a more genuinely democratic state. They demanded and received new presidential elections in which the president was actually elected by the people rather than being placed in power by a military coup. Since the elections, democratic reforms have appeared, and newspapers have actually started to be critical of the government. But even now problems remain. The Korean Central Intelligence Agency was charged with interfering with elections in May 1995, and the National Security Law, which makes it possible for anyone to be arrested on suspicion of subverting the government, is still in force. When Chung Ju Yung, chief executive of Hyundai Corporation, ran against Kim Young Sam and lost, Yung faced a prison term for violating campaign laws, and Hyundai was prohibited from participating in the world bond market.

Many of the issues that dominate South Korean politics, however, are local rather than national. Locally prominent wealthy families not only control much of the economy, but are able to elect their members to the National Assembly and to local offices. Many issues debated in the National Assembly are squabbles over local issues rather than attempts to work out viable long-term national policies, but this situation is also a result of the strong leadership that the president takes in the national policy arena. On June 27, 1995, elections were held for the first time for 5,700 local government positions that had previously been appointed by the president. In a campaign that fortunately lacked violence, 140 arrests were made of persons suspected of trying to bribe voters (*Economist* 1995b, 25). President Kim Young

Sam's party, the Democratic Liberal Party (DLP), won only five of fifteen major gubernatorial and mayoral races, while the liberal Democratic Party (DP) won four and the conservative United Liberal Democratic Party (ULD) won three, with the remainder going to other small parties. Kim Jong Pil, chairman of the ULD, tries to press President Kim to be tougher on the North and on internal dissidents. In fact, the number of political prisoners in South Korea may have actually increased in recent years, and now, according to Amnesty International, they number almost five hundred. The continuing struggle to broaden democratic reforms provides a clear indication of the depth of authoritarianism still left in Korean culture, even in South Korea.

Political Institutions of North and South Korea

North Korea

As do many other authoritarian political regimes, including the former Soviet Union, North Korea attempts to hide a totalitarian state behind a veil of democratic rhetoric. The *Democratic People's Republic of Korea* (DPEK) has two government structures, a formal (in name only) democratic structure and an actual totalitarian structure. We shall examine them both to contrast totalitarian ideals with reality.

The formal structure of the Democratic People's Republic of Korea (DPRK) is based on a constitution which guarantees political rights to the citizens and a democratically elected government. The *Constitution of the Democratic People's Republic of Korea* (April 9, 1992) provides for separate legislative, executive, and judicial functions. The *Supreme People's Assembly* (SPA), according to the Constitution, "is the highest organ of power in the Democratic People's Republic of Korea." The SPA is composed of one delegate for every 30,000 citizens and currently seats 687 delegates elected by the people for one-year terms. The constitutionally provided powers of the *SPA* are far greater than those of legislatures in most modern democracies. They include the power to (1) amend the Constitution, (2) elect and recall all major national legislative, executive, and judicial government officers, including the President of the Republic, and (3) establish all state policy.

The Constitution further stipulates that "The permanent body when the Supreme People's Assembly is not in session is the *Standing Committee of the Supreme People's Assembly*," which includes 15 members selected by the Supreme People's Assembly. Both the SPA and the *Standing Committee* have a Chairman, Vice-chairman, and secretary, and the officers of the SPA are the same individuals who are the officers of the Standing Committee. The Standing Committee is empowered by the Constitution to adopt measures when the SPA is not in session, convene the SPA, conduct the SPA's elections, and provide judicial review.

Under the formal Constitution, the President of the DPRK is elected by universal secret ballot for a five-year term. As head of state and head of the executive branch of government, the president is empowered to call a national referendum, negotiate and ratify treaties, command the armed forces, issue presidential decrees, and proclaim martial law in time of emergency.

The constitution of the DPRK specifies a number of other offices and official bodies. The Prime Minister, who is appointed by the President with consent of SPA, assists the President in his or her duties. The *State Council* (SC) deliberates on executive policies, including basic plans for state affairs, declarations of war, budgets, and amendments to the Constitution. The SC is composed of the President, Prime Minister, and 15 to 30 members appointed by the President. The *Executive Ministries* includes the executive departments and commissions of government, among which are the Ministries for the Armed Forces, Foreign Affairs, Public Security, Light Industry, State Planning, and Economic Affairs.

The DPRK *National Defense Committee* (NDC) is separate from the Armed Forces Ministry and has a prominent place in the Constitution. It is the supreme military council of the nation. It has a Chairman, a Vice Chairman, and a variable number of members. The NDC guides armed forces in all matters, declares war, and mobilizes the country for war. The Constitution seems to be filled with committees, such as the *Central People's Committee* (CPC), which acts in an executive policy planning capacity, the *Executive Council,* which advises the President, and the *Administration Council,* which is composed of the heads of the ministries. At the regional and local levels, *Local People's Assemblies* and *Local Administrative and Economic Committees* carry out the directives of the national agencies.

North Korea's constitution also provides for a system of higher and lower courts, which are to "interpret the law and ensure justice." The Central Court is the highest court. It supervises activities of other courts and receives guidance from the Central People's Committee.

The formal constitutional government of North Korea, presented in diagram form, looks something like this:

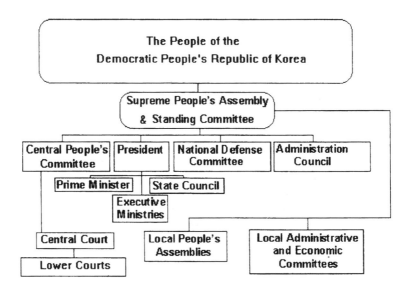

The diagram depicts the formal governmental structure of the government of North Korea, but it has virtually no relation to how the DPRK actually operates.

Today North Korea is a single-party totalitarian dictatorship. All dictatorships feature rule by one dominant person who is surrounded by a small group of influential associates. A diagram which illustrates how the DPRK actually operates looks something like this:

Actual Operating Structure of the Government of the DPRK

The diagram above indicates that the President is, in fact, a dictator who rules through a small governmental elite, and the people, at the bottom of the structure, take directions from the government rather than give direction to it. Some dictators base their power primarily upon the strength of their own personalities, like Uganda's Idi Amin, while others, like Fidel Castro of Cuba, dominate a strongly ideological political party. Kim Il Sung became dictator of North Korea in the 1940s by overcoming opponents within Korea's ruling communist party, the KWP. His son, Kim Jong Il, succeeded him upon his death in 1994. Kim Jong Il rules both party and government with a combination of personal ability, a cadre of loyal followers assembled by himself and his father, and an authoritarian party ideology, but the strength of his power base is not yet clear. In a pattern similar to other communist dictatorships, such as the former Soviet Union, the Korean government features a system of *interlocking directorates*. This means that (1) there are two actually active political organizations in North Korean society: the organization of the dominant party (the WPK), and the organization of the government, and (2) the leading figures in both party and government organizations are the same people. In the case of North Korea, therefore, Kim Jong Il now holds the most important positions in both the WPK and the government.

The KWP's ideology combines elements of communism, periodic denunciations of Japan and the United States, and the concept of *Juche*. *Juche* means self-sufficiency, especially economic and political independence from other countries, and "socialist economic construction," an economic program that entails three technical, cultural, and ideological "revolutions." In these "revolutions," the North Korean government attempts to get popular support for state-planned economic policies which have largely failed to compete technologically and economically with South Korea and Western democracies. Under the guidance of Kim Jong Il, *Juche* has taken on a militaristic flavor, and economic slogans feature martial themes, such as "battles" for development and economic "war" (Yang 1994, 183). Moving to reinforce the family dictatorship, Kim Jong Il has incorporated into the *Juche* idea the notion that the Korean people have not only a physical body, but a sociopolitical body whose father was Kim Il Sung and is now himself, Kim Jong Il.

Although anti-Americanism is occasionally inflamed by dictatorial rhetoric, overtures for diplomatic and economic agreements with the United States have been made from time to time. Anti-Japanese sentiment has also been exploited intermittently as a rhetorical tool, while the government peridically attempts to normalize diplomatic relations with Japan.

South Korea

While the North has lived under dictatorial leadership for forty years, the democratic Republic of Korea (RK) in the south, in Yang's words (1994, 191), has had "seven regimes, two military coups, one major student revolution with a series of off and on student anti-government protests and riots, not to mention an almost unceasing number of major and minor political crises."

The Rhee regime, which dominated Korean politics from 1948 to 1960, was conservative. It advocated democracy in theory, unification with the North, and close ties with America, and it opposed communism and new ties with Japan. From April 1960 to May 1961, two interim governments briefly enjoyed an era of "democratism," which liberalized debates on what had been considered closed questions of unification and relations with the United States and Japan, but a flood of student demonstrations poured forth ending in a military coup in May 1961. The new leader, Park Chung Hee, reinstated conservative attitudes about unification and foreign relations and launched vigorous and successful new programs of economic development. Park's regime was strongly anti-communist but more favorably disposed than his predecessors to economic ties with the Japanese. As time progressed Park became increasingly authoritarian. He had himself proclaimed "President-Dictator" in 1972 but generated strong hostility and was assassinated. Chun Doo Hwan then seized power and embarked on a program of "progressive conservatism" which was antagonistic to communism, and more open to all sorts of exchanges with foreign countries. Anxious about subversion from the North, Chun used the KCIA to suppress opposition ruthlessly, and became both feared and hated. His hand-picked usccessor, Roh Tae Woo, assumed power in 1988. Woo was much more pragmatic and less ideological than his predecessors in his attitude toward unification and relations with America and Japan. He allowed some efforts towards democratization, although the country was kept under military rule.

Kim Young Sam was elected President in 1992, replacing military regimes with a government more democratic than those of his predecessors. Kim has guaranteed basic civil rights and continues to press for an open electoral process, al-

though the authoritarian cultural predisposition of the people has made this difficult. Working under a slogan of globalization, Kim has led South Korea to an economic boom that has impressed other nations around the world.

Whereas the structure of the government of South Korea is democratic, the
authoritarian tendency in Korean culture has led to a concentration of power in
the presidency. While this does not mean that South Korea, like its northern neighbor, has two government structures, it does mean that practice has varied from the
constitution so much at certain times that a second, actual form of government has
also existed alongside the formal structure in South Korea. In South Korea, the
President has been so powerful the government has sometimes been democratic in
name only. The formal structure of the government is established by the constitution which was adopted on July 12, 1948 and has been amended nine times, including major modifications made in 1962.

The National Assembly holds the legislative power in South Korea. The Assembly, whose 299 members are elected by proportional representation by district
for four-year terms, is constitutionally empowered to pass laws, establish a national
budget, set tax rates, and consent to the ratification of treaties and declarations of
war. In practice, however, these powers have been limited by presidents who have
insisted on having final authority in budget and defense matters.

The President is the chief executive and head of state, charged with promul-
gating the laws. Elected for a four-year term, the President appoints the members
of the State Council, the Prime Minister and Deputy Prime Ministers, and the
heads of the government departments, which include ministries such as Culture,
Construction, Education, Transportation, National Defense, and Labor. The President is also commander-in-chief of the armed forces. The Prime Minister assists
the President in administering the executive ministries. Officially, the State Council prepares plans and policies, drafts amendments to the constitution, declares
war, grants pardons, and has many other duties, but in practice, the Council normally voices the views of the President in these matters.

The South Korean judiciary is headed by a Supreme Court and a Constitutional Court. The Supreme Court is the court of final appeal in all cases except
those that require review of law to determine its constitutionality (judicial review).
The Supreme Court's justices are appointed by the President with the consent of
the National Assembly. Ten of the eleven Supreme Court justices are limited to two
six-year terms, while the Chief Justice has a single six-year term. The Constitutional
Court has, at least formally, the power of judicial review. It is composed of nine ad-
judicators, three selected by the National Assembly, three chosen by the Chief Justice of the Supreme Court, and three chosen by the President. They serve for re-
newable six-year terms. Six of the nine members must agree in order to declare a
law unconstitutional.

Comparing Politics in North and South Korea

We shall compare the governments and politics of North and South Korea, as we
did with Israel and the United States of America. We shall first summarize the features of both countries, placing descriptions of major factors side by side in a table

so that similarities and differences may be noted. Then we shall draw conclusions from our summary. Examine the entries in the table below.

Having summarized the main features of the two political systems, we may now draw some conclusions. First, that a country or people has a particular politi-

Category	North Korea	South Korea
Ethnicity	Asian, primarily Korean	Same as North Korea
History to 1945	Succession of Dynasties until 1910, domination by Japanese from 1910–1945	Same as North Korea
History since 1945	Rule by Kim Il Sung and WPK from 1945–1994, and by Kim Jong Il and the WPK since 1994	American protectorate, 1945–1948, Semidemocratic, and military regimes 1948–1989, democratic regimes from 1989 to present
Political Culture	Class stratification with party elite ruling	Class stratification with family clans controlling wealth and elections
	Authoritarian political and family practices	Democratic political and hierarchical family practices
	Intense nationalism, single party (WPK) dominance	Intense nationalism, multiparty system
	Socialist: wealth concentration in ruling class, large lower class	Capitalist state, growing middle class
Government Structure	Formal constitutional: democracy with separation of powers and popular elections; President, Supreme People's Assembly, Central People's Committee, Central Court, Various Ministries	Increasingly democratic republic with President, Prime Minister, National Assembly, Supreme Court, Constitutional Court, Various Ministries
	Actual: totalitarian dictatorship; power flows from top down	Power flows from bottom up and from top down
Political Behavior	Active party loyalty, spy on others, watch foreigners, devote free time to public projects, no free speech or press, no strikes or demonstrations	Increasing participation in elections, which now involve nearly 6000 offices; three major political parties vying for power, occasional strikes and demonstrations, national Security Law still in force, 500 political prisoners

cal culture does not mean that it will adopt a particular type of government structure, but underlying cultural tendencies, such as authoritarianism, remain a powerful influence upon political life. The governments of North and South Korea were set up in 1945 by foreign powers, mainly the U.S.S.R. and the U.S. Despite the common culture, a democratic regime was eventually instituted in the South, and a totalitarian regime in the North, and both regimes have survived well into the 1990s. The underlying features of the common political culture, however, showed up in both regimes, for even though South Korea has always technically been a democracy, at times the military regimes which governed it were nearly as ruthless as the government of the DPRK. The Southern regimes remained authoritarian, however, as distinct from the totalitarian regime in the North. In addition, nationalism has remained strong in both nations, both in terms of a continuing desire for unification and for tendencies towards competing against the United States and Japan. The totalitarian regime in the North has relied much more upon communist ideology and personality cult leadership in gaining control than have the governments of the South.

Both countries have retained class divisions, but the free market economy in the South is quickly giving rise to prosperity for a new middle class. In the North, the elites have formed within the WPK while in the South, influential families who control major corporations have more influence. Both countries, each in its own way, have had two government structures: an ideal one and a real one. In North Korea, the contrast between the ideal, formal government structure, which is thoroughly democratic, and the real operating government structure, which is totalitarian, is evident to even the casual observer. The need to have a formal democratic constitutional structure at all belies the fact that the government of North Korea is founded upon a giant lie: that the government is operated of, by, and for the people. In South Korea, the lie is not so great, for attempts to make the government actually democratic are finally becoming successful.

Cognitive dissonance is the disturbing perception that what appears to be true is really not true. Cognitive dissonance is more severe and widespread in the North than in the South, but it enters people's consciousness as cracks appear in the ideological facades of authoritarian regimes. The results of people responding to cognitive dissonance, being told they are living in a democracy when actually the state is authoritarian, are now widely acted upon in the South, but it is too early to tell when this will happen in the North.

Although many other implications and conclusions may be drawn, perhaps one worthy of final note concerns political behavior. The widespread participation in politics now prevalent in South Korea is currently having a profound effect upon political culture. The tendency towards authoritarianism once prevalent equally in North and South is beginning to fade away in the South. It may not be long, as this process continues, before the two countries no longer share an authoritarian culture. When this happens, values in many aspects of life will change, and the North Koreans and South Koreans will be, in their political identities, two distinct peoples.

6

Schools, Sects, and Approaches to the Study of Politics

The difference between our age and the past is in our way of seeing. Everywhere in the buildings of the past is relationship among parts: contrast, tensions, balance. Compare the buildings of today and we see no such patterns. We see fragmentation, mismatched systems, uncertainty.

—Jonathan Hale *The Old Way of Seeing*, 1994

Some Basic Problems and Challenges for the *Science* of Politics

We call the time in which we now live the era of eclecticism because, beyond the idea that political science is the search for knowledge about politics, there is little profession-wide consensus on either method or subject matter. People calling themselves political scientists still *disagree* widely on two vital and basic questions:

- What is valid information (truth) concerning politics?
- How do we go about finding it?

These questions are known to philosophers as concerns of *epistemology* (the study of what can be known) and *metaphysics* (the study of how knowledge can be accumulated). The controversies that surround these two questions have appeared throughout the history of political science and continue today. Political science is by no means unique in this respect. Jonathan Hale has noted the lack of consistency in contemporary architecture, and many professions and disciplines are presently examining their most fundamental beliefs and approaches to finding the truth.

To understand the complexity of the problems involved in developing a political science hermeneutic, it is helpful to examine the strengths and weaknesses of a fundamental aspect of the process of acquiring knowledge in science: the inductive–deductive dialectic.

Political science, like all science, is dialectical. This means that there is a continuous evolving interaction among the attributes of the search for knowledge. Meaning flows from a chain of insights passed back and forth from one part of the brain to another, from one insight to another, from one experiment to another, from one person to another, and from one discipline to another. To provide you with an idea of how the dialectical process applies to all aspects of the discipline, we shall illustrate dialectical process first from classical writing, then from logic and the conduct of scientific investigation today.

The most famous classical demonstration of dialectic as a method for discovering truth is found in the dialogues of Plato, written in the fourth century BCE, which we have discussed in previous chapters. In the dialogues, Socrates, Plato's mentor, seeks understanding through a process of questions and answers. A speaker (such as Socrates) asks a question, "What is justice?" Another person (such as Thrasymachus) answers, "The interest of the powerful." The first person then responds to the second person's answer, attempting to find a problem in the second person's logic. If the second person's statement is persuasive, the two go on to the next statement or stage in the discussion, attempting to build upon what they have agreed in order to gain more understanding. The dialectic is the process of evolution and change that occurs in the perception of truth held by the two speakers as the argument progresses. The back and forth action of the statements, objections, counter-objections, and confirmations eventually yields a conclusion about the subject at hand.

Socratic dialectic, like much traditional philosophy, is *deductive* in nature. This means that it begins with a *general* principle and then uses logic to deduce *specific* conclusions from the general premise. For example, Socrates states the general principle that reason is a higher capacity than courage or bodily strength, and from this principle he *deduces* that people who have the most highly developed intelligence should rule those who are bold and strong.

The first steps of any investigation in science, however, are normally *inductive.* This means that science studies specific phenomena and then induces general principles from what has been observed. Aristotle's study of governments, for example, was inductive. He studied about 350 individual Greek city-states and then developed a classification of governments and drew conclusions from his classification. From observation of specific governments, then, Aristotle *induced* the properties of good governments and bad governments.

In all science, induction and deduction work together in a dialectical relationship to produce knowledge. Suppose that political scientists are trying to find the cause of voter apathy in local elections They survey hundreds of *specific* registered voters across the country about their participation in *specific* local elections. The patterns they observe allow them to *induce* a certain general conclusion, such as "voters are more likely to vote in local elections when tax increases are at issue." Having induced this general principle, they may then examine a particular subsequent local election, such as an election for Mayor in Dallas, and *deduce* the proposition that if there is no tax increase on the ballot, voter turnout in the election will be relatively low. They can then test their deduction by determining if there is a tax increase on the ballot, and whether voter turnout is high or low.

A dialectical pattern is evident among the three major activities of political science: investigation, interpretation, and application. Investigation results in data. Data are interpreted. The interpretation leads both to further investigation and to application. Application leads to further interpretation and application.

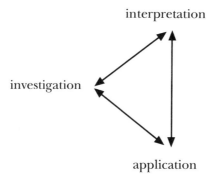

Although political scientists of all sorts employ the induction–deduction dialectic as a normal procedure for advancing our knowledge of politics, philosophers of science have found some important problems inherent in this procedure itself. The contributions of Thomas Kuhn and Karl Popper provide good examples.

Two points made by philosopher Karl Popper have stirred considerable controversy within the discipline. First, Popper argues that the structure of logic underpinning the process of induction is faulty. Induction proceeds on the belief that general principles can be found by examining individual phenomena and discovering patterns among them. Suppose that I observe, for example, a cow eating grass. I then observe several more cows eating grass. I find more and more cows, and find that they all eat grass. I induce the general principle, "cows eat grass." I expect then to feel confident that I can thereafter deduce, upon encountering a new cow, that it will also eat grass. Popper points out that my conclusion is in error. Even if every cow I find does eat grass, there may be one somewhere which does not. In fact, no matter how many cows I find eating grass, there is still the possibility of finding one that does not. Inductively discovered principles, therefore, are not reliable for deduction. The whole process, followed daily by physical scientists and social scientists, is theoretically unreliable.

Popper points out a second problem with the way in which political science is normally conducted: observation is not value-free. Some political scientists had claimed that they observed only facts (statements about phenomena that can be supported by empirical [sensory] observations), instead of stating values (statements about the desirability or usefulness of phenomena). In other words, facts concern what *exists,* and values concern what *should be.* Popper was fond of mocking scientists who believed they could achieve a value-free science by starting his college classes with a command to his students: "Observe!" They would sheepishly look around at one another wondering what it was they were supposed to observe. Popper's point is that, when we observe, we constantly make choices about what to observe and how to observe it, and that these choices unavoidably involve value choices. Science, therefore, is never value-free.

Thomas Kuhn pointed out another problem with one of the major assumptions of both traditional and behavioral political science. Scientists had long believed that scientific progress comes from collecting facts and testing theories. When new facts are discovered that contradict current theories, new theories are devised and tested. Kuhn noted, however, that although much progress is made in precisely this manner in day to day science, the truly great scientific breakthroughs come not from finding errors and making incremental progress, but from the creative ideas of geniuses who see basic relationships in an entirely new way. One good example comes from the theories of Ptolemy and Copernicus. Ptolemy believed that the sun and planets revolve around the earth. Through many centuries astronomers continued to believe this theory even though many of their observations did not seem to confirm it. Instead of coming up with new theories, they kept adding caveats to Ptolemy's theory. It was only when Copernicus made a giant leap to a whole new theory, the idea that the earth and planets revolve around the sun, that science was truly able to progress. Kuhn's point is that, contrary to popular belief, merely adding more facts to the pile of knowledge does not necessarily result in scientific progress. Adding facts does, Kuhn maintains, further "normal science" in which important discoveries which aid our understanding are made. Popper and Kuhn together have helped demonstrate, therefore, both the strengths and weaknesses of the dialectical process of the scientific method.

Before proceeding to observation of today's leading approaches to the study of politics, it is worth noting that political science is still struggling with some epistemological difficulties that are now nearly a century old. In a 1925 article entitled "Recent Advances in Political Methods," Charles Merriam, a leader of a then new scientific movement in political science, outlined four of the most important problems in attempting to study politics with the scientific method. The first problem is "the difficulty of isolating political phenomena sufficiently to determine precisely the causal relations between them." For example, to what extent do attitudes affect voting patterns? Is it possible to isolate the influence of certain attitudes from others, and from other factors in the environment, to determine the cause of a vote for a given candidate? The second problem Merriam lists is "the difficulty of separating the personality of the observer from the social situation of which he is a part." How, for example, can we frame survey questions so that they do not bias the respondent towards a particular answer? If we ask, for example, "Do you think the government is wasting too much money?" the way we have phrased the question may lead respondents to answer in the affirmative, which may not accurately express the respondent's actual belief.

Merriam's third problem is "the difficulty of obtaining the mechanism for accurate measurement of the phenomena of politics." How reliable, for example, are polls? Can we trust what people tell us is actually what they will do? How else can we get good, objective measurements of other influences upon politics, such as economics, ethnicity, family relationship? Merriam's fourth problem, finally, is "the absence of what in natural science is called the controlled experiment." While we can test rats in a laboratory, and hold constant the environment for a series of different stimuli, in the human political arena many factors change all at once. It is relatively difficult to conduct experiments under these complex conditions.

By 1996, some aspects of the problems Merriam mentioned have been resolved, as we shall see. Some of Merriam's concerns, however, remain. The progress of the discipline toward solving these problems, and the challenges that remain, are the subjects of this chapter and are discussed further in the remainder of this book.

Approaches to Politics:
Gabriel Almond's Schools and Sects

Contemporary political science forms a complex and intricate web of beliefs, approaches, methods, and philosophies. To understand how they are similar to and differ from one another, we must seek some way to place them into intelligible categories. One of the more interesting and widely discussed categorizations of the divergent forces in political science is "Separate Tables: Schools and Sects in Political Science." Written by Stanford professor Gabriel Almond in 1988, this typology divides the discipline into four categories, two ideological (left and right) and two methodological (hard and soft), which are still very much in evidence in the discipline in the late 1990s, and are likely to be so well into the twenty-first century. Using these sets of categories, Almond divides the discipline into four ideological-methodological groups: the "soft left," the "soft right," the "hard left," and the "hard right."

	Left	**Right**
Soft	Soft Left	Soft Right
Hard	Hard Left	Hard Right

"Soft" methodologies are descriptive and philosophical. They describe political movements historically and analyze the attributes of political institutions philosophically. A biographical study of the Presidency of Jimmy Carter would be an example of a "soft" study. "Hard" methodologies are quantitative. They gather data that can be analyzed mathematically and statistically. Hard methodologies study directly observable behavior such as voting and political campaigns. They use methods similar to those of economics and psychology.

Almond's methodological categories "hard" and "soft" parallel the long-standing division between behavioralists and traditionalists. Behavioralists are "hard" political scientists because they attempt to produce quantifiable (hard) data. Traditionalists employ methodologies called "soft" because their findings describe politics in qualitative, not mathematically expressed, ways. Almond uses the term "right" to refer to approaches that focus on power and rational thinking, and the term "left" to describe perspectives that concern social, economic, or political equality. The student should be aware that there are many groups in each of Almond's four categories, and this chapter provides only examples of each.

The Soft Right

Traditional Political Analysis

The first political science programs were traditionalist in content. They were heavily influenced by the German model, which emphasized history, economics, and law, and focused upon describing institutions of government and evaluating their effects upon the political process. The goal of the traditional approach is to improve government through understanding the way it works. Traditional studies, therefore, describe government institutions, their constitutions and structures, and then offer observations on the way the institutions serve the "public interest," and affect the values of freedom, equality, equity, justice, and order in society. Among the elements commonly found in political studies are:

- History
- Biography, leadership, management, or personality
- Institutions
- Constitutions, law, and legislation
- Issues
- Philosophies, theories, methods, and concepts like freedom, justice, and equality

The earliest examples of the traditional approach appear in the form of political histories such as Thucydides' *History of the Peloponnesian War,* which describes the war between Athens and Sparta in the fifth century BCE. Thucydides lists the events of the war in detail, including the speeches given at major debates and celebrations, and concludes that "What made war inevitable was the growth of Athenian power and the fear which this caused in Sparta."

Roy Macridis, attempting to make the study of comparative politics more truly comparative, published an effective critique of the traditional approach to comparative politics in his 1955 book, The *Study of Comparative Politics.* Macridis found that the traditional approach, as it had been practiced in the field of comparative politics to that time, was essentially noncomparative, descriptive, parochial, static, and monographic.

Macridis points out that supposedly comparative traditional studies only claim to be comparative, but that even though they may present the constitutions, institutions, and political practices of several nations, they fail to construct criteria for comparison and then to apply these criteria to the countries studied. These studies, therefore, were essentially only descriptive, typically focusing on either the historical growth of specific institutions or on the legal framework of a nation's power structure, including its constitution and laws. When Macridis claims that traditional studies are parochial, he means that most of them had focused on Western Europe, and that relatively little had been done in studying the politics of the rest of the world. Since 1955, there have been many "area studies" of countries in all parts of the world, but some commentators claim that Western Europe is still overrepresented in studies of comparative government.

When Macridis says that traditional studies were "essentially static," he means that traditional studies had ceased to be innovative in their methodology and they continued to look again and again upon institutions from the same limited methodology:

> In general the traditional approach has ignored the dynamic factors that account for growth and change. It has concentrated on what we have called political anatomy. After the evolutionary premises of some of the original works in the nineteenth century were abandoned, students of political institutions apparently lost all interest in the formulation of other theories in the light of which change could be comparatively studied. (Macridis 1955, 11)

Macridis' final criticism of traditional studies in the field of comparative government is that, "The most important studies of foreign systems, aside from basic texts, have taken the form of monographs that have concentrated on the study of the political institutions of one system or on the discussion of a particular institution in one system." For Macridis, and others engaged in the behavioral movement, simply to describe the institutions of other nations is not enough. The development of criteria to definitively compare a series of nations, or all nations, was needed. Political scientists such as Gabriel Almond and David Easton, whose contributions have been discussed in previous chapters, responded to Macridis' call with new methodological approaches such as systems analysis and structure-functionalism, which will be described later in this chapter. Before proceeding, we shall examine two other individuals, Leo Strauss and Eric Voegelin, who have become very famous within the discipline of political science by using traditional methods, and who, responding to critics like Macridis, challenged the value-free emphasis of the behavioralist movement.

Leo Strauss and Eric Voegelin

Standing above, or perhaps beyond, the rest on the "soft right" of political science is Leo Strauss. From his professorship at the University of Chicago during the middle decades of the twentieth century Strauss formed a school of thought that is unique in the discipline. It approaches politics so differently, in fact, that "Straussians" and other political scientists often find little upon which they can agree. In *Natural Right and History*, Strauss proclaims that modernism, relativism, and skepticism have poisoned Western culture. Modernism, to Strauss, is a trend in modern thinking which has given up the pursuit of truth. Claiming that all observations are valid only in relation to a particular place and time (relativism), modern science denies the existence of fixed, eternal truth, applicable at all times and all places (skepticism). But modern thought, Strauss believes, is wrong. Moral truths may, in fact, be found by clarification of the classical texts, especially those of Plato and Aristotle. These texts, carefully examined, reveal an objective moral order in which, by use of our reason, we may discern the existence of natural rights which ensure the protection and dignity of every human being. The essence of Strauss's method is to attempt to understand the texts of the ancients, not in terms of our attitudes today, but only as the authors of the texts themselves would have understood them. In *What is Political Philosophy* (1959, 68), Strauss declares that

> [T]he seemingly infinite variety of ways in which a given teaching can be understood does not do away with the fact that the originator of the doctrine understood it in only one way, provided he was not confused. The indefinitely large variety of equally legitimate interpretations of a doctrine of the past is due to conscious or unconscious attempts to understand its author better than he did himself. But there is only one way of understanding him as he understood himself.

Modern approaches to politics, claims Strauss, mistakenly deny the existence of natural right, which to Strauss creates the foundation for relations in society. Natural right is a concept that derives from the natural order of the universe the principles of the innate dignity of human beings and their universal equality before the law. The rejection of natural rights by the modern world leads to nihilism, or the loss of all value. When political science gave up the search for objective truth, Strauss (1959, 68) argues, it lost its value as a discipline. Condemning the "scientific" study of politics, Strauss announces that, "Generally speaking, one may wonder whether the new political science has brought to light anything of political importance which intelligent political practitioners with a deep knowledge of history, nay intelligent and educated journalists, to say nothing of the old political science at its best, did not know at least as well beforehand."

Eric Voegelin's *The New Science of Politics* (1952) also helped to revive study of classical authors. Voegelin believed, as we explained in Chapter 3, that representation is the central issue of politics. By this, Voegelin meant not merely the manner in which a member of the House of Representatives represents her or his constituents. More important, however, is the manner in which the values and interests of the members of society are represented in political processes and institutions. Voegelin called "gnostic," those modern political movements, like Nazism and Marxism, which mistakenly attempt to resolve artificially the long-standing problems of politics, and in so doing attempt to establish social patterns on earth in a manner which misrepresents human ability to live together. Gnosticism is the easy and wrong answer to the difficulties of life. Gnostic movements start when someone announces himself or herself as having the answer to life's political problems. This answer rejects the difficult way of faith, which calls upon people to rest in the beneficence of God. Gnostic movements attempt to "immanentize the eschaton." The eschaton is the final fulfillment of meaning in history. In Christianity it is described in the book of Revelation, in which Christ returns to free the earth of evil and establish a permanent kingdom of peace. To immanentize the eschaton is to try to bring final salvation from life's problems, however they may be conceived, to earth here and now. For Voegelin, Karl Marx immanentized the eschaton by proclaiming that the communist movement would one day bring an order of peace in which politics would be so minimal that the government would "wither away." Adolf Hitler's conception of the Third Reich could also be an example of a vision of an immanentized eschaton in which the Aryan race subjugated or eliminated all other peoples, who were viewed as inferior. The problem with gnostic visions is that they often, as in the cases of Hitler and Stalin, lead to tragic results, including the deaths of millions of innocent people. Ironically, the result of Gnosticism is the destruction of the very goals it is trying to achieve because Gnosticism, so full of spiritual symbols, kills the vitality of spiritual life:

> The death of the spirit is the price of progress. Nietzsche revealed this mystery of the Western apocalypse when he announced that God was dead and that He had been murdered. This Gnostic murder is constantly committed by the men who sacrifice God to civilization. The more fervently all human energies are thrown into the great enterprise of salvation through world-immanent action, the farther the human beings who engage in this enterprise move away from the life of the spirit. And since the life of the spirit is the source of order in man and society, the very success of a gnostic civilization is the cause of its decline. (Voegelin 1952, 131)

Studies of the State

Strauss and Voegelin fall into Almond's category "soft right" because their research methods are traditional in that they examine the perennial questions of history and philosophy, and the conclusions of their research are conservative, that is, they point toward the reawakening of long-held values. Traditionalist methods are also evident in other schools of thought that may be classified as "soft right." Believing that behavioral methods such as systems analysis and structural-functional analysis reduce political societies to so many parts that it is difficult to understand the unity of political systems, some specialists in comparative studies have recently given new attention to the state as a unit of analysis. In so doing, these specialists have to a large extent revived the traditional approach. Although many analytical concepts are used in conducting them, the new studies of the state continue the legacy of the traditionalist approach by focusing upon the state as the central entity in politics and government. More than just a government, they assert, the state is a cohesive set of systems that determine political life. The state is not merely an institution that responds to other forces in society but is a creative and vital source of important initiatives. These theorists believe that studying the substantially autonomous elites (groups that hold political or economic power that direct states, such as corporate executives or military leaders) will lead to explanations of domestic and international political events. In "Putting States in Their Place: State Systems and State Theory," Lancaster University (United Kingdom) political scientist Bob Jessup identifies "six crucial factors about the state or state system" that are most often examined by "state-centered theorists":

- Geo-political position
- Military
- Internal powers
- External powers
- State managers
- Pathologies

The *geo-political position* of a state is the status which a state holds in the hierarchy of nations because of the relative importance of its location. A state's geo-political position changes from time to time in history. Venice, Italy, for example, developed great wealth by taking advantage of being in a central location for trade in the Mediterranean in the late Middle Ages. Venice lost its geo-political importance, however, when other great European trading cities developed at the end of the Middle Ages. Holland, Spain, Portugal, France, England, and the Untied States came to power in turn, using the geo-political advantages of their locations to develop military and commercial empires. Geo-political power changes from one century to the next. Panama's importance to world trade will always be significant because the Panama Canal shortens the ocean voyage from the Atlantic to the Pacific, but is less so at the end of the twentieth century than it was at the end of the nineteenth because forms of freight movement other than ocean shipping are now more readily available.

The *role of the military* is of central importance in the daily affairs of most countries. In the United States, even after the end of the Cold War, defense appropriations continue to account for a significant part of the national budget. Even Switzerland, which has a long tradition of neutrality in the wars in Europe, requires its male citizens to participate in military preparedness activities at times throughout their adult lives. The role of the military is especially important in Middle Eastern countries where wars have erupted frequently in the twentieth century. Political scientists study the *direct* influences of the military upon the state, such as military leaders in civilian positions and the potential for a military coup, and *indirect* influences, such as the prestige of military careers or the potential for human rights violations by members of military units.

The *direct internal powers* of the state are the executive, legislative, and judicial powers that help organize society. The state may use the direct force of military or police. During the civil rights demonstrations and antiwar protests of the 1960s, the national guard was called upon by presidents and governors to quell demonstrations that led to violence. The state may also call upon quietly existing but substantial *indirect* internal powers such as a sense of obligation on the part of the people to obey laws, pay taxes, and serve in the military. Political leaders use the media to strengthen these indirect sources of power.

The *external powers* of the state are those exercised in international relations, such as the use or threat of use of the armed forces or economic sanctions, or the ability to give foreign aid. Its natural, human, and economic resources have given the United States an exceptional ability to employ military, diplomatic, and economic external powers since World War II, making the United States the world's most powerful nation for the last half of the twentieth century.

States are led by elite groups that state theorists call *state managers*. Not all state managers actually hold government positions. Some may be private individuals who are wealthy or widely popular. In some countries like Kuwait, a hereditary aristocracy manages state affairs. In others, such as Iran, religious leaders have extraordinary influence. In Japan, the executives of major corporations have substantial influence on government policy. Political scientists who study state managers are interested in the state's decisionmaking process, how elites gain their positions of influence, and how they relate to one another to form a power structure that guides the society as a whole.

The *pathologies* of state systems, which are the aspects or elements of the system that do not work well, reveal much about the distribution of power in society. In any state, some elements of the system seem to work better than others, and the relative efficiency of units changes over time. In the United States, for example, citizens were more impressed with public secondary schools in the 1950s, except for those attending segregated schools, than they are in the 1990s. Some state systems are infested with so much corruption that they are susceptible to continuous regime changes through elections or revolutions. State analysts attempt to identify the factors that lead to increases in both stability and instability.

The Soft Left

Feminism

In Gabriel Almond's construct, feminism would be found among the perspectives of the soft left. In an article entitled "Feminism and Politics," Diana Coole describes two waves of feminism in modernity. The first wave is a movement to assert women's political rights which has continued since it first appeared in the seventeenth century. The second wave is an intellectual movement which represents a unique perspective on politics; it is more radical than the first wave, and seeks a transformation of Western culture. As Coole points out, "Feminism is, then, both an intellectual perspective and a social movement; its theories and its practice are interwoven." Feminism has gained much support for its theories from psychoanalytical thought. According to Coole (1990, 30), women are universally given primary responsibility for the care of children, and, therefore, women profoundly affect their children in both positive and negative ways:

> The girl who is like her mother and is strongly identified with her, gains a secure sense of her sexual identity but a weak sense of her own autonomy and ego-boundaries, owing to the difficulty of separation. The boy, on the other hand, is always treated as different and must gain a sense of his sexual identity from the absent father; his masculinity is predicated on his being not-female. The result is a weak and abstract sense of masculinity but a stronger notion of self-identity. From these early differences we see subsequent gendered proclivities for different types of knowledge and being. Females evidence a capacity for empathetic relationships, for cooperation and caring; they feel at home in the world and relate strongly to their environment. Men, on the other hand, are more strongly attracted to modes of abstract thought which reflect their own sense of separation from the world. They distrust subjectivity and favour rational, objective, impersonal forms of knowledge and association. They fear that which is associated with femininity and pursue projects of domination over it.

Perhaps one of the most important contributions of feminism as an intellectual movement is its assertion that ideas of what is masculine and what is feminine can change over time. Societies can become more masculine or feminine. Women may always bear children, but the implications of this fact for their role in politics is purely a matter of culture and is not physiologically determined. Femininity, therefore, is socially and not biologically acquired. Coole points out that some feminists have criticized value-neutral political analysis because it tends to support the status quo, which equates to male domination. She notes that feminism favors neither empiricism nor rationalism. Feminine thinking is more empathic, engaged, and open than masculine thinking, which is power-based.

Feminists have a wide variety of views, from moderate positions which seek to broaden the range of opportunities for women, to radical perspectives which, according to Coole (1990, 27), see "patriarchy as the most pervasive feature of social life."

In addition to the controversy that radical feminist views have generated, feminists have made a profound and revolutionary contribution to the study of politics. Coole (1990, 32) defines this transformational contribution as the idea that "politics cannot be confined to the macro-levels of state processes; that politics is defined not by proximity to a particular *institution* but by a kind of relationship, namely one in which power and domination/subordination are present." This realization, that politics is not confined to governments, but is ubiquitous in all personal relationships, broadens the scope of political science from a discipline that looks only at the workings of activities related to governments to a study of the political nature of all human relationships.

Coole notes further that feminist writers have challenged not only traditional views of the nature of politics, but perspectives on scientific methodology as well. She explains that the scientific method incorporates masculine (rational) attitudes that may be used not only to discover facts about political life, but to dominate political life as well. To the extent that political science is dominated by theories of power and the state, and both the state and the positions of power in the world are dominated by men, then the scientific method becomes a tool of patriarchy.

Feminists are not yet a leading influence within political science, but many in the discipline expect them to make a continually growing contribution. The recent trend towards more empirical political research in relation to women is, ironically, as Coole notes, helping to reinforce a masculine method that feminists reject.

Political Psychology

The potential applications of psychology to politics have only begun to be explored. The father of the discipline of psychology, Sigmund Freud, provided a dramatic response to other schools of political thought, especially Marxism, at the turn of the century. Karl Marx, following a course initiated by Jean Jacques Rousseau, had believed that human beings were naturally capable of living in peace, and that class conflict in society is primarily the result of faulty institutions. Freud thoroughly and profoundly rejected Marx's view. Freud proposed that the human psyche is composed of the ego (rational consciousness), the superego (conscience, or the capacity of moral choice), and the id (subconscious desires). For Freud, the id, rather than the ego or the superego, is the controlling element. As human beings we may see ourselves as rational, moral creatures, but in actuality we serve our subconscious desires for sex, comfort, and power.

In *Civilization and Its Discontents*, written on the eve of Hitler's reign of terror in Germany, Freud presented a pessimistic view of humanity's ability to reform itself in any fundamental way. He contrasted two human drives, one for love and community and the other for death and destruction, and noted that these drives are perpetually in conflict with each other within individual human beings, and that they recurrently express themselves in society in crime, violence, and war. Since Freud's monumental writings, the study of political psychology has made notable contributions to the discipline. We shall discuss a few of the most famous works briefly here, and note some recent developments in Chapter 15.

Immediately after World War II, revelation of the atrocities that had been committed in Nazi Germany and under Stalin's communism led to an intense interest in finding the root causes of mass violence. The *Authoritarian Personality* (1950), a famous study by a research team headed by Theodore Adorno, developed a measurement called the F scale to determine the extent of authoritarian tendencies in an individual's personality. The scale measured the following attitudes:

1. *Conventionalism.* Rigid adherence to conventional, middle-class values.
2. *Authoritarian submission.* Submissive, uncritical attitude toward leaders.
3. *Authoritarian aggression.* Tendency to be on the lookout for, and to condemn, reject, and punish people who violate conventional values.
4. *Anti-intraception.* Opposition to the subjective, the imaginative, the tenderminded.
5. *Superstition and stereotypy.* The belief in mystical determinants of the individual's fate; the disposition to think in rigid categories.
6. *Power and "toughness."* Preoccupation with the dominance–submission, strong–weak, leader–follower dimension; identification with power figures; overemphasis upon the conventional attributes of the ego; exaggerated assertion of strength and toughness.
7. *Destructiveness and cynicism.* Generalized hostility, vilification of the human.
8. *Projectivity.* The disposition to believe that wild and dangerous things go on in the world; the projection outwards of unconscious emotional impulses.
9. *Sex.* Exaggerated concern with sexual "goings-on." (Adorno 1982, 157)

Adorno's research suggested that authoritarian personalities, which are found in all societies, were susceptible to mass movements and likely to support dictatorships. It pointed in a new direction for preventing the problems of Nazism and communism: finding ways to help authoritarian personalities become more at home in and less aggressive towards society.

Erich Fromm's *Escape from Freedom* explored and expanded some of the concepts addressed by Adorno. For Fromm, two primary human tendencies combine to produce authoritarian movements. The first is masochism, in which the individual has "feelings of inferiority, powerlessness, [and] individual insignificance" (Fromm 1960, 42). Fromm (1960, 143–44) finds, ironically, that:

> Besides these masochistic trends, the very opposite of them, namely, *sadistic* tendencies, are regularly to be found in the same kind of characters. They vary in strength, are more or less conscious, yet are never missing. We find three kinds of sadistic tendencies, more or less closely knit together. One is to make others dependent on oneself and to have absolute and unrestricted power over them. . . . Another consists of the impulse . . . to exploit them, to use them, to steal

from them. . . . A third kind of sadistic tendency is the wish to make others suffer or to see them suffer.

From these studies on authoritarian personality, political psychology has taken off in many directions. Robert Jervis, for example, wrote a fascinating study of the psychology of decisionmaking in international relations. Jervis found that one of the greatest problems that leaders face in foreign policy is their tendency to shape information that they receive into their own preconceived theories. Policymakers during the Vietnam war, for example, originally assumed that a timely, efficient, and nonnuclear victory over the guerrilla forces of North Vietnam was possible, and held that belief long after the evidence demonstrated otherwise.

What qualities constitute effective presidential leadership is a recurring topic in political psychology. Many commentators have discussed, for example, Richard Nixon's paranoia, Jimmy Carter's penchant for understanding the operations of government in minute detail, and Ronald Reagan's focus on ideological concepts and lack of interest in administration. James David Barber (1972) classified presidents into personality types, according to whether they were active or passive, positive or negative in pursuit of their goals. Active-positive presidents, for example, like Franklin Roosevelt, believe the President should take a strong role in making policy and directing the course of the nation, and they enjoy their jobs. Passive-negative presidents, like Calvin Coolidge, see the Presidency as an institution that should respond to the actions of Congress, and they seem to take little satisfaction in the daily duties of the Presidency. Recent studies of the Presidency incorporate psychological concepts to attempt to predict presidential actions based upon personality and management styles.

Critical Theory

Critical theory attempts to diagnose the problems in society in order to help find a cure. Karl Marx is given credit by some commentators for being the first critical theorist because he recognized that the alienation of labor was the basis of class conflict and described how that conflict was to be resolved. Marx's view was optimistic. He believed that the developing processes of interaction in society would bring forth the overthrow of the middle class by the laboring class, which would then institute a just and fair society. Marx is viewed by critical theorists as someone who subscribed to a theory of *social rationalization,* which is a process by which society appropriates nature to meet its needs, and builds social structures of authority and influence on the basis of who is best able to put nature's resources to use. Max Weber, an influential twentieth-century sociologist, also believed in social rationalization, but was more pessimistic than Marx. Weber saw society degenerating into an ever more complex set of bureaucracies established supposedly to help people meet their ever increasing needs. For Weber, then, social rationalization is a process by which society, as it develops from medieval to modern forms, instead of depending upon tradition to form its social arrangements, turns to reasoned principles and uses these principles to build structures of status and authority.

According to the critical theory of Theodore Adorno, Herbert Marcuse, and others of the "Frankfurt School," a group of scholars centered in Frankfurt, Germany, objectivity in political science is inappropriate. All students of politics, whether they admit it or not, are unavoidably involved in the struggle between the rich and the poor. Political science is impossible without ideological commitment. Theory and practice cannot be separated, nor can science and politics. Both theory and practice, further, can be explained only by economic analysis because economic conditions determine societal relations. The primacy of economics in political life defines, more than any other factor, the perspective of the left side of Almond's methodological spectrum. For the "hard left," as well as the "soft left," the class struggle between the wealthy and the poor is the ultimate basis of all political action.

A theorist who has gained substantial attention for further developing a concept of social rationalization is Jurgen Habermas. Habermas' book *The Structural Transformation of the Public Sphere* (1962) argues that the public sphere has collapsed. In his commentary on Habermas entitled *Jurgen Habermas, Critic in the Public Sphere* (1991, 6), Robert Holub explains that

> The collapse occurs because of the intervention of the state into private affairs and the penetration of society into the state. Since the rise of the public sphere depended upon a clear separation between the private realm and public power, their mutual interpenetration inevitably destroys it. The role that the public sphere had played in the intellectual life of society is then assumed by other institutions that reproduce the image of a public sphere in a distorted guise. . . . As we progress into the twentieth century, the free exchange of ideas among equals becomes transformed into less democratic communicative forms, such as public relations. Party politics and the manipulation of the mass media lead to what Habermas calls a 'refeudalization' of the public sphere, where representation and appearances outweigh rational debate.

Habermas set out to understand how capitalist societies developed, and to understand their weaknesses and failures. Habermas finds that, because of its process of social rationalization, capitalist society has established economic and administrative institutions that threaten the development of culture. Habermas believes that instrumental rationality, which is a way of thinking that focuses on how to achieve goals efficiently, is superseded in importance by communicative rationality, which brings into public discussion, not only the question of how to meet objectives, but also the value to society of the objectives being met. Communicative rationality is conducive to mutual understanding, and leads to forms of consensus that build stable and peaceful societies. Although Habermas is concerned first not to judge the values of modern societies, but to explore the evolution of communicative rationality within them, he is critical of modern capitalism, seeing its injustices and inequalities as problems for theorists to help solve.

The Hard Right

Rational Actor Theory and Decisionmaking Analysis

Much analysis of public policy is conducted according to what is called the *rational actor theory*. Its precepts are found in the writings of the soft left, hard right, and soft right as well as the hard left. It is included in the section on the hard right because it is here, among hard right theorists, that it has been most highly developed. Rational actor theory assumes that people will normally act rationally, which means in particular that they will act to maximize what they perceive to be their own best interests.

A "contemporary classic" example of rational actor analysis, with a critique of the rational actor approach, is found in Graham Allison's *Essence of Decision: Explaining the Cuban Missile Crisis* (1971). The Cuban missile crisis marked the peak of the Cold War. On October 14, 1962, the United States discovered that Soviet strategic nuclear weapons had been placed in Cuba. The United States responded with a naval blockade of Cuba, challenging the entry of Soviet ships and setting the stage for a possible nuclear war. The Soviet Union responded by withdrawing the missiles from Cuba, averting a nuclear confrontation.

The analyst of international relations, using the rational actor model, examines the history of an incident or series of interactions, and attempts to explain why the events took place as they did by finding a rational pattern in them. In *Essence of Decision,* Allison applies the rational actor model and two alternative models (organizational process and governmental politics) to explain the crisis, and then compares the strengths and weaknesses of the three models. Applying the rational actor model to the Cuban missile crisis, Allison identifies the options open to both the Americans and the Soviets, outlines the comparative costs and benefits of each possible action as each party saw them, and discovers in the pattern of events the reasoning process that each side used in making its decision. Allison notes that this approach seems quite reasonable. It assumes that most people will act in a rational manner most of the time, and that government policies are most often the result of rationally ordered decisions, made by the officials responsible for making them. But Allison uncovers a problem with the model. According to Allison, rational actor theorists:

- Examine a situation,
- Identify what seem to be the logical choices for the actors in the situation,
- Examine the choices selected by the actors, and
- Find a rationale for the choices the actors selected.

The problem with this process, according to Allison, is that rational actor theorists keep looking for a rational explanation for an event until they find one. Their analysis has no way of taking into account whether their "rational" explanation had anything at all to do with what actually happened. Rational actor theorists, therefore, apply a synthetic answer for events after the fact, an answer that seems reasonable, but may in fact have had nothing to do with the actions being studied. Allison (1971, 11) gives an example of how this error was made by rational actor theorists Arnold Horelick and Myron Rush, who had tried to answer the question, "Why did the Soviets place missiles in Cuba?"

> The most widely cited explanation of the Soviet emplacement of missiles in Cuba has been produced by Rand sovietologists, Arnold Horelick and Myron Rush. They conclude that 'the introduction of strategic missiles into Cuba was motivated chiefly by the Soviet leaders' desire to overcome . . . the existing large margin of United States strategic superiority.' How do they reach this conclu-

sion: In Sherlock Holmes style, they magnify several salient characteristics of the action and use these features as criteria against which to test alternative hypotheses about Soviet objectives.

Allison (1971, 11) then notes that University of Chicago political scientist Hans Morgenthau made the same mistake in his rational actor analysis of the causes of World War I:

> According to Hans Morgenthau, "The first World War had its origins exclusively in the fear of a disturbance of the European balance of power. In the pre-World War I period, the Triple Entente was a delicate counterweight to the Triple Alliance. If either bloc could have gained a decisive advantage in the Balkans, it would have achieved a decisive advantage in the balance of power . . ." How is Morgenthau able to resolve this problem so confidently: By imposing on the data a "rational outline."

To determine if there are viable alternatives to the rational actor theory for explaining the Cuban missile crisis, Allison defines and applies two other approaches. The first is the *Organizational Process Model*. The organizational process analyst views political events as the products of large organizations rather than as the choices of individual decisionmakers. Analysts have shown, through a series of studies, that bureaucracies have sets of procedures that produce results different from what one would naturally expect from individual decisionmakers. Organizations produce change incrementally, according to recognized procedures. When applied to specific situations, these procedures may have consequences that do not appear rational at all. One interesting question about the Cuban missile crisis is, "Why did the Soviets place missiles in Cuba when they had previously been pursuing a policy of détente and much of their effort continued to be in the direction of détente?" For organization process analysts, the explanation, according to Allison, is simple. One part of the Soviet bureaucracy was pursuing détente while another part was attempting to increase Soviet influence in Cuba in order to enlarge the Soviet share of the balance of power. This explanation of Soviet behavior, according to Allison, is at least as good if not better than the explanation offered by the rational actor model.

Another alternative approach is the *Governmental Politics Model*, in which "events in foreign affairs are understood . . . neither as choices nor as outputs . . . [but] as a *resultant* of various bargaining games among players in the national government." In the Departments of State, Defense, and Commerce, for example, competing interests attempt to influence decisions, and the policies finally announced are the result of compromises among these competing interests.

Allison (1971, 7) provides an excellent metaphor to explain the differences among the three models he sets forth:

> Imagine a chess game in which the observer could see only a screen upon which moves in the game were projected, with no information about how the pieces came to be moved. Initially, most observers would assume . . . that an individual chess player was moving the pieces. . . . But a pattern of moves can be imagined that would lead some observers . . . to consider a loose alliance of semi-independent organizations, each of which moved its set of pieces according to stan-

dard operating procedures. . . . [I]t is conceivable, furthermore, that a pattern of play might suggest [that] a number of distinct players, with distinct objectives but shared power over the pieces, could be determining the moves as the resultant of collegial bargaining. For example, the black rook's move might contribute to the loss of a black knight with no comparable gains for the black team, but with the black rook becoming the principal guardian of the palace on that side of the board.

Allison's work has challenged political scientists to refine their methodologies, and many advances have been produced since *The Cuban Missile Crisis* was published in 1971. Having introduced one of the leading concepts of hard right theorists, rational actor theory, we continue our discussion with a discussion of a hard right theory that has become, in the 1980s and 1990s, one of the most prominent methodologies in political science: public choice theory.

Public Choice Theory

At the forefront of the hard right is a group of studies known by three different names: "formal theory," "rational choice theory," or "public choice theory." Public choice theory follows techniques developed in economics. In public choice studies, voters are viewed as participants in a political marketplace. A founding father of the public choice school in political science, James Buchanan (1972, 12), explains that

> The critically important bridge between the behavior of persons who act in the marketplace and the behavior of persons who act in political process must be analyzed. The "theory of public choice" can be interpreted as the construction of such a bridge. The approach requires only the simple assumption that the same individuals act in both relationships.

Albert Weale (1990, 196–97) describes public choice theory in more detail:

> Rational choice theory regards politics as a particular set of institutions forming a process for amalgamating individual preferences into a collective choice of policy or outcome. . . . There is no assumption in rational choice approaches that these preferences are motivated entirely by selfish considerations. . . . There is an assumption, however, that whatever preferences persons have, they will want to maximize the chance of achieving their most favoured outcome, or, at least the outcome that seems most achievable in the circumstances in which they are placed. This maximizing assumption is crucial. . . . Instead of asking how, in practice, preferences are amalgamated or how ideally preferences ought to be amalgamated, it asks instead: under what conditions will preferences be amalgamated in a characteristic way? Two characteristics have been of particular concern to rational choice theorists. The first is that of stability. . . . [N]o individual in the system is able to change the outcome from the sum of individual choices, given that none of the other individuals is prepared to change their choices. . . . [The second,] optimality, is the principle that everyone is as well-off as they can be, in the sense that no one can be made better off without making someone else worse off.

Public choice theorists assume that voters, like people who have money to spend in an economic marketplace, will act in a rational manner. This means that they, as a group (an aggregate), will make choices that tend to maximize gain, especially short-term gain. Public choice analysts assume that free market economic and political systems are alike in providing for the most efficient allocation of resources. Politicians, voters, and lobbyists strive for benefits in the form of executive, legislative, and judicial power.

The objective of public choice theory is to analyze the rational choices (votes, campaign contributions, etc.) of voters and their aggregate consequences. Buchanan provides just this kind of analysis in his study of problems in the British health system. Buchanan finds that the British health system is failing because more demands are placed on the system than it is prepared to meet (Buchanan 1972, 33). Buchanan argues that the problems plaguing the British health system stem from the British people, who act simultaneously through the government and the private market place to have their health needs met. The British people, through their government, have set up the National Health Service to regulate the provision of health care services, and they have set limits to the extent and availability of those services. At the same time, as individuals, they demand more services than the National Health Service is capable of providing. Buchanan (1972, 28) explains that

> The individuals who are the demanders and those who are the suppliers are, of course, basically the same persons acting in two separate roles, and the facts themselves suggest the inconsistency. My central point is that this inconsistency does not in any way reflect irrationality on the part of individual decision-makers, but that it arises exclusively from the institutional setting for choice on the two sides of the account.

Buchanan proceeds to demonstrate how the National Health Service provides services at a low direct cost that drives up demand for services. Thus, the institutional arrangements made by the National Health Service create an artificial contradiction within the individual who acts in the public sphere, voting for representatives who will limit funds to the National Health Service, and who also acts in the private sphere by demanding more services than the National Health Service can provide.

Game Theory

Game theory is one of the approaches to understanding politics that has developed within the field of formal theory. Some people view politics as a game, and they correctly point to similarities between games and politics. Politics is a contest with rules, winners, losers, tactics, and strategies. It is perhaps analogous to poker. How you play the hand you hold is often more important than the hand itself, and winning depends upon your ability to assess what others are likely to do. Politics is not, however, like croquet, in the sense that croquet is played for fun without serious consequences, nor is it like professional football games, which have as their objective merely to entertain and prove who has the better team.

Game theorists attempt to represent the possibilities inherent in political action by constructing "games," which are scenarios which allow for the precise description of the choice of action that a political actor has in a particular situation. The prisoner's dilemma is a game strategy situation which mimics actual political situations. The prisoners in this scenario are hypothetical felons who find themselves with an opportunity to bargain with a hypothetical district attorney. Making this comparison enables political scientists a better understanding of the costs, benefits, and options for political action in real life. The following description of the prisoner's dilemma was written by Peter Ordeshook in his book *Game Theory and Political Theory: An Introduction* (1986). The prisoner's dilemma presents two choices for each of two prisoners. One choice is more risky, assumes a lack of cooperation with the opposing side, and has a higher reward, while the second choice is less risky, is based upon a sense of cooperation, and has a lower reward. Many political choices seem to follow this pattern. The prisoner's dilemma according to Ordeshook (1986, 206–207) follows this scenario: Suppose that two prisoners,

> who are factually guilty of a felony, are locked in separate cells by the district attorney [DA]. Contemplating their fates, they each perceive two strategies: (s1) stonewall the DA and admit nothing, and (s2) turn state's evidence and confess all. The DA, however, sees an opportunity to extract a confession if he keeps the prisoners from communicating with each other and if he implements the following incentives: Realizing that if neither prisoner confesses, a conviction on the felony is at best doubtful, he nevertheless promises to make life miserable with several lesser offenses and a 10-year sentence at one of the state's less luxurious incarceration facilities. With a confession, he can ensure a felony conviction, and if only one prisoner turns states evidence, then the DA promises him parole in eight years, while threatening the less cooperative felon with twenty years and no hope of parole. Of course, if both confess, then both are convicted and the DA regards himself as less bound by any promises made with respect to securing a confession (a confession is now a cheap commodity) and both felons receive 15-year sentences.

The diagram below is Ordeshook's illustration of the possible outcomes if different choices are made by each of the prisoners. The numbers in the boxes represent the relative gains and losses that each player may expect under each combination of options. In the upper right box, for example, Prisoner 1 does not confess, while Prisoner 2 confesses. Prisoner 1 loses 20 years of his life to prison, while Prisoner 2 loses only eight.

		Prisoner 2	
		S1 (don't confess)	S2 (confess)
Prisoner 1	S1	−10, −10	−20, −8
	S2	−8, −20	−15, −15

Game theory allows decisionmakers to categorize all of the possible outcomes of different decisions made within a particular situation. They thereby gain a clear comprehensive view of their options, allowing them to make better-informed decisions.

Political scientists borrowed game theory from economists, who used it to understand fluctuations in market conditions. Political scientists use game theory primarily to analyze decisions. Most decisions in politics are made with less than complete knowledge of how people in different interest groups, parties, or nations may respond. An example will help illustrate how game theory is conducted.

Suppose that a group of terrorists seize an airliner and threaten to blown up the plane and its one hundred occupants if certain demands are not met. The terrorists demand that fifty specified "political prisoners" be released, and that the terrorists themselves are guaranteed safe passage to a neutral country where they will be granted asylum. A government representative is assigned responsibility and authority for dealing with the terrorists. We shall simplify the situation, which may in fact involve many options, for the purpose of demonstrating game theory. The government shall have two basic choices: (1) to comply with the terrorist demands, or (2) refuse to comply with the demands. The terrorists have two choices: (1) kill the hostages, or (2) free the hostages. These choices are illustrated in the diagram below.

		terrorist options	
		kill the hostages	free the hostages
government options	comply with demands	1 A −1	1 B 0
	refuse to comply with demands	0 C 0	0 D 1

The numbers in the boxes refer to the consequences of the decisions. The government's gains and losses are represented by numbers in the lower left corners of the boxes, and the terrorists' gains and losses are represented by numbers in the upper right corners. Look at the box labeled "B." The scenario portrayed in box B is that the government complies with the demand of the terrorists and the terrorists free the hostages. If this happens, the government will achieve an objective, which is to free the hostages, but only at the cost of complying with terrorist demands, which may encourage terrorists to attempt this type of action in the future. The government's gains and losses cancel each other out, and this result is represented by a 0 in the lower left hand corner of box B. The terrorists, in the box B scenario, achieve their primary objective, which is to free the political prisoners and suffer no loss in freeing the hostages, so the terrorists' success is represented in box B as a 1. Looking at all boxes one at a time, the whole pattern of likely choices and consequences becomes clear.

Our example of a hypothetical dispute between the government and the terrorists is rather simple. Surprisingly, though, this is why game theory may be especially helpful in solving problems. Let us suppose that, instead of two viable options, each side to the dispute has seven viable options, which might include, for the terrorists, such things as freeing some of the hostages. The game theory matrix would now have forty-nine boxes (7×7) instead of four (2×2). Many more combinations of results are now possible. Game theory helps analysts systematically think through all the possible combinations of decisions and the possible costs and consequences of those decisions.

Game theorists have identified three different types of games. A *zero-sum* game is one in which there is always a winner and a loser. If two people toss a coin to see who keeps the coin, the results will be heads or tails, one wins and one loses, the sum of the loss for one (-1) and the gain for the other (1) is zero. In a *zero-difference* game the parties succeed or fail together. Suppose, for example, that John and Wyn are writing a report, due the next day, which has two sections, section A and section B. Both people are capable of writing both sections. To divide the work, they agree that in the evening John will write section A and Wyn will write section B. John, wanting some peace and quiet, decides to leave his house and go to his cottage at the lake, where there is no telephone. When he gets to the cottage he realizes that he can't remember which section of the report he has agreed to write. Wyn, at her own home, has the same difficulty, and cannot remember which section to write. If they write different sections of the report, they will both "win" the game. If, however, they both write the same section of the report, the report will not be complete, and they will both lose the game.

A third type of game is an *inefficient* game. Suppose that Chris is baking cake and Molly is baking cookies. Chris owns an oven but does not have a mixer. Molly has a mixer but no oven. Chris knows he can mix the cake ingredients by hand, but would like to borrow Molly's mixer for just a half hour, and use the oven all the rest of the afternoon. Molly also needs the oven all afternoon, but will try to borrow Chris' and keep it for as long as she can, offering the mixer in trade. If Chris keeps the use of the oven all afternoon, he will lose the use of the mixer. If, however, he gives up the oven for a while, he is afraid he will have a hard time getting it back, because he knows how badly Molly wants to bake cookies. If the two can come to an agreement, they will both gain the use of the oven and the mixer. This situation is an inefficient game because the lack of agreement between the two players will definitely result in an inefficient solution, that is, one in which neither gains or loses proportionately from the situation, but both will lose in some way if an agreement is not reached.

Systems Analysis

Systems analysis is the legacy of David Easton, who defines politics as the "authoritative allocation of values," and a system as "any set of variables regardless of the degree of interrelationship among them" (Easton 1966, 143–154). A political system, therefore, is a set of variables which together authoritatively allocate values. This means that any set of variables (people, institutions, groups) capable of making decisions about values may be called a political system. Easton intends this definition to refer primarily to governments, because governments, more than other institutions in the modern age, are the agents which authoritatively allocate values. It is important to note that this is not universally true. For most of the middle ages, for example, it could be argued that the Church was the primary agent for the authoritative allocation of values. Aristotle, in fact, begins a discussion of politics in his *Politics* with a discussion of families, which are micrcosmic political systems and certainly allocate values. A strength of systems analysis is that it can be used to understand political systems at all levels. Political systems may include, for example, a social club, a local church, a national religious denomination, a school district, a city council, a regional planning commission, Congress, or the North Atlantic Treaty Organization (NATO).

Conducting systems analysis begins with an understanding of the standard components of any political system, which include:

- *People, groups,* or *populations* who interact in the system;
- *Gatekeepers,* that is, those who set the agenda for making decisions;
- *Authorities,* or those who speak for the system;
- *Inputs,* including
  - *Demands* for actions and services and
  - *Supports* that help maintain and strengthen the system;
- *Outputs,* or decisions made by the system;
- *Intrasocietal* (inside the system) *environments;*
- *Extrasocietal* (outside the system) *environments;* and
- *Disturbances,* or things that cause stress in the system.

Once the elements of a system have been identified, a *flow model,* a diagram which illustrates the relationships among the elements of the system, may be constructed. In addition to the basic elements listed above, a flow model will also include

- Major *transactions* (one-way actions) among the participants;
- *Exchanges* (two-way interactions) with other internal and external systems of the environment;
- A *feedback loop,* or the manner in which outputs return to the system as new inputs;
- The *covariance,* or manner, in which changes in some elements in the system act in response to changes in other elements of the system; and
- The *interdependence* of some elements of the system upon each other.

A flow model of the political system of a local school district might be diagrammed in the manner of the example presented on the following page. The diagram represents, of course, a mere outline of the information which the system analysis would produce.

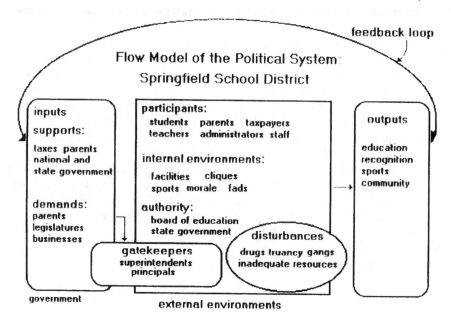

Flow Model of the Political System:
Springfield School District

Systems analysis then proceeds to consider other factors, such as:

• Levels and types of *stress* in the system; the way the system handles stress
• The *critical range,* or limits, of the system's ability to handle stress
• The *openness* of the system to change
• *Adaptibility* to new demands, stresses, and conditions
• *Objectives* or purposes of the system
• The system's *potential* and *limitations* in respect to fulfilling its objectives
• *Effectiveness* of the system in accomplishing its objectives
• *Efficiency* of the system in converting inputs to outputs

Systems analysis is particularly useful in comparing political systems in different countries because, while every system carries out the same functions, every political system handles those functions in different ways.

Structural-Functionalism

Gabriel Almond introduced structural and functional analysis to the study of comparative government in *The Politics of the Developing Areas* (1960). The political structures of any nation include political and legal institutions, such as executive, legislative, and judicial agencies, and the rules, such as the constitution and principal laws under which the institutions operate. The political structures of the United States, for example, are first described in the Constitution, which establishes a federal system in which national, state, and local governments operate. The national government's institutions, including the Presidency, the executive departments and agencies, Congress, the Supreme Court and other federal courts, operate under fundamental organizational principles, also described in the Constitution, which include checks and balances such as the President's veto power and judicial review.

A foundational principle of structural-functional analysis, as Almond points out, is that even though political structures differ from one country to the next, they all carry out the same basic functions. Almond presents four *input functions,* things which support a political system, and three *output functions,* things that the political system produces. Almond's four input functions are political socialization and recruitment; interest articulation; interest aggregation; and political communication.

Political socialization is the manner in which people learn the political values of their culture. Most political socialization is accomplished through mediating institutions such as families, schools, churches, clubs, and businesses. For example, for many years voting studies have indicated that a primary influence upon a person's choice of political party is the party of his or her parents. Families teach ideas and outlooks which are carried into the political arena by children brought up under them. The primary task of functional analysis, when studying the political systems of nations, is to determine the relative importance of various mediating institutions in shaping the political values and preferences of a nation. In some nations, such as Iran, people will be strongly influenced by a dominant religion. In other places, the political values of a person's social class will be more important.

Political recruitment is an extension of political socialization. It is the process whereby society equips people for political roles by providing them with education and experience necessary to participation in the activities of government.

Interest articulation refers to the ways in which interests may be expressed. Functional analysis attempts to determine which groups are more effective at expressing their views than other groups, and the reasons for their relative effectiveness. Sometimes unwritten rules of expression are more important than the written laws of society in determining effectiveness of interest articulation. Because of these unwritten rules, some groups have less influence in the politics of the society than others. Native Americans provide an example of unwritten rules which limit interest articulation. The culture of many Native Americans is based on the concept of flowing with nature rather than trying to fight against it. Their religious beliefs incline them to quiet respect rather than aggressive confrontation. Their leaders are aware that because of their beliefs they are much less aggressive than other groups in politics, such as Christian fundamentalists, and that their articulation of their values in political issues is, therefore, sometimes less effective.

Interest aggregation, Almond's third input function, is the process by which interests compete, cooperate, and compromise to distribute the resources and make the rules of society. The American pattern is for interests to aggregate in political parties *before* elections. During the nominating process, presidential candidates attempt to draw into their parties as much support from as many groups as possible in order to form a coalition of interests large enough to get the 270 electoral college votes necessary for election. Great Britain, and other nations with parliamentary systems, however, aggregate interest *after* elections. After election of the members of Parliament (MPs), the MPs elect one of their number as Prime Minister. When no political party elects a majority of the members of Parliament, which is often the case, the party with the largest number of members must then make bargains with other parties and form coalitions which have sufficient votes to elect a Prime Minister. Interest aggregation takes place as parties agree to support each other's interests in the process of forming a majority coalition.

Political communication, the fourth input function, is the means by which political values in society are communicated. The primary concern of functional analysis with regard to political communication is the extent of openness in the system. Functionalist analysts inquire about the extent of freedom of the press, the extent to which the major information services and media are either owned by a small group of people or dispersed among many people with a broad range of views. The first question functional analysts ask is, "Is there freedom of the press?" But they do not stop here. In the United States we enjoy freedom of the press. But some commentators say that our abilities to influence opinion are far from equal. They point out that the major media organizations, newspapers, television, and radio stations, are in the hands of a few powerful people. We note that individual citizens, like Ross Perot, may have a substantial effect upon a presidential election. But is such access available only to the wealthy?

Almond's three *output* functions are *rule making, rule application,* and *rule adjudication. Rule making* is a function, in democracies, first, of legislatures, and, second, of executive agencies that implement the programs passed by legislatures. Rules may be made, however, by parents, school boards, city councils, state legislatures, and international organizations. Functionalist analysts identify the people who make the rules, examine the manner in which they are selected, describe the amount of authority they have, and estimate the extent of bargaining and compromise they must do.

Rule application is normally an executive function. Bureaucracies apply general rules to specific circumstances. The Department of Transportation, for example, makes regulations to apply the laws that Congress has passed to govern management of airports, highways, and navigable waters. Functionalist analysts describe the primary types of rule application structures, such as government department and regulatory agencies like the Interstate Commerce Commission. They then describe how a nation's customs and political culture affect the rule application process. Some bureaucracies apply rules efficiently, with a view to effective customer service. Others work through complicated procedures (known as red tape), and still others provide service only when bribes are paid. Corruption and inefficiency can often be a critical impediment, such as in Zaire in 1995 when government operations were unable to respond quickly to the epidemic of the deadly ebola virus.

Rule adjudication, the final output function, is the responsibility of a judiciary. Functional analysts first compile a description of the court system, then examine the character, qualifications, and cultural attributes of the participants in the judicial system, such as the judges, lawyers, and court administrators. The judicial process is examined next, including, for example, the extent to which most disputes are settled formally, through the courts, or in other settings. The analysts scrutinize the implications of such phenomena as a large number of lawyers in the general population and the extent to which the judicial system enjoys the respect of the people.

Communications Theory

Karl Deutsch applied cybernetics, the systematic study of human communication, to politics in *The Nerves of Government: Models of Human Communication and Control* (1963). According to Deutsch, the political system is a "self-conscious network" that is continuously self-responsive, which means that changes in one part of a system lead to adjustments in other parts of the system and to the system as a whole. Deutsch proposes that communication is the key to politics, and he compares communications systems in politics to the nervous system in the human body. Communications networks which produce political decisions are the eyes, ears, and nose of the corporate political body. Political systems are also "learning nets" or "self-modifying communications networks" (Deutsch 1963, 80). Deutsch defines a learning net as "any system characterized by a relevant degree of organization, communication, and control, regardless of the particular processes by which its messages are transmitted and its functions carried out" (Deutsch 1963, 80). Information rather than political power is the essence of politics. Nations are essentially information networks in which power, instead of being an ongoing function of political systems, is normally employed only as a last resort.

Messages are the basic units of communication, and are, therefore, the focus of cybernetic analysis. Messages are symbols which hold meaning, and are exchanged in many verbal and nonverbal forms.

For Deutsch and the cyberneticists, what really counts is the process of decisionmaking, rather than the implementation of the decisions. They believe that relatively small amounts of information, when used in decisionmaking, keep extensive organizations moving by providing needed direction. Deutsch compares the decisionmaking process in government to the steering mechanism in a ship. The small mechanism determines the direction the giant vessel will take. When Congress passes a wide ranging tax reform law, for example, and it is signed by the President, only 535 people have produced a decision that will affect the personal lives of 260 million people.

Excessively rigid ideologies, such as extreme conservatism or extreme liberalism, induce a sort of selective deafness in the communications abilities of those who adhere to them because these ideologies exclude certain types of accurate and valid information. Some communists long believed, for example, that the internal economic structures of capitalist systems were naturally bound to self-destruct as a result of inevitable revolutions by the working class. For decades, their ideology blinded them to the fact that, while communist revolutions did occur, they were by no means inevitable.

According to cybernetics, a political system's viability depends upon the system's ability to

- *Absorb* information,
- *Process* it expeditiously,
- *Respond* appropriately, and
- *Evaluate* its own response.

Cyberneticists evaluate systems according to the above capacities by systematically describing:

- The individuals who are responsible for making decisions, their positions, and responsibilities;
- The laws, regulations, or rules that govern making decisions;
- The steps in normal process through which the organization's decisions are made; and
- Examples of decisions made by the organization's leadership, and the manner in which the decisions were made.

The Hard Left

Dependency Theory

Political analysts of the hard left combine either a liberal or a radical ideology with a quantitative methodology. One example of an approach used by the hard left is "dependency theory," which applies a scientific methodology to propositions derived from a socialist analysis of the international political and economic system. Christopher Chase-Dunn, applying dependency theory, has attempted to demonstrate objectively that world capitalism consists of four interrelated classes:

1. The capitalist center (capitalists in the U.S., Japan, and Western Europe)
2. The periphery of the center (exploited underclasses of the capitalist world)
3. The center of the periphery (dependent bourgeoisie in Latin America, Africa, and Third World countries)
4. The periphery of the periphery (rural far Eastern and other peasant populations)

According to dependency theory, capitalist systems control the centers of economic activity. From this position, they continuously exploit the less developed countries of the periphery by bringing resources from the periphery to the center in a pattern which keeps the periphery continually dependent upon the center. According to dependency theorists, only a transformation of the international regime from capitalism to socialism will eliminate dependency.

Gabriel Almond, the structure-function theorist mentioned earlier, is very critical of dependency theory. The portion of his response to dependency theory which follows below is exemplary of the discussion that is a continuous, necessary, and vibrant part of the discipline of political science.

> The analytic structure of dependency theory is relatively simple and straightforward. World capitalism consists of four interrelated classes. . . . By comparison with Marxism and Leninism, dependency theory is incomplete and inconclusive. While it speaks of revolution and socialism as alternatives to the capitalist world system, the strategy, whether Marxist, Leninist, or some other, is left to implication. Marxist and Leninist theories are predictive theories. . . . De-

pendency theory is not very good Marxism or very good Leninism. Marx was far too good a historian and social scientist to have treated the world political economy as divisible into four class formations. The social periphery of metropolitan capitalism would not qualify as a Marxist proletariat, nor would the peripheral social groups of the dependent countries. A Marxist Revolution would have to occur in the capitalist industrialized world, and not in the backward, predominantly rural, agricultural periphery. . . . The dependency approach can best be characterized as a propaganda fragment of an ideology, a polemic against mainstream development theory. (Almond 1990, 231–233)

Almond's critique of dependency theory is an example of the philosophical and methodological controversies that abound in the era of eclecticism. Having discussed a dozen general approaches to the study of politics, we now turn to some of the quantitative methods frequently used in the discipline.

Quantitative Methods

7

> *Statistics happen.*
> —Anonymous

The Basics of Scientific Knowledge

Chapter 6, *Schools, Sects, and Approaches to the Study of Politics,* contained a discussion of the *general* philosophical approaches within which we find the principles of interpretation that help us make sense out of politics. In the present chapter we shall examine some quantitative methods commonly used for analyzing politics. Quantitative methodology includes methods of study in which observations about politics are collected as data and then placed into categories that can be analyzed numerically. Paradigms of political exegesis are *specific* detailed methods of critical interpretation of political events. We are, therefore, about to study ways of conducting numerical analyses which help us to interpret political events.

Science, as it is understood at the end of the twentieth century, is the process of observing, categorizing, and analyzing empirical data. Relationships among empirical phenomena are discovered through counting, measuring, classifying, and organizing. Many of the qualitative approaches and perspectives on politics discussed in the previous chapter disregard quantitative measures in describing and evaluating political activities, and many of them are normative, that is, they bring value judgments to bear upon the subject matter. Quantitative measurements normally attempt to reduce the effects of normative judgments in the study of politics to a bare minimum, if not eliminate them altogether, in order to produce facts, which are observations that may be verified through recognized procedures.

Some commentators have argued that it is impossible to eliminate normative concerns completely from the study of politics. They claim, following the ideas of Karl Popper, that the act of choosing a subject to study itself involves a value judgment. Although quantitative political scientists are aware of these concerns, they attempt to reduce the effect of bias in their measurements as much as possible to make their studies as value-free and objective as possible.

In addition to being nonnormative, scientific knowledge has several other characteristics. First, scientific knowledge is replicable. This means that phenomena observed under a particular set of conditions will behave in the same manner whenever those same conditions exist. If two measurements of the same phenomena yield different results, then some significant variable in the process must have changed.

Scientific knowledge is also generalizable. The object of science is to discover principles or laws that apply from one situation to another, so that causes of phenomena can be found and future events may be predicted.

Finally, as we discussed in the introduction and in the previous chapter, science proceeds through a dialectical process of induction and deduction through which specific observations are generalized into principles from which further specific observations may be anticipated.

The Basics of Social Science Research

Science is conducted primarily through the testing of hypotheses. A research hypothesis is a preliminary educated guess about the anticipated results of a scientific experiment. An hypothesis gives direction and purpose to a study before it has begun. If you do not know what it is you are trying to accomplish, how can you accomplish anything? An hypothesis is a declarative sentence that states that a specific *relationship* exists between two or more variables. *Variables* are the phenomena being observed, such as negative campaign ads or votes. A political scientist, for example, might develop the following research hypothesis: "Candidates who use negative campaign advertising are more likely to win elections." This hypothesis states that there is a specific relationship between two variables: (1) negative campaign advertising and (2) votes in elections. The hypothesis may or may not be true, but it serves as a starting place, giving direction to the inquiry.

The *dependent* variable is the phenomenon that is affected by other variables. In our example, voter turnout is the *dependent* variable. The *independent* variable is the phenomenon that may have some effect upon the dependent variable. Campaign advertising, therefore, is the independent variable in our example.

Antecedent variables are phenomena which act upon or relate to independent variables. In our example, "candidates who use negative campaign advertising are more likely to win elections," antecedent variables could be factors that affect how negative the campaign ads are, such as the results of polls which show voter's reactions to previous ads, or the philosophy of the campaign manager concerning negative ads. Candidates who run negative campaign ads run the risk of going too far, creating sympathy for those they are trying to discredit.

Intervening variables are variables other than the independent variable which affect the dependent variable directly. In our example, since usually days or weeks pass between the time campaign ads are published or broadcast and the time of the election, the response to the ad by the opposing candidate might be an intervening variable. Another intervening variable might be an endorsement of a particular candidate by an influential person.

Our example hypothesis, in a diagram that represents the relationships among the variables, looks like this:

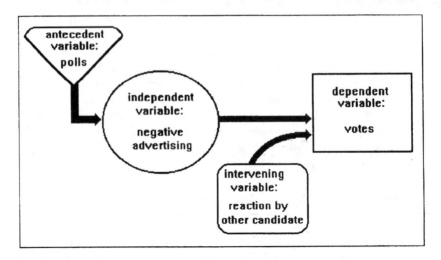

Identifying the dependent, independent, antecedent, and intervening variables helps researchers to define carefully the relationships they are examining. Hypotheses are constructed to find out what relationship, if any, exists between the independent and dependent variables. The hypothesis also states the nature of the relationship between the two variables. Relationships between variables are called correlations. Correlations between variables are of various types. Direct correlations are ones in which, as the independent variable increases or decreases, the dependent variable increases or decreases right along with it. If, for example, candidates who are taller than average tend to be elected more often than candidates who are shorter than average, then a direct correlation is observed between the height of the candidate and getting elected. Inverse correlations are those in which, as one variable increases, the other variable decreases. If voters go to the polls less often when it rains, then rain and voting have an inverse correlation to one another. In a logarithmic correlation, one variable will increase or decrease at a different rate than the other variable in such a manner that eventually, as one variable increases, the other ceases to increase, or virtually ceases to increase. Suppose, for example, that a study of state legislative candidates finds that the more education candidates have, up through four-years of college (sixteen years of education or a bachelor's degree), the more likely they are to be elected; but candidates who have advanced degrees are no more likely to be elected than candidates who have just a bachelor's degree.

An hypothesis is said to be "true" if the relationship that is specified in the hypothesis is indeed found to exist between the variables that are being studied. Hypotheses are constructed for the sole purpose of testing whether or not they are true. Hypotheses are used to develop theories which help to explain how certain conditions lead to certain behaviors or results.

Testing a hypothesis requires the researcher to *measure* the amount of change in the dependent variable as change is observed in the independent variable. This requires making accurate measurements of the dependent and independent variables as they vary over time or in different circumstances.

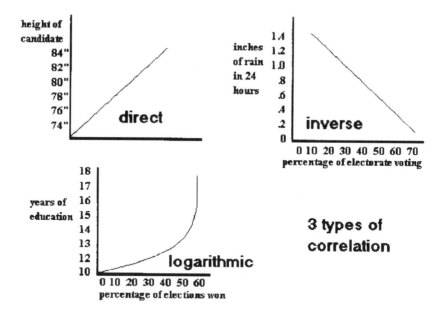

Measurement of variables begins with a determination of the appropriate level of measurement. There are four levels of measurement: nominal, ordinal, interval, and ratio. *Nominal* measurements are for types of information that are in no sequential or rank order; they are simply different. For example, if one is analyzing voter information by state of residence, some categories might be Washington, Oregon, California, Wyoming, and Montana. *Ordinal* data are data for which one category is more or less than another, but the differences between categories are not exact, similar, or stable. For instance, "children" (ages 1–18), "adults" (ages 19–65), and "senior citizens" (ages 66–100) are categories that apply to age groupings that demonstrate an increase in age, but the number of years that defines each category is not the same. *Interval* data have an arbitrary zero point, like years on a calendar, temperature, or the labels "liberal" and "conservative" on a political spectrum.

Ratio data are data for which the zero point actually represents an absence of the phenomena being studied. If one is comparing the number of votes received by two candidates, the variable zero votes forms a baseline of comparison, and we may accurately say that a particular candidate has received twice or three times as many votes as another candidate, because we are using ratio data. If we were using interval data, such as a spectrum of ideology, we cannot say that one candidate is twice as conservative as another, because no point on our ideological spectrum is objectively fixed. In ratio data, therefore, in contrast to nominal, ordinal, or interval data, the values that are quantified can be multiplied and divided.

To be called accurate, measurements must be *valid,* that is, they must measure the effects they are supposed to measure instead of measuring something else. Accurate measurements must also be *reliable,* which means that the same results can be obtained under similar circumstances when measurements are made at different times.

When doing nominal level analysis, validity is made possible only when the categories of analysis are exhaustive and mutually exclusive. To be exhaustive, there must be a category for every data element. In our example, there must be a state of residence for every voter. To be mutually exclusive means that a data element can be assigned to only one category, and, therefore, in our example, residence should be defined so that voters may be a resident of only one state. If, therefore, some voters in the study have two or more homes in different states, a primary residence would need to be selected for each of these voters.

Accurate measurements require that the effects of antecedent and intervening variables upon the dependent variable be determined, and this is one of the most difficult areas of political science research. If a candidate issues a set of negative campaign advertisements (the independent variable), and that same week she is endorsed by an influential person (the intervening variable), how can a researcher tell if a rise in the polls after these events is due to the advertising (the independent variable), the endorsement (the intervening variable), both, or neither? Such variables can be measured if a study is properly constructed to test varying responses of voters over a period of time.

There are several kinds of validity. Face validity concerns whether a measurement seems reasonable. An instrument lacks face validity if it appears there are good reasons to question it. Content validity concerns the comprehensiveness of the measurement. A measurement has content validity if all the relevant aspects of the specified subject are included in the research. Construct validity is obtained when a correlation is demonstrated between a measure of one concept and the measure of another concept. For example, if measurements of efficacy, the sense that a person's actions actually make a difference, and measurements of voter turnout demonstrate a significant correlation, then the comparison of efficacy and voter turnout has construct validity.

Reliability, the second major aspect of effective measurement, concerns whether or not the measurement provides the same result when it is repeated. A measurement of opinions about universally available health care, for example, should provide the same results on rainy days or sunny days, and from one week to the next with the same group of people, if nothing has happened to make the people change their minds.

The reliability of political science studies is difficult to determine for several reasons. Many problems may occur to make the data collected inaccurate. Persons answering questions may give false or misleading answers because they secretly resent the intrusion of the questions, because they wish to conceal their ignorance, or because they misunderstand the questions. The persons who are conducting the survey may be careless or fill in false answers merely to complete the assignment. Data entry provides another opportunity for mistakes. When the data are transferred to computers, mistakes are likely.

Hypotheses help us to select specific aspects of a problem or question and explore them one at a time. Hypotheses that are too vague and general are difficult to test. In our example, we have proposed the following hypothesis: "Candidates

Reprinted by permission: Tribune Media Services.

who use negative campaign advertising are more likely to win elections." This hypothesis is so vague that it will be difficult to test. What is meant, for example, by "negative advertising"? A more specific hypothesis is needed, such as: "Candidates whose advertising includes more references to faults of opponents than strengths of the candidate are more likely to win elections than candidates whose advertising contains more references to the candidate's strengths than to the faults of the other candidate." Further, even if all the elections that we sample are ones in which our hypothesis is confirmed, we have only a correlation between negative campaigning and voting, not a *causal* relationship. Our example hypothesis, that "candidates who use negative campaign advertising are more likely to win elections" is, therefore, a relational hypothesis, not a causal hypothesis. Relational hypotheses indicate whether or not two phenomena are related to one another in a specific way, without demonstrating that one causes the other.

Devising a good hypothesis is a difficult matter. Good hypotheses are

- Plausible: they appear to be reasonable.
- Specific: they are precisely stated in clearly defined terms.
- Generalizable: they are applicable to other situations.
- Empirical: they are nonnormative.
- Testable: they can be tested empirically to determine if they are true.

As mentioned earlier, causal hypotheses are difficult to prove in political science. It is one thing to demonstrate that negative campaign ads are associated with votes for a candidate (direct correlation), but it is more difficult to prove that the ads caused the votes to be cast (causation). One way that political scientists, and scientists of all types, deal with the difficulty of proving causation is the null hypothesis. A null hypothesis is an hypothesis established precisely for the purpose of refuting it. The null hypothesis allows the researcher to make a statement of greater certainty. If we wanted to try, for example, to prove that negative campaign ads are associated with an increase in voter turnout, we would begin by testing a null hypothesis: "Negative campaign ads are not associated with an increase in voter turnout." If we can find a case in which voter turnout increases as negative campaign ads increase, we will have disproved the null hypothesis. We will not have proven that voter turnout *always* increases as negative campaign ads increase, but we will have taken the first step by showing that negative campaign ads *can* be associated with an increase in voter turnout. Science thus proceeds by disproving successively specific null hypotheses.

Several difficulties frequently occur when testing hypotheses in political science. Sometimes sufficient data are not available. Necessary records are not consistent or accurate, or perhaps they have been compiled according to different systems or categories. Another problem is the multiplicity and ambiguity of variables. If we want to find out what influences presidential decisions, for example, we may need to try to sort out the competing influences of advisors, public opinion, the attitudes of senators, Supreme Court opinions, or the actions of foreign nations.

A third problem with the scientific study of politics has to do with the nature of knowledge itself. Testing hypotheses, an approach fundamental to the scientific method, is an inductive process and, therefore, shares the problems of induction in general. In *The Logic of Discovery* (1934), Karl Popper pointed out that to show that some examples of a certain phenomenon behave in a certain manner is not to demonstrate that others will also. Even if all known political candidates have spent money to obtain office, for example, there may be a candidate in the future who will win an election without spending money. Even if all known national leaders have been effective orators, it is still possible that in the future a national leader will arise who cannot speak at all.

Further, according to Popper, scientific observation is always selective. We must choose what to observe, and what context we shall observe it in, before the actual observation takes place. Therefore, hypotheses do not describe reality, but only specific contexts of reality.

Before proceeding with a discussion of some quantitative methodologies, we shall explain how to conduct a literature review, which, for a variety of reasons, is a necessary component of every quantitative study.

Literature Reviews

There are six steps in any research project:

1. Find a topic (identification).
2. Clearly define the topic (topic definition).
3. Find out what is already known about the topic (literature review).

4. Figure out how to discover something new about the topic (methods plan).
5. Conduct the process of discovery (research).
6. Record and examine the results for validity, reliability, accuracy, and meaning (analysis and quality control).

The process of social science research is recursive. This means that, even though all of the above steps must be taken at some point, they are not necessarily taken in order. For example, when researchers are finding out what is already known about a topic before they do their research, the information they discover helps them to define more clearly their topic, or may even lead them to select a new topic altogether.

A literature review is a written summary of what is already known about a selected topic. Analysts conduct literature reviews in order to find out what has already been discovered before they begin their own research project so that they can benefit from what others have learned and not simply rediscover things that are already known. The literature examined in a literature review normally consists of published research studies, unpublished research reports, government documents, and other similar materials. It normally includes two types of information: the subject matter of the research project and the project's methodology. For example, if the subject matter of a project is state legislators' attitudes on gun control, researchers would include in their literature review the most recent information on state legislators and gun control, but they would also include information on methods of studying legislators' attitudes, such as interviews or content analysis (which will be discussed later).

A literature review is a form of secondary data analysis. This means that, rather than going directly to voters or politicians, as the primary research techniques that we will be discussing next do, secondary research takes materials already prepared by someone else and draws more information from them by combining information from different sources or by examining the data in them in a different way.

A research question helps the analyst clearly define exactly what he or she wants to know. Research questions, therefore, help analysts to focus their literature reviews. A research question may ask, for example, "What is the extent of registered voters' knowledge of Supreme Court decisions about abortion?" Research questions should be confined to a narrowly defined topic. Once the researcher has formulated a research question, stated an hypothesis, and supported the inquiry with a literature review, he or she is ready to conduct the research. Political scientists use a wide variety of research methods selected primarily for their appropriateness to the topic being studied. Several of the most common methods will be presented in this chapter.

Content Analysis

Content analysis is a method of analyzing written documents that allows researchers to transform nonquantitative data into quantitative data by counting and categorizing certain variables within the data. Content analysts look for certain types of words or references in the texts, and categorize them or count them. A content analysis of presidential speeches, for example, might record the number of times a selected president (or several presidents) refers to civil rights or the economy or foreign policy issues or his or her mother. This analysis can then be used as one indication of the relative importance of selected issues to presidents. Other content analyses determine if the news media have an ideological bias, or if published reports demonstrate a preoccupation with ethnic or religious issues.

Content analyses of "events data," focus on a particular event or a series of events over time. A number of content analyses have examined the major wars of this century and have attempted to identify factors that are common in situations of war. Compilations of events data, such as the *World Handbook of Political and Social Indicators,* provide a listing of the important political events (elections, coups, wars) for most countries of the world. These listings help to compare trends in selected types of events from one country to another. Press reports, statistics, televised and radio media reports, personal records, newspapers, and magazines provide inexhaustible mines of data for content analysis. Government documents are an especially rich source of material for political scientists. Different types of government documents include: presidential papers; the Code of Federal Regulations; the Congressional Record; federal, state, and local election returns; historical records; judicial decisions; and legal records.

In her study of gender and statewide elections, Kim Fridkin Kahn (1994, 167–169), a political scientist at Arizona State University, used a content analysis:

> A content analysis of 26 U.S. Senate races and 21 gubernatorial races between male and female candidates was conducted to assess whether the media differentiate between male and female candidates in their coverage of statewide campaigns. . . . For the content analysis of news coverage, every day from September 1 through the day of the election was analyzed. Any item in the newspaper that mentioned either candidate was analyzed including news articles, columns, editorials, and "news analysis" articles. . . . I analyzed news characteristics known to be significant for a candidate's success [such as perceptions of] a candidate's viability. . . . Second, content was assessed by anticipated differences between male and female candidates. The content analysis also reveals consistent differences in the coverage of issues for male and female candidates—in both gubernatorial and senatorial campaigns. Women routinely receive less issue coverage than their male counterparts, and in some instances, these differences are quite dramatic.

Surveys

Public Opinion Polls are the primary indicators of the strength and vitality of democracy. They reveal and describe the political climate. Survey results appear in virtually every issue of all national news magazines. In an article entitled "Little Interest in the News" published in *Editor & Publisher* magazine, (March 4, 1995, 14–15), the author declares "Latest Times Mirror Center Poll reveals no more than

25% of the public has paid close attention to the major news stories." This poll is typical of samples of public opinion taken daily to determine attitudes of people on a wide range of subjects. The article went on to say:

> No more than one-quarter of the public paid very close attention to the earthquake in Japan (25%), violence at abortion clinics (24%), the U.S. economy (23%), or even the O.J. Simpson trial (23%), according to the latest News Interest Index from the Times Mirror Center for the People & the Press. But even if people report they are not very closely watching the O.J. Simpson trial, 64% of respondents knew the name of the judge in that case, Lance Ito, while only 52% could name Newt Gingrich as speaker of the House of Representatives.

The lack of interest in the news indicated by the Times Mirror Poll described above is further supported by a similar article entitled, "Disengaged Freshmen," published in *The Chronicle of Higher Education* (January 13, 1995, A29):

Interest in Politics Among First-Year Students Is at a 29-year Low, Survey Finds.

The rise of Newt Gingrich, the down-to-the-wire duel between Oliver North and Charles S. Robb, the toppling of icons like Thomas S. Foley: It would be hard to imagine a more politically interesting year than 1994.

Yet, if a new survey is to be believed, few college freshmen were paying much attention. Only 31.9% of them said that "keeping up with political affairs" was a very important goal for them. The figure is the lowest recorded in the 29-year history of an annual survey of freshmen conducted by the Higher Education Research Institute at the University of California at Los Angeles. In 1990, 42.4 percent of the freshmen said that keeping up with politics was very important or essential. In 1966, the first year of the survey, 57.8 percent said it was that important.

"There seems to be a massive disengagement from politics," said Alexander W. Astin, a professor of higher education at U.C.L.A., and director of the freshman study.

Surveys have been used for many years to determine voter attitudes on a wide variety of questions. In their classic study, *The American Voter* (1960), Campbell, Converse, Miller, and Stokes presented an exposition of voting patterns which examined a number of influences upon voting behavior, including economics, personality, and social class. In recent years a large amount of survey data about every major issue in American politics has accumulated. The *Inter-University Consortium for Political and Social Research* (ICPSR) at the University of Michigan has become the foremost center for public opinion survey research and analysis in the United States. *American National Election Studies,* a database of information on national elections, has been collecting information every two years for forty years. The *Gallup Poll* has been conducted for more than fifty years. The data from these and other polls are being used now to see how patterns of voting change over time.

The skillful use of polls is of substantial value to candidates in helping them win elections. Campaign consultants earn large fees by helping candidates avoid unpopular stands on issues and take strong stands on issues that are likely to gain them votes. Guided by their consultants, candidates are then also able to allocate their media advertising budgets to selected campaign issues and to selected popu-

SHOE JEFF MacNELLY

Reprinted by permission: Tribune Media Services.

lations, emphasizing themes specifically tailored to appeal to different interest groups.

A poll, most simply, is a device for counting preferences. A survey is a series of statements or questions that define a set of preferences to be polled. If a poll is conducted on the subject of gun control, for example, analysts will construct a survey consisting of a series of questions such as "Do you think the sale of automatic weapons should be outlawed?" or "Do you think that handgun registration should include a requirement of a waiting period?"

Conducting a survey requires first preparing a research design, which is a plan for proceeding with the project. A plan for a survey must include at least the following elements:

- A *research question* (what you want to know),
- A *research hypothesis* (what you expect to find),
- An *instrument* (a questionnaire containing the questions you want to ask), and
- A *sample plan* (a plan for selecting people whose views you want to know about).

The sample plan will identify

- *The population* (the people to be studied),
- *Elements* (individual units of the population),
- *Sampling frame* (the group from which elements will be selected), and
- *The sample* (the number and characteristics of the portion of the population selected for study).

Consider the following example of a survey research design:

Research Question: "Are the registered voters of Santa Fe in favor of an ordinance which will restrict the size and design of advertising signs?"

Research Hypothesis:	Sixty percent of the registered voters of Santa Fe will be in favor of an ordinance which will restrict the size and design of advertising signs.
Population:	Registered voters in Santa Fe
Elements:	Individual registered voters
Sampling Frame:	Two hundred registered voters in Santa Fe selected at random from voter registration lists
Sample:	Of the 200 registered voters in Santa Fe selected at random from voter registration lists, those who answer the survey questions when called on the telephone
Instrument:	A ten-question questionnaire to be administered by telephone

The *sampling frame* is the part of the population from which a sample is drawn. *Strata* are groups of similar elements within a population, such as men, women, minorities, or people attending school. There are ways of classifying the population within the sampling frame. *Stratified samples* include numbers of respondents belonging to a particular stratum of the population that is not in proportion to the general population. A stratified sample, for example, may include more Hispanics than the general population if the views of that group are of particular interest.

How large must a sample be in order to represent the population accurately? This question is difficult to answer, but three general principles apply. The first is that a large sample is more likely, simply by chance, to be representative of a population than a small sample. The second is that the goal of a representative sample is to include within it representatives of all of the strata that are included in the whole population. The third, which partly contradicts the first, is that the sample should not be excessively large because the survey will then be unnecessarily laborious or expensive. These three principles may be applied, by way of illustration, to taking a sample of fabric for draperies for your home. Examine the illustration below:

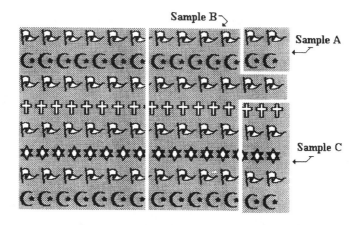

Suppose that you are newly married and wish to buy some fabric for draperies. You find the fabric pictured above and want to take a sample home to your wife or husband, to get her or his approval. If you select Sample A, you will not be able to show your spouse the entire pattern represented in the fabric. If you take home Sample B, you will pay for more fabric than you need to allow your spouse to see the entire pattern. Taking home Sample C allows you to show your spouse the entire pattern at less cost than Sample B.

The sampling instrument for a public opinion survey is the questionnaire which lists the questions that will be asked. The research question for the project is the primary guide for constructing survey questions. The number of questions included in a questionnaire must be sufficient to find out precisely what the researcher wants to know, and yet not so long that people, who ordinarily do not like to fill out questionnaires, will refuse to fill them out. Short surveys with a small number of questions are more likely to be answered completely than long questionnaires.

Surveys consist of two types of questions, closed and open. In *open* questions, respondents are not provided a fixed list of choices but may answer anything that they want. They may be asked, for example, "What would you like the city to do about the downtown parking problem?" The advantage of open questions is that the survey may discover ideas or attitudes of which the survey taker is not aware. Open questions, or open-ended questions, however, generate such varied responses that they are not easy to quantify.

Closed questions restrict the respondent to a specific set of answers, such as "Agree, Disagree, or Don't know." Closed questions have the advantage that they are easy to quantify. A number value can be assigned to each answer, and totals can be made of answers to different types. Closed questions are often formatted in such a way that the results can be quantified and analyzed statistically. Two common formats for questions are known as the Likert and Guttman scales.

A Likert scale has several response options which present a sequential set of choices. A Likert scale question might be stated like this:

"Tighter security measures are needed at airports to reduce the possibility of terrorist attacks." (select one of the following):

☐ Strongly Agree   ☐ Agree   ☐ Not Sure   ☐ Disagree

☐ Strongly Disagree

Guttmann scale multiple choice questions provide discrimination among a range of answers by creating a series of statements with which it is increasingly difficult to agree or disagree. If a respondent selects one item on the scale of questions, she or he is likely also to agree with the items higher on the scale. Examine the example at the top of page 179.

A Guttman scale allows the researcher to identify and categorize levels of empathy and antipathy towards government welfare payments or beliefs on virtually any issue.

Select the one answer with which you agree most completely. Welfare payments should be made:

☐ Whenever anyone asks for one

☐ Whenever someone can demonstrate a need for the money

☐ When need is demonstrated but the welfare payment is temporary

☐ Only when a substantial mental or physical disability prevents a person from obtaining the necessities of life, such as food and shelter

☐ Never under any circumstances

Basic Survey Analysis Statistics

Once researchers collect the survey data, they analyze it with statistics that describe the data, compare components of the data, and evaluate the data. There are many statistical procedures specially designed to carry out each of these three categories of tasks.

For the purpose of giving an idea of how statistics are compiled from surveys, we shall look at some elementary examples. Let's suppose that we want to know the views of college students in the Town of Delaware, Ohio, on the topic of security at airports. We shall conduct telephone interviews to gather our data and ask 100 students, selected at random from the Ohio Wesleyan University phone book, some Likert scale questions. Since not all the people we call will answer our questions, we shall prepare a list of 200 names, and proceed through the list until 100 students have replied. Our first question (which we used in a previous example), looks like this:

"Tighter security measures are needed at airports to reduce the possibility of terrorist attacks." (select one of the following):

☐ Strongly Agree   ☐ Agree   ☐ Not Sure   ☐ Disagree

☐ Strongly Disagree

Having secured the answers we sought, we proceed to analyze the data to identify patterns within it. The first step is to assign a numerical value to each response as follows:

Response Options	Assigned Value	Response Options	Assigned Value
Strongly Agree	1	Disagree	4
Agree	2	Strongly Disagree	5
Not Sure	3		

The next step is to determine the number of responses for each answer to each question. The following results are from a hypothetical sample of 100 respondents.

Response Options	Assigned Value (v)	Frequency (f) [Number of Responses]	Products (p) [v × f]	p/f
Strongly Agree	1	21	21	
Agree	2	31	62	
Not Sure	3	17	51	
Disagree	4	19	76	
Strongly Disagree	5	12	60	
Totals		100	270	2.7

We then: 1. Multiply the assigned value (v) by the frequency (f),
2. Total the products (p), and
3. Divide the product total by the frequency total.

Having completed these steps, we arrive, in our example, at the number 2.7, which is the mean (average) response value. This tells us that the average response to the stated question, on a scale from 1 to 5, in which 1 is strongly agree and 5 is strongly disagree, is 2.7. In other words, the average respondent tends to agree slightly with the statement "Tighter security measures are needed at airports to reduce the possibility of terrorist attacks."

The mean, or average, is one way to get a statistical sense of how a group as a whole has responded to a question. Students should be aware of a problem with the calculation as it was just explained: the concepts being dealt with are fluid and inexact. The Likert scale produces what is technically interval data, and it is assigned values and treated statistically as if it is ratio data. Even though this procedure is technically incorrect, it allows social scientists to make statistical generalizations that still have some value.

Statistics allow social scientists to determine measures of central tendency in opinions and attitudes, that is, the extent to which opinions are spread across a continuum or are gathered together at the center. A frequently used measure of central tendency is the *standard deviation,* which provides a single number that indicates how different from one another the responses to the question are. In order to calculate the standard deviation (S) for the question above, we will follow these steps:

• Assign a *value* to each response (Strongly Agree = 1, for example, as in our example question).

• Find the *mean* for the question (in our example the mean is 2.7).

- Find the *difference* between each value and the mean.
- *Square* the differences in step 2.
- *Multiply* the squared differences by the frequency of each value.
- *Add* the values in step 4.
- *Divide* the values in step 5 by the number of respondents.
- Find the *square root* of the value in step 6.

Our calculation of the *standard deviation* of *Question 1,* therefore, looks like this:

Step 1	Step 2	Step 3	Step 4	Step 5	Step 6	Step 7	Step 8
Assign a value to each response and the frequency of each response	Find the mean	Subtract the value from the mean	Square the results of step 3	Multiply the results of step 4 by the frequency	Sum of values of step 5	Step 6 divided by number of respondents (100 in our example)	Square root of Step 7
Strongly Agree Value = 1 Frequency = 21	2.7	1.7	2.89	60.69			
Agree Value = 2 Frequency = 31	2.7	.7	.49	15.19			
Not Sure Value = 3 Frequency = 17	2.7	−.3	.09	1.53			
Disagree Value = 4 Frequency = 19	2.7	−1.3	1.69	32.11			
Strongly Disagree Value = 5 Frequency = 12	2.7	−2.3	5.29	63.48			
Totals					173	1.73	**1.315**

The standard deviation for the sample above is 1.315. To understand the significance of this standard deviation, we need to know that public opinion samples usually correspond to what is known as a "normal distribution," which, when graphically represented, is a "bell curve." In a normal distribution, 68.26% of the responses will fall between (1) the mean *minus* one standard deviation (2.7 − 1.315, or 1.385 in our example), and (2) the mean *plus* one standard deviation (2.7 + 1.315, or 4.015 in our example). In other words, in a normal distribution, about two thirds of the respondents to our example ("Tighter security measures are needed at airports to reduce the possibility of terrorist attacks.") will express an opinion that is between 1.385 and 4.015. Another one third of the respondents will score less than 1.385 or more than 4.015.

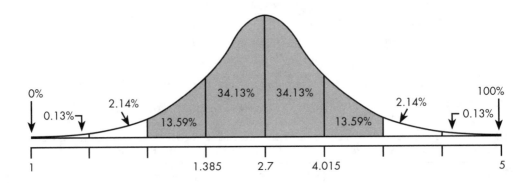

for our example: mean = 2.7
standard deviation = 1.315
68.26% of respondents score between 1.385 and 4.015
31.74% of respondents score between 0 and 1.385
or between 4.015 and 5.0

Remember that the assigned values for our example are 1 for strongly agree and 5 for strongly disagree. Our analysis tells us, therefore, that, since almost one third of the respondents scored in the narrow ranges at the ends of the scales (from 1 to 1.385 and from 4.015 to 5), the scores are fairly widely dispersed.

After assessing the dispersion in the responses questions, social scientists measure *relationships* in the data. Let's suppose that in our questionnaire we asked the political party affiliation of the respondents. Breaking down the responses into answers from Democrats, Republicans, Independents, and Others, we have the following result:

Response Options	Assigned Value (v)	Total Responses (f)	Democratic Responses	Republican Responses	Independent Responses	Other Responses
Strongly Agree	1	21	10	3	7	1
Agree	2	31	15	2	14	0
Not Sure	3	17	4	6	6	1
Disagree	4	19	4	11	4	0
Strongly Disagree	5	12	2	4	6	0
Totals		100	35	26	37	2

The table constitutes a *correlation matrix*. These data in column chart form are as follows:

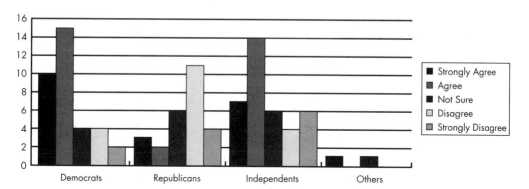

Just by looking at the table, and perhaps more easily by looking at the column chart, we can see that the Democrats in our hypothetical example tend to agree with the need for more airport security more than Republicans or Independents. Social scientists have a number of statistical tools to quantify these correlations. Some of them, like the statistic known as Kendall's Tau, formulate correlations on a scale from +1.0 to –1.0. A strong positive correlation, for example, between being a Democrat and agreeing with increased airport security, would appear as a score close to +1, such as +0.8 or +0.9. A strong negative correlation between being a Republican and agreeing with increased airport security would appear as a score close to –1, such as –0.8 or –0.9. A score close to 0 indicates a weak correlation. A score of precisely 0 indicates no correlation between the variables in the data. A score of +1 (or –1) means a perfect correlation. A perfect correlation would mean, in our example, that all Democrats in the sample agreed strongly with the need for more airport security.

Correlation statistics like Kendall's Tau are calculated with formulas that use the statistics in correlation matrices. Correlations can be found not only between such things as party affiliation (or gender or ethnicity) and answers to specific questions, but between answers to different questions. For example, if the survey asked one question about airport security and another question about capital punishment, correlation statistics could show if people who favor increased airport security also tend to favor capital punishment.

A popular method of indicating relationships among sets of data is known as *regression* analysis. Regression analyses require data to be placed in a graph in which the values of the independent variable are placed in relation to an X axis and the values of the dependent variable are placed along the Y axis. The points formed in the diagram form a regression line, which expresses the nature of the relationship among the variables.

A problem that always arises when statistically analyzing survey results relates to the validity and reliability of the data. Not only do social scientists need to know what the data indicate, but they also need to know if they can depend on their results. Tests of *statistical significance* have been formulated for this purpose. A chi-square (X^2) is a commonly used measure of statistical significance. A X^2 is calculated according to a formula that indicates, when compared to statistical tables, the likelihood that the data are statistically significant. A X^2, for example, might indicate that there are only five chances in 100 that the results of a survey are not statistically significant. This would mean that the survey results are likely to be statistically significant.

Advanced Statistical Methods

Data analysis techniques range from simply adding up numbers of elections, votes, or interest groups to highly sophisticated formulas. Each statistical method has a particular purpose. Most formulas and statistical methods have been devised to increase the accuracy of measurements or confidence in the reliability and validity of measurements, and many of the methods commonly used in political science have been adapted from economics. These methods require extensive time to explain and are more appropriate to a course on research methods than to an introduction to political science, but a few examples will be briefly mentioned here.

Larry Bartels and Henry Brady (1993), in their review of recent developments in quantitative methodology, identify four data analysis techniques as having been applied in new and interesting ways in the last few years. The first of these techniques, the "Box-Tiao Intervention Method," is a process of comparing the effects of some political and economic phenomena on others. It has been used, for example, to show the influence of the ideology of a governing party on unemployment rates and the influence of war on economic growth rates. *Vector autogression*, another method of relating political variables to one another, has been used to study political-economic processes such as the preparation of Great Britain's government budget. *Cointegration and error correction methods* are used to study equilibrium in political systems. Equilibrium is achieved under normal market conditions when important political and economic factors are in correct relation to one another. For example, an equilibrium of socioeconomic conditions and presidential popularity is established when there is a direct and stable relationship between the perceived quality of life in society and the popularity of the president who is in office. Cointegration and error correction methods have been used to determine how unusual political events, such as foreign crises and scandals, may upset this equilibrium. Finally, the *Kalman Filter,* developed in engineering, is a method of estimating a "state space model," which helps find the errors in projections of political events. This method has been used to determine and improve the accuracy of public opinion polls such as the New York Times/CBS poll.

Experiments

Experimentation is the fundamental method of acquiring knowledge in the physical sciences. As a research method it has one primary and substantial advantage: experiments allow the researcher to control the variables, permitting the scientist to determine more easily the effect of the independent variable upon the dependent variable. In the social sciences experiments are more difficult to conduct than in the physical sciences because the research subjects are human beings, and the number of variables is typically large. In spite of these difficulties, however, political scientists are now successfully conducting more experiments than they have in the past.

Experiments in the social sciences are set up according to several different basic designs. The first is the simple post-test measurement. For example, a lecture on political ideologies may be followed by a test of the knowledge of the participants about ideology. The test-retest method is more accurate. The effects of a speech upon the attitudes of the people in an audience, for example, might be measured by having the members of the audience complete a survey, listen to the speech, and then complete the survey again. Researchers could then measure the differences in opinion registered before and after the survey. If no pretest is given, the researcher cannot be sure of the level of knowledge or the respondents' attitudes before the test was given, and the effects of the lecture or speech, then, are less certain.

The alternative-form type of experiment uses two different measures of the same concept. If research concerns liberal and conservative attitudes, for example, the analyst could measure attitudes on defense spending in one questionnaire and then measure attitudes on abortion in a separate questionnaire. The split-halves device is similar to the alternative forms measurement, except that two measures of the concept are applied (questions about defense and abortion in the same questionnaire, for example) at the same time.

Kim Fridkin Kahn (1994, 162) has used experimental methods in her studies of the effects of sex stereotypes in statewide campaigns:

> Do gender differences in news coverage and the candidates' sex influence people's perceptions of gubernatorial and senatorial candidates? To investigate this question, I conducted a series of experiments in which I manipulated both the type of coverage a candidate received and the candidate's sex. The results of these experiments suggest that people's perceptions of male and female candidates are influenced by patterns of news coverage and by people's sex stereotypes.
>
> This study suggests that women are uniquely advantaged in certain campaign environments while disadvantaged in others. . . . During the 1992 senatorial campaigns, for instance, the end of the Cold War made foreign policy issues less central and the concurrent presidential campaign made such issues as health care reform more prominent. Similarly, congressional scandals—like the White House banking scandal—made traits like integrity and trustworthiness especially relevant. The 1992 campaign, then, placed a premium on women's stereotypical strengths ("female" issues and "female" traits), thereby creating a favorable electoral setting for women candidates for the U.S. Senate. Given that people's sex stereotypes and patterns of news coverage make certain campaign environments especially desirable for women candidates, women should consider the prevailing political climate when seeking statewide office.

As we have already mentioned, a number of problems are commonly associated with experimental designs. More specifically, they include:

1. *Control of variables:* Can the environment be controlled to rule out other factors?
2. *Time passage:* People get tired, or for some other reason take a different attitude.
3. *Varying acts of measurement:* Poll takers may record responses differently.
4. *Statistical regression:* Someone who is on the high end of a test score range may register a high score only temporarily.
5. *Experimental mortality:* Subjects drop out.
6. *Instrument decay:* The instrument may not be used as carefully the second time.
7. *Selection error:* Control and experimental groups may not be equivalent.

To overcome these problems, a number of complex methodologies have been developed. Multigroup designs, for example, test multiple independent variables against the same dependent variable. Factorial designs may test the effects of several independent variables in different combinations. A simple "2 x 2" factorial design, for example, might test combinations of four possibilities that result from two different actions a candidate could take in conducting a campaign: distributing a brochure and mailing out personal letters to selected party activists. The chart below illustrates the four resultant possibilities:

	Send Personal Letter	**Do Not Send Personal Letter**
Send Brochure	(1) Both brochure and letter	(2) Brochure but no letter
Do Not Send Brochure	(3) Letter but no brochure	(4) Neither letter nor brochure

A factorial design based upon the choices set forth in the chart would test the results of voter activity according each of the four situations.

This factorial design is designed as part of a field experiment, which is an experiment conducted within a natural setting (in this case, an actual political campaign). For each subject in the study, the researchers would have to be able to determine (1) who acted as a result of receiving information from the candidate (such as voting, making a contribution, or volunteering to assist in the campaign), and (2) to which of the four combinations of brochures and letters the voters had been exposed.

In her studies of the effects of sex stereotypes in statewide campaigns, Kim Fridkin Kahn (1994, 174–5) used a 2 × 4 factorial design, which, of course, results in eight categories of analysis.

> To investigate the impact of gender differences in coverage and the candidate's sex on people's evaluations of statewide candidates, I conducted a series of experiments. . . . I used a two-by-four factorial design, and the manipulated variables are the sex of the candidate (male or female) and the type of news coverage (male encumbent coverage, female encumbent coverage, male challenger coverage, female challenger coverage). . . . Selected residents of two local communities participated in these experiments, and each experimental session

lasted approximately one hour. Volunteers came to a research setting at a major university campus to participate in the study, where they were randomly assigned to one of the experimental conditions. In each condition, the participants read a newspaper page that included the article about the statewide candidate as well as two other political articles. After reading the entire newspaper page, the participants completed a questionnaire.

Dozens of different types of experimental designs, using different combinations of strategies, are used in political science research. After reviewing more than 2,000 political science publications, Larry M. Bartels and Henry E. Brady, in their publication "The State of Quantitative Political Methodology" (1993, 122), conclude the following about experiments: "In the past decade, political scientists have found many new and exciting ways to do experimental work. Samples are more representative and treatments are more realistic, increasing greatly the external validity of experimental work."

Bartels and Brady outline a number of these developments, including the experiments conducted by Michael Levine and Charles Plott (1977, 1978), which demonstrated that the work and decisions of committees can be altered by manipulating their agendas. Another study cited by Bartels and Brady is the work of Richard Johnston (1992) which demonstrated how, in Canadian elections, voters' perceptions of a free trade agreement changed when particular candidates' names were attached to the title of the agreement. When voters asked about "[Prime Minister] *Mulroney's* free trade agreement" their answers were either more positive or negative, depending upon Mulroney's popularity at the time, than the answers of voters who were asked about a "free trade agreement." In another experiment, Frolich and Oppenheimer demonstrated that, under circumstances in which students set the rules under which their group will operate, acceptance of the rule is facilitated by participation in formulating the rule (Bartels and Brady 1993, 123).

Nonexperimental Designs

Political scientists have used a wide variety of nonexperimental designs. Cross-sectional designs, for example, sample a cross-section of the population. Suppose that you want to determine if sermons in which pastors advocate political participation actually cause people to vote more often. Comparing voting records of people who have and who have not heard sermons could be one way of doing this. One of the main problems would be in isolating other variables. For example, did the people listening to the sermons previously vote more than those who did not?

Panel studies are cross-sectional designs done over time in which measurements are taken of the same variables on the same units at different times. Panel studies are like experiments, except that the researcher just lets the variable happen without introducing it. In an experimental design, for example, a group of voters could be subjected to a particular set of sermons selected by the researchers. In a panel study, however, the researcher would accumulate data on two series of voters' voting records, and then wait as one group is exposed to the sermons, while the other is not. Finally the voting records of the two groups would be tested again.

A time series design takes multiple measures of a variable over a period of time. It may be used in experimental and nonexperimental designs. In a time series design of the effects of sermons on voting patterns, an experimental design could be constructed in which two groups of people's voting patterns are measured over a period of four years. The control group would not be exposed to sermons, and the experimental group would hear sermons at selected intervals.

Interviews

Interviews are used in studies in which it is important to get some depth in the observations taken, or to allow respondents to express views not anticipated by the interviewer. *Elite interviewing* selects a certain type of individual to interview, such as labor leaders, congresspersons, or persons with blue eyes. The elite can be any group of people specially selected for the purposes of the study. We may want the views of state court judges, for example, if we were to conduct a study on the effects of limited jail space on the lengths of sentences that are given to people convicted of crimes. Interviews of any kind require considerable skill and preparation. Elite interviews, for example, often require the development of standardized questions that are asked in a manner that does not sound like a set of standardized questions. This is because respondants often expect to be treated like individuals, and sometimes resent being asked standard questions.

Case Studies

Case studies, which are in-depth examinations of particular situations, are conducted for the insights they reveal about the situations in question and are generally on political affairs. In his case study of the role of ethnicity in political developments surrounding the independence of Estonia after the demise of the Soviet Union, Andrus Park offers an explanation of the events that he selected. He identifies political trends, provides an explanation of economic, social, and other factors associated with those trends, and draws conclusions from his findings. In 1989, at the time the independence process began, Estonia's population was approximately 62% Estonian, 30% Russian, and 8% other groups, including Ukrainians, Belarussians, and Finns. Previous to independence, however, the Russian population had enjoyed advantages which would no longer be honored in the new system ruled by the Estonian majority. Park's case study (1994, 69–87) includes the following comments:

> In this article I argue that Estonia's ethnic developments in 1991–93 were characterized by the following features: after the independence declaration, there was (at least on the surface) a decline in the intensity of ethnic tensions; many

public signs of ethnic conflict were displayed less vividly in 1991–93 than in 1988–91. . . . [T]here were two main directions of international pressures in regard to Estonia's citizenship and the minorities policy in 1991–93; the governments of the Western countries and the main interstate organization were mostly friendly, while Russia was sharply critical. The Western media and human rights organizations also often expressed disapproval of Estonia's policies; compared with many other post-communist states (Moldova, former Yugoslavia, the Transcaucasian states, even former Czecho-Slovakia) the minorities and citizenship policy in Estonia in 1991–93 appeared to be quite successful: the visible signs of ethnic tensions diminished . . . violence or active separatism on ethnic grounds was avoided . . . Estonia's integration into European and other international organizations was generally successful.

Case studies have gained increasing acceptance in recent years. They are flexible in that they may be used to study one particular phenomena or a single instance of a combination of phenomena. Even though it is difficult to form generalizations confidently directly from the results of case studies, they provide opportunities for testing hypotheses that are generated from theories.

Case studies are excellent educational tools. Law students gain much of their knowledge of legal precedents by reading the decisions and testimony of many actual cases filed in the courts. Business schools were pioneers in developing administrative case studies to help students understand actual management situations. Courses in public administration adopt the case study method as a primary teaching tool less often than business or law schools, but case studies have also become a common feature of many public administration courses.

Direct Observation

A number of other techniques are used for data collection. *Direct observation* of political phenomena is conducted by trained observers who carefully record selected behaviors. Observation may be structured, that is, a definite list of phenomena are noted, such as number of political contacts, political allusions in speech, or appeals to certain groups of voters. Or observation may be unstructured, in which case observation attempts to take in every action in a certain setting that may possibly be significant. In either case, successful observation for purposes of social science research always follows clear guidelines and standard procedures.

While political scientists may make more use of direct observation in the future because it provides many opportunities for creative thinking which may lead to new discoveries, thus far analysts have been reluctant to use it widely for several reasons. First, observation data is said to be qualitative, and, therefore, subjective in nature. Although much of the data can be quantified, qualitative considerations are hard to avoid. Another problem is that political events can be difficult, time consuming, and expensive to observe, and an entire event such as an election may require several observers whose activities are highly coordinated and regulated.

Focus Groups

Focus group methods are similar to direct observation techniques in that they produce qualitative data and are often used when little is known about the subject under study. Although substantial research exists on many topics in political science, research from which background knowledge can be drawn, there remain areas for which little is known. Focus groups are an excellent way to begin research into a new area because they provide opportunities for careful consideration of a topic in a setting that encourages creative thinking.

In a focus group, a moderator guides several carefully selected participants in a discussion of the topic under consideration. Let's suppose that a new religious group, with practices that are unusual, has moved to a community, and the researcher wants to know how the newcomers have affected the local political climate. A focus group can help a researcher more carefully define both areas of topical concentration and methods for carrying on further research with respect to the newcomers in the community. To conduct a focus group, a moderator should be prepared with a clear conception of the goals and objectives that she or he wishes to accomplish, and a list of issues or questions to discuss which form a general guideline, not a strict agenda for the discussion. The moderator should guide the group by helping it stay on track, but she is there to help motivate discussion more than to define its direction. The moderator continually helps to clarify issues under discussion and to draw out the implications of observations made by participants in the group. An assistant to the moderator should take careful notes.

A major advantage of focus groups, compared to surveys, is that surveys will only take in the answers to the specific questions asked, whereas focus groups provide the opportunity to make sure that the correct questions are being asked in the first place.

8

American Government: Political Analysis

Hypothesis is a tool which can cause trouble if not used properly. We must be ready to abandon our hypothesis as soon as it is shown to be inconsistent with the facts.

—William I. B. Beveridge

A Closer Look at Selected Issues in Political Analysis

Chapters 6 and 7 of this text explored the most well-known approaches to political analysis. To understand more completely how political scientists analyze politics, in this chapter we shall explore a few examples of approaches to political analysis in greater detail.

Dozens of studies of American political institutions are published every year, and many of them contain what is normally called *traditional* political analysis. One such recent study is Janet M. Martin's *Lessons from the Hill: The Legislative Journey of an Education Program* (1993). In this examination of federal legislation involving a federal school dropout prevention program, Martin describes in detail the stages that the legislation passed through on its way to finally becoming law in May 1990. She then draws conclusions about the national legislative process. Martin concludes that conventional attitudes about the effectiveness and responsiveness of Congress are unduly negative, and that the hard, often unseen work of senators and representatives produces many benefits for American society. In that Congress often receives low ratings in public opinion polls, Martin's conclusions are important, for she reveals that much of Congress' valuable work does not receive appropriate recognition:

> Congress may appear to be slow in responding, but it is nonetheless a responsive institution. . . . The inherent tension created in a system of separation of powers with a bicameral legislature was designed to guarantee that the national government's actions would be deliberative and well thought out. The dropout issue had been on the congressional agenda since at least the Ninety-eighth Congress. Over the course of several years, the issue began to capture the attention of many members of Congress, including key subcommittee and committee chairs. The new interest paralleled a growing public realization that the dropout problem was serious, having long-term economic consequences for the United States, and therefore a matter demanding national attention. . . . The story of the school dropout program is indeed the story of much of the day-to-day work in Congress—unseen, unreported, and generally unknown. (Martin 1993, 153–160)

Reprinted by permission: Tribune Media Services.

One important approach to political analysis not previously discussed in this text is Yale political scientist Robert Dahl's *Modern Political Analysis* (1971). Dahl set out to examine the relationship between power and political systems, especially the conditions that affect the stability of democracy. Finding that the word "democracy" has many different meanings in different countries around the world, he formulated a list of seven desirable characteristics of governments and invented a new term for governments which have them: "polyarchy." The seven characteristics of polyarchy are:

1. Control over government decisions about policy is constitutionally vested in elected officials.
2. Elected officials are chosen and peacefully removed in frequent, fair, and free elections in which coercion is absent or quite limited.
3. Virtually all adults have the right to vote.
4. Most adults also have the right to run for public offices in these elections.
5. Citizens possess a right, effectively enforced by judicial and administrative officials, to freedom of expression, including criticism of and opposition to the leaders or party in office.
6. They have access and an effectively enforced right to gain access to sources of information that are not monopolized by the government of the state or by any other single group.
7. They possess an effectively enforced right to form and join political organizations, including political parties and interest groups. (Dahl 1991, 71)

Having established a definition of polyarchy, Dahl is able to examine governments around the world to see the extent to which they exhibit the characteristics of polyarchy. The findings of such analyses, of course, change over time as the attributes of particular governments change. Dahl's approach is, therefore, helpful in comparative analysis, that is, comparing not only different nations, but also nations as they develop politically over time.

Although there are many more examples of political analyses and frameworks for political analyses that could be listed here, the limited space available forces us to be very selective. An improved understanding of contemporary political science often comes by way of introduction to an important current controversy in political analysis through an example of a typical recently published political analysis. We have selected for review two separate issues which together provide readers with a sense of the types of issues currently being explored by political analysts. The first issue, the current controversy about the usefulness of *public choice theory,* has been selected because public choice theory has received more attention than any other single method in recent years. Next, we have selected an article which analyzes the question of whether or not men and women have different voting patterns. The selected article, entitled "Gender and Citizen Participation: Is There a Different Voice?" (*American Journal of Political Science,* May 1995) was chosen because women's issues are increasingly gaining attention in every area of the discipline.

Pathologies of Rational Choice Theory

Rational choice theory is described in Chapter 6, and students may wish to review that chapter before proceeding. The increasing importance of rational choice theory is hard to overestimate. As one recent report states:

> Outside economics . . . the field in which rational-choice thinking has had by far the greatest impact is political science. No department wishing to make a name for itself in the field can be without a contingent of formal theorists. New Ph.D.s with training in rational choice routinely receive multiple job offers from leading universities. More and more books and journal articles are written from a rational choice perspective; according to one estimate, rational choice work made up 40 percent of the pieces in the 1992 volume of the *American Political Science Review.* (Coughlin 1994, A9)

Donald Green and Ian Shapiro have generated a storm of controversy about rational choice theory with their book *Pathologies of Rational Choice Theory, A Critique of Applications in Political Science* (1994), which claims that for all the attention public choice theory has received, it has actually provided relatively little new empirical information about politics. Students should be aware both that such controversies are not rare in political science, and that Green and Shapiro's analysis is by no means the last word to be said on the subject. Controversies such as these have led to the demise of some approaches and to the strengthening of others, and, in the end, to the benefit of the profession as a whole. The authors begin by describing initial observations that led them to conduct their study:

> Since the publication of Kenneth Arrow's *Social Choice and Individual Values* in 1951 there has been an explosion of rational choice scholarship in political science, but there exists in it a curious disjunction that provides both the occasion

and motivation for this book. On the one hand, great strides have been made in the theoretical elaboration of rational actor models. . . . On the other hand, successful empirical applications of rational choice models have been few and far between. . . . Our question was, What has been learned about politics? We focused our attention, therefore, on the empirical rational choice literatures and gradually came to the view that exceedingly little has been learned. (Green and Shapiro 1994, 1–2)

The authors then proceed to describe the development of rational choice theory, noting that its adherents have developed a variety of methods, models, and theories, but that rational choice theorists tend to agree on certain basic assumptions. These assumptions include:

- *Utility maximization:* the tendency for people to attempt to achieve effectiveness and efficiency when making choices;
- *Consistency:* the tendency for people to follow the same general patterns when ordering choices;
- *Maximization of expected values:* the tendency for people to attempt to get maximum gain when making choices;
- *Individuals:* a deliberate focus by analysts on individuals as opposed to families, groups, communities, or species; and
- *Continuity:* the tendency for people to establish stable patterns of actions because individuals make the same types of choices over time. (Green and Shapiro 1994, 14–17)

Green and Shapiro then outline two classes of what they call the "methodological pathologies," or problems inherent in the methodology of rational choice theory. The first class consists of ordinary mistakes in calculation or application of techniques. Although this type of problem is evident in the work of political science, it is not of immediate interest to Green and Shapiro, and they pass over it quickly. Instead, they move directly to the second class of problems, which they call a "syndrome of fundamental and recurrent methodological failings rooted in the universalist aspirations that motivate so much rational choice theorizing" (Green and Shapiro 1994, 33). Universalist aspiration is the desire to apply a methodology to political situations which originate in any place or time. These universalist aspirations lead, according to Green and Shapiro, to three basic groups of methodological failings.

The first group is called "post-hoc theory development." By this the authors mean that rational choice theorists often first examine a given set of facts and then attempt to demonstrate that the facts support their theory. This process then gives rise to bending or arranging the theory to fit the facts. Green and Shapiro cite Ordeshook (1993), who maintains that when public choice theorists are faced with a question to which they have difficulty responding, they simply make their model more complex. The more complex the models become, however, the less useful they are in explaining political phenomena.

Green and Shapiro's second group of methodological pathologies concerns formulating tests. Sometimes the models become so complex that it is difficult to isolate accurately the effects of important variables, and predictions based on the theory, therefore, become "slippery." Unanticipated results are found in experiments, and the theories become more complex to satisfy the requirements of the results. A related problem is that sometimes the empirical tests that are employed are not appropriate for the hypotheses they are supposed to test.

The third area of pathology concerns selecting and interpreting evidence. Some of Green and Shapiro's most serious claims fall in this category. First, they note that all too often investigators state an hypothesis and then go looking for the evidence with which to confirm it. Usually, some evidence can be found. The point is, however, that science is best served when a search is made for evidence that disproves the hypothesis, and this approach is too seldom taken. A related problem is that some rational choice theorists, in their attempts to imagine evidence that will confirm their hypotheses, almost forget the difference between evidence that is real and evidence that is imaginary, a practice that Green and Shapiro call "projecting evidence from theory" (Green and Shapiro 1994, 43). Finally, the authors cite what they call "arbitrary domain restriction." "On occasion, rational choice theorists will concede that there are domains—such as voter turnout and organized collective action—in which no plausible variant of the theory appears to work. Some theorists are then inclined to withdraw, choosing to concentrate on applications in which these theories appear to have better success" (Green and Shapiro 1994, 44).

The authors continue from this point to give detailed examples of these and other problems, and then to address anticipated objections to their study. It must be noted, however, that the controversy is far from over. Rational choice theorists, as may be expected, disagree with Green and Shapiro's analysis. As Ellen Coughlin notes, the public choice theorists "respond that the demand for empirical proof is premature, that the models themselves are still being refined, and that Mr. Green and Mr. Shapiro fail to point to any other theory that explains things better" (Coughlin 1994, A16).

An Issue in Political Analysis

Gender and Citizen Participation: Is There a Different Voice?

Although as we have seen there is no such thing as a "typical" article in political analysis because so many approaches and techniques are used, the following discussion of gender issues is not atypical of articles that may be found in political science journals in the 1990s. It has been selected because it uses quantitative methods and because its topic, gender issues, is frequently discussed in the political science literature. As you read this article, consider the following questions and be prepared to answer them in class discussion:

1. What is the research question?
2. What is the hypothesis?
3. Are the research question and hypothesis properly structured?

4. Are the research question and hypothesis significant and worth investigating?
5. What research methods are used? Are they appropriate to the topic being studied?
6. What are the results or findings of the study? Are they convincing?
7. Is further study needed?

Gender and Citizen Participation:
Is There a Different Voice?*

Kay Lehman Schlozman, Boston College
Nancy Burns, The University of Michigan
Sidney Verba, Harvard University
Jesse Donahue, Boston College

Theory: Gender differences are considered in relation to citizen participation, an aspect of politics subject to more speculation than data when it comes to what Carol Gilligan so aptly termed "a different voice."

Hypotheses: Male and female activists specialize in different forms of activity, derive different gratifications from taking part, and bring different policy concerns to their participation.

Methods: Tabular and logit analysis of survey data from the Citizen Participation Study.

Results: We find, overall, more similarity than difference between women and men. Gender differences are not necessarily what we might have expected. Although women are slightly less active than men, there is substantial similarity in the overall pattern of the participatory acts they undertake. With respect to the gratifications attendant to participation, women and men are similar in terms of how they recalled the reasons for their activity. Men and women address similar issues; when it comes to the content of participation, however, men and women do speak with different voices, with educational issues and abortion weighing especially heavily in the policy agendas of female activists.

In investigating the nature and extent of gender differences in ways of thinking and in behavior, scholars often ask whether, in Carol Gilligan's resonant phrase, men and women speak "in a different voice."[1] Because issues of representation among citizens are so fundamental in a democracy, whether men and women speak with different voices is a particularly important question when it comes to politics. In this paper we use data from an unusual national survey to ask whether women and men differ as citizen activists—in the forms of their participation, in the rewards they seek, and in their issue-concerns.

Little systematic information has been available that bears directly on whether men and women differ in the kinds of activity they undertake, their motivations for taking part, or the policy concerns behind their participation. However, several bodies of literature—feminist theory, historical accounts of women's organizational and political involvements, and analyses in political science of citizen and elite political behavior—are helpful in developing

* The authors would like to thank the National Science Foundation, the Spencer Foundation, the Ford Foundation, the Hewlett Foundation, and the Kellogg Foundation for generous support. We are also grateful to Danny Schlozman for research assistance in a time of need. The data used in this article along with the SPSS documentation necessary to replicate the analysis will be available from the Interuniversity Consortium for Political and Social Research after 1 June 1995.

Schlozman, Kay L., Nancy Burns, Sidney Verba, and Jesse Donahue. "Gender and Citizen Participation: Is There a Different Voice?" In *American Journal of Political Science,* Vol. 39, No. 2, May 1995, Pp. 267–93

[1] We appropriate the phrase from the title of Gilligan's (1982) book, not because we seek to consider gender differences in moral choices or moral reasoning or because we wish to enter into the scholarly debate that has surrounded Gilligan's work, but because her metaphor captures so aptly the question of gender difference.

expectations about men's and women's voices as political activists. We do have systematic evidence in political science about gender differences with respect to many aspects of political behavior—for example, public opinion or the priorities of state legislators. With certain leaps, these studies can provide the basis for hypothesizing about gender differences among activists. With respect to the issues considered here, however, the literature does not provide direct evidence based on systematic samples. We provide that evidence here.

GENDER AND PARTICIPATORY VOICE: EXPECTATIONS FROM THE LITERATURE

Let us review what these various bodies of inquiry suggest about the possibilities for gender differences in citizen voice. Feminist theory provides important background for consideration of these matters.

Many feminist theorists emphasize that, compared to men, women speak and act in ways that are more altruistic, more communal, more peaceful, and more nurturing.[2] Particularly relevant is Ruddick's (1989) influential discussion of maternal thinking, thinking that emerges from protecting and nurturing children (see also Bassin, Honey, and Maher 1994). If these orientations are brought to politics, then we would expect women activists to be more likely than men to anchor their participation in concern for the good of the community; to be active on behalf of issues involving children and families, human welfare, broadly shared interests such as consumer or environmental concerns, and international peace; and to derive civic gratifications from their participation.

Historical inquiries generate complementary expectations. The literature on social feminism and women's involvements in the period just before the granting of suffrage emphasizes the extent to which that work was charitably oriented and motivated by communal orientations (Flexner 1975; Baker 1984; Kraditor 1968; Stoper and Johnson 1977). Historians have also alerted us to the important role of women's involvement in organizations both as an incubator for other forms of political participation and as a form of community participation in its own right (Lerner 1979; Scott 1984, 1991; Baker 1984; Giddings 1984; and Cott 1990). In this vein, feminist scholars among political scientists have frequently argued that, in concentrating upon voting and other forms of electoral involvement, political scientists have neglected forms of participation that are especially congenial to women.[3] According to this view, which is supported by case studies of women's grassroots organizations (for example, Acklesberg 1984), women's participation is centered in political organizations, in grassroots and local activities, and in ad hoc rather than formal involvements. In short, we expect women and men to bring distinctive concerns to citizen participation and to specialize in different kinds of activity.

[2] See, for example, Elshtain (1981), Sapiro (1981), and Eisler (1990). For a cautionary note, see Dietz (1985) and Tronto (1987).

[3] For excellent examples of this point of view, see the discussion in Randall (1987, 50 ff.) and Acklesberg (1994). Some critics (for example, Boals 1975, 171–175; and Baker 1984, 646–647) take this point even further, arguing that our definition of politics should be extended to include all activities undertaken to benefit the community—regardless of whether they involve public authority.

Mainstream political science has developed a reputation for slighting nonelectoral forms of citizen participation because the single best source of continuing survey data is the biennial National Election Study. Because it is anchored in national elections, the NES naturally emphasizes voting and other forms of electoral participation.

In political science, the most relevant systematic analyses of citizen participation have focused on gender differences in the amount rather than the nature of participation—finding that women now equal or surpass men in voter turnout (for example, Wirls 1986; and Beckwith 1986) and that the disparity between men and women in terms of citizen activity is quite narrow (Andersen 1975; Welch 1977; Clark and Clark 1986; and Schlozman, Burns, and Verba 1994). These studies are somewhat less helpful in determining whether men and women differ in national or local focus of their activity and the particular acts in which they specialize. Work using data from the biennial National Election Studies—which focus on national politics and electorally based participation—suggest small and inconsistent gender differences in particular forms of citizen activity. (See, among others, Beckwith 1986; and Rosenstone and Hansen 1993, 141). Using data more appropriate for investigating some of these distinctions, Verba and Nie find that, compared to men, women are slightly less likely to be affiliated with an organization (1972, 181) and slightly more likely to be completely inactive (1972, 97). Unfortunately, they do not differentiate local from nationally focused activity. Extending these findings, Verba, Nie, Kim, and Shabad (1978, 235) observe in an important footnote, "We had expected to find a different sex-related participatory pattern for campaign and communal activity. We found, however, no systematic differences between the acts." In short, existing studies based on systematic samples find little evidence for gender specialization in particular forms of activity.

When it comes to the policy concerns animating citizens' activity and the rewards attendant to it, studies based on systematic samples are suggestive but less directly relevant. Although this literature only rarely connects political orientations to political participation, assessments of the gender gap in political attitudes, partisan identification, and vote choices find evidence for distinctive gender voices (Frankovic 1982; Goertzel 1983; Klein 1985; Shapiro and Mahajan 1986; Wirls 1986; Conover 1988; Kenski 1988; Miller 1988; Mueller 1988; Welch and Sigelman 1989; Conover and Sapiro 1993; and Bendyna and Lake 1994). Over the past 15 years, men have consistently been somewhat more Republican than women in both their electoral choices and their party leanings. Gender differences, some of them long documented in opinion polls, also exist in regard to attitudes on issues. The issues on which women's and men's opinions differ most consistently and most markedly are not women's issues—issues that affect men and women differently, for example, women's rights, abortion, or during the 1970s, the Equal Rights Amendment. Instead, consistent with the expectations derived from feminist theory, the disparities in opinion appear with respect to international aggression, the use of violence, and government welfare policies. We must be somewhat cautious in making inferences to citizen activity from these studies, however, for this literature does not connect these gender differences in opinions to political action.[4]

For systematic studies that link policy preferences to the content of involvement, we must move from the level of the mass public to the level of political elites. Unlike respondents in public-opinion surveys, who are presented a preselected

[4] Exceptions include Klein (1984) as well as Welch and Hibbing (1992, p. 197), who show that men are more likely than women to "cast ego-centric economic votes."

agenda of policy concerns, citizen activists retain considerable control over whether, and about what, to be active. Analogously, public officials have discretion over the translation of their policy opinions into political action. Their choices about the committees on which they sit, the bills they cosponsor, and the subjects they speak on manifest their issue priorities.

Recent studies of public officials—especially legislators in both the state houses and the U.S. Congress—find gender differences.[5] Compared to their male fellow partisans, female representatives tend to have distinctive attitudes; and their attitudes are reflected in their behavior and legislative priorities. Most notably, consistent with feminist theory, women legislators are more likely to champion measures concerning women, children and families.

Studies of political elites also suggest that men and women differ in the rewards that they derive from political participation, with women more likely than men to cite civic concerns and men more likely to cite material rewards. For example, in her study of delegates to the 1972 presidential nominating conventions, Kirkpatrick (1976, chap. 12) found women delegates in both parties to be less ambitious for elected office than their male counterparts. In her study of state legislators, Kirkpatrick (1974, 143–145) found women in the state houses to be more comfortable with a conception of politics as an arena characterized by problem solving in search of the common good rather than by self-interested conflict. We must once again urge caution in making inferences, however, for these are data about political

elites, and we are asking questions about citizens.

With certain important exceptions, the theoretical and critical literature and studies based on systematic samples converge in suggesting that, if there are differences between women and men in the nature of their political activity, they would conform to the following patterns:

1. Men and women activists specialize in different forms of participation with women more likely to engage in informal, grassroots, and organizationally based activities and to focus their energies at the local level.

2. Men and women derive different gratifications from taking part—with men more likely to emphasize material, as opposed to civic, rewards.

3. Men and women bring different clusters of policy concerns to their participation with women's activity more likely than men's to be inspired by issues involving children and families; broad public interests such as consumer or environmental concerns; the use of violence in the home, the streets, or the international arena; and the protection of human rights and the fulfillment of basic human needs.

THE CITIZEN PARTICIPATION STUDY

We employ data from the Citizen Participation Study, a large-scale, two-stage survey of the voluntary activity of the American public. The first stage consisted of over 15,000 telephone interviews of a random sample of the American public conducted during the last six months of 1989. These 20-minute screener interviews provided a profile of political and nonpolitical activity as well as basic demographic in-

---

[5] The literature is substantial, much of it recent. Complementary perspectives and extensive bibliographical references can be found in, among others, Kelly, Saint-Germain, and Horn (1991); Welch and Thomas (1991); Mandel and Dodson (1992); Mezey (1994); Tamerius (1993); and Thomas (1994).

formation. In the spring of 1990, we conducted longer, in-person interviews with a stratified sample of 2,517 of the original 15,000 respondents chosen so as to produce a disproportionate number of both activists as well as African-Americans and Latinos. The data in this paper are drawn from the 2,517 respondents in the follow-up survey. The data are weighted to create an effective random sample. We use the weighted sample throughout. All data can, therefore, be interpreted as if the sample were a random sample.[6]

For several reasons, this study is unusually well suited for probing the questions we have posed here. First, the Citizen Participation Study is based on a very broad construction of what constitutes participation allowing, for the first time, empirical testing of the contention that women and men specialize in different kinds of voluntary activity. With respect to politics, the survey asked about an array of citizen activities: modes of participation that require money as well as those that demand inputs of time; unconventional as well as conventional activity; electoral activities as well as more direct forms of the communication of messages to public officials; and activities done alone as well as those undertaken jointly. Furthermore, the survey was particularly unusual in including voluntary activity outside of politics in churches, secular charities, and nonpolitical organizations.

Whenever a respondent indicated having been active in a particular way, we asked a series of questions designed to measure the relative importance of a range of possible rewards in animating the activity. We also inquired whether there

was any issue or problem, "ranging from public policy issues to community, family, and personal concerns" that led to the activity. We later coded the verbatim answers into categories of issue concerns. These data permit us to investigate in a way that has never before been possible the roots of citizen activity and to make systematic comparisons between women and men in terms of the gratifications attendant to their participation and the issue concerns behind it.

Gender Differences in Participation

Do women and men specialize in different modes of voluntary involvement? Figure 1 presents data on the proportion of women and men who engage in a range of political acts. What is striking about Figure 1 is how little gender specialization there is in types of political activity. Indeed, rank-ordering the activities by frequency yields identical lists. In terms of the amount of activity for several of the activities including voting,[7] the gender differences in participation are neither substantively nor statistically significant. There are statistically significant disparities for four activities—working informally to deal with a community problem, making campaign contribu-

---

[6] A more detailed description of the sample, the weighting scheme that creates an effective random sample, a listing of the relevant measures, and data on the effective numbers of cases can be found in Verba, Schlozman, Brady, and Nie (1993).

[7] As in all surveys, the figures for voter turnout are exaggerated. Data from polls taken just after the election, for example, show the opposite result with respect to gender: for example, the 1990 *Statistical Abstract* gives figures from a large government-sponsored survey that 56.4% of men and 58.3% of women reported going to the polls in 1988. With respect to level of turnout, these figures are still inflated, but are closer to the actual turnout than the figures from our survey. With respect to gender difference, there is evidence from vote validation studies (Traugott and Katosh 1979) that men are slightly more likely to misrepresent having gone to the polls than women are. Unfortunately, we have no analogous method of ascertaining the extent of, or gender bias in, overreporting for other activities.

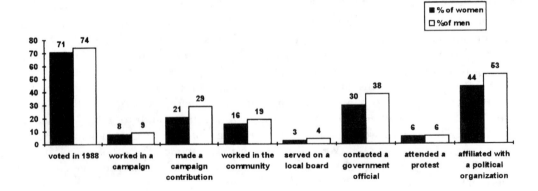

Figure 1. Political Participation by Gender

tions,[8] contacting public officials, and affiliation with (membership in or contributions to) organizations that take stands in politics. In each of these cases, men are somewhat more active than women.

In terms of specific acts, the differences in participation do not suggest that women will specialize in ad hoc, informal, local, grassroots activity. Although there is gender parity with respect to attendance at demonstrations, marches, or protests, the gap is larger for informal community activity than for working in electoral campaigns or community activity in the more formal setting of a local governing board. Women are also slightly less likely than men to be affiliated with any organization, political or nonpolitical: 82% of male and 77% of female respondents indicated involvement in an organization. For organizations that take stands in politics, the gap is wider.

[8] Men are more likely than women to make campaign donations, and to give larger amounts. In Schlozman, Burns, and Verba (1994) we discuss the significance of this disparity, as well as other differences in levels of activity, and the extent to which they can be explained by access to politically relevant resources.

Additional data not included on Figure 1 question the notion that women are local specialists. Each time a respondent indicated having engaged in a political act, we asked a series of follow-up questions about the activity including whether it was national, state, or local. Women were only slightly more likely than men to confine their political activity to subnational politics. Among those who engaged in some political activity beyond voting, 53% of the women, as opposed to 49% of the men, had no activity at the national level.

Voluntary Activity outside Politics

Figure 2 embellishes these findings by presenting data about voluntary activity in realms outside of politics—nonpolitical organizations and charities as well as religious institutions. Figure 2 suggests, for voluntary participation in the secular domain in nonpolitical organizations and charities, no real gender specialization. What is striking, however, is that women are clearly more active than men in an arena that is rarely mentioned in discussions of gender differences in participa-

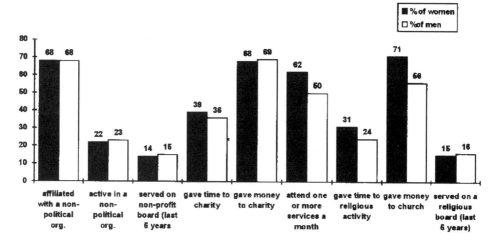

Figure 2. Non-Political Activity by Gender

tion—religious institutions.[9] Not only are women more likely than men to attend services regularly, they are more likely to give time to educational, charitable, or social activities associated with their church or synagogue and to contribute money to their religion.

In short, for voluntary activity both inside and outside politics, the similarity between women and men in the patterns and levels of their involvement stands out. Where there are differences, they do not support the expectations developed in the literature. Women's activities—at least in 1990—were not more locally based, more ad hoc, more grassroots, or more organizationally focused than men's activities. In many instances, they were less so.

THE REWARDS OF PARTICIPATION

Although men and women do not undertake significantly different civic activities, they might take part in politics for different reasons and thereby create a different citizen voice. We looked at this question from the perspective of the activists by asking them how *they* interpret their participation, in particular, their recollections of reasons for their activity.[10] As we indicated, we might expect women to be more likely than men to cite civic concerns and less likely than men to indicate seeking material rewards.

In order to capture the broad range of possible gratifications that can flow from voluntary activity, we presented respondents who indicated having participated with a long list of possible motivations for that activity. We asked them to recall

[9] Luker (1984) and Mansbridge (1986) make the point that advocates of a conservative social agenda have been successful by using Catholic and conservative Protestant churches as a base for recruiting women issue activists. However, none of those who advocate a broadened definition of what constitutes politics mention religious activity as a domain in which women predominate.

[10] For a detailed analysis of the issue including a discussion of the methodological issues associated with asking respondents to reconstruct their reasons for activity and extensive bibliographic references, see Schlozman, Verba, and Brady (1994).

whether each reason was very, somewhat, or not too important in the decision to become active—or, in the case of ongoing participation like organizational affiliation or membership on a local governing board, in keeping them active. The theoretical underpinnings of the lists derive from James Q. Wilson's (1973, especially chaps. 2–3) typology of the incentives provided by political organizations,[11] modified to reflect pretest experience about the language and categories that citizen activists actually use in explaining and interpreting their activity. In asking respondents to recollect their motivations for getting involved, we attempted, insofar as possible, to make a complete matrix—that is, to ask each reason-item for each voluntary act, but we were not always able to do so. In assigning items to categories of analysis, we attempted to use items germane to many kinds of participation and to include only items that were unambiguous as indicators of the theoretical dimension in question.

We consider selective benefits of three types—material benefits, social gratifications, and civic gratifications—as well as the desire to influence a collective policy. *Selective gratifications* may be material or intangible. *Material benefits*, such as jobs, career advancement, or help with a personal or family problem, were the lubricant of the classic urban machine. They continue to figure importantly in contemporary discussions of congressional constituency service and incentives for joining organizations. *Social gratifications*, such as the enjoyment of working with others or the excitement of politics, cannot be enjoyed apart from the activity itself. Without taking part, there is no way to partake of the fun, gain the recognition, or enjoy other social benefits. Similarly, *civic gratifications*, such as satisfying a sense of duty or a desire to contribute to the welfare of the community, also derive from the act itself. *Collective outcomes* are the enactment implementation of desired public policies or the election of a favored candidate.

Table 1 reports the proportion of activists who say that a gratification in one of the four categories was very important in their decisions to undertake six kinds of activity: vote, work in a campaign, make a campaign contribution, contact an official on a matter affecting themselves or their families, contact an official about an issue affecting the nation, and become active with others in an informal community effort. Some gender differences in Table 1 reach statistical significance, but the differences are neither very substantial in magnitude nor consistent across gratifications or political acts. In fact, what is most apparent about Table 1 is how little difference there is between men and women in the gratifications cited.

Much more striking are the differences across political acts. In discussing voting, respondents—whether male or female—referred frequently to civic rewards and only rarely to material ones.[12] With respect to the gratifications attendant to working in a campaign, social gratifications assume greater prominence—again for both women and men. This suggests that the nature of the act rather than the sex of the participant determines the rewards associated with it. Since men and women choose to engage in the same kinds of participatory acts, the consequent rewards accruing to them are necessarily similar.

---

[11] Other typologies of the gratifications attendant to organizational support have many elements in common with Wilson's. See for example, Salisbury (1969); or Knoke (1991).

[12] This is consistent with the findings of those who study turnout as a rational process. For discussion and extensive bibliography, see Schlozman, Verba, and Brady (1994).

Table 1. Gratifications from Political Participation Percentage Mentioning as "Very Important"[a]

	Material		Social		Civic		Policy	
	Women	Men	Women	Men	Women	Men	Women	Men
Vote	7	6	21	19	95	91**	60	62
Work in a campaign	25	24	47	50	85	84	44	52
Campaign contribution	17	20	28	18	79	80	46	47
Particularized contact	86	67**	26	22	43	38	17	21
Contact on a national issue	16	32**	10	13	87	88	80	79
Informal community activity	17	17	36	34	89	82*	38	39

[a] Items included in scales are listed in the Appendix.

$* p < .05; ** p < .01; *** p < .001.$

THE ISSUE-AGENDA OF PARTICIPATION

Women and men might speak in different voices as citizen activists by bringing different sets of issue concerns to their participation. Women and men would thereby offer different agendas for politics.

The Scope of the Agenda

We first investigate the scope of the issues behind women's and men's political activity—probing whether men are less likely than women to bring to politics concerns related narrowly to themselves or their families. Each time a respondent indicated having engaged in a particular activity, we asked whether there was any particular issue or problem—"ranging from public-policy issues to community, family, and personal concerns"—that led to the activity. Across all 3,600 political acts discussed, respondents in 63% of cases provided a comprehensible, codeable answer about the policy concerns that animated the ac-

tivity.[13] Analyzing the substantive concerns behind this issue-based activity allows us to characterize the participatory input from women and men.

Since we wish to assess whether women and men differ in the likelihood of mentioning a concern limited to the individual and the family rather than issues with a broader referent, we focus on contacts with public officials, the only activity for which sizable numbers of respondents said that their concern was narrowly personal. (With regard to all other participatory acts, for the overwhelming majority of participants, the referent was broader.) There is virtually no difference between men and women who contact public officials in terms of whether the matter raised is germane only to themselves or their families, or a policy issue of more general concern. Discussing their most recent contact, 22%

[13] Only 47% of voters—in contrast to 84% of those active in their communities, 87% of contactors, and 95% of protesters—cited at least one identifiable public policy issue as the basis of their activity.

Table 2. Percentage of Issue-Based Participation Motivated by Concern about Particular Issues

Variable	Women	Men
Basic human needs	10	9
Taxes	12	15*
Economic issues (except taxes)	9	11
Abortion	14	7***
Social issues (except abortion)	2	2
Education	20	13***
Children or youth (except education)	5	4
Crime or drugs	9	7
Environment	8	10
Foreign policy	5	8**
Women	1	a
Number of respondents	1,327	1,191
Number of issue-based acts	1,162	1,235

a Less than 1%.

* $p < .05$; ** $p < .01$; *** $p < .001$.

of the men and 21% of the women indicated that the subject was a matter of particularized concern. Of the female contactors, 35% indicated that the issue affects the whole community and 25% that it affects the entire nation (or world); the analogous figures for male contactors are 38% and 22% respectively.

The Content of the Agenda

More important to the assessment of the earlier claims than the scope of the policy concerns behind political activity is their subject matter. Table 2 compares women and men respondents with respect to the issue concerns that animate their participation. The issue-based political act is the unit of analysis, and the figures represent the proportion of all issue-based activity

for which the respondent mentioned, among other things, a particular set of policy concerns.[14]

[14] In coding the open-ended responses, we created over 60 relatively narrow categories. In analyzing the data, we have combined these narrow categories in various ways. The components of the categories in Table 2 are as follows:
Basic human needs: various government benefits (welfare, AFDC, food stamps, housing subsidies, Social Security, Medicare, and Medicaid); unemployment (either as an economic issue or in terms of the respondent's own circumstances); housing or homelessness; health or health care; poverty or hunger; aid to the handicapped or handicapped rights.
Taxes: all references to taxes at any governmental level.
Economic issues: local or national economic performance; inflation; budget issues or the budget deficit; government spending; other economic issues.
Abortion: all references to abortion whether pro-life, pro-choice, or ambiguous.
Social issues: traditional morality; pornography; family

The actual issues associated with activity reveal more similarity than difference between women and men. Both groups bring a diverse set of issues to participation. Moreover, their issue agendas are similar, though not identical.[15] Contrary to expectation, we find no statistically significant gender difference in how importantly issues involving basic human needs, children, or youth (except for education), the

environment, or crime or drugs figure in issue-based participation. Where there are disparities, they do not always conform to the expectations generated by the literature discussed earlier. Men are slightly more likely to mention taxes and foreign policy or international issues. When we looked more carefully at the exact content of the foreign policy concerns, we found that, contrary to expectation, there is no gender difference in the likelihood that issue-based activity is inspired by concerns about international peace and cooperation, arms control, or international human rights. A mere 1% of women's and men's issue-based activity is animated by these concerns.

With respect to education and abortion, the gender differences are more substantial. Concern about education animates at least in part 20% of women's issue-based activity, in contrast to 13% of men's. For abortion, the analogous figures are 14% and 8% respectively. Neither of these is an issue like gun control for which men and women have traditionally held differing opinions. Education, however, falls into the domain of issues of care that were the traditional bailiwick of the social feminists and that have traditionally taken precedence among the priorities of women legislators.

Because the availability of abortion is germane to women's lives in a way that it is not relevant to men's, it is the sole item on the list that qualifies as a "women's issue." In interpreting these figures, we must recall that they conflate activists who are pro-choice with those who are pro-life. Elsewhere in our questionnaire we asked a standard survey question about attitudes towards abortion. The center of gravity on this issue leans decidedly in the direction of support for the availability of abortion—with men somewhat more pro-

---

planning, teenage pregnancy, sex education, or contraception; school prayer; gay rights or homosexuality.
Education: educational issues (school reform, school voucher plans, etc.); problems or issues related to schooling of family members; guaranteed student loans.
Children or youth: recreation for children or youth; day care; other issues affecting young.
Crime or drugs: crime; gangs; safety in the streets; drugs.
Environment: specific environmental issues (e.g., clean air, toxic wastes) or environmental concerns in general; wildlife preservation; animal rights.
Foreign policy: relations with particular nations or to foreign policy in general; defense policy or defense spending; peace, arms control, or international human rights issues.
Women's issues: women's rights; domestic violence; rape; women's health and reproductive issues (excluding abortion).
Note that the categories vary in the extent to which they encompass respondents with quite different issue-positions. For example, activists on the abortion issue are polarized in their opinions. In contrast, activists who cited concerns about the environment tend to be in overall agreement with one another. These activists' opponents might be, for example, activists with concerns about economic development and performance.
It should also be noted that the categories in Table 2 are not exhaustive. Issue concerns ranging from gun control to drunk driving have been omitted from the table. If the universe of issue concerns had been included, the figures in each column would add to more than 100%. A single political act is often inspired by more than one issue concern. The contactor who expressed concern about "public housing, teenage pregnancy, and the child care bill" would have been coded as mentioning three separate issues.
[15] Hansen (1994) finds a similar result when men and women are asked what they consider to be the most important issue facing the country.

choice than women.[16] For both women and men, however, activity on abortion comes disproportionately from the pro-life side.[17] In response to the survey question 35% of women expressed pro-life views; yet 53% of their political activity motivated by concern about the abortion issue emanated from respondents who reported pro-life attitudes. For men the figures are 26% and 43% respectively.[18]

In contrast to the circumstance with respect to abortion, there is no division of opinion among those who mentioned women's issues. All the messages on women's issues indicated support for women's rights or greater attention to such problems as rape or domestic violence. (Interestingly, not one respondent mentioned sexual harassment in these 1990 interviews.) What is most noteworthy, however,

---

[16] The data are as follows:
(1) A woman should always be able to obtain an abortion as a matter of choice.
(7) By law abortion should never be permitted.

	1	2	3	4	5	6	7
Men	40%	11%	9%	13%	6%	10%	10%
Women	36%	9%	8%	12%	7%	9%	19%

Women in legislatures—who, unlike women activists, place women's rights issues among their policy priorities—are not as divided in their attitudes about abortion as are women in the mass public and are distinctly less pro-life in their opinions than their fellow legislators who are male (Thomas 1994, 65).

[17] In order to ensure that the direction of opinion on abortion expressed in the survey item could be used as a guide to the direction of opinion expressed through activity on abortion, we conducted the following experiment. We coded the actual verbatims for abortion activists as to whether the activity was pro-life, pro-choice, or ambiguous in direction. In no case that a direction was specified in connection with abortion-related activity did that direction contradict the opinion elicited by the survey item.

[18] Abortion figures more importantly in the activity of those who are pro-life than of those who are pro-choice: abortion was mentioned in connection with 24% of the issue-based activity of pro-life women and 12% of the activity of pro-life men; in contrast, abortion was discussed in relation to 11% of the activity of pro-choice women and 6% of the activity of pro-choice men.

is just how rarely these issues were raised in connection with activity. Women discussed these issues in connection with 1% of their issue-based activity, and men barely mentioned them at all. In short, what is most apparent is not that the government hears more from women than from men about women's issues or that the content of the messages is uniformly in support of equality between the sexes, but rather that public officials hear so little on the subject.

These findings hold up when we compare men and women within groups defined by their race or ethnicity. As shown in Table 3, education figures prominently among the issue concerns of women and men—whether they are Latino, African-American, or white. In each case, however, it weighs even more heavily in the issue-based activity of women than men. Analogously, abortion figures more importantly in the issue priorities of women than men, regardless of race or ethnicity. There are, however, important differences across groups defined by their race or ethnicity. Abortion occupies more space in the political agendas of white activists than of African-Americans or Latinos. In contrast, issues of basic human need as well as crime or drugs weigh more heavily among the issue concerns of Latinos or African-Americans than of whites. When it comes to issues involving civil rights or minorities, there are differences between, on one hand, Anglo-Whites and, on the other, African-Americans or Latinos, for whom these issues figure more importantly in issue-based activity. There is a gender difference as well: issues connected to civil rights or minorities are higher among the issue priorities of African-American and Latino men than women.

For policy issues expressed through activity by men and women differentiated by socioeconomic advantage, the findings are more complex. In Table 4 we compare

Table 3. Percentage of Issue-Based Political Activity Motivated by Concern about Particular Issues

	White		Black		Latino	
	Women	Men	Women	Men	Women	Men
Basic human needs	9	8	19	21	20	13
Taxes	12	16**	9	8	5	9
Economic issues (except taxes)	9	12*	5	7	1	6
Abortion	15	8***	6	3	6	3
Social issues (except abortion)	2	1	2	2	1	2
Education	20	13***	19	14	24	16
Children or youth (except education)	4	3	8	10	15	2
Crime or drugs	7	5	27	23	16	18
Environment	9	11	1	2	6	10
Foreign policy	6	8	1	7*	6	8
Women	1	a	1	1	0	0
Civil rights or minorities	1	1	5	7	3	8
Number of respondents	1,068	1,006	141	92	85	56
Number of issue-based acts	1,009	1,076	103	90	31	41

a Less than 1%.

* p < .05; ** p < .01; *** p < .001.

men and women who are relatively advantaged (who have had at least a year of college education and whose family incomes were $50,000 or more) with those who are much less advantaged (who have no more than a high school education and whose family incomes were no more than $20,000). Educational concerns figure importantly in the issue-based activity of both advantaged and disadvantaged respondents. Once again, however, they occupy greater space in women's activity than in men's. Abortion weighs more heavily in the issue-based activity of the advantaged,

for whom there is no gender gap, than in the activity of the disadvantaged, for whom there is a gender disparity in abortion-related activity. Disadvantaged respondents, both female and male, are more concerned with issues of basic human need. Among the advantaged, however, there is no difference between women and men in the extent to which these issues figure in issue-based activity. In contrast, among the disadvantaged issues of basic human need occupy much more space in the issue concerns for women than for men. A similar pattern

Table 4. Percentage of Issue-Based Political Activity Motivated by Concern about Particular Issues

Variable	Advantaged[a]		Disadvantaged[b]	
	Women	Men	Women	Men
Basic human needs	9	9	27	12**
Taxes	8	16**	13	15
Economic issues (except taxes)	14	15	4	5
Abortion	13	12	6	0**
Social Issues (except abortion)	1	1	6	0**
Education	24	14***	17	8
Children or youth (except education)	5	3	9	5
Crime or drugs	8	5	15	6*
Environment	5	10*	0	4
Foreign policy	7	9	2	4
Women's issues	2	c	c	0
Number of respondents	197	228	297	182
Number of issue-based acts	326	338	113	72

[a] Advantaged: At least one year of college and family income at least $50,000.
[b] Disadvantaged: No college education and family income less than $20,000.
[c] Less than 1%.
* $p < .05$; ** $p < .01$; *** $p < .001$.

tains for issues associated with drugs and crime. Concern about crime and drugs figures much more importantly on the agenda of issues that inspire activity for disadvantaged women than for disadvanned men or for the advantaged of either summary, among more advantaged he gender differences are rela '9: among those less well off,

is the fact that advantaged men o be concerned with taxes than ad .1.

there is a decided focus of attention among women on issues associated with poverty and poor living conditions.

Putting Children First: Further Analysis

Across all the groups and all the aspects of citizen involvement we have considered, the most notable manifestation of a different citizen voice is the relative space occupied by issues surrounding education in the bundle of issue concerns of women. Feminist theory alerts us to the potential implications for politics of the fact that women bear a disproportionate share of the responsibility for raising children. Following this line of inquiry, we can investigate whether women's special concern with children's issues is the exclusive bailiwick of mothers or whether women activists pay greater attention to these issues regardless of whether they have children.

In Table 5, we present the results of a logit analysis in which the dependent variable combines two categories that were separate on Table 3 to Table 5: activity involving education or other concerns about

Table 5. Logit Analysis of the Sources of Participation in Children's Issues

Variable	Coefficient	Standard Error
Constant	−3.02	(0.21)
Woman	0.36***	(0.12)
Preschool children	−0.05	(0.18)
School-aged children	0.75***	(0.14)
Education	0.36***	(0.04)
Income	−0.01	(0.02)
Free time	−0.03	(0.02)
N	2,278	
2 * Log-likelihood Pre	−1,957	
Post	−1,822	

$* p < .05; ** p < .01; *** p < .001.$

Predicted Values from the Logit Analysis

Probability of Participating on Children's Issues

A woman with no children	0.12
A man with no children	0.10
A woman with preschool children	0.12
A man with preschool children	0.09
A woman with school-aged children	0.23
A man with school-aged children	0.19
A woman with preschool and school-aged children	0.22
A man with preschool and school-aged children	0.18

the young such as day care or recreational opportunities. We include among the independent variables not only gender and the presence of preschool and school-age children in the household but also three variables related to the propensity to participate—education, income, and free time.[20] We report the interpretations of the coefficients at the bottom of Table 5.

The results suggest that there is always a small difference between men and women when it comes to participating about children and education, a difference that is larger for respondents with children than for those without. The largest effect, however, is not a gender-based effect indicating something about a differential propensity to take on—or to be assigned—responsibility for being caring and active when it comes to children. Instead, the most substantial effect comes from the fact of having school-aged children in the first place. Note that what matters is not simply having children, but having *school-aged* children. In our data, women are more likely to have school-aged children living at home with them than are men; that difference is the source of most of the gender difference in activism about children and education that we report in our tables.

[20] On the definitions of these variables and the predictors of political participation, see Brady, Verba, and Schlozman (1995); and Schlozman, Burns, and Verba (1994).

We use a logit model because the dependent variable is dichotomous and because we believe that the assumptions of a logit model are more appropriate here. Note that, unlike ordinary least squares, the coefficients cannot be interpreted simply as the effect on the dependent variable of a one-unit change in one of the explanatory variables. A logit model includes the assumption that all of the variables work interactively—that the effects of each explanatory variable depend on the values of the others. Thus, we cannot know about the effects of having preschool children in the house, for example, without knowing whether the person has school-age children at home.

CONCLUSION

Across disciplines scholars have been probing the extent, nature, and roots of differences between women and men, an enterprise that is often described—as we have done here—by reference to Carol Gilligan's apt metaphor, the search for "a different voice." Greater headway is possible, however, if instead of asking flatly whether men and women differ, we qualify the question in several ways. First we must recognize the significance of the cleavages of race, class, family status, employment status that differentiate the experiences of both men and women (Moraga and Anzaldua 1983; hooks 1984; Aptheker 1989). What is characteristic of gender differences among African-Americans may not obtain for whites. Similarly, what we found for the poor may not apply to the affluent, and so on. Hence, we must ask, "Which men? Which women?"

Surely, the extent and nature of gender differences will also vary across domains of endeavor. There is no reason to expect that we can generalize from the committee hearing room to the board room, school room, locker room, operating room, and living room. Gender differences in moral reasoning or rates of violent crime do not necessarily tell us much about the realm of politics. Finally, even within a particular realm of activity, there may be no uniformity across different aspects of behavior. For example, patterns of gender similarity or difference characteristic of congressional roll call voting may not be relevant when it comes to paths of political recruitment or styles of campaigning for the House. In short, ask not "Is there a different voice?" but "With respect to what is there a different voice?"

Armed with inferences drawn from several bodies of theoretical and empirical literature and unusually rich data, we began this enterprise expecting to find gender differences among activists in terms of the activities in which they specialize, the gratifications they reap from taking part, and the issues that animate their participation. Probe as we might, we were surprised to find much more *similarity* than difference between men and women on all these dimensions. Across a wide variety of participatory acts, we found few significant disparities in men's and women's levels of participation. Where differences existed, they confounded the expectations generated by the literature: women do not participate disproportionately in grassroots, organizational, local, ad hoc political activities. In terms of the rewards of participation, men have no monopoly on material benefits, and both men and women are likely to cite altruistic and civic gratifications. Furthermore, the contours of women's and men's participatory agendas bear striking similarity. When we considered the issue priorities expressed through participation for subgroups defined by their race or ethnicity or their condition of socioeconomic disadvantage, however, we found some notable group differences. This reinforces a point made earlier, that we must be sensitive to the differences among women and among men as well as to the aggregate differences between women and men.

By and large, gender differences in issue priorities that arise among citizen activists do not appear with respect either to women's rights or to the issues on which women and men have traditionally expressed different opinions in surveys. We found differences in relative issue emphasis with respect to abortion, education, and, among the disadvantaged, basic human needs and, to a lesser extent, crime or drugs. We were led to inquire how to interpret these distinctive issue emphases—as the result of particular life circumstances that men or women are disproportionately likely to experience, or the result of distinctively masculine or feminine responses to those circumstances. Our results suggest that both are important.

In the aggregate, the conditions of men's and women's lives differ: women assume a disproportionate share of the child-rearing responsibilities in almost all households and are much more likely than men to raise children on their own; furthermore, women are substantially more likely than men to be poor. Analysis showed that, when it comes to being active on issues related to education, what really matters is having school-aged children; however, gender retains a significant, though smaller, effect. With respect to emphasis upon issues of basic human need, it is not, by and large, simply being poor that has an effect but being poor and female. In comparison with disadvantaged men, disadvantaged women—who our data show to be much more likely to have responsibility for children and to depend on government benefits for support—place a much higher priority on basic human need in their issue-based activity. Given the special impact that abortion policies have on women's lives, it would seem logical to root the relative importance women participants place on abortion in their life circumstances. As we have seen, however, women's (and men's) activity on abortion emanates disproportionately from those who are pro-life.

Making progress in understanding big questions requires both bold theorizing and systematic evidence. With results that are often surprising, this paper has presented significant new data about gender differences in an aspect of politics about which the evidence has not kept pace with the theorizing. Our data tell only part of the story of whether women and men activists speak with different voices, however. Long, in-depth interviews might reveal gender differences that do not emerge from survey data—for example, in the nature of the discourse used to discuss political participation or in the propensity to engage in conflictual rather than cooperative endeavors. Just as we have built on the findings of previous scholars, we invite others to use other methods to elaborate upon our results.

Appendix

Indicators of Gratifications Derived from Participation

Material benefits
The chance to further my job or career.
I might want to get help from an official on a personal or family problem.
I might want to run for office someday.
I might want to get a job with the government some day.
Social gratifications
I find it exciting.
The chance to be with people I enjoy.
The chance to meet important and influential people.
The chance for recognition from people I respect.
I did not want to say no to someone who asked.
Civic gratifications
My duty as a citizen.
I am the kind of person who does my share.
The chance to make the community or nation a better place to live.
Collective outcomes
The chance to influence government policy.

REFERENCES

Acklesberg, Martha A. 1994. "Broadening the Study of Women's Participation." Paper presented at the CAWP Conference.

———. 1984. "Women's Collaborative Activities and City Life: Politics and Policy." In *Political Women: Current Roles in State and Local Government*, ed. Janet A. Flammang. Beverly Hills: Sage.

Andersen, Kristi. 1975. "Working Women and Political Participation, 1952–1972." *American Journal of Political Science* 10:439–55.

Aptheker, Bettina. 1989. *Tapestries of Life: Women's Work, Women's Consciousness, and the Meaning of Daily Life*. Amherst: University of Massachusetts Press.

Baker, Paula. 1984. "The Domestication of Politics: Women and American Political Society, 1780–1920." *American Historical Review* 89:620–47.

Bassin, Donna, Margaret Honey, and Meryle Maher Kaplan, eds. 1994. *Representations of Motherhood*. New Haven: Yale University Press.

Beckwith, Karen. 1986. *American Women and Political Participation: The Impacts of Work, Generation, and Feminism*. New York: Greenwood Press.

Bendyna, Mary E., and Celinda C. Lake. 1994. "Gender and Voting in the 1992 Presidential Election." In *The Year of the Woman: Myths and Realities*, ed. Elizabeth Adell Cook, Sue Thomas, and Clyde Wilcox. Boulder: Westview Press.

Boals, Kay. 1975. "The Politics of Male-Female Relations: The Functions of Feminist Scholarship." *Signs* 1:161–74.

Brady, Henry, Sidney Verba, and Kay Lehman Schlozman. 1995. "Beyond SES: A Resource Model of Political Participation." *American Political Science Review*. Forthcoming.

Clark, Cal, and Janet Clark. 1986. "Models of Gender and Political Participation in the United States." *Women and Politics* 6:5–25.

Conover, Pamela Johnston. 1988. "Feminists and the Gender Gap." *Journal of Politics* 50:985–1010.

Conover, Pamela Johnston, and Virginia Sapiro. 1993. "Gender, Feminist Consciousness, and War." *American Journal of Political Science* 37:1079–99.

Cott, Nancy F. 1990. "Across the Great Divide: Women in Politics Before and After 1920." In *Women and Political Change*, ed. Patricia Gurin and Louise A. Tilly. New York: Russell Sage.

Dietz, Mary G. 1985. "Citizenship with a Feminist Face." *Political Theory* 13:19–37.

Eisler, Riane. 1990. "The Gaia Tradition and the Partnership Future: An Ecofeminist Manifesto." In *Reweaving the World*, ed. Irene Diamond and Gloria Feman Orenstein. San Francisco: Sierra Club Books.

Elshtain, Jean Bethke. 1981. *Public Man, Private Woman*. Princeton, NJ: Princeton University Press.

Flexner, Eleanor. 1975. *Century of Struggle: The Women's Rights Movement in the United States.* Cambridge: Harvard University Press.

Frankovic, Kathleen A. 1982. "Sex and Politics—New Alignments, Old Issues." *PS* 15:439–48.

Giddings, Paula. 1984. *When and Where I Enter: The Impact of Black Women on Race and Sex in America.* New York: Morrow.

Gilligan, Carol. 1982. *In a Different Voice.* Cambridge: Harvard University Press.

Goertzel, Ted. 1983. "The Gender Gap: Sex, Family Income, and Political Opinions in the 1980s." *Journal of Political and Military Sociology* 11:209–22.

Hansen, Susan B. 1994. "Talking about Politics: Gender and Contextual Effects on Political Discourse." University of Pittsburgh. Unpublished manuscript.

hooks, bell. 1984. *Feminist Theory: From Margin to Center.* Boston: South End.

Kelly, Rita Mae, Michelle A. Saint-Germain, and Jody D. Horn. 1991. "Female Public Officials: A Different Voice?" In *American Feminism: New Issues for a Mature Movement,* ed. Janet K. Boles. Newbury Park, CA: Sage Publications.

Kenski, Henry C. 1988. "The Gender Factor in a Changing Electorate." In *The Politics of the Gender Gap,* ed. Carol M. Mueller. Newbury Park, CA: Sage Publications.

Kirkpatrick, Jeane J. 1974. *Political Woman.* New York: Basic Books.

———. 1976. *The New Presidential Elite.* New York: Russell Sage Foundation and Twentieth Century Fund.

Klein, Ethel. 1984. *Gender Politics.* Cambridge: Harvard University Press.

———. 1985. "The Gender Gap: Different Issues. Different Answers." *Brookings Review* 3:33–37.

Knoke, David. 1990. *Organizing for Collective Action.* Hawthorne, NY: Aldine deGruyter.

Kraditor, Aileen S. 1965. *The Ideas of the Women's Suffrage Movement.* New York: W.W. Norton.

Lerner, Gerda. 1979. *The Majority Finds its Past: Placing Women in History.* New York: Oxford University Press.

Luker, Kristin. 1984. *Abortion and the Politics of Motherhood.* Berkeley: University of California Press.

Mandel, Ruth B., and Debra L. Dodson. 1992. "Do Women Officeholders Make a Difference?" In *The American Woman 1992–93: A Status Report,* ed. Paula Ries and Anne J. Stone. New York: W.W. Norton.

Mansbridge, Jane J. 1986. *Why We Lost the ERA.* Chicago: University of Chicago Press.

Mezey, Susan Gluck. 1994. "Increasing the Number of Women in Office: Does It Matter?" In *The Year of the Woman: Myths and Realities,* ed. Elizabeth Adell Cook, Sue Thomas, and Clyde Wilcox. Boulder: Westview Press.

Miller, Arthur. 1988. "Gender and the Vote: 1984." In *The Politics of the Gender Gap,* ed. Carol M. Mueller. Newbury Park, CA: Sage Publications.

Moraga, Cherrie, and Gloria Anzaldua, eds. 1983. *This Bridge Is Called My Back: Writings by Radical Women of Color.* New York: Kitchen Table.

Mueller, Carol M., ed. 1988. *The Politics of the Gender Gap.* Newbury Park, CA: Sage Publications.

Randall, Vicky. 1987. *Women and Politics: An International Perspective.* Chicago: University of Chicago Press.

Rosenstone, Steven J., and John Mark Hansen. 1993. *Mobilization, Participation, and Democracy in America.* New York: Macmillan.

Ruddick, Sara. 1989. *Maternal Thinking.* Boston: Beacon Press.

Salisbury, Robert. 1969. "An Exchange Theory of Interest Groups." *Midwest Journal of Political Science* 13:1–32.

Sapiro, Virgina. 1981. "When Are Interests Interesting?: The Problem of Political Representation of Women." *American Political Science Review* 75:701–16.

Schlozman, Kay Lehman, Sidney Verba, and Henry Brady. 1994. "Participation's Not a Paradox: The View from American Activists." *British Journal of Political Science.* Forthcoming.

Schlozman, Kay Lehman, Nancy E. Burns and Sidney Verba. 1994. "Gender and Political Participation: The Role of Resources." *Journal of Politics* 56:963–90.

Scott, Anne Firor. 1984. *Making the Invisible Woman Visible.* Urbana: University of Illinois Press.

———. 1991. *Natural Allies: Women's Associations in American History.* Urbana: University of Illinois Press.

Shapiro, Robert Y., and Harpreet Mahajan. 1986. "Gender Differences in Policy Preferences: A Summary of Trends from the 1960s to the 1980s." *Public Opinion Quarterly* 50:42–61.

Stoper, Emily, and Roberta Ann Johnson. 1977.

"The Weaker Sex and the Better Half: The Idea of Women's Moral Superiority in the American Feminist Movement." *Polity* 10:192–217.

Tamerius, Karin L. 1993. "Does Sex Matter?: Women Representing Women's Interests in Congress." Paper delivered at the annual meeting of the Midwest Political Science Association, Chicago.

Thomas, Sue. 1994. *How Women Legislate*. New York: Oxford University Press.

Traugott, Michael W., and John P. Katosh. 1979. "Response Validity in Surveys of Voting Behavior." *Public Opinion Quarterly* 43:359–77.

Tronto, Joan C. 1987. "Beyond Gender Difference to a Theory of Care." *Signs* 12:644–63.

Verba, Sidney, and Norman H. Nie. 1972. *Participation in America*. New York: Harper and Row.

Verba, Sidney, Norman H. Nie, Jae-on Kim, and Goldie Shabad. 1978. "Men and Women: Sex-Related Differences in Political Activity." In *Participation and Political Equity*, ed. Sidney Verba, Norman H. Nie, and Jae-on Kim. Cambridge: Cambridge University Press.

Verba, Sidney, Kay Lehman Schlozman, Henry Brady, and Norman Nie. 1993. "Citizen Activity: Who Participates? What Do They Say?" *American Political Science Review* 87:303–18.

Welch, Susan. 1977. "Women as Political Animals? A Test of Some Explanations for Male-Female Political Participation Differences." *American Journal of Political Science* 21:711–30.

Welch, Susan and John Hibbing. 1992. "Financial Conditions, Gender, and Voting in American National Elections." *American Journal of Political Science* 36:197–213.

Welch, Susan and Lee Sigelman. 1989. "A Black Gender Gap?" *Social Science Quarterly* 70:120–33.

Welch, Susan, and Sue Thomas. 1991. "Do Women in Public Office Make a Difference?" In *Gender and Policymaking*, ed. Susan J. Carroll, Debra Dodson, and Ruth B. Mandel. New Brunswick, NJ: Center for the American Woman and Politics, Eagleton Institute of Politics, Rutgers University.

Wilson, James Q. 1973. *Political Organizations*. New York: Basic Books.

Wirls, Daniel. 1986. "Reinterpreting the Gender Gap." *Public Opinion Quarterly* 50:316–30.

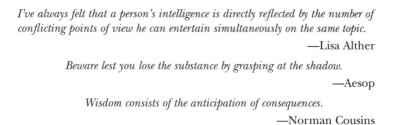

American Government: Policy Analysis

9

I've always felt that a person's intelligence is directly reflected by the number of conflicting points of view he can entertain simultaneously on the same topic.

—Lisa Alther

Beware lest you lose the substance by grasping at the shadow.

—Aesop

Wisdom consists of the anticipation of consequences.

—Norman Cousins

An Introduction to Policy Analysis

Once a branch of public administration, public policy analysis has now become a separate and growing field within political science. Policy analysts are hired by governments, interest groups, and educational institutions to study society's problems and help find solutions to them. A *policy* is a general rule or principle that is intended to guide specific actions in a variety of circumstances. A high school policy of discouraging smoking may, for example, prohibit smoking inside a building, provide for classes on the harmful effects of smoking, or provide smoke-free activities for students. Although policies are made by mothers and fathers, churches, clubs, and many others, *public* policy refers to policies made by an agency of government. More specifically, public policy refers to the decisions that governments make which direct their administrators to act in a certain way in a given set of circumstances.

Analysis is the process of

- Breaking down or taking apart the object of investigation, and examining the content and character of the constituent parts,
- Examining the relations of the various parts to one another,
- Describing interactions and the effects of the interactions of the parts on each other and on external phenomena, and
- Describing and evaluating the whole object in light of the knowledge of the parts. (Scott and Garrison 1995)

Public policy analysis, therefore, is the process of examining the internal and external characteristics, interaction, and effects of the components of a government's decision to act—according to a set principle or rule—in a given set of circumstances. Public policy analysis, therefore, studies the development, content, implementation, and effects of public policy. Public policy analysts use a variety of methods, many of them learned from economists to whom government economic policy is very important.

Policy analysis papers are written at all levels of government every day. Public officials are constantly challenged to initiate new policies or change old ones. They want to know how effective their current policy is, if they have a formal policy at all. They then want to know what options are available to them, what changes they might make to improve current policy, and what the consequences of those changes will be. Policies are reviewed under a number of circumstances. Policy analyses are sometimes conducted as part of the routine agency budgeting processes. They help decisionmakers decide what policies should be continued or discontinued. They may be very narrow in scope, such as deciding the hours of operation of facilities at city parks. Or they may be very broad in scope, such as deciding how the nation will provide health care or defense for its citizens. Historically, a famous treatise on how to formulate and conduct public policy was *The Prince,* by Niccolo Machiavelli (1513), discussed in Chapter 2. *The Prince* contained advice for government rulers on how to remain in power. Advocating a policy of deception, Machiavelli says (1513, XVIII) in part:

> How laudable it is for a prince to keep good faith and live with integrity . . . [however] a prince being thus obliged to know well how to act as a beast must imitate the fox and the lion, for the lion cannot protect himself from traps, and the fox cannot defend himself from wolves. One must therefore be a fox to recognize traps, and a lion to frighten wolves. Those who wish to be only lions do not understand this. Therefore, a prudent ruler ought not to keep faith when by so doing it would be against his best interest, and when the reasons which made him bind himself no longer exist. If men were all good, this precept would not be a good one; but as they are bad, and would not observe their faith with you, so you are not bound to keep faith with them. . . . It is not, therefore, necessary for a prince to have all the above-named [good] qualities, but it is very necessary to seem to have them.

Machiavelli's advice does *not* conform to standards of ethical conduct accepted in the profession of policy analysis today. He does, however, establish ground rules for the development of specific policies based upon an analysis of the problems of political life as he sees them. In the remainder of this chapter we shall mention some well known comments upon the process of making public policy, and then present, as an example, a recently published policy analysis: a study of teenage fathers and child support payments.

Public policies are made within the framework of a government system. Systems within which policy decisions are made always include three general categories of actors: *policy makers* (the people who make the policies, such as Congress), *policy implementers,* (the people who carry out the policies, such as the departments and agencies of the federal government), and *policy constituents* (the people who are affected by the policies, such as interest groups and the general population).

These three elements of the policy making process form what are known as "policy making triangles," which, in the case of the federal government, have become known as "iron triangles" because the three groups together are so powerful with regard to a specific area of policy that they effectively control the process. For example an "iron triangle" related to farm policy may include members of House and Senate agriculture committees, officials of the Agriculture Department, and interest groups such as the United Farm Workers union and associations of meat, dairy, and grain farmers. President Reagan, frustrated with the ability of iron triangles to hamper a president's ability to change government policies, stated in his Farewell Address that a major source of the power of iron triangles is their "ability to focus debate and overwhelming resources—like campaign money and letter writing campaigns—on issues that don't command broad and intense national attention."

Very simply, policies are made up and put into effect to solve problems. If no problem exists or is likely to develop, then no policy is necessary. National health policies, for example, are formulated when costs of health care are beyond the reach of part of the population, or when different groups contest the safety of certain medical procedures. Political scientists and other policy analysts, therefore, share a very practical purpose. They want to know what policy or policies will likely be most effective and efficient in solving any given problem. All policy analysis, therefore, shares the same basic list of considerations, and all policy analysis follows, more or less, the same basic steps or stages. A summary of the common accepted stages prepared by Stella Z. Theodoulou (1995, 86), political scientist at California State University, Northridge, is as follows:

1. *Problem Recognition and Issue Identification:* This stage draws the attention of policy makers to a problem that might require governmental action; problems, if legitimate, then become issues.
2. *Agenda Setting:* The issue is given the status of a serious matter.
3. *Policy Formulation:* Proposals are developed for dealing with issues.
4. *Policy Adoption:* Efforts are made to obtain enough support for a proposal to make it to the government's stated policy.
5. *Policy Implementation:* The policy mandate is aimed at through public programs and the federal bureaucracy, often with citizen, state, and local government cooperation.
6. *Policy Analysis and Evaluation:* This involves examining the consequences of policy actions, including whether the policy has worked.

The process of policy analysis, which is carried on within Theodoulou's stages 3 and 6 above, also is conducted in a series of steps, although by no means are they always done in the same order. In fact, the process of proceeding through the stages above and the steps below is recursive, meaning that as people work through one step or stage they revert back again to previous stages to account for new insights learned along the way. Steps 1 and 2 below are commonly reversed, that is, policy analysis may begin with either a problem that government needs to address or an existing policy that was designed to solve a specific problem. To conduct a policy analysis, it is necessary to:

1. *Select and clearly define* a specific existing *government policy.*
2. Identify and then carefully *define* the social, governmental, economic, or other *problem* the existing policy (if there is one) was designed to solve.

3. Describe the economic, social, and political *environments* in which the problem arose and the existing policy was developed.
4. Evaluate the *effectiveness* of the current policy or lack of policy in dealing with the problem.
5. Identify *alternative policies* that could be adopted to solve the selected problem.
6. Estimate the economic, social, environmental, and political *costs and benefits* of each alternative policy.
7. Provide a *summary comparison* of all policies examined.
8. Write a *recommendation* which identifies the most beneficial policy to be adopted (optional, depending upon the purpose of the analysis).

Students must be aware that the steps listed above represent an ideal scientific method of determining the proper course of public policy, but that many commentators have noted that this practice is rarely followed in the course of everyday life in government. Probably the most famous of these critiques is Charles E. Lindblom's *The Science of Muddling Through*. According to traditional policy analysis theory, Lindblom contends, policy makers are supposed to follow a "rational-comprehensive" approach (like the approach outlined above). This rational-comprehensive approach may be outlined as follows:

1a. Clarification of values or objectives distinct from and usually prerequisite to empirical analysis of alternative policies.
2a. Policy-formulation is, therefore, approached through means-end analysis: First the ends are isolated, then the means to achieve them are sought.
3a. The test of a "good" policy is that it can be shown to be the most appropriate means to the desired ends.
4a. Analysis is comprehensive; every important relevant factor is taken into account.
5a. Theory is often heavily relied upon. (Lindblom 1995, 116)

Lindblom proceeds to explain that policy makers, in real life, rarely follow the pattern set forth above. They are too busy solving too many problems, which are not separate and distinct but highly interrelated. Instead, a different approach is in fact followed, an approach he calls "successive limited comparisons," in which instead of looking at all the possibilities in a comprehensive way, policy makers rely upon their own personal experience, comparing two, three, or a few options to each other at a time, eliminating those that do not fare well in the successive comparisons. In this approach, the policy making process looks quite different:

1b. Selection of value goals and empirical analysis of the needed action are not distinct from one another but are closely intertwined.
2b. Since means and ends are not distinct, means-ends analysis is often inappropriate or limited.
3b. The test of a "good" policy is typically that various analysts find themselves directly agreeing on a policy (without their agreeing that it is the most appropriate means to an agreed objective).

4b. Analysis is drastically limited: i) Important possible outcomes are neglected. ii) Important alternative potential policies are neglected. iii) Important affected values are neglected.

5b. A succession of comparison greatly reduces or eliminates reliance on theory (Lindblom 1995, 116–117).

Political scientists like Lindblom have studied many aspects of the policy making process. The pioneering study of policy analysis within political science was Lerner and Laswell's *The Policy Sciences* (1951). Lasswell listed six basic characteristics of what he perceived as a newly emergent field of inquiry:

- "Interdisciplinary" . . . policy analysis takes in data from the social and physical sciences.
- "Empirical" . . . it uses quantitative methodologies.
- "Megapolicy" . . . it focuses upon the "fundamental problems of man in society, rather than upon the topical issues of the moment."
- "Theoretical complexity" . . . simple theories may be inadequate.
- "Applied" . . . policy research is for concrete, current problems, not abstract eventualities.
- "Normative/prescriptive" . . . it will support democratic government.
  (Lerner and Lasswell 1992, 227)

In an excellent compendium of the major works of public policy analysis, Stella Theodoulou has summarized approaches to public policy, models of who makes policy, and types of public policy. The three approaches she lists are systems theory (promoted by David Easton and others as described in Chapter 6), structural functionalism (also described in Chapter 6), and policy cycle analysis. Theodoulou maintains that the policy cycle approach "views the policy process as a cycle that is deliberative, staged, recursive, and administrative. Policy making is thus seen as a dynamic ongoing process confirming the importance of policy as a learning system" (Theodoulou 1995, 5).

Among the models of policy analysis that have appeared in the literature, Theodoulou finds group theory, elite theory, corporatism and subgovernments theory to be of particular importance. Elite theory espouses the idea that certain key individuals or groups of individuals hold a predominant place in the policy making process. Corporatism emphasizes the role of industries and economic systems in setting government policy. According to Theodoulou, group theory is based upon a pluralist interpretation of politics: "The central argument of both group theory and pluralism is that societies consist of a large number of social, ethnic, or economic groups, who are more or less well organized. These groups, in political competition with each other, put pressure on the government to produce policies favorable to them" (Theodoulou 1995, 5). The subgovernments model also emphasizes the influence of interest groups upon public policy. Subgovernments are "coalitions of members of Congress, the bureaucracy, and interest groups. . . . [which] tend to develop around those specialized areas of policy that have a low level of public interest and awareness" (Theodoulou 1995, 6). The subgovernment model, notes Theodoulou, has become outmoded in recent years as analysts have found the policy making process more complex than the model represents.

Theodoulou has summarized a number of the interesting ways in which policy has been categorized into different types and forms, three of which shall be mentioned here. Theodore Lowi finds that policies either regulate actions, distribute benefits (monetary or in other forms, such as permissions), or redistribute government benefits. Murray Edelman finds that policies are either material (money, or other tangible items) or symbolic (values such as freedom and justice). For James Anderson, policies are either substantial (that is, they provide actual tangible benefits or penalties) or procedural, which means they detail the manner in which something is to be done.

Having provided a brief introduction to public policy analysis, we now proceed to an example of a recent analysis, Maureen A. Pirog-Good and David H. Good's "Child Support Enforcement for Teenage Fathers: Problems and Prospects." This article is selected because it is typical of much policy analysis in its approach and presentation, and because it is an issue with which students are becoming increasingly familiar.

Reprinted by permission: Tribune Media Services.

When reading this article, consider the following questions and be prepared to discuss them in class:

1. How clearly and accurately have the authors identified a problem for policy analysis?
2. How clearly have the authors described current government policy concerning the problem they have identified?
3. How clearly and comprehensively have the authors examined alternative solutions to the problem they have identified?
4. What methods of analysis did the authors employ?
5. Are the methods of analysis appropriate to the subject matter?
6. What conclusions do the authors have to offer?
7. Are the conclusions offered justified by the evidence and the analysis that the authors present?

Child Support Enforcement for Teenage Fathers: Problems and Prospects

Maureen A. Pirog-Good
David H. Good

Abstract

Data from the NLSY (National Longitudinal Survey of Labor Market Experiences—Youth Cohort) indicate that about 7.3 percent of teenage males become fathers and that very few of these fathers live with their children. Father absence and the concurrent increase in female-headed households are closely associated with the impoverishment of children. Most absent teen fathers never come into contact with the child support enforcement program, and the extent to which they financially support their children informally is not well understood. While the income of absent teen fathers is low in the teen years, it increases over time, as does the potential for collecting child support. Nevertheless, men who were absent teen fathers earn less in early adulthood than men who deferred parenting until age 20 or later and teen fathers who lived with their children. Early establishment of paternity and greater standardization in the treatment of adolescent fathers by the child support enforcement program are recommended. Further, the substantial and persistent income deficit experienced by adolescent fathers who live apart from their children raises an interesting dilemma. While children may benefit financially and psychosocially from living with two parents, the lower income of men who were absent teenage fathers may make them poor marital prospects. This raises doubts about the recent recommendations of some scholars that we should bring back the shotgun wedding.

INTRODUCTION

While we know a great deal about adolescent mothers, relatively little is known about adolescent fathers, their educational and labor market outcomes, and their interactions with and impacts on their children. A growing literature on fathers, not specifically teen fathers, suggests that under certain circumstances, fathers promote the cognitive, educational, emotional, and developmental outcomes of their children, particularly boys [for reviews of the literature, see Radin, 1981; Lamb, 1981; or Lamb et al., 1987]. In light of these potential benefits, some have suggested that we should bring back the shotgun wedding [Chase-Lansdale and Vinovskis, 1987]. Others, however, have argued forcefully that it is irresponsible to encourage the highly unstable marriages of young adults [Furstenberg, 1988]. Legislative changes in the mid- and late 1980s have represented a compromise between these two positions by ensuring that more and more fathers take responsibility for their children through our nation's Child Support Enforcement (CSE) program. As

Maureen A. Pirog-Good and David H. Good, "Child Support Enforcement for Teenage Fathers: Problems and Prospects." In *Journal of Policy Analysis and Management,* Vol. 14, No. 1, 25–42 (1995).

the rate of births to young men between the ages of 15 and 19 is increasing dramatically, with a 12-percent increase between 1988 and 1989 alone [National Center for Health Statistics, 1991], it is important to clarify the extent to which teen fathers can assume financial responsibility for their children.

This article addresses this issue by identifying the ages at which young men become fathers and looking at their ability to pay child support. Using data from the National Longitudinal Survey of Labor Market Experiences—Youth Cohort (NLSY), this article further distinguishes the labor market experiences of adolescent fathers who live continually with their children from those who are the targets of the CSE program: young men who regularly or intermittently live apart from their children. Treatment of teen fathers by the CSE program is described, and the wholesale application of more rigorous CSE enforcement for this population is discussed in light of the short- and long-term potential of teen fathers to contribute to their children's economic well-being.

THE CSE PROGRAM AND
TEENAGE FATHERS

Nearly half of the children born today will live in a single-parent household before reaching their 18th birthday, and most of them will be potentially eligible to receive child support [Bumpass and Sweet, 1989]. The CSE program, Title IV-D of the Social Security Act, was enacted in 1975 to establish and enforce the support obligations of these children. States take the primary responsibility for administering the CSE program, although the federal government shares the administrative costs; monitors, evaluates, and provides technical assistance; and, under certain conditions, directly assists in locating absent parents and

obtaining support. Amendments to Title IV-D in 1984 and the Family Support Act of 1988 have provided states with a wider range of policy instruments to use in establishing paternities and support orders and enforcing those orders. An estimate of the number of teen fathers who come into contact with the CSE program and their movement through this system are described below.

Approximately 203,000 males become fathers each year after their 15th birthday and before age 20.[1] The percentage of these fathers who come into contact with the CSE program is undoubtedly less than the 30 percent rate for all unmarried fathers reported by the U.S. House of Representatives [1991, p. 720]. The paternity adjudication rate of 20 percent for teenage mothers in Wisconsin calculated by Danziger and Nichols-Casebolt [1988] is probably much closer, given that their figure is based solely on teens. If this rate is applied to teenage fathers, it suggests that approximately 40,600 young men become involved in paternity and child support proceedings each year.[2]

For teen fathers, movement through the CSE system begins with the establishment of paternity. Paternity can be established via criminal or civil proceedings, and can be contested by the putative father or established voluntarily in either type of proceeding. In contested cases, blood tests can be mandated, often pro-

[1] This figure was estimated using the birth rate of 22.4 births per 1000 males 15–19 years of age provided in National Center for Health Statistics [1991]. This rate was applied to the total number of 15–19-year-old males in the United States (resident population) from the U.S. Bureau of the Census [1990].

[2] Similar figures are given by Adams et al. [1989]. Unfortunately, all these figures are based on births to teenage mothers, not fathers. Data on the percentage of births to teenage men resulting in a paternity adjudication are not available at the state, regional, or federal level. Thus, the 40,600 figure should be viewed as a best estimate.

longing the paternity proceedings. One researcher found that when establishing paternity for teenage fathers, procedural delays are pervasive, generally ranging between 18 months and 5 years [Wattenberg, 1988]. Another study found that 84 percent of the paternity cases of teen fathers are contested and typically take over a year to adjudicate [Pirog-Good, 1988].

The court system does not work well for adolescent fathers. Even if a paternity defendant cannot afford an attorney, his right to court-appointed counsel is far from settled as a national issue [Kohn, 1987]. However, if the teenage father has not reached the age of majority (age 18 in most states), courts may appoint a guardian *ad litem*—usually a lawyer or one of the defendant's parents, depending on the state in which the paternity case is adjudicated. Unfortunately, guardians *ad litem* are not routinely available in paternity cases [Wattenberg, 1988; Pirog-Good, 1992]. Also, in civil paternity proceedings, a default judgment can be entered. Even if the alleged father does not appear in court, cooperate, contest, or acknowledge paternity, the court can find him to be the father. One survey found a variety of explanations for default judgments, including that the defendant does not understand his rights, cannot afford counsel, and is intimidated by the system—explanations that are likely to be especially true for teenagers [Kohn, 1987].

Some jurisdictions are reluctant to prosecute paternity cases while the absent parent is a minor. Nine states indicate that some teen fathers are so young that the states do not attempt to establish paternity [Pirog-Good, 1992]. A ten-state survey found that some paternities involving teen fathers were not adjudicated because the custodial parent either did not need or want paternal involvement, the CSE program could not locate the absent parent,

the potential for collection and cost recovery was low, a guardian *ad litem* was needed, or there were unresolved issues concerning counsel for indigent defendants [Kohn, 1987]. However, the probability of ever establishing a paternity diminishes with time [McLanahan, Monson, and Brown, 1992; Danziger and Nichols-Casebolt, 1988]. Thus, deferring paternity adjudications of teen fathers reduces the likelihood of ever legally establishing paternity.

Once paternity is established, the amount of the child support award must be determined. At the support stage, there is no body of state law suggesting that very young fathers should be held to a different standard because of their age [Danziger and Nichols-Casebolt, 1988]. In fact, national legislation continues to press states toward greater consistency in the amount of support awarded through state guidelines mandated by the 1984 amendments to Title IV-D. As a consequence of the 1988 Family Support Act, there is now a rebuttable presumption that the amount of child support awarded be the amount specified in a state's guidelines.

Factors considered in determining the amount of the child support award vary from state to state. In general, the obliger's ability to pay and the cost of raising the child figure prominently in this determination. However, even though a teen father may be unemployed and enrolled in school full-time, support may be ordered to establish the principle of the fathers' obligation to provide monetary support to his child.[3] More than half of all states have required some teen fathers

---

[3] For example, the Colorado child support guidelines (revised August 1987) indicate that a specific amount of child support should always be ordered, no matter how minimal, so as to establish the absent parent's obligation to provide monetary support.

under age 16 to pay child support [Pirog-Good, 1992].

While the use of state guidelines may have reduced within-state variation in the amounts of support awarded, there remains considerable variation across states for obligers in identical economic circumstances. For example, using 1989 state guidelines, an absent father earning $720 per month would be required to pay $27/month in New York but $325/month in Indiana for two children [Pirog-Good, 1993a]. The extent to which judges and CSE administrators are willing to relax state guidelines for teenage fathers, particularly in states where high support awards are the norm, is simply not known.

The limited available evidence suggests that, before the Family Support Act, the weekly support obligations of teenage fathers ranged from $0 to $50. Some jurisdictions did not require support from teenage fathers, while others routinely sought token awards of $5 to $15 per week [Kohn, 1987]. One study of 333 teenage fathers found average support awards of $21.40 in 1984 [Pirog-Good 1988]. A second larger study of 1,250 young (but not necessarily teenage) fathers found an average weekly award of $25.20 between 1980 and 1985 [Danziger and Nichols-Casebolt, 1988].

After a child support order has been obtained, the CSE program enforces that order. Since 1984, there has been enormous growth in the tools available to CSE program administrators for support collection. These tools now include automatic wage withholding, delinquency notices, regular billings, liens on personal and real property, reporting of arrearage to credit bureaus, seizure and sale of property, garnishment of wages, federal and state tax garnishment, the interception of unemployment benefits, civil or criminal contempt-of-court charges for nonsup-

port, and incarceration. Unfortunately, little is actually known about the effectiveness of these tools in procuring support from teenagers.

To summarize, the treatment of teenage fathers by the CSE program is not well understood at a national level. Although there is greater uniformity in the amount of child support ordered within states, across-state variation is the norm. With regard to the establishment of paternity and support orders and the enforcement of child support for teen fathers, within-state uniformity is the exception. State and local jurisdictions are denied the benefit of a well-articulated national policy on the treatment of teenage fathers. This lack of direction undoubtedly stems in large part from our lack of information about the characteristics of the teenage father population, knowledge that we attempt to provide in this article. The data and methods used in this study are described in the next section, which is followed by a description of the size of the teenage father population, their ability to pay child support, and the ramifications of different collection strategies.

THE DATA AND METHODS

In this study, we use the National Longitudinal Survey of Labor Market Experiences—Youth Cohort (NLSY). It is a nationally representative, thirteen-year panel including data on 6,403 males who were 14–21 years of age in 1979, the initial survey year. Data through 1991 are currently available. Annual response rates are high, with 90.5 percent of respondents interviewed in 1991 [Center for Human Resource Research, 1992]. Because the NLSY oversampled blacks, Hispanics, and poor whites, the data contain a larger absolute number of teenage fathers than would be present in a purely random survey. Although the number of teen fathers varies across survey years, there are approximately 650 teenage fathers who can be identified in the NLSY. This study utilizes the NLSY weights for each respondent in each survey year. These weights reflect the probability of each person's inclusion in the sample, allowing us to generate national estimates from the data.

The NLSY is conducted with well-trained interviewers and focuses primarily on less sensitive issues such as labor market experiences, rather than on more personal issues such as fertility. Nevertheless, enough data on fertility are available for the purposes of our analysis. The fertility data are not without problems, however. A 1983 study of the NLSY fertility data found discrepancies that could not be resolved for 28 percent of the male respondents who had reported a live birth as of the 1982 survey. The most common inconsistency was the acknowledgment of the birth of a child for the first time in 1982, even though the child had been born before the 1981 survey [Mott, 1983]. In the present study, the male fertility data were used simply to determine if the respondent had a biological child in his teen years. Hence, a serious problem was not presented by the late reporting of births, which was likely due to new knowledge of births, as well as delayed willingness on the part of some respondents to acknowledge paternity. Since the youngest respondent turned 20 in 1985, there were at least six years to capture late reports of births to teens.

On the other hand, a 1985 study of the NLSY male fertility data suggests that births to males ages 20–24 in 1982 may have been underreported by as much as 15 percent, with underreporting more pronounced among black respondents [Mott, 1985]. Although some of the young men who became fathers in 1982 waited until *after* 1982 to report that they had fathered a child, others *never* reported this fact. Unfortunately, we know of no obvious way in which to correct for births that were never reported. There are two implications of the underreporting problem for this research. First, the sample of young men who acknowledged births is undoubtedly biased in favor of fathers who have taken responsibility for their children. Second, the differences between teen fathers and young men who deferred parenting are likely to be understated since it is likely that some young men who were teen fathers were erroneously included with the young men who deferred parenting. Further, because underreporting was most pronounced among nonwhites, differences between nonwhite teen fathers and other nonwhites will be the most seriously understated.

Several additional methodological points merit elaboration. First, the presence or absence of a teen father was assessed for each child born during the respondent's teen years. A father was considered to be present for a given child when he was reported to be living with the child during each of the four years following the child's birth. If he was not living with the child during any of the four years, he was considered absent. In a few cases, either because the child was born before the beginning of the survey or because the respondent was not administered the survey for a particular year, the respondent was considered to be present as long as he was present for all years for which data were available, and data were available for the fourth year. Further, to be considered present, a father must be present for a four-year period for every child born during his teen years. These criteria resulted in the identification of 236 teen fathers as present, 414 as absent, and 20 as missing.

Our choice of the four-year period was

driven by two objectives. On the one hand, we wanted to be able to include information about the very young fathers in our sample, yet at the same time, we wanted to subject each father to the same hazard.[4] Were we to choose a shorter period, we would lose several cases where the child was born prior to the beginning of the survey. Were we to choose a longer period, we would lose several cases where the fifth-year data were not yet available for the youngest cohort of teen fathers in the NLSY. In addition, using a longer period would have tilted the sample toward the behavior of 25+-year-olds, where divorce and separation are much more likely to occur for both teen and nonteen fathers. We also rejected using information about living arrangements only during the respondent's teen years since this would subject the teens to differential hazards. It would exaggerate the likelihood that the older teen fathers were much more likely to remain with their children than the younger teen fathers, because it would subject 19-year-old fathers to the hazard of divorce or separation for less than one year, while it would subject the youngest teen father in our sample to this hazard for more than eight years.

The definition of income also requires some elaboration. Our definition includes

earnings from wages, salary, commissions, and tips from all jobs, where employment in the formal and informal sectors is not distinguished. Also included in our definition of income are military earnings, profits from businesses owned by the respondent, and unearned income (dividends, interest, and so forth). We used this definition because it provides the most comprehensive representation of the resources available for fathers to share with their children. One possible alternative would exclude business profits and unearned income from income as these sources of income would be more difficult for a child support office to attach. Nevertheless, we felt that it was important to identify all the financial resources of young men, regardless of the difficulty of securing this income as child support. Further, we used the income earned over a calendar year to describe the annual income of each respondent at his age on June 30 of the calendar year, and all incomes were measured in real terms using 1982–1984 as the base period. Consequently, the 1983 poverty threshold was used in determining whether the incomes of adolescent fathers were below the poverty line.

Since our objective is to identify the short- and long-term consequences of teenage paternity, it was essential to summarize the income data from individuals at different ages. One standard way to deal with this situation is to aggregate individuals of similar ages together, for instance, young men ages 16–17, and use sample means to summarize the age-income data. However, this approach muddies the age-income profiles. For example, young men who were nearly 17 and who had just turned 17 would be placed in different age categories, even though their earning powers are presumably quite similar. This is particularly problematic because earn-

---

[4] Our use of the term *hazard* is consistent with the survival analysis literature to describe the probability that a failure (in our case, an absent teen father) will occur at some time. Practicality dictates that we measure this phenomena over an *interval* rather than at an instant in time. Obviously, for an individual at a given level of risk of failure, the longer the measurement period, the higher this probability. Consequently, we must use a time interval of the same length for all individuals. Were we to do otherwise, two individuals at the same level of risk would, on average, result in different probabilities of failure over their respective intervals. (We call this the differential hazards problem.) It is essential to be sensitive to this potential problem and use the same length time period for all individuals.

ing power is changing rapidly over the period of interest. Although we wanted to summarize the income data, we wanted to impose as few restrictions on the shape of the age-income profiles as possible. We chose to do this by modeling the age-income profiles using regression analysis with a tenth-order Taylor series expansion about the sample mean ages. While not commonly used in the social sciences, this approach is common in the engineering response function literature [Box and Draper, 1987]. Sensitivity analysis indicated that very little structure was imposed by the tenth-order series on the age-income profiles we generated. Higher order series produced virtually identical results. Further, this approach substantially smoothed the age-income profile, but made it virtually impossible to extrapolate beyond the range of the sample. In fact, only three months after and end of our sample (age 32), confidence intervals for the expected income increased dramatically to over $50,000 wide. Although the tenth-order polynomial introduced substantial collinearity among regressors, the predicted values of the dependent variable, income, were quite stable.

TEENAGE FATHERS AND THEIR ABILITY TO PAY CHILD SUPPORT

All Teen Fathers and Absent Teen Fathers

Examination of the weighted NLSY data reveals that at least 7.3 percent of all males become fathers prior to the age of 20 in the United States. Further, 57.0 percent of these young men do not live with their children. Figure 1a indicates the percentage of all young men who become teen fathers and absent teen fathers between the ages of 14 and 20. Ninety-five percent confidence intervals for both series are

represented by the dotted lines. Figures 1b and 1c provide the same information for whites and nonwhites, respectively. Figure 1a illustrates that most males who become teen fathers do so between the ages of 17 and 20.

By the age of 17, only 0.79 percent of the male population has become a teen father and 0.52 percent of the male population can be classified as absent teen fathers. Even when analysis is restricted to males who eventually became teen fathers, only 10.8 percent of all teen fathers and 12.4 percent of absent teen fathers achieve this status before age 17. However, as seen in Figures 1b and 1c, these patterns are substantially different for whites and nonwhites.[5] Only 5.8 percent of white males become teen fathers, in contrast to 15.1 percent of nonwhites. Further, very early parenting—having a child before age 17—is more than eight times more common among minorities than whites. Fully 2.9 percent of nonwhite males become parents before age 17. Moreover, this race differential in early parenting is undoubtedly understated, as births to black males are the most seriously underreported in the NLSY.

The fact that teen fatherhood is much more common among older teens, both whites and minorities, is somewhat heartening, given that the youngest fathers are the least likely to possess the maturity and financial ability to contribute to the support of their children. Further, due to the length of time required to adjudicate pa-

[5] Nonwhites include blacks and individuals of other races. There were insufficient observations on individuals of other races to perform separate analyses. For our analyses, there were 4,323 white males, 1,589 black males, and 361 males of other races with complete information. Once these data are weighted using the NLSY weights to generate nationally representative statistics, white, black, and other males constitute 82.7, 13.8, and 2.9 percent of the sample, respectively.

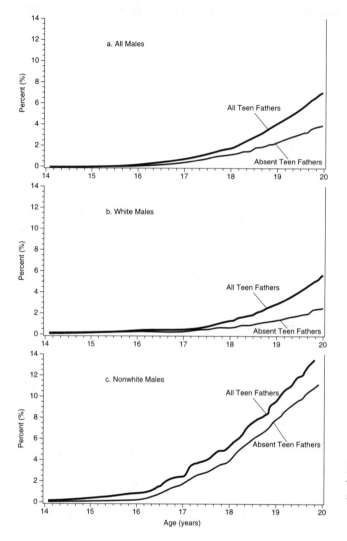

Figure 1. Percentage of men
who become teenage fathers
and absent teenage fathers.
(a) All males. (b) White males.
(c) Nonwhite males.

ternity cases, the CSE program probably has to deal with very few young men who are legally prohibited from holding most jobs because of their age. However, some very young putative fathers will come into contact with the CSE program; consequently, it is important for CSE jurisdictions to establish and implement guidelines to safeguard the rights of very young teenage fathers. This will become more important given the increasing trends toward adolescent paternity and the use of

expedited paternity processes mandated by the Family Support Act.

All Teens Fathers and Males Who Delay Parenting Until Age 20 or Later

To determine the extent to which young fathers can support their children, the age-income profile of teenage fathers was compared to the age-income profile of young men who never became teen fathers. Figure 2a provides this information for all males, while comparable information for whites and nonwhites is given in Figures 2b and 2c. Dotted lines provide 95-percent confidence intervals for the average in each series.

First, Figure 2a shows that the average income of all teenage males before age 16 is quite minimal, and, consequently, rigorous enforcement of child support orders can be questioned on both practical and ethical grounds. Second, teenage fathers enter the labor force earlier than their nonfather peers. Between the ages of 17 and 22, teenage fathers have higher incomes than their nonfather peers. This may reflect an attempt by the teen fathers to support their children. Alternatively, the characteristics or environments of some young men may incline them to enter the labor force as well as have children. Third, teenage fathers consistently have lower average incomes after age 23 than the young men who were never teen fathers. These differences in income are

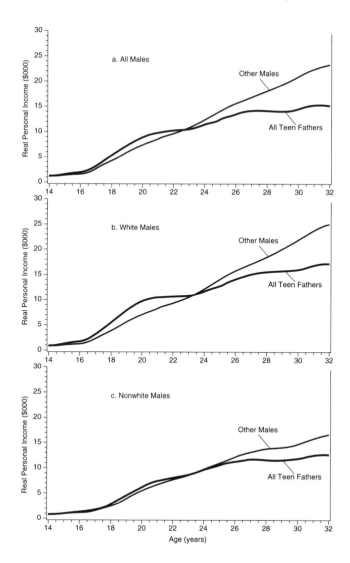

Figure 2. Age-income profiles for teenage fathers and other males. (a) All males. (b) White males. (c) Nonwhite males.

quite large. On average, by age 30, teen fathers earn only $13,783—roughly two thirds of the earnings of males who delay parenting until age 20 or later. By age 32, this difference increases to nearly 40 percent or $8,475 per year.

This early labor force entrance and lower income after age 23 are consistent with the fact that teen fathers complete fewer years of education than do their nonfather peers. The NLSY data used for this study show that by age 23, only 64.7 percent of teen fathers have a high school diploma or GED compared to 84.9 percent of other young men ($p < 0.0001$). On average, by age 23, teen fathers have completed 12.35 years of formal schooling, 2.14 fewer years than men who deferred parenting until after age twenty ($p < 0.0001$). This larger human capital investment of nonfathers eventually translates into higher incomes for this group.

Figures 2b and 2c show somewhat different patterns for whites and nonwhites. The pattern for whites parallels that of all males but is slightly more pronounced. White teen fathers initially have larger incomes than other white males until age 23. By age 32, white teen fathers earn on average only $17,100, compared to $25,672 for other white males. For minorities, however, the age-income profiles of teen fathers and other males are much more similar to one another. The averages are statistically indistinguishable until age 26, when the incomes of nonwhite teen fathers fall short of the incomes of other nonwhite men. Still, by age 32, the average income of nonwhite teen fathers is $4,692 less than the $16,509 income of other nonwhite males. The fact that the incomes of minority teen fathers and other minority males are similar until age 26 most likely results from fewer work opportunities being available for this population. Moreover, readers should recall that income dif-

ferentials between teen fathers and nonteen fathers (all, whites, and nonwhites) are likely to be larger than reported here because of the underreporting of teenage paternity, particularly among nonwhites.

Thus, Figure 2 clearly indicates that the price of teen fatherhood (in terms of forgone income) is lower for nonwhite males than whites. At age 32, white teen fathers earn $8,572 less or 66.6 percent of the income of other white males, whereas nonwhite teen fathers earn $4,692 less, or 71.6 percent of the income of nonwhite males who delay parenting until age 20 or later. An appropriate policy response to this price differential is unclear. One way to raise the price of teen fatherhood might involve initially limiting the labor market opportunities of teen fathers. However, this approach is objectionable for two reasons. First, teen fathers should be encouraged to regularly provide some economic support for their children, and limiting job opportunities would conflict with this objective. Second, raising the price of teen fatherhood for nonwhites by limiting their job opportunities would rightfully meet with cries of injustice, as discrimination in the labor market is undoubtedly one of the reasons why the price of teen fatherhood is lower for nonwhite males. It would appear that if we want to raise the price of adolescent paternity for teen fathers, we must search for nonpecuniary approaches, perhaps requiring parenting classes and more shared responsibilities for child care.

Teen Fathers Who Live with and Apart from Their Children

Unfortunately, from the perspective of collecting child support, teenage fathers are not a homogeneous lot. Fathers who live apart from their children have different labor market experiences than do fathers who live with their children. This is demonstrated by comparing the age-income profile of absent teen fathers with that of teen fathers who live with their children, as shown in Figure 3a. Figures 3b and 3c provide the same comparisons for whites and nonwhites, respectively. Again, 95-percent confidence intervals for average incomes are represented in both series by dotted lines.

Figure 3a shows that the incomes of young fathers who live with or apart from their children are statistically indistin-guishable until they reach 17.4 years of age, after which males living with their children have higher average incomes. By age 25, men who live apart from their children have incomes of only $10,288, or approximately 70 percent of the incomes of present fathers. By age 30, this difference increases to $4,477, leaving absent fathers only 73 percent of the income of men living with their children.

Because Figures 3b and 3c deal only with white and nonwhite teen fathers, the

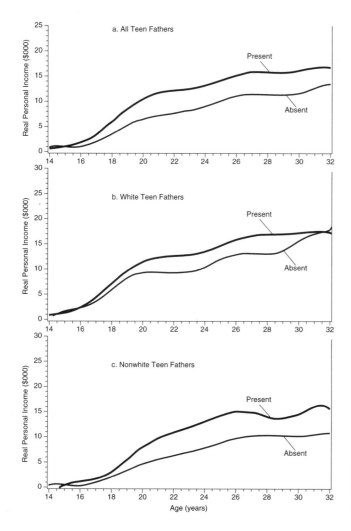

Figure 3. Age-income profiles for present and absent teenage fathers. (a) All males. (b) White males. (c) Nonwhite males.

number of observations on which the age-income profiles are based is necessarily smaller than in Figure 3a or earlier figures. The smaller sample sizes, particularly for absent white fathers and present nonwhite fathers, result in larger confidence intervals surrounding the age-income profiles. Nevertheless, the patterns for whites and nonwhites are remarkably similar. Men who live with their children generally have higher incomes than men living apart from their children. However, these income differentials are more pronounced among nonwhites. For example, for nonwhite males between the ages of 20 and 30, the income of absent teen fathers is as little as 58.6 percent and never exceeds 75.7 percent of the income of teen fathers who live with their children. In contrast, over this same time interval, the income of absent white fathers ranges between 71.8 percent and 93.8 percent of the income of white fathers living with their children.

These findings are consistent with the hypothesis of Wilson [1987] that some men are absent fathers because they are financially incapable of supporting a family. If this thesis is correct, it would explain why a much higher percentage of minority males live apart from their children. An alternative explanation is that some characteristics of absent teen fathers make them inclined to remain apart from their children and underemployed. In either case, the implications of these findings for the CSE program are discouraging. If young men who are the least capable of providing financially for their children are more likely to be absent fathers, this self-selectivity will necessarily make it more difficult for the CSE program to collect child support.

That the income of absent fathers typically falls short of the income of men who live with their children does not necessar-

ily imply that they are not attempting to earn additional income to support their offspring. To examine their motivation, differences in the incomes of absent and present teenage fathers before and after the birth of their children were compared. In Figure 4, zero on the horizontal axis refers to the point of birth, with positive and negative values referring to the number of years after and before the birth of the first child, respectively.

Several interesting conclusions can be drawn from Figure 4a. First, the increase in income at the point of the birth is statistically significant for men who live apart from their children (though at only the 10 percent level). On average, the annual income of absent fathers one month after the birth is $1,788 or 45.6 percent greater than it has been one month before the birth. This suggests that even absent fathers attempt and are somewhat successful at earning additional income to provide for their children. In comparison, the increase in income at the point of birth is not statistically significant for men who live with their children. This finding probably reflects better opportunities or planning on the part of these young men, whose incomes exceed those of absent fathers as early as 22 months *before* the first birth. Second, men who live with their children have higher incomes before the birth and during the 10-year period after the first birth. Three months after the birth and continuing thereafter, the income of absent fathers is roughly two thirds the income of men who live with their children. These differences are not inconsequential. Following the birth of the child, men who live with their children have incomes sufficient to support a family of three at 111 percent of the 1983 poverty threshold for a family of three. At the same time, the income of absent fathers is only 70.9 percent of the poverty threshold

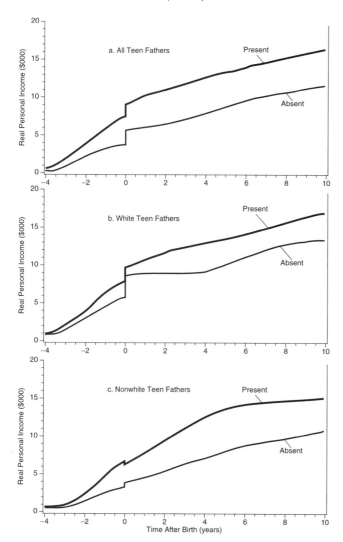

Figure 4. Earnings profiles before and after first teenage birth. (a) All teen fathers. (b) White teen fathers. (c) Nonwhite teen fathers.

for a family of three. Not until nearly four years after the birth is the income of absent fathers adequate to support a family of three at the poverty threshold.

Figures 4b and 4c provide the same information for whites and nonwhites, respectively. For whites, the profiles generally follow the same pattern described above, although at higher levels of income. For the 10-year period following birth, absent fathers generally earn 75–80 percent of the income of present teen fa-

thers. Still, the white absent teen father's average income of $8,715 one year after birth and $10,050 five years after the child's birth is adequate to support a family of three at the poverty threshold level of $8,015, reflecting the higher incomes of white teen fathers in general. In stark contrast in Figure 4c, nonwhite absent fathers earn an average of only $4,423 (55.3 percent of present teen fathers) one year after the birth of the child, partially reflecting their younger age. Not until approximately five years after the first child's birth do nonwhite absent fathers earn enough to support a family of three at the poverty level. These differences between white and nonwhite absent fathers may explain why a much smaller percentage of white teen fathers live apart from their children. The NLSY data indicate that, at age 19, only 46.7 percent of white teen fathers are absent parents, in contrast to 81.7 percent of minority fathers.

Overall, these results suggest that while the typical absent teen father earns income and can provide some support for his children, the magnitude of the support award deserves serious consideration given the heterogeneity of individual income levels. A total of 52.3 percent of absent teenage fathers lived in poverty households at the time of the birth of their first child. The strict enforcement of significant support orders will push the households of even more teenage fathers below the poverty threshold. Under the Wisconsin model, the amount of child support awarded is equivalent to 17 percent of gross income for one child, and 25, 29, 31, and 34 percent, respectively, for two, three, four, or five more children. Strictly applying even this modest guideline for support awards would push an additional 2.3 percent of the households of teen fathers into poverty. Alternatively, a flat support award of $25 per week would increase the percentage of teen father households in poverty by 5.1 percent to 57.5 percent. Thus, because of the low economic resources of the households of many absent teenage fathers, rigorous CSE enforcement may result in merely shifting poverty, along with its societal burdens, from one household to another. Providing disincentives to prospective teen fathers and fairness to the children of teenage males must be weighed against the likely increases in poverty in teen fa-

ther households that will result from collecting child support from adolescent males.

Practically speaking, the income available for child support is very limited for very young fathers. At age 16, the annual income of absent fathers is $896. Even if every dollar of income were used for child support, this would equal only $17.23 per week. Further, if child support is viewed as an income tax by absent parents, then given the low earnings of very young absent fathers, even moderate child support awards may seriously discourage work among this population. Hence, if we wish to encourage very young fathers to take financial responsibility for their children by establishing token awards, the size of these awards must be quite low. However, although the income of absent teen fathers remains typically lower than that of other men, it increases during the late teens and early twenties. By age 20, the annual income of absent fathers is $6,488, and by age 23 it is $8,258. Hence, establishment of paternity and frequent modifications of support awards to reflect the increases in earnings of young fathers should be encouraged.

DISCUSSION

Despite the underreporting of births to adolescent males in the NLSY, our results confirm that teenage fatherhood, and in particular *absent* teenage fatherhood, is a serious social problem. The majority of programs that deal with teen parenting, such as supplemental education programs, are directed toward mothers. We suggest that teen fathers merit special attention. Further, absent adolescent fatherhood poses a serious dilemma. On the one hand we want these individuals to be responsible for their actions. On the other hand, they are clearly unable to provide the same kind of financial support that we would expect of adults. This has a variety of implications for the operation of the CSE program.

The 1988 Family Support Act set goals for the number of paternities established by states, with financial penalties for states failing to meet these goals. It makes no distinctions in cases dealing with adolescent fathers. The increased emphasis on paternity establishment should be supported and encouraged even for minor putative fathers, given that the probability of ever establishing paternity declines over time. By failing to establish paternity, children cannot obtain child support orders, are denied Social Security and Worker's Compensation coverage in the event of injury or death of the absent parent, and may be denied access to potentially important medical records [Children's Defense Fund, 1987].

Since the benefits of establishing paternity are numerous, it is shocking that paternity is established for such a small percentage of absent teenage fathers. The vast majority of absent teenage fathers fail to come into contact with the CSE program [U.S. House of Representatives, 1991; Danziger and Nichols-Casebolt, 1988]. Whether or not these fathers make private arrangements with the mothers of their children to provide support is not well documented. It is likely that paternity is never established for many children simply because their custodial parents are unaware of the benefits of paternity establishment and services provided by the CSE program. Outreach services to middle and high schools should clarify the services available for teen parents. More research is needed to ascertain the well-being of the children of the vast majority of teenage fathers who fall outside the purview of the CSE program.

When a paternity case is adjudicated for an absent father who is a teenager, local jurisdictions must make the putative father aware of the implications of paternity establishment, his right to contest the paternity, and his right, if it exists, to a guardian *ad litem* or court-appointed counsel. When the defendant has a right to a guardian *ad litem* or court-appointed legal counsel, these rights must be safeguarded. Further, a national resolution to the debate concerning the right to court-appointed legal representation for indigent defendants is clearly warranted.

Our study suggests that judges should have considerable discretion when setting the amount of child support awards. While greater uniformity in the amount of support awards is generally desirable, departures from state guidelines should not be discouraged for teenage fathers. Such departures will avoid setting unrealistically high support awards that may contribute to the early departure of our youth from schools and the shifting of poverty from household to household. This is particularly important given that the majority of absent teenage fathers already live in poor households. Further, the impacts of token child support awards for teenage fathers on their support compliance during adulthood are simply not known. Research on this topic is needed.

Attention should also be focused on the few CSE programs across the country that have adopted innovative approaches in their dealings with teen fathers [for a description of several of these programs, see Association of Maternal and Child Health Programs, 1991]. For example, the Teen Alternative Parenting Program (TAPP) in Marion County, Indiana, allows young fathers to use in-kind credits for the payment of child support. Each father signs one or more 90-day contracts in which a certain amount of child support will be considered "paid" if the youth completes a week of school without any unexcused absences, attends parenting classes, babysits his child, and/or attends GED, vocational education, or training classes. The emphasis on child care and developing good parenting skills in TAPP explicitly acknowledges that fathers, even young absent fathers, can contribute in many ways to the development of their children [Pirog-Good, 1993b]. In a program offered through the Department of Social Services on behalf of the New York City CSE program, teen fathers volunteer to receive education and training and counseling on parenting, budgeting, and sex education. In exchange for these services, the fathers provide items such as diapers or milk toward the support of their children. Yet another possibility is to suspend child support payments for in-school fathers until the summer and Christmas recesses when they might be expected to work to support their child, labor market conditions permitting. The success and replicability of these approaches should become an objective of the CSE program at a national level.

If an alleged absent father has not been informed of his right to contest paternity or informed of his right, if it exists, to court-appointed counsel or a guardian *ad litem,* or if the amount of child support ordered is unrealistically high, then vigorous enforcement of child support orders raises very serious ethical problems. However, provided that the rights of teenage fathers are protected when establishing paternity and that reasonable support award amounts are mandated, child support orders should be enforced. If a teenage father has the ability to pay child support and refuses, the enforcement techniques used for adults should be applied to juveniles. However, the CSE program would clearly benefit from research designed to determine the short- and long-run effec-

tiveness of the myriad of policy instruments available to elicit child support. Further, such research should clearly distinguish between the adult and juvenile populations of obligers as the effectiveness of these instruments are likely to be very different for these populations.

Finally, the lower income of absent fathers implies that there are fewer resources for the CSE program to tap and that the potential financial benefits of the marriage of mothers and absent fathers discussed by Chase-Lansdale and Vinovskis [1987] may be overstated. Also, the lower income of absent fathers lends some support to the notion that some men do not form families because they cannot afford to support themselves and their children. However, our research does not address whether the low income of absent fathers is a consequence of poor economic opportunities and whether low income is why some men remain apart from their children. Nevertheless, these hypotheses are clearly consistent with our data. Alternatively, it is also possible that the characteristics of absent fathers incline them to perform poorly in the labor market and remain absent from their children. This distinction is critical and should be researched further, particularly given the recent emphasis on work programs for absent parents whose children are supported by AFDC.

Support from the Office of Adolescent Pregnancy Programs, U.S. Department of Health and Human Services, is gratefully acknowledged. Work on this article was conducted in part while Maureen A. Pirog-Good was a visiting scholar at the Institute for Research on Poverty at the University of Wisconsin-Madison and while David H. Good was a visiting scholar at the LaFollette School of Public Affairs at the University of Wisconsin-Madison.

MAUREEN A. PIROG-GOOD is Associate Professor in the School of Public and Environmental Affairs, Indiana University.

DAVID H. GOOD is Associate Professor in the School of Public and Environmental Affairs, Indiana University.

REFERENCES

Adams, Charles, David Landsbergen, and Larry Cobler (1989), "Welfare Reform and Paternity Establishment: A Social Experiment." Presented at the 1989 meeting of the Association for Public Policy Analysis and Management.

Association of Maternal and Child Health Programs (1991), *Adolescent Fathers: Directory of Services* (Washington, DC: National Center for Education in Maternal and Child Health).

Bumpass, Larry L. and James A. Sweet (1989), "Children's Experience in Single-Parent Families: Implications of Cohabitation and Marital Transition," *Family Planning Perspectives* 21(6), pp. 256–259.

Box, George and N. R. Draper (1987), *Empirical Model Building and Response Surfaces* (New York: Wiley).

Center for Human Resource Research (1992), *NLS Update: The National Longitudinal Surveys of Labor Market Experience* (Fall), pp. 1–2.

Chase-Lansdale, P. Lindsay, and Maris A. Vinovskis (1987), "Should We Discourage Teenage Marriage?" *The Public Interest* 87 (Spring), pp. 23–37.

Children's Defense Fund (1987), *Child Support and Teen Parents*. Adolescent Pregnancy Prevention Clearinghouse.

Danziger, Sandra K. and Ann Nichols-Casebolt (1988), "Teen Parents and Child Support: Eligibility, Participation and Payment," *Journal of Social Service Research* 11(2-3), pp. 1–20.

Furstenberg, Frank F., Jr. (1988), "Bringing Back the Shotgun Wedding," *The Public Interest* 90 (Winter), pp. 121–127.

Kohn, Margaret A. (1987), *Child Support Enforcement and Young Unwed Fathers* (Washington, DC: National Legal Resource Center for Child Advocacy and Protection, American Bar Association) pp. 1–65.

Lamb Michael E. (1981), "Fathers and Child Development: An Integrative Overview," in Michael E. Lamb (ed.), *The Role of the Father in Child Development* (New York: Wiley), pp. 1–70.

Lamb, Michael E., Eric L. Charnov, and James A. Levine (1987), "A Biosocial Perspective on Paternal Behavior and Involvement," in Jane B. Lancaster, Jeanne Altman, Alice S. Rossi, and Lonnie R. Sherrod (eds.), *Parenting Across the Lifespan: Biosocial Dimensions* (New York: Aldine de Gruyter), pp. 111–142.

McLanahan, Sara, Renee Monson, and Pat Brown (1992), "Paternity Establishment for AFDC Mothers: Three Wisconsin Counties," in *Paternity Establishment: A Public Policy Conference, Vol. 2: Studies of the Circumstances of Mothers and Fathers.* Institute for Research on Poverty Special Report 56B, University of Wisconsin-Madison, pp. 157–190.

Mott, Frank L. (1983), "Fertility-Related Data in the 1982 National Longitudinal Surveys of Work Experience of Youth: An Evaluation of Data Quality and Some Preliminary Analytical Results" (Columbus, OH: Center of Human Resource Research, Ohio State University).

Mott, Frank L. (1985), "Evaluation of Fertility Data and Preliminary Analytical Results from the 1983 (5th Round) Survey of the National Longitudinal Surveys of Work Experience of Youth" (Columbus, OH: Center for Human Resource Research, Ohio State University).

National Center for Health Statistics (1991), *Advance Report of Final Natality Statistics, 1989.* Monthly Vital Statistics Report 40(8), suppl. (Hyattsville, MD: Public Health Service).

Pirog-Good, Maureen A. (1988), "Teenage Paternity, Child Support and Crime," *Social Science Quarterly* 69(3), pp. 527–546.

Pirog-Good, Maureen A. (1992), "Teen Fathers and the Child Support Enforcement System," in *Paternity Establishment: A Public Policy Conference, Vol. 2: Studies of the Circumstances of Mothers and Fathers.* Institute for Research on Poverty Special Report 56B, University of Wisconsin-Madison, pp. 157–190.

Pirog-Good, Maureen A. (1993a), "Child Support Guidelines and the Economic Well-Being of Our Nation's Children," *Family Relations* 24(4), pp. 453–462.

Pirog-Good, Maureen A. (1993b), "In-Kind Contributions as Child Support: The Teen Alternative Parenting Program," in Theadora Ooms and Robert Lerman (eds.), *Young Unwed Fathers: Changing Roles and Emerging Policies* (Philadelphia, PA: Temple University Press), pp. 251–266.

Radin, Norma (1981), "The Role of the Father in Cognitive, Academic, and Intellectual Development," in Michael E. Lamb (ed.), *The Role of Father in Child Development* (New York: Wiley), pp. 379–428.

U.S. Bureau of the Census (1990), *U.S. Population Estimates, by Age, Sex, Race, and Hispanic Origin: 1989.* Current Population Reports Series P-25, No. 1057 (Washington, DC: GPO).

U.S. House of Representatives, Committee on Ways and Means (1991), *Background Material and Data on Programs within the Jurisdiction of the Committee on Ways and Means* (Washington, DC).

Wattenberg, Esther (1988), "Young, Unmarried Parents and Paternity Decisions: What Is Known and Not Known." Paper prepared for the Child Support Research Conference, Department of Health and Human Services, Washington, DC.

Wilson, William J. (1987), *The Truly Disadvantaged* (Chicago: University of Chicago Press).

10 American Government: Constitutional Law

> *A people which is able to say everything becomes able to do everything.*
>
> —Napoleon Bonaparte
>
> *We are rapidly entering the age of no privacy, where everyone is open to surveillance at all times; where there are no secrets from government.*
>
> —William O. Douglas

An Introduction to Constitutional Law

American constitutional law is the study of the Constitution of the United States of America, laws passed pursuant to the mandates and protections of the Constitution, and decisions of Courts interpreting the Constitution. Constitutional law is studied in law schools in preparation for legal practice in state and national courts and is studied by political scientists as a vital part of the governmental and political process. Constitutional law defines who we are as a society, what we value, and what we consider to be fundamental fairness. Constitutional law determines our freedoms and obligations and provides the standards against which we are judged if we infringe upon the values of the community. It is our ultimate refuge if we are oppressed or falsely accused.

The published writings on constitutional law in the United States alone would fill a large library, and the same could be said of many other nations. Political scientists who study constitutional law examine the decisions of the Supreme Court primarily, but other materials such as treaties, legislation, and other court decisions are studied as well. Topics normally covered include:

- Fundamental freedoms of the first amendment: religion, speech, press, assembly, and issues in fundamental freedoms, including abortion and obscenity
- Amendments beyond the Bill of Rights
- Anti-trust laws
- Citizenship
- Civil rights and discrimination
- Congressional powers
- Due process of law

- Elections
- Equal protection of the laws
- Federalism
- Incorporation of the Bill of Rights: its application to the States
- Interstate commerce
- Jurisdiction of the courts
- Labor rights and laws
- Military operations and war
- Obligations of contracts

- Other freedoms, including search and seizure, self-incrimination immunity, cruel and unusual punishment immunity, and right to counsel
- Political questions beyond the Court's jurisdiction
- Presidential powers

- Separation of powers
- State executive powers
- State judicial powers
- State legislative powers
- Taxing and spending powers of governments
- Treaties and executive agreements

A close look at one of these topics should help us gain an initial understanding of how constitutional law progresses through a series of Supreme Court decisions. We have selected the issue of abortion because, of all of the issues of vast importance (civil rights, religious freedom) that have been addressed by the Supreme Court, it is the most widely contested and still unresolved issue of the last third of the twentieth century.

A Brief History of the Abortion Issue in the United States Supreme Court

The practice of abortion extends back through centuries, and an American history of abortion as a legal issue begins at least with the framing of the Constitution. Although the Constitution does not mention the word abortion, it also does not mention many aspects of life, such as computers, automatic weapons, and prayer, that fall within the bounds of constitutional protection or restriction. Of direct importance to the issue of abortion, however, are at least the following sections of the Constitution:

- Article I, Section 8 : The Congress shall have Power . . . To make all Laws which shall be necessary and proper for carrying into Execution the foregoing powers, and all other Powers vested by this Constitution in the government of the United States, or in any Department or Officer thereof.
- Article III Section 2: In all Cases affecting Ambassadors, or other public Ministers and Consuls, and those in which a State shall be a party, the Supreme Court shall have original Jurisdiction. In all the other cases before mentioned, the Supreme Court shall have appellate jurisdiction, both as to Law and Fact, with such Exceptions, and under such Regulations as Congress shall make.
- Article VI : This Constitution, and the Laws of the United States which shall be made in Pursuance thereof; and all Treaties made, or which shall be made, under the authority of the United States, shall be the supreme Law of the Land; and the Judges in every State shall be bound thereby, anything in the Constitution or Laws of any State to the contrary notwithstanding.

- Amendment IX: The enumeration in the Constitution of certain rights, shall not be construed to deny or disparage others retained by the people.
- Amendment X: The powers not delegated to the United States by the Constitution, nor prohibited to the States, are reserved to the States respectively, or to the people.
- Amendment XIV: No state shall make or enforce any law which shall abridge the privileges or immunities of citizens of the United States; nor shall any State deprive any person of life, liberty, or property, without due process of law; nor deny to any person within its jurisdiction the equal protection of the laws.

With these articles of the Constitution in mind, we shall consider some of the most important cases in the history of the controversy over abortion in order to see how the Supreme Court gradually shapes and forms constitutional law. Supreme court cases not only define the course of law, but the language in which laws are written provides a fascinating window through which to view prevailing social attitudes within a specific period in time. Notice the content, language, and attitude displayed in Justice Holmes' rendition of the facts of the case in his decision in *Buck v. Bell* (1927). If this decision were to be written today, how would its content be different?

> Carrie Buck is a feeble minded white woman who was committed to the State Colony above mentioned in due form. She is the daughter of a feeble minded mother in the same institution, and the mother of an illegitimate feeble minded child. She was eighteen years old at the time of the trial of her case in the Circuit Court, in the latter part of 1924. An Act of Virginia, approved March 20, 1924, recites that the health of the patient and the welfare of society may be promoted in certain cases by the sterilization of mental defectives, under careful safeguard, &c.; that the sterilization may be effected in males by vasectomy and in females by salpingectomy, without serious pain or substantial danger to life; that the Commonwealth is supporting in various institutions many defective persons who if now discharged would become a menace but if incapable of procreating might be discharged with safety and become self-supporting with benefit to themselves and to society; and that experience has shown that heredity plays an important part in the transmission of insanity, imbecility, &c. The statute then enacts that whenever the superintendent of certain institutions including the above named State Colony shall be of opinion that it is best for the interests of the patients and of society that an inmate under his care should be sexually sterilized, he may have the operation performed upon any patient afflicted with hereditary forms of insanity, imbecility, &c.; on complying with the very careful provisions by which the act protects the patients from possible abuse.

Justice Holmes concluded in his decision that the Virginia law which allowed involuntary sterilization was reasonable in its protection of the interests of society, and of the rights of individuals, and that Carrie Buck could, therefore, be involuntarily sterilized. The thrust of this decision is to limit the rights of individuals in favor of the rights of society. In the decades after this decision, in many areas of law, the Court began to gradually move toward favoring individual rights. In the area of reproductive rights, the major cases begin with *Griswold v. Connecticut* (1965). Griswold, who was the Executive Director of the Planned Parenthood League of Connecticut, was convicted of violating a Connecticut statute that made it a criminal offense to use contraceptives or to provide information about contraceptives to married people. When his conviction was upheld in appeals courts, Griswold appealed to the Supreme Court, claiming that the Constitution guarantees a right of privacy which includes the use of medical means to prevent conception. The first issue for the Court to decide, then, was whether a right of privacy did exist. In his decision for the Court, Justice William O. Douglas first notes that although the word "privacy" appears nowhere in the Constitution, it is still possible that a constitutionally protected right of privacy exists:

> The association of people is not mentioned in the Constitution nor in the Bill of Rights. The right to educate a child in a school of the parent's choice—whether public or private or parochial—is also not mentioned. Nor is the right to study any particular subject or any foreign language. Yet the First Amendment has been construed to include certain of those rights. . . . In NAACP v. Alabama, 357 U.S. 449, 462, we protected the "freedom to associate and privacy in one's associations," noting that freedom of association was a peripheral First Amendment right . . . . In other words, the First Amendment has a penumbra where privacy is protected from governmental intrusion.

Justice Douglas here employs a metaphor. A penumbra, in astronomy, is the visible glow that forms around the sun or moon during an eclipse. If the Bill of Rights has a penumbra, then, it is said to emanate rights not explicitly mentioned in it. The right of privacy, Justice Douglas decides, is an emanation of the Bill of Rights just as a glow emanates from the sun during an eclipse. Having decided that the right to privacy is constitutionally protected, the Court must next decide whether or not the right to privacy includes the right to use contraception.

> The present case, then, concerns a relationship lying within the zone of privacy created by several fundamental constitutional guarantees. And it concerns a law which, in forbidding the use of contraceptives rather than regulating their manufacture or sale, seeks to achieve its goals by means of having a maximum destructive impact upon that relationship. Such a law cannot stand in light of the familiar principle, so often applied by this Court, that a "governmental purpose to control or prevent activities constitutionally subject to state regulation may not be achieved by means which sweep unnecessarily broad and thereby invade the area of unprotected freedoms." . . . Would we allow the police to search the sacred precincts of marital bedrooms for telltale signs of the use of contraceptives? The very idea is repulsive to the notions of privacy surrounding the marriage relationship.

The Griswold decision established a right of privacy, and included in that right freedoms related to procreation. Looming on the horizon was the question of a woman's right to terminate a pregnancy, which had been denied by some of the states. Knowing that a decision on this controversy was unavoidable, Justice Harry Blackmun spent the summer of 1972 at the Mayo Clinic, where he studied the biological aspects of abortion. His decision in *Roe v. Wade* (1973) is now the most well known case in the Court's history.

Having previously decided that a right to privacy exists, and that it covers the area of contraception, the Court was next confronted by three basic questions:

1. Does the right to privacy include the right to abort a human fetus?
2. Is this right absolute, or may it be regulated by the state in some circumstances to protect rights of society or the fetus?
3. If the right is not absolute, what kinds of regulations may the state apply?

The Court always makes decisions on questions such as these within the context of a particular case that has come before it. *Roe v. Wade* involved a woman who had violated Texas abortion statutes, which made it a criminal offense to perform or procure an abortion except for one which was necessary to protect the health and safety of the mother. In respect to the first basic question, Justice Blackmun's decision affirmed that "The right of privacy . . . is broad enough to encompass a woman's decision whether or not to terminate her pregnancy."

With respect to the second question, concerning whether or not the right is absolute, Justice Blackmun declared:

> [S]ome amici [briefs filed by interested parties not directly involved in the case] argue that the woman's right is absolute and that she is entitled to terminate her pregnancy at whatever time, in whatever way, and for whatever reason she alone chooses. With this we do not agree. . . . [A] state may properly assert important interests in safeguarding health, in maintaining medical standards, and in protecting potential life. . . . The privacy right involved, therefore, cannot be said to be absolute.

If the right to an abortion is not absolute, then what restrictions may be imposed? The Roe decision first swept aside the proposition that human life begins at conception and that a fetus, therefore, has a constitutional right to life from the moment of conception. "We do not agree that, by adopting one theory of life, Texas may override the rights of the pregnant woman that are at stake." At what point, then, may a state regulate abortion? Blackmun reasoned as follows:

> With respect to the State's important and legitimate interest in the health of the mother, the "compelling" point, in the light of present medical knowledge, is at approximately the end of the first trimester [the first three months of pregnancy]. This is so because of the now established fact . . . that until the end of the first trimester mortality in abortion is less than mortality in normal childbirth. It follows that, from and after this point, a State may regulate the abortion procedure to the extent that the regulation reasonably relates to the preservation and protection of maternal health.

Blackmun continued to say that during the third trimester the fetus is viable outside the womb, and that the state may regulate abortions to save a fetus during that period. The Court's rule in *Roe v. Wade*, therefore, set up a schedule for admissible state restriction of abortions:

- First trimester: no restrictions (except as may concern the quality of acceptable medical procedures, etc.).
- Second trimester: restrictions for the purpose of preserving the health of the mother.

- Third trimester: the state may regulate in the interests of the fetus or the mother.

In an associated case, *Roe v. Bolton* (1973), the Court declared unconstitutional restrictions on places used to perform abortions, allowing abortion clinics to operate. Since 1973 numerous cases have been heard by the Court on related issues, some of them altering, in one way or another, the substance of the Roe decision. We shall summarize some of these decisions.

In *Planned Parenthood v. Danforth* (1976), the Court invalidated a Missouri law which required the husband's consent before a married woman could have an abortion, and insisted that parents of unwed girls could not have an absolute veto over their daughter's abortion decision. In *Maher v. Roe* (1977), the Court decided that states are not required to pay for abortions for poor women. In *Colautti v. Franklin* (1979), a Pennsylvania law requiring doctors to choose the abortion method most likely to save the life of the fetus was declared unconstitutional. *Bellotti v. Baird* (1979) established that, if a state law requires the parent's consent for a minor's abortion, the law must provide an alternative form of permission, such as permission from a judge.

In 1976, Congressman Henry Hyde of Illinois attached an amendment to the Labor-HEW appropriations bill for that year that stated, "None of the funds contained in this Act shall be used to perform abortions except where the life of the mother would be endangered if the fetus were carried to term." This amendment was upheld by the Court in *Harris v. McRae* (1980). The decision in *Akron v. Akron Center for Reproductive Health* (1983) invalidated an Akron ordinance's requirement of parental consent, a 24-hour waiting period, and the provision that all second-trimester abortions be performed in a hospital. In *Thornburgh v. American College of Obstetricians and Gynecologists* (1986), the Court invalidated a Pennsylvania requirement that women be provided "informed consent" information which was meant to discourage abortions.

Due to retirement of some of the Court's liberal justices, and the appointment of conservative justices by Presidents Reagan and Bush, decisions in the 1980s started to become more accepting of state regulation of abortions. *Webster v. Reproductive Health Services* (1989) had the appearance of a slight turning point for the court, for it upheld certain elements of a Missouri law restricting abortions. The preamble of the law made a statement that the Court had struck down in the past: "The life of each human being begins at conception." The Court said that in this particular law this statement was merely an expression of belief which had no regulatory effect and, therefore, was permissible. The Court also upheld the Missouri law's provisions that state funds could not be used for abortions, that public officials could not perform or assist in performing abortions, and that fetal viability testing was mandatory.

In *Planned Parenthood of Southeastern Pennsylvania v. Casey*, the Court rejected the formula of *Roe v. Wade*, which allowed states different alternatives in each trimester. Still upholding Roe's protection of a right to an abortion, the Court instituted a more flexible policy that said that state regulations will be valid if they do not impose an "undo burden" on women by creating "substantial obstacles" to her in her attempt to get an abortion. Substantial obstacles, according to this decision, include a husband's permission, but not provisions such as:

- Informing patients of the dangers of abortions,
- A 24-hour waiting period,
- Consent of parents *or* a judge for minors, or
- Reporting information on abortions to the state.

The case reprinted in this text presents an interesting example, not only of a recent development in the abortion controversy, but also of a situation in which different constitutional rights at times collide. In *NOW v. Scheidler* (1994), a law intended to restrict racketeering (the Racketeer Influenced and Corrupt Organizations [RICO] chapter of the Organized Crime Control Act of 1970) is used by abortion advocates to curtail violence against abortion clinics conducted by abortion opponents. Printed below are:

- A summary of the Brief of the Petitioners, the written argument presented by NOW and others who have brought the case in order to get the respondents to end their disruption of abortion clinics
- A summary of the Brief of the Respondents, the written argument presented by the people charged with violating RICO, including Joseph Scheidler
- The Opinion of the Court, delivered by Chief Justice William Rehnquist
- A concurring opinion by Justice Souter

As you read this case, consider the following questions, and be prepared to discuss them in class:

1. Who are the participants, on both sides, in the case?
2. What actually happened, that is, what are the facts of the case?
3. What constitutional issue(s) is raised in the case?
4. What arguments are presented by the petitioners?
5. What arguments are presented by the respondents?
6. What is the decision of the Court?
7. What are the constitutional grounds of the Court's decision?

National Organization for Women, Inc. v. Joseph M. Scheidler, et al.

SUMMARY OF ARGUMENT (petitioners)

The economic motive requirement that the Seventh Circuit imposed on § 1962(c) finds no support in the text of RICO. The creation of this non-textual requirement contravenes Congress's directive that RICO is to be interpreted broadly. Examination of the Organized Crime Control Act ("OCCA"), of which RICO is a part, underscores the breadth of RICO's provisions by revealing the contrast between RICO and other, more limited portions of the OCCA.

While there is no need to look beyond RICO's plain and unambiguous text, the legislative history of RICO supports its plain language. Congress expressly rejected versions of the bill that would have limited RICO to profitseeking enterprises or to predicate acts motivated by financial concerns.

For more than a decade, this Court has rebuffed lower courts' attempts to engraft unwritten requirements onto RICO. This Court's decisions underscore the impropriety of imposing limitations not found in the definitions of "enterprise" and "racketeering activity." Congress defined the terms "enterprise" and "racketeering activity" clearly and precisely, avoiding any need to look for hidden meanings in them or to judicially amend the terms, as the lower courts did.

The economic motive requirement that the Seventh Circuit has imposed is vague, uncertain and problematic. It would invite the weighing of subjective racial, religious, political, psychological and social motivations that have no place in RICO cases. Such a requirement would severely hamper the effectiveness of RICO, render already complex cases unmanageable and impose tremendous burdens on the courts.

In enacting RICO, the economic elements that concerned Congress were the effect of concerted criminal conduct on businesses and interstate commerce, not the motives of the perpetrators of criminal acts. In this case, there is no question that the defendants' highly-organized, nationwide campaign of terrorism against clinics that perform abortions has injured the business and property of these clinics and their patients. This is the only economic requirement that RICO imposes.

However, if the Court were to open the Pandora's box of economic motives, there are ample facts contained in the Complaint and RICO Case Statement to permit NOW and the clinics to proceed with discovery and trial. The well-pled facts show that the defendants' motives include the desire for the substantial economic benefits that they receive from their wrongful conduct. Most of the defendants had low-paying jobs before being elevated into positions in the enterprise that compensate them lucratively. The defendants' unlawful work is done for money, and most of the defendants have no business outside their employment by the enterprise or its member organizations.

The defendants and their enterprise profit from their acts of violence, and they have hidden portions of the proceeds received in support of their violent crimes to keep these assets safe from court fines and civil judgments. This in itself indicates economic motive. The defendants and their enterprise have other economic aspects, as well, for they operate with all the accoutrements of profit-seeking businesses, including budgets, employees, staff, and modern equipment.

The lower court dismissed this case on a Rule 12(b)(6) motion. While there is no principled or practical reason to enmesh the courts in an inquiry about motives, if the Court were to affirm the Seventh Circuit's economic motive requirement, NOW and the clinics should be given the opportunity to prove that it has been satisfied. The complaint alleged economic purposes and benefits that should not have been ignored when the lower court created this requirement.

SUMMARY OF THE ARGUMENT (respondents)

Reading the text of RICO in conjunction with its legislative history, which we believe this Court is compelled to do in light of its previous method of interpreting the statute and its interpretive jurisprudence in the analogous area of antitrust law, this Court should determine that dismissal of the Petitioners' Complaint is warranted.

RICO does not apply to social and political protest activities that are not, as an objective matter, directed toward an economic goal. Because the Petitioners have failed to allege, and after years of discovery they have been unable to assert, that any of the Respondents directed their actions toward financial objectives, they have failed to satisfy that test. This is particularly true with regard to Respondent Migliorino, who was affirmatively alleged to have been a mere "volunteer" in her pro-life activities in opposition to abortion.

In addition, most of the conduct alleged against Migliorino is presumptively protected under the First Amendment, and as to the remaining allegations, they fail to assert that any of that conduct was directed toward "wrongful" goals, thus precluding a finding of "extortion" under the Hobbs Act, the only RICO predicate asserted by the Petitioners.

Lastly, the Petitioners have failed to assert any valid conspiracy claim against Migliorino under RICO.

This Court should affirm, in its entirety, the Court of Appeals judgment, dismissing the Complaint of the Petitioners.

OPINION OF THE COURT

Chief Justice Rehnquist delivered the opinion of the Court.

[1a] We are required once again to interpret the provisions of the Racketeer Influenced and Corrupt Organizations (RICO) chapter of the Organized Crime Control Act of 1970 (OCCA), Pub L 91-452, Title IX, 84 Stat 941, as amended, 18 USC §§ 1961–1968 (1988 ed and Supp IV) [18 USCS §§ 1961–1968]. Section 1962(c) prohibits any person associated with an enterprise from conducting its af-

fairs through a pattern of racketeering activity. We granted certiorari to determine whether RICO requires proof that either the racketeering enterprise or the predicate acts of racketeering were motivated by an economic purpose. We hold that RICO requires no such economic motive.

I

Petitioner National Organization For Women, Inc. (NOW) is a national non-profit organization that supports the legal availability of abortion; petitioners

Delaware Women's Health Organization, Inc. (DWHO) and Summit Women's Health Organization, Inc. (SWHO) are health care centers that perform abortions and other medical procedures. Respondents are a coalition of antiabortion groups called the Pro-Life Action Network (PLAN), Joseph Scheidler and other individuals and organizations that oppose legal abortion, and a medical laboratory that formerly provided services to the two petitioner health care centers.[1]

Petitioners sued respondents in the United States District Court for the Northern District of Illinois, alleging violations of the Sherman Act, 26 Stat 209, as amended, 15 USC § 1 *et seq.* [15 USCS §§ 1 *et seq.*], and RICO's §§ 1962(a), (c), and (d), as well as several pendent state-law claims stemming from the activities of antiabortion protesters at the clinics. According to respondent Scheidler's congressional testimony, these protesters aim to shut down the clinics and persuade women not to have abortions. See, *e.g.*, Abortion Clinic Violence, Oversight Hearings before the Subcommittee on Civil and Constitutional Rights of the House Committee on the Judiciary, 99th Cong, 1st and 2d Sess, 55 (1987) (statement of Joseph M. Scheidler, Executive Director, Pro-Life Action League). Petitioners sought injunctive relief, along with treble damages, costs, and attorneys' fees. They later amended complaint, and pursuant to local rules, filed a "RICO Case Statement" that further detailed the enterprise, the pattern of racketeering, the victims of the racketeering activity, and the participants involved.

The amended complaint alleged that respondents were members of a nationwide conspiracy to shut down abortion clinics through a pattern of racketeering activity including extortion in violation of the Hobbs Act, 18 USC § 1951 [18 USCS § 1951].[2] Section 1951(b)(2) defines extortion as "the obtaining of property from another, with his consent, induced by wrongful use of actual or threatened force, violence, or fear, or under color of official right." Petitioners alleged that respondents conspired to use threatened or actual force, violence or fear to induce clinic employees, doctors, and patients to give up their jobs, give up their economic right to practice medicine, and give up their right to obtain medical services at the clinics. App 66, Second Amended Complaint ¶ 97. Petitioners claimed that this conspiracy "has injured the business and/or property interests of the [petitioners]." *Id.*, at 72, ¶ 104. According to the amended complaint, PLAN constitutes the alleged racketeering "enterprise" for purposes of § 1962(c). *Id.*, at 72–73, ¶¶ 107–109.

The District Court dismissed the case pursuant to Federal Rule of Civil Procedure 12(b)(6). Citing *Eastern Railroad Presidents Conference v Noerr Motor Freight, Inc.*, 365 US 127, 5 L Ed 2d 464, 81 S Ct 523 (1961), it held that since the activities alleged "involve[d] political opponents, not commercial competitors, and political ob-

---

[1] The other respondents named in the complaint include the following: John Patrick Ryan, Randall A. Terry, Andrew Scholberg, Conrad Wojnar, Timothy Murphy, Monica Migliorino, Vital-Med Laboratories, Inc., Pro-Life Action League, Inc. (PLAL), Pro-Life Direct Action League, Inc. (PDAL), Operation Rescue, and Project Life.

[2] The Hobbs Act, 18 USC § 1951(a) [18 USCS § 1951(a) provides: "Whoever in any way or degree obstructs, delays, or affects commerce or the movement of any article or commodity in commerce, by robbery or extortion or attempts or conspires so to do, or commits or threatens physical violence to any person or property in furtherance of a plan or purpose to do anything in violation of this section shall be fined not more than $10,000 or imprisoned not more than twenty years, or both." Respondents contend that petitioners are unable to show that their actions violated the Hobbs Act. We do not reach that issue, and express no opinion upon it.

jectives, not marketplace goals," the Sherman Act did not apply. 765 F Supp 937, 941 (ND Ill 1991). It dismissed petitioners' RICO claims under § 1962(a) because the "income" alleged by petitioners consisted of voluntary donations from persons opposed to abortion which "in no way were derived from the pattern of racketeering alleged in the complaint." *Ibid.* The District Court then concluded that petitioners failed to state a claim under § 1962(c) since "an economic motive requirement exists to the extent that some profit-generating purpose must be alleged in order to state a RICO claim." *Id.,* at 943. Finally, it dismissed petitioners' RICO conspiracy claim under § 1962(d) since petitioners' other RICO claims could not stand.

The Court of Appeals affirmed 968 F2d 612 (CA7 1992). As to the RICO counts, it agreed with the District Court that the voluntary contributions received by respondents did not constitute income derived from racketeering activities for purposes of § 1962(a). *Id.,* at 625. It adopted the analysis of the Court of Appeals for the Second Circuit in *United States v Ivic,* 700 F2d 51 (CA2 1983), which found an "economic motive" requirement implicit in the "enterprise" element of the offense. The Court of Appeals determined that "noneconomic crimes committed in furtherance of noneconomic motives are not within the ambit of RICO." 968 F2d, at 629. Consequently, petitioners failed to state a claim under § 1962(c). The Court of Appeals also affirmed dismissal of the RICO conspiracy claim under § 1962(d).

We granted certiorari, 508 US ——, 125 L Ed 2d 659, 113 S Ct 2958 (1993), to resolve a conflict among the courts of appeals on the putative economic motive requirement of 18 USC § 1962(c) and (d) [18 USCS § 1962(c) and (d)]. Compare *United States v Ivic,* supra, and *United States v Flynn,* 852 F2d 1045, 1052 (CA8) ("For

purposes of RICO, an enterprise must be directed toward an economic goal"), cert denied, 488 US 974, 102 L Ed 2d 546, 109 S Ct 511 (1988), with *Northeast Women's Center, Inc. v McMonagle,* 886 F2d 1342 (CA3), cert denied, 493 US 901, 107 L Ed 2d 210, 110 S Ct 261 (1989) (because the predicate offense does not require economic motive, RICO requires no additional economic motive).

II

[2, 3, 4a] We first address the threshold question raised by respondents of whether petitioners have standing to bring their claim. Standing represents a jurisdictional requirement which remains open to review at all stages of the litigation. *Bender v Williamsport Area School Dist.,* 475 US 534, 546–547 89 L Ed 2d 501, 106 S Ct 1326 (1986). Respondents are correct that only DWHO and SWHO, and not NOW, have sued under RICO.[3] Despite the fact that the clinics attempted to bring the RICO claim as class actions, DWHO and SWHO must themselves have standing. *Simon v Eastern Ky. Welfare Rights Organization,* 426 US 26, 40, n 20, 48 L Ed 2d 450, 96 S Ct 1917 (1976) citing *Warth v Seldin,* 422 US 490, 502, 45 L Ed 2d 343, 95 S Ct 2197 (1975). Respondents are wrong, however, in asserting that the complaint alleges no "injury" to DWHO and SWHO "fairly traceable to the defendant's allegedly unlawful conduct." *Allen v Wright,* 468 US 737, 751, 82 L Ed 2d 556, 104 S Ct 3315 (1984).

---

[3] NOW sought class certification for itself, its women members who use or may use the targeted health centers, and other women who use or may use the services of such centers. The District Court did not certify the class, apparently deferring its ruling until resolution of the motions to dismiss. All pending motions were dismissed as moot when the court granted respondents' motion to dismiss. 765 F Supp 937, 945 (ND Ill 1991).

[4b] We have held that "[a]t the pleading stage, general factual allegations of injury resulting from the defendant's conduct may suffice, for on a motion to dismiss we presume that general allegations embrace those specific facts that are necessary to support the claim." *Lujan v Defenders of Wildlife,* 504 US ——, ——, 119 L Ed 2d 351, 112 S Ct 2130 (1992) (citations omitted). The District Court dismissed petitioners' claim at the pleading stage pursuant to Federal Rule of Civil Procedure 12(b)(6), so their complaint must be sustained if relief could be granted "under any set of facts that could be proved consistent with the allegations." *Hishon v King & Spalding,* 467 US 69, 73, 81 L Ed 2d 59, 104 S Ct 2229 (1984). DWHO and SWHO alleged in their complaint that the respondents conspired to use force to induce clinic staff and patients to stop working and obtain medical services elsewhere. App 66, Second Amended Complaint ¶ 97. Petitioners claimed that this conspiracy "has injured the business and/or property interests of the [petitioners]." *Id.,* at 72, ¶ 104. In addition, petitioners claimed that respondent Scheidler threatened DWHO's clinic administrator with reprisals if she refused to quit her job at the clinic. *Id.,* at 68, ¶ 98(g). Paragraphs 106 and 110 of petitioners' complaint incorporate these allegations into the § 1962(c) claim. *Id.,* at 72, 73. Nothing more is needed to confer standing on DWHO and SWHO at the pleading stage.

III

[1b] We turn to the question of whether the racketeering enterprise or the racketeering predicate acts must be accompanied by an underlying economic motive. Section 1962(c) makes it unlawful "for any person employed by or associated with any enterprise engaged in, or the activities of which affect, interstate or foreign com-

merce, to conduct or participate, directly or indirectly, in the conduct of such enterprise's affairs through a pattern of racketeering activity or collection of unlawful debt." Section 1961(1) defines "pattern of racketeering activity" to include conduct that is "chargeable" or "indictable" under a host of state and federal laws.[4] RICO broadly defines "enterprise" in § 1961(4) to "includ[e] any individual, partnership, corporation, association, or other legal entity, and any union or group of individuals associated in fact although not a legal en-

---

[4] Section 1961(1) provides: " 'racketeering activity' means (A) any act or threat involving murder, kidnaping, gambling, arson, robbery, bribery, extortion, dealing in obscene matter, or dealing in narcotic or other dangerous drugs, which is chargeable under State law and punishable by imprisonment for more than one year; (B) any act which is indictable under any of the following provisions of title 18, United States Code: Section 201 (relating to bribery), section 224 (relating to sports bribery), sections 471, 472, and 473 (relating to counterfeiting), section 659 (relating to theft from interstate shipment) if the act indictable under section 659 is felonious, section 664 (relating to embezzlement from pension and welfare funds), sections 891-894 (relating to extortionate credit transactions), section 1029 (relating to fraud and related activity in connection with access devices), section 1084 (relating to the transmission of gambling information), section 1341 (relating to mail fraud), section 1343 (relating to wire fraud), section 1344 (relating to financial institution fraud), sections 1461-1465 (relating to obscene matter), section 1503 (relating to obstruction of justice), section 1510 (relating to obstruction of criminal investigations), section 1511 (relating to the obstruction of State or local law enforcement), section 1512 (relating to tampering with a witness, victim, or an informant), section 1513 (relating to retaliating against a witness, victim, or an informant), section 1951 (relating to interference with commerce, robbery, or extortion), section 1952 (relating to racketeering) . . . (C) any act which is indictable under title 29, United States Code, section 186 (dealing with restrictions on payments and loans to labor organizations) or section 501(c) (relating to embezzlement from union funds), or (D) any offense involving fraud connected with a case under title 11, fraud in the sale of securities, or the felonious manufacture, importation, receiving, concealment, buying, selling, or otherwise dealing in narcotic or other dangerous drugs, punishable under any law of the United States."

tity." Nowhere in either § 1962(c), or in the RICO definitions in § 1961, is there any indication that an economic motive is required.

The phrase "any enterprise engaged in, or the activities of which affect, interstate or foreign commerce" comes the closest of any language in subsection (c) to suggesting a need for an economic motive. Arguably an enterprise engaged in interstate or foreign commerce would have a profit-seeking motive, but the language in § 1962(c) does not stop there; it includes enterprises whose activities "affect" interstate or foreign commerce. Webster's Third New International Dictionary 35 (1969), defines "affect" as "to have a detrimental influence on—used especially in the phrase *affecting commerce.*" An enterprise surely can have a detrimental influence on interstate or foreign commerce without having its own profit-seeking motives.

The Court of Appeals thought that the use of the term "enterprise" in §§ 1962(a) and (b), where it is arguably more tied in with economic motivation, should be applied to restrict the breadth of use of that term in § 1962(c). 968 F2d, at 629. Respondents agree, and point to our comment in *Sedima, S. P. R. L. v Imrex Co.,* 473 US 479, 489, 87 L Ed 2d 346, 105 S Ct 3275 (1985), regarding the term "violation," that "[w]e should not lightly infer that Congress intended the term [violation] to have wholly different meanings in neighboring subsections."

We do not believe that the usage of the term "enterprise" in subsections (a) and (b) leads to the inference that an economic motive is required in subsection (c). The term "enterprise" in subsections (a) and (b) plays a different role in the structure of those subsections than it does in subsection (c). Section 1962(a) provides that it "shall be unlawful for any person who has received any income derived, directly or indirectly, from a pattern of racketeering activity . . . to use or invest, directly or indirectly, any part of such income, or the proceeds of such income, in acquisition of any interest in, or the establishment or operation of, any enterprise which is engaged in, or the activities of which affect, interstate or foreign commerce." Correspondingly, § 1962(b) states that it "shall be unlawful for any person through a pattern of racketeering activity or through collection of an unlawful debt to acquire or maintain, directly or indirectly, any interest in or control of any enterprise which is engaged in, or the activities of which affect, interstate or foreign commerce." The "enterprise" referred to in subsections (a) and (b) is thus something acquired through the use of illegal activities or by money obtained from illegal activities. The enterprise in these subsections is the victim of unlawful activity and may very well be a "profit-seeking" entity that represents a property interest and may be acquired. But the statutory language in subsections (a) and (b) does not mandate that the enterprise be a "profit-seeking" entity; it simply requires that the enterprise be an entity that was acquired through illegal activity or the money generated from illegal activity.

By contrast, the "enterprise" in subsection (c) connotes generally the vehicle through which the unlawful pattern of racketeering activity is committed, rather than the victim of that activity. Subsection (c) makes it unlawful for "any person employed by or associated with any enterprise . . . to conduct or participate . . . in the conduct of such enterprise's affairs through a pattern of racketeering activity. . . ." Consequently, since the enterprise in subsection (c) is not being acquired, it need not have a property interest that can be acquired nor an economic motive for engaging in illegal activity; it need only be an association in fact that engages in a pattern of racketeering activity.[5] Nothing in subsections (a) and (b) directs us to a contrary conclusion.

The Court of Appeals also relied on the reasoning of *United States v Bagaric*, 706 F2d 42 (CA2), cert denied, 464 US 840, 78 L Ed 2d 128, 104 S Ct 133, 104 S Ct 134, (1983), to support its conclusion that subsection (c) requires an economic motive. In upholding the dismissal of a RICO claim against a political terrorist group, the *Bagaric* court relied in part on the congressional statement of findings which prefaces RICO and refers to the activities of groups that " 'drain[ ] billions of dollars from America's economy by unlawful conduct and the illegal use of force, fraud, and corruption.' " 706 F2d, at 57, n 13 (quoting OCCA, 84 Stat 922). The Court of Appeals for the Second Circuit decided that the sort of activity thus condemned required an economic motive.

We do not think this is so. Respondents and the two courts of appeals, we think, overlook the fact that predicate acts, such as the alleged extortion, may not benefit the protestors financially but still may drain money from the economy by harming businesses such as the clinics which are petitioners in this case.

We also think that the quoted statement of congressional findings is a rather thin reed upon which to base a requirement of economic motive neither expressed nor, we think, fairly implied in the operative sections of the Act. As we said in *H. J. Inc. v Northwestern Bell Telephone Co.*, 492 US

229, 248, 106 L Ed 2d 195, 109 S Ct 2893 (1989), "[t]he occasion for Congress' action was the perceived need to combat organized crime. But Congress for cogent reasons chose to enact a more general statute, one which, although it had organized crime as its focus, was not limited in application to organized crime."

In *United States v Turkette*, 452 US 576, 69 L Ed 2d 246, 101 S Ct 2524 (1981), we faced the analogous question of whether "enterprise" as used in § 1961(4) should be confined to "legitimate" enterprises. Looking to the statutory language, we found that "[t]here is no restriction upon the associations embraced by the definition: an enterprise includes any union or group of individuals associated in fact." *Id.*, at 580, 69 L Ed 2d 246, 101 S Ct 2524. Accordingly, we resolved that § 1961(4)'s definition of enterprise "appears to include both legitimate and illegitimate enterprises within its scope; it no more excludes criminal enterprises than it does legitimate ones." *Id.*, at 580-581, 69 L Ed 2d 246, 101 S Ct 2524. We noted that Congress could easily have narrowed the sweep of the term "enterprise" by inserting a single word, "legitimate." *Id.*, at 581, 69 L Ed 2d 246, 101 S Ct 2524. Instead, Congress did nothing to indicate that "enterprise" should exclude those entities whose sole purpose was criminal.

The parallel to the present case is apparent. Congress has not, either in the definitional section or in the operative language, required that an "enterprise" in § 1962(c) have an economic motive.

The Court of Appeals also found persuasive guidelines for RICO prosecutions issued by the Department of Justice in 1981. The guidelines provided that a RICO indictment should not charge an association as an enterprise, unless the association exists " 'for the purpose of maintaining operations directed toward an

---

[5] One commentator uses the terms "prize," "instrument," "victim," and "perpetrator" to describe the four separate roles the enterprise may play in section 1962. See Blakey, The RICO Civil Fraud Action in Context: Reflections on *Bennett v Berg*, 58 Notre Dame L Rev 237, 307-325 (1982).

economic goal . . . .' " The Second Circuit, in *United States v Ivic, supra,* believed these guidelines were entitled to deference under administrative law principles. See 700 F2d, at 64. Whatever may be the appropriate deference afforded to such internal rules, see, *e.g., Crandon v United States,* 494 US 152, 177, 108 L Ed 2d 132, 110 S Ct 997 (1990) (Scalia, J., concurring in judgment), for our purposes we need note only that the Department of Justice amended its guidelines in 1984. The amended guidelines provide that an association-in-fact enterprise must be "directed toward an economic *or other identifiable goal.*" US Dept. of Justice, United States Attorney's Manual § 9-110.360 (Mar. 9, 1984) (emphasis added).

Both parties rely on legislative history to support their positions. We believe the statutory language is unambiguous, and find in the parties' submissions respecting legislative history no such "clearly expressed legislative intent to the contrary" that would warrant a different construction. *Reves v Ernst & Young,* 507 US ——, 122 L Ed 2d 525, 113 S Ct 1163, (1993), citing *United State v Turkette,* 452 US 576, 580, 69 L Ed 2d 246, 101 S Ct 2524 (1981), quoting *Consumer Product Safety Comm'n v GTE Sylvania, Inc.,* 447 US 102, 108, 64 L Ed 2d 766, 100 S Ct 2051 (1980).

[1c, 5, 6a] Respondents finally argue that the result here should be controlled by the rule of lenity in criminal cases. But the rule of lenity applies only when an ambiguity is present; "it is not used to beget one. . . . The rule comes into operation at the end of the process of construing what Congress has expressed, not at the beginning as an overriding consideration of being lenient to wrongdoers." *Turkette, supra,* at 587-588, n 10, 69 L Ed 2d 246, 101 S Ct 2524 (quoting *Callanan v United States,* 364 US 587, 596, 5 L Ed 2d 312, 81 S Ct 321 (1961) (footnote omitted)). We

simply do not think there is an ambiguity here which would suffice to invoke the rule of lenity. "[T]he fact that RICO has been applied in situations not expressly anticipated by Congress does not demonstrate ambiguity. It demonstrates breadth." *Sedima,* 473 US, at 499, 87 L Ed 2d 346, 105 S Ct, 3275 (quoting *Haroco, Inc. v American Nat. Bank & Trust Co. of Chicago,* 747 F2d 384, 398 (CA7 1984)).[6]

[1d] We therefore hold that petitioners may maintain this action if respondents conducted the enterprise through a pattern of racketeering activity. The questions of whether the respondents committed the requisite predicate acts, and whether the commission of these acts fell into a pattern, are not before us. We hold only that RICO contains no economic motive requirement.

The judgment of the Court of Appeals is accordingly reversed.

SEPARATE OPINION

Justice Souter, with whom Justice Kennedy joins, concurring.

I join the Court's opinion and write separately to explain why the First Amendment does not require reading an economic-motive requirement into the RICO, and to stress that the Court's opinion does

---

[6] [6b] Several of the respondents, and several amici argue that application of RICO to antiabortion protesters could chill legitimate expression protected by the First Amendment. However, the question presented for review asked simply whether the Court should create an unwritten requirement limiting RICO to cases where either the enterprise or racketeering activity has an overriding economic motive. None of the respondents made a constitutional argument as to the proper construction of RICO in the Court of Appeals, and their constitutional argument here is directed almost entirely to the nature of their activities, rather than to the construction of RICO. We therefore decline to address the First Amendment question argued by respondents and the *amici.*

not bar First Amendment challenges to RICO's application in particular cases.

Several respondents and *amici* argue that we should avoid the First Amendment issues that could arise from allowing RICO to be applied to protest organizations by construing the statute to require economic motivation, just as we have previously interpreted other generally applicable statutes so as to avoid First Amendment problems. See, e.g, *Eastern Railroad Presidents Conference v Noerr Motor Freight, Inc.*, 365 US 127, 138, 5 L Ed 2d 464, 81 S Ct 523 (1961) (holding that antitrust laws do not apply to businesses combining to lobby the government, even where such conduct has an anticompetitive purpose and an anticompetitive effect, because the alternative "would raise important constitutional questions" under the First Amendment); see also *Lucas v Alexander*, 279 US 573, 577, 73 L Ed 851, 49 S Ct 426, 61 ALR 906 (1929) (a law "must be construed with an eye to possible constitutional limitations so as to avoid doubts as to its validity"). The argument is meritless in this case, though, for this principle of statutory construction applies only when the meaning of a statute is in doubt, see *Noerr, supra,* and here "the statutory language is unambiguous," *ante,* at ——, 127 L Ed 2d, at 111.

Even if the meaning of RICO were open to debate, however, it would not follow that the statute ought to be read to include an economic-motive requirement, since such a requirement would correspond only poorly to free-speech concerns. Respondents and *amici* complain that, unless so limited, the statute permits an ideological organization's opponents to label its vigorous expression as RICO predicate acts, thereby availing themselves of powerful remedial provisions that could destroy the organization. But an economic-motive requirement would protect too much with respect to First Amendment interests, since it would keep RICO from reaching ideological entities whose members commit acts of violence we need not fear chilling. An economic-motive requirement might also prove to be underprotective, in that entities engaging in vigorous but fully protected expression might fail the proposed economic-motive test (for even protest movements need money) and so be left exposed to harassing RICO suits.

An economic-motive requirement is, finally, unnecessary, because legitimate free-speech claims may be raised and addressed in individual RICO cases as they arise. Accordingly, it is important to stress that nothing in the Court's opinion precludes a RICO defendant from raising the First Amendment in its defense in a particular case. Conduct alleged to amount to Hobbs Act extortion, for example, or one of the other, somewhat elastic RICO predicate acts may turn out to be fully protected First Amendment activity, entitling the defendant to dismissal on that basis. See *NAACP v Claiborne Hardware, Co.*, 458 US 886, 917, 73 L Ed 2d 1215, 102 S Ct 3409 (1982) (holding that a state common-law prohibition on malicious interference with business could not, under the circumstances, be constitutionally applied to a civil-rights boycott of white merchants). And even in a case where a RICO violation has been validly established, the First Amendment may limit the relief that can be granted against an organization otherwise engaging in protected expression. See *NAACP v Alabama ex rel. Patterson*, 357 US 449, 2 L Ed 2d, 1488, 78 S Ct 1163 (1958) (invalidating under the First Amendment a court order compelling production of the NAACP's membership lists, issued to enforce Alabama's requirements for out-of-state corporations doing business in the State). See also *NAACP v*

Claiborne Hardware, Co., supra, at 930-932, 73 L Ed 2d 1215, 102 S Ct 3409 (discussing First Amendment limits on the assessment of derivative liability against ideological organizations); *Oregon Natural Resources Council v Mohla,* 944 F2d 531 (CA9 1991) (applying a heightened pleading standard to a complaint based on presumptively protected First Amendment conduct).

This is not the place to catalog the speech issues that could arise in a RICO action against a protest group, and I express no view on the possibility of a First Amendment claim by the respondents in this case (since, as the Court observes, such claims are outside the question presented, see *ante,* at ——, n 6, 127 L Ed 2d, at 111). But I think it prudent to notice that RICO actions could deter protected advocacy and to caution courts applying RICO to bear in mind the First Amendment interests that could be at stake.

11

Comparative Government and Politics

All concrete has four constituents: cement, sand, aggregate, and water. The proportions change, depending on whether you are putting down a floor or erecting a supporting column. And reinforcing may be added. I would think good government should have a few basic constituents that would vary depending on whether the country is mobilizing for war or legislating to fight a depression.

—James Swanson

Further Thoughts on Comparative Government and Politics

In this chapter, we continue the discussion of comparative politics that we started in Chapter 5 to present some important trends in this subfield of the discipline in greater detail. As we have noted, in 1955 Roy C. Macridis inspired substantial changes within the discipline when he criticized what he perceived as the traditional approach to comparative politics. The traditional approach, said Macridis, is essentially noncomparative, descriptive, parochial, static, and monographic, by which he meant that the typical traditional "comparative" government study merely described without evaluating or analyzing its subject and was, therefore, merely descriptive. Further, traditional political science usually described only one institution within one country, and so the study was monographic and noncomparative. In addition, Macridis complained that American political scientists tended to study mostly European countries and to limit their focus to only one period, producing a discipline of comparative politics which was both parochial and static.

Since Macridis' article, much has happened within the study of comparative politics. It has expanded its investigations into every area of the world and has adopted a variety of new methods and approaches. Ronald Rogowski (1993, 431) has identified five trends that characterized the study of comparative politics in the 1980s. In the 1980s, Rogowski declares, comparative political science placed increased emphasis on:

1. The relationship of economics to politics,
2. The international context of domestic politics and institutions,
3. Interest groups,
4. State structures, and
5. Nationalism and ethnic cleavages.

We shall mention a few of the most interesting of the many developments which Rogowski describes. The new political economy examines the discrepancies in resources among nations and the increasing importance of economic trends in shaping national policies. The effects of the international environment upon domestic policy is a subject of increasing interest. New studies have concentrated upon the effects of governmental policy on economic growth, the social sources of policy, and the consequences of failure of economic policies on political systems. An interesting example of such work, Rogowski explains, is Robert H. Bates' *Markets and States in Tropical Africa: The Political Basis of Agricultural Politics* (1981). According to Rogowski (1993, 432):

> Bates's (1981) pathbreaking work on what, to the ill-informed, would have seemed a soporific topic, namely post-independence African agricultural policy, demonstrated conclusively, if sometimes obliquely (a) that the African economic disaster was self-inflicted and (b) that, in general, policies of Soviet-style rapid industrialization at the expense of the countryside of more moderate import-substituting industrialization (ISI) were doomed. With but two significant exceptions (Cote d'Ivoire and Kenya), the independent governments of land-rich Africa had ruthlessly taxed domestic farmers to gain the investment capital that would supposedly permit rapid industrialization; and they had attempted to stimulate industrial growth through tariffs, quotas, and an over-valued currency. Instead, these policies had yielded—in ways that Bates showed to be absolutely predictable from the most rudimentary economics—black markets, smuggling, declines in agricultural production, flight from the land, monopolistic and uncompetitive industries, massive corruption, and an increasing reliance on imported foodstuffs. An early side effect of Bates's crucial book was near-total abandonment of two important streams of previous theorizing about development, namely (a) culturalism and (b) the "dependency" and "world-systems" analyses.

Other recent efforts have studied the effects of military technology and trade upon governmental systems. Looking back to history, Perry Anderson (1974), for example, has argued that the authoritarian regimes of the Middle Ages were the only political organizations that could have survived during these times because only they could develop the armies that were needed to fend off frequent attack from many directions. Changes in trade patterns also affect political regimes. Great Britain's government, for example, changed during the course of its empire from feudalism to democracy, as the base of its economy changed from agriculture to international commerce.

Corporatism is another prominent theme in recent literature. Corporatism is the inclusion of specific important associations of economic interests within the institutional structure that makes the decisions for society. Interest groups in labor and industry form informal and formal partnerships to push policy decisions in certain directions. As governments increasingly turn their attention to economic matters, the influence of these groups upon governmental decisions increases in turn.

Ethnic diversity within nations and in particular regions, such as the former Soviet Union and the Middle East, have drawn substantial attention in the past decade. These conflicts pose many problems for economic theories. Donald Horowitz (1985) has done some interesting investigation into systems with ranked and unranked ethnicities. Ranked ethnicities occur in societies in which some ethnic groups are at the top of the economic and social strata while others find themselves at the bottom. In unranked systems, people from the major ethnic groups share positions in all occupations. Horowitz finds that ranked systems tend to be relatively stable over long periods, but when change comes it is often violent. Unranked systems tend to have more ongoing controversy, but internal conflicts are normally less violent.

A Case in Comparative Policy Analysis—
Skocpol's Revolution and State Construction

States and Social Revolutions, A Comparative Analysis of France, Russia and China (1979, 1994) by Harvard University political scientist Theda Skocpol achieves the highest goals of comparative analysis because it derives from its comparisons a general social theory, which may then be tested in similar comparisons of other nations. One of Skocpol's findings is that state construction, the process of consolidating political power that leads to establishing a more or less permanent modern state, is advanced considerably by the necessity of preparing for a foreign war. Like all such major works, Skocpol's book has been criticized by other political scientists who, examining it closely, came to different conclusions, or identified different factors as being more important. In the article included in this chapter, "The National Causes of State Construction in France, Russia and China," Rosemary H.T. O'Kane of the University of Keele in the United Kingdom examines the same three countries that Skocpol studied and finds that civil war, not foreign war, is the major factor in state construction. O'Kane comes to the important conclusion that "the fundamental basis of permanent state building in post-revolutionary society is the establishment of central control over the revolutionary forces of internal coercion" (O'Kane 1995, 3).

Before proceeding to O'Kane's article, we shall summarize Skocpol's analysis. Skocpol begins by explaining that revolutions are infrequent, but important events in the development of most nations, and that existing theories that have attempted to explain them are inadequate.

> I shall argue that, in contrast to the modes of explanation used by the currently prevalent theories, social revolutions should be analyzed from a structural perspective, with special attention devoted to international contexts and to developments at home and abroad that affect the breakdown of the state organizations of old regimes and the buildup of new, revolutionary state organizations. Furthermore, I shall argue that comparative historical analysis is the most appropriate way to develop explanations of revolutions that are at once historically grounded and generalizable beyond unique cases. (Skocpol 1979, 5–6)

Skocpol then proceeds to analyze "four major families" of theories of revolution, telling why they are inadequate. The first family is Marxism. "Marx understood revolutions not as isolated episodes of violence or conflict but as class-based movements growing out of objective structural contradictions within historically developing and inherently conflict-ridden societies" (Skocpol 1979, 7). The second family of approaches that Skocpol identifies are "aggregate-psychological theories," an example of which is Ted Gurr's *Why Men Rebel*. Skocpol (1979, 9) notes that Gurr's theory is

> simple enough in essence: Political violence occurs when many people in society become angry . . . and people become angry when there occurs a gap between the valued things and opportunities they feel entitled to and the things and opportunities they actually get—a condition known as "relative deprivation."

The third type of approach is the "systems/value consensus" group, which includes Chalmers Johnson's *Revolutionary Change*. Johnson sees society as a system of "internally consistent institutions" which express a set of coordinated values. Revolutions represent, above all, a change in the basic value system of society. Instability occurs whenever a society's value system and the environment that they find themselves in become "dis-synchronized." If the governing authorities respond with policies that resynchronize values and the environment, revolution may be avoided, but if they fail to do this, violence is the result.

The fourth family of theories of revolutions is the political-conflict approach, exemplified by Charles Tilly's *From Mobilization to Revolution*. Tilly denies Ted Gurr's thesis that revolutions occur because a segment of the population experiences relative deprivation. Instead, revolution occurs when, as a part of the normal political process, the general population is given a choice between the ruling government and another faction that is trying to displace it, and the population chooses the revolting faction.

Skocpol finds that the four families of existing explanations of revolutions share some important inadequacies, and that three other important principles are needed for a satisfactory analysis. "In the first place, an adequate understanding of social revolutions requires that the analyst take a nonvoluntarist, structural perspective on their causes and processes. But all existing approaches theorize on the basis of a voluntarist image of how revolutions happen" (Skocpol 1979, 14). Skocpol's structuralist viewpoint considers that structures, that is, the institutions and economic and social arrangements of society, such as slavery, serfdom, medieval guilds, and the stock market, determine what happens in society. Voluntarists, on the other hand, see individuals acting on the basis of personal values, needs, or desires, without particular regard to the structure of society. "In the second place," Skocpol proceeds, "social revolutions cannot be explained without systematic reference to *inter*national structures and world-historical developments. Existing theories, however, focus primarily or exclusively upon *intra*national conflicts and processes of mobilization" (Skocpol 1979, 14). Here we see the argument between Skocpol and the author of the article included in this text, Rosemary O'Kane. O'Kane returns the focus of revolution back from *inter*national conflicts to *intra*national ones.

Skocpol (1979, 14) then states her third principle, again explaining why previous theories are inadequate:

In the third place, in order to explain the causes and outcomes of social revolutions, it is essential to conceive of states as administrative and coercive organizations—organizations that are potentially autonomous from (though of course conditioned by) socioeconomic interests and structures. But currently prevalent theories of revolution instead either analytically collapse state and society or they reduce political and state actions to representations of socioeconomic forces and interests.

Having rejected previous theories as, in and of themselves inadequate, Skocpol presents her own framework for analysis of the causes of revolution. She rejects Gurr's aggregate-psychological theories and Johnson's systems/value consensus approach and adopts instead a combination of Marxist class analysis and political-conflict theory:

> The Marxist conception of class relations as rooted in the control of productive property and the appropriation of economic surpluses from direct producers by nonproducers is, in my view, an indispensable theoretical tool for identifying one sort of basic contradiction in society. . . . [C]lass analysis must be supplemented by the ideas of political-conflict theorists . . . . When and how can subordinate classes fight successfully against those who exploit them? And when and how do dominant classes have the capacity for collective political action? For answering these questions, the political conflict argument that collective action is based upon group organization and access to resources, often including coercive resources, is especially fruitful. (Skocpol 1979, 13–14)

In the article you are about to read, Rosemary O'Kane explains how Skocpol applies a structuralist comparative method to France, Russia, and China, and then argues that factors that Skocpol did not consider which bring a sound comparative analysis to a somewhat different conclusion. As you read the article, consider the following questions:

1. What point is Skocpol trying to make?
2. What method does Skocpol use to make her argument?
3. According to O'Kane, what are the strengths of Skocpol's argument?
4. According to O'Kane, what are the weaknesses of Skocpol's argument?
5. According to O'Kane, what are the causes of state construction?
6. What method does O'Kane use to make her argument?
7. What are the strengths of O'Kane's argument?
8. What are the weaknesses of O'Kane's argument?

The National Causes of State Construction in France, Russia and China

Rosemary H. T. O'Kane (University of Keele)

General lessons about state construction are drawn from concentration on the 'Terror' years of three post-revolutionary regimes: the Jacobin in France, 1793–4; the Bolshevik in Russia, 1918–21; and the Chinese, 1950–3. These three cases are chosen in order to develop a direct challenge to Skocpol's claims about state building in *States and Social Revolutions*. The findings show that early state building is not, primarily, a rational, centralizing, mobilizing, response to war and foreign war in particular. It is civil war which is of greater importance to an understanding of the development of revolutionary states and it is only after civil war is over that permanent state construction can begin. Comparison for differences, as well as similarity, at this crucial point at the end of civil war shows that, along with the importance of practical domestic policies as a basis for support, the essential foundation for the post-revolutionary state is central control over the revolutionary forces of internal coercion.

In recent years Skocpol's theory of social revolution has captured center stage, seemingly pushing all other theories into the wings.[1] The theory has attracted such a following both because of its emphasis on the state and state building after the revolution and because of its consideration of international factors. At the same time, the theory has also attracted considerable criticism, particularly in respect of the explanations offered for the differing outcomes of the French, Russian, and Chinese revolutions, on which the study is based.[2] Skocpol contrasts the 'professional-bureaucratic state' involving 'national markets and capitalist private property' in France, with 'the development-oriented party—states' in, loosely, their industrial (Russia) or agrarian (Chinese) varieties.[3] Attention has not, however, focused on the early stage of state building. Following a 'liberal' phase in which each state failed to achieve consolidation, these modern states began, according to Skocpol, with the coming to power of the Jacobins in France in 1793, the Bolsheviks in Russia in October 1917, and the Chinese Communists in China in 1949.

> In all three revolutionary situations, political leaderships and regimes—the Jacobin and then the Napoleonic in France, the Bolshevik in Russia, and the Communist in China—emerged to reestablish national order, to consolidate the socioeconomic transformations wrought by the class upheavals from below, and to enhance each country's power and autonomy over and against international competitors.[4]

The factor which Skocpol singles out as similar for each of these consolidating regimes is the pressing need to mobilize

Rosemary H. T. O'Kane, "The National Causes of State Construction in France, Russia and China." *Political Studies* 43(1995) 2–21. Reprinted by permission, Blackwell Publishers.

[1] T. Skocpol, *States and Social Revolutions: A Comparative Analysis of France, Russia and China* (Cambridge, Cambridge University Press, 1979).

[2] See S. Taylor, *Social Science and Revolutions* (London, Macmillan, 1984), M. S. Kimmel, *Revolution: A Sociological Approach* (Oxford, Polity, 1990) and P. Calvert, *Revolution and Counter-Revolution* (Buckingham, Open University Press, 1990).

[3] Skocpol, *States and Social Revolutions*, p. 162.

[4] Skocpol, *States and Social Revolutions*, pp. 163–4.

for war. Whilst 'war' for Skocpol includes both foreign and civil war, in line with her general international interest, it is foreign war to which she gives the greater emphasis. It will be argued here that it is not foreign war but civil war which is central to an understanding of state formation and this will be demonstrated through examination of the same three cases of revolution (France, Russia, and China) which Skocpol employs to build her generalization. Crucially, it will be shown that permanent state construction cannot begin until after the civil war has ended and that even at this stage there is no guarantee that state construction will succeed. Through moving the focus of enquiry away from the start of Jacobin, Bolshevik, and Chinese Communist rule towards the critical period at the end of civil war, the crucial lesson emerges that, along with the advantages of practical policies which carry popular support, the fundamental basis of permanent state building in postrevolutionary society is the establishment of central control over the revolutionary forces of internal coercion.

SKOCPOL ON WAR AND STATE CENTRALIZATION: COMPARISON FOR SIMILARITY

The Jacobins, Bolsheviks, and Chinese Communists, each 'state-building leaderships' were, in Skocpol's view, 'the people who created administrative and military organizations and political institutions to take the place of prerevolutionary monarchies.' What they created were 'centralized, bureaucratic state structures.'[5]

In respect of France, Skocpol argues for the importance of involvement in foreign war and the consequent need for centralized mobilization to win the war, as follows:

> Ultimately it was the French declaration of war in Austria in April 1792—involving the nation in the first of a series of international conflicts that were to embroil Europe until 1815—that delivered the coup de grace for the liberal phase of 1789–91. This act set in motion the processes of government centralization and popular political mobilization that were to culminate first in the Montagnard Term of 1793–4, and then in the Napoleonic Dictatorship.[6]

To emphasize this crucial importance of war she continues:

> [U]nder the aegis of mobilization for war and military intervention in unstable internal politics, a centralized bureaucratic state had been constructed, to be bequeathed to a consolidated French nation. Thus warfare was far from extrinsic to the development and fate of the French Revolution; rather it was central and constitutive.[7]

For Russia, the Bolsheviks had to 'begin at once to rebuild administrative and military organizations and to enforce ever more centralized discipline within the Party.'[8] Again foreign war is central to Skocpol's argument. The First World War had devastated the country and after the Bolsheviks had negotiated their withdrawal from it in March 1918 and Germany had been defeated by the Allies in November, 'counter-revolutionary regimes based upon armies led by former tsarist officers had sprung up in Siberia and the south, and Western expeditionary forces scattered around the periphery of European and Asian Russia were initiating attempts at foreign intervention.'[9]

In response to these threats of war, Skocpol explains that along with the Red

---

[5] Skocpol, *States and Social Revolutions*, p. 168. She makes it quite clear that by 'military organizations' is meant the army. (See, for example, p. 163.)

[6] Skocpol, *States and Social Revolutions*, pp. 185–6.

[7] Skocpol, *States and Social Revolutions*, p. 186.

[8] Skocpol, *States and Social Revolutions*, p. 215.

[9] Skocpol, *States and Social Revolutions*, p. 215.

Army the Bolsheviks developed the Cheka. The Cheka, set up immediately after the October Revolution 'for combatting counter-revolutionary subversion,' and subject only to the control of the 'central Party leaders,' quickly took a role in the economy because of the total devastation caused by the First World War. The Cheka were crucial to Red Army victories, using force to obtain supplies from the rural areas and enforcing rationing in the urban areas. 'The Civil War years also witnessed the establishment of a bureaucratic and Party-supervised civil administration and the centralization and extreme extension of state controls over the Russian economy.'[10]

In China, it is argued that the Nationalists under Tchiang Kai-chek, having failed to consolidate power, were replaced by the mobilizing, centralizing communists. Again it is mobilization for war, the war with Japan from 1937–45 being given special prominence, which is viewed as the factor propelling the Communists to victory over the Nationalists in the ensuing years, bringing the Communists consolidated power and the 'establishment of the People's Republic of China' in 1949.[11] Discussing the important land reforms in the Communist areas between 1946–49, which potentially challenge her emphasis on foreign wars, she argues that social reforms essentially took place in response to war. 'In short, the Chinese Communist Party's quest for rural resources to make possible military victories against Japan, the warlords, and the Nationalists finally resulted in social revolution in the Chinese countryside.'[12]

This same link between mobilization for war and the need to develop a centralized administration for supplies is also made for France. As in China and Russia, in France modern state centralization developed primarily in response to the war effort: 'The chief purpose and most enduring achievement of the Montagnard dictatorship was to expand, invigorate and supply the national armies of France.'[13] Skocpol draws attention to the *levée en masse*, 'One of the first measures adopted (in August 1793) by the Committee of Public Safety,' under which all unmarried men, aged under 25, were conscripted and everyone else was mobilized in the war effort. In support of her argument that the development of a centralized state was the consequence of this war mobilization she quotes Sydenham: the 'regulation of the economy was soon as extensive as the bureaucracy of the day and the power of coercion could make it.'[14] Whilst Robespierre may have been overthrown, Napoleon 'legally confirm[ed] the status quo of the social and economic accomplishments of the Revolution' and 'reintroduce[d] administrative centralization.'[15]

INITIAL CONTENTION

Whilst the view that war leads to centralization is persuasive, there are a number of problems with Skocpol's argument. The fact that war was going on and leaderships responded to it does not prove that these responses became permanent. For example Brinton describes the Jacobin and Bolshevik reigns of terror as 'rough and ready

---

[10] Skocpol, *States and Social Revolutions*, p. 218, and for the above see p. 215–6.

[11] Skocpol, *States and Social Revolutions*, p. 263.

[12] Skocpol, *States and Social Revolutions*, p. 262.

[13] Skocpol, *States and Social Revolutions*, p. 189, and for quotation below.

[14] See M. J. Sydenham, *The French Revolution* (New York, Capricorn, 1966), p. 167 quoted in Skocpol, *States and Social Revolutions*, p. 189.

[15] Skocpol, *States and Social Revolutions*, p. 195.

centralization.'[16] In order to demonstrate that state building is taking place it is necessary to examine the inception, development, and sometimes disappearance of new organizations and structures, to consider policy-decisions and the implementation of laws and also to show how these affected the modern state in the longer term.

Skocpol gives very little attention to the process of state building, construing it as 'doing.' For France the only legislation mentioned is the *levée en masse;* no bureaucratic organizations, or ministries, are mentioned by name and the claim that the 'Montagnard dictatorships' chief purpose' was 'to expand, invigorate, and supply the national armies of France' is asserted, not proven. In the Russian case, again, no ministries are actually mentioned, nor consideration made of how legislation affected the development of centralization, what exactly the balance between the Cheka (coercion) and the government and administration was, or how the relationship may have changed and developed. In respect of China the case is so noticeably different from the other two, because the discussion is mostly concerned with events before Mao came to power in 1949, that it is difficult to see where comparison is to be made. This case, however, is the only one for which Skocpol actually considers figures on the growth of bureaucracy in the new postrevolutionary regime.[17] Nevertheless, there is no specific discussion of the growth of ministries and the only policies mentioned for the early 1950s are offered in support

of the claim that China was copying Soviet measures. By this point the importance of the war is forgotten, ironically in spite of China's involvement in the Korean War from 1950–3, which is given only passing reference.[18]

It is also perfectly clear that whilst foreign war, as an international factor, is given prominence in Skocpol's accounts, civil war is important to her argument: in Russia, response to the problems of foreign war leads to civil war: in China, civil war follows the defeat of Japan, with the Communists at war with the Nationalists from 1927 and even during the period of the United Front. The revolts of the sansculottes in Paris and of the urban workers in Russia also play a part in her argument. Furthermore, all this takes place against a background of continuing peasant revolt. In stressing foreign war as the primary factor propelling the Jacobin, Bolshevik and Maoist regimes to modern state building, Skocpol seems to press the importance of international over national factors.

THE PRIMARY IMPORTANCE OF CIVIL WAR: FRANCE

What Skocpol refers to as the Montagnard Government,' which began in March 1793 after the Jacobins gained control over the National Convention and displaced the previous domination of the Girondins, is normally referred to as the Reign of Terror. The Jacobins came to power at a point of both national and international crisis and the policies and organizations of the regime were more coercive than administrative. The most famous revolutionary organization of the Montagnard Government was the Committee of Public Safety which was set up on 6 April 1793 and headed, from July, by Robespierre. The

[16] Brinton, *The Anatomy of Revolution* (New York, Vintage, 1965), pp. 171–2. For a recent study of reigns of terror, in broad agreement on this point, see R. H. T. O'Kane, *The Revolutionary Reign of Terror: The Role of Violence in Political Change* (Aldershot, Edward Elgar, 1991).

[17] See Skocpol, *States and Social Revolutions*, p. 263.

[18] See Skocpol, *States and Social Revolutions*, p. 276.

Committee had charge of both internal and external affairs. Prior to this, on 9 March, the Committee of General Security had been set up to take charge of internal security. On the same day that the Committee of General Security was founded Representatives on Mission (82 deputies of the Convention) were sent to the Departments. On the following day, the Paris Revolutionary Tribunal was set up, and on 21 March a law was introduced to begin the organization of surveillance committees (or 'revolutionary committees') in the French communes. The crucial Law of Suspects, aimed at controlling counter-revolution, was also introduced in March, though strengthened in September.[19]

What had provoked the development of these organizations and instruments of Terror had been the outbreak, in March 1793, of civil war in the Vendée. By April it was in full swing throughout the West. Civil war then began to erupt elsewhere. From May, anti-Jacobin rebellions (the Federalist Revolts) began to break out, first in Lyon, hit by crisis in the silk industry and facing starvation, and then in Marseilles and Bordeaux. By the summer, sixty departments were embroiled in civil war though, outside the West, full-scale rebellion was largely concentrated in these three towns.[20]

The importance of civil war as the prime cause of the reign of terror is supported by the evidence offered by Greer in the classic work on the Terror. Examining the geographical incidence of executions Greer finds a very strong association between the most intense civil war areas and the total percentage of executions: 52 per cent in the West—the areas around the

Vendée which included Loire-Inferieure (3548), Maine-et-Loire (1886), Vendée (1616)—and 19 percent (1880) in the Rhône Valley, where Lyon is situated. In all, 76 per cent of all executions occurred in the departments where insurrections involving a thousand or more people occurred. Seine (Paris), at 2639 executions, is the fifth and the only other centre where official executions reached totals over 509.[21] Greer further supports his emphasis on civil war through consideration of the peak of the Terror. The steep rise in victims in December and January, he argues, 'represents the punishment of rebels' as the Jacobins won their decisive victories from November, when Lyon was taken, until the end of December, by which time the civil war in the West was effectively at an end, though outbreaks of rebellion continued in the Vendée into the spring. The continuation of executions into the spring of 1794 Greer puts down mainly to the delays in capturing and trying rebels involved in these civil wars.[22]

Compared with civil war, the evidence shows that foreign war played a relatively small part. Whilst for the frontier zones some 22 per cent of all crimes recorded were for 'intelligence with the enemy' only the two northern regions, Pas de Calais

[19] For the relevant documents and events see D. G. Wright, *Revolution and Terror in France* (Harlow, Longman, 1974).

[20] M. Lyons, *Revolution in Toulouse: An Essay on Provincial Terrorism* (Berne, Peter Lang, 1978), p. 41.

[21] For the above, see D. Greer, *The Incidence of Terror During the French Revolution: A Statistical Interpretation* (Gloucester, MA, Peter Smith, 1966), pp. 40, 70 and 147, Table III. The crime for which 72.25 per cent of the 17,000 official recorded victims met their death was 'sedition.' The substantial majority were convicted under the September 1793 Law of Suspects.

[22] Greer, *The Incidence of Terror During the French Revolution*, p. 115. R. Louie, 'The incidence of the terror: a critique of a statistical interpretation,' *French Historical Studies*, 3 (1974), 379–89 has confirmed that when divided by the population for each area, the official victims of the Terror remain highest in the civil war areas. (Greer's work first appeared in 1935.) For general and more recent support see D. M. G. Sutherland, *France 1789–1815: Revolution and Counterrevolution* (London, Fontana, 1985), p. 219.

and Nord, had relatively high levels of executions with 392 and 157, respectively. These figures are clearly a long way from those of the top five departments where executions ranged from 3548 to 1616.[23]

The spark for counter-revolution in the Vendée had been the decision, on 24 February, to conscript 300,000 men in response to the crisis of foreign war. The tinder, however, had been dried by the problems of supply and the threat of starvation. In September 1792 a short-lived uprising had developed in the Vendée and calm had been restored only because of the promise afforded by the September elections.[24] With expectations disappointed, grievances again intensified. The problem of distribution and the threat of famine which it caused also lay behind the wider domestic insurrection which thrust the Jacobin regime deeply into crisis. Throughout 1793–4 large towns in particular, especially Paris, were on the edge of famine.[25]

THE PEOPLE'S ARMIES, ECONOMIC POLICIES, AND DECENTRALIZATION

With the outbreak of civil war, by April 1793 demands began to be made for 'people's armies' to fight internal uprisings. They began to be enrolled in May. The decree to set them up was proclaimed on 4 June 1793 and the law to enact this decree was passed in September 1793. These armies were set up under the Committee of Public Safety though, in practice, they generally took their orders from the Committee of General Security and the local surveillance committees. Membership of the armies was entirely voluntary. Under the act, these revolutionary armies were intended to control counter-revolutionaries, to defend the revolutionary laws, to protect public safety and to 'supply the urban markets and ensure the circulation of provisions, merchandise and people.'[26] The most important and also the most notorious of these revolutionary armies was the Paris People's Army, formed on 5 September under Ronsin.

It is a common error to suppose, and a supposition made by Skocpol, that the conventional army was used to suppress counter-revolution in the major areas of civil war.[27] This was the case in some areas, Toulon for example, but usually it was the Paris People's Army which did the suppressing. The Paris Army was particularly important in Lyon and in the West. Indeed, a third of Ronsin's army were fighting in Lyon, taken on 5 Frimaire (25 November 1793).[28] The Paris and other people's armies also played a part in the war effort, requisitioning foodstuffs and metals and materials from churches, but far more important was their task of protecting the passage of food (grain in particular) and ensuring its supply. Permanent garrisons of these civil soldiers were stationed at more than two-thirds of the grain stores, positioned on major rivers

---

[23] Greer, *The Incidence of Terror During the French Revolution*, p. 147, Table III and p. 153, Table IV.

[24] Wright, *Revolution and Terror in France*, p. 57.

[25] See M. J. Sydenham, *The First French Republic 1792–1804* (London, Batsford, 1974), pp. 20–1.

[26] R. Cobb, *The People's Armies—the Armées Revolutionnaires: Instrument of the Terror in the Departments April 1793 to Floreal Year II* (New Haven, Yale University Press, 1987), p. 160. For the above see also pp. 40, 19–30, 339 and 195. Skocpol (p. 37) portrays the people's armies as completely spontaneous and makes no mention of their legalization.

[27] See, for example, J. R. Adelman, *Revolution, Armies and War: A Political History* (Boulder, CO, Lynne Rienner, 1985), p. 4.

[28] See Cobb, *The People's Armies*, ch. 3, see especially section IV on Lyon, and p. 554.

and roads. The major task of the Paris army was to ensure the supply and protect the passage of grain and other foodstuffs to Paris and, following the introduction of the Law of the General Maximum on 29 September 1793, to 'lend force to the control of prices.'[29]

A maximum on grain prices was first introduced on 4 March 1793. Laws against hoarding to back up requisitioning for the war effort were introduced in July 1793 and on 23 August the *levée en masse,* stressed by Skocpol, was decreed. The General Maximum of September fixed a ceiling on both prices and wages. This legislation was directed towards needs at home. As Kemp argues, 'the immediate need was to check the rise in prices and speculation and ensure a supply of basic foods and other essentials for the civilian population.'[30] Importantly, prices were to be fixed by the districts and wages were to be set by town councils.

In October the Subsistence Commission headed by Lindet and answerable to the Committee of Public Safety was set up to prepare lists of maximum prices. The staff of the Subsistence Commission soon grew to over 500.[31] State-owned factories were set up to manufacture ammunition, and foreign trade was controlled by the state between November 1793 until March 1794. However, supply for civilians (food rationing and control and regulation of food production) remained with the districts and was not the responsibility of the Subsistence Commission.[32] This runs contrary to Skocpol's centralizing view. In April 1794 the law against hoarding was abolished and the government lost interest in violations of the Maximum in all foods other than bread. On 23 July a list of maximum wage rates, representing a substantial wage cut for workers, was published by the Paris Commune. This led to the uprising in Paris which opened the way, on the night of 9 Thermidor (27–28 July), for the end of the Jacobin regime.

Events after the fall of Robespierre also fail to support Skocpol's claim for 'reintroduced administrative centralization.' A new constitution was introduced which installed the Directory. This was a period of 'failed consolidation' characterized by 'shaky bureaucracy' and a series of coups d'état, culminating in Napoleon Bonaparte's coup on the 18 Brumaire Year VIII (7 November 1799).[33] The constitution of Year III was replaced by the constitution of Year VIII, which in turn was replaced by the constitution of Year X (3 August 1802). At the time, that is eight years after Thermidor, Roederer remarked: 'Hardly any institutions nor yet any formed or rooted habits.'[34] It fell to Napoleon after a military coup—imposed coercive centralization—to construct the 'masses of

[29] Cobb, *The People's Armies*, pp. 276–83.

[30] T. Kemp, *Economic Forces in French History* (London, Dennis Dobson, 1971), p. 94.

[31] See A. Soboul, *The French Revolution 1787–1799,* vol. 1, *From the storming of the Bastille to the fall of the Girondins,* vol. 2, *From the Jacobin dictatorship to Napoleon* (London, NLB, 1974), p. 390 and Sutherland, *France* 1789–1815, p. 203.

[32] See Sydenham, *The First French Republic* 1792–1804, p. 187 and Soboul, *The French Revolution* 1787–1799, pp. 390–l and for what follows pp. 391–3.

[33] Sutherland, *France* 1789–1815, p. 325 (title of ch. 9). This view of the Jacobin regime as a period of temporary government is also supported by the frequent declarations of the revolutionaries themselves. See M. P. Carter. 'The French Revolution: Jacobin terror' in D. C. Rapoport and Y. Alexander (eds). *The Mortality of Terrorism: Religious and Secular Justifications* (New York, Pergamon, 1982), ch. 6, pp. 146–7.

[34] Sutherland, *France* 1789–1815, p. 362. For 'masses of granite' see p. 366.

granite,' as he described them, to build the lasting state. Napoleon essentially lost his exalted position through defeat in war but his administrative rock remained.

THE PRIMARY IMPORTANCE OF CIVIL WAR: RUSSIA

This lesson about the primary importance of civil war is even more obvious for the Bolsheviks between 1918–21. What is more, though the Bolsheviks succeeded where the Jacobins failed in hanging on to power after the civil war had been brought under control, the early years of Bolshevik rule also saw, as in France, a period of emergency government where terror organizations were crucial.

On the fall of the Provisional Government in November 1917, a new temporary central government was set up, the Council of People's Commissars—Sovnarkom—with Lenin its Chairman. Local government continued under the workers', peasants', and soldiers' councils (soviets) with a new kind of dual power retained within the All-Russian Central Executive Committee (VTsIK) of the Congress of Soviets which had first met in June 1917. Whilst Bolsheviks were now present on both VTsIK and Sovnarkom, as had not been the case under the dual power of the Provisional Government and Soviets, rivalry between the two central organizations of state still continued. Five days after the overthrow of the Provisional Government, Sovnarkom decreed itself powers of legislation. The important clause for the development of Sovnarkom's power read 'measures of extreme urgency may be put into force on the sole authority of Sovnarkom.'[35] On 20 December 1917, the All-

Russian Extraordinary Commission for Combatting Counter-revolution and Sabotage was set up under Sovnarkom.[36] This Cheka or Vecheka (the acronym for its full Russian title) was to become the instrument of the Terror. As an 'extraordinary' organization it was not intended to be permanent.[37] The Cheka took over the police functions of the Military Revolutionary Councils. These MRCs were then replaced by the Worker-Peasant Red Army following a decree of the Sovnarkom on 28 January 1918.[38] Whereas the MRCs had been accountable to the soviets, the Red Army was under the authority of Sovnarkom. With the setting up of the Red Army, therefore, the soviets lost further power.

The Cheka grew with the civil war. As Greer had found for France, Leggett found that in Russia the toll of victims highly correlated with the areas of civil war.[39] In February 1918, there were 120 staff at the Cheka headquarters; by 10

---

[35] For the above see E. H. Carr, *The Bolshevik Revolution*, vol. 1 (Penguin, Harmondsworth, 1966), p. 156 and p. 222.

[36] G. Leggett, *The Cheka: Lenin's Political Police* (Oxford, Clarendon, 1981), p. 129, claims that it was by an 'ad hoc committee which claimed affiliation to Sovnarkom but was never established by it,' but Carr, *The Bolshevik Revolution* 1917–23, vol. 1, p. 167 simply points out that the decree seems to have been kept secret and was not published until December 1927. For the text of the decree see J. Bunyan and H. H. Fisher, *The Bolshevik Revolution* 1917–18 (Stanford, Stanford University Press, 1965), pp. 297–8.

[37] Bunyan and Fisher, *The Bolshevik Revolution* 1917–18, pp. 292–7.

[38] See Rigby, *Lenin's Government*, p. 60 and Bunyan and Fisher, *The Bolshevik Revolution* 1917–18, pp. 568–9. Truly effective soviet based people's militias never developed and over time the Chekas took on ordinary police duties too. See Leggett, *The Cheka*, pp. 122–3.

[39] Leggett, *The Cheka*, Appendix C. Latsis's official records are only 22 deaths to July 1918 compared to 12,733 from July 1918–December 1920 (Leggett, p. 464). The actual total for the whole of the Terror, Leggett puts at around 140,000, but accepts that the total for this early period is low (p. 467). The evidence available is not adequate for statistical analysis, comparable with Greer's.

June 1918 they numbered 1,000. By January 1919, in addition to the Petrograd and Moscow Chekas there were 40 Provincial, 365 District, and 34 Frontier Chekas. The Cheka troop corps, first formed in March, had grown to 20,000, making in all a total of 37,000 personnel under the Cheka Establishment. By December 1921, Cheka numbers had reached their peak of 143,000.[40]

Against a background of peasant uprisings, the civil war essentially consisted of three White army advances, led by Admiral Kolchak in Siberia (defeated July 1919), General Denikin in the south (from July 1919, reversed November 1920), General Yudenich in the northwest (May 1919, peace December 1919), and a fourth attack led by Marshal Pilsudski from Poland into the Ukraine (April 1920, armistice October 1920).[41] Peasant uprisings, which seemed under control in the summer of 1920, then began to break out again. The Tambov rebellion began in August 1920 and revolt soon spread with a form of guerrilla warfare led by the outlaw and ex-Left Social Revolutionary, Antonov. Coinciding with the Polish war and revived civil war action in the Don and Ukraine (Wrangel's and the anarchist Makhno's forces), the Tambov rebellion was not suppressed until April 1921, in spite of 3,500 Cheka troops being sent in to fight the rebels in September 1920.[42] Towards the end of 1920, worker rebellions also began to break out in the Red areas, including Moscow and Petrograd, and soldiers too

became rebellious.[43] During the month of February 1921, throughout Russia 118 independent risings were reported by the Cheka, culminating in the famous rebellion in Kronstadt, stronghold of the Bolshevik revolution.[44]

Compared with the civil war, foreign war was of relatively little importance. Mawdsley argues that 'the "fourteen-power" anti-Bolshevik Allied alliance that was featured in Soviet propaganda was a myth.'[45] Whilst war against Germany continued the Allies' main concern was to win the war, and after the Armistice in November 1918 the Allies proved unable to reach a coordinated plan. The best they achieved was reached on 22 January 1919, but from then on Bradley characterizes the action of the Allies as 'uninformed, impulsive and fraught with disagreement.'[46] The Allies played some small part in territories on the edges of Soviet territory (such as Murmansk and Vladivostok in the North) and offered some financial and organizational help, but the war which threw the RSFSR into crisis was above all a civil war.

As in France, the need to get food to the cities was a crucial pressure on the government. On the day after the Bolsheviks came to power, stocks of grain in Petrograd (the capital city until 10 March 1918) were at starvation levels, with less than sufficient rations to supply the population of

---

[40] For the above figures, in order, see Carr, *The Bolshevik Revolution*, vol. 1, p. 169 and Leggett, *The Cheka*, p. 100 and p. 346.

[41] See J. F. N. Bradley, *Civil War in Russia 1917–20* (London, Batsford, 1975), p. 55. This last case was strictly a foreign war. The Polish war is not discussed by Skocpol.

[42] Leggett, *The Cheka*, p. 331.

[43] Indeed, between late 1920 and March 1921, 2,000–3,000 soldiers of the Moscow garrison were shot. R. Sakwa, *Soviet Communists in Power: A Study of Moscow During the Civil War 1918–21* (London, Macmillan, 1988), p. 241.

[44] Leggett, *The Cheka*, p. 325.

[45] E. Mawdsley, *The Russian Civil War* (Boston, Allen and Unwin, 1987), pp. 283–4. As an example of the Bolshevik's view, see L. Trotsky, *Terrorism and Communism* (Michigan, Ann Arbor, 1963), p. 50.

[46] Bradley, *Civil War in Russia 1917–20*, p. 68. For reactions after the Brest-Litovsk Treaty see p. 55.

the city with half a pound of bread each. The Brest-Litovsk Peace Treaty added to the problems.[47]

Bolshevik economic policy certainly went far beyond anything attempted in France. Collectively, the policy is known as 'war communism.' For agriculture, it involved 'the forcible collection of food supplies in grain-producing provinces in order to feed the starving cities.'[48] This was organized under Narkomprod, the Commissariat for Food Supply which, in a way similar to policy in France, set up guarding posts at critical points on the rail, road, and waterway networks, where foodstuffs could be confiscated and those suspected of profiteering could be placed in the hands of the Cheka. From December 1918 a revolutionary tax, which became a tax in kind, began to be levied, calculated on the basis of supposed family need with everything above that requisitioned. Prices were fixed but this later gave way to rationing.[49]

For industry, the 'war communist' policies began in June 1918 with nationalization; by the end of the year all areas of industry had been nationalized. (Banks had already been nationalized after the October takeover.) Vesenkha, the Council of National Economy, which had been set up within weeks of the October Revolution became the state organization for the central planning of industry, fixing prices, setting targets for production for export and

home consumption. Vesenkha's importance declined in 1919 as its powers became overshadowed by the Council of Labour and Defence (STO).[50] Labour conscription was introduced and from March 1920 it was stepped up under STO and fell more heavily on industrial workers.[51] Wage fixing began to be introduced from February 1919. By 1920, however, rationing gave way to wages in kind and a money economy effectively ceased to exist as inflation drove it out of existence.[52]

Under the pressures brought by the resurgence and escalation of peasant rebellions from August 1920, war communism 'collapsed.'[53] Food shortages were the major factor. Compared with January–March 1920, grain procured from the provinces had fallen to less than half and grain from Siberia failed to reach the central, Bolshevik areas because of transport disruptions, peasant riots, and banditry.[54] By January 1921, bread rations in Moscow, Petrograd, Kronstadt, and Ivanovo-Voznesensk were reduced by over one third and growing social disorder and worker demands were the inevitable consequence. Through February, protests and uprisings broke out all over Russia. In Moscow, the metalworkers Union Conference of 2–4 February 1921 passed a resolution de-

[47] See Rigby, *Lenin's Government*, p. 16. As a consequence of the Peace Treaty, the Ukraine passed to Germany. As the major wheat growing area, this seriously exacerbated the food crisis in Moscow and Petrograd. See A. B. Ulam, *Lenin and the Bolsheviks* (London, Fontana, 1969), p. 532.

[48] Decree quoted in Leggett, *The Cheka*, p. 64.

[49] For the above, see Carr, *The Bolshevik Revolution*, vol. 2, pp. 159–65 and vol. 1, pp. 248–50 and p. 233. From May 1919 food rations for children under 14 were given free of charge. Collective farms also made their first appearance in 1919.

[50] See Carr, *The Bolshevik Revolution*, vol. 2, pp. 79 and 198.

[51] See Malle, *The Economic Organization of War Communism*, pp. 479 and 502 and Carr, *The Bolshevik Revolution*, vol. 2, pp. 202 and 210.

[52] The purchasing price of money in circulation at 1 July 1921 was worth little over 1 per cent of what it had been worth at 1 November 1917. (See Carr, *The Bolshevik Revolution*, vol. 2, p. 259.) Between 65–70 per cent of food needed for subsistence in the RSFSR as a whole was supplied by the black market (see Malle, *The Economic Organization of War Communism*, p. 504).

[53] Sakwa, *Soviet Communists in Power*, p. 240.

[54] Malle, *The Economic Organization of War Communism*, p. 513.

manding free trade and a 'fixed tax in kind' to replace forced requisitioning. Strikes and demonstrations erupted throughout February and on 23 February, 10,000 workers took part in a demonstration. Following obstruction to production in the factories the (mostly Menshevik) trade union leaders were arrested.[55] In March 1921, the Kronstadt Rebellion, as elsewhere, erupted in reaction to food shortages, resentment over food requisitioning, labour compulsion, and the Cheka's brutality. On 17 March, the Bolsheviks defeated the Kronstadt rebels.

THE HOLD ON POWER AT THE END OF CIVIL WAR: JACOBINS AND BOLSHEVIKS COMPARED

Faced with economic collapse and escalating social disorder similar to that faced by the Jacobins, the Bolsheviks succeeded in hanging on to power whilst the Jacobins lost control. Having argued for the importance of similarity in respect of war mobilization, to explain this contrast between Bolsheviks and Jacobins Skocpol elaborates the differences between these cases in the following way:

> The Bolsheviks managed to execute economic policy changes (including concessions to market-oriented interests and peasant smallholders) and remain in national political power. Why could they do it and not the Montagnards in 1794? As the 'party of the proletariat,' operating in a twentieth-century society that had already had large-scale, modern industries, the Bolsheviks enjoyed two advantages: they possessed both an ideological self-justification and a realistic organizational basis for a political mission that could sustain their movement in state power beyond the military defence of the Revolution. The Bolsheviks could 'fall back' on state-controlled industries and could devote

themselves after 1921 to devising ways to use state power to expand those industries and the numbers of factory workers employed in them. By contrast, the Montagnards in France, even if they had been consistently willing to conceive of themselves as the 'party of the *sansculottes*' did not have objectively available to them any expansionist economic mission to sustain them in state power beyond the military victories of 1793–4. . . . More important, a French economy consisting almost entirely of small-scale agricultural and commercial units (and some non-mechanized industrial enterprises) simply could not be directed from above by a political party. There were no 'commanding heights' for the state to manage; and even foreign models of large-scale industry were entirely lacking at that point of world history.[56]

There is no doubt that Lenin's introduction of the New Economic Policy at the Tenth Party Congress in March 1921 played a crucial part in the Bolsheviks' capacity to retain power. The introduction of NEP amounted to the reintroduction of the market and represented, therefore, a reversal of war communism. Its most important measure was the replacement of the 'tax in kind' which took everything above a calculated basic family need with a new tax calculated on the basis of a percentage of crop production. This responded to the demands for a 'fixed tax in kind.' This tax was to be graduated, falling most heavily on the rich and least on the poor, but it permitted peasants to retain a surplus above family needs which could be sold on the market. To facilitate this sale of surplus, restrictions on movements of goods for trade were removed in May and so, in effect, the black market became legal.

The incentives offered by NEP for peasant production began to reap rewards in the spring of 1922, and the favourable

---

[55] For the above see Sakwa, *Soviet Communists in Power*, pp. 241–5.

[56] Skocpol, *States and Social Revolutions*, pp. 192–3.

weather of that summer brought the best harvest since the outbreak of the revolution. In March 1922, the new tax in kind was reduced to a standard 10 per cent. The decree of May 1922 also made peasants' tenure of their land secure.[57] Essentially directed at agriculture, NEP also had a bearing on industry where it was less successful in increasing production. In the summer of 1921, a series of measures effected a Bolshevik form of privatization as state control gave way to commercialism in the form of leases and trusts.[58] A free labour market was reintroduced and a money wage system reemerged with wages related to productivity. Wage-fixing gave way to a minimum wage.

The changes introduced by NEP clearly constituted such a radical departure from war communism that it is difficult to support the view that 'ideological self-justification' was one of the two crucial differences between the Bolsheviks and the Jacobins. A willingness to adopt a material economic response was certainly central to Marxist-Leninist thinking, but the reversal of war communism in practical response to demands indicated flexibility, not dogmatism.[59] There is also no disputing that international conditions in respect of world trade and inter-state relations differed at the times of the Russian and French revolutions. Over 128 years it would be odd indeed had they not

changed. It is not so clear, however, that the relative lack of industrial enterprises in France in 1789 made the difference to the Jacobins' chances of hanging on to power. There is some evidence against this view in the development of state owned armament industries and the potential for nationalization of mines which was not acted upon in France.[60] More importantly, the comparative lessons of NEP suggest that practical policies did not rest solely on the potential for state control of industry. As consideration of war communism has shown, rural policies were at least as important as industrial ones to the Bolsheviks' hold on power at the end of the civil war.[61]

It is, undoubtedly, also true that the Jacobins lacked Communist Party-type organization.[62] Again, however, it is not so clear that party organization was decisive for the Bolsheviks during the civil war. Certainly, the importance of the party grew through the civil war. From early 1919 the Politburo, the Political Bureau of the Communist Party Central Committee, began to develop as a sort of 'court of appeal' against Sovnarkom decisions.[63] Lenin, Trotsky, and Stalin were amongst its

[57] For above see Carr, *The Bolshevik Revolution*, vol. 2, p. 282, 285, and 294.

[58] For details of leases and trusts see Carr, *The Bolshevik Revolution*, vol. 2, pp. 298–309, and for the following see p. 310 and pp. 318–22.

[59] For support see N. Harding, 'Socialism, society and the organic labour state,' in Harding (ed.), *The State in Socialist Society* (Oxford, Macmillan, 1984). For a full discussion of the changes brought by NEP see L. H. Siegelbaum, *Soviet State and Society between Revolutions, 1918–29* (Cambridge, Cambridge University Press, 1992).

[60] See Soboul, *The French Revolution 1787–1799*, pp. 390–1.

[61] Consideration of NEP in Russia suggests, for France, that peasants could have been encouraged to increase production and to sell their surplus more readily through the use of incentives combined with the redistribution of the land in favour of the peasants who worked on it. Such ideas were not, however, compatible with the Committee of Public Safety's thinking. Indeed anyone advocating radical 'agrarian law' ran the risk of execution (see Kemp, *Economic Forces in French History*, p. 88).

[62] F. Fehér, *The Frozen Revolution: An Essay on Jacobinism* (Cambridge, Cambridge University Press, 1987), p. 67, has argued that the structure of Jacobin clubs indicates an early form of political party, though he argues that the Jacobin idea of a general will prevented it acting as such.

[63] Rigby, *Lenin's Government*, p. 183.

five members. As local soviets were weakened by the pressures of the civil war and the strength of the Cheka, local party committees came to play an important role in the provinces. Even by the end of the civil war, however, membership of the party was still relatively small and given the vast size of the RSFSR and the problems of communication, the party control achieved was far from total.[64] The collapse of war communism illustrates the party's failure to control the mode of production. The Cheka played the major role in extracting and maintaining supplies from 1918 and, crucially, it was Sovnarkom which held executive power over Russia during the Civil War. The central planks of Communist party control were laid down at the Tenth Party Congress in March 1921, that is, at exactly the same time as NEP was introduced.

There were three aspects to the development of central party control in Russia: the removal of political opposition in the form of parties and trade unions, the imposition of discipline within the Communist Party and the decline of Sovnarkom. By the summer of 1918, the opposition parties, the Anarchists, Mensheviks, and Social Revolutionaries (Right and Left), had been suppressed, though throughout the civil war they had remained in the Congress of Soviets (the December 1920 All-Russian Congress of Soviets being the last to admit members from those parties). Within the trade unions, oppositions had played a crucial and visible role in the crisis which had broken out in the summer of 1920 which reached its peak in February 1921, and the issue of trade unions had given rise to heated debates within the Bolshevik Party.[65] Lenin's decision at the Tenth Party Congress to liberalize the economy whilst strengthening the party at the expense of oppositions was, therefore, crucial to central party-state control. From March 1921 rival platforms within the Communist Party, permitted by a statute of 1919, were also banned and party discipline made far more draconian. The first 'purge' of party members was initiated in October 1921 when, in all, 24 per cent of party members were expelled.[66] From mid-1921 onwards, party organization (Politburo and Central Committee) began to displace Sovnarkom as the center of government.[67] The temporary government of Sovnarkom which had presided over the period of civil war gave way to the permanent government of Communist Party rule. The RSFSR adopted its modern title of The Union of Soviet Socialist Republics in December 1922.

THE END OF CIVIL WAR— LESSONS FROM RUSSIA TO FRANCE ON STATE CONSTRUCTION

The foundations for the consolidated 'modern' state of the Soviet Union were laid, then, not in November 1917 as Skocpol holds but in March 1921 after the civil war had ended. As in France, the years of civil war were years of emergency government. This is obscured by Skocpol's stress on international war which for France continued to 1815 and for Russia was effectively ended by March 1918. This international emphasis, by stressing the growth of the army, conceals the importance to these emergency governments of

[64] Mawdsley, *The Russian Civil War,* p. 274.

[65] See Sakwa, *Soviet Communists in Power,* pp. 247–64.

[66] Carr, *The Bolshevik Revolution,* vol. 2, p. 208 and pp. 211–3.

[67] Rigby, *Lenin's Government,* pp. 191–213, argues that Lenin (Trotsky too) was against the dominance of the party organs (Politburo and the Central Committee) over Sovnarkom.

the internal security organizations, and so obscures a crucial factor in Bolshevik success and Jacobin failure. Whilst Lenin succeeded in bringing the Cheka under central control, Robespierre failed to gain control over the Committee of General Security. Sovnarkom's legitimacy had been undermined by the violence of the civil war and the terrorism of the Cheka in particular.[68] In the very summary nature of their powers, the Chekas operated outside the controls of law.[69] By virtue of the change in emphasis from compulsion to the market, with the introduction of NEP at the Tenth Party Congress in March 1921, the importance of the Cheka for obtaining supplies was reduced. Following debates in the press over the excesses of the Cheka, its powers were cut in June 1921. The Cheka ceased to be an 'Extraordinary Commission' and became subordinate to the Department of Internal Affairs. The GPU replaced the Cheka in February 1922.[70]

By contrast, in France the end of the civil war was followed by a series of laws and actions taken by the Committee of Public Safety (or by Robespierre and any other members of the Committee when in Paris) which failed to impose central control over the revolutionary coercive forces. The first was the law of 14 Frimaire, introduced on 4 December 1793 by the Committee of Public Safety, which removed power from the Departments and under section 18 of the law disbanded all the de-

partmental and local people's armies, with the exception only of the Paris army. In February 1794, the laws of 8 and 13 Ventôse were introduced to set up a bureaucracy for the organization of punishment and arrest.[71] The Representatives on Mission, accountable to the Committee of General Security, were opposed to centralization but from February the Committee of Public Safety began to recall those 'who showed themselves to be lusting after blood.'[72] The split between the Indulgents (led by Danton) and the Hébertistes (led by Héberte and including Ronsin, the head of the Parisian Army) which is usually put down to in-fighting amongst the Jacobins, essentially developed over the Terror. The Indulgents objected to the excesses of Ronsin's Army (in Lyon they were involved in massacres)[73] and the scale of executions carried out by the Representatives on Mission. On 13–14 March the Hébertistes were arrested and on 24 March they were executed. Fouché, Representative on Mission in Lyon, was recalled on 21 March and, with Ronsin executed, the Paris Army was disbanded on 28 March.[74]

Without the Paris army, the force for ensuring supplies to Paris and for policing the Maximum had gone. Unlike Lenin, at

---

[68] See Rigby, *Lenin's Government*, pp. 173–4 and Leggett, *The Cheka*, p. 202.

[69] In Moscow, where party control ought to have been feasible—certainly more so in relation to areas more distant from the capital—Sakwa argues that the Cheka 'emerged as an almost autonomous fiefdom despite several attempts by the Moscow party organization and the national leadership to bring it under control' (Sakwa, *Soviet Communists in Power*, p. 271).

[70] See Leggett, *The Cheka*, p. 343 and Carr, *The Bolshevik Revolution*, vol. 1, p. 187–8.

[71] For the above see Sutherland, *France 1789–1815*, pp. 235–6 and Cobb, *The People's Armies*, p. 524.

[72] Soboul, *The French Revolution 1787–1799*, p. 397. See also C. Lucas, *The Structure of the Terror: The Example of Javogues and the Loire* (London, Oxford University Press, 1973), p. 388.

[73] Cobb, *The People's Armies*, p. 368.

[74] See Sutherland, *France 1789–1815*, p. 240. Ronsin's execution and the disbandment of the Paris revolutionary army has been linked to a military plot to remove Robespierre from power. Cobb, *The People's Armies*, pp. 567–617, after detailed consideration, however, takes the view that rumor of a plot was in fact used by the government to get rid of the Paris army whilst at the same time maintaining its image of revolutionary zeal.

this point, Robespierre had neither viable economic policies nor central control over revolutionary coercion. Without policies to satisfy demands he could not afford to relax coercion to the level demanded by the Indulgents. At the beginning of April, the Dantonists, too, were arrested and executed. In the same month, the Committee of Public Safety set up its own special police, the Bureau de Surveillance in charge of internal policing, in direct threat to the Committee of General Security.[75]

On 8 May, the provincial revolutionary tribunals were suppressed and all counter-revolutionary crimes were from then on to be tried by the Paris Revolutionary Tribunal. On 10 June, the Law of 22 Prairial was passed,[76] under which representatives on mission with continuing records of excessive use of terror were to return to Paris and all suspects were, in future, to be tried in Paris. The Law of 22 Prairial which, theoretically, ended the decentralized system of revolutionary tribunals, was never allowed to operate properly. The Committee of General Security, in charge of gathering information on suspects, chose to bring large groups of people under a whole range of different charges from the relatively minor to the highly serious, and condemn them as a group rather than trying them each in turn.[77] The effect was highly damaging for Robespierre's government, made worse by the Committee

of General Security's ridiculing of Robespierre's Fête of the Supreme Being on 20 Prairial (8 June).[78] This appeal to Virtue, in such contrast to Lenin's practical policies, grated against the continuing terror. With Ronsin's army disbanded, protests against supply shortages, prices, and wages escalated once again, culminating in the rising in Paris which precipitated Robespierre's downfall.

Whilst Robespierre and the Committee of Public Safety failed to gain central control over the Committee of General Security, Lenin and Sovnarkom succeeded in gaining control over the Cheka. With a centralized police and secret police force in place, in Russia, the permanent state could be established.

CHINA: THE TEST CASE

The importance to state construction of civil war and the development of centralized internal coercion is confirmed by the case of China between 1950–3, the year before permanent state structures were established in 1954. Significantly, here too the move towards permanent state construction began only after the civil war was over. Skocpol draws no special attention to these years, in spite of quoting Schurmann on the effects of land reform and the slide

---

[75] Being in charge of internal policing, retention of power for the Committee of General Security rested on the continuation of the Terror. See Sutherland, *France 1789–1815*, p. 242 and Soboul, *The French Revolution 1787–1799*, vol. 1, p. 409.

[76] The Law of 22 Prairial was introduced after assassination attempts had been made on both Robespierre and Collot d'Herbois. For details of the law see Sutherland, *France 1789–1815*, p. 242.

[77] See Soboul, *The French Revolution 1787–1799*, p. 406. Prison conspiracies were used as an excuse to do this.

[78] See Sutherland, *France 1789–1815*, p. 242–3 and Wright, *Revolution and Terror in France*, p. 89 and Document 24. Robespierre's vision, heavily inspired by Rousseau's ideas of the general will and the social contract, was for a fundamental change to the way people thought, turned in direction towards the public good [Norman Hampson, 'From regeneration to terror: the ideology of the French revolution,' in Noel O'Sullivan (ed.), *Terrorism, Ideology and Revolution* (Brighton, Harvester Wheatsheaf, 1986), ch. 3, pp. 62–3]. The worship of the Supreme Being was to replace the old hierarchical Catholic religion. The new civil religion with faith in human nature was to retain its spiritual and ethical content but to lose all the diverse aspects of Catholicism which made it a source of power separate and, therefore, in revolutionaries' eyes, in opposition to the state.

into terror for lack of party control at village level.[79]

China differs from Russia and France in two crucial respects. Firstly, full scale civil war preceded the takeover in 1949 rather than erupting after it. Full scale civil war reemerged between the Guomindang and the Communists in 1946 after Japan's defeat in World War Two. Secondly, the revolutionaries had a fully organized and experienced communist guerilla army, and experience of political administration in the soviets in the liberated areas. Thus, the Chinese communists came to power with considerable advantages in establishing a new revolutionary government.[80] After the victory in 1949, China was divided into six military areas. Military administration dominated civilian administration until 1954. In September 1949, the Chinese People's Political Consultative Conference, under Mao's chairmanship, enacted the 'Organic Law' under which the civilian administration was established for the new People's Republic. Mao was Chairman of the People's Republic as well as Chairman of the CCP and Chou en-lai became the Premier of the new Government Administrative Council. This new government had 24 ministries, 11 of which were headed by non-Communist Party members. Three of the six vice-chairmen of the Republic were also noncommunists.[81]

Though the Communists had won the civil war in 1949, counter-revolution remained a serious threat with the Guomindang left in control of the islands of Formosa, Quemoy, and Matsu. With the outbreak of the Korean War in late June 1950, furthermore, the United States made Taiwan a military protectorate. This threat of counter-revolution in combination with foreign intervention raised the serious possibility of a renewed civil war backed by a powerful foreign state. Guomindang air raids into China continued well into 1950 and in the big cities secret drug dealing and gambling organizations were operated through connections with the old Guomindang secret police.[82] Under the auspices of the Ministry of Security (Gonganqu), which was headed by General Luo Rui-qing, a secret police force was established to hunt out these gangsters and political opponents, to bring them to trial and punishment and to destroy the secret societies through which they worked. The secret police network permeated deep into society. In the cities, every local committee (each one governing around 100 households) and in the countryside, every local administration unit (xiang) had a public security section.[83] Beginning in 1951 and continuing through 1952, the police set up mass movements with public cooperation to eliminate counter-revolutionaries. These movements (Yundong) were mobilizations for the reenforcement of new values through discussion, posters, and marches. These Yundong received both training and advice from Soviet technicians and an organized system of repression developed with special prisons and camps. As Chesneaux remarks, 'This apparatus was solid and durable, even if it did not attain

---

[79] See F. H. Schurmann, *Ideology and Organization in Communist China* (Berkeley, University of California Press, 1966), pp. 431–2, mentioned in Skocpol, *States and Social Revolutions*, p. 262.

[80] See O'Kane, *The Revolutionary Reign of Terror*, p. 209.

[81] For above see M. Meisner, *Mao's China: A History of the People's Republic* (New York, Free, 1977), pp. 70–2.

[82] For the above see J. Chesneaux, *China: The People's Republic 1949–1976* (Brighton, Harvester, 1979), p. 34, Meisner, *Mao's China*, p. 80 and B. Brugger, *China: Liberation and Transformation* 1942–1962 (London, Croom Helm, 1981), p. 63.

[83] Meisner, *Mao's China*, p. 77.

the size and harshness of the Soviet Gulag.'[84]

Thought reform and a centralized secret police system did not, however, provide the only conditions for state construction. A crucial programme for economic and social reform was also implemented, and it was here that terror went seriously out of control.[85] The Agrarian Reform Law was introduced in June 1950. It was designed to apply to the newly liberated areas, recently brought under Communist control. The reforms included the confiscation of landlord properties and requisitioning of supplies with compensation. The confiscated land was redistributed to the poor peasants. The system of village community politics established in the liberated areas before 1949 was used to enforce the law. Special 'people's tribunals' were set up for the purpose.[86] In some villages public confession was enough but in others landlords were shot and even lynched. With China fully engaged in the Korean War, by November 1950 agrarian policy became tougher, especially in the central south area (Wuhan) where land reforms met resistance.[87] In 1951–2 the people's tribunals moved to the cities. Corrupt government officials and capitalists, involved in tax evasion, for example, were also brought to trial.

At the beginning of 1953, the people's tribunals were disbanded. Though the threat from the Korean War was by then diminishing, the War was not ended until the middle of 1953, that is, after the Terror had been brought to an end.[88] Fear of counter-revolution at home, however, was under control. As Meisner remarks, 'Three years after the establishment of the People's Republic the goal of a strong state had been realized—and it was a state (like all states) which rested on a powerful army and an extensive police apparatus as well as on a broad base of popular support.[89] The broad base of support had been gained through real achievements. The mobilization campaign had pushed changes on at so rapid a pace that industrial production had nearly trebled between 1949 and 1952. In agriculture, cereal production had risen from 113 million tons in 1949 to 164 million in 1952, an especially impressive figure given that 150 million tons had been the best pre-war figure.[90] Politically too the local party organization had been strengthened within the villages and state control over the economy had been expanded significantly.[91] However, only after the revolutionary Terror had come to an end, and Stalin had died (March 1953), did China begin clearly to develop its political and economic system according to the Soviet model. In 1953, the Five Year Plan of 'tran-

[84] Chesneaux, *China: The People's Republic*, p. 41. For expansion on Yundong see Brugger, *China: Liberation and Transformation*, pp. 80–5.

[85] For details of the reform see *Keesing's Contemporary Archives*, 1950 (London, Keesing's), p. 10855. In February 1951 the reform programme was developed in accordance with Mao's ideas of 'new democracy,' the first stage of socialism rather than socialism itself. See N. Smart, *Mao* (Glasgow, Fontana/Collins, 1974), ch. 6. *The New Democracy* was published by Mao in 1940.

[86] H. McAleavy, *The Modern History of China* (London, Weidenfeld and Nicolson, 1972), p. 339.

[87] Brugger, *China: Liberation and Transformation*, p. 72.

[88] McAleavy, *The Modern History of China*, p. 340 estimates the number of executions during the Terror to be 'unlikely to have been much lower than one million.'

[89] Meisner, *Mao's China*, p. 92. Between 1950–5 the people's militia was expanded from 5 million to 12.8 million and from the militia recruits were produced for the People's Liberation Army in Korea. Brugger, *China: Liberation and Transformation*, p. 75.

[90] Chesneaux, *China: The People's Republic*, pp. 44–7.

[91] Brugger, *China: Liberation and Transformation*, pp. 84–5.

sition to socialism,' essentially favoring heavy industry, was adopted and in 1954 a new constitution was introduced.[92] Under this 1954 constitution, the Government Administrative Council gained the new name of the State Council and ruled as a central organization over a county (xien) and village (xiang) local government network. The regional military control established in 1949 was combined within the civil administration. This had been made possible through the growth of the Communist Party between 1949–52 both within the civil administration and the army.[93]

The differences between the outcomes in China and Russia Skocpol ascribes to 'two sets of world-historical and international contextual factors: (1) political influence upon China from previously revolutionized Soviet Russia; and (2) enhanced possibilities in the twentieth century for state-propelled national industrialization.'[94] Skocpol admits that the Chinese case was essentially an agricultural rather than an industrial based revolution and that China and Russia had fallen out by 1957 and parted company by 1958. She also argues that the outcome of the Chinese revolution differed from that of the Russian revolution in being far more egalitarian and successful in its agricultural policies.[95] It is clear that the very special mass mobilization character of Maoism was central not only to the development of the peasant egalitarianism which, Skocpol argues, characterizes modern China but also, as analysis of 1949–54 has shown, to the development of a highly effective state police system.

[92] Chesneaux, *China: The People's Republic,* pp. 56–68.

[93] Meisner, *Mao's China,* p. 72 and for above see also p. 71.

[94] Skocpol, *States and Social Revolutions,* p. 266.

[95] Skocpol, *States and Social Revolutions,* p. 281.

CONCLUSION: GENERAL COMPARATIVE LESSONS

In all three revolutions, the French, Russian and Chinese, civil war was of greater significance for state building than was foreign war. Permanent state construction could only begin once the civil war was over. Comparison between the three cases at this crucial point, the end of the civil war, showed that success in modern centralized state building relied on a number of factors, only in part taken into account by Skocpol. Some support was found for the advantages of party organization, though party-states did not begin immediately the Bolsheviks and Chinese Communists came to power. Party organization was, at best, a secondary factor in explaining the Jacobin's failure either to construct a permanent state or to lay the foundations for one eventually to be built by Napoleon. Policies were important, though consideration of what the leaders were 'doing' demonstrated the importance of agricultural policies over industrial ones for all three cases. In particular, I have stressed the importance of practical policies which had support from those directly affected. This showed the importance of flexibility rather than ideological dogmatism. In stressing agricultural issues over industrial ones, and domestic economic problems as crucial to these regimes, national considerations were given prominence over international ones.

In addition to the need to achieve support from practical policies, concentration on civil war has also revealed an essential basis for state-building which Skocpol failed to analyze: centralized control over the revolutionary forces of internal coercion. A new revolutionary army may be needed to win foreign wars, but at home it is a new revolutionary system of internal security that is needed, under state control. This might well be at odds with the final goal of a stateless communist society. It is, however, consistent with Marx's view of 'state power' defined in his analysis of the 1848 revolutions: he defined it in terms of the police, army, courts, and bureaucracy with the police declared to be the 'ultimate expression of the old state.'[96] It fits too with Trotsky's declaration at Brest-Litovsk that 'Every state is founded on force,' accepted by Weber in his classic definition of the state as a 'human community that (successfully) claims the *monopoly of the legitimate use of physical force* within a given territory.'[97] The analysis here, however, has challenged Weber. In addition to highlighting the specific importance of revolutions to an understanding of the state, it has drawn attention away from the monopoly of existing coercive forces to the development of new revolutionary forces of coercion within a territory and their need to be brought under central control.

---

[96] K. Marx, *The Revolution of 1848: Political Writings Vol. 1* (Harmondsworth, Penguin, 1973), p. 205.

[97] H. H. Gerth and C. W. Mills, *From Max Weber: Essays in Sociology* (London, Routledge and Kegan Paul, 1970), p. 78.

International Relations

12

He who is seated in authority soon learns to think security, and not progress, the highest lesson of statecraft.

—James Russell Lowell

The state represents violence in a concentrated and organized form. The individual has a soul, but as the state is a soulless machine, it can never be weaned from violence to which it owes its very existence.

—Mohandas Gandhi

An Introduction to International Relations

The study of international relations may be separated, as Jacek Kugler's (1993) recent synopsis has done, into two broad categories of study. The first is conflict and conflict resolution in the international arena, which examines how peace may be achieved and war avoided. The second is international political economy, which is the study of how economic relations within and between nations affects both national and international political systems.

The study of conflict and conflict resolution in international politics has an historical tradition reaching back at least as far as ancient Greece. This tradition has historically been dominated by the debate between realists, who argue that the strong defense of national interests provides the only form of security in a dangerous world, and idealists, who believe that international organizations and other cooperative efforts are the best way to ensure peace. Greek historian Thucydides's *History of the Peloponnesian War,* is a remarkable chronicle of the decades long struggle for supremacy between Athens and Sparta. Thucydides's work is the foundational classic work in international relations because it not only catalogs facts about what occurred but also attempts to make sense of the conflicts among the nation-states as they existed at that time, and because the basic elements of that historical struggle have appeared over and over again in history and do so until this day. There are many striking similarities between the situation that Thucydides describes (two superpowers, their alliances, and the balance of power that at first worked and then failed) and the contest between the United States and the Soviet Union during the twentieth century's Cold War. Note what Thucydides says about the reasons for the start of the Peloponnesian War: "What made war inevitable was the growth of Athenian power and the fear which this caused in Sparta." The similarities are so intriguing that American defense planners seriously studied Thucydides's history for insights that could be applied to the Cold War conflict. Because Thucydides recorded the events of the Peloponnesian War as objectively as he could, and because he implies that international conflict is a natural, inevitable part of human existence, thereby rejecting the notion that universal peace is achievable through the improvement of human nature or better social conventions, Thucydides is known as a realist.

Continuing through the history of international relations we find many prescriptions for world peace, but perhaps the most famous exponent of idealism in international relations before modern times was Dante Aligheri (1265–1321). Dante lived in a medieval Italy that was beset by constant petty wars among feudal kingdoms. Looking back through history he noted that the only time of lasting peace was in the days of the Roman Empire. The Roman Catholic Church ("catholic" means universal) had expected to bring about the universal peaceful dominion of Christ, but that attempt had failed. Since the Roman Empire had achieved international peace, something which no other international order has done, Dante reasoned that it must be necessary to recreate an empire, a world government under a secular leader who could again bring peace to the world. Dante's book *Monarchy* (1958, 13–14) offers arguments typical of medieval deductive logic:

> Again, a son's condition is most perfect when the son, as far as his nature allows, reproduces the perfection of the father. Mankind is the son of the heavens, which is perfect in all its works. . . . Therefore mankind's condition is most perfect when it reproduces the perfection of the heavens, so far as human nature allows. And just as the heavens are governed and directed in every movement by a single mover, which is God (as human reasoning in philosophy amply demonstrates), so, if our argument has been correct, mankind is at its best when all its movements and intentions are governed by one Prince as its sole mover and with one law for its direction. Hence it is obvious that the world's well-being demands a Monarch or single government known as the Empire. This is the argument that led Boethius to sigh: 'How happy you would be, O mankind, if your minds were ruled by the love that rules the heavens.'

Because Dante believed that universal peace is achievable either through a transformation of human nature or by building better government institutions, he is known as an idealist.

Many more philosophers and historians have attempted to shed some light on the problems of conflict among nations. Three more historical figures deserve at least brief mention here because their works have been central to the realist-idealist debate: realists Niccolo Machiavelli, Karl von Clausewitz, and idealist Woodrow Wilson. Niccolo Machiavelli is known as the father of modern realism. His work *The Prince* discussed political power not in terms of God's authority, as other philosophers before him had done, but in terms of how, from Machiavelli's own practical experience in a dangerous and violent world, power is accumulated and secured. He wrote *The Prince* as an exile from government, in an attempt to gain the favor of Lorenzo de Medici, ruler of Florence. In an introductory letter to Lorenzo, Machiavelli states: "Now, I am anxious to offer myself to Your Magnificence with some token of devotion to you, and I have not found among my belongings anything as dear to me or that I value as much as my understanding of the deeds of great men, won by me from a long acquaintance with contemporary affairs and a continuous study of the ancient world."

Any student of armed conflict among nations will soon become familiar with the work of Prussian General Karl von Clausewitz (1780–1831), whose book *On War* is still read with more than historical interest in military strategy classes. Clausewitz was not especially original in his thought, but his exposition and clarification of the problems of war popularized his definitions for the key military concepts of strategy and tactics: ". . . tactics teaches the use of the armed forces in engagements, and strategy the use of engagements to obtain the object of the war" (Clausewitz 1962, 141). Clausewitz is most famous, however, for his concept that war is a continuation or extension of politics:

> War is therefore a continuation of policy by other means. It is not merely a political act but a real political instrument, a continuation of political intercourse, a conduct of political intercourse by other means. What still remains peculiar to war relates merely to the peculiar character of the means it employs . . . for the political design is the object, while war is the means, and the means can never be thought of apart from the object. (1962, 83)

Woodrow Wilson must be noted again as the leading figure in twentieth century idealism for his efforts to found the League of Nations. The Charter of the League of Nations, which its organizers hoped would be able to at least control if not abolish war, states, in part:

THE COVENANT OF THE LEAGUE OF NATIONS
THE HIGH CONTRACTING PARTIES
In order to promote international co-operation and to achieve international peace and security:
   by the acceptance of obligations not to resort to war;
   by the prescription of open, just and honourable relations between nations;
   by the firm establishment of the understandings of international law as the actual
      rule of conduct among Governments;
   and by the maintenance of justice and a scrupulous respect for all treaty obligations
      in the dealings of organised peoples with one another.
Agree to this Covenant of the League of Nations.
[Article 12] 1. The Members of the League agree that if there should arise between them any dispute likely to lead to a rupture they will submit the matter either to arbitration or to inquiry by the Council, and they agree in no case to resort to war until three months after the award by the arbitrators or the report by the Council.

The study of conflict and conflict resolution in international politics since World War II has been dominated by the realist school. Realists such as Henry Kissinger and Zbigniew Bzrezinski not only developed international political theory in universities but were able to apply their ideas as advisors to presidents as well. They believe that war is a normal aspect of international relations because nations' vital economic and strategic interests often conflict, and nations will always attempt to promote their own interests, whenever they find it necessary, at the expense of others. The United States, according to the realists, can most successfully avoid war by actively promoting its own long-term interests, which include a stable, peaceful international political environment, with the support of a strong defense.

Robert Keohane and Joseph Nye at Harvard University propounded what came to be known as neorealism in the 1970s. Neorealism examined not only the activities of nation-states as rational actors attempting to maximize their national interests, but described trends such as the increasing role of transnational organizations and multinational corporations in the international realm as well.

Political scientists study conflict resolution under a number of different subject headings within international relations, the most important of which are international organization and international law. Many different types of international organizations are of interest to political scientists. The most well known is the United Nations (U.N.), which was established immediately after World War II to provide a forum for all nations to discuss mutual problems and conflicts that may arise among them. Headquartered in New York City, the United Nations did not fulfill the expectations of some who thought it might provide the basis for a unified world order. The U.N. has, however, played an increasingly important role in resolving conflicts in many places around the world. Other international organizations include military alliances such as the North Atlantic Treaty Organization (N.A.T.O.), economic alliances such as the Organization of Petroleum Exporting Countries (O.P.E.C), private social service agencies such as the International Red Cross, and private political organizations such as Amnesty International. Sometimes, as in the following cartoon, international organizations are faulted for not exerting the force that they could in order to stop wars such as the one in Bosnia.

The discipline of international law studies the agreements that nations make among themselves to regulate political, economic, resource, and environmental

Peters
Dayton Daily News

Reprinted by permission: Tribune Media Services.

matters. The International Court of Justice at the Hague arbitrates disputes voluntarily brought before it by nations that are unable to resolve them by themselves.

Kuglar describes a number of theories about conflict resolution that have been widely discussed in the last three decades. The first is balance of power theory. According to the many variations of this theory, international systems are anarchical, that is, there is no world government over the nations, which all act independently. International relations become stable when a balance of power is achieved among the major powers or power-blocks in the system. Going all the way back to the days of Athens and Sparta during the Peloponnesian War, the same patterns, according to some balance of power theorists, are evident. When a party within a major alliance changes its loyalty, the balance of power is upset and war may result. During the Peloponnesian War, for example, the small cities of Epidamnus and Corcyra quickly created a major regional conflict when they attempted to gain the assistance of the more powerful cities of Corinth, Athens, and Sparta.

Competing with balance of power theories for the attention of political scientists, notes Kuglar, is the power preponderance perspective. Power preponderance theory proposes that the world's nations collectively relate to one another in a hierarchical and not in an anarchical way. In other words, instead of a realm in which each state is independent and there is no governing body, the international order is characterized by states having different levels of military power and economic influence. At the top of the hierarchy is the hegemon, the leading world power, which is currently the United States. Below that nation are the "great powers," or those with the capability of becoming a hegemon. At different times great powers have included nations such as France, China, Germany, and Austria-Hungary. Power preponderance theory denies the principle of realist theory that claims that nations always attempt to maximize their power, pointing out that if this were true, hegemons would always try to become world empires. Instead, hegemons appear to be satisfied with a preponderance of power.

Two other important approaches are the collective security perspective and nuclear deterrence. According to Kuglar, collective security was advocated by Woodrow Wilson after World War I. Wilson argued for a League of Nations in which the major powers would collectively control international affairs in a manner that would mutually assure their security. Wilson hoped that collective security would succeed where less formal balance of power arrangements had failed. Although the League of Nations failed in its attempts to achieve peace, and World War II was even more ferocious than World War I, proponents of collective security argue that world conditions are much different today, and that collective security institutions such as the United Nations increasingly offer a viable alternative to war.

Nuclear deterrence includes, among other ideas, the concept of mutually assured destruction (MAD). Proponents of MAD argue that the best way to deter nuclear war is to have enough nuclear weapons to assure the total or nearly complete destruction of the other side. Peace is maintained under conditions in which the dominant competitors for power in the international system assure each other of destruction if nuclear war breaks out. This situation provides no incentive for either side to start a nuclear war. Opponents of MAD argue that it will work only as long as rational people who do not make mistakes have control of the nuclear weapons, and irrational and imperfect people have frequently come to power.

The second major area of international relations is international political economy. Since 1970, many books have been written about the increasing amount of international economic interdependence that has been brought about by new developments in technology and the ability to transport goods cheaply to foreign markets. In his letter to students who read this book, United States trade representative Mickey Kantor outlines some of the major issues in global political economy today, and presents some thoughts on how to deal with them:

THE UNITED STATES TRADE REPRESENTATIVE
Executive Office of the President
Washington, D.C. 20506

JUL 14 1995

Mr. Greg Scott
Assistant Professor
University of Central Oklahoma
100 North University Drive
Edmond, Oklahoma 73034-5209

Dear Mr. Scott:

Thank you for the opportunity to send greetings to your students. The values they will learn in school -- hard work, an open mind, tolerance, curiosity -- will sustain them for their whole lives. The learning and wisdom they will gain is in itself a good thing. But it is also immensely important as we approach the challenges of a new century. Education is more important than ever to getting a job and building a good life because of a rapidly changing world.

The world students today are entering is much different from the one I knew when I was a student at Vanderbilt University.

The end of the Cold War has radically changed the way we must think about our national security. A new global economy has emerged, where goods, services, and information speed around the globe. When I was in school the U.S. economy was largely self-contained. Now, our success is linked to the success of the global economy. The nations of the world are truly interdependent.

If you buy a car today, it could be assembled in this country from parts made in Mexico or Taiwan, be advertised by a British firm, insured by an American firm and sold, hopefully, around the world.

Competition is now a global matter. Companies compete with other firms around the world. Often, workers within the same company are competing against each other from different parts of the globe.

Our age offers immense potential for greater freedom and prosperity. But the new interdependence of this era contains both reward and risk. It is marked by both opportunities and challenges.

Mr. Greg Scott
Page 2

We must give Americans the tools to succeed and prosper in this new economy. All Americans must have the opportunity to receive the best education they can get. We must ensure that we build a new relationship between government and the people; a relationship where government is not a savior, but not on the sidelines either, working instead as a partner as we fight to restore the American Dream.

But the renewal of our nation and the success in making the most of those opportunities must come from inside each of us first. It must come from a renewed commitment to those values that bind us as a nation. That renewal must occur in our government and it must occur in our homes and communities.

Our renewal begins with a willingness to accept personal responsibility to make the most of the opportunities you received in your education. Each one of us carries the responsibility to give back to our communities -- with time, talent and energy. Our renewal must include honoring the basic values of this country: family, work, tolerance, fairness, and community.

Only by meeting these challenges will we renew our nation and restore the American Dream.

I wish all of your students the best of luck in their future endeavors.

Sincerely,

Michael Kantor

At the beginning of this decade, Steve Smith reviewed the course of developments in the study of international relations and identified some trends which he believed would be evident in the discipline in the decades to come. He first identifies "seven main problems and anomalies in the field" which have been encountered in the past few decades:

1. Ethnocentricity: the United States and Great Britain dominate the field.
2. Lack of consensus on methodology.
3. Failure of the discipline to achieve a continuously cumulative body of knowledge.
4. Failure to integrate values and facts into a meaningful product.
5. Failure to evaluate recent changes in the nature of the state.
6. Lack of attention in international relations to domestic politics.
7. Failure to understand adequately the international arena as a system. (Smith 1990, 151–53)

Smith continues, listing six areas that he expects to be important in the 1990s:

1. Feminism and international relations.
2. Critical theory and international relations.
3. The subject needs to become less hegemonic (Anglo-American).
4. Linkage between international economics and international politics.
5. Work linking the explanation of the policy making process within the state to the foreign policy behavior of states.
6. The relationship between unit-level and system-level causes of unit behavior. (Smith 1990, 154)

An Issue in International Relations: Democracy and War

The last years of the twentieth century resemble the final years of previous centuries in at least one respect. People who reflect upon the course of history try to find reason for hope that the century ahead will be better than the one just reaching its conclusion. In the last decade of the twentieth century, few events have given people around the world more hope for a brighter future than the fall of the Soviet Union, not because a human attempt to reconstruct society failed, but because the dangerous power struggle of the Cold War seems at last at an end. Seeking reason for hope, many analysts have examined history and found that democratic regimes do not fight each other. This thought is very hopeful when combined with Harvard Professor Samuel Huntington's conclusion that the trend in many countries around the world is strongly toward democratization. In a recent article in Foreign Affairs, however, Edward D. Mansfield and Jack Snyder, political scientists at Columbia University, review the record and find that democracies are, in fact, not immune to going to war, and that much caution must be exercised to avoid the perilous effects of transitions from nondemocratic regimes to democratic ones. In the following article, Mansfield and Snyder raise some concerns that will be central to discussions of international relations for the next decade.

As you read this article, consider the following questions:

1. What misconception do Mansfield and Snyder believe is pervasive in today's thinking about international relations?
2. How do the authors' views differ from other analysts?
3. What is the substance of Mansfield's and Snyder's argument?
4. What methods of analysis do the authors employ?
5. How successful are the authors in supporting their arguments?

Democratization and War

Edward D. Mansfield and Jack Snyder

DANGERS OF TRANSITION

The idea that democracies never fight wars against each other has become an axiom for many scholars. It is, as one scholar puts it, "as close as anything we have to an empirical law in international relations." This "law" is invoked by American statesmen to justify a foreign policy that encourages democratization abroad. In his 1994 State of the Union address, President Clinton asserted that no two democracies had ever gone to war with each other, thus explaining why promoting democracy abroad was a pillar of his foreign policy.

It is probably true that a world in which more countries were mature, stable democracies would be safer and preferable for the United States. But countries do not become mature democracies overnight. They usually go through a rocky transition, where mass politics mixes with authoritarian elite politics in a volatile way. Statistical evidence covering the past two centuries shows that in this transitional phase of democratization, countries become more aggressive and war-prone, not less, and they do fight wars with democratic states. In fact, formerly authoritarian states where democratic participation is on the rise are more likely to fight wars than are stable democracies or autocracies. States that make the biggest leap, from total autocracy to extensive mass democracy—like contemporary Russia—are about twice as likely to fight wars in the decade after democratization as are states that remain autocracies.

This historical pattern of democratization, belligerent nationalism, and war is already emerging in some of today's new or partial democracies, especially some formerly communist states. Two pairs of states—Serbia and Croatia, and Armenia and Azerbaijan—have found themselves at war while experimenting with varying degrees of electoral democracy. The electorate of Russia's partial democracy cast nearly a quarter of its votes for the party of radical nationalist Vladimir Zhirinovsky. Even mainstream Russian politicians have adopted an imperial tone in their dealings with neighboring former Soviet republics, and military force has been used ruthlessly in Chechnya.

The following evidence should raise questions about the Clinton administration's policy of promoting peace by promoting democratization. The expectation that the spread of democracy will probably contribute to peace in the long run, once new democracies mature, provides little comfort to those who might face a heightened risk of war in the short run. Pushing nuclear-armed great powers like Russia or China toward democratization is like spinning a roulette wheel: many of the outcomes are undesirable. Of course, in most cases the initial steps on the road to democratization will not be produced by any conscious policy of the United States. The roulette wheel is already spinning for Russia and perhaps will be soon for China. Washington and the international community need to think not so much about encouraging or discouraging democratization as about helping to smooth the transition in ways that minimize its risks.

Edward D. Mansfield is Associate Professor of Political Science at Columbia University and author of *Power, Trade, and War.* Jack Snyder, Professor of Political Science and Director of the Institute of War and Peace Studies at Columbia University, is the author of *Myths of Empire.* A longer version of this article will appear in the Summer 1995 issue of *International Security.*

THE EVIDENCE

Our statistical analysis relies on the classifications of regimes and wars from 1811 to 1980 used by most scholars studying the peace among democracies. Starting with these standard data, we classify each state as a democracy, an autocracy, or a mixed regime—that is, a state with features of both democracies and autocracies. This classification is based on several criteria, including the constitutional constraints on the chief executive, the competitiveness of domestic politics, the openness of the process for selecting the chief executive, and the strength of the rules governing participation in politics. Democratizing states are those that made any regime change in a democratic direction—that is, from autocracy to democracy, from a mixed regime to democracy, or from autocracy to a mixed regime. We analyze wars between states as well as wars between a state and a nonstate group, such as liberation movements in colonies, but we do not include civil wars.[1]

---

[1] On the definition of war and the data on war used in this analysis, see Melvin Small and J. David Singer, *Resort to Arms: International and Civil Wars, 1816–1980,* Beverly Hills: Sage, 1982.

Because we view democratization as a gradual process, rather than a sudden change, we test whether a transition toward democracy occurring over one, five, and ten years is associated with the subsequent onset of war. To assess the strength of the relationship between democratization and war, we construct a series of contingency tables. Based on those tables, we compare the probability that a democratizing state subsequently goes to war with the probabilities of war for states in transition toward autocracy and for states undergoing no regime change. The results of all of these tests show that *democratizing states were more likely to fight wars than were states that had undergone no change in regime.* This relationship is weakest one year into democratization and strongest at ten years. During any given ten-year period, a state experiencing no regime change had about one chance in six of fighting a war in the following decade. In the decade following democratization, a state's chance of fighting a war was about one in four. When we analyze the components of our measure of democratization separately, the results are similar. On average, an increase in the openness of the selection process for the chief executive doubled the likelihood of war. Increas-

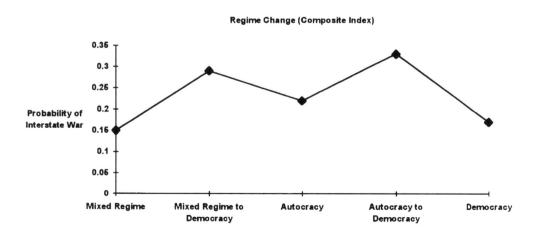

Regime Change (Composite Index)

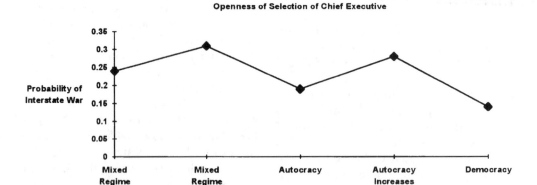

ing the competitiveness of political participation or increasing the constraints on a country's chief executive (both aspects of democratization) also made war more likely. On average, these changes increased the likelihood of war by about 90 percent and 35 percent respectively.

The statistical results are even more dramatic when we analyze cases in which the process of democratization culminated in very high levels of mass participation in politics. States changing from a mixed regime to democracy were on average about 50 percent more likely to become engaged in war (and about two-thirds more likely to go to war with another nation-state) than states that remained mixed regimes.

The effect was greater still for those states making the largest leap, from full autocracy to high levels of democracy. Such states were on average about two-thirds more likely to become involved in any type of war (and about twice as likely to become involved in an interstate war) than states that remained autocracies. Though this evidence shows that democratization is dangerous, its reversal offers no easy solutions. On average, changes toward autocracy also yielded an increase in the probability of war, though a smaller one than changes toward democracy, com-

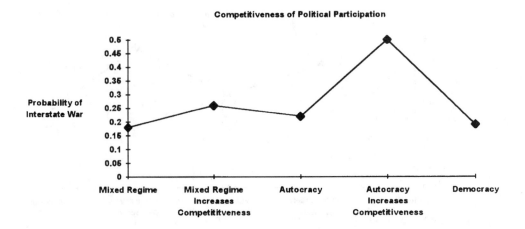

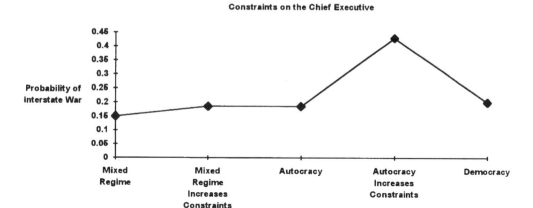

Constraints on the Chief Executive

NATIONALISM AND
DEMOCRATIZATION

The connection between democratization and nationalism is striking in both the historical record and today's headlines. We did not measure nationalism directly in our statistical tests. Nonetheless, historical and contemporary evidence strongly suggests that rising nationalism often goes hand in hand with rising democracy. It is no accident that the end of the Cold War brought both a wave of democratization and a revival of nationalist sentiment in the former communist states.

In eighteenth-century Britain and France, when nationalism first emerged as an explicit political doctrine, it meant self-rule by the people. It was the rallying cry of commoners and rising commercial classes against rule by aristocratic elites, who were charged with the sin of ruling in their own interests, rather than those of the nation. Indeed, dynastic rulers and imperial courts had hardly been interested in promoting nationalism as a banner of solidarity in their realms. They typically ruled over a linguistically and culturally diverse conglomeration of subjects and claimed to

pared to states experiencing no regime change.

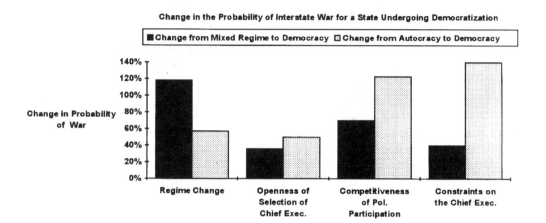

govern by divine right, not in the interest of the nation. Often, these rulers were more closely tied by kinship, language, or culture to elites in other states than to their own subjects. The position of the communist ruling class was strikingly similar: a transnational elite that ruled over an amalgamation of peoples and claimed legitimacy from the communist party's role as the vanguard of history, not from the consent of the governed. Popular forces challenging either traditional dynastic rulers or communist elites naturally tended to combine demands for national self-determination and democratic rule.

This concoction of nationalism and incipient democratization has been an intoxicating brew, leading in case after case to ill-conceived wars of expansion. The earliest instance remains one of the most dramatic. In the French Revolution, the radical Brissotin parliamentary faction polarized politics by harping on the king's slow response to the threat of war with other dynastic states. In the ensuing wars of the French Revolution, citizens flocked to join the revolutionary armies to defend popular self-rule and the French nation. Even after the revolution turned profoundly antidemocratic, Napoleon was able to harness this popular nationalism to the task of conquering Europe, substituting the popularity of empire for the substance of democratic rule.

After this experience, Europe's ruling elites decided to band together in 1815 in the Concert of Europe to contain the twin evils of nationalism and democratization. In this scheme, Europe's crowned heads tried to unite in squelching demands for constitutions, electoral and social democracy, and national self-determination. For a time nationalism and democratization were both held back, and Europe enjoyed a period of relative peace.

But in the long run, the strategy failed in the face of the economic changes strengthening popular forces in Western and Central Europe. British and French politicians soon saw that they would have to rule by coopting nationalist and democratic demands, rather than suppressing them. Once the specter of revolution returned to Europe in 1848, this reversal of political tactics was complete, and it led quickly to the Crimean War. British Foreign Secretary Palmerston and French Emperor Napoleon III both tried to manage the clamor for a broader political arena by giving democrats what they wanted in foreign affairs—a "liberal" war to free imprisoned nations from autocratic rule and, incidentally, to expand commerce.

But this was just the dress rehearsal for history's most potent combination of mass politics and rising nationalism, which occurred in Germany around the turn of the twentieth century. Chancellor Otto von Bismarck, counting on the conservative votes of a docile peasantry, granted universal suffrage in the newly unified Reich after 1870, but in foreign and military affairs, he kept the elected Reichstag subordinate to the cabinet appointed by the kaiser. Like the sorcerer's apprentice, however, Bismarck underestimated the forces he was unleashing. With the rise of an industrial society, Bismarck's successors could not control this truncated democracy, where over 90 percent of the population voted. Everyone was highly politicized, yet nobody could achieve their aims through the limited powers of the Reichstag. As a result, people organized direct pressure groups outside of electoral party politics. Some of these clamored for economic benefits, but many of them found it tactically useful to cloak their narrow interests in a broader vision of the nation's interests. This mass nationalist sentiment exerted constant pressure on German diplomacy in the Wilhelmine years before 1914 and pushed its vacillating elites toward war.

Democratization and nationalism also became linked in Japan on the eve of the Manchurian invasion in 1931. During the 1920s Japan expanded its suffrage and experimented with two-party electoral competition, though a council of military elder statesmen still made the ultimate decisions about who would govern. These semi-elected governments of the 1920s supported free trade, favored naval arms control, and usually tried to rein in the Japanese army's schemes to undermine the Open Door policy in China. During the 1920s, Young Turks in the army developed a populist, nationalist doctrine featuring a centrally planned economy within an autarkic, industrialized, expanded empire, while scapegoating Japan's alleged internal and external enemies, including leftist workers, rich capitalists, liberals, democrats, Americans, and Russians. After the economic crash of the late 1920s, this nationalist formula became persuasive, and the Japanese military had little trouble gaining popular support for imperial expansion and the emasculation of democracy. As in so many previous cases, nationalism proved to be a way for militarist elite groups to appear populist in a democratizing society while obstructing the advance to full democracy.

The interconnection among nationalism, democratization, and war is even clearer in new states. In today's "Weimar Russia," voters disgruntled by economic distress backed belligerent nationalists like Zhirinovsky, put ostensible liberals like President Boris Yeltsin and Foreign Minister Andrei Kozyrev on the defensive on ethnic and foreign policy issues, and contributed to the climate that led to war in

Chechnya. In "Wilhelmine Serbia," the political and military elites of the old regime, facing inexorable pressure for democratization, cynically but successfully created a new basis for legitimacy through nationalist propaganda and military action, and they recently won elections that were only partially manipulated. Until its recent decree suspending the activities of the main opposition party, Armenia had moved quite far toward full democracy while at the same time supporting an invasion of its ethnic foes in Azerbaijan. The Azeris have been less successful in sustaining momentum toward democracy. However, in Azerbaijan's one relatively free and fair presidential election, the winner, Abulfaz Ali Elchibey, attacked the incumbent for being insufficiently nationalist and populist. Elchibey's platform emphasized Turkic identity and the strengthening of the Azeri nation-state to try to mount a counteroffensive against the Armenians. In other ethnically divided societies, where holding an election is like taking a census, democratization has often become an opportunity to exercise the tyranny of the majority.

THE SORCERER'S APPRENTICE

Although democratization in many cases leads to war, that does not mean that the average voter wants war. Public opinion in democratizing states often starts off highly averse to the costs and risks of war. In that sense, the public opinion polls taken in Russia in early 1994 were typical. Respondents said, for example, that Russian policy should make sure the rights of Russians in neighboring states were not infringed, but not at the cost of military intervention. Public opinion often becomes more belligerent, however, as a result of propaganda and military action presented as faits accomplis by elites. This mass opinion, once aroused, may no longer be controllable.

For example, Napoleon III successfully exploited the domestic prestige from France's share of the victory in the Crimean War to consolidate his rule, despite the popular reluctance and war-weariness that had accompanied the war. Having learned this lesson well, Napoleon tried this tactic again in 1859. On the eve of his military intervention in the Italian struggle with Austria, he admitted to his ministers that "on the domestic front, the war will at first awaken great fears; traders and speculators of every stripe will shriek, but national sentiment will [banish] this domestic fright; the nation will be put to the test once more in a struggle that will stir many a heart, recall the memory of heroic times, and bring together under the mantle of glory the parties that are steadily drifting away from one another day after day."[2] Napoleon was trying not just to follow opinion but to make public opinion bellicose, in order to stir a national feeling that would enhance the state's ability to govern a split and stalemated political arena.

Much the same has happened in contemporary Serbia. Despite the memories of Ustashe atrocities in World War II, intermarriage rates between Croats and Serbs living in Croatia were as high as one in three during the 1980s. Opinion has been bellicized by propaganda campaigns in state-controlled media that, for example, carried purely invented reports of rapes of Serbian women in Kosovo, and even more so by the fait accompli of launching the war itself.

In short, democratizing states are war-prone not because war is popular with the mass public, but because domestic pressures create incentives for elites to drum up nationalist sentiment.

THE CAUSES OF DEMOCRATIC WARS

Democratization typically creates a syndrome of weak central authority, unstable domestic coalitions, and high-energy mass politics. It brings new social groups and classes onto the political stage. Political leaders, finding no way to reconcile incompatible interests, resort to short-sighted bargains or reckless gambles in order to maintain their governing coalitions. Elites need to gain mass allies to defend their weakened positions. Both the newly ambitious elites and the embattled old ruling groups often use appeals to nationalism to stay astride their unmanageable political coalitions.

Needing public support, they rouse the masses with nationalist propaganda but find that their mass allies, once mobilized by passionate appeals, are difficult to control. So are the powerful remnants of the old order—the military, for example—which promote militarism because it strengthens them institutionally. This is particularly true because democratization weakens the central government's ability to keep policy coherent and consistent. Governing a society that is democratizing is like driving a car while throwing away the steering wheel, stepping on the gas, and fighting over which passenger will be in the driver's seat. The result, often, is war.

Political Stalemate and Imperialist Coalitions

Democratization creates a wider spectrum of politically significant groups with diverse and incompatible interests. In the

---

[2] Alain Plessis, *The Rise and Fall of the Second Empire, 1852–1871,* Cambridge: Cambridge University Press, 1985, pp. 146–47.

period when the great powers were first democratizing, kings, aristocrats, peasants, and artisans shared the historical stage with industrialists, an urban working class, and a middle-class intelligentsia. Similarly, in the postcommunist world, former party apparatchiks, atavistic heavy industrialists, and downwardly mobile military officers share the stage with populist demagogues, free-market entrepreneurs, disgruntled workers, and newly mobilized ethnic groups. In principle, mature democratic institutions can integrate even the widest spectrum of interests through competition for the favor of the average voter. But where political parties and representative institutions are still in their infancy, the diversity of interests may make political coalitions difficult to maintain. Often the solution is a belligerent nationalist coalition.

In Britain during the period leading up to the Crimean War, neither the Whigs nor Tories could form a lasting governing coalition because so many groups refused to enter stable political alliances. None of the old elites would coalesce with the parliamentary bloc of radicals elected by urban middle-class and Irish voters. Moreover, protectionist Tories would not unite with free-trading Whigs and Peelite Tories. The social and political mid-Victorian equipoise between traditional and modern Britain created a temporary political stalemate. Lord Palmerston's pseudo-liberal imperialism turned out to be the only successful formula for creating a durable ruling coalition during this transitional period of democratization.

The stalemate in Wilhelmine-era electoral politics was even more serious. In principle, coalitions of the left and right might have formed a two-party system to vie for the favor of the average voter, thus moderating policy. In fact, both left and right were too internally divided to mount

effective coalitions with internally consistent policies. Progressives dreamed of a bloc extending "from Bassermann to Bebel," from the liberal-democratic middle classes through the Marxist working classes, but the differences between labor and capital chronically barred this development. Conservatives had more success in forging a "marriage of iron and rye," but fundamental differences between military-feudal Junkers and Ruhr industrialists over issues ranging from the distribution of tax burdens to military strategy made their policies incoherent. Germany wound up with plans for a big army and a costly navy, and nobody willing to pay for it.

In more recent times, incipient democratization has likewise caused political impasses by widening the political spectrum to include too many irreconcilable political forces. In the final days of Yugoslavia, efforts by moderates like former Prime Minister Ante Markovic to promote a federalist, democratic, economic reformist platform were hindered not only by ethnic divisions but also by the cleavage between market-oriented business interests on the one hand and party bosses and military officers on the other. Similarly, in Russia, the difficulty of reconciling liberal, neocommunist, and nationalist political platforms and the social interests behind them has led to parliamentary stalemate, attempts to break the stalemate by presidential decree, tanks in the streets, and the resort to freelancing by breakaway regions, the military, and spontaneous privatizers of state property. One interpretation of Yeltsin's decision to use force in Chechnya is that he felt it necessary to show that he could act decisively to prevent the unraveling of central authority, with respect not only to ethnic separatists but also to other ungovernable groups in a democratizing society. Chechnya, it was hoped, would allow

Yeltsin to demonstrate his ability to coerce Russian society while at the same time exploiting a potentially popular nationalist issue.

Inflexible Interests and Short Time Horizons

Groups threatened by social change and democratization, including still-powerful elites, are often compelled to take an inflexible view of their interests, especially when their assets cannot be readily adapted to changing political and economic conditions. In extreme cases, there may be only one solution that will maintain the social position of the group. For Prussian landowners, it was agricultural protection in a nondemocratic state; for the Japanese military, it was organizational autonomy in an autarkic empire; for the Serbian military and party elites, it was a Serbian nationalist state. Since military bureaucracies and imperial interest groups occupied key positions in many authoritarian great powers, whether monarchal or communist, most interests threatened by democratization have been bound up with military programs and the state's international mission. Compromises that may lead down the slippery slope to social extinction or irrelevance have little appeal to such groups. This adds to the difficulty of finding an exit from the domestic political impasse and may make powerful domestic groups impervious to the international risks of their strategies.

Competing for Popular Support

The trouble intensifies when elites in a democratizing society try to recruit mass allies to their cause. Threatened elite groups have an overwhelming incentive to mobilize mass backers on the elites' terms, using whatever special resources they might retain. These resources have included monopolies of information (the

Wilhelmine navy's unique "expertise" in making strategic assessments), propaganda assets (the Japanese army's public relations blitz justifying the invasion of Manchuria), patronage (Lord Palmerston's gifts of foreign service postings to the sons of cooperative journalists), wealth (the Krupp steel company's bankrolling of mass nationalist and militarist leagues), organizational skills and networks (the Japanese army's exploitation of rural reservist organizations to build a social base), and the ability to use the control of traditional political institutions to shape the political agenda and structure the terms of political bargains (the Wilhelmine ruling elite's agreement to eliminate anti-Catholic legislation in exchange for Catholic support in the Reichstag on the naval budget).

This elite mobilization of mass groups takes place in a highly competitive setting. Elite groups mobilize mass support to neutralize mass threats (for instance, creating patriotic leagues to counter workers' movements) and counter other elite groups' successful efforts at mass mobilization (such as the German Navy League, a political counterweight to the Junker-backed Agrarian League). The elites' resources allow them to influence the direction of mass political participation, but the imperative to compete for mass favor makes it difficult for a single elite group to control the outcome of this process. For example, mass groups that gain access to politics through elite-supported nationalist organizations often try to outbid their erstwhile sponsors. By 1911, German popular nationalist lobbies were in a position to claim that if Germany's foreign foes were really as threatening as the ruling elites had portrayed them, then the government had sold out German interests in reaching a compromise with France over the Moroccan dispute. In this way, elite mobilization of the masses adds to the ungovernability and political impasse of democratizing states.

Ideology takes on particular significance in the competition for mass support. New entrants to the political process, lacking established habits and good information, may be uncertain where their political interests lie. Ideology can yield big payoffs, particularly when there is no efficient free marketplace of ideas to counter false claims with reliable facts. Elites try out all sorts of ideological appeals depending on the social position they are defending, the nature of the mass group they want to recruit, and the kinds of appeals that seem politically plausible. A nearly universal element of these ideological appeals, however, is nationalism, which has the advantage of positing a community of interest uniting elites and masses. This distracts attention from class cleavages that divide elites from the masses they are trying to recruit.

The Weakening of Central Authority

The political impasse and recklessness of democratizing states is deepened by the weakening of the state's authority. The autocrat can no longer dictate to elite interest groups or mass groups. Meanwhile, democratic institutions lack the strength to integrate these contending interests and views. Parties are weak and lack mass loyalty. Elections are rigged or intermittent. Institutions of public political participation are distrusted because they are subject to manipulation by elites and arbitrary constraints imposed by the state, which fears the outcome of unfettered competition.

Among the great powers, the problem was not excessive authoritarian power at the center, but the opposite. The Aberdeen coalition that brought Britain into the Crimean War was a makeshift cabinet headed by a weak leader with no substantial constituency. Likewise, on the eve of the Franco-Prussian War, Napoleon III's regime was in the process of caving in to its liberal opponents, who dominated the parliament elected in 1869. As Europe's armies prepared to hurtle from their starting gates in July 1914, Austrian leaders, perplexed by the contradictions between the German chancellor's policy and that of the German military, asked, "Who rules in Berlin?" Similarly, the 1931 Manchurian incident was a fait accompli by the local Japanese military; Tokyo was not even informed. The return to imperial thinking in Moscow today is the result of Yeltsin's weakness, not his strength. As the well-informed Moscow analyst Sergei Karaganov recently argued, the breakdown of the Leninist state "has created an environment where elite interests influence [foreign] policy directly."[3]

In each of these cases, the weak central leadership resorts to the same strategies as do the more parochial elite interests, using nationalist ideological appeals and special-interest payoffs to maintain their short-run viability, despite the long-run risks that these strategies may unleash.

Prestige Strategies

One of the simplest but riskiest strategies for a hard-pressed regime in a democratizing country is to shore up its prestige at home by seeking victories abroad. During the Chechen intervention, newspaper commentators in Moscow and the West were reminded of Russian Interior Minister Viacheslav Plehve's fateful remark in 1904, on the eve of the disastrous Russo-Japanese War, that what the tsar needed

---

[3] Karaganov, "Russia's Elites," in Robert Blackwill and Sergei Karaganov, *Damage Limitation*, Washington: Brassey's, 1994, p. 42.

was "a short, victorious war" to boost his prestige. Though this strategy often backfires, it is a perennial temptation as a means for coping with the political strains of democratization. German Chancellor Johannes Miquel, who revitalized the imperialist-protectionist "coalition of iron and rye" at the turn of the century, told his colleagues that "successes in foreign policy would make a good impression in the Reichstag debates, and political divisions would thus be moderated."[4] The targets of such strategies often share this analysis. Richard Cobden, for example, argued that military victories abroad would confer enough prestige on the military-feudal landed elite to allow them to raise food tariffs and snuff out democracy: "Let John Bull have a great military triumph, and we shall have to take off our hats as we pass the Horse Guards for the rest of our lives."[5]

Prestige strategies make the country vulnerable to slights to its reputation. Napoleon III, for example, was easily goaded into a fateful declaration of war in 1870 by Bismarck's insulting editorial work on a leaked telegram from the kaiser. For those who want to avoid such diplomatic provocations, the lesson is to make sure that compromises forced on the leaders of democratizing states do not take away the fig leaves needed to sustain their domestic prestige.

MANAGING THE DANGERS

Though mature democratic states have virtually never fought wars against each other, promoting democracy may not promote peace because states are especially war-prone during the transition toward

democracy. This does not mean, however, that democratization should be squelched in the interests of peace. Many states are now democratizing or on the verge of it, and stemming that turbulent tide, even if it were desirable, may not be possible. Our statistical tests show that movements toward autocracy, including reversals of democratization, are only somewhat less likely to result in war than democratization itself. Consequently, the task is to draw on an understanding of the process of democratization to keep its unwanted side effects to a minimum.

Of course, democratization does not always lead to extreme forms of aggressive nationalism, just as it does not always lead to war. But it makes those outcomes more likely. Cases where states democratized without triggering a nationalist mobilization are particularly interesting, since they may hold clues about how to prevent such unwanted side effects. Among the great powers, the obvious successes were the democratization of Germany and Japan after 1945, due to occupation by liberal democracies and the favorable international setting provided by the Marshall Plan, the Bretton Woods economic system, and the democratic military alliance against the Soviet threat. More recently, numerous Latin American states have democratized without nationalism or war. The recent border skirmishes between Peru and Ecuador, however, coincide with democratizing trends in both states and a nationalist turn in Ecuadorian political discourse. Moreover, all three previous wars between that pair over the past two centuries occurred in periods of partial democratization.

In such cases, however, the cure is probably more democracy, not less. In "Wilhelmine Argentina," the Falkland Islands/Malvinas War came when the military junta needed a nationalist victory to stave

[4] J. C. G. Rohl, *Germany without Bismarck,* Berkeley: University of California Press, 1967, p. 250.

[5] Letter to John Bright, October 1, 1854, quoted in John Morley, *The Life of Richard Cobden,* abridged ed., London: Thomas Nelson, pp. 311–12.

off pressure for the return of democracy; the arrival of full democracy has produced more pacific policies. Among the East European states, nationalist politics has been unsuccessful in the most fully democratic ones—Poland, the Czech Republic, and Hungary—as protest votes have gone to former communists. Nationalism has figured more prominently in the politics of the less democratic formerly communist states that are nonetheless partially democratizing. States like Turkmenistan that remain outright autocracies have no nationalist mobilization—indeed no political mobilization of any kind. In those recent cases, in contrast to some of our statistical results, the rule seems to be: go fully democratic, or don't go at all.

In any given case, other factors may override the relative bellicosity of democratizing states. These might include the power of the democratizing state, the strength of the potential deterrent coalition of states constraining it, the attractiveness of more peaceful options available to the democratizing state, and the nature of the groups making up its ruling coalition. What is needed is to identify the conditions that lead to relatively peaceful democratization and try to create those circumstances.

One of the major findings of scholarship on democratization in Latin America is that the process goes most smoothly when elites threatened by the transition—especially the military—are given a golden parachute. Above all, they need a guarantee that they will not wind up in jail if they relinquish power. The history of the democratizing great powers broadens this insight. Democratization was least likely to lead to war when the old elites saw a reasonably bright future for themselves in the new social order. British aristocrats, for example, had more of their wealth invested in commerce and industry than in agricul-

ture, so they had many interests in common with the rising middle classes. They could face democratization with relative equanimity. In contrast, Prussia's capital-starved, small-scale Junker landholders had no choice but to rely on agricultural protection and military careers.

In today's context, finding benign, productive employment for the erstwhile communist nomenklatura, military officer corps, nuclear scientists, and smokestack industrialists ought to rank high on the list of priorities. Policies aimed at giving them a stake in the privatization process and subsidizing the conversion of their skills to new, peaceful tasks in a market economy seem like a step in the right direction. According to some interpretations, Russian Defense Minister Pavel Grachev was eager to use force to solve the Chechen confrontation in order to show that Russian military power was still useful and that increased investment in the Russian army would pay big dividends. Instead of pursuing this reckless path, the Russian military elite needs to be convinced that its prestige, housing, pensions, and technical competence will improve if and only if it transforms itself into a Western-style military, subordinate to civilian authority and resorting to force only in accordance with prevailing international norms. Not only do old elites need to be kept happy, they also need to be kept weak. Pacts should not prop up the remnants of the authoritarian system, but rather create a niche for them in the new system.

Another top priority must be creating a free, competitive, and responsible marketplace of ideas in the newly democratizing states. Most of the war-prone democratizing great powers had pluralistic public debates, but the debates were skewed to favor groups with money, privileged access to the media, and proprietary control over information ranging from archives to intelligence about the military balance. Pluralism is not enough. Without a level playing field, pluralism simply creates the incentive and opportunity for privileged groups to propound self-serving myths, which historically have often taken a nationalist turn. One of the rays of hope in the Chechen affair was the alacrity with which Russian journalists exposed the costs of the fighting and the lies of the government and the military. Though elites should get a golden parachute regarding their pecuniary interests, they should be given no quarter on the battlefield of ideas. Mythmaking should be held up to the utmost scrutiny by aggressive journalists who maintain their credibility by scrupulously distinguishing fact from opinion and tirelessly verifying their sources. Promoting this kind of journalistic infrastructure is probably the most highly leveraged investment the West can make in a peaceful democratic transition.

Finally, the kind of ruling coalition that emerges in the course of democratization depends a great deal on the incentives created by the international environment. Both Germany and Japan started on the path toward liberal, stable democratization in the mid-1920s, encouraged by abundant opportunities for trade with and investment by the advanced democracies and by credible security treaties that defused nationalist scaremongering in domestic politics. When the international supports for free trade and democracy were yanked out in the late 1920s, their liberal coalitions collapsed. For China, whose democratization may occur in the context of expanding economic ties with the West, a steady Western commercial partnership and security presence is likely to play a major role in shaping the incentives of proto-democratic coalition politics.

In the long run, the enlargement of the zone of stable democracy will probably enhance prospects for peace. In the short run, much work remains to be done to minimize the dangers of the turbulent transition.

Political Theory

13

A belief is not true because it is useful.

—Henri Frederic Amiel

Not everything that is more difficult is more meritorious.

—Saint Thomas Aquinas

An Introduction to the Varieties of Political Theory

Political theory, understood most simply, is thoughtful reflection upon politics, and as such is among the most ancient human intellectual activities. Today political theory has two roles within the discipline of political science. Its first role, philosophically speaking, is called epistemology: to define the *questions* that the discipline should study. Its second role is metaphysical, that is, to define the *methods* to be used to find answers to the selected questions. Political theory continually seeks to develop "theories" (connected series of concepts used to explain something) concerning political behavior, and the methodologies that test and apply these theories. After at least twenty-five centuries of these attempts, consensus within the discipline has been achieved on neither the questions that should be studied nor the answers to the questions most often asked. This does not mean, however, that little has been accomplished.

In the 1990s, political science has accepted, if only temporarily, the lack of cohesion that has resulted from the proliferation of views, values, and approaches to the study of politics. Today political theory is studied within four categories:

- Political methodology
- Formal political theory
- History of political philosophy
- Normative political theory

Political methodology, as a field of study, attempts to improve the ways in which information about politics is collected, analyzed, and interpreted. Observations about politics are collected as data and are quantified by being placed into categories that can be analyzed numerically. Among the most important data collection methods are surveys, experiments, and "events data." *Formal political theory* has developed from the "scientific" approach to politics, notably positivism and behavioralism. Formal theory applies quantitative techniques, developed primarily in

303

economics, to political science. It attempts to quantify the actions of voters, interest groups, office holders, and other political actors within a political system which
is viewed as an open marketplace of freely selected political choices. Political
Methodology and Formal Theory are described in detail in Chapters 6 and 7, and
recent developments in these subfields are described in Chapter 15.

The *history of political philosophy* is the study of the political "great thinkers." In
political theory classes in the United States, these thinkers normally include a series of Western (European) writers, such as Plato, Aristotle, Cicero, St. Augustine,
St. Thomas Aquinas, Machiavelli, Thomas Hobbes, John Locke, Jean-Jacques
Rousseau, G. W. F. Hegel, Karl Marx, and John Stuart Mill. Occasionally non-West-
ern thinkers such as Mao Zedong and Mohandas Gandhi are included in these
studies, a practice encouraged in recent years by an emphasis upon multiculturalism, which attempts to consider the viewpoints of a variety of cultures, ideologies,
and religions. The objective of studying the history of political philosophy is to
learn lessons of value for understanding politics today. Many of the major figures
of the history of political philosophy are discussed in Chapters 2, 3, and 4.

The word "normative" refers to political values such as freedom, justice,
equality, law, dignity, and rights. *Normative political theory* is the study of how these
values are expressed in different political systems. Normative political theory continues today to discuss the same great issues such as equality, freedom, and justice,
that have been the subjects of famous writers throughout the history of political
philosophy.

In the 1950s, behavioralists, believing that a science of politics should study
facts instead of values, nearly succeeded in eliminating normative political philosophy from serious consideration by the discipline, but in recent years normative
studies have not only survived but have become an increasingly active forum for debate of concepts such as justice, freedom, and equality. One of the factors giving
rise to the rebirth of normative political thought has been dissatisfaction with behavioral political science. John Horton (1990, 129) provides an explanation of this
trend:

> In the case of Political Science [after the Vietnam war], the increasingly obvious
> sham of its 'scientific' pretensions, its complacent ethnocentricity and its com-
> plicity with American imperialism did much to undermine its credibility. Yet
> more important were developments within philosophy, especially in the USA
> where most of the leading figures in the resurgence of political philosophy in
> the late 1960s and 1970s emerged from philosophy departments or philosoph-
> ically inclined law departments. At this time the locus of philosophical devel-
> opment decisively shifted from Oxford to the USA, where it has subsequently re-
> mained.

New "schools" or "sects" of political philosophy have developed within the discipline in the last several decades. Some of the most influential in recent years have
been those established or inspired by thinkers such as Leo Strauss, Jurgen Habermas, Eric Voegelin, and John Rawls. These figures have been discussed in previous
chapters. In this chapter we shall devote attention to a topic of current interest in
normative political thought: postmodernism. This theoretical perspective on poli-

tics and other matters is defined and described in Carleton College political theorist Catherine Zuckert's 1995 article "The Postmodern Problem," which is included at the end of this chapter. To understand Zuckert's article, it is necessary to know something about the major philosophers to whom she refers, individuals whose works contributed substantially to the development of postmodernism. Before proceeding to Zuckert's article, therefore, we shall briefly describe the works of some of the authors Zuckert mentions.

Precursors to and Patrons of Postmodernism

Immanuel Kant (1724–1804) was one of the most influential philosophers of all time. Kant distinguished between the phenomenal world, the world that we experience with our senses, and the noumenal world, the world of things in themselves which we cannot experience. In making this distinction, Kant contributed to a long historical metaphysical discussion of epistemology, or the study of what can be known. Of particular importance to political philosophers is the heart of Kant's ethics, his "categorical imperative" which he defines in *Groundwork of the Metaphysics of Morals* (1785). The principle of the categorical imperative is that each person should "act only according to the maxim of action that you can at the same time will to be a universal law." Suppose, for example, that you propose to steal your neighbor's car. Can you will that obtaining articles by theft should be a universal law? If you cannot, you should change your behavior to conform to a principle that you would want to see universally applied. For Kant, moral law commands that we act rationally, that is, in our own long-term best interests. This command represents an imperative which becomes categorical by applying it to all possible situations. Kant assumes that the value of human existence is, universally, the foundation of morality. The categorical imperative means, therefore, that you should "act so that you treat humanity, whether in your person or in that of another, always as an end and never as a means only." Kant, therefore, will not allow that any principle that you wish to universalize will meet the conditions of the categorical imperative. For example, Kant would reject Friedrich Nietzsche's principle that the strong should dominate the weak because it treats part of humanity as means rather than ends.

If at his death in 1900, Prussian philosopher Friedrich Nietzsche (1844–1900) could have spoken a benediction for the nineteenth century, he would have called it sick. If the century could have responded, it might have placed a mirror before the German philosopher, and asked him if he was not merely projecting his own infirmity onto humanity, for Nietzsche had taken opium to relieve his migraine headaches and eventually died of what was probably syphilis after years of extreme mental instability. These problems, however, did not keep him from writing a condemnation of Western civilization and a vision for a new future that have had profound effects upon philosophy.

Nietzsche's philosophy has not yet ceased to shock and bewilder defenders of traditional Western culture, which he attacked with vigor and vituperation. For Nietzsche, Western civilization, at the close of the nineteenth century, had reached a state of almost total degeneration, a process that had started in ancient Greece. Before the time of Socrates (480–399 BCE), intelligent, creative, and, above all, powerful men were honored by ordinary people. *Oedipus Rex* and the other great Greek tragedies of the pre-Socratic era expressed, for Nietzsche, an appreciation for the true character of life. In Nietzsche's interpretation, these tragedies portrayed life as inherently irrational and capricious. The true hero within them is not the naive optimist but rather the hard core pessimist who grasps the absurdity of life and bends it to his own will.

The degeneration of culture began in Greece with Socrates and his student Plato, who together proposed the idea, which Nietzsche found ridiculous and deceitful, that reason governs the universe. Even Socrates and Plato, however, could not surpass the damage done to Western civilization by Christianity, which Nietzsche called "Platonism for the people." For Nietzsche, Christianity was one of two forms of morality which vied for dominance of the world: slave morality and master morality. Christianity was the ultimate slave morality because it advocated meekness, altruism, and submission to authority. Such values produce weak, cowardly, and soft people, who perpetuate "defective, diseased, degenerating forms of life." The pre-Socratic Greeks had built a master morality with which they dominated inferior cultures. Western civilization, however, from Socrates forward, had followed Plato and Christianity and had thereby sunk into degradation.

In *Thus Spake Zarathustra* (1885) Nietzsche proclaimed that God is dead. A confirmed atheist, Nietzsche believed that God was once alive because people, particularly Christians, believed in him. God is now dead because modern science has demonstrated that there is no evidence for the existence of God and that God, therefore, must have been created by people who wanted to believe in him. Nietzsche hoped and believed that the death of God meant the death of Christian morality.

Christianity, further, promoted the rise of democracy, which to Nietzsche was rule by the mediocre, since most people are lazy and stupid. Western civilization in the nineteenth century had allowed the mediocre to rule not only through democracies but through the influence of public opinion upon the policies of monarchies as well. The values of democracy, such as equality, do not elevate the lowly. Instead, they bring the people who might have been great down to the lowest common denominator of education and culture.

With the death of God, man could discover his own creative possibilities because he could finally discover his own will to power, which would obliterate both Christianity and democracy. The will to power is the creative force that generates life. The will to power does not press man to seek out objective concepts of reality, truth, and goodness, because they do not exist. The will to power moves people to create their own forms and concepts of existence.

Nietzsche's ontology, his philosophy of what exists, is the aspect of his philosophy that has had the greatest direct effect on postmodernism. For Nietzsche, there is no objectively identifiable reality. Only differing perspectives of reality exist, and powerful people will create their own realities. In the future these powerful men who create their own realities will become what Nietzsche called supermen. The superman will be the totally actualized human being who has created all things new for himself. The superman will be totally free and, living within the eternal return of time, will create new forms of philosophy which will transcend traditional concepts of good and evil and generate new forms of culture which will surpass Christianity and democracy.

Ironically, Nietzsche thought that the superman may discover that the past, present, and future exist in a continuous state, a form understood to primitive peoples as the myth of the eternal return (described in Chapter 2). Nietzsche had always believed that philosophers of the nineteenth century had misunderstood the meaning of history. In *The Use and Abuse of History* (1874) Nietzsche argued against Hegel's idea of the meaning of history. For Hegel (1770–1831), history was the unfolding of reason, a process guided by a spiritual rationality, which had found its final fulfillment in Hegel's own time. For Nietzsche, history was anything but rational; in fact, it was highly irrational. Looking back through time, he found neither reason in history nor the likelihood of an ultimate end to history. The superman would continuously create new realities, and history, as his contemporaries saw it, would disappear.

Edmund Husserl (1859–1938) is known as the "father of phenomenology." He believed that, since all we know of the world is what we perceive in our minds, knowledge of the world is limited to a knowledge of the phenomena of the mind. Husserl proposed that the goal of the phenomenologist is to perceive the essence of an object. Essences cannot be derived from an object, he claimed, but can only be seen in the object's appearances. Correct phenomenological perception of an object is completely objective. This means that it is the same for all people and is also, therefore, completely scientific in that it represents accurate observations of phenomena.

Martin Heidegger (1889–1976) conducted a quest for being (the study of ontology) which for him was the essential true object of philosophy. He succeeded to Husserl's chair at the University of Freiberg and dedicated his most important work, *Being and Time*, to Husserl. Heidegger proposed that being cannot be calculated, measured, or objectified. Being can be understood only through a meditative process which involves a poetic mode of thinking. Understanding of life as being is primarily an interpretive task. Interpretation is done, however, not as other philosophers and scientists do it, by attempting to look outward to an external reality. Rather, Heidegger finds the quest for knowledge to be wrapped up in what he called *Dasein*, or "being there," which is to experience one's self as an integral part of one's surroundings. To be authentic, a person must accept and face up to the possibilities of the future even in view of the uncertainty of one's circumstances. Heidegger studied Nietzsche carefully and supported the Nazis in the early 1930s. Although he later denounced them, his career was marred by this association.

Jacques Derrida was born July 15, 1930, in El Biar, Nigeria, and since 1984 has directed the *Ecole des Hautes Etudes en Sciences Sociales* in Paris. He is a leading figure in the poststructuralist, deconstructionist movement, a school of philosophy which seeks to discover the multiple meanings and underlying assumptions in contemporary social thought. Derrida builds upon Nietzsche's and Heidegger's thought, with insights from Marx and Freud. Derrida holds that language is inadequate to represent reality. He scrutinizes texts for multiple meanings, which he finds as *dif-*

ferences in the meanings of words in the texts. To deconstruct a text is, therefore, to find the differences in meanings of the words in it, and to understand the implications of those differences.

The Problem of Postmodernism

In the following article, Catherine Zuckert describes these thinkers in greater detail, and some others, like Leo Strauss, who has been discussed previously in this text. ***Warning!*** Students who have not previously read philosophy often expect to read it as they would a novel. Philosophy, however, is unusually dense and rich, and can be as rewarding as a great novel, but it usually requires more time and patience. Reading this material will not be easy, but it is intelligible even to introductory students. Read it slowly, think about what you read, and write down questions to ask your instructor. Also consider the following questions and be prepared to discuss them in class:

1. What is postmodernism?
2. How do postmodernists analyze literature?
3. How do postmodernists analyze politics?
4. What new perspectives or insights do postmodernists have to offer for the study of politics?
5. What are the problems or limitations of postmodernism for the study of politics?

The Postmodern Problem

Catherine Zuckert

Postmodern is a term much bandied-about these days, so it may be useful to begin this article by defining it a bit more precisely. Literally, it means *after the modern,* and that is generally how it is used. What is understood to be "modern" differs somewhat, however, in art and architecture, literature, and philosophy—three areas where postmodern developments run rampant. In architecture, *modern* referred primarily to designs such as those inspired by the Bauhaus that were strictly, if not starkly, functional. In architecture *postmodern* thus refers to a reintroduction of decorative elements that are not simply functional and a mixture of past styles. In literature, on the other hand, *modernism* was associated not with function, but with nonuse, with purely aesthetic, as opposed to moral, political, or historical value. Exemplified by the poetry of T. S. Eliot, modernism gave rise to the New Critical claim that texts ought to be read solely in their own terms, not in terms of their context, biographical sources, or broader teaching. Both literature and criticism served and were designed to serve, more or less explicitly, to keep the barbarians at bay.

In philosophy and political philosophy, *postmodern* also means that which comes after the modern. But here the modern has a much wider historical and substantive scope; it does not refer simply to the twentieth century or even nineteenth- and twentieth-century styles and developments. *Modern* includes the entire effort, beginning with Machiavelli and Descartes, to acquire and use knowledge to improve the human condition. Scholars disagree, in fact, about where the modern begins—does it have a Christian element, for example—and whether its essential characteristic is power seeking or liberty, but they virtually all agree that it ends with Nietzsche. The collection of essays entitled *Nietzsche as Postmodernist: Essays Pro and Contra* indicates the status of his thought; it brings the modern to an end and thus points toward, if it does not itself begin, something new.[1]

What is called *postmodern* in philosophy, I submit, constitutes a response—or, to speak more precisely, a variety of responses—to a problem first enunciated by Nietzsche and modified or extended by Heidegger's critique of Nietzsche. In describing "the postmodern problem," I shall thus first describe the dilemma Nietzsche and Heidegger have bequeathed us and then examine the difficulties involved in two attempts to respond to it. Both philosophically and politically, Leo Strauss and Jacques Derrida mark the extreme limits of the possibilities. An examination of their opposed reactions to the dilemma thus brings out the issues at stake.

Nietzsche announced the problem in his very first book, *The Birth of Tragedy*: the search for knowledge, the philosophy that has been the distinguishing characteristic of what we call Western civilization, has culminated in modern times in the work of Immanuel Kant; to be more precise, solely in the knowledge that we do not

---

Catherine Zuckert is a professor of political science at Carleton College in Northfield, Minnesota. Her *Postmodern Platos: Nietzsche, Heidegger, Gadamer, Strauss, and Derrida* is forthcoming from the University of Chicago Press in 1996.

Perspectives on Political Science 24(2), 87–94 (Spring 1995). Reprinted with permission of the Helen Dwight Reid Educational Foundation. Published by Heldref Publications, 1319 Eighteenth St., N.W., Washington, D.C. 20036-1802. Copyright 1995.

[1] Clayton Koelb, ed., *Nietzsche as Postmodern: Essays Pro and Contra* (Albany, N.Y.: State University of New York Press, 1990).

know, that we can never know the things-in-themselves. We know only what we construct. One of those constructs, Nietzsche himself goes on to argue in his later works, is our notion of "self." In fact, we are bundles and masses of drives, not all of which are conscious, according to Nietzsche's ungrateful student Sigmund Freud, and none of which are, according to Nietzsche himself, strictly speaking rational.

If the search for wisdom does not produce wisdom or knowledge, the question arises, what good is it? In *The Birth of Tragedy* Nietzsche takes Socrates to represent the promise that human beings cannot only plumb the depths of existence but also use the knowledge they acquire to correct it. This is the promise of philosophy that has proved to be false. The problem does not apply simply to the field of philosophy as understood in the nineteenth and twentieth centuries, moreover. Even by Nietzsche's time and surely in the twentieth century, modern natural scientists have also had to admit that they do not have knowledge, strictly speaking, certainly not of the things-in-themselves. What scientists claim to know is how to produce certain effects, to show what works. But, as Nietzsche pointed out in an essay he wrote shortly after *The Birth of Tragedy*, "On the Uses and Disadvantages of History for Life," the standard of what is useful is explicitly or implicitly what is good for human life. If, as a result of a century or more of scientific and historical research, we no longer believe that there are natural species; if, in other words, we no longer believe that there *is* an essential difference between human beings and animals, what, then, is our measure of effectiveness?

The outcome or end of the history of philosophy, Nietzsche announces, would appear to be profoundly disillusioning. Nietzsche himself expressed that disillu-

sionment most powerfully and poignantly in his famous announcement that "God is dead." "We have killed him." Toward the end of his life, Nietzsche himself concluded, however, that the knowledge we had acquired—that we knew only that we did not know—need not be deadly. On the contrary, the discovery that all the things we thought we knew were human projections or constructions means that we can now do consciously and intentionally what philosophers had been doing unconsciously or at least covertly in the past—giving meaning to the world and their own existence. He called these new philosophical value-givers "supermen," and he predicted in *The Genealogy of Morals* that their attempts to impose their own values on the world would produce two centuries or more of violent, ideological struggle.

In the 1930s the philosopher who was arguably Nietzsche's greatest student and critic, Martin Heidegger, suggested that Nietzsche had articulated the truth of our time. Two great, ideological superpowers, the Soviet Union and the United States, were competing for worldwide dominion. His own nation, Germany, was caught in the pincers. Not just political life, but everything in the twentieth century was an expression of a will to power. Individualism and collectivism were merely two sides or expressions of the same drive to reduce everything into material—Heidegger would later call it "standing reserve"—that had no inherent value, structure, or form of its own, and that could, therefore, be transformed at will. *But,* Heidegger insisted, Nietzsche's truth was only that, the truth of our times. It was not an eternal "metaphysical" truth applying to all times, places, and things, as Nietzsche himself sometimes suggested. And, Heidegger thought, Nietzsche's truth pointed to a broader, more fundamental, more important truth, the truth of Being—or the need to inquire about it. As the practical technological results of Nietzsche's will to power showed, everything could be transformed into "standing reserve." That is, there is no necessity that everything or anything exists in itself or be intelligible. The ground or reason for our existence and knowledge is itself completely mysterious. But once we perceive the non-necessity of it, once we perceive the mystery, we can—and, Heidegger hopes, we will—come to cherish and seek to preserve our existence, the shared life-experience or "world" of our particular people in its particular time and place. Although Heidegger initially embraced a politics of resolution and with it the Nazi party, on the basis of his famous analysis of *Being and Time,* in his later works he advocated an explicitly more poetic and passive stance of "letting things be."

The problem with which Nietzsche and Heidegger leave us and to which postmodern thinkers seek to respond thus has two parts: First, if it is true, as Nietzsche argued, that the search for knowledge or philosophy culminates only in the knowledge that we do not know, what is the character and value of that activity—of the Western philosophical tradition? Second, if centuries of philosophical and scientific investigations have shown that we do not know and cannot discover any eternal or necessary order in the universe, how do we avoid what seem to be the equally undesirable practical alternatives: the Nietzschean politics of the drive for total mastery of the world or the apolitical, poetic passivity of the late Heidegger who finally urged that "only a god can save us"?

Let me turn first to a brief account of the response that a thinker who is not usually considered to be postmodern gave to these questions, that is, to Leo Strauss. As a partial justification for treating him under this rubric, I should perhaps refer

to the authority of Stanley Rosen.[2] The better justification is probably a letter Strauss wrote to Karl Loewith in 1935 in which Strauss states: "Nietzsche so dominated and bewitched me between my 22nd and 30th years, that I literally believed everything that I understood of him. . . ."[3] By 1935 Strauss had already separated himself somewhat from Nietzsche. His thirtieth year, or the end of the time during which he was bewitched by Nietzsche, coincides roughly with the publication of *Spinoza's Critique of Religion* in which Strauss argued that modern rationalism did not and could not disprove revelation; that is, in Nietzschean terms, God was not necessarily dead. What Strauss says both in his letter to Loewith and in his later correspondence with Hans Georg Gadamer is that Nietzsche set the problem or problems from which Strauss began.[4]

What then was Strauss's response to Nietzsche's announcement that philosophy had culminated only in the knowledge that we did not and could not know? Nietzsche had associated that problem with Socrates in his first book on *The Birth of Tragedy;* the end of philosophy was the end of the vision or the promise Socrates had embodied that human beings could acquire knowledge and use it to correct existence. The search for knowledge served

[2] "According to Strauss, modern thought in all its forms is determined by the idea of progress, . . . and hence is rooted from the outset in the Enlightenment. Strauss's critique of modernity is thus a critique of the Enlightenment, similar to that of Nietzsche, but also entirely typical of what has frequently been called 'post-modernism.' " Alan Udoff, ed., "Leo Strauss and the Quarrel between Ancients and the Moderns," in *Leo Strauss' Thought: Toward a Critical Engagement* (Boulder: Lynne Rienner, 1991), 166.

[3] "Correspondence," *Independent Journal of Philosophy 5/6* (1988): 183.

[4] "Correspondence concerning *Wahrheit und Methode," Independent Journal of Philosophy* 2 (1978): 5–12.

for centuries to justify human existence, that is, to make human life worth living. According to Gotthold Lessing, who was also a source or author for the young Strauss, it was the search rather than what was found that was truly worthwhile.[5] The problem in modern times was that this search had been shown to be fruitless; it could no longer serve, therefore, to justify human suffering or to provoke further striving.

Strauss responded to the question Nietzsche had raised about the character of philosophy and thereby the value of the Western tradition with a study of what he called "the problem of Socrates"—a problem he announced in the introduction to his book on *Socrates and Aristophanes* that had been explicitly raised by Nietzsche.[6] In *The Birth of Tragedy*, Strauss observed, Nietzsche had leveled Aristophanes' critique at Plato's Socrates. But, in a series of studies of Aristophanes, Xenophon, and Plato, Strauss showed that the Socrates presented by his students differed from the philosopher lampooned by the comic poet in two decisive respects: First, Xenophon's and Plato's Socrates clearly recognized the difference between the human and the nonhuman things. Second, Xenophon's and Plato's Socrates also recognized the need to preserve the political conditions necessary for the perpetuation of his own philosophical activity. The Socrates depicted by Xenophon and Plato was not simply a moralist, as Aristotle suggested in his *Metaphysics;* on the contrary, both his students show that Socrates continued his studies of nature after his "turn"

to the study of the *logoi* described in the *Oeconomicus* and the *Phaedo.* Xenophon's Socrates did not parade the results of his investigations of nature very openly, Strauss suggests in his commentary on *Xenophon's Socratic Discourse*, because it was not clear to him that nature was altogether friendly to human beings—or rational. For Xenophon there seemed to be some question whether the philosophical or the political was the best way of life. For Plato there was no question; it was the philosophical. In the *Republic* Plato's Socrates argues that as a result of their love of truth, above all, people with philosophical natures will possess all other virtues as well. *Only* philosophers are happy, according to Plato, but they *are* happy. And, in order to be happy, it is not necessary that they possess the truth; they need merely seek it. As Socrates says in the *Apology* (38a), the unexamined life is not worth living; to talk every day about virtue and the other things about which you hear me talking and examining myself and others is the greatest good to man.[7] In sum, Strauss's studies of the three original sources convinced him that the philosophy represented by Socrates did not consist so much in the investigation of first principles and the articulation of cosmological doctrines as Aristotle and his successors thought; philosophy was rather a way of life, the only truly satisfying and happy way of life. And its possibility did not depend upon the possession of absolute or certain knowledge. On the contrary, all we could ever expect to achieve would be imperfect knowledge, partial knowledge that we could hope to expand. In *What is Political Philosophy?* he explains:

---

[5] *Birth of Tragedy*, sec. 15; Leo Strauss, "Exoteric Teaching," reprinted in *The Rebirth of Classical Political Rationalism*, ed. Thomas L. Pangle (Chicago: University of Chicago Press, 1989), 63–71.

[6] Leo Strauss, *Socrates and Aristophanes* (New York: Basic, 1968), 6.

[7] Cf. *The City and Man* (Chicago: Rand McNally, 1964), 13–23, 50–138; *Socrates and Aristophanes; Xenophon's Socratic Discourse* (Ithaca, N.Y.: Cornell University Press, 1970); *Xenophon's Socrates* (Ithaca, N.Y.: Cornell University Press, 1972).

Socrates was so far from being committed to a specific cosmology that his knowledge was knowledge of ignorance. Knowledge of ignorance is not ignorance. It is knowledge of the elusive character of the truth, of the whole. . . . The whole eludes us but we know parts. . . . The knowledge which we possess is characterized by a fundamental dualism which has never been overcome. At one pole we find knowledge of homogeneity: above all in arithmetic. . . . At the opposite pole we find knowledge of heterogeneity, and in particular of heterogeneous ends; the highest form of this kind of knowledge is the art of the statesman. The latter kind of knowledge is superior to the former [because] . . . it is knowledge of what makes human life complete or whole. . . . But this knowledge— the political art in the highest sense—is not knowledge of the whole. It seems that knowledge of *the* whole would have to combine somehow political knowledge in the highest sense with knowledge of homogeneity. And this combination is not at our disposal. . . . Philosophy . . . could appear as Sisyphean or ugly, when one contrasts its achievement with its goal. Yet it is necessarily accompanied, sustained and elevated by *eros*. It is graced by nature's grace.[8]

In his analysis of Nietzsche's *Beyond Good and Evil*, Strauss suggests that Plato's Socrates is, indeed, very much like Nietzsche's philosopher of the future. Nietzsche did not perceive the similarity, because he read the dialogues too much in

terms of the distinction Aristotle introduced between Socrates the moralist and Plato the theorist of the ideas. There is, however, an important difference. When Nietzsche lists the virtues of his philosopher of the future, he adds solitude and compassion to the Platonic virtues of wisdom and courage. That is, he drops moderation and justice.[9] In considering the differences between Socrates and the superman, we thus approach Strauss's response to the second problem Nietzsche bequeathed us, that is, the political consequences of our lack of absolute, complete, or certain knowledge.

Strauss points to the fundamental difference between Socrates and Nietzsche's philosopher of the future when he observes that, famous as he is for asking "What is . . . ?" questions, there are two "what is" questions Plato's Socrates never asks: What is soul? and What is god? The reason he does not ask these questions, I believe, is that there is no good or simple answer to them. The popular notion of god combines the notion of cause with the source of moral order or justice, and the two functions of god have incompatible ontological requirements. The notion of soul combines intellect with life—two very different qualities. But, as Socrates suggests in the *Republic* and liberal political theorists like Alexis de Tocqueville have argued since, belief in some kind of god and the immortality of the soul is an almost essential foundation of a decent political order. Nietzsche himself, by way of contrast, is famous for having declared that God is dead and that there is no such thing as a soul, immortal or otherwise. We are complexes of irrational drives. In

---

[8] Leo Strauss, *What Is Political Philosophy? and Other Studies* (Glencoe, Ill.: Free Press, 1959), 38–40. Thus in his "Restatement on Xenophon's *Hiero,*" Strauss writes: "Philosophy as such is nothing other than the real consciousness of the problems, that is to say, of the fundamental and comprehensive problems. It is impossible to think about these problems without being attracted toward . . . one or the other of certain rare typical solutions. However, as long as there is no wisdom, but only the search for wisdom, the evidence of all these solutions is necessarily smaller than the evidence of the problems. As a result, the philosopher ceases to be a philosopher from the moment that his 'subjective certitude' of the truth of a solution becomes stronger than the consciousness that he may have of the problematical character of this solution" (116).

[9] Thomas L. Pangle, ed., "Note on the Plan of Nietzsche's *Beyond Good and Evil*," in *Studies in Platonic Political Philosophy*, (Chicago: University of Chicago Press, 1983), 174–91.

contrast to Nietzsche, Strauss suggests, Socrates showed his moderation and justice by not publicly and directly calling into question the opinions necessary to maintain political order. The political moderation of the philosopher consists primarily in his restraining his speech.

Strauss's response to the question concerning the political ramifications or effects of our lack of knowledge can be put more schematically, however. If human beings do not and probably never will possess knowledge, all we have are opinions. Our lives, our communities are based on opinions—especially about what is right or wrong, advantageous and harmful, just and unjust—that represent, at best, partial truths and that can, therefore, be discredited by openly being brought into question. All political communities are, in other words, like Socrates' famous cave. A few philosophically minded individuals may fight their way through the images projected by the opinion makers, but they never will be able to lead all their people after them. What the so-called modern Enlightenment did was to replace one set of popular prejudices with another; it did not make people generally more rational or more knowledgeable.

Contrary to Nietzsche's proclamation that true philosophers are legislators (*Beyond Good and Evil* 211), Strauss pointed out, Plato showed that philosophers never want to rule. They have no interest in honor (which is merely a matter of popular opinion) or desire for wealth. They would be the only just rulers precisely because they can get nothing they want for themselves by ruling. What this means in effect is that all people who actually seek and exercise political power *are* apt to be unjust. The best possible or practicable political order, according to Strauss's Plato, is constituted by the rule of law, laws that combine reason with consent (and force

to back them up), administered by citizens who have proved to be of good character and sound judgment. The best possible form of government is a limited government; because in contrast to the "city in speech" of the *Republic,* all actual governments are going to be partial and therefore somewhat unjust. At the conclusion of his analysis of "The Three Waves of Modernity," Strauss thus observes:

> The theory of liberal democracy, as well as of communism, originated in the first and second waves of modernity; the political implication of the third wave proved to be fascism. Yet this undeniable fact does not permit us to return to the earlier forms of modern thought: the critique of modern rationalism or of the modern belief in reason by Nietzsche cannot be dismissed or forgotten. This is the deepest reason for the crisis of liberal democracy. The theoretical crisis does not necessarily lead to a practical crisis, for the superiority of liberal democracy to communism, Stalinist or post-Stalinist, is obvious enough. *And above all, liberal democracy, in contradistinction to communism and fascism, derives powerful support from a way of thinking which cannot be called modern at all: the premodern thought of our western tradition.*[10]

Like Heidegger, Strauss thought that the unfettering of technological progress from all moral and political control was disastrous, but unlike Heidegger, he did not think that it was possible or prudent for people simply to turn their backs on technology. Like Heidegger, Strauss thought that the institution of a world-state would involve an attempt to level all distinctions among human beings. It was important, therefore, to defend liberal democratic nation-states, and technology was a necessary part of defense.[11] As Strauss

[10] Hilail Gildin, ed., "The Three Waves of Modernity," in *An Introduction to Political Philosophy: Ten Essays by Leo Strauss* (Detroit, Mich.: Wayne State University Press, 1989), 98. The emphasis is mine.

[11] Cf. Leo Strauss, *Thoughts on Machiavelli* (Glencoe, Ill.: Free Press, 1958), 299.

saw it, neither the drive for world mastery advocated by Nietzsche nor the poetico-religious passivity advocated by the late Heidegger were practically or politically desirable or necessary.

Let me turn now to what I have suggested is the left border or extreme defining the "space" or territory covered by postmodernism in the works of Jacques Derrida. At first glance, I will admit, no two thinkers might appear to have less in common than Strauss and Derrida. Whereas Strauss explicitly seeks to revive the Western tradition in the face of the radical critique leveled by Nietzsche and Heidegger, Derrida wants to carry that critique even further.[12] Strauss was politically conservative; Derrida's sympathies are evidently with the radical Left. The first and necessary step in reading any book, according to Strauss, is to understand it as its author did; Derrida is famous for arguing that the author's intention does not control the meaning of the text. Strauss reads Plato in terms of the "age-old quarrel between poetry and philosophy"; Derrida denies that there is a fundamental difference between *mythos* and *logos*.[13] Strauss argues that Plato's Socrates represents a way of life, not a set of doctrines; following Heidegger, Derrida treats the history of philosophy from Socrates onward as the history of "metaphysics" or "onto-theology." Whereas Strauss emphasizes the tension between politics and philosophy, Derrida suggests that we ought to regard all attempts to articulate and so establish order—poetic or rhetorical as well as scientific or philosophical—to be essentially "political."

In light of the apparently polar opposition, the similarities between Strauss and Derrida are, therefore, both surprising and striking. Both men trace the origins of their own thought, at least in part, to their experiences as persecuted Jews. Because both Strauss and Derrida argue that a careful reading shows that some—or perhaps in the case of Derrida all—texts have multiple meanings, both have been described as "Talmudic" commentators. Both argue that what an author does not say is often as, if not more, important than what he does; it is necessary to read between the lines. Both suggest in the case of Plato that careful reading of the dialogues shows that all the apparent arguments and doctrines are undercut. Both suggest that Plato shows that Socrates let the city of Athens kill him to prove in deed, as it were, that philosophy does not threaten to undermine the legal order. Both also suggest that the explicit teachings of the dialogues have a political function or purpose. But neither thinks that Plato's philosophy—or that of anyone else—should be understood simply in political terms. On the contrary, both Strauss and Derrida insist that philosophers, in general, and Nietzsche and Heidegger, in particular, should *not* be judged solely in terms of their political associations or effects; but both also argue that Nietzsche and Heidegger *were implicated* in the rise of National Socialism.[14] Endorsing some aspects of the radical critique of the tradition by Nietzsche and Heidegger, both Strauss and Derrida seek to avoid the disastrous political results of that critique. Avoiding those results appears, at least at

---

[12] Jacques Derrida, *Of Grammatology*, trans. Gayatri Chakravorty Spivak (Baltimore: Johns Hopkins University Press, 1974), 19.

[13] Jacques Derrida, "Plato's Pharmacy," in *Dissemination*, trans. Barbara Johnson (Chicago: University of Chicago Press, 1981), 61–171.

[14] Strauss, "Three Waves"; *What is Political Philosophy?*, 54–55; *Studies*, 30; Jacques Derrida, *The Ear of the Other*, trans. Peggy Kamuf (New York: Schocken, 1985); *Of Spirit*, trans. Geoffrey Bennington and Rachel Bowlby (Chicago: University of Chicago Press, 1987).

times, to be the major purpose of both of their works. Because both Strauss and Derrida find Nietzsche's analysis of the limits of reason to be basically sound, both conclude that everything is not and never will be wholly intelligible; on the contrary, they both argue, in opposition to Hegel, that there are aspects of "things" that are not and never will be captured by, or expressible in, *logos*. Finally, in opposition to Nietzsche and Heidegger as well as to Hegel, both Strauss and Derrida argue that there is no necessary direction or "end" to "history."

There is the convergence in the midst of the divergence between Strauss and Derrida, because, as Strauss says of Gadamer, beginning at the same place, they subsequently marched in almost entirely different directions. That is why I am suggesting they indicate the limits or extreme boundaries of the postmodern horizon. What I mean by the common beginning point are the problems left by Nietzsche and Heidegger. So, we should now turn to Derrida's responses.

With regard to philosophy, Derrida agrees with Nietzsche that his predecessors have shown that we cannot know anything in the traditional sense. There are no eternal, atemporal, aspatial "truths" or "ideas."

Like Heidegger and Strauss before him, Derrida's thought begins with insights he gleaned from Edmund Husserl. (One might say, in passing, that it is Husserl's failure to provide the foundation for science that he sought that sends Heidegger, Strauss, and Derrida back to the problem posed by Nietzsche concerning the limits of reason.) But, Derrida's studies of Husserl took him in a very different direction from that which Heidegger and Strauss pursued. If, as Husserl argued, science arises from and so depends upon prescientific experience, then, both Hei-

degger and Strauss concluded, it is necessary to engage in what Heidegger called the "de-struction" of the philosophical tradition, that is, to clear an accumulation of theoretical terms and conceptions that stand between us and the original experience we want to recapture. Because *consciousness* and *self-consciousness* are both terms that arise only in modern philosophy, Heidegger and Strauss jettisoned the phenomenological reductions, whereby Husserl himself attempted to reconstruct the basic elements of our consciousness and proceeded directly to study the Greek origins of philosophy—philosophy before it had become encrusted by or with a tradition, and so philosophy that was closer to the prephilosophical or prescientific experience out of which it developed.

Derrida, by way of contrast, proceeds through Husserl's reductions. Early in his *Logical Investigations,* Husserl distinguished signs that merely point to a meaning to be found elsewhere, from concepts, which contain their own meaning. We necessarily use signs in communicating with others, Husserl admitted. That is, all language is essentially indicative. But, he suggested, we do not need to use signs in our own thinking or internal soliloquy. There we can proceed through or in terms of pure concepts, that is, nonspatial, nontemporal ideas, which have been the object of pure knowledge since Plato.

What reflection on the experience of internal soliloquy actually shows, Derrida argues, is that there is neither a unitary "self" nor any eternally present "ideas" for it to contemplate. Self-consciousness, that is, consciousness of oneself as a self, entails a certain division or doubling of itself within the self, so that a part separates itself in order to look back at itself. Likewise, the notion of atemporal, aspatial ideas that infinitely can be recalled or recollected entails a certain deferral or reserve in the contents of the human mind. If they are subject to recall or recollection, these ideas are not always present to consciousness. They do not, in other words, have Being in the traditional sense of presence that Heidegger had explicated.

Derrida's study of Husserl's reduction of the basic objects or experiences of consciousness thus led him to his famous notion of *difference,* the claim that all the contents of what used to be called consciousness—ideas, verbal signs for ideas, and the things to which these ideas and words refer—are characterized by an internal division that generates different things or meanings over time by deferring some of the meaning or effects of the division. Derrida combined this insight, which he explains in a book entitled *Speech and Phenomena,* with another he took from Husserl's study of the *Origins of Geometry.* Husserl wrote his book partly in response to Heidegger's contention that, to recapture the prescientific experience upon which science was based, it would be necessary to engage in historical studies, to formulate his famous contention that what we call "thinking" ought to be described, rather, as a kind of "writing."[15]

For a science like geometry to be constituted, Husserl showed, it was necessary for mathematicians to write down their findings. If they did not write down the proofs they discovered, those proofs would remain buried, so to speak, in the heads of the inventors. They would not and could not be passed down to posterity. But, Derrida pointed out in the introduction he wrote to his translation of the *Origins,* what

is written down can always be erased. If the transmission of knowledge over time entails writing, there cannot be any essentially eternal ideas. All are subject to being erased. Moreover, as Plato's Socrates complains in the *Phaedrus,* anything that is written down becomes separated from its author or "father," who is no longer there to explain it. As a result of being written down, Derrida thus concludes, everything loses something of its original meaning, some aspects of what the author had in mind when he or she wrote. All we have, all that is left, are marks or "traces" of the intended meaning of an "author" or "source" who is no longer present, even if he or she is still alive, because we all change over time. In order to acquire a full meaning, to survive rather than gradually to fade away, these traces have to be reinscribed on the minds of readers in new books or articles. But in these minds or books, these marks or ideas will necessarily be put into a new context and thereby acquire a new meaning. The process is ongoing. And it is not limited to human productions or works of art. Following Heidegger who described all the beings as "traces" of Being, Derrida regards all "things" in the world as such traces or leavings from the past. There is no origin or end to the process of reinscription, in which some marks are erased by being crossed over by others, and others are deepened by repetition, because it is impossible "to write on a blank slate." Writing presupposes something or someone already there to impress or inscribe.

Understood as a trace left from the past, all existence could be said to be "historical"; but, Derrida emphasizes in explicit opposition to Heidegger, there is no necessary direction, no beginning or end to this "history." As he playfully illustrates in *The Post Card,* authors write

[15] Edmund Husserl's *Origin of Geometry: An Introduction,* trans. John P. Leavey, Jr. (Stony Brook, N.Y.: Nicolas Hays, 1978); *Speech and Phenomena,* trans. David Allison (Evanston, Ill.: Northwestern University Press, 1973).

down their "will," so to speak, in an attempt to have it outlive and outlast them, to preform if not to predict the future. But they cannot control the fate or reception of their writings; there is always a chance that they will become lost or be erased. The fate or meaning of past "writings," which is to say the tradition we inherit, is no more entirely under the control of the recipients than it is of the would-be fathers or ancestors. Authors who deny their debts to past thinkers tend, like Freud, to reproduce the logic or movement of past arguments without recognizing it. History is thus like a huge postal operation in which things are constantly being sent back and forth, emitted and received, with continual additions and corrections or losses. Nothing ever has a set, stable, or unchanging meaning or existence. Derrida's post is, in other words, very much like Nietzsche's becoming. It is explicitly constituted by a play of interrelations or differences of "power" that is not controlled or directed by any will. Philosophy as traditionally understood, that is, as the search for knowledge of an eternal truth or enduring intelligible order, is simply impossible, because there is no such truth or order to be found.

And, to turn to Derrida's response to the second problem bequeathed to us by Nietzsche and Heidegger—the political effects of the discovery that we have and can have no certain knowledge—he insists that his "deconstruction" of the Western philosophical tradition has practico-political effects. Some of his students, most preeminently Rodolphe Gasche and Christopher Norris, have pointed out that Derrida's *difference* has a great deal in common with the transcendental principles of Kantian philosophy, inasmuch as *difference* specifies the conditions, which cannot in themselves be observed or experienced, for all the thoughts and experiences we do

have.[16] But, Derrida himself repeatedly insists, "deconstruction . . . is not a discursive or theoretical affair, but a practico-political one, and it is always produced within the structures (somewhat quickly and summarily) said to be institutional."[17] Having moved beyond all such "metaphysical distinctions," Derrida does not think that "theory" can be divided from "practice," anymore than mind can be completely separated from body.

As Nietzsche showed, philosophers have not been able to find any enduring, eternal order or meaning in the world. But, Derrida argues, contrary to Nietzsche, that it is impossible for anyone to impose such an order or meaning upon it, because the "will" is always divided against itself and all traces of its past works are constantly both losing their old meaning and gaining new ones. There is, in other words, no such "thing" or effective force as Nietzsche's will to power.[18]

Nor is there a direction and end to his-

16 Roldolphe Gasche, *The Tain of the Mirror* (Cambridge, Mass.: Harvard University Press, 1986); Christopher Norris, *Derrida* (Cambridge, Mass.: Harvard University Press, 1987); Richard Rorty, "Is Derrida a Transcendental Philosopher?" in *Derrida: A Critical Reader,* ed. David Wood (Cambridge: Blackwell, 1992), 235–46.

17 "Du Tout," reprinted in *The Post Card,* trans. Alan Bass (Chicago: University of Chicago Press, 1987), 508.

18 In *Of Grammatology,* Derrida thus urges: "To save Nietzsche from a reading of the Heideggerian type [in terms primarily of the "will to power"], it seems that *we must above all not attempt to restore or make explicit a less naive 'ontology'* [which, I believe, is what Derrida would think Strauss is doing]. . . . [R]ather than protect Nietzsche from the Heideggerian reading, we should perhaps offer him up to it completely, underwriting that interpretation without reserve; in a *certain* way and up to the point where, the content of the Nietzschean discourse being almost lost for the question of being, its form regains its absolute strangeness . . . [and] invokes a different type of reading, more faithful to his type of writing: Nietzsche has *written* . . . that writing—and first of all his own—is not originarily [*sic*] subordinate to the logos and to truth" (19; my emphases).

tory as Heidegger maintained. There is and ought to be more openness—to the Other, to the non-West, to the utterly unexpected.

Derrida makes the political consequences of his understanding of history most explicit in a talk he gave in 1990 at the prospect of the reemergence of a unified Europe (something, I might add, Nietzsche had called for in *Beyond Good and Evil*). There had been an attempt to unify or re-unify Europe in 1939, Derrida reminded his listeners. That attempt had been blocked by the Western democratic nations in the name of another idea of Europe, and their victory had placed barriers or divisions that were just now coming down. The reopening of these partitions is what gives rise to the same mixture of hope and anxiety that could be felt at the earlier prospect of reunification, because with the hope also comes the danger—realized today in what was Yugoslavia—of a return to old forms of religious fanaticism, nationalism, or racism.

"Europe" has never and never will be simply one thing, Derrida suggests. It has always been composed of different nations speaking different languages under different governments. The unity of "Europe" has a geographical foundation, but it is primarily cultural or spiritual. Especially since the nineteenth century, Europeans like Paul Valery, Husserl, and Heidegger have regarded "Europe" as the intellectual leader of the world. At the same time, they have feared that this intellect or its grounds are being eroded. To keep it alive, Derrida suggests, it is necessary to see the European intellect as looking forward, in advance, to the West, into the unknown. We who come later, we have a double, a contradictory, and hence a perhaps impossible responsibility. We must seek to preserve our heritage, because we remember that among the worst

abuses have been those undertaken under the banner of the completely "new," the attempts to wipe the slate clean and begin entirely anew—for example, the terrors of the French Revolution and Stalin's new economic order. But, in order to preserve our heritage, we must at the same time be open and willing to see it disrupted by the emergence of the new.

We cannot, to take the Heideggerian example, turn our backs on technology; we must, rather, be attentive to the novel dangers it poses to our freedom. According to Derrida, "We bear the responsibility for this heritage. . . . We did not choose this responsibility; it imposes itself upon us . . ." (28). And the responsibility—or the response that is called for, because Derrida denies a juridical notion of "responsibility"—is always twofold or divided. He emphasizes:

> [O]*n the one hand,* European cultural identity cannot be dispersed (and when I say "cannot," this should also be taken as "must not") . . . into a myriad of provinces, into a multiplicity of self-enclosed idioms or petty little nationalisms. . . . But, *on the other hand,* it cannot and must not accept the capital of a centralizing authority that, by means of trans-European cultural mechanisms, by means of publishing, journalistic, and academic concentrations—be they state-run or not—would control and standardize . . . artistic discourses and practices . . . to philosophical or aesthetic norms [or] . . . pursuit of ratings and commercial profitability. (38–39)

> [But] if it is necessary to make sure that a centralizing hegemony . . . not be reconstituted, it is also necessary . . . not to cultivate for their own sake minority differences, untranslatable idiolects, national antagonisms, or the chauvinism of idiom. (44)

"Europe" does not and should not constitute a cultural or a political hegemony. The political universalism for which it is and ought to be responsible is that of "human rights and international law—

which logically presupposes that it [be] the first to denounce divergences between the principle of these rights (whose reaffirmation must be and can only be unconditional) and the concrete conditions of their implementation. . . . The task is always at once urgent and infinite" (52). There are myriad old and new threats to rights. The "duty to recall what has been promised under the name Europe, to re-identify Europe" thus "also dictates opening Europe . . . onto that which is not, never was, and never will be Europe." It "dictates welcoming foreigners in order not only to integrate them but to recognize and accept their alterity. . . ." It "dictates assuming the European, and *uniquely* European, heritage of an idea of democracy, while also recognizing that this idea, like that of international law, is never simply given, that its status is not even that of a regulative idea in the Kantian sense, but rather something that remains to be thought and *to come;* not something that is certain to happen tomorrow, . . . but a democracy that must have the structure of a promise . . ." (76–77).[19]

In conclusion, let me try briefly to bring Strauss and Derrida together in order to sketch the contours or outlines of what I take to be the space or the problem called *postmodernism.* That problem concerns, first, the status and character of philosophy, and the status of philosophy, it turns out, has very much to do with the status of nature or natural differences. Strauss responds to Nietzsche's call for a transformation of nature, especially human nature, by arguing that, if it is possible for a human being like Socrates to live a per-

fectly satisfying life, it is not necessary to change human nature or to risk all the disastrous political consequences of that attempt. In his studies of Socrates, Strauss emphasizes the "turn" in the ancient philosopher's thought when he became aware of the differences between the human and the nonhuman things. What is important, what we must recapture from the prephilosophical experience out of which philosophy emerged, is this insight into the heterogeneous character of the whole. That insight is captured and preserved in Socrates' famous question, "What is . . . ?" It is the basis for his examination of the opinions of others, because the insight into the differences among the kinds of things is first captured in language. That insight and the "what is" questions to which it gives rise are much more important, much more fundamental than the Platonic "theory of the ideas." Strauss does not attempt to resuscitate either this theory or the Aristotelian cosmology that seemed to follow from it. On the contrary, in the history of "Natural Law" he gives in his *Studies,* he suggests that Aristotle took the first step away from the Platonic notion of natural right, a step that was then broadened by the Stoics and Aquinas. Both in this essay and in *Natural Right and History,* he suggests that the most important function of a teaching about nature, especially human nature, is that it provides a foundation for political morality.[20] *The* problematic results of modern political philosophy began to emerge, therefore, most clearly after Kant separated morality entirely from nature.

Derrida locates the beginning of "the ends of man" in exactly the same place—in Kant's break with what Derrida calls *an-*

---

[19] Quotations from Jacques Derrida, *The Other Heading: Reflections on Today's Europe,* trans. Pascale-Anne Brault and Michael B. Naas (Bloomington, Ind.: Indiana University Press, 1992).

[20] Strauss, *Studies,* 137–46; Leo Strauss, *Natural Right and History* (Chicago: University of Chicago Press, 1953).

thropomorphism.[21] Unlike Strauss, however, Derrida celebrates this move. If we no longer see evidence of a natural order composed of eternal species, it becomes philosophically necessary to understand what distinguishes "man" in terms other than his nature. The three previous attempts to bring "man" to an end that Derrida describes in the works of Hegel, Husserl, and Heidegger all constitute attempts to redefine what is distinctively human in solely intellectual terms—*Geist,* the transcendental ego, or *Dasein,* the only being for whom its own being is a question. And in complete contrast to Strauss, Derrida celebrates this move. Distinctions on the basis of "nature" have been used to exclude, if not to oppress, certain groups on the basis of their race or sex.

Strauss has a response to this Derridean critique, I believe. Although he admits, sotto voce, that the concept of "nature" is problematic, he would object to Derrida's *difference* as a philosophical construct that serves, like most modern scientific theories, to obscure the differences among things we all continue to be able to observe on the surface—the differences between nature and art, for example, or human beings and others. Like other modern philosophers, Derrida fails to take account of the prephilosophical foundations of his own thought.

The philosophical differences between Strauss and Derrida are clearly related to, if they do not simply produce, political differences as well. But the political differences between Strauss and Derrida are not merely those of a conservative as opposed to a liberal egalitarian. Like Nietzsche, Strauss appears to want to reintroduce a notion of natural differences in order to support a teaching about the relative merits or hierarchy of the different possible forms or ways of human life. Only the philosopher is happy; but for philosophers and nonphilosophers to continue to exist, he insists, political order is necessary. And the maintenance of political order requires a public teaching or agreement about what the best way of life is that will not be philosophical or grounded in truth. Because political associations or communities are based on *opinions* about what is right or wrong, on which all human beings will not and should never simply agree, political societies are necessarily partial and closed. Any attempt to create a world-state, therefore, would necessarily result in a tyrannically imposed uniformity. (In this respect, I might note, Strauss agrees with Heidegger, although they understand both the limits and the sources of these limits somewhat differently.)

Derrida challenges the notion that all polities are or must be closed. *The* promise of European civilization, the promise of the Enlightenment, he reminds his readers, is the *open* society. Like Nietzsche, Heidegger, and Strauss, Derrida is worried about the powerfully homogenizing trends in modern life. He would, therefore, also seek to preserve different cultural and historical traditions as well as independent nation-states. Like many contemporary thinkers on the Left, he is particularly concerned about the insidious, standardizing, pacifying effect of the media. He would respond to the danger with critique, however, rather than by instituting public or other forms of control.

In sum, the postmodern problem is, first, what kinds of beings are we, we who think and write? If the concept of "nature" is no longer tenable, how are we to understand ourselves? Second, if it is true that we cannot survive without joining forces

---

[21] Jacques Derrida, "The Ends of Man," in *Margins of Philosophy,* trans. Alan Bass (Chicago: University of Chicago Press, 1982).

somehow with others, how much diversity or difference can we tolerate in our associations? Are we always necessarily at war, if only implicitly and in groups rather than, à la Hobbes, as individuals? And, third, if the only locus of intelligent life that we know from experience is the human being, and if human beings are, both individually and as a race, finite; is all truth, as Heidegger argues, necessarily limited in time and space, or do we have some grounds still to aspire, as Strauss would urge us, to come to know some kind of eternal truth, if only in the form of unsolvable problems?

14

Political Science and Politics Around the World

The problem is to find a form of association which will defend and protect with the whole common force the person and goods of each associate, and in which each, while uniting himself with all, may still obey himself alone, and remain as free as before.

—Jean-Jacques Rousseau

Introduction

In 1991, David Easton, John G. Gunnell, and Luigi Graziano published a compendium of articles which examined the state of the discipline of political science in numerous countries around the world. In their study they noted that, whereas in 1949 there were only four national political science associations, by 1991 the number had risen to more than fifty. The authors point first to the positive aspect of this development, that this growth has enriched and broadened the profession. They also note, however, that the profession's expansion has "fostered fragmentation, communication overload, multiple approaches, conflicting schools, and one suspects, considerable overlap and duplication." Due to these trends, they note further, "Political scientists as a whole are no longer as certain about their 'progress' as they were formerly or as imbued with as confident a sense of direction" (Easton 1991, 1). Easton, Gunnell, and Graziano hereby sound the call of both the promise and the peril of contemporary political science. Much is happening, and much is left to accomplish. Perhaps it is appropriate to begin our brief tour of political science around the world with a quick reference to Aristotle, to recall that great philosopher's definition of democracy, and to be reminded that in some respects the concerns of political science today have changed little since Aristotle's time.

As we have noted before, when Aristotle used the term "democracy" he meant not the rule of the largest class in the interests of all the people (a form of government which he called "polity") but mob rule, the rule of the largest, poorest class of people acting in their own interests alone. Democracy, as he defined it, was at least potentially the worst of all forms of government. But for most Western political scientists today democracy means something else. Democracy today means at least that government rule is an expression of the will of the majority and is limited to protect the rights of minorities. At the end of the twentieth century, democracy is also increasingly commonly understood to include a capitalist, or free-market economy.

A review of international literature in the 1990s reveals that, if there is a predominant preoccupation within the discipline as it is practiced around the world, it is with the development, the solidification, the stabilization of democracy. The fall of the Soviet empire at the dawn of the decade brought forth many books and articles speculating on the future of democracy. Two popular books of this genre were Samuel Huntington's *The Third Wave* (1991) and Francis Fukuyama's *The Last Man and the End of History* (1992). Huntington's book identifies three waves of democracy (described in Chapter 3 of this text) and argues that a third wave has recently begun which may lead to far more widespread democratization in the remaining autocratic states, or there may be a reappearance of authoritarianism before the work of democracy proceeds again. Fukuyama, in a work which builds upon the philosophy of nineteenth century philosopher G. W. F. Hegel, asserts that "history" is the developing struggle among classes and their ideologies for control of the world. Because capitalist democracy has now, in the wake of the dissolution of the former Soviet Union, demonstrated its supremacy over communism, the last great ideological battle has been concluded, and history is, therefore, over.

Other political scientists, however, are not at all confident that democracy has already won the final battle. They are studying democracy with renewed vigor in many different settings, seeking clues to its vitality, success, disintegration, or decline. This chapter touches upon only a few of the many efforts political scientists are making throughout the world to understand not only democracy, but all aspects of political life. Democracy has been selected as the focus of this chapter because of the continuing intensive efforts that analysts make to understand its past, its current varieties, and its future.

It is fair to conclude, based on the reports of political scientists around the world, that political science is coincident with democracy. This should not surprise anyone who reflects upon the thought that, if political science is the objective and critical evaluation of politics and government, then a certain democratic freedom is necessary to political science's progress.

Summing up their thoughts on this subject after reviewing trends in European political science at the beginning of this decade, Kenneth Newton and Josep M. Valles declare that the studies that have been done support the conclusion that "political science can only emerge and develop on democratic societies" and, further, that "like democracy itself, political science flourishes most strongly in relatively affluent societies" (Newton and Valles 1991, 227–228). Extending these findings to their ultimate conclusions, Newton and Valles declare that "as political science is genuinely alive only in democracy, so is democracy genuinely alive only with political science." They are aware, however, that determining the impact of political science upon society is a most difficult task, especially because political scientists do not appear to have a very great direct affect upon politics in most democracies.

With these thoughts about political science and democracy in mind, we now present a brief tour of political science in a dozen countries around the world. The student is reminded that dozens more countries have similar stories, and the trend around the world is for political science to increase its vitality and popularity. Study of the development of political science in countries around the world immediately reveals that the development of the discipline in each country is inextricably linked with the development of the country itself. We shall begin our tour with Canada.

Canada

Although Canada has developed in many ways under the influence of its neighbor to the south, Canadians quickly, proudly, and justly point to their unique and independent accomplishments. Like the United States and Mexico, Canada was competed for by European nations, primarily England, France, and Spain, who sought to claim, exploit, and colonize North America after the discoveries of Columbus. The battle for Canada was finally won by the British in 1763 when France lost the Seven Years War. Canada was granted Dominion status, as a part of the British Commonwealth, under the British North America Act of 1867, when the provinces of Quebec, Ontario, Nova Scotia, and New Brunswick were united. Until 1931, the British crown continued to exercise executive authority through an appointed governor general, while the legislative power fell to a Parliament consisting of a Senate and a House of Commons. In that year, the British Statute of Westminster recognized Canada as an autonomous state within the Commonwealth, and its constitution was "patriated" on April 17, 1982. The two primary political parties are the Liberals and the Progressive Conservatives, which have taken turns in power for the past several decades. Jean Chretian was installed as Prime Minister in November 1993. Canada still has a governor general who fulfills a symbolic role in state ceremonies, and who is a Canadian citizen appointed by the British crown on the advice of Canada's actual chief executive, the prime minister.

With more than 3.8 million square miles, Canada is the second largest country in land area in the world. Today Canada is divided into ten provinces. More than two-thirds of its people live in a 100-mile wide strip along the border of the United States. Canada's population of 27 million includes six million French-speaking people, eighty percent of whom live in Quebec. Canada's official languages are French and English. Movements for establishment of Quebec as a separate country have occurred from time to time. In 1992, a proposal which would have given Quebec substantial independence, but not autonomy, and increased self-governance to native peoples, was rejected in a national referendum and in a 1995 national referendum a proposal for independence for Quebec was narrowly defeated.

Political science first achieved official recognition as an academic discipline in Canada when chairs in political science (modeled after similar chairs at Cambridge and Oxford universities in England) were installed at the University of Toronto in 1888 and at Queen's University in 1889. At first political science in Canada was strongly tied to the British model, which emphasized legal and historical studies, in contrast to departments in the United States, which were more heavily influenced by continental European scholars from an early date. The influence of American scholarship in Canada was also unmistakable, however, due in large to Canada's proximity to American graduate programs and professional activities. According to Trent and Stein (1991), the idea of a Canadian Political Science Association (CPSA) was conceived in 1912 by a group of twelve Canadian professors visiting a meeting of the American Political Science Association (APSA) which had been formed in 1903. The CPSA held its first annual meeting in Ottawa in September 1912. The CPSA, unlike the APSA, "had a distinct interdisciplinary orientation, and included economists, lawyers, historians, and political scientists among its members" (Trent and Stein 1991, 62). The CPSA got off to a weak start and ceased to meet after World War I, but was rejuvenated by Harold Innis of the University of Toronto in 1929. In that same year, Innis also initiated production of the *Canadian Journal of Economics and Political Science.*

Political scientists became much more active in Canada in the 1930s, when some of the discipline's radicals helped to found the Cooperative Commonwealth Federation (CCF), the first Canadian democratic socialist party. Canadian political scientists also gained national recognition in the 1930s for their participation in the Rowell-Sirois Commission on Dominion-Provincial Relations, which addressed problems arising out of the Great Depression.

Departments of political science grew substantially in number and size after World War II, and by the beginning of the 1980s about 775 political scientists taught in 45 departments throughout the country (Trent and Stein 1991). The *Canadian Journal of Political Science* was established in 1968. In Quebec, political science proceeded more slowly because both the provincial authorities and the Roman Catholic Church feared that a new social and political science would undermine their authority. In spite of this, however, R. P. Levesque managed to establish the Department of Political Science at Laval University in 1954.

In 1982, Trent and Stein (113) described Canadian political science in much the same terms that were used by Americans to depict political science in the United States at that time. They maintained that the eclecticism of the Canadian discipline had led to certain deficiencies in the knowledge accumulated by the discipline as a whole. Political science, they declared, is characterized by:

- An approach to knowledge that is primarily synthetic, evolutionary, and cumulative knowledge rather than dialectical or discontinuous.
- Greater innovativeness in case studies and theoretical applications than in pure theoretical contributions.
- [An approach which] fosters partial rather than holistic and sectoral rather than systemic studies.

Today Canadian political science is making many notable contributions. The University of Toronto is regarded as one of the finest educational institutions on the continent, and its department of political science continues to produce highly regarded scholarship. Several other Canadian universities have also won international recognition.

The United Kingdom

The government of the United Kingdom of Great Britain and Northern Ireland is technically a constitutional monarchy, for it presently has a ruling queen, Elizabeth II, and a royal family, but it is controlled by a democratic parliamentary government which includes the powerful House of Commons and the largely but not entirely ceremonial House of Lords. The North Atlantic island territory of the United Kingdom was once controlled by the Roman Empire, and Roman roads dating from around the birth of Christ can still be seen there. Conquering the Angles and the Saxons in the Battle of Hastings in 1066, the French Normans established a royal line from which today's democracy eventually developed. The Magna Charta, reluctantly signed in 1215 by King John, gave to the nobles a share in governing the country. Through the centuries, the British people added a Bill of Rights, a House of Commons, and a long tradition of rule by law to their government practices, gradually establishing a parliamentary system which has been copied, if in revised form, by many other countries around the world.

The peak of Britain's power occurred during the reign of Queen Victoria (1837–1901). During her sixty-three year rule, the British Commonwealth extended to every part of the world. After World War II, numerous independence movements caused Britain, willingly or not, to grant her colonies their independence.

The parliamentary system of Great Britain is founded upon the basis of tradition and custom rather than a written constitution. There is no separation of powers as in the American system. The prime minister, a member of the House of Commons, is elected by the membership of that body and is, therefore, both the chief executive and the chief legislative official. Since World War II, the Labour Party and the Conservative Party have traded turns running the government. The Labour Party governed under Prime Ministers Clement Attlee, Harold Wilson, and James Callaghan, from 1945 to 1951, 1964 to 1970, and 1974 to 1979. The Conservative Party governed under Prime Ministers Winston Churchill, Anthony Eden, Harold MacMillan, Sir Alec Douglas-Home, Edward Heath, Margaret Thatcher, and John Major, from 1951 to 1964, 1970 to 1974, and 1979 to present.

British political science claims as its heritage many of the great treatises of political philosophy, such as those written by Thomas Hobbes, John Locke, Jeremy Bentham, Edmund Burke, James Mill, and John Stuart Mill, among others. The tradition at Oxford and Cambridge, two leading British universities with histories reaching back into the middle ages, was one of historical-philosophical analysis rather than quantitative science. This antiscientific disposition was challenged by the more scientific inclinations of the London School of Economics, established in 1895 with Graham Wallas as its first Professor of Political Science. Wallas favored the French model called the *Ecole Libre des Sciences Politiques,* which wanted to form the study of politics on a scientific basis for the benefit of society. Wallas believed that the political scientist was to be "not a philosopher but a social engineer" (Weiner 1971, 67). But Wallas and his scientific and behaviorally minded colleagues were not able to capture the mainstream of British political science. According to commentator Jack Hayward, "In surveying the pre-history of British political science before the mid-twentieth century, the allergy to social science of most of its leading practitioners has emerged unambiguously" (Hayward 1991, 309). Hayward claims that British political science was traditional and antiempirical in the 1950s, was enthusiastically technocratically reformist in the 1960s and early 1970s, and has been skeptically professional since 1975 (Hayward 1991, 310). Hayward notes further that British political science purposefully rejected the solidification of behaviorlism that was taking place in America in the 1960s and 1970s: "The British response to American political science [in the years 1961–74] was a classic case of dynamic conservatism: changing enough so as to keep things basically the same" (Hayward 1991, 313).

Political scientist Bernard Crick voiced typical British criticisms of behavioralism in his widely read book *The American Science of Politics*. The British aversion to behavioral and scientific studies was in some quarters so strong that the label "political scientist" has been avoided by some in scholarly publication. Facing this difficulty in describing British contributions to the study of politics, Jack Hayward (1982, 355) substitutes the term "politist":

> I shall adopt the locution "politist" because it conveys (to me at least) the increasing aspiration to become a social scientist, particularly among the younger members of the profession, without laying claim to having as yet finally attained it. Ironically, in the light of its parents, the Webbs, the London School of Economics and Political Science Department of Government—in conjunction with the other great pillar of British political studies, Oxford—has been a stronghold of hostility to 'political science" in Britain since Michael Oakeshott's succession to Harold Laski in mid-century. . . .

The British, by and large, also rejected the Marxist approaches being adopted in some of the American and European universities. Although their methods remained predominantly conservative from an American point of view, the British did, however, continue to develop one of the most active political science professions in the world. The United Kingdom Political Studies Association was established in 1950. The Social Science Research Council, established in 1965, encouraged the development of political science departments in universities and the creation of journals for the publication of research. *Political Studies* and the *British Journal of Political Science,* which are among the most important British journals, are widely known in other countries.

Political scientists in Great Britain have often provided direct help in government. Bernard Crick's *Reform of Parliament* (1964) was the result of a study that brought together political scientists and legislators and resulted in changes in the procedures and committee structures of Parliament. In contributing to government, however, British political scientists have often had to overcome attitudes of the more pragmatically inclined politicians. Hayward notes that, "The state-sustaining function that has usually been an implicit purpose of political science is ironically combined in Britain with the fact that practical men of affairs think they have little to learn from academics in political matters" (Hayward 1991, 320). Another problem mentioned frequently by British political scientists is that the British have a tradition of secrecy in the executive branch of government which excludes political scientists from much information available to them in the United States.

In addition to famous political philosophers of centuries past, British political science has produced a number of others who have made internationally important contributions. Ernest Barker, for example, whose editions of the political works of the ancient Greek philosophers are still widely read, was the first person to hold the Cambridge Chair of Political Science. Students of law around the world are likely to be familiar with Blackstone's treatises on law, which were the basic legal texts for the British Commonwealth for decades, and A. V. Dicey's *Introduction to the Study of the Law of the Constitution* was highly influential because it highlighted the central place of law in British society.

The 1980s was a decade of some difficulty for British political science. Approximately 1,000 political scientists were identified as working in the universities of Great Britain in 1987, but university budgets, which had been on the decline for a decade, caused a lack of opportunities that led many in the field to seek employment in the United States. As the 1990s progress, however, the British continue to play an important role in analyzing the contributions that political scientists make elsewhere, as well as in conducting their own studies of governmental processes.

Even though British political science, considered as a whole for the last half of the twentieth century, has been more traditional in orientation than American political science, it is important not to underestimate British contributions to behavioral as well as traditional studies. In the 1990s, political scientists in the United Kingdom are using all the methodologies known to the discipline in their quest for knowledge. Rosemary H. T. O'Kane's 1995 article, "The National Causes of State Construction in France, Russia, and China" (*Political Studies* 43: 2–21), for example, has been included in this text as an example of recent scholarship in comparative government. British scholar Adrian Leftwich, further, has edited one of the most important reviews of recent trends in political science around the world (*New Developments in Political Science: An International Review of Achievements and Prospects,* 1990). In fact, an examination of the recent publications reveals that British political scientists are publishing widely, not only in their own journals, but in American journals as well, and their contribution to the discipline may well excel that of any other nation except the United States.

Continental Europe

Political science on the European continent has taken a different tack from the course of the discipline in the United Kingdom. The European Economic Community is perhaps only the most obvious of many expressions of a general movement to combine efforts and resources to forge a stronger and more unified Europe. Britain has, in some cultural respects, tried to remain relatively distant from this movement, in spite of its participation in the European Economic Community (EEC). Encouraged by the unification movement, scholars from several European countries have attempted to create a sense of community among European political scientists. Organized by Jean Blondel, Hans Daalder, Stein Rokkan, and Rudolf Wildenmann, a group of leading scholars, encouraged by a Ford Foundation grant, established in 1970 the *European Consortium for Political Research* (Newton 1991, 445). By 1990, this new association had 139 members from 15 European countries and was actively engaged in publishing books, journals, and newsletters.

France

The French Revolution of 1789 has a special place in the history of politics for its revolutionary idealism and its violence. After large numbers of aristocrats were executed by leaders of the peasants, the revolutionaries turned on each other, and the revolt that began with the hope of making people free and equal resulted in the reign of one of history's great despots, Napoleon. Since the Revolution, France has had five Republics. The first followed the revolution and was dissolved by Napoleon. The second was established after the Revolution of 1848, the third lasted from 1870 to 1940, the fourth had a brief life beginning in 1946, and the fifth, which continues today, was founded in 1958 by General Charles de Gaulle. Under the Constitution adopted in 1958 and amended in 1962, the President is a strong executive official who can dissolve the National Assembly, hold national referenda, and assume legislative and executive authority in times of emergency. France also has a premier, who has limited administrative and official functions, and a Council of Ministers, whose members are appointed by the President. Jacques Chirac became President in May 1995. The Premier, Edouard Balladur of the Rally for the Republic Party, assumed office in March 1993.

The study of politics in France was largely subsumed in the disciplines of law, history, philosophy, and sociology until the French Political Science Association and the *Revue Française de Science Politique* were both established in 1950. The *Fondation Nationale des Sciences Politiques*, in Paris, established "to ensure the progress and diffusion in France and abroad of political, economic and social studies" (Dreyfus 1982, 431), has helped the profession gain attention and respect. The French university system is tightly controlled by the central government, which decided to strengthen the discipline from 1960 to 1980, during which time 40 chairs and more than 100 lectureships and assistantships were created (Dreyfus 1982, 429). According to Francois G. Dreyfus' article entitled "Political Science in France" (1982, 435), French political science has been divided into several fields, but the major emphasis is on "institutional studies" led by Duguit, Hauriou, Carre de Malberg, Marcel Prelot, and Georges Burdeau.

Perhaps the most original and well-known French contributions to political science have been the electoral studies which originated with the work of Andre Siegfried. Siegfried's *Tableau Politique de la France de l'Ouest sous la Troisieme Republique* (1913) was the founding document of what became known as the *ecological school*. Participants in these electoral studies pioneered the use of use of aggregate data, which combines information about many individuals to analyze voting patterns. Another member of this school, Jean Stoetzel, met George Gallup at Columbia University in 1938 and returned to France to found the *Institut Francais d'Opinion Publique* (IFOP) (Ysmal 1994, 367). A student of electoral politics, Herbert Tingsten achieved international recognition with *Political Behaviour* in 1937. According to Newton and Valles, the advances in these studies are so original that "the school of electoral sociology in France owes nothing to American election studies" (Newton and Valles 1991, 235).

In many other areas as well, French political science continues to produce substantial works of scholarship. Raymond Aron's *Peace and War* is merely one example from the field of international relations. Encountering a number of problems in the development of the discipline, the French, much like their American counterparts, have produced an exceptional amount of self-critical literature, which may well bear fruit in the years ahead. As noted in numerous places in this text, the ability to be self-critical demonstrates strength rather than weakness in the discipline. In 1982, Pierre Favre (1982, 161) characterized the development of political science in France in the following terms:

> Three traits appear to characterize the present situation of political science in France: (1) the subjects studied by political science remain few if one compares them with the list of what is usually included in the proper subject matter of this discipline; (2) French political science is divided into very individualized specialties which communicate little with each other; (3) political science in France has little scientific legitimacy to the extent that many works emanating from diverse sociological or historical schools deny it the capacity to deal with politics and propose other approaches to political subject matter.

Another critic of French political science is Jean Leca of the *Institute of Political Science* at Paris, who points out a number of biases in current French practice. First, political science in France has been taught in conjunction with studies which are intended primarily for training managers for the French civil service. This emphasis on practitioners is said to have impeded the development of a science of politics.

Another problem, according to Leca (1991, 334), is that "French political science has some trouble asserting its identity [as a discipline] and being recognized by others." One of the results of the lack of a strong identity is an "historical bias," a result of influence from the Annales school of economic history. The Annales school, according to Leca, held the view that "the only political science is political history . . . in particular the view that any sequence of events is unique and must be studied in itself without reference to an overall explanatory framework of sociological generalizations." These beliefs led to the antiscientific conclusion "that history is unique, cannot be replicated or used as an experiment to test generalizations" (Leca 1991, 334). Another antiscientific bias has been introduced into the discipline in France by young philosophers who find job prospects more plentiful in political science than in philosophy, and who tend to produce for the most part commentaries on the great philosophers.

And finally, Leca (1991, 332) identified an economic bias in the discipline, pointing out that "the overwhelming majority of French political scientists, lacking an adequate training in micro-economics and formal theory, do not go for the sophisticated exercises familiar to many of their European and American colleagues."

Germany

On October 3, 1990, the Federal Republic of Germany became once again the nation of a unified German people. More than a century earlier, in 1871, a loose association of German speaking provinces was united by Otto von Bismark into the German Empire, which was replaced after its defeat in World War I by the Weimar

Republic (1919–1933). Beset by the depression and constant political turmoil, the Weimar Republic fell prey to Adolph Hitler's Nazi Party, which joined forces with Japan and Italy to fight the Allies (United States, British Commonwealth, France, and the Soviet Union) in World War II. After its defeat in World War II, in July of 1945, Germany was divided into British, French, Soviet and United states zones of occupation. The Federal Republic of Germany (FRG), to be known as West Germany and encompassing the British, French, and American zones, was established with a democratic parliamentary government on May 23, 1949. The German Democratic Republic (GDR), known as East Germany, was established as a communist government in the Soviet zone on October 7, 1949. By the 1960s, West Germany had recovered, with the help of Western nations, from the devastation of the war to become the strongest industrial nation in Europe, but East Germany, under the Soviet Union's control, continually lagged behind economically and in many other ways. Today, the Federal Republic has a president, Roman Herzog, and a Federal Chancellor, Helmut Kohl, both of the Christian Democratic Union party.

The Deutsche Hochschule fuer Politik (German Academy for Politics) was founded in 1920 but was closed by the Nazis. In 1948 it was reestablished in West Berlin and became a part of the Free University of Berlin in 1959. A Department of Political Science was established at the Free University of Berlin in 1970 and departments and chairs established at Freiburg, Muenchen, Marburg, Frankfurt, Heidelberg, and Hamburg.

During the second world war, almost 3,000 German intellectuals emigrated to the United States. Among them were people who became prominent political scientists, such as Hannah Arendt, Karl Deutsch, Lewis Edinger, Heinz Eulau, Gottfried Dietze, Arnold Heidenheimer, Carl J. Friedrich, Otto Kirchheimer, Henry Kissinger, Gerhard Lowenberg, Karl Lowenstein, Peter Merkl, Hans Morgenthau, Franz and Sigmund Neumann, Herbert Spiro, Leo Strauss, and Eric Voegelin (Beyme 1982).

The loss of most of the best students of politics that Germany had to offer combined with another factor to shape the course of the development of the discipline in West Germany after the war. Universal shock and abhorrence of the authoritarian extremes and atrocities of the Nazi regime fostered anticommunist and prodemocratic attitudes, and the efforts of German political science turned towards understanding and strengthening basic democratic processes. These developments led Hans Kastendiek (1987) to conclude that German academic development has been tied to politics even more than in most other countries.

Under these circumstances it was particularly difficult for German political science to form its own new identity. This task was made even harder by traditional approaches and attitudes in the major universities, which were biased towards normative theory and against scientific approaches (Beyme 1991).

Another problem for the encouragement of originality and innovation in political science in Germany is the strong control of the government over university life. The government appoints a limited number of full professors and limits assistant professorships to five years. Those assistant professors who do not receive a professorship at the end of this time must seek employment elsewhere (Kastendiek 1987).

In the 1960s, the United States, which the German people had held in high regard, lost influence because of the Vietnam war. In German universities a conservative tradition of political philosophy took up the battle against American behavioralism. The traditional normative philosophical and historical disciplines of *Staatsrechtslehre* (public law) and *Staatswissenschaften* (state craft) continued to dominate the study of politics. This conservative movement also impeded quantitative studies. German departments did not prepare their students to conduct quantitative analysis. Another problem for the establishment of behavioral political science was the reemergence of Marxism in the 1960s in the form of the Frankfurt school of critical studies and neo-Marxism, which applies class conflict principles to current political problems.

By the 1980s, four schools of thought competed for influence in Germany: the normative-ontological school represented by Arnold Bergstraesser and Eric Voegelin; mainstream political science, which included Carl J. Friedrich; behaviorists such as Otto Stammer; and Marxist orientations such as those of Adorno and Habermas (Beyme 1982).

Today West German political science boasts one of the largest memberships in the international political science association. Its growth shows promise, especially if it can overcome two problems: a lack of sufficient financial support of the government, and a decline in student interest. Ironically, both of these problems are the direct result of Germany's achievement of democratic stability.

Before closing this discussion, it is important to say a word or two about East German political science, if it may be called political science, as it was under Soviet domination. Roder and Franke are two communist East German political scientists who described their country's political science in an article published in the *International Handbook of Political Science* (1982). To the extent that their article is an accurate portrayal of the status of political science in East Germany under Soviet rule (and it may not accurately represent all of East German political science), it demonstrates how ideology may not only impede but halt the advancement of worthwhile knowledge altogether. Roder and Franke render a pathetic litany of Marxist ideology that, except as a reminder to the rest of the world of the tragedy of totalitarianism, would not normally be accepted for publication by a journal which otherwise attracted reputable scholarship. Rather than describe the results of studies that have been undertaken, they merely recite discredited communist ideology. Note the following selection:

> The changing character of the classes, their interests, and their position within the historical process and the type of state power will, in the course of development of society, result in a change in the historically concrete character of political relations . . . . A characteristic phenomenon of developed socialism is the general social activity of the working people, who participate with high responsibility and competence in management and planning of social development. The main direction, along which the socialist state power develops, is the further development and perfection of socialist democracy. (Roder and Franke 1982, 177–178)

If we accept Roder and Franke's presentation as representative of East German political science before reunification, we may conclude that normally acceptable political science did not exist in East Germany at that time. It is still too early to tell what contribution the former East Germans will make to Germany's newly developing political science, but it is likely that many of them are happy to make, at long last, genuine contributions to the discipline in the newly unified Germany.

Italy

Italian history is recorded in detail even before the legendary establishment of Rome by Romulus in 753 BCE. Although the separate states that now constitute Italy became unified in 1861 (CE), the Italian Republic was not created until a national referendum in 1946. Before this time, the House of Savoy led the people symbolically through a parliamentary monarchy. The Italian Republic has a president, a parliament, and an independent judiciary; its constitution went into effect on January 1, 1948. Luigi Scalfaro of the Italian Popular Party (formerly the Christian Democratic Party) was inaugurated as president of the Republic on May 25, 1992. The president has a seven-year term and is selected by an electoral college consisting of both houses of parliament plus delegates named by the regional assemblies. The president appoints the prime minister, and may dissolve Parliament upon advice from the prime minister. The Parliament has a Senate and a Chamber of Deputies, which have equal legislative powers. The Christian Democratic Party (DC) dominated Italian politics from World War II until 1994, when a new coalition came to power headed by billionaire businessman Silvio Berlusconi, who has since left office after a series of scandals in his administration. The Communist Party, now declining in popularity, was for many years a powerful if not dominant influence.

To give credit where it is due, political science begins in Italy at least with Cicero, the Roman statesman and author who predated by a century the arrival of Jesus Christ. St. Thomas Aquinas' *Summa Theologica* is one of many leading treatises of the Middle Ages. Machiavelli's masterful if unsentimental *The Prince*, a product of the dawn of the sixteenth century, remains the classic exposition of political realism. In this century, two masters of politics, economics, and sociology are the contemporary grandfathers of Italian political science: Gaetano Mosca and Wifredo Pareto. Mosca's *Elementi di scienza politica* (1896), according to Leonardo Morlino (1991, 343), "may symbolically be considered to mark the birth of Italian political science." Italians themselves, however, note that these two seminal thinkers did not immediately attract a stable set of followers locally, and, therefore, the development of political science in Italy was delayed until after World War II (Graziano 1987, 42).

In the 1950s, however, political science came alive in Italy as in few other European countries, and Italy today ranks high on the list of contributors to international political science. Two of the most important Italian political scientists in the last half of this century are Giovanni Sartori and Noberto Bobbio. Sartori is given credit for introducing American behavioral political science to Italy, and Bobbio led Italian efforts to establish political science as an independent discipline. Bobbio demonstrated the importance of the works of Mosca and Pareto and helped define the particular role and contribution of political science within the social sciences and the humanities (Morlino 1991). Sartori and Bobbio both fought against the antiscientific bias of traditional Italian scholarship and culture (Graziano 1987). Graziano notes that, while Italian culture has traditionally focused on the "why" questions of philosophy and the meaning of life, science in general and political science in particular has to do with the "how" questions.

In addition to making a place for behavioral political science in the face of a dominant tradition of political philosophy, Sartori, Bobbio, and others had to assert the value of their behavioral methods in the face of the popularity of Marxism, with its emphasis on changing society in the interests of subjugated classes. Many Italians are Marxist in orientation, and in the postwar period the communist party was very popular. Marxism provided an ideological lens through which to view reality. But, for the behavioralists, the application of Marxist principles to Italian society was "not supported by scientific knowledge" (Graziano 1987, 45). Although they promoted empirical research and behavioral political science, Sartori and Bobbio still hoped that political science would have practical value in helping to solve the problems of society (Graziano 1987).

The *Societa Italiana di Scienza Politica* (SISP), the Italian political science association and the journal *Rivista Italiana di Scienza Politica* have helped to place behavioral political science on a firm foundation (Morlino 1991). Today, some of the major departments of political science in Italy are at Turin, Padua, Pavia, Genoa, Bologna, Florence, Perugia, Rome, and Palermo. Departments most often range from one to ten positions, not large by American standards. In 1971, Sartori held the only chair in political science, but today there are several more.

Graziano (1987, 42) identifies four factors which have led to the development of political science in Italy:

- The conscious effort by a few authoritative scholars to rescue political science from academic oblivion and reestablish it as a distinct field of study, methodologically and substantively autonomous from such older disciplines as public law, history, and political philosophy.
- The social and economic development of Italian society, which by the 1960s had changed beyond recognition.
- The push from the outside, especially the impact of American political science in the age of behavioralism.
- Changes in the Italian university structure, which allowed for the development of . . . teaching positions in political science.

One thing that has done much to further the growth of Italian political science has been the substantial exchange of scholars and educational programs between the United States and Italy. Graziano notes that from 1949 to 1982, the Fulbright Program sent 4,373 Italians to the United States, and 3,942 Americans to Italy. It is interesting to note also that, although there are some notable American specialists in Italian politics, there is not yet a notable Italian specialist in American politics (Graziano 1987). With all its recent successes, Graziano notes that Italian research has progressed well in the "input" side (political parties and interest groups), but not much on the output side (international relations) and that Italians have done little to study the political systems of other countries.

Russia

No other story has affected international politics in the twentieth century to the same extent as the rise and the fall of the Union of Soviet Socialist Republics. Now splintered into independent states, the former Soviet Union's member states are still making front page headlines as they struggle to find a place in an increasingly democratic and capitalist world. The Russian empire that established a powerful set of Czars in the nineteenth century collapsed with the onset of World War I. The Russian Revolution, led by V. I. Lenin, established what soon became a totalitarian state. Under the rule of Josef Stalin (1925–1952) between 20 and 40 million people, suspected of being enemies of the state, were eliminated. The communist regimes which followed eventually relaxed the terror, but the collapse of the system in 1990 was a surprise to virtually everyone. Mikhail Gorbechev was named General Secretary of the Communist Party in 1985, and began a series of reforms, including policies of openness to the outside world and to new ideas (glasnost), and restructuring of government to more democratic methods and processes (perestroika). The Russian Federation, or Russia, has a new government today, created after the dissolution of the Soviet Union, with a constitution approved by referendum on December 12, 1993. Boris Yeltsin, who led a democratic reform movement under the Soviet Union, became President on June 12, 1991. The 1993 constitution provides that the president, who may have a maximum of two four-year terms, will prepare domestic and foreign policy guidelines and nominate a prime minister. The Federation Council is the upper house of the legislature, and the Duma is the lower house. The Council is made up of two representatives from each of the 89 territories of the confederation, plus other local representatives. The Duma has 450 members, half elected by proportional representation from lists of party delegates, and half from single-member constituencies.

The internal politics of Russia are anything but stable. Opposition parties, especially those conservative parties that play upon the nostalgia of times when things were more stable economically, have aroused the concern of Western leaders. Vladimir Zhirinovosky is perhaps the most notable of these opposition leaders. His often inflammatory rhetoric has given him a reputation for being an extremist, and some fear that he will return Russia to authoritarian rule if given the chance. His appeal for strong government action, however, in a time of economic chaos and severe deprivation for many, hits a resounding note with many Russians. In response to a request from the author, Zhirinovosky has written a letter specifically for this book, and for American students of political science. It is printed here in the original Russian, and a translation follows.

Since the fall of the former Soviet Union, much has transpired culturally and politically in Russia. A dramatic increase in commercial and academic exchange has helped to place the discipline of political science, like many other endeavors in the country, on a new footing. At the time of publication of this book, trends for the discipline as a whole in Russia had not been clearly identified, as they have been for some of the former Soviet states. New programs are being established, but a predominant orientation is not yet apparent. Some of the trends that are evident

ФЕДЕРАЛЬНОЕ СОБРАНИЕ — ПАРЛАМЕНТ РОССИЙСКОЙ ФЕДЕРАЦИИ

ГОСУДАРСТВЕННАЯ ДУМА

ФРАКЦИЯ ЛИБЕРАЛЬНО-ДЕМОКРАТИЧЕСКОЙ ПАРТИИ РОССИИ

103009, г. Москва, ул. Охотный ряд, д. 1   тел.: 292-80-01, 292-37-95

№ 52-598   « 14 » апреля   1995 года

Грег Скотту

Уважаемый господин Грег Скотт!

Направляю Вам ответ на Ваше письмо.

Председатель фракции ЛДПР   В.В. Жириновский

Уважаемый господин Грег Скотт!

Благодарю за Ваше письмо, в котором Вы просите написать несколько слов в качестве советов для студентов изучающих политологию.

Мой жизненный опыт и участие в политической деятельности позволяют утверждать, что политиков порождает сама жизнь, хотя она не может сделать из каждого человека политического деятеля. Если сослаться на мой собственный опыт, то все, что я достиг в жизни, мне пришлось добиваться самому, без посторонней помощи, полагаясь исключительно на свои силы, волю, упорство, способности. Эти качества и черты характера помогли и мне (и, думаю, многим другим) стать политиками.

Политик, как я считаю, должен быть в высшей степени образованным человеком, обладать широкими познаниями в различных сферах знаний, быть немножко журналистом, писателем, лидером, оратором, знать иностранные языки, разбираться в разнообразных экономических, политических, духовных проблемах. То, что я много учился, много изучил, помогло мне стать политиком. К сожалению, Россией часто управляли либо малограмотные, либо просто весьма недалекие и ограниченные люди.

Для политика необходим также жизненный опыт, накопленная житейская мудрость. Прежде чем пойти в большую политику, я, например, прошел серьезную жизненную школу, хорошо узнал жизнь людей в городах и сельской местности. Всю нашу страну, ее регионы, народы я знаю уже давно. Все это позволило мне накопить тот опыт, который необходим для политика.

Политику необходимо обладать высоким искусством политической деятельности и руководства, что также является своего рода талантом. В данном случае характеризовать самого себя весьма не просто. Самовосхваление не лучшее качество любого человека, тем более политика.

И еще одна черта необходима, как мне кажется, политику - это, в хорошем смысле слова, фанатизм, беспредельная увлеченность политической деятельностью. Уже в 30 лет я увлекся политикой по-настоящему, мечтал о новой политической партии, об избрании в Парламент, о возможности стать министром, главой государства. Для меня это желание вобщем-то не было фанатизмом. Но, фанатизм, пожалуй, был в стремлении, чтобы цель, идея, приверженцем которой я стал, осуществилась.

Государственный деятель, политик должен понимать, что политика это самая ответственная работа, связаная с жизнью миллионов людей. В политике иногда возникают ситуации, когда нужно спасать страну, когда от решения высшего государственного лица зависит судьба всей Планеты.

Я уже глубоко вошел в политику и другого пути у меня нет. Это моя жизнь, моя судьба. И если у меня сейчас есть фанатизм, то я его выражу в словах: Я пришел в политику, чтобы спасти свою страну, спасти Россию!

С уважением   В. Жириновский

MISTER GREG SCOTT

ASSISTANT PROFESSOR
OF THE UNIVERSITY OF
CENTRAL OKLAHOMA

100 NORTH UNIVERSITY DRIVE,
EDMOND, OKLAHOMA 73034-5209
(405) 341-2980
FAX: (405) 330-3523

DEAR MISTER GREG SCOTT!

Thank you for your letter where you ask me to write shortly some advices for political science students.

My life experience and taking part in political activities may affirm that the political figures are born by life itself, although not everybody can be a politican Refering to my own experience I want to say that everything I've achieved, I've achieved by myself without somebodies help, reliing on my will, presistence and abilities. These qualities and features of character helped me and I think many others to be political figures.

A political figure, as I believe, hase to be a well-aducated person, possess wide knowledge in different spheres, be a journalist in a way, a writer, a leader, an orator, know some foreign languages, understand any kind of economic, politic and spiritual problems.

The fact that I studied a lot helped me to be a political figure. To my great regret Russia was often ruled by half-educate or none to clever and narrow-minded people.

It's very important for a political figure to have a life experience and knowledge of life. Before going to a big policy I traveled a serious life school, knew the life of the people in towns and in villages. I know my country, its regiones, its peoples for a long time. All these facts let me accumulate the experience which is necessary for a political figure.

A political figure has to possess the high skill of political activities and leader ship, which is something like a talent. In the present case it's difficult to define me myself.

Self-praising is not the best quality of any person, espesially when we speak about the political figure.

And me more feature is indispensable for the political figure: this is fanaticism in a good sence of the word, I mean infinite keenness on political activites.

-2-

For 30 years I have been taking a great interest in policy seriosly, dreamed of a new political party, about the ellection in Parlament, about the chance to be Minister, the head of the State. My fanaticism was the aspiration for my dream to be true.

The statesman has to understand that policy is the most responsible work closely connected with the life of million of people. Sometimes in policy there are situations, when you have to save the country, when the fate of the whole world depends on the decision of the highest stateman.

I came into the policy deeply, and I haven't another way. This is my life, this is my destiny. And if I have some fanaticism then I want to express it in the following words: I came into policy to save my country, to save my Russia.

at this date include attempts to understand the processes of democracy, business, and journalism; increased exchanges of scholars through the Fulbright and other programs; struggles to overcome bureaucracy as a way of life; and a deeper and broader attempt to understand and overcome authoritarianism.

On the other hand, some very interesting analyses have been published of political science as it was during the last years of the Soviet Union. These studies are of great importance to political science because they illustrate the problems and potentials of political science in nondemocratic states. It is, for example, most interesting to compare Russia and Poland, where some meaningful attempts to conduct political science were actually being carried out, and with East Germany, where substantive and viable political science had become extinct.

Arch Brown, a commentator on the development of Soviet political science, has helped Western scholars become aware that much more was happening in political science in the last years of the Soviet Union than they had previously supposed. Brown notes that perhaps the beginnings of honest attempts at objective political science in Russia began when Fedor Burlatskii, an associate of Yuri Andropov and later head of the Department of Philosophy at the Institute of Social Sciences in Moscow, published his pathbreaking discussion of political science in the official newspaper *Pravda* in 1965. In his article Burlatskii differentiated "political science" from other "political sciences," which had included history, economics, and law, and argued that a communist political science that could tackle some of the problems of soviet society, especially in the area of international relations, had not been sufficiently studied to that point (Brown 1986, 444–448). It is interesting to note that, perhaps in response to Burlatskii's efforts, in 1978 the "Soviet Association of Political (State) Sciences" changed its name to "Soviet Association of Political Sciences" and the Soviet Union opened its doors to other political scientists by hosting the Eleventh World Congress of the International Political Science Association in Moscow in 1979. The extent of the new Soviet openness to political science, even in the 1970s, is evident in the breadth and scope of studies that Burlatskii and his colleague Shakhnazarov were prepared to undertake. These studies included the actual role of the communist party and its effects upon the state and society (Brown 1986, 454).

Authoritarian states often perceive criticism in any form to be dangerous, and since objective analysis normally leads to criticism of policies, it is viewed as dangerous to the state. Brown argues, however, that at least from the late 1960s, the rulers of the Soviet Union, needing perhaps more desperately than before to find viable economic policies, were for the first time looking favorably upon political and economic analysis. According to Brown (1986, 449):

> Western scholars readily assume that academic institutions are more enlightened and receptive to change than the higher echelons of a ruling Communist Party, but this has by no means invariably been the case in the Soviet Union. It was, quite clearly, in the interest of the party leadership to have available specialists who had studied political institutions in their multifaceted complexity and who were experts on particular parts of the world, since they would be of value in a policy advisory capacity and as producers of well-qualified recruits for relevant branches of the party and state apparatus. With such needs in mind the Institute of World Economy and International Relations (IMEMO) had been founded in 1956, the Institute of Economics of the World Socialist System and the Africa Institute in 1960, and the Latin America Institute in 1961 . . . Far East Institute in 1966, and the USA Institute founded in 1967.

Perhaps the most poignant lesson for political scientists in democracies to learn from Brown's analysis is the danger of oversimplifying the workings of political systems, and of operating under preconceptions which are not substantiated by research. And Brown (1986, 473) drives the point home by noting "how absurd an oversimplification it is to view the USSR as an extreme monolith in which policy and doctrine flow only in one direction—form the top downward."

Poland

Poland was an advanced and powerful kingdom in the fifteenth century and remained prominent until it was conquered first by Austria, then Prussia, and finally Russia in the late eighteenth century. At the end of World War I, Poland became an independent Republic, but its brief experiment with democracy ended in 1926 when Marshal Jozef Pilsudski became military dictator. In September 1939, Germany entered Poland after reaching an agreement for joint occupation with the Soviet Union. The Germans betrayed Russian trust in June 1941 and assumed control of all of Poland. At the end of the war, the Soviet Union assumed control of the country through a Polish communist regime, and the communist People's Republic of Poland was thereby established in 1947. The constitution of July 1952 was revised in April 1989, when Poland assumed independence from the former Soviet Union. In August of 1980, some seventeen thousand workers went on strike at the Lenin Shipyard at Gdansk, an action which began the rise of the Solidarity Movement led by Lech Walesa, who became President of the Polish Republic in December 1990, following the country's independence from Soviet control. Walesa, leader of the Polish United Worker's Party, succeeded General Wojciech Jaruzelski, who had headed the communist state.

Poland became the seventh national member, and the first socialist member, of the IPSA in 1950, and the Polish Political Science Association (PPSA) was organized in 1955. In 1982, Kazimierz Opalek described Polish political science as being focused on problems of the socialist state and the functioning of the communist party. Klaus Zeimer has detailed the transition of political science from the communist regime to the current democratic government. It is most interesting to note that Polish political science was more advanced during Soviet rule than most, perhaps all, other Soviet-dominated countries. According to Zeimer (1994, 483):

> Poland was probably the first country of the former Soviet-dominated bloc where empirical social science research had been implanted. Polish political scientists have for many years been familiar with Western approaches to political science and possessed highly sophisticated methodology. But the publication and the practical importance of this empirical research was extremely politically determined.

Polish political scientists responded to a need by government officials to understand the strength of the solidarity movement, and support for the government. In a poll conducted in the early 1980s, "a ranking of 'confidence in institutions'" gave the Church 82.4 percent, the military 65.4 percent, the Communist Party 37 percent, television 27.2 percent, and the then underground Solidarity movement 12.7 percent. "One of the surprises of the survey was the low degree of confidence in underground Solidarity . . . which quite evidently had ceased to be identified with the 'legal' 'Solidarity' of 1980/81" (Klaus Zeimer 1994, 485). According to Zeimer (1994, 485), the poll included numerous other surprises as well, especially two seemingly contradictory attitudes. The first was "a high inclination towards authoritarianism especially among workers." The second was "an astonishingly high degree of approval for peaceful forms of protest against the government and a harsh critique of repression against participants in protest actions." Poland during the 1980s, therefore, was a country of many paradoxes. Perhaps one of the most important is Zeimer's conclusion that, although it was possible to criticize the government orally, it was nearly impossible to publish critical material legally.

As the 1990s progress, Zeimer expects a promising future for Polish political science. He notes in conclusion that, "As in other ex-communist countries Poland is experiencing an extremely difficult time of transition from 'real socialism' towards a postcommunist system. The conditions for social research have changed very favourably in almost all of these countries, of which Poland probably has the longest experience in empirical research" (Zeimer 1994, 497).

Latvia

Our fourth and final examination of a country which was a part of the former Soviet empire is Latvia. Bordered on the east by Russia, on the north by Estonia, and on the south by Lithuania, Latvia has finally won an independence that seemed merely a dream for decades. Although Latvians make up a slim majority of the population, Russians account for more than a third, and other ethnic groups compose the rest. It is an industrial and agricultural nation. Before Soviet domination, Latvia had a turbulent political history. Having beaten back Bolshevik attempts to control it in 1917 and 1919, Latvia had a democratic government recognized by the League of Nations until a military coup in 1934 brought it under authoritarian control. It was forced to incorporate into the Soviet Union on August 5, 1940. The Republic of Latvia emerged as a sovereign state on August 21, 1991, after fifty-one years of Soviet dominance. On a 74 percent vote in a referendum in March 1991, independence for Latvia was affirmed. Guntis Ulmanis was elected to a three year term as president and Valdis Birkavs was named prime minister in July 1993. The Saemia, or parliament, has 100 members chosen in direct elections for three-year terms. One of the greatest problems during the transition from Soviet domination and socialism to independence and capitalism is that the Russian Latvians, who make up a third of the population, were in control of most of the Latvian economy before independence.

Latvian political scientist Einars Semanis (1994) has described the development of political science amidst the upheaval of the transition. Like in some of the Soviet-dominated countries, social science as it is known in the West was virtually nonexistent. According to Semanis, it was the new political freedom and not the desire to conduct science for its own sake, that gave birth to political science in Latvia. As Semanis (1994, 181) tells the story:

> It all began in September 1989, when students from all the higher educational establishments staged a large demonstration in the centre of Riga, the capital of Latvia. The demonstration was cast as an enormous funeral service for orthodox Marxism-Leninism accompanied by ironic slogans such as "Party, army and the Soviet nation are forever united," "Lenin is alive for ever," "The victory of communism is inevitable," and so on and so forth. There was a coffin full of orthodox Marxist-Leninist literature, and the students were displaying pictures of Marx, Lenin, Stalin, Brezhnev, Gorbechev, and other Soviet leaders. The university authorities received a number of complaints from students and faculty alike, particularly from within the natural sciences. This marked the symbolic end of totalitarian education within the natural sciences; the social scientists had lost whatever legitimacy they had previously enjoyed.

With the old educational system dissolved, there was much confusion and a new set of programs evolved. Under the Soviet regime, the study of politics had been known as politology to differentiate it from western political science and to emphasize its Marxist foundations. Advancing from politology was made possible by the introduction of numerous speakers and textbooks from Western countries. It took some time to publish adequate texts in Latvian. As Semanis notes, the help of people from universities in other countries such as the University of Oslo, Norway, was most valuable in making the transition. Finding qualified professors to teach in Latvian departments was another concern. There was a shortage of scholars to fill positions in political science, because the ones available had generally been trained as generalists in other disciplines and many did not know the new methodologies of Western political science. Latvian scholars took advantage of grants for study at other institutions, especially the London School of Economics, the University of Gothenberg, and the University of Oslo. The University of Latvia is the only institution in that country to grant a doctorate in political science, and its first candidate defended his dissertation in 1994. A council of international experts was assembled to read the dissertation to ensure that it met international standards.

Semanis is concerned about the challenges facing Latvian political science. He finds that recruiting and retaining qualified teachers is the greatest problem, partly because university positions in Latvia are neither well paid nor as well respected as they are in other countries. Of even greater concern, because Latvia is a relatively new and unstable democratic state, is the role that the discipline can play in helping society understand and adjust to the challenges of democracy.

China

With more than a billion people, the People's Republic of China (PRC) has the largest population of any nation in the world. Its political history and concern with politics is as old as that of Greece. The series of dynasties that unified China politically goes back at least as far as the Ch'in dynasty, established in 221 BCE. The last (Manchu) dynasty fell in 1912, and a republic was established under Sun Yat-sen, but a series of civil wars ensued. Chaing Kai-shek established the Kuomintang (Nationalist Party) and managed to maintain power in opposition to communists from 1928 until 1949 when communists, under Mao Zedong, forced the nationalists to take refuge on the island of Taiwan. For four decades the nationalist Chinese on Taiwan waged a diplomatic war with the communist Chinese on the mainland for recognition as the legitimate representative of all the Chinese people, but the nationalists lost the struggle in 1979 when the United States, joining other nations, recognized the PRC as the representative of the Chinese people. Taiwan now uncomfortably awaits formal union with the mainland.

From time to time under Mao Zedong, the totalitarian Chinese communist state ruthlessly suppressed opposition. In 1958, Mao's Great Leap Forward attempted to form peasants into agricultural-industrial cooperatives, but the attempt failed. In 1965 and 1966, Mao instigated the Cultural Revolution, which was an attempt to root out revisionist elements in communist society in favor of traditional communists. A series of struggles for political leadership followed Mao's death on September 9, 1976. China's most recent constitution (1982) defines the PRC as "a socialist state under the people's democratic dictatorship led by the working class and based on the alliance of workers and peasants." Americans became acutely aware of internal attempts to liberalize China in April 1989, when student protests in Tiananmen Square in Beijing, the capital, were crushed.

Political science in China has developed as a combination of Western and traditional Chinese studies. In the 1840s, Western countries brought missionaries and other aspects of Western culture to China. Capital Academy (now Peking University) offered China's first university course on politics in 1903. The *Chinese Social and Political Science Review* was first published in 1916, and the Chinese Political Science Association was established in 1932. By 1948, forty Chinese colleges featured political science departments with professors who had trained at the leading American universities and were publishing widely in professional journals (Baoxu 1984). The academic freedom that allowed this publication to take place did not last long. In 1952, Mao's communist regime abolished the disciplines of political science and sociology, charging that (1) "reactionary" Western capitalist methodologies were being used in the discipline rather than Marxism-Leninism, (2) under socialism there would be no major social problems to study, and (3) if the Soviet Union could get along without these disciplines, so could China (Fu 1991, 229). Lacking enough internally trained scholars to teach Marxist approaches, scholars were brought in from the Soviet Union.

By the 1960s, a need to have Chinese Marxists independent of Soviet Marxists led to the reestablishment of political science departments, but only for the purpose of teaching Marxist doctrine. Zhao Baoxu, a communist professor of political science at the Department of International Politics at Peking University, notes that in 1964 departments of politics were established at Peking University, the Chinese People's University, and Fudan University (Baoxu 1984, 748). Apologizing for the errors of previous regimes, in 1984 Baoxu explained (1984, 749):

> In effect, we fell into blindness and made mistakes because for almost 30 years no scientific study of political science took place. We neglected to carry out serious scientific research on important problems related to the Chinese political system, such as the structure of government, the limits of power of their branches, their mutual relationships, the relationship between the Party and the government, the bureaucracy, the policy-making process, and the protection of the democratic rights of the people.

Baoxu (1984) reports that efforts made to correct previous mistakes included creation of the Chinese Political Science Association (CPSA) and the Political Science Research Institute within the Chinese Academy of Social Sciences (CASS), and encouragement of development of political science departments in other universities. Communist Chinese political scientists still have difficulty, however, in pursuing objective political science while upholding the ideology of the regime sufficiently to escape censorship or persecution. Baoxu (1984, 755) summarizes the problem in the following manner:

> To uphold Marxism-Leninism, we first must be clear about what constituted a
> correct attitude toward Marxism. Is it treating Marxism dogmatically by reciting
> quotations from the classical writers or is it conducting investigations and re-
> search of actual conditions realistically and creatively from which to derive sci-
> entific conclusions? . . . Socialism is a magnificent ideal of humankind. . . . So-
> cialism must be continually perfected and developed. . . . [I]f no scientific
> research in political science is carried out, how can socialism be "upheld"? . . .
> In order to support the dictatorship of the proletariat, it is also necessary to con-
> duct scientific research on this question and to summarize the historical lessons
> of the past. . . . To uphold the leadership of the Party, we must also carry out
> major political science research. (Baoxu 1984, 755)

This is where political science stands in China today: attempting to break
through the constraints of ideology to do critical analysis, while upholding the
ideals of the communist state.

South Africa

Today's Republic of South Africa is the result of a long and still not fully resolved
conflict among European colonists and the varied indigenous tribal groupings of
the southernmost extremes of the African continent. Although the slave trade
darkened the shores of Western coastal Africa from the beginning of the 1600s,
Dutch settlers, along with some German and French Huguenots, had staked a substantial claim to the southern region by the end of that century, becoming known
as Afrikaners. During the next two centuries, British settlers moved in, resulting in
conflicts that finally ended in the British victory of the Boer (Afrikaan) War in
1910. The British then formed a Commonwealth government, the Union of South
Africa, which assumed full political independence from British rule in 1934. In
1990, the population was composed of 4.3 million whites (2.6 million Afrikaaners
and 1.7 million English), 19 million blacks (native Africans of numerous tribes), 3
million coloureds (South African term for people of mixed parentage), and
800,000 Asians.

Before World War II, the minority white population, supported by colonial
armies, maintained control of the political and economic systems of the country
and its substantial natural resources, including gold, diamonds, copper, asbestos,
chrome, platinum, and vanadium. After World War II, fear of the black majority
prompted the whites to institute the policy of apartheid, which meant segregation
in housing, education, and other public facilities and exclusion of nonwhites from
participation in making government policy. Frederik Willem De Klerk led the National Party's control of the government in the last days of apartheid.

Apartheid sparked protest movements at home and economic sanctions from
other countries around the world. In 1978, Steven Biko, a leader of the protest
movement, died under mysterious circumstances while in police custody, becoming a martyr and symbol of black and coloured resistance to the government. Nelson Mandela assumed leadership of the African National Congress after Biko's
death and, after serving many years in jail for his protest activities, was released in

1990 as apartheid was abandoned. He became president of the Republic of South Africa on May 10, 1994, a month after the current interim constitution went into effect. Although the black majority and groups other than the white minority now have a voice in government, many very difficult problems remain. For example, deep divisions remain among competing groups of blacks, especially the African National Congress and the Zulu tribe, and while the literacy rate for whites is 98%, it is only 32% for the nonwhite population.

In 1990, as the transition from apartheid to democratic government was beginning, Dr. Rupert Taylor of the Department of Political Studies at University of the Witwatersrand conducted a thorough and intriguing review of the discipline of political science in South Africa. He notes, first, that, while a study of the discipline in the early 1970s had shown it to be "underdeveloped," by the 1990s, political science had gained substantial recognition in university departments. Beginning in the 1960s, a set of major reforms within the university system had advanced the growth of political science as a subject of study. Among these developments, according to Taylor (1990), was the establishment of new universities, including the University of Port Elizabeth (1964) and Rand Afrikaans University (1966). Student enrollment increased from 59,000 to 215,000 in the period from 1968 to 1985, and the teaching staff grew from 3,067 to 9,009 during that same period. In 1988, according to other reports, 97 political scientists were teaching in twenty South African universities. The Political Science Association of South Africa (PSPSA), founded in 1973, had 224 members in 1990, and the journal *Politikon* has already established a strong international reputation. Although the number of political scientists in South Africa is small by American standards, there are indications that South African political scientists are unusually professionally active. For example, in one survey, three quarters of the respondents said that they had published at least one journal article, and South African political scientists are more than twice as likely to read professional journals as their American counterparts.

The methods and perspectives of South African political scientists are quite similar to those of American political scientists. A majority (55%) of South African political scientists claim as their perspective the American mainstream, including

> Positivist/empiricist 15%
> Systems theory 15%
> Behavioralist 14%
> Pluralism 11%
> Political philosophy 7%
> Normative theory 6%
> Eclectic 6% (Taylor 1990, 120)

Marxists, however, make up the remaining 26%, which indicates a continuing concern to help the oppressed majority obtain appropriate participation in economic as well as political activity.

According to other polls of political scientists, oddly enough, the person most frequently named as having made the most important contribution to South African political science is Heribert Adam, a sociologist at Simon Fraser University in Vancouver, Canada. Deon Geldenhuys is said to be the South African who has made the greatest contribution to South African political science. The works of American political scientists are well known and discussed. South Africans, when asked to name political scientists who have made substantial contributions to the discipline, most often mention David Easton, Hans Morgenthau, Robert Dahl, Gabriel Almond, Harold Laski, Harold Lasswell, Samuel Huntington, K. J. Holsti, Arend Lijphart, and Theda Skocpol (Taylor 1990).

For all its new advances, however, political science in South Africa has some major problems to overcome. The first is integrating black and minority political scientists into the discipline. According to Rupert Taylor (1990, 116), "the typical South African political scientist is a white Afrikaner male around forty years old, with a masters degree or doctorate, holding a university position."

Another problem which is also common to the discipline in other countries is the lack of time and resources to do research. Taylor explains that professors are overworked, with too few teachers to serve the growing number of students. In spite of these problems, however, South African political scientists press on, hoping to advance knowledge in the discipline and to help shed light on some of their country's most pressing problems. According to one survey, South African political scientists name as important subjects for future research agendas the following items:

- Post-apartheid economic and social politics (26%)
- Conflict resolution (25%)
- Constitutional reform (17%)
- Policy studies (9%)
- Attitude/opinion surveys (9%) (Taylor 1990, 123)

These research topics clearly indicate a response by South African political scientists to the evolving crisis and potentials of their society.

India

India has vast cultural diversity, with more than 1,600 different languages and dialects. More than 80 percent of the population is Hindu, but the Muslim population accounts for more than 10 percent. Caste discrimination, a long-standing Hindu tradition throughout India, is illegal today, but it is still practiced in some rural areas. India is still underdeveloped in many ways economically, and agriculture is the basis of existence for 70% of the people.

In 1526, the Mogul dynasty brought together Buddhist, Moslem, and Hindu states within India into one unified polity. The British East India Company created the first European settlements in the 1600s, and, after a series of internal wars, India came under British control in 1786. India's independence from British colonial rule was hard won. It came on August 15, 1947, when Britain promulgated the Indian Independence Act. Mohondas Gandhi, leader of the independence movement, was assassinated on January 30, 1948, and his death brought on widespread rioting. On July 26, 1950, India became a democratic republic with Jawahar Lal

Nehru, leader of the Indian National Congress, as the first Prime Minister. The constitution of 1950 called for a republican form of government for a union of 25 states and 7 territories. The president is chosen for a five-year term by an electoral college composed of the elected members of both houses of parliament and the state legislatures. The upper house of the legislature is the Rajya Sabhahe, or Council of States. The lower house is the Lok Sabha, or House of the People. The prime minister is elected by parliamentary members of the majority party and leads a government that is responsible to the legislature.

Jawahar Lal Nehru died in 1964 and was succeeded by Bahadur Shastri, who, in the early 1970s, led India to war with the Muslim nation of Pakistan, from which it had been separated by the British prior to independence. Shastri's successor was Indira Gandhi, Nehru's daughter. She was assassinated by two of her Sikh bodyguards, who were angry about the government's repression of a Sikh uprising four months before. Rajiv, Indira Gandhi's son, succeeded her but was driven from office in 1989 due to charges of incompetence and corruption. The President of the Republic of India today is Dr. Shankar Dayal Sharma, who was elected in July 1992. The Prime Minister is Pamulaparti Venkata Narasimha Rao, who assumed office in June 1991.

Indian political scientist V. R. Mehta (1987) notes that Indian political science developed from the discipline of history. Early efforts at studying politics conformed to the country's efforts to achieve independence, and some political scientists attempted to establish an independent political science for India. The *Indian Journal of Political Science* and the Indian Political Science Association were created as a part of these independence efforts in the 1920s and 1930s.

By the 1950s, Indian political scientists, like their counterparts in many other countries, found themselves observing with fascination the American behavioral movement. In response to this movement, in the 1960s the University Grants Commission and the Indian Council of Social Science Research invested substantial support in electoral studies (Mehta 1987). But problems quickly arose from behavioralist attempts to understand Indian politics within the context of India's many distinct cultural traditions and history. In the 1960s, a movement to convert higher education courses from English to regional languages was successful. Although it was implemented over a series of years, it broke down the unanimity of communication in university communities and made the production of a unified body of knowledge much more difficult. Many students coming out of these programs were not proficient in the English language and, therefore, did not have the ability to utilize much current research (Narain and Mathur 1982).

Mehta (1987) notes that the rational, scientific thinking of behavioral political scientists conflicts with the mystical, philosophical traditions of a culture steeped in Hinduism. As Mehta (1987, 275) explains:

> The liberal model implicit in behavioral analysis was that of consensus in which groups and interests compete with each other for a larger share of the cake, within a framework of assumptions and values which all have in common. The role of politics was to mediate in this bargaining process so that a maximum number of interests is served. The state was neutral, and its role was that of an umpire, to see that the parties did not hurt each other. . . . An application of

> this model neglected the important structural as well as psychological factors which made the situation vastly different from that of America. . . . [A] leader like Indira Gandhi . . . is radically different from a leader who will merely conciliate bargaining interests. Instead, this leader acquires a charisma which symbolizes the dreams and hopes of the people. . . . The chief ministers and the party bosses become marginal to this new relationship of the leader and the masses.

The response of Indian political scientists to the problems inherent in American political science, however, may bring forth positive results for the international political science community as researchers like Mehta seek to develop new methods and theories that better explain the conditions in which they find themselves.

Another aspect of Indian experience in the development of political science and academic life is interesting because it is so *similar* to the American experience. Iqbal Narain and P. C. Mathur (1982, 196) explain that Indian universities are having difficulty finding the correct balance between research and teaching:

> Partly as a corollary of the ever-growing student enrollment, a balanced partnership between research and teaching could not develop even in university departments, let alone postgraduate and undergraduate colleges. Worse still, the two regard each other as dichotomous. We are thus far from a situation in which the latest research feeds into and enriches teaching and in which research stereotypes are given an intellectual jolt in the classroom. The poverty of political science in India can be in part traced to the fact that the world of research and the world of teaching have, by and large, been kept apart from each other. This is what perhaps also explains the paradox of outdated textbooks coexisting with the most up-to-date research in substantive and methodological terms.

Narain and Mathur's comments are also, unfortunately, directly applicable to some universities in the United States.

Mexico

Proclaiming independence from Spain in 1810, the Mexican people established a Republic in 1822, which was governed by General Antonio Lopez de Santa Anna from 1833 to 1855. Following a struggle for control of the country, Archduke Maximillian of Austria was made emperor of Mexico by Napoleon II of France in 1865, but two years later was overthrown and executed by Benito Juarez. In 1877, General Porfirio Diaz led a regressive administration that was overthrown in the revolution of 1910. The nation's current constitution was adopted February 5, 1917.

The population of Mexico stands at about 81 million, most of whom are of Mestizo (mixed Indian and Spanish) descent. Mexico has thirty-one states, each with a constitution, governor, and legislative chamber. The national government has a legislature composed of a senate and Chamber of Deputies, often dominated by strong presidential leadership. The Institutional Revolutionary Party (PRI) has dominated the political scene for several decades. Among the most influential opposition parties are the rightist National Action Party (PAN) and the leftist Na-

tional Democratic Front (FDN). The current president is Ernesto Zedillo of the Institutional Revolutionary Party, who assumed office in 1994 for a six-year term.

In an article entitled "Political Science in Mexico" (1994), Enrique Suarez-
Iniguez, professor of political science at the National University of Mexico, describes the development and current condition of Mexican political science. The
two primary historical influences on the development of Mexican political science
are (1) research done by American professors Frank Tannenbaum, Robert C. Scott,
Raymond Vernon, and Frank Brandenburg, and (2) the *Escuela di Ciencias Politcas
y Sociales* (School of Political and Social Sciences) founded in 1951 by Lucio Mendi-
eta y Nunez at the National University of Mexico (UNAM) (Suarez-Iniguez 1994).
Nunez created programs at the *Escuela di Ciencias Politcas y Social* that were similar
to programs at the Universities of London, Paris, and Louvin. The UNAM founded
the Division of Graduate Studies in 1967, and invited internationally known scholars such as Eric Fromm, Herbert Marcuse, and Susan Sontag to speak. By 1988, the
Department had enrolled 848 students, but despite the discipline's progress, Enrique Suarez-Iniguez seemed disappointed to note that by 1985 only 16 of Mexico's
247 colleges offered a baccalaureate major in political science and less than one
Mexican student in 200 was enrolled in a course in political science or public administration. Suarez-Iniguez (1994, 33) describes the methodological perspectives
of Mexican political scientists in these terms:

> Behavioralism has not been very important in Mexico, and, as a result, David
> Easton's classification of U.S. political science (formal, traditional, behavioral-
> ist, and post-behavioralist) are not relevant. . . . Up until now, Marxism has been
> the predominant school of thought in Mexico. Nevertheless, most researchers
> are not Marxist. How can this be explained? Marxism has played a *hegemonic*
> role in teaching and research. There are journals devoted to it; it appears in di-
> verse forms; and it implies political activism. It also has a justifying ideological
> element. . . . The freedom to criticize Marxism is now prevalent, although or-
> thodox Marxists are scandalized. The crisis of Marxism and what has happened
> in Eastern Europe has accelerated this process and has given it just value to ide-
> ologies.

Suarez-Iniguez's comments about the future of political science are typical of comments of political scientists in some other countries, and they thereby demonstrate
that the discipline as a whole is, in one respect, at the same place around the globe.
International political science is still strongly influenced by American leadership,
but this leadership will diminish as a new international consensus gradually forms
about acceptable methods. In addition, political scientists will have to compete
more vigorously for what now appear in many countries to be diminishing social
science resources.

15

New Developments in American Political Science

Mr. Speer was killed one evening in 1835 when the axle on the rail car he controlled broke. The accident threw him from his seat atop the car, which crushed him as it overturned. Speer's untimely death—and those of many conductors of the time—occurred because the first train designers couldn't see beyond standard vehicle designs. Early train cars required conductors to ride on top of the car like stage coach drivers: the invention that came first—the stage coach—limited the designers' creativity.

—Beth Azar

Political Science as Creative Expression

Chapter 1 characterized political science as an expression of human creativity. In this final chapter, we hope to help you think more creatively both about politics and about ways in which you might study politics, by providing examples of the thousands of creative efforts currently being undertaken within the discipline. To this end, we shall provide dozens of examples of studies recently undertaken, covering virtually every area of the discipline as it is practiced in the United States.

Before proceeding, however, we shall sound a note of caution about our own approach. In an article entitled "Breaking Through Barriers to Creativity" (1995), Beth Azar (quoted above) summarized the results of recent psychological studies that indicate that, although knowledge of the creative efforts of others is helpful in gaining understanding of any subject, this same knowledge serves to limit our creativity because our minds are all too ready to imitate what others have done. In political science we certainly need to learn from what others have done, and this book is dedicated to that end. But we also encourage you to look beyond the ideas presented throughout this book, especially in this chapter, and come up with new questions, perspectives, and directions of your own. As you read in this chapter about the innovative and engaging studies currently being done by others, try to learn the lessons others have to teach. But, and this is the difficult part, try to retain a critical distance from them sufficient to allow the incendiary potential of your own creativity to reveal new insights about the political world.

The discipline of political science today covers a wide variety of subject areas, from international relations to public administration to voting studies. The American Political Science Association (APSA), the national professional organization founded to promote the development of political science, holds annual meetings at which many activities occur, including general addresses, meetings of section members, and presentations of papers at scores of panels. The annual meeting is held in a different city each year. The 1994 meeting was in New York, the 1995 meeting was in Chicago, and the 1996 meeting was in San Francisco.

In addition to the APSA, there are national political science associations in more than fifty foreign countries, other national and international associations that political scientists attend, such as the International Studies Association, and numerous social sciences associations. There are also several regional political science associations within the United States, such as the Midwest Political Science Association (MPSA) and the Southwest Political Science Association (SWPSA), which hold meetings every year in their regions, and also publish journals. In addition, each state has its own political science association.

At association meetings at all levels, political scientists present papers at panel sessions which other members attend. The purpose of the paper presentations is to give those who have written the papers the opportunity to share their research with other political scientists and receive comments and criticism before their papers are submitted to journals to be published. A typical panel includes:

- A chairperson, who calls the session to order, allots time to each paper presentation, and sometimes comments on the papers presented;
- From one to five political scientists who make brief (normally ten- to thirty-minute presentations) oral presentations of the contents of their papers; and
- One or two discussants, who are association members or guests who have read the papers presented before the meeting, and who give oral evaluations of the papers presented, outlining specific strengths and weaknesses.

Political science today has become so complex that it is carried out through dozens of subject-matter specialties. A convenient way to introduce these specialties is to examine some of the papers and other activities of the program divisions of the APSA. Program divisions are organized units, which represent subgroups of the association, established to provide a forum for persons with similar interests to share their views. New divisions develop as members organize to find a formal place within the discipline, to meet each other, and to encourage research in common interests. The names of the 47 program divisions which participated in the program at the APSA 1995 annual meeting are presented in the first boxed list below.

Program divisions often coincide with organized *sections* of the APSA, such as the section on Politics and History or the section on Religion and Politics, which are subunits of the Association, within which newsletters are circulated and discussions are carried on. It is difficult to group these divisions into broader categories, because many of them are concerned with a variety of interests. Foreign Policy Analysis, for example, could easily be classified under either "policy analysis" or "international relations." The larger categories presented here, therefore, are by no means absolute or conventional, but have been constructed especially for the purposes of this text so that similar activities may be discussed sequentially. The second boxed list below presents a summary of the program divisions grouped into six categories, as they are discussed in this chapter.

Our goal is more to inspire than to inform. After reading this chapter, we hope that you will have gained an appreciation for the depth and breadth of creativity in the discipline. We have *not*, therefore, systematically and uniformly reviewed the history or activities of each program division, a task which would require a book in itself. Instead, we have highlighted different activities and projects in each section, providing historical background in some, notes on famous participants in others, and discussions of major works in still others. Some sections receive more attention than others, not because of their relative importance, but because they have not received as much attention elsewhere in this text. For each program section we have provided examples of panels and papers presented at the APSA's 1995 annual meeting to illustrate the topics disscussed.

List of Program Divisions of the APSA by Section Number

1. Political Thought and Philosophy: Historical Approaches
2. Normative Political Theory
3. Foundations of Political Theory
4. Formal Political Theory
5. Political Methodology
6. Legislative Behavior
7. Presidency Research
8. Public Opinion and Participation
9. Elections and Electoral Behavior
10. Political Organizations and Parties
11. Law and Courts
12. Constitutional Law and Jurisprudence
13. Public Administration
14. Federalism and Intergovernmental Relations
15. Urban Politics
16. State Politics and Policy
17. Public Policy
18. Political Economy
19. Women and Politics
20. Race, Gender, and Ethnicity
21. Politics and History
22. Comparative Politics
23. Comparative Politics of Developing Countries
24. Communist Politics and After
25. Comparative Politics of Advanced Industrial States
26. Politics and Society in Western Europe
27. International Collaboration
28. International Security
29. International Security and Arms Control
30. International Political Economy
31. Foreign Policy Analysis
32. Representation and Electoral Systems
33. Conflict Processes
34. Politics and the Life Sciences
35. Religion and Politics
36. Applied Political Science
37. Science, Technology, Environment, and Politics
38. Computers and Multimedia
39. Political Communication
40. Transformational Politics
41. New Political Science
42. Political Psychology
43. Politics and Literature
44. Internships and Experiential Education
45. Teaching and Learning in Political Science
46. Domestic Sources of Foreign Policy
47. Program Committee Panels

Program Divisions of Political Science by Subject Category

Part 1. Approaches to Politics, Theory, and Methodology
    Political Thought and Philosophy: Historical Approaches
    Normative Political Theory
    Foundations of Political Theory
    Formal Political Theory
    Political Methodology
    New Political Science
    Political Psychology
    Transformational Politics
    Political Economy
    International Political Economy

Part 2. Political Behavior
    Elections and Electoral Behavior
    Public Opinion and Participation
    Political Organizations and Parties
    Urban Politics
    Political Communication
    Religion and Politics
    Women and Politics
    Race, Gender, and Ethnicity

Part 3. Political Institutions, Law, Administration, and Policy Analysis
    Legislative Behavior
    Representation and Electoral Systems
    Presidency Research
    Federalism and Intergovernmental Relations
    Public Administration
    Law and Courts
    Constitutional Law and Jurisprudence

    Public Policy
    State Politics and Policy

Part 4. Comparative Politics and Area Studies
    Comparative Politics
    Comparative Politics of Developing Countries
    Communist Politics and After
    Comparative Politics of Advanced Industrial States
    Politics and Society in Western Europe

Part 5. International Relations
    Conflict Processes
    International Collaboration
    International Security
    International Security and Arms Control
    Foreign Policy Analysis

Part 6. The Discipline of Political Science and its Applications
    Applied Political Science
    Politics and Life Sciences
    Science, Technology, Environment, and Politics
    Computers and Multimedia
    Politics and History
    Politics and Literature
    Teaching and Learning in Political Science
    Internships and Experiential Education
    Program Committee Panels

Part 1. Approaches to Politics, Theory, and Methodology (Political Thought, Philosophy, and Theory)

The study of political philosophy was thrust virtually to the margins of the discipline during the behavioral revolution of the 1950s and 1960s. Since that time, however, writers like Leo Strauss, Eric Voegelin, John Rawls, and Jurgen Habermas have inspired a renewed interest in the study of politics as philosophical discourse. This interest is sufficiently strong today that three APSA program divisions are devoted to these studies: *Political Thought and Philosophy: Historical Approaches; Normative Political Theory;* and the *Foundations of Political Theory.* They all study the same subjects, but with somewhat different emphases.

Political Thought and Philosophy: Historical Approaches

Participants in this section are most likely to study the great political thinkers, such as Plato, Aristotle, Machiavelli, Hobbes, and Locke, and to be particularly interested in the historical development of the seminal concepts of political philosophy, such as freedom, justice, and order, during particular periods over the course of centuries. At a recent meeting of the APSA, three of the numerous panels within this program division had the following titles: Freedom and Democracy: Machiavelli and Rousseau; Liberal Citizenship and Patriarchy; and Liberalism, Democracy, and the Future of East-Central Europe. Three of the dozens of papers on panels included "Women and Courage in Greek and Jewish Political Thought" by Nancy L. Schwartz of Wesleyan University; "Tolerance, Toleration, and the Liberal Tradition" by Andrew Murphy of the University of Wisconsin; and "The Genesis of Hate: Liberalism as Cause or Defense" by James M. Glass of the University of Maryland.

Mary Dietz of the University of Minnesota, who has been an organizer of programs for this division, explains that the members of this section are interested in the interpretation and historical study of the texts of political thought as well as the "problem of relevance," that is, the extent to which the historical masterpieces of political thought are pertinent for understanding politics today. Some members of this section are concerned with the decline of truly historical analysis of the classic texts in favor of studies of twentieth century works of political philosophy. Among the many recent books of interest to members of this section are James Miller's *The Passion of Michel Foucault,* J. G. A. Pocock's *The Machiavellian Moment,* and A. MacIntyre's *After Virtue.*

Arelene W. Saxonhouse (1993, 3) posed one of the questions that members of this section want students of political science to ponder: "Are the texts we study and assign to our students culture and time bound, reproducing the white, patriarchal past in a multicultural present, or are they to be preserved as the focus of common discourse lest we and our students drown in a sea of relativism?"

Normative Political Theory

Participants in the Normative Political Theory division are also concerned with the great texts of political thought, but the focus of the division is more on normative (value) choices that are ubiquitous in politics than on specifically historical approaches to the subject matter. William Galston (1993, 28–30) has written an excellent summary of developments in normative political thought in which he identifies six major recent trends:

• Diminished interest in Marxism
• Increased interest in postmodernism

- A lively communitarian response to liberalism
- A renewed interest in the state
- A revived interest in pragmatism
- Increased interest in feminist thought

Normative Political Theory panels at the 1995 annual meeting of the APSA included: Jewish Themes in Modern Political Theory; American Liberalism at Century's End; and Rawlsian Justice Revisited. Among the many papers presented at the meeting were "Rush Limbaugh, Jacques Derrida, and the Gamble of Reform-minded Cynicism" by Ken Cmiel of the University of Iowa; "The Fetishism of Modernities" by Bernard Yack of the University of Wisconsin, Madison; and "Phenomenology and Body Politics" by Hwa Yol Jung of Moravian College.

Foundations of Political Theory

Susan Hekman of the University of Texas at Arlington, who has organized panels for the Foundations of Political Theory program division, explains that this division was formed as an alternative to the other political theory sections, so that points of view which were not given sufficient opportunity for expression previously, such as the methodology of the social sciences, identity politics and feminism, would find a forum. Edward Portis of Texas A&M University, who has also been active in organizing events in this section, notes that this division's programs have had the effect of welcoming political theorists and philosophers who had been alienated by the behavioral revolution back into an active role in the association.

The Foundations of Political Theory section discusses a wide variety of topics, including issues of proper methodologies for social and political science and the relevance to current politics of theoretical positions, such as liberalism, Marxism, feminism, postmodernism, and identity politics. Another focus of this section is the nature of political change and its relation to the discipline of political science. Recent panels have included The Moral Geography of Politics; Democracy and Environmentalism; and Political Philosophy at the Edge. Papers presented included "The Politics of Conscience" by Melissa A. Orlie of the University of Illinois, Urbana-Champaign; "Avoiding Scylla: Configuring Individuality Aesthetically" by Morton Schoolman of the State University of New York at Albany; and "Liberalism and Pluralism: An Uneasy Alliance" by Alan Ryan of Princeton University.

Formal Political Theory

Formal political theory is the name given within the association to quantitative studies, those investigations that measure political phenomena precisely and mathematically. The works of this section are also known as public choice theory, rational choice theory, or positive theory. Lalman, Oppenheimer, and Swistak, in their review of developments in formal theory, describe the unique features of this branch of the discipline. They report that, rather than concentrating on one aspect of the political science, such as the judiciary or intergovernmental relations, formal theorists investigate general trends across many areas of the discipline. In addition, formal theory consists largely of making mathematical analyses based on rational actor models (Lalman, Oppenheimer, and Swistak 1993).

Much recent work within this section is being done in the area of game theory, discussed earlier in this book. Among the panels in this division presented at a recent APSA meeting were Topics in Time Series Analysis; Modeling Choice; and Ecological Inference. Papers presented at the meeting included "Quantal Response Equilibria in Extensive Form Games" by Richard McKelvey and Thomas Palfrey, both of the California Institute of Technology; "Statistical Models for Inferring Individual Voter Instability from Aggregate Electoral Volatility" by Chris Achen of the University of Michigan; and "Rationality and Comparative Method" by Junko Kato of the University of Tokyo. Of special recent interest to members of the Formal Political Theory Section is Green and Shapiro's *Pathologies of Rational Choice*, discussed in Chapter 8.

Political Methodology

While the formal theory program division focuses specifically on quantitative methodology, the political methodology division examines the broader question of what methodologies are appropriate for studying politics. Political scientists in this section are concerned about the strength and validity of various methodologies, what they tell us and what they do not tell us about politics. At the 1995 annual meeting of the APSA, among the panels presented were: On the Stability of Social Interactions; New Games: Modeling International Relations After the Cold War; and Formal Models of Executive Politics. Among the papers presented were "Theory of Social Order" by Sun-Ki Chai of the University of Arizona; "Poison Games and the Condorcet Jury Theorem" by Roger Meyerson of Northwestern University; and "Coalition Dynamics" by Daniel A. Diermeier of Stanford University.

New Political Science

In addition to the political theory and methodology program divisions, there are several other program divisions that are, from different perspectives and points of view, particularly interested in how political science is conducted, how the political process is viewed, and how values figure in the process of studying politics. In 1967, The Caucus for a New Political Science was organized in the APSA. Donald M. Freeman (1991, 30–31) describes the origin of the Caucus as follows:

> That year [1967] the antibehavioralists organized the Caucus for a New Political Science, an opposition movement determined to challenge "the establishment." The event had significance. Change was in the air. . . . Caucus members were opposed to things as they were [concern with the Vietnam War, and with civil rights movement was widespread]. Political science, the caucus argued, was either uncritically proestablishment (as a product of pseudo-scientific objectivity) or irrelevant and without the capacity to help solve the nation's problems . . . . The caucus "party" so frightened the APSA establishment "party" that the constitution was changed to settle elections and policy-related questions by mailed ballot. The business meetings were initially so volatile

that the APSA employed the American Arbitration Association to assist in running them. . . . The caucus lives on as a sort of moon to the APSA sun. Its business meetings and organized panels are a substantial part of the "courtesy listings" in the program at each convention and some of the nation's leading political scientists are active in its deliberations. For the last decade, the caucus has been little more than an interest group within the political science community.

It is interesting that just as the behavioralist movement was itself once a protest movement that finally found a legitimate place within the profession, so the reaction to the behavioralist movement, in the form of the Caucus for a New Political Science and other groups, has now asserted its place within the discipline in the face of the dominance of the behavioralists. Recent panel topics for this section included Repositioning Class in Struggles for Liberation, Liberalism and the Governance of Bodies, and Nationalism and Modernity. Papers presented in this program division included "The Art of Negative Campaigning in American Elections" by Kerwin Swint of Kennesaw State College; "The Material and Political Force of Racial Imaginings" by Cedric Robinson of the University of California at Santa Barbara, and "Desiring Revolution: Marx and the Question of Pleasure" by Bradley Macdonald of Colorado State University.

Political Psychology

Political psychology was introduced in Chapter 6. Richard Lau of Rutgers University, who has organized programs in this section, notes that issues of recent interest to members of this section include the nature of voting decisions, the nature of survey responses, the personalities of political leaders, and the nature of group-based political responses. Among recently presented panels are Voters' Information Processing, Psychological Processes in Political Attitudes, and Psychological Processes in Political Communication. Papers presented recently included: "Political Advertising and Political Mood: An Experimental Study of Children's Political Attitudes" by Wendy Rahn and Rebecca Hirshon, both of the University of Wisconsin, Madison; "The Case of Black Conservatives: Do They Lead, Follow, or Are They in the Way" by Christopher Mobley of Purdue University; and "Evaluating Measures of Racism from an African American Perspective" by David Moskowitz of the University of North Carolina at Charlotte.

Transformational Politics

One of the wonderful things about political science is that people with special interests can work to organize sections of the APSA within which they can share the results of their research. One such group has organized the section on transformational politics, which focuses upon the nature of political change and the expressions of change in terms of transformations in society that occur as change progresses. Recent panels in this program division have been entitled Transforming Democracy: The Politics of Community and Responsibility; Transforming Environmental Consciousness: Theory, Policy, and Political Action; and The State and the

Transformation of the Principle of Sovereignty. Papers recently delivered within this division included: "Reassessing Chairman Mao" by Su Shaozhi, Fellow of the Princeton China Initiative; "The United States and the My Lai Massacre in Vietnam" by Arthur N. Gilber of the University of Denver; and "Gaia Politics for a 21st Century Polity" by Christopher B. Jones of Eastern Oregon State College.

Political Economy

The relationship between economics and politics has always been important to political scientists. What is now known as classical political economy was developed by British scholars, among whom was nineteenth century-writer John Stuart Mill. The focus of the discipline for classical scholars was the encouragement of commerce among nations, sponsored by England during the span of the British Empire. These scholars believed that the free-market system, regulated at times by import and export duties, was the key to economic growth and, consequently, the welfare of all nations. In the twentieth century, neoclassical political economy applied the concepts of free-market trade to the United States and other Western nations. A key principle of neoclassical economics is that the free market is the most efficient method of creating incentives to produce what society needs, and of distributing those benefits to those who participate in society. Neoclassical economists lately have been increasingly preoccupied with the causes and effects of market failure. Competing with neoclassical thought is Marxist political economy, which sees the capitalist open market system as the chief instrument of Western imperialism, that is, the economic subjugation of weak and less developed nations by the dominant industrial societies.

Miriam Golden of the University of California at Los Angeles has organized panels for this program division. She notes that among the many topics of ongoing interest in this field are the general relationship between politics and economics, the impact of economic phenomena on political processes, and the use of economic theory to analyze political phenomena. Professor Golden notes that two of the most prominent methodological perspectives within this field are rational choice theory and historical institutionalism. Among panels recently presented within this program division are The Post-Corporalist Political Economy of Europe, The Politics of Strategic Industrial Policy, and Ideology and Interests in the History of Trade. Among the papers recently presented are "Rational Choice Theory and Fundamentalism" by Kristen Monroe of the University of California at Irvine; "Is Communalism Rational: The Logic of Hindu-Muslim Relations in India" by Ashutosh Varshney of Harvard University; and "Deflation Through Revaluation: A British Tragedy in Three Acts" by Randall Kroszner of the University of Chicago.

International Political Economy

James Caporaso, in his review of recent developments in international political economy, cites several approaches that have attracted substantial interest in recent years. One of these is strategic trade theory. Sometimes called the "new international economics," strategic trade theory discusses how governments relate to trade between countries. Unlike traditional theory, which assumes perfect competition in the international arena, strategic trade theory investigates the comparative trade advantages of different nations, how governments may affect these advantages, and how governments focus on strategic sectors of commerce rather than on the macroeconomic picture as a whole. Marxist political economy is still carried on by those who view the capitalist system as inherently imperialistic. They are most concerned with relieving inequities in the underdeveloped nations. As noted in Chapter 14, although the fall of the Soviet empire has given rise to speculation that Marxism as an international movement is quickly dying, a concern for relations among wealthy and poor nations remains strong among economists in other nations such as China and Mexico. In addition, insights from Marxism continue to be studied by political scientists in the United States as well. Among the panels recently presented in this program division are Liberalism and the Illicit Global Economy, International Trade and Domestic Politics, and The Political Economy of Regionalism. Among papers recently presented are "Global Hazards: The Illicit Export of Environmental Harm" by Jennifer Clapp of York University; "Law and Place: A Global Perspective on the Rejection, Relocation, and Reinvention of Government" by Alfred Aman of Indiana University; and "The Externalization of Domestic Regulation: Intellectual Property Rights Reform in a Global Era" by Paul N. Doremus of the Office of Technology Assessment.

Part 2.   Political Behavior

Elections and Electoral Behavior

The most notable institutional development in studies of electoral behavior was the creation in 1946 of the Survey Research Center (SRC) at the University of Michigan. In 1948, the SRC was joined by the Institute for Social Research (ISR), later known as the Center for Political Studies. The work of Angus Campbell and associates at the SRC in Michigan has been responsible for a cumulative series of American National Election Surveys, which have formed the core of U.S. voting studies since 1948. In their recent assessment of the state of the discipline and current developments in the study of elections and behavior, Russell Dalton and Martin Wattenburg note that the sociological approach, which relied heavily on comparing census statistics to voting patterns, dominated research efforts until researchers at Columbia University and the University of Michigan began to explore the psychological bases of voting behavior in the 1950s and 1960s (Dalton and Wattenburg 1993). They note the special contribution made by *The American Voter* (Campbell et al. 1960), which "introduced an explicitly social psychological model of the vote" (Dalton and Wattenburg 1993, 197). *The American Voter* constitutes an extensive critique of the assumption in traditional liberal theories of representative government that voters rationally choose candidates on the basis of the alternative party platforms. Campbell and colleagues stressed that, according to data in the series of American national Election surveys, the electorate was only marginally informed about, interested in, and influenced by political issues. The model specifies three necessary conditions for issue voting: citizens must have an opinion about the issue; they must feel that the issue is important; and they must be able to distinguish between alternative polities offered by the parties. In the mid-1950's, according to *The American Voter,* only a fifth to a third of the American electorate met these criteria on any given issue. According to Campbell *et al.,* the key concept was party identification, which seemed to be highly stable (although not unchangeable). It appeared to develop early in life prior to policy preferences and it appeared to strengthen over time.

The primary challenge to Campbell's study was *The Changing American Voter* (1976) by Norman H. Nie, Sidney Verba, and John Petrocik. This study argued that *The American Voter* was essentially the product of the time in which it was written, and was deficient for understanding electoral behavior in the 1970s. Nie, Verba, and Petrocik argued that after *The American Voter* was written, voters developed relatively consistent attitude structures and were able to assess the proximity of their attitudes to those of other candidates, enabling prospective issue voting to play a larger role.

Recently presented panels in the Elections and Electoral Behavior program division of the APSA include The Current American Revolution, The Vulnerable American Politician, and Consequences of Political Knowledge. Papers recently presented include: "The Effectiveness of Negative Campaigning" by Gerald Pomper and Richard R. Lau, both of Rutgers University; "Duck or Punch? A Psychologically Informed Model of Candidate Strategies" by Adam Simon of the University of California at Los Angeles; and "White Southern Ethics and the Republican Alignment" by Charles Leonard of the University of Missouri at St. Louis.

Public Opinion and Participation

Those who have studied public opinion and participation were among the champions of the behavioral revolution of the 1950s and 1960s. Among the "classic" works in this area are Philip Converse's 1964 essay, "The Nature of Belief Systems in Mass Publics," in *Ideology and Discontent* edited by David Apter; *The American Voter,* 1960 (Angus Campbell, Philip Converse, Warren E. Miller, and Donald E. Stokes); and Sidney Verba and Norman Nie, *Political Participation in America,* 1972. Stephen E. Bennett of the University of Cincinnati, who has chaired the Public Opinion and Participation Section of the American Political Science Association notes that:

> In terms of public opinion, the most important issue of late has been the quality of public opinion. How much do people know about public affairs, and what level of sophistication do they bring to bear on political questions? There are also concerns about linkages between public opinion and electoral outcomes. In terms of political participation, we're seeing a lot of work dealing with what difference different levels of participation make to what governments at all levels do. Survey research is still the dominant means of acquiring information about public opinion and political participation, although focus groups are being more and more used. In terms of theoretical perspective, diversity reigns supreme.
>
> Public opinion work [in the future] will drift back toward issues dealt with by the first generation of empirical researchers, namely, trying to tie more carefully empirical research to normative democratic theories. Participation research has to resolve the issues surrounding rational choice. This field will also divide over

issues of measurement: how do we tap opinions, etc. The next decade will see a substantial generational turnover in leadership. We've been watching the slow but inevitable departure of the generation of scholars who have dominated these fields since the 1960s. The big question, in my mind, is whether the next generation will fixate on methodological issues. Most of our key concepts date back fifty years, and very little attention has been given to improving our core measuring instruments.

Recent books in the field include Benjamin Page and Robert Shapiro, *The Rational Public*, 1991; Eric R. A. N. Smith, *The Unchanging American Voter*, 1989; and Paul Snider Man and Thomas Piazza, *The Scar of Race*, 1993. Panels recently presented in the Public Opinion and Participation program division include The Dynamics of Political Reasoning; Ideology and Political Beliefs; and Gender, Race, and Public Opinion. Papers recently presented include: "Theories of Political Literacy" by Carol Cassel of the University of Alabama; "Public Opinion and Hillary Clinton as First Lady" by Barbara Burrell of the University of Wisconsin; and "Consensus Cues in Political Persuasion" by Diana Mutz and Mira Sotriovic, both of the University of Wisconsin.

Political Organizations and Parties

In his review and summary of developments in political parties research, William Crotty notes that political parties research is a long-standing and traditional area of political science, which has produced a wealth of data and analysis. Currently, so many different techniques are used in the field, says Crotty, that the "only common bond is that the research deals in some manner with an aspect of political parties or a topic of immediate concern to the understanding of party operations." Crotty (1991, 137–45) continues with some observations about this subfield that hold true for many other subfields in political science as well: "There has been no dominant theoretical perspective in the study of political parties, and in fact most of the research is self-consciously empirical and theoretical. This condition is not likely to change in the foreseeable future."

Among the panels presented at the 1995 annual meeting of the American Political Science Association were Political Action Committees, Party Activists, and Grassroots Mobilization. Among the many papers presented at that meeting were "Change Comes to Steeltown: Local Political Parties as Instruments of Power" by Melanie J Blumberg, University of Akron, William C. Binning, Youngstown State University, and John C. Green, University of Akron; "Was 1994 a Return to Party-Centered Campaigning?" by Diana Dwyre of the University of Maryland at Baltimore County; and "Social Movements and Theories of American Politics" by Andrew McFarland of the University of Illinois at Chicago.

Urban Politics

Urban politics, as a subfield, is the study of the challenges and problems of America's cities. Kenneth Mladenka and Bryan Jones (1991, 288) report that three works of major importance in urban politics—Banfield's *Political Influence*, Dahl's *Who*

Governs? and Sayre and Kaufman's *Governing New York City*—helped bring to the pluralist school of political thought the empirical methods of behavioral political science.

Mladenka and Jones accentuate the importance of urban studies due to the enormous problems that cities face around the world today. Because of their belief in the importance of these studies, they take more care than commentators in other parts of the discipline to outline carefully some of the shortcomings that the study of urban politics has been experiencing. Students reading these criticisms should note, not only that substantial progress in the study of urban politics has been made, but that similar criticisms could be made of most if not all of the other sections of the discipline, if this text could devote the space to them.

Mladenka and Jones (1991, 291) note several problems with the current state of urban political research. First, they point out that there is "a mismatch between urban theory and the supporting data." This mismatch occurs because urban theory is trying to be comprehensive, and this attempt has brought about an interdisciplinary approach that has had many benefits. However, there have been problems as well. "There is a pronounced tendency to try to study it all—economics, politics, culture. To accommodate these overarching concerns, theories have become increasingly abstract . . . [and] too little rigorous empirical work is being produced." The result, ironically, is that "The interdisciplinary approach has succeeded too well." One further problem noted by Mladenka and Jones (1991, 292), which might be said of some other areas of study as well from time to time, is that "Urbanists are prone to an infatuation with the latest scholarly fad. The political economy approach is the dominant perspective in the study of urban politics today." Perhaps one result of these problems, the authors find, is that "Urban scholarship does not fare well in the pages of the major political science journals" and this fact would further "suggest that the study of urban politics is not well integrated into mainstream political science" (Mladenka and Jones 1991, 287).

It is important to note at this point that political scientists in other areas of the discipline have also complained from time to time of not receiving sufficient attention from or acceptance in the major journals. Political scientists are human, and the editors of journals are as susceptible to bias as anyone. These editors do, however, devote many hours of time, almost always for no compensation, in attempting to provide fair treatment to many submissions competing for attention. The competition for publication may justly be termed highly intense. Please note that Mladenka and Jones are not blaming journal editors for a lack of publication in the area of urban studies, but instead are placing the responsibility on the urban specialists. In fact, this sort of modesty and willingness to assume responsibility is characteristic of the vast majority of political scientists.

Among panels recently presented in the program division of urban politics are The Politics of Urban Education, Black Mayors and the Challenges of Urban Leadership, and Urban Government Structure and Municipal Reform. Among papers recently presented are "Moving and Shaking to the Rhythm of Local Economic Development" by Bob Jessup of Lancaster University; "Who Will Govern Metropolitan America" by John Stuart Hall of Arizona State University; and "We Win, You Lose! Black, Latino, and Asian Socioeconomic and Political Outcomes in

Urban Politics" by Paula D. McClain and Steven C. Tauber, both of the University of Virginia.

Political Communication

The world of communications is being continually revolutionized by advances in technology, which in turn have profound impacts upon politics. Copy machines helped underground newspapers influence public opinion in the Soviet bloc countries prior to the fall of the Soviet Union. Observers of the 1989 popular revolt in China note how protesters used electronic mail and the internet to inform the rest of the world of their struggle when other forms of communication were too dangerous for the protesters to use. Panels presented at a recent APSA meeting in the field of political communication reflect the vast variety of studies now being conducted, including The Political Impact of Call-in Talk Shows, Psychological Processes in Political Communication, and Mass Media and the Policy Process. Among the papers presented were: "The Rise of Cooperative Muckraking" by Trevor Thrall of the Massachusetts Institute of Technology; "Race and Poverty in America: Public Misperceptions and the News Media" by Martin Gilens of Yale University; and "Episodes, Incidents, and Eruptions: How the U.S. Networks Cover the Post-Cold War World" by Pippa Norris of Harvard University.

Religion and Politics

The section on Religion and Politics is one of many success stories in the history of the development of the APSA. In the 1970s, Professor Hubert Morken, then of Oral Roberts University and now at Regent University, worked actively with several others, among whom were Corwin Smidt, Lyman Kellstedt, and Paul Weber, to form a study group called the Caucus for Faith and Politics. As with several other sections, the members of this group strove to demonstrate both that religion and politics is a valid subject of study and that enough people are interested in the topic to make program development worthwhile. As their efforts progressed, some of the most eminent political scientists in the country, such as Aaron Wildavsky and Daniel Elazar, began to take an interest, or to develop further previously initiated works in the subject. Today the section on religion and politics is among the largest, in terms of registered members, within the association. Professor Kenneth D. Wald of the University of Florida, whose work *Religion and Politics in the United States* (3rd ed., 1996) is one of the leading texts in the field, has made some observations about the development of interest in religion and politics as a field of study:

> Because the field of religion and politics is so new, it is still attempting to establish its relevance and legitimacy to the larger enterprise of political science. Thus individual scholars are busy mapping the terrain, identifying the interesting questions and only beginning to answer them. The sheer diversity of the field—its inclusiveness of every major approach in the discipline—also tends to minimize the degree to which scholars study the same phenomenon.
>
> First, many scholars are simply trying to determine the extent of religious in-

fluence, broadly conceived, on the major aspects of American political activity. This includes mass behavior, public policy formulation, and the broad political culture. The questions are, "How much impact does religion exert?" and "Under what circumstances?" Similar work is conducted by comparativists. The second major area is the continuing quest to determine the proper role of religion in modern society. This concern with normative questions encompasses a range of issues—the role of religion under the First Amendment, the contribution of religion to violence, the nature of religious discourse in a liberal democracy, religion as an antidote to the excesses of liberal individualism and a resource to help overcome the oppression of women and other racial and ethnic minorities. To some extent, we are in our infancy as far as assessing religious commitment in the mass public, and a considerable body of work is going into that effort.

The fundamental challenge to the field, in my view, is to integrate our work with the discipline at large—be it work on American politics, comparative politics, or political theory. This means we need to persuade the discipline that religion is a useful realm in which to explore important and interesting questions and that we need to treat religion in politics as a species of a larger category such as cultural politics. This perception rests on my assumption that we ought not to become a self-contained ghetto with our own journals but should try whenever possible to bring our views to the attention of the profession.

Many organized sections of the American Political Science Association have newsletters which inform members of current events and often provide a forum for the exchange of views. Some sections also have related groups with special interests that have meetings and circulate newsletters. Within the membership of those interested in religion and politics, one such subgroup is known as Christians in Political Science. In a recent edition of this group's newsletter, which also has the title *Christians in Political Science,* editor Brent F. Nelsen presents a controversy which has arisen over Mark Noll's recent book, *The Scandal of the Evangelical Mind.* After Nelsen's explanation, responses to the subject from several political scientists are printed. The following excerpt is from Nelsen's (1995, 1) presentation of the subject.

> Wheaton College historian Mark Noll has generated a small storm in Christian intellectual circles with his recent book, *The Scandal of the Evangelical Mind* (Eerdmans, 1994). The book, which *Christianity Today* named 1994 Book of the Year, argues that the Evangelical tradition in America, especially in the 20th century, has not encouraged "the effort to think like a Christian—to think within a specifically Christian framework—across the whole spectrum of modern learning, including economics and political science, literary criticism and imaginative writing, historical inquiry and philosophical studies, linguistics and the history of science, social theory and the arts." Rather than affirm the life of the mind as an avenue of worship, modern Evangelicals have largely shunned rigorous intellectual activity for the relative safety of anti-intellectual populism and revivalism. This, Noll argues, is a scandal.

Professor Martin Marty's *Fundamentalism Project,* another book that has received substantial interest from political scientists lately, describes fundamentalist movements across the world. Liberation theology, which has been influenced by Marxist thought and has been very influential in South America, is now being studied to see in what ways it has been affected by the fall of the Soviet Union. Among the panels presented at the 1995 annual meeting of the APSA were Religion and the 1994 Elections, The Catholic Church and Global Politics, and Religion and Politics in a Neo-Liberal Latin America. Among the many papers presented in this section were "The Bishops Take Cairo: Domestic Catholic Influence in an International Setting" by Lisa L. Ferrari of Georgetown University; "Religion and Politics in Contemporary Central America" by Anne M. Hallum of Stetson University; and "Filled with Spirit and Power: The Significance of Issue Framing Among Protestant Clergy" by Laura R. Olson of the University of Wisconsin at Madison.

Women and Politics

The subject of women and politics is currently so popular that papers dealing with it are found throughout the presentations of most of the APSA organized sections. Christine DiStefano of the University of Washington at Seattle, who has helped to organize programs within this division, has identified some of the fascinating questions that are currently being raised:

- How are women faring in political regimes undergoing processes of democratization?
- Why do women seem to be losing political ground in previously socialist regimes?
- What are the specific needs of women in developing economies?
- To what extent do development plans address women's economic needs?
- How will current debates about "welfare reform" impact on poor women in the U.S.?
- How might we get beyond the current impasse on abortion in the U.S.?
- To what extent do women leaders and legislators display gender-specific modes of behavior?
- What kinds of policies are key in the effort to promote gender equity?
- How are women's experiences, needs, and aspirations shaped not only by gender but also by class, race, ethnicity, and sexuality?
- What are the prospects for a unified international women's movement?
- How do we explain the nearly universal phenomenon of women's political subordination to men?
- What are the culturally specific components of subordination?

Professor DiStefano has also listed a number of the books currently of interest to students interested in the study of women and politics:

- Susan Carroll, *Women as Candidates in American Politics* (1985)
- Carole Pateman, *The Sexual Contract* (1980)
- Nancy Hartsock, *Money, Sex, and Power* (1985)

- Jane Mansbridge, *Why We Lost the ERA* (1986)
- Joyce Gelb, *Feminism and Politics* (1989)
- Joni Lovenduski, *Toward the Emasculation of Political Science: The Impact of Feminism* (1981)
- Zillah Eisenstein, *The Female Body and the Law* (1988)
- Robert Darcy, Susan Welch and Janet Clark, *Women, Elections, and Representation* (1994)
- Susan Moller Okin, *Justice, Gender, and the Family* (1989)
- Vicky Randall, *Women and Politics* (1987)
- Jo Freeman, *The Politics of Women's Liberation* (1975)

Among the panels recently presented in this program division are Women, Equality, and Citizenship; The Impact of Women in Legislative Politics; and Promises Unfulfilled: Liberalism and Economic Equality for Women. Among the numerous papers recently presented are "Women Mentoring Women: Generating a Feminist Vision Across Generations" by Susan Clarke of the University of Colorado; "The Increasing Presence of Women in Government and Their Influence on Liberalizing Society" by Valerie O'Regan of the University of California at Riverside; and "Women, Warriors, and Equality" by Mary Lou Kendrigan of Lansing Community College.

Race, Gender, and Ethnicity

Like the Women and Politics program division, the issues of interest to the Race, Gender and Ethnicity division are discussed in a variety of panels throughout the APSA program. Professor Katherine Tate of the Ohio State University notes that among the many issues of interest to members of this section are

- How do minority groups, including women, gain political inclusion and win political incorporation?
- Does gender or race or ethnicity matter in politics: Do women and minority legislators legislate differently?
- Do different electoral systems inhibit or enhance minority voting power?

Professor Tate also notes that among the books and articles of particular interest in this section are Sue Thomas' *Women as Legislators,* and Bubo and Gilliam's 1990 APSR article, "Black Empowerment."

Among this section's panels presented at the 1995 APSA meeting are Federal Indian Policy, Indian Sovereignty, and the Limits of the Liberal State; Race, Radicalism and Ideology; and Affirmative Action: An International Perspective. Among the papers presented are "The Effects of Candidates' Gender on Electoral Success" by Paul B. Raymond of the University of Southern Indiana, "Tough but Caring; Elected Women and Criminal Justice Policy" by Janet Boles of Marquette University, and "Sentencing Behavior of Black Judges Elected From Majority-Black Subdistricts" by Jason Kirksey of Oklahoma State University.

Part 3. Political Institutions, Law, Administration, and Policy Analysis

Legislative Behavior

Michael L. Mezey explains that, while functionalism, which studied the functions of legislative bodies as a whole within various societies, was once the predominant methodology in this subfield, most legislative studies now focus on the activities of individual legislators. Mezey (1993, 335) reports that "Typically, legislative behavior is explained in terms of the purposes of the legislator, and questions of structure and performance are approached from the perspective of the members' goal-seeking behavior." Roger Davidson (1991, 29) reports that legislative studies have been influenced by what is known as the "new institutionalism," which studies "how legislative structure dictates certain decision sequences and policy forms."

Among legislative behavior panels presented recently at the APSA are Change and Reform in State Legislatures, Legislative Careers and Political Ambition, and The 1994 Congressional Elections. Among the papers presented in this division are "Minority Groups in Congress: The Black, Women's, and Hispanic Caucus" by Charles E. Menifield of the University of Missouri; "The Role of the Mass Media in Americans' Distaste for Congress" by Elizabeth Theiss-Morse and John R. Hibbing, both of the University of Nebraska; and "Conceptualizing Legislative Activity" by Grant Reeher of Syracuse University.

Representation and Electoral Systems

Representation and electoral systems studies focus on how representatives to legislative bodies gain and retain their seats, and how they represent the people who elected them. The program presented at a recent APSA meeting included panels entitled The Future of Voting Rights in the Wake of Shaw v. Reno and its Progeny, Electoral Systems in Comparative Perspective, and Consequences of the Voting Rights Act. Papers presented at the same meeting included: "Voting Rights in a New Key: Using Seats/Votes Models to Evaluate African-American Representation" by Thomas Cavanaugh of Yale University; "One Person, N Votes: An Assessment of Alternative Voting Schemes as a Possible Remedy for Geographically Dispersed Districts" by Byron D. Orey of the Southern Regional Council; and "The New Electoral System in the Japanese Lower House" by John Hickman of Berry College.

Presidency Research

The presidency has long been one of the favorite subjects of study for students of political science. Two leading presidential scholars, Professors Stephen Wayne of Georgetown University and Paul Quirk of the University of Illinois at Urbana-Champaign, note that among the topics currently being investigated by scholars are

- Presidential influence
- Presidential psychology
- The public and rhetorical dimensions of the office
- The link between elections and governance
- Presidential influence in congress
- The sources of presidential popularity
- Presidential strategy and success in controlling the bureaucracy

Professor Wayne led organizational efforts for the Presidency Research section. Among his scholarly works is the continuing series *The Road to the White House* (1996), which prepares college students to understand presidential elections. Discussing the basic approach of scholars in the presidency research section, Wayne notes that analysts take a "presidency-centered approach" which focuses upon the "president's ability to stimulate the system to produce policy responses to issue dilemmas." Within the section's discussion, Wayne notes, "We continue to debate methodology, psychology, the nature of the system and the president's role in it, and the relevancy of some theoretical approaches." Professor Quirk adds that studies of the presidency had, until recently, "been neglected due to the difficulty of doing methodologically rigorous work" but that this work is now being done to the benefit of the profession. Quirk also notes that, "The main issue in this field concerns the President's relations with other institutions or groups, such as Congress and the public. Each of these relationship raises very different questions, and the field is therefore highly fragmented theoretically and methodologically."

Among classic and recent works of interest in the field mentioned by Wayne and Quirk are Richard Neustadt's *Presidential Power* (1960), Samuel Kernell's *Going Public: New Strategies for Presidential Leadership* (1986), Stephen Skowronek's *The Politics Presidents Make* (1993), Charles O. Jones' *The Presidency in a Separated System* (1994), Paul Brace and Barbara Hinkley, *Follow the Leader: Opinion Polls and Modern Presidents* (1992), and Mark Peterson, *Legislating Together* (1990). Presidency research panels presented at a recent APSA meeting include Roundtable on Studying the White House Over Time, Presidents and Public Communication, and Perspectives on Presidential Policy-Making. Papers presented include "Reconceiving Theories of Power: Masculinism in Executive Politics" by Georgia Duerst-Lahti of Beloit College; "Bargaining with the President: A Baysean Model of a Simple Game" by Terry Sullivan of the University of North Carolina; and "Presidential Vetoes and Event Count Models" by Todd Shields of the University of Arkansas.

Federalism and Intergovernmental Relations

Federalism is the system of government in which various levels of government, national, state, and local, each have independent powers and share power in governing the society as a whole. Intergovernmental relations is the study of how the powers and programs of these various units are coordinated and how they relate to one another and coordinate their many activities on a daily basis. Susan MacManus

(1991, 203) describes three events that generated a revival of interest in federalism and intergovernmental relations that began in the 1980s:

- The fiscal problems of local governments in the late 1970s (New York City's fiscal crisis and California's Proposition 13 movement);
- The Reagan Presidency and its special brand of "New" Federalism; and
- The nation's bicentennial.

MacManus (1991, 204) also describes progress and problems in exploring methodologies for the study of federalism and intergovernmental relations, noting that, "At the center of the debate is the perennial question of which government has (or should have) the authority for various functional responsibilities."

Among the panels recently presented in this program division are Education and the American Federal Order, The Battle for Natural Resources: Indian Tribes, State Government, and Local Communities; and Roundtable on Local Government Responsibility and Responsiveness. Among papers delivered are "Educational Goals 2000: Efficiency, Equity, and Centralization" by Jonathan Parker of the University of North Carolina at Chapel Hill; "The Political Economy of Russian Federalism, 1990–1995" by Steve L. Solnik of Columbia University; and "'Operative Federalism': Health Care Reforms in the States" by Marian Lief Paley of the University of Delaware.

Public Administration

In 1887, founding father of American public administration Woodrow Wilson wrote (1993, 33–40):

> There is scarcely a single duty of government which was once simple which is not now complex; government once had but a few masters; it now has scores of masters. Majorities formerly only underwent government; they now conduct government. Where government once might follow the whims of a court, it must now follow the veins of a nation. . . . This is why there should be a science of administration which shall seek to straighten the paths of government, to make its business less unbusinesslike, to strengthen and purify its organization, and to crown its duties with dutifulness. . . . Most important to be observed is the truth already so much and so fortunately insisted upon by our civil-service reformers; namely, that administration lies outside the proper shores of politics. Administrative questions are not political questions. Although politics sets the tasks for administration, it should not be suffered to manipulate its offices.

In this passage, Wilson hails the dawn of modern public administration, a new profession, calling for a professional education that has arisen to face boldly the challenge of carrying out policies made by presidents and legislators. A century later, however, Christopher Hood (1990, 107) wrote the following about the same discipline: "Public Administration—the study of institutional arrangements for provision of public services—is a subject which has often been declared to be in a condition of chaos and decline." How has this discipline come from the optimism of Wilson to the pessimism of Hood? The story is not only fascinating, but its lessons are of vital importance to the health and vitality of government in America and elsewhere.

Public administration is almost a discipline by itself. In some universities it stands alone as a separate department or is placed in the same department with business administration. According to University of Wisconsin political scientist Donald Kettl (1993), the modern *practice* of public administration may be traced to reports written by Alexander Hamilton when he was Secretary of the Treasury. Woodrow Wilson, as Kettl notes, however, is given credit for being the father of the *study* of public administration. Wilson made famous what became known as the "policy–administration dichotomy." This dichotomy, quoted in the passage above, states that *policy* ought to consist of the decisions made by elected officials, most notably legislatures, and *administration* should be a separate set of activities in which policy decisions are carried out by appointed officials in government agencies. For Wilson, effective government results when legislators and administrators perceive a clear line between decisionmaking (policy) and implementation (administration).

As the twentieth century progressed, public administration became separated from political science as it developed its own methods and goals. As distinct from the study of politics, public administration became an educational channel for training future government administrators. It was not long before public administration began to adopt methods and practices newly developed in business administration. Frederick Taylor's "scientific management" studies, published just after the turn of the century, in which new techniques of improving efficiency were developed, encouraged this trend. The "public management" movement emerged as public administration increasingly turned from politics to management efficiency as the appropriate subject for study. Organizational behavior, decisionmaking, and financial management became central elements in public management curriculums. In resistance to this trend, however, were studies which described administration as an inherently political activity. The most famous of these was Graham Allison's discussion of the Cuban Missile Crisis (1969), discussed in Chapter 6.

Kettl notes that in recent years a number of trends have surfaced within the field of public administration. Institutional theory, for example, developed within public management programs and placed a newly intensified focus upon the behavior of organizations. Institutional theory examines internal administrative, personnel, budgeting, accounting, and other policies, attempting to determine the constraints that these phenomena place upon the decisions and productivity of organizations.

Several of the new approaches have developed from related studies in the field of economics. Kettl explains that these are based upon an assumption that bureaucrats are rational and act to maximize the utility of their positions and resources. Principal-agent theory, for example, examines the relationship between elected officials, who act as principals (decisionmakers), and administrators and consultants, who act as their agents (those who carry out decisions). A problem in implementing policy often results because the agents have more information on many subjects than do the principals. Principals, therefore, have difficulty in selecting competent and trustworthy agents. Principal-agent theory examines the effects of these relationships upon the processes and products of public organizations.

Other economics-based approaches include bureaucratic-outcomes theory, institutional-choice theory, and transaction-cost theory. Bureaucratic-outcomes theory has helped to define how policy makers are able to use incentives and sanctions to change the manner in which bureaucracies operate. Institutional-choice theory examines the manner in which groups with political power are able to change the rules that direct the bureaucracy. Transaction-cost theory analyzes the network of relationships among organizations and the manner in which the network provides for its member units a framework for mutual support.

Public bureaucracy theory examines bureaucratic organizations rather than administration. Kettl (1993) notes that the three basic principles of this movement are that (1) bureaucracy, as a set of institutions in society, matters; (2) that bureaucracy operates within a network of political forces; and (3) bureaucracies are important because of their roles within the state.

With all the progress that has been made in the discipline of public administration, as described by Donald Kettl, what are the problems that led Christopher Hood to describe the discipline as being in a state of "chaos and decline"? Hood's comments are not directed at a lack of progress in understanding the functions or process of administration. Instead, his concern is that so many competing schools of thought, with their own methodological approaches, have grown up from within or have been borrowed from other disciplines, that the discipline of public administration has no single methodological foundation on which to rest, and there is a lack of agreement even over general operating principles. Hood's case may be a bit overstated, yet his analysis helps to identify some of the major developments in the field. Hood (1990, 112–113) identifies several types of "theoretical development" that he observed taking place in the 1970s and 1980s.

[1] The policy approach . . . concerned with ways of improving public policy by better analytic techniques [was] showing signs of intellectual fatigue by the 1980s.

[2] Organizational sociology [became] fragmented into a variety of different approaches—for example, 'corporate culture' . . . 'population ecology' . . . 'institutional' . . . and the radical organization theory approach.

[3] The New Public Administration approach claimed that values such as equity and equality should be paramount in public administration, and that administrators should not simply obey whatever goals elected officials choose to set. The New Public Administration movement was short-lived and its doctrines soon became under attack as a formula for elitism and a politically irresponsible bureaucracy.

A review of panels and papers presented at recent APSA meetings will easily demonstrate that the field of public administration is addressing not only its traditional concerns, such as the role of policy making in relation to administration, but also new methodologies and problems. Recent panels in public administration include Institutional Consequences of Policy Choices, Bureaucracy and Democracy, and Empirical Research on the Public Service. Papers presented include "Femocrats in Government: Center-Periphery Constellations in Public Administration" by Janneke van der Ros of Lillehammer College, "The Napoleonic State Tradition" by James Hollifield of Auburn University, and "Forest Management Policies in India: The Role of Citizen Participation" by Rumki Basu of the University of Delhi.

Public Policy

We have described public policy analysis in Chapter 9, but there are so many analyses currently being conducted that a few more examples deserve mention here. Paul Sabatier has identified four types of policy research conducted by political scientists since the mid-1970s:

1. *Substantive area research*. This seeks to understand the politics of a specific policy area, such as health, education, transportation, natural resources, or foreign policy. Most of the work in this tradition has consisted of detailed, largely atheoretical case studies.
2. *Evaluation and impact studies*. Most evaluation [of the effectiveness and efficiency of public politics] research is based on contributions from other disciplines, particularly welfare economics.
3. *Policy process* [how policies are developed and implemented].
4. *Policy design*. . . . this approach has recently focused on such topics as the efficacy of different types of policy instruments. (Sabatier 1995, 10–11)

Public policy panels presented at the 1995 Annual Meeting of the APSA include Issues in Aging Policy, Causes and Consequences of Federal Budget Reform, and The Future of Entitlements. Papers presented include " 'Cyber-Crats Among Cyber-Orgs?': Public Organizations—A 'Paradox of Participation' in Regulating Transnational Networks" by Chris C. Demchak of the University of Arizona, "Explaining the Budget Deficit" by Daniel Hofrenning of St. Olaf College, and "Alternatives to the Balanced Budget Amendment" by Roy T. Meyers of the University of Maryland, Baltimore County.

State Politics and Policy

Students of state politics and policy study all of the subjects that are studied by other political scientists on the national level, such as administration, policy making, political participation, voting behavior, and representation. Ronald E. Weber has recently summarized progress in this field. According to Weber (1991, 255), analysts of state politics have

> advanced remarkably during the past twenty-five years . . . from a period when the study of roll call voting and party cohesion in individual state legislatures was considered seminal work to one where it is possible to examine state legislative elections and behavior across both time and space . . . from an era when statistics like Spearman's Rho and Chi Square were considered the bread and butter techniques in this field to one in which two-stage, generalized, least-squares regression and probit analysis techniques are highly likely to be the most appropriate ones to explore the research questions of the field.

Panels recently presented in this program division include Diversity and Representation in State Politics, Assessing New Education Policy Tools, and Setting the Policy Agenda: The Role of Governors. Papers presented include: "Reinvent State Government or Reorganize It? Governors' Proposals for Administrative Reform in the 1990s" by Dan Durning of the University of Georgia; "Was Susan B. Anthony Wrong? State public Policy and the Representation of Women's Interests" by Susan B. Hansen of the University of Pittsburgh; and "An Economic and Moral Threshold Model of Welfare Effects" by David Dodenhoff and Anthony Woodlief, both of the University of Michigan.

Law and Courts

With candor, humor, and some of the frustration that has also been expressed about other fields of interest within political science, Eliot Slotnik (1991, 67) describes recent developments in the study of judicial politics, one of the areas of interest within the study of law and courts:

> The subfield of judicial politics is, perhaps, the most schizophrenic of the recognized sub-areas within our discipline. If that overstates my premise, few, I think, would dispute the fact that we have the earmarks of multiple personalities and that the internal tensions abounding in the field in which we labor are more substantial than in those areas mined by our colleagues. Our roots are multidisciplinary, and we owe a great deal to fields as diverse as history, psychology, statistics, literature, philosophy, anthropology, economics, sociology and others. At the same time, we are in no sense simply a result or a residual of these other disciplines. Indeed, within political science, we predate most other areas of study, as our work was generally pursued under the label "public law."

The United States Supreme Court is the primary focus of judicial politics research. Important works in this field include, according to Slotnik, Pritchett's *The Roosevelt Court* (1948). Among the studies in which the primary question was, "[W]hat makes judges behave as they do? . . . [T]he classic breakthrough came in Peltason's 1955 study, *Federal Courts in the Political Process*. Peltason's process orientation spawned numerous efforts that moved judicial politics research in several directions simultaneously, and numerous case studies of facets of the judicial process would follow" (Slotnik 1991, 67).

Judicial studies have, since the 1960s, increasingly turned to quantitative methods. Several large data collections have been established for use in judicial research, including the Civil Litigation Research Project Data Archive, the U.S. Supreme Court Judicial Data Base, and the U.S. Supreme Court Judicial Data Base: Phase II (Slotnik 1991).

Professor Lee Epstein of Washington University at St. Louis, who has organized activities of the Law and Courts Program Division, notes that among topics of continuing and current interest to scholars in this division are theoretical approaches to decisionmaking, the role of courts and law in the transitional regimes in eastern Europe, the relationship of courts to public opinion, and the impact of court decisions and public compliance with them. Epstein also notes that, along with more traditional methods, theories grounded in social psychology, rational choice approaches, and statistical models are being increasingly utilized to understand how court systems operate and influence public affairs.

Panels in law and politics recently presented include The Dynamics of Supreme Court Decision Making, Litigation for Gay Rights, and Comparative Judicial Perspectives. Papers presented include "The Role of the General and the Particular in Law: The Case of Battered Women Who Kill in Self-Defense" by Nancy Crowe of the University of Chicago; "Mobilizing Law for Social Change: Sexual Harassment Decisions" by Anna-Maria Marshall of Northwestern University; and "Litigating for Gay Rights: Strategy and Tactics" Robin M. Wolpert of Georgetown University.

Constitutional Law and Jurisprudence

Allied to the Law and Courts program division is the division on Constitutional Law and Jurisprudence. Constitutional law is directed, of course, to the fundamental laws that define our political duties and freedoms. Jurisprudence is the study of the philosophy of law. Professor David O'Brien of the University of Virginia is a leading constitutional scholar, among whose best known works is *Storm Center: The Supreme Court in American Politics* (4th ed., 1996). O'Brien notes that among general areas currently of interest to scholars in this field are freedom of speech and feminist legal theory. Most recently, scholars are developing new investigations into comparative constitutional law and judicial politics and state constitutional law. Among leading works in this field is Henry Abraham's *Freedom and the Court* (6th ed., 1994) and Gerald Rosenberg's *The Hollow Hope* (1991).

Recent APSA panels in this field include The Practice of Constitutional Rights, Constitutional Politics and Sexual Identity, and The Crisis of Labor and the State. Papers presented include "Abortion Rhetoric" by Eileen McDonagh of Northeastern University; "Citizen Review of the Constitution: The First Amendment and Prayer at High School Graduations" by Phyllis Farley Rippey of Western Illinois University; and "'Dred Scott' and the Problem of Constitutional Evil" by Mark A. Graber of the University of Maryland.

Part 4.   Comparative Politics and Area Studies

Comparative Politics

Because this text has already provided an introduction to comparative politics in Chapters 5 and 11, relatively little will be said about this field in this chapter. This is not to underestimate the field's importance, however. Recent developments in this field include new investigations into the effects of military technology and trade on political systems, corporatism, and ethnic diversity within nations.

Panels presented in this program section include: Rational Choice in Comparative Contexts, The 1993 Political Change in Japan and Its Consequences, and The Political Mobilization of Culture and Its Containment. Papers presented include: "Consequences of the Adoption of NAFTA for Mexican Politics" by Charles L. Davis of the University of Kentucky, "The Kurdish Political Movements: A Critical Analysis" by Abbas Manafy of New Mexico Highlands University, and "Political Equilibrium and Policy Stasis in Thailand" by Danny Unger of Georgetown University.

Comparative Politics of Developing Countries

The political patterns of developing nations have proven a challenging laboratory for the application of many methodologies, some of which were explored in Chapter 6. The work going on in this section is wide ranging, and promises interesting applications for American politics as well. Panels presented in this program section include: The State and Reform in African Politics, The Authoritarian Holdouts: Middle East and Asia, and Consolidating Democracy in Low Income Countries. Papers presented include: "Learning, Jail, and Exile in Uruguay" by Astrid Arraras of Princeton University; "The Social Bases of State Decay and Post Patrimonial Politics in Africa" by William Reno of Florida International University; and "The Colonial Antecedents of the Welfare State in the Arab World" by Lisa Anderson of Columbia University.

Communist Politics and After

In the previous chapter, we noted the activities of political scientists in Eastern Europe as they struggle to understand the political problems involved in the transition from communist to capitalist regimes. In this program division, American scholars join the efforts of their European colleagues. Panels presented in this program section include: The Political Economy of Reforming Communism, The International Politics of Interdependence in the Former Soviet Union, and Media's Role in East European Democratization. Papers presented include: "Water Resource Allocation in Central Asia: Institutions and Externalities" by Erika Weinthal of Columbia University, "Is Pandora's Box Half Empty or Half Full? A Critical Evaluation of the Ethnic Domino Theory" by Stephen Saideman of the University of Vermont, and "National Role Conception in Belarussian Nuclear Weapons Policy" by Suzette R. Grillot of the University of Georgia.

Comparative Politics of Advanced Industrial States

A counterpart to the study of developing nations, which we just discussed, is the study of advanced industrial nations. Many of the methods used in this section have been discussed previously. Panels presented in this program section include: Comparative Analyses of Bureaucratic Control, Right Wing Populism in Comparative Perspective, and Social Democracy in a Conservative Age. Papers presented include: "Republicanism and the Extreme Right in Italy and France" by Catherine Fieschi of McGill University, "When Waves Collide: The Meeting of the New and Old Women's Movements in Switzerland" by Lee Ann Banaszak of the Pennsylvania State University, and "The Political Asylum Debates in Germany: Extreme Politics in a Moderate Party System" by Ted Permutter of New York University.

Politics and Society in Western Europe

The rich variety of materials that are available for the study of Western Europe are, as we have already seen, producing some interesting insights about politics. As cooperative efforts with Western European political scientists continue, much more progress is expected. Panels presented in this program section include: Rethinking Perspectives on the European Union, Changing Concepts of Citizenship, and Switzerland: From Homeland to Outlier of Liberalism. Papers presented include: "Public Support for European Integration: A Longitudinal Analysis" by Andreas Sobish of John Carroll University, and David Patterson of Southern Methodist University; "The End of Social Democracy as We Knew It" by Jens Borchert of the University of Goettingen; and "Subnational Transborder Cooperation in Western Europe: Debordering the State" by Mathias Albert and Lothar Brock, both of JW Goethe-Universitat.

Part 5.   International Relations

Several program divisions of the APSA, as well as much of the program of the International Studies Association, are devoted to the study of international relations. Because the study of international relations has also been explored in Chapter 13, it will be given relatively little attention here. This does not imply, however, that the field is not vitally significant, and that many fascinating developments are not currently taking place.

Conflict Processes

The nature of conflict and how to handle or contain it have long been central themes is in the study of international relations. Professor Michael Ward of the University of Colorado, who has organized activities of the Conflict Processes Section of the APSA, notes that among the central issues of this section are the problems of ethnonational conflict and the relationship between democracy and peace. He notes further that among the broad range of methodologies currently used are both deductive and empirical approaches. Game theory is often used in conflict analysis, and statistical methods such as regression are popular. Ward expects that in the future even more game theory analyses will be combined with detailed empirical studies and that more interdisciplinary work will be done with geographers and economists.

APSA Panels presented in this program section include: Democracy and War, War Termination and the Impact of War, and The International Diffusion of Ethnic Conflict. Papers presented include: "Democratic War" by Alex Mintz of Texas A&M University, "Theory and Practice in Ethnic Conflict Management: Conceptualizing and Measuring Objectives Over Time" by Marc Howard Ross of Bryn Mawr College, and "The Organization of African Unity and African Conflicts: The Effectiveness of Conflict Management" by Mi Yung Yoon of Hanover College.

International Collaboration

On the other side of the coin of conflict studies are the investigations into international collaboration, which concerns ways in which nations can cooperate to solve problems and create new opportunities. Panels presented in this program section include: Formal Theories of International Cooperation, Law and Rule Making in the European Union, and Regional Environmental Cooperation. Papers presented include: "Coping as a Strategy" by Edward A Kolodziej of the University of Illinois, "Causes and Counterfactuals in Social Science" by James Fearon of the University of Chicago, and "The Fallacy of the International Food-Aid Regime" by Polly J. Diven of Grand Valley State University.

International Security

David Mares of the University of California at San Diego, who has organized activities of the International Security and Conflict Section, notes that among the issues of current interest to scholars in this field are the relationship between democracy and international conflict, ethnic conflict, the proliferation of weapons of mass destruction, and the nature of international security after the cold war. Mares notes that among the better known works in this field are Kenneth Waltz's *Theory of International Politics* (1979), Thomas Schelling's *The Strategy of Conflict* (1960), and Bruce Russett's *Grasping the Democratic Peace* (1993).

Panels presented in this program section include: Testing the Democratic Peace, Coping With Conflict, and Rethinking Realism in a Post-Cold War World. Papers presented include: "Identity and Insecurity in a Small State" by Mark Laffey of the University of Minnesota, "The Cultural Construction of Crisis: A Feminist Reading of Missiles in Cuba" by Jutta Weldes of Kent State University, and "Colonizing Cyberspace: National Security and the Internet" by Diana Saco of the University of Minnesota.

International Security and Arms Control

Professor Joyce Kaufman of the Immaculate Heart College Center, who has organized APSA programs in this section, notes that within this section,

> The primary topic pertains to security in the post-Cold War world. The discussion includes rethinking the concept of security, and the idea of "threat," since these notions have both changed dramatically. The section has also been focusing a great deal on regional and ethnic conflicts, as the primary threat to global peace and security in the post-Cold War world.

Panels presented in this program section include: Sources of Civilian Control, Weapons Proliferation, and How Terrorism Ends. Papers presented include: "A Structural Theory of Civil-Military Relations" by Michael Desch of Harvard University, "Agency and Organizations: The Politics of Military Bias" by Deborah Avant of the State University of New York at Albany, and "How Terrorism Ends: A Historical Trajectory, 1947 to the Present" by Bruce Hoffman of St. Andrews University.

Foreign Policy Analysis

Deborah J. Gerner (1991, 125) has summarized recent developments in the study of foreign policy generally. According to Gerner, the field lacks an accepted methodology, but there is a common core of concerns on which scholars focus their studies:

> The central focus of foreign policy is on the intentions, statements, and actions of an actor—generally a state—that are directed toward the external world and the responses to these intentions, statements, and actions, but unpacking what this focus actually means is a complex task. Foreign policy can be *descriptive,* attempting to establish the actual facts regarding foreign policy decisions made, policies declared publicly by actors, and the relationships among state and non-state international actors. Alternatively, foreign policy *analysis* can attempt to answer the question: Why do states take the actions they do? Such research may focus on the *inputs* that affect the foreign policy process: external, societal, governmental, role and individual factors; or it can examine the *process* by which foreign policy is formulated through theories of decision-making. Finally, foreign policy *evaluation* considers the consequences of foreign policy actions.

Panels presented in this program section include: Eagle Come Home: The Domestic Face of U.S. Foreign Policy, Roundtable on the Vietnam War: 40 Years Later, and Human Rights and Foreign Policy. Papers presented include: "Clinton's Chinese Puzzle: Domestic Politics and Economic Sanctions to Promote Human Rights" by T. Clifton Morgan of Rice University; "Is Anyone Listening? Does Anyone Understand? International Relations Theory and The Problem of Policy Relevance" by Joseph Lepgold of Georgetown University; and "French Jacobinism" The Challenge of American Multiculturalism" by Martin Schain of New York University.

Domestic Sources of Foreign Policy

The Domestic Sources of Foreign Policy program division examines in particular the relationship between domestic politics, such as the state of the economy or the rise of extremist movements, on decisions that are made in foreign policy. Panels presented in this program section include: Public Opinion and Domestic Pressures in U.S. Foreign Policy Making; Assessing Public Opinion on Foreign Policy, 1974–1994; and Public Opinion, Political Polling, and the 1994 Election.

Part 6. The Discipline of Political Science and Its Applications

Applied Political Science

Nolan Jones, of the National Governors Association, who has been an active participant in the Applied Political Science Section of the APSA, notes that among the important concerns currently being addressed in this section are the following questions:

- How can political science affect the public policy debate on social issues?
- How does the role of a political scientist differ from that of a public administrator?
- What does the political scientist offer that is different from the public administrator?

It is interesting to note, as mentioned in Chapter 14, that these questions are of great interest to European political scientists because in some countires in Europe political scientists have a greater role in determining public policy than political scientists do in the United States. Christensen's "The Political Scientist as a Management Consultant," according to Jones, has been widely read and discussed.

Panels presented in this program section include: The Policy Relevance of Contemporary Theories of International Relations and Foreign Policy and Budget Policy and Politics 1995: The GOP Takes Charge. Papers presented include: "Establishing Orthodoxy: Electoral Effects on Budget Reform" by James Saturno of the Congressional Research Service and "Institutional and Representational Alternatives to the Balanced Budget-Constitutional Amendment" by Roy Meyers of the University of Maryland, Baltimore County.

Politics and the Life Sciences

Professor John M. Strate of Wayne State University, who has organized APSA programs for the Politics and the Life Sciences program division, notes that "a host of issues in biomedicine and biotechnology (prenatal diagnosis, fetal tissue transplants, the human genome project, surrogate parenting, genetic engineering, neonatal care, euthanasia, agricultural biotechnology, etc.)" are becoming increasingly interesting because of their political and ethical implications. The nature of the dilemmas presented by new biological research are so profound that they involve discussing, as Strate notes, the "fundamental questions about human nature and politics, including issues of political evolution, structure, leadership, nationalism, race, and gender."

Panels presented in this program section include: Public Policy at the End of Life, Rationing Medicine in the American System, and Biotechnology and Reproductive Rights. Papers presented include: "Fetal Egg Use in Assisted Reproduction: Ethical and Policy Issues" by Andrea Bonnicksen of Northern Illinois University and "Health Care Rationing: From an Aging Perspective" by Janie Steckenrider of Loyola Marymount University.

Science, Technology, Environment, and Politics

Another physical sciences-focused program division, which has an even broader scope in science issues, is entitled Science, Technology, Environment, and Politics. Professor Richard Worthington of Pomona College, who has organized activities in this section, notes that even though the section has been developed only in the last decade, new scholars are increasingly becoming interested, indicating that the subfield has a bright future. Worthington notes further that some of the topics currently being studied include "citizen participation in technology decisions, ideologies of sustainable development, and the politics of risk-benefit analysis."

Panels presented in this program section include: Democratic Theory and Ecological Practice; The Political Economy of Nature and Natural Resources: National-International Linkages; and Challenges to Governance from Scientific, Technical, and Environmental Change. Papers presented include: "Individual Protest, Community Mobilization, and the NIMBY Syndrome" by Heather Elliot of Yale University; "Commoditization of Nature: Conservation, Preservation, and International Regimes" by Ronald J. Herring of Cornell University; and "The Political Economy of Logging in Southeast Asia: Clientelism, Contracts, and Reform" by Michael Ross of Princeton University.

Computers and Multimedia

Because technology is increasingly affecting all aspects of political science, including, teaching, research, and publishing, a program division has been established within which to discuss the ongoing flow of developments in communications technology and what they mean to political scientists. Panels presented in this program section include Technologies Galore for the Political Science Classroom, Issues Involved in Cruising the Infobahn, and Electronic Publishing Outlook. Papers presented include "Using 'Capitol Hill' CD ROM to Teach Undergraduate Political Science Courses" by Cynthia Opheim and Willard Stouffer, both of Southwest Texas State University; "International Interdependencies, Global Realities, and the 28800 Modem" by Charles Mitchell of Graphic Arts; and "An On-Line Electronic Publishing System for Political Science" by William Ball of Trenton State College.

Politics and History

Yale University's Professor Stephen Skowronek, President of the Politics and History Section of the APSA, notes that rapid growth in recent years has made this section one of the association's largest. Skowronek points out an ironic trend, that history has become more interesting to political scientists as historians have become

MIXED MEDIA

Reprinted by permission: Tribune Media Services.

less interested in politics. As this text has discussed previously, the roots of political science in history are strong, and today it seems that they are not only alive but growing with renewed vitality. According to Skowronek, among the issues of greatest current interest related to scholars exploring history and politics are

- Comparative state-building,
- The development of the welfare state,
- History of social movements,
- Race and gender issues as they have affected American political development,
- The formation of political identities,
- Roads not taken or alternative pathways of development,
- Transitions to democracy,
- The end of liberalism, and
- Constitutional development.

Panels presented in this program section include: Race Politics: The Long View, Roundtable on Eldon Eisenbach's *The Lost Promise of Progressivism,* and Imagining Politics in History. Papers presented include: "Defining the Feminist Citizen: The Interwar Debate" by Candace Bredbenner of Arizona State University, "Party Out of Power: Democratic Strategies After 1896" by Kenneth Finegold of Eastern Washington University, and "Liberalism and Neo-Liberalism: How Many French Revolutions?" by Andrew Gould of the University of Notre Dame.

Politics and Literature

In recent years political scientists have been exploring the creative opportunities available in related disciplines that have always had insights about politics to share. Literature is full of political situations, as anyone who has read Shakespeare or Jonathan Swift or who has seen the films *Mr. Smith Goes to Washington, Advise and Consent, The Candidate,* or *Power* knows.

Professor Catherine Zuckert of Carleton College is one of the original organizers of this new section. She notes that examples of works reflecting interest in the study of literature and politics are Irving Howe's *Politics and the Novel,* Harry Jaffa and Allan Blooms' *Shakespeare's Politics* (1964), and Wilson Carey McWilliams' *The Idea of Fraternity in America* (1973). In the June 1995 edition of *PS: Political Science and Politics* (189), Zuckert provides a summary of the development of the section:

> The emergence of an Organized Section devoted to the study of politics and literature is indicative of the evolution of the discipline during the last generation. In the 1960s, political science was in the midst of the behavioral revolution. In an effort to make the study of politics *scientific,* researchers sought quantifiable data and did studies that could be replicated. Unfortunately for the behavioralists, the major political events of that decade, including the civil rights movement and the war in Vietnam, could not be studied solely in quantitative or pos-

itivistic terms. . . . The questions that led political scientists to look to works of art for enlightenment concern the aspects of human life that are most difficult, if not impossible, to study and observe externally or objectively—the attitudes, emotions, and opinions that shape and are shaped by people's circumstances, especially their political circumstances. . . . Chief among the issues that escape the positivist paradigm and attract political scientists to the study of literature have been the moral dimensions of politics.

Panels presented in this program section include: The Politics of Machiavellian Comedy, Greek Light and Modern Shadows, and Identifying Good and Evil. Papers presented include: "The Politics of Evil in Popular Culture" by John S. Nelson of the University of Iowa, "Aristophanes' Acharnians: The Justice of A Separate Peace" by Stephanie Nelson of the University of Chicago, and "Odysseus and the Problem of Individualism" by Richard Ruderman of the University of North Texas.

Teaching and Learning in Political Science

The primary duty of most political scientists is teaching. This program division recognizes the role of teaching in the profession and helps members explore ways to improve the teaching of political science. Panels presented in this program section include: Teaching Democracy Through Community Involvement and Team Teaching and Assessment in Political Science. Papers presented include: "Shall We Dance?: Applying the Theory of Multiple Intelligences to American Government Courses" by David G. Lawrence of Westmont College; and "Team Teaching a Senior Seminar Course with a Person with Disabilities" by Fred Smoller and Arthur Blaser, both of Chapman University.

Internships and Experiential Education

According to John C. Berg of Suffolk University, the first chair of the section on Internships and Experiential Education, the section

was recognized in 1993, following a long campaign by a group of political scientists who were involved in internships and who had met each other through the National Society for Experiential Education. The section sought both "to stimulate the use of all experiential teaching techniques," not only internships but simulations, field work, etc., and also to "maintain academic quality in experiential programs." It organized such panels as Learning by Doing: Mock Trials and Learning by Doing: Internships and Service.

The section experienced a crisis one year after its founding when the APSA increased the minimum membership cutoff from 100 and 250. After considerable discussion, in 1995 it changed its name (and its focus) to "Organized Section on Undergraduate Education." It intends to continue to promote experiential techniques, but to look as well at the improvement of all other methods of teaching. The section hopes to become a home for the considerable number of political scientists who have a strong commitment to teaching, a group that has not always been well represented in the annual meeting of the APSA.

Program Committee Panels

In addition to the regular program division panels, the APSA program committee establishes special panels. At the 1995 meeting, one of these panels entitled, "Looking Back on Theodore Lowi's *The End of Liberalism*," examined some of the important contributions of Cornell University political scientist and former President of the APSA, Theodore Lowi. Another panel entitled "Foundations and the Study of American Politics" explored some of the fundamental concepts of the discipline.

A Concluding Comment: Creativity

To end this book we return to our starting point. Of the many expressions of human creativity, science is one of the most interesting and fruitful, and of the sciences, political science is one of the most meaningful. Science proceeds, as Einstein liked to say, by both inspiration and perspiration, and more by the latter than by the former. If this book has been successful, you, the reader, are eager and ready to launch or continue your own efforts to understand politics, for your own personal satisfaction, or through pursuing your interests as a professional. May your efforts be rewarded with enjoyment, satisfaction, and success!

Bibliography

Adams, Abigail. 1992. "Letter to Her Husband John Adams, 31 March 1776." In *Feminism: The Essential Historical Writings*. Ed. Miriam Schneir. New York: Vintage Books.

Adams, John. 1851. "Thoughts on Government." In *The Works of John Adams*. Ed. Charles Francis Adams. Vol. 14. Boston: Little, Brown.

Adorno, T.W. et al. 1982. *The Authoritarian Personality*. New York: W.W. Norton.

Alighieri, Dante. 1958. *Monarchy and Three Political Letters*. Trans. Donald Nicholl. New York: Noonday Press.

Allison, Graham. 1971. *Essence of Decision Explaining the Cuban Missile Crisis*. Boston: Little, Brown.

Almond, Gabriel, and G. Bingham Powell. 1966. *Comparative Politics: A Developmental Approach*. Boston: Little, Brown.

Almond, Gabriel. 1990. *A Discipline Divided, Schools and Sects in Political Science*. Newbury Park, Calif.: Sage Publications.

Arendt, Hannah. 1958. *The Origins of Totalitarianism*. New York: Meridian Books.

Aristophanes. 1969. *The Acharnians*. Trans. Douglas Parker. Ann Arbor: University of Michigan Press.

Aristotle. 1958. *The Politics of Aristotle*. Trans. Ernest Barker. New York: Oxford University Press.

Aronoff, Myron. 1993. "The Origins of Israeli Political Culture." In *Israeli Democracy Under Stress*. Ed. Ehud Sprinzak and Larry Diamond. Boulder, Colo.: Lynne Rienner Publishers.

Azar, Beth. 1995. "Breaking Through Barriers to Creativity." *APA Monitor* 26 (8): 1.

Baoxu, Zhao. 1984. "The Revival of Political Science in China." Trans. David Chu. *PS: Political Science and Politics* (fall): 744–757.

Barber, James David. 1972. *The Presidential Character: Predicting Performance in the White House*. Englewood Cliffs, N.J.: Prentice Hall.

Bartels, Larry M., and Henry E. Brady. 1993. "The State of Quantitative Political Methodology." In *Political Science: The State of the Discipline II*. Ed. Ada W. Finifter. Washington, D. C.: American Political Science Association.

Bary, William Theodore de, Wing-tsit Chan, and Burton Wilson, comps. 1966. *Sources of Chinese Tradition*. New York: Columbia University Press.

Bell, Daniel. 1968. "The End of Ideology in the West." In *The End of Ideology Debate*. Ed. Chaim I Waxman. New York: Funk & Wagnalls.

Beyme, Klaus von. 1982. "Federal Republic of Germany." In *International Handbook of Political Science*. Ed. William G. Andrews. Westport, Conn.: Greenwood Press.

Beyme, Klaus von. 1994. "German Political Science: The State of the Art." *European Journal of Political Science* 20: 263–278.

Brown, Archie. 1986. "Political Science in the USSR." *International Political Science Review* 7: 443–481.

Buchanan, James. 1972a. "Toward Analysis of Closed Behavioral Systems." In *Theory of Public Choice.* Ed. James M. Buchanan and Robert D. Tollison. Ann Arbor: University of Michigan Press.

Buchanan, James. 1972b. "The Inconsistencies of the National Health Service." In *Theory of Public Choice.* Ed. James M. Buchanan and Robert D. Tollison. Ann Arbor: University of Michigan Press.

Burke, Edmund. 1961. "Reflections on the Revolution in France." In *Reflections on the Revolution in France and The Rights of Man.* Garden City, New York: Dolphin Books.

Burke, Edmund. 1992. "On Election to Parliament." In *The Democracy Reader.* Ed. Diane Ravitch and Abigail Thernstrom. New York: Harper Collins.

Carson, Rachel. 1962. *Silent Spring.* Boston: Houghton Mifflin.

Chan, Nyein. 1992. "The Dream of a People." In *The Democracy Reader.* Ed. Diane Ravitch and Abigail Thernstrom. New York: Harper Collins.

Chilcote, Ronald H. 1994. *Theories of Comparative Politics: The Search for A Paradigm Reconsidered.* Boulder, Colo.: Westview Press.

Churchill, Winston. 1992. "Speech at Fulton, Missouri." In *The Democracy Reader.* Ed. Diane Ravitch and Abigail Thernstrom. New York: Harper Collins.

Clausewitz, Karl von. 1962. *War, Politics, and Power.* Trans. Edward M. Collins. Chicago: Regnery Gateway.

Cone, James H. 1969. *Black Theology and Black Power.* New York: Seabury.

Coole, Diana. 1990. "Feminism and Politics." In *New Developments in Political Science: An International Review of Achievements and Prospects.* Ed. Adrian Leftwich. Brookfield, Ver.: Edward Elgar Publishing.

Coughlin, Ellen K. 1994. "How Rational is Rational Choice?" *The Chronicle of Higher Education,* 7 December, A9.

Crick, Bernard. 1960. *The American Science of Politics: Its Origins and Conditions.* Berkeley: University of California Press.

Crick, Bernard. 1992. *In Defense of Politics.* 4th ed. Chicago: University of Chicago Press.

Crotty, William, Ed. 1991. *Political Science: Looking to the Future.* Vol. 4. *American Institutions.* Evanston, Ill.: Northwestern University Press.

Cumings, Bruce. 1990. *The Two Koreas: On the Road to Reunification?* New York: Foreign Policy Association.

Dacey, John S. 1989. *Fundamentals of Creative Thinking.* Lexington, Mass.: Lexington Books.

Dahl, Robert A. 1961. "The Behavioral Approach in Political Science: Epitaph for a Monument to a Successful Protest." *American Political Science Review* 55: 763–72.

Dahl, Robert A. 1991. *Modern Political Analysis.* 5th ed. Englewood Cliffs, N.J.: Prentice Hall.

Dahl, Robert. 1995. "Participation and the Problem of Civic Understanding." In *Rights and the Common Good: The Communitarian Perspective.* Ed. Amitai Etzioni. New York: St. Martin's Press.

Dalton, Russell J., and Martin P. Wattenburg. 1993. "The Not So Simple Act of Voting." In *Political Science: The State of the Discipline II*. Ed. Ada W. Finifter. Washington, D.C.: American Political Science Association.

Davidson, Roger H. 1991. "Legislative Research: Mirror of A Discipline." In *Political Science Looking to the Future*. Ed. William Crotty. Vol. 4. *American Institutions*. Evanston, Ill.: Northwestern University Press.

Debs, Eugene V. 1989. "Revolutionary Unionism." In *American Political Thought*. 2nd ed. Ed. Kenneth M. Dolbeare. Chatham, N.J.: Chatham House.

Deutsch, Karl. 1963. *The Nerves of Government: Models of Human Communication and Control*. New York: Free Press.

Dreyfus, Francois G. 1982. "Political Science in France." *Government and Opposition* 17: 429–443.

Drucker, H. M. 1974. *The Political Uses of Ideology*. New York: Barnes & Noble.

Easton, David. 1966. "Categories for the Systems Analysis of Politics." In *Varieties of Political Theory*. Ed. David Easton. Englewood Cliffs, N.J.: Prentice Hall.

Easton, David. 1993. "Political Science in the United States: Past and Present." In *Discipline and History: Political Science in the United States: Part 4*. Ed. James Farr and Raymond Seidelman. Ann Arbor: University of Michigan Press.

Easton, David, John G. Gunnell, and Luigi Graziano, Eds. 1991. *The Development of Political Science: A Comparative Survey*. London and New York: Routledge.

Easton, David. 1991. *Political Science in the United States Past and Present*. London and New York: Routledge.

Elazar, Daniel J. 1986. *Israel: Building a New Society*. Bloomington: Indiana University Press.

Eliade, Mircea. 1971. *Myth of the Eternal Return or Cosmos and History*. Princeton: Princeton University Press.

Ellis, Richard J. 1992. "Rival Visions of Equality in American Political Culture." *The Review of Politics* 54: 253–280.

Erikson, Erik H. 1982. *The Life Cycle Completed: A Review*. New York: W.W. Norton.

Estes, Clarissa Pinkola. 1992. *Women Who Run with the Wolves: Myths and Stories of the Wild Woman Archetype*. New York: Ballantine Books.

Etzioni, Amitai. 1995. *Rights and the Common Good: The Communitarian Perspective*. New York: St. Martin's Press.

Farr, James, and Raymond Seidelman. 1993. "Introduction." In *Discipline and History: Political Science in the United States: Part II*. Ed. James Farr and Raymond Seidelman. Ann Arbor: University of Michigan Press.

Favre, Pierre. 1982. "France." In *International Handbook of Political Science*. Ed. William G. Andrews. Westport, Conn.: Greenwood Press.

Feuer, Lewis S. 1975. *Ideology and the Ideologists*. New York: Harper & Row.

Flathman, Richard. 1987. *The Philosophy and Politics of Freedom*. Chicago: University of Chicago Press.

Freeman, Donald M. 1991. "The Making of a Discipline." In *Political Science: Looking to the Future*. Ed. William Crotty. Vol. 1. *The Theory and Practice of Political Science*. Evanston, Ill.: Northwestern University Press.

Friedan, Betty. 1963. *The Feminine Mystique*. New York: Dell Books.

Friedan, Betty. 1966. "The National Organization for Women Organizing Statement." In *It Changed My Life*. New York: Random House.

Fromm, Erich. 1960. *Escape from Freedom*. New York: Holt, Rinehart, and Winston.

Fu, Zhengyuan. 1991. "The Sociology of Political Science in the People's Republic of China." In *The Development of Political Science: A Comparative Survey*. Ed. David Easton, John G. Gunnell, and Luigi Graziano. New York: Routledge.

Fulghum, Robert. 1988. *All I Really Need to Know I Learned in Kindergarten: Uncommon Thoughts on Common Things*. New York: Ivy Books.

Galston, William. 1993. "Political Theory in the 1980s: Perplexity Amidst Diversity." In *Political Science: The State of the Discipline II*. Ed. Ada W. Finifter. Washington, D.C.: American Political Science Association.

George, John, and Laird Wilcox. 1992. *Nazis, Communists, Klansmen, and Others on the Fringe: Political Extremism in America*. Buffalo, N.Y.: Prometheus Books.

Gerner, Deborah J. 1991. "Foreign Policy Analysis: Renaissance, Routine, or Rubbish?" In *Political Science: Looking to the Future*. Ed. William Crotty. Vol. 2, *Comparative Politics, Policy, and International Relations*. Evanston, Ill.: Northwestern University Press.

Gilder, George. 1981. *Wealth and Poverty*. New York: Basic Books.

Goldman, Emma. 1907. "Anarchism: What It Really Stands For." In *American Political Thought*. 3rd ed. Ed. Kenneth M. Dolbeare. Chatham, New Jersey: Chatham House, 1996, 392–401.

Goodspeed, Edgar J., Trans. 1950. "The Martrydom of Polycarp." In *The Apostolic Fathers: An American Translation*. New York: Harper & Brothers.

Graziano, Luigi. 1987. "The Development and Institutionalization of Political Science in Italy." *International Political Science Review* 8: 41–57.

Great Commission Prayer League. n.d. *The Fundamentals of the Faith as Expressed in the Articles of Belief of the Niagara Bible Conference*. Chicago: Great Commission Prayer League.

Green, Donald P., and Ian Shapiro. 1994. *Pathologies of Rational Choice Theory, A Critique of Applications in Political Science*. New Haven: Yale University Press.

Grotius, Hugo. 1715. *Of the Rights of War and Peace*. London: D. Brown, T. Ward, and W. Meares.

Haddow, Anna. 1969. "Early American Political Science." In *Political Science in American Colleges and Universities 1636–1900*. Ed. William Anderson. New York: Octagon Books.

Hahm, Pyong-Choon. 1967. *The Korean Political Tradition and Law*. Seoul: Hollym Corporation.

Hayward, Jack. 1991. "Political Science in Britain." *European Journal of Political Research* 20: 301–322.

Hayward, Jack. 1982. "United Kingdom." In *International Handbook of Political Science*. Ed. William G. Andrews. Westport, Conn.: Greenwood Press.

Hilberg, Raul. 1985. *The Destruction of the European Jews*. New York: Holmes and Meier.

Hitler, Adolf. 1939. *Mein Kampf*. Ed. John Chamberlain, et al. New York: Reynal & Hitchcock.

Holloway, Harry, and John George. 1979. *Public Opinion: Coalitions, Elites and Masses*. New York: St. Martin's.

Holub, Robert. 1991. *Jurgen Habermas: Critic in the Public Sphere*. London: Routledge.

Hood, Christopher. 1990. "Public Administration: Lost an Empire, Not Yet Found a Role?" In *New Developments in Political Science: An International Review of Achievements and Prospects.* Ed. Adrian Leftwich. Brookfield, Ver.: Edward Elgar Publishing.

Hoover, Kenneth R. 1994. *Ideology and Political Life.* Belmont, Calif.: Wadsworth Publishing.

Horton, John. 1990. "Weight or Lightness? Political Philosophy and its Prospects." In *New Developments in Political Science: An International Review of Achievements and Prospects.* Ed. Adrian Leftwich. Brookfield, Ver.: Edward Elgar Publishing.

Hunter, James Davidson. 1991. *Culture Wars.* New York: Basic Books.

Huntington, Samuel P. 1991. *The Third Wave: Democratization In the Late Twentieth Century.* Norman: University of Oklahoma Press.

Jefferson, Thomas. 1944. "Letter to James Madison." In *The Life and Selected Writings of Thomas Jefferson.* Ed. Adrienne Koch and William Pedden. New York: Modern Library.

Jessup, Bob. 1990. "Putting States In Their Place: State Systems and State Theory." In *New Developments in Political Science: An International Review of Achievements and Prospects.* Ed. Adrian Leftwich. Brookfield, Ver.: Edward Elgar Publishing.

Kahn, Kim Fridkin. 1994. "Does Gender Make a Difference? An Experimental Examination of Sex Stereotypes and Press Patterns in Statewide Campaigns." *American Journal Of Political Science* 38: 162–195.

Kastendiek, Hans. 1987. "Political Development and Political Science in West Germany." *International Political Science Review* 8 (1): 25–40.

Kepel, Giles. 1994. *The Revenge of God: The Resurgence of Islam, Christianity, and Judaism in the Modern World.* Trans. Alan Braley. University Park, Penn.: Pennsylvania State University Press.

Kettl, Donald. 1993. "Public Administration: The State of the Field." In *Political Science: The State of the Discipline II.* Ed. Ada W. Finifter. Washington, D.C.: American Political Science Association.

Kristol, Irving. 1978. *Two Cheers for Capitalism.* New York: Basic Books.

Kristol, Irving. 1979. "Confessions of a True, Self Confessed—Perhaps the Only— 'Neoconservative.' " *Public Opinion* October/November 1979.

Lalman, David, Joe Oppenheimer, and Piotr Swistak. 1993. "Formal Rational Choice Theory: A Cumulative Science of Politics." In *Political Science: The State of the Discipline II.* Ed. Ada W. Finifter. Washington, D.C.: American Political Science Association.

Lane, Jan-Erik, and Svante Ersson. 1990. "Comparative Politics: From Political Sociology to Comparative Public Policy." In *New Developments in Political Science: An International Review of Achievements and Prospects.* Ed. Adrian Leftwich. Brookfield, Ver.: Edward Elgar Publishing.

League of Nations. 1993. "The Covenant of the League of Nations." In *The League of Nations.* Ed. Ruth B. Henig. New York: Barnes and Noble.

Leca, J. 1991. "Some Problems and Difficulties in the Social Organization of the Discipline." *European Journal of Political Science* 20:323–340.

Lenin, V. I. 1990. *Imperialism, The Highest Stage of Capitalism: A Popular Outline.* New York: International Publishers.

Lerner, Daniel, and Harold Lasswell, Eds. 1951. *The Policy Sciences*. Stanford: Stanford University Press.

Lieber, Francis. 1881. "An Inaugural Address Delivered on the 17th of February, 1858, on Assuming the Chair of History and Political Science, in Columbia College, New York." In *Miscellaneous Writings*. Vol.1. Philadelphia: J.B. Lippincott.

Lincoln, Abraham. 1990. "On Slavery." In *Lincoln on Democracy*. Ed. Mario Cuomo and Harold Holzer. New York: Harper Collins.

Lindblom, Charles E. 1995. "The 'Science' of Muddling Through." In *Public Policy, The Essential Readings*. Ed. Stella Z. Theodoulou and Matthew A. Cahn. Englewood Cliffs, New Jersey: Prentice Hall.

Lippincott, Benjamin E. 1993. "The Bias of American Political Science." In *Discipline and History: Political Science in the United States*. Ed. James Farr and Raymond Seidelman. Ann Arbor: University of Michigan Press.

Lippman, Walter. 1947. *The Good Society*. Boston: Little, Brown.

Lovelock, J. E. 1979. *Gaia: A New Look at Life on Earth*. Oxford: Oxford University Press.

Lowi, Theodore J. 1993. *The State in Political Science: How We Become What We Study*. Ann Arbor: University of Michigan Press.

Machiavelli, Niccolo. 1979. *The Prince*. In *The Portable Machiavelli*. Trans. Peter Bondanella and Mark Musa. New York: Viking Press.

MacManus, Susan A. 1991. "Federalism and Intergovernmental Relations: The Centralization versus Decentralization Debate Continues." In *Political Science: Looking to the Future*. Ed. William Crotty. Vol. 4. *American Institutions*. Evanston, Ill.: Northwestern University Press.

Macridis, Roy C. 1955. *The Study of Comparative Politics*. New York: Random House.

Marx, Karl, and Friedrich Engels. 1959. "The Communist Manifesto." In *Marx & Engels, Basic Writings on Politics & Philosophy*. Ed. Lewis S. Feuer. New York: Anchor Books.

Marx, Karl. 1959. "The German Ideology." In *Marx & Engels, Basic Writings on Politics & Philosophy*. Ed. Lewis S. Feuer. New York: Anchor Books.

May, Rollo. 1975. *The Courage to Create*. New York: Norton.

Mehta, V. R. 1987. "Political Science in India: In Search of an Identity." *Government and Opposition* 22: 270–81.

Merriam, Charles E. 1993. "Recent Advances in Political Methods." In *Discipline and History: Political Science in the United States: Part 2*. Ed. James Farr and Raymond Seidelman. Ann Arbor: University of Michigan Press.

Mezey, Michael L. 1993. "Legislatures: Individual Purpose and Institutional Performance." In *Political Science: The State of the Discipline II*. Ed. Ada W. Finifter. Washington, D.C.: American Political Science Association.

Michaels, Robert. 1915. *Political Parties: A Sociological Study of the Oligarchical Tendencies of Modern Democracy*. Trans. Eden and Cedar Paul. New York: Free Press of Glencoe.

Mill, John Stuart. 1951. "On Liberty." In *Utilitarianism, Liberty, and Representative Government*. New York: E.P. Dutton.

Mladenka, Kenneth R., and Bryan D. Jones. 1991. "Urban Politics and Political Science." In *Political Science: Looking to the Future*. Ed. William Crotty. Vol. 4. *American Institutions*. Evanston, Illinois: Northwestern University Press.

Morlino, Leonardo. 1991. "Political Science in Italy: Tradition and Empiricism." *European Journal of Political Research* 20: 341–358.

Narain, and P. C. Mathur. 1982. "India." In *International Handbook of Political Science*. Ed. William G. Andrews. Wesport, Conn.: Greenwood Press.

National Conference of Catholic Bishops. 1986. *Economic Justice for All: Pastoral Letter on Catholic Social Teaching and the U.S. Economy*. Washington, D.C.:United States Catholic Conference.

Nelsen, Brent F. 1995. *Christians in Political Science Newsletter* 4 (2): 1.

Newton, Kenneth, and Josep M. Valles. 1991. "Introduction: Political Science in Western Europe, 1960–1990." *European Journal of Political Research* 20: 227–238.

Nozick, Robert. 1974. *Anarchy, State, and Utopia*. New York: Basic Books.

O'Brien, David. 1990. *Storm Center: The Supreme Court in American Politics*. New York: W.W. Norton.

O'Kane, Rosemary H. T. 1995. "The National Causes of State Construction in France, Russia and China." *Political Studies* 43: 2–21.

Opalek, Kazimierz. 1982. "Poland." In *International Handbook of Political Science*. Ed. William G. Andrews. Westport, Conn.: Greenwood Press.

Ordeshook, Peter C. 1993. "The Development of Contemporary Political Theory." In *Political Economy: Institutions, Competition, and Representation*. Ed. William A. Barnett, Melvin J. Hinich, and Norman J. Schofield. Cambridge: Cambridge University Press.

Paehlke, Robert C. 1989. *Environmentalism and the Future of Progressive Politics*. New Haven: Yale University Press.

Paine, Thomas. 1989. "Common Sense." In *American Political Thought*. 2nd ed. Ed. Kenneth M. Dolbeare. Chatham, N.J.: Chatham House.

Park, Andrus. "Ethnicity and Independence: The Case of Estonia in Comparative Perspective." *Europe-Asia Studies* 46: 69–87.

Plato. 1967. *The Republic of Plato*. Trans. Francis MacDonald Cornford. New York: Oxford University Press.

Powell, G. Bingham Jr. 1986. "American Voter Turnout in Comparative Perspective." *American Political Science Review* 80: 38.

Rawls, John. 1971. *A Theory of Justice*. Cambridge, Mass.: Belknap Press.

Rogowski, Ronald. 1993. "Comparative Politics." In *Political Science: The State of the Discipline II*. Ed. Ada W. Finifter. Washington, D.C.: American Political Science Association.

Roosevelt, Franklin D. 1990. "Economic Bill of Rights." In *The U.S. Constitution*. Ed. Bertell Ollmann and Jonathan Birnbaum. New York: New York University Press.

Rushdooney, Rousas John. 1973. *The Institutes of Biblical Law*. Presbyterian and Reformed Publishing.

Sabatier, Paul A. 1995. "Political Science and Public Policy." In *Public Policy: The Essential Readings*. Ed. Stella Z. Theodoulou and Matthew A. Cahn. Englewood Cliffs, N.J.: Prentice Hall.

Sand, George. 1992. "The Intimate Journal of George Sand, entry for 13 June 1837." In *Feminism: The Essential Historical Writings*. Ed. Miriam Schneir. New York: Vintage Books.

Sargent, Lyman Tower. 1993. *Contemporary Political Ideologies: A Comparative Analysis*. 9th ed. Belmont, Calif.: Wadsworth.

Sartori, Giovanni. 1994. "Compare Why and How; Comparing, Miscomparing, and the Comparative Method." In *Comparing Nations: Concepts, Strategies, Substance*. Ed. Mattei Dogan and Ali Kazancigil. Cambridge: Blackwell.

Saxonhouse, Arelene W. 1993. "Texts and Canons: The Status of the 'Great Books' in Political Theory." In *Political Science: The State of the Discipline II*. Ed. Ada W. Finifter. Washington, D.C.: American Political Science Association.

Schaeffer, Francis. 1981. *A Christian Manifesto*. Westchester, Ill.: Crossway Books.

Schlafly, Phyllis. 1977. *The Power of the Positive Woman*. New York: Arlington House.

Scott, Gregory M., and Stephen M. Garrison. 1995. *The Political Science Student Writer's Manual*. Englewood Cliffs, N.J.: Prentice Hall.

Seeley, Sir John Robert. 1896. *Introduction to Political Science*. London: Macmillan.

Semanis, Einars. 1994. "Academic Political Science in Latvia: The First Steps." *Scandanavian Political Studies* 17 (2): 181–191.

Skidmore, Max J. 1993. *Ideologies: Politics in Action*. 2nd ed. Fort Worth: Harcourt Brace Jovanovich.

Skocpol, Theda. 1979. *States and Social Revolutions: A Comparative Analysis of France, Russia, and China*. Cambridge: Cambridge University Press.

Slotnick, Eliot E. 1991. "Judicial Politics." In *Political Science: Looking to the Future*. Ed. William Crotty. Vol. 4. *American Institutions*. Evanston, Ill.: Northwestern University Press.

Smith, Adam. 1985. *The Wealth of Nations*. New York: Viking/Penguin.

Smith, Steve. 1990. "International Relations." In *New Developments in Political Science: An International Review of Achievements and Prospects*. Ed. Adrian Leftwich. Brookfield, Ver.: Edward Elgar Publishing.

Sowell, Thomas. 1987. *A Conflict of Visions: Ideological Origins of Political Struggles*. New York: Quill/William Morrow.

Spicker, Paul. 1992. "Equality versus Solidarity." *Government and Opposition* 27 (1): 66–77.

Standing Bear, Luther. 1933. *What the Indian Means to America*. Lincoln: University of Nebraska Press.

Stanton, Elizabeth Cady. 1992. "Declaration of Sentiments and Resolutions, Seneca Falls, July 19, 1848." In *Feminism, The Essential Historical Writings*. Ed. Miriam Schneir. New York: Vintage Books.

Stone, I. F. 1988. *The Trial of Socrates*. Boston: Little, Brown.

Strauss, Leo. 1959. *What is Political Philosophy*. New York: Free Press.

Students for a Democratic Society. 1962. *The Port Huron Statement*.

Suarez-Iniguez, Enrique. 1994. "Political Science in Mexico." *Perspectives on Political Science* 23 (1): 31–35.

Taylor, Rupert. "The State of Political Science in South Africa: A Survey of the Profession." *Politikon* 17 (2): 115–127.

The Economist 1 July 1995, 25.

The Economist 3 June 1995, 3.

Theodoulou, Stella Z. 1995a. "How Public Policy is Made." In *Public Policy: The Essential Readings*. Ed. Stella Z. Theodoulou and Matthew A. Cahn. Englewood Cliffs, N.J.: Prentice Hall.

Theodoulou, Stella Z. 1995b. "The Contemporary Language of Public Policy: A Starting Point." In *Public Policy: The Essential Readings*. Ed. Stella Z. Theodoulou and Matthew A. Cahn. Englewood Cliffs, N.J.: Prentice Hall.

Thompson, John B. 1984. *Studies in the Theory of Ideology*. Berkeley: University of California Press.

Thoreau, Henry David. 1965. *Walden, or Life in the Woods and Civil Disobedience*. New York: Harper & Row.

Thucydides. 1986. *History of the Peloponnesian War*. Trans. Rex Warner. New York: Penguin.

Tocqueville, Alexis de. 1945. *Democracy in America*. New York: Vintage Books.

Torgerson, Douglas 1992. "Priest and Jester In Policy Sciences: Developing the Focus of Inquiry." *Policy Sciences* 25 (3): 225–35.

Trent, John E., and Michael Stein. 1991. "The Interaction of The State and Political Science in Canada: A Preliminary Mapping." In *The Development of Political Science: A Comparative Survey*. Ed. David Easton, John G. Gunnell and Luigi Graziano. London: Routledge.

Voegelin, Eric. 1952. *The New Science of Politics*. Chicago: University of Chicago Press.

Wald, Kenneth. 1996. *Religion and Politics in the United States*. 3rd. ed. Washington, D.C.: Congressional Quarterly, Inc.

Walzer, Michael. 1985. *Exodus and Revolution*. New York: Basic Books.

Weale, Albert. 1990. "Rational Choice and Political Analysis." In *New Developments in Political Science: An International Review of Achievements and Prospects*. Ed. Adrian Leftwich. Brookfield, Ver.: Edward Elgar Publishing.

Weber, Max. 1946. "Bureaucracy." In *Essays in Sociology*. Trans. H. Gerth and C. Wright Mills. Oxford: Oxford University Press.

Weber, Ronald E. 1991. "The Study of State and Local Politics: A Preliminary Exploration of Its Contributions to Empirical Political Theory." In *Political Science: Looking to the Future*. Ed. William Crotty. Vol. 4. *American Institutions*. Evanston, Ill.: Northwestern University Press.

Weiner, C. 1971. *Between Two Worlds: The Political Thought of Graham Wallas*. Oxford: Clarendon Press.

Wilcox, Laird, and John George. 1994. *Be Reasonable*. Buffalo, N.Y.: Prometheus Books.

Willoughby, W.W. 1993. "The American Political Science Association." In *Discipline and History Political Science in the United States: Part 1*. Ed. James Farr and Raymond Seidelman. Ann Arbor: University of Michigan Press.

Wilson, Woodrow. 1993. "The Study of Administration." In *Discipline and History Political Science in the United States: Part 1*. Ed. James Farr and Raymond Seidelman. Ann Arbor: University of Michigan Press.

Wuthnow, Robert. 1990. "Quid Obscurum: The Changing Terrain of Church-State Relations." In *Religion and American Politics: From the Colonial Period to the 1980s*. Ed. Mark A. Noll. New York: Oxford University Press.

Yang, Sung Chul. 1994. *The North and South Korean Political Systems: A Comparative Analysis.* Boulder, Colo.: Westview Press.

Ysmal, Colette. 1994. "The History of Electoral Studies in France." In *European Journal of Political Research* 25 (3): 367–377.

Zeimer, Klaus. 1994. "Polish Political Science and the Transformation from Communism." *European Journal of Political Research* 25 (4): 483–498.

Zuckert, Catherine. 1995. "Why Political Scientists Want to Study Literature." *PS: Political Science and Politics* 28 (2): 189–190.

Glossary

Amicus curiae brief   A "friend of the court" brief filed by an individual or organization not directly involved in the case.

Anarchism   The belief that all political authority is inherently oppressive and that government should be reduced to a minimum.

Antinomianism   A belief that faith without adherence to law is sufficient for religious practice.

APSA   American Political Science Association.

Aristocracy   For Aristotle, government by the best or most capable people; in common terms, government by a privileged, hereditary ruling class.

Authoritarianism   Rule without popular consent, requiring obedience to law but not necessarily active support for a regime.

Autocratic   Having unrestricted power.

Autonomous   Self-governing; independent.

Bicameral legislature   A legislature that is divided into two branches or houses.

Bourgeoisie   For Karl Marx, the capitalist middle class.

Brief   A compilation of facts, arguments, and points of law concerning a specific law case, prepared by an attorney and submitted to the court.

Capitalism   An economic system in which the means of production and distribution are privately owned and operated for profit.

Case study   A detailed examination of a representative individual or group.

Class stratification   The differentiation of classes within a society for political or economic purposes.

Cognitive dissonance   A perceived discrepancy between what is stated to be reality and what is reality in fact.

Communism   A collectivist social system in which the means of production are owned by the state and in which the products of society are distributed according to need.

Communitarian	One who advocates communal life, in which possessions are shared by commune members.
Conservatism	An ideology normally associated with resistance to changes in culture, and less government intervention in the social and economic life of the nation.
Constitutionalism	A belief in a system of government limited and controlled by a constitution, or contract, drawn up and agreed to by its citizens.
Corporatism	An approach to the study of politics focusing on the activities of economic interests.
Cybernetics	The study of government that focuses on how information is transmitted and received.
Deductive logic	Reasoning from a general premise to a specific conclusion.
Democracy	A system of government in which the majority governs and in which the rights of minorities are protected.
Détente	The relaxing of tension between nations.
Dialectic	A process of arriving at the truth in which succeeding propositions transform each other.
Eclectic	Combining a variety of approaches or methods.
Empiricism	The idea that all knowledge results from sense experience; a scientific method that relies on direct observation.
Epistemology	The study of what knowledge is.
Ethnocentricity	A tendency to believe that one's own race is superior to other races; a focus of attention upon one race, to the exclusion of others.
Fascism	A totalitarian political system in which power is concentrated in the hands of a dictator who keeps rigid control of society and promotes a belligerent nationalism.
Flow model	A diagram illustrating the relationships among elements of a system.
Gaia hypothesis	James Lovelock's conservationist concept of the earth as a living entity needing the same sort of nurture that all organisms require.
Game theory	A method of understanding and predicting socio-political attitudes and events through devising mathematical models of social behavior.
Green	In politics, a name for those policies, politicians, and activists who advocate environmental responsibility in policy decisions.

Hard left	In Gabriel Almond's methodological approach to the study of politics, the mode that stresses the scientific analysis of quantitative data in the interests of promoting social, economic, and political equality.
Hard right	The method of studying politics, in Gabriel Almond's research, that stresses the scientific analysis of quantitative data and rational thinking and focuses on the study of power.
Humanism	The concept that humanity, and not a deity, is and should be the central focus of concern in philosophy, politics, the arts, etc.
Ideology	The combined beliefs and doctrines that reveal an individual's or a culture's value system.
Inductive logic	Reasoning from a series of specific observations to a general principle.
Inefficient game	In game theory, a game in which no player completely achieves a desired end.
Intrasocietal	The environment existing inside the structure of a given society.
Iron curtain	Those countries of Eastern Europe dominated by the Soviet Union.
Iron law of oligarchy	The principle stating that all associations eventually become dominated by a minority of their members.
Iron triangle	The interrelationship of government agencies, congressional committees, and political action groups as they influence policy.
Irrationalist	One who believes that human behavior is determined by factors other than reason.
Knesset	The legislative body of the Israeli government.
Literature review	In a research project, the task of canvassing publications, usually professional journals, in order to find information about a specific topic.
Millenarian	Member of any of many religious movements that challenged the church after the year A.D. 1000.
Millennium	A time period of 1,000 years.
Moderate	Within reasonable limits; in politics, one who is opposed to extremely liberal or conservative views.
Monarchy	A political system in which power is held by a hereditary aristocracy, headed by a king or queen.
Myth	A story or narrative intended to explain a natural or social phenomenon beyond normal human understanding.

Nazism	The political movement led in Germany by Adolf Hitler, combining nationalism with antisemitism.
Negative freedom	Isaiah Berlin's phrase for the freedom from obligation or restraint on one's actions.
Neoconservatism	A conservative reaction to liberal and radical movements of the 1960s.
Normative theory	Any theory attempting to assign value judgments to its conclusions, as opposed to quantitative theory, which attempts to produce value-free results.
Oligarchy	Government of the many by and in the interests of the few.
Orthodox	"Right belief," holding the basic beliefs of the faith.
Paradigm	A model or example.
Patrician	A member of the wealthy class or aristocracy.
Phenomenology	The study of the development of human consciousness and how it attempts to assimilate sensory data.
Plebeian	In common use, of the common people, as opposed to the aristocracy.
Politics	Ordering societal relations.
Polity	For Aristotle, government by the many in the interests of all.
Positive freedom	Isaiah Berlin's phrase for the freedom to do what one wills.
Pragmatism	The notion that ideas and concepts should be judged by their practical consequences instead of their correspondence to abstract or ideal criteria.
Progressivism	Any doctrine calling for changes within a system, to be made in the light of recent findings or achievements.
Proletariat	The urban, industrial working class.
Quantification	Determining or measuring quantity or amount.
Radical	One calling for substantial change in institutions, society, political systems, etc.
Rational actor theory	In public policy analysis, the theory that people and institutions tend to act in ways which they perceive to be in their own best interests.
Rationalism	The belief that reasoned observation is the proper foundation for problem solving.
Reactionary	One who holds extremely conservative views.
Republic	A government that derives its power from the consent of the people, who control policy by electing government officeholders.

Sample plan	An essential step in setting up a survey; the task of establishing which elements of the general population are to be asked to participate in the survey.
Sampling frame	That specific part of a population from which a sample is drawn for a survey.
Social contract	The agreement, either formally stated or implied, among members of a society that allows for the establishment and continuance of the social structure and the government.
Socialism	An economic system in which the state owns the means of production.
Soft left	In Gabriel Almond's terms, a methodological approach to the study of politics which favors philosophical and descriptive analysis of political in the interests of social, economic, or political equality.
Soft right	The analytical mode described by Gabriel Almond that takes a philosophical or descriptive rather than a quantitative approach to the study of power and rational thinking in politics.
Soviet Bloc	Those Eastern European countries dominated by Soviet communism from 1945 to 1990.
Structural-functionalism	A method of studying political systems introduced by Gabriel Almond in which various elements of a political system are analyzed according to the types of tasks they perform.
Subjectivism	A theory of knowledge in which truth is individually determined by each person's preferences or perceptions.
Totalitarianism	A type of authoritarian government in which the state demands active support of its policies.
Typology	A classification of phenomena according to differing characteristics.
Utopia	An ideal social environment.
Validity	In statistics, the characteristic that a measuring instrument, such as a survey, has when it actually measures what it purports to measure.
Variables	The elements of an equation, experiment, or formula that are under study and subject to change in accordance with changes in their environment.

Index

Public policy
  analysis: American Government, 217–240
  APSA Program Division, 375
  constituents, 218
  cycle analysis, 221
  design, 375
  implementers, 218
  makers, 218
  making triangles, 218–219
  policy analysis, 217
  process, 375
"Public sphere," Habermas, 151
Pure negative freedom, 54
Puritans, New Haven Colony, 53
"Putting States in Their Place: State Systems
    and State Theory," Jessup, 145–147

Q

Qualities associated with creativity, 9–11
Quantitative methodologies, 166–190,
    303–304
  Almond's, "hard" methodologies, 141,
    151–165
  APSA Program Division on Formal Political
    Theory, 358–359
  basics of social science research, 168–169
  Germany, quantitative analysis, 333
  judicial studies, data collections, 376
  public choice theory, 154–158, 193, 379
  regression of statistics, 379
  surveys, 174–184, 303
Queens. *See* Monarchs and monarchy
Questionnaires, surveys, 178
Quirk, Paul, 371

R

Race, Gender, and Ethnicity, APSA Program
    Division, 369–370
Racism, 91–92, 347, 349
Racketeer Influenced and Corrupt
    Organizations (RICO) Act, 247
"The Radical Right," 81, 86–88
Radicals and radicalism, 81, 87–88, 100
Rajya Sabhahe, India, 350
Ranked ethnicities, 260
Ranney, Austin, 3
Rao, Pamulaparti Venkata Narasimha, 350
Raphael, "School of Athens," 28–29
Ratio data, research, 169, 180
Rational actor theory, 151–154
Rational choice theory, 193–195, 361. *See also*
    Quantitative methodologies
  APSA Program Division on Formal Political
    Theory, 358–359

Rational choice theory (*cont.*)
  game theory, 155–158, 379
  "hard right," Almond's schools and sects,
    154–155
Rational-comprehensive approach, policy
    analysis, 220–221
Rationality, instrumental and communicative,
    151
Rationalization, social, 150–151
Rawls, John, 64–65
Reactionaries and reactionism, 81, 86–88
Readings
  *Child Support Enforcement for Teenage Fathers:
    Problems and Prospects,* Pirog-Good and
    Good, 222–240
  Democratization and War, Mansfield and
    Snyder, 282–302
  *Gender and Citizen Participation: Is There a
    Different Voice,* Schlozman, Burns, Verba,
    and Donahue, 195–216
  *National Organization for Women, Inc. v.
    Joseph M. Scheidler, et al.* (1994), 247–257
  The Postmodern Problem, Zuckert, 308–322
  "The National Causes of State Construction
    in France, Russia and China," O'Kane,
    260–281
Reagan, Ronald, 85, 150, 219
Realism and realists
  American realist movement, 41
  Bzrezinski, Zbigniev, 284
  Clausewitz, Karl von, 283–284
  international relations, 282–283, 285
  Kissinger, Henry, 284
  Machiavelli, Niccolo, 283
  modern political realism, 36
  neorealism, international relations, 285
  power preponderance theory, 286
Reality, Nietzsche, 306
"Real socialism," 343–344
"Recent Advances in Political Methods,"
    Merriam, 15, 17, 41, 140
Recruitment, political, structural-
    functionalism, 161
Reflections on the Revolution in France, Burke,
    83, 85
Reform of Parliament, Crick, 328
Regression analysis, surveys, 183
Reinsch, Paul S., 40
Relational hypotheses, basics of research,
    171
Relational quality of politics, 3
Relationships, data, 167, 182
Relativism, 143
Reliability of data and measurements,
    169–170, 183